Modern Collector's Dolls

The current values in this book should be used only as a guide. They are not intended to set prices, which vary from one section of the country to another. Auction prices as well as dealer prices vary greatly and are affected by condition as well as demand. Neither the Author nor the Publisher assumes responsibility for any losses that might be incurred as a result of consulting this guide.

Additional copies of this book may be ordered from:

Collector Books
P.O. Box 3009
Paducah, KY 42001

@$19.95 Add $2.00 for postage and handling.

FIRST EDITION

Modern Collector's Dolls

by

Patricia R. Smith

PHOTOGRAPHY BY DWIGHT F. SMITH

EDITED BY DOROTHY WESTBROOK

COLLECTOR BOOKS

A Division of Schroeder Publishing Co., Inc.

ACKNOWLEDGMENTS

My special thanks go to my good friend, Reva Hill, who spent many hours helping me search for collectable dolls. Her good nature never failed. At one point of this project, Reva gave me five days a week, for six weeks, of her time and help. I could not have started nor finished this book, without her help.

A good photographer is hard to find and the most valued in the eyes of one who needs him. My photographer was always valued by me, as he is my husband, Dwight F. Smith. I certainly acknowledge my thanks to him.

I would like to give my special thanks to Earlene Johnston for her help in research and for her introduction to people who sell dolls but mainly for loaning me some of her own prized collection of modern dolls.

To Dorothy Westbrook for her editing and encouragment.

I would also like to express my thanks to Sue and Alvin Allin. They loaned me their "star" dolls when I found I was unable to locate them for my own collection. The Allin's operate the only Antique and Modern doll museum in the midwest.

Dolls on loan have been acknowledged with the picture. All other dolls belong to the author.

All photographs are by Dwight F. Smith, with the exception of the "Annabelle" by Alexander. That photo was by Mrs. Edith Goldsworthy, of Long Beach, California.

About the Author
PATRICIA R. SMITH

SCHOOLS: Page School for Girls, Los Angeles, California
St. Mary's, Santa Barbara, California
Nevada State, Nevada
St. Theresa, Kansas City, Missouri

DEGREE'S: Pedogogy
Adult Psychology
Child Psychology
Dogmatic Theology
Apologetics
Literary Methods

OTHER: "Famous Artists" Course, studying art layout and design. A commissioned artist, who specializes in "faces" and religious art.
Studied with "Famous Writers School" in Connecticut on fiction aspects.

WORK: Has worked in Occupational Therapy Departments in Psychiatric Wards. As Assistant Advertising Director for large catalog order firm. Member of Ad Club. Worked as substitute teacher in local school system.

PUBLISHED: Articles and short stories on such varied subjects as: "Teen-age Dating", "How to Sculpture A Face", "Comparative Religions", "The Art Of Being A Wife", "Safety Afloat", "That Life-Jacket May Save You", "What It Is All About (USCGAUX)", "The Day That Tim Drowned", "What Is Religion?", "The Ins and Outs of Ceramics", "You Can Paint".

HOBBIES: Archery, Boating, Sewing, Collecting dolls.

ORGANIZATIONS: National Field Archers Ass'n, U.S. Coast Guard Auxiliary, Council of Catholic Women, Lake of the Ozarks Yachting Assn'n. Independence Gay Ninety's Doll Club. National Federation of Doll Clubs.

DEDICATION

To the real live "dolls" in my life, Bunny and Linda Moore of Houston, Texas; Terry Mitchell and Dawn Swope of Independence, Missouri.

To the memory of my mother, Delia Rosa Crellin, who would have loved to share the countless hours of research.

To my aunt, Dorothy Bell Gamble, who started me on this entire project.

But mainly to my husband, Dwight F. Smith, for his sense of humor, his interest and his love.

Contents

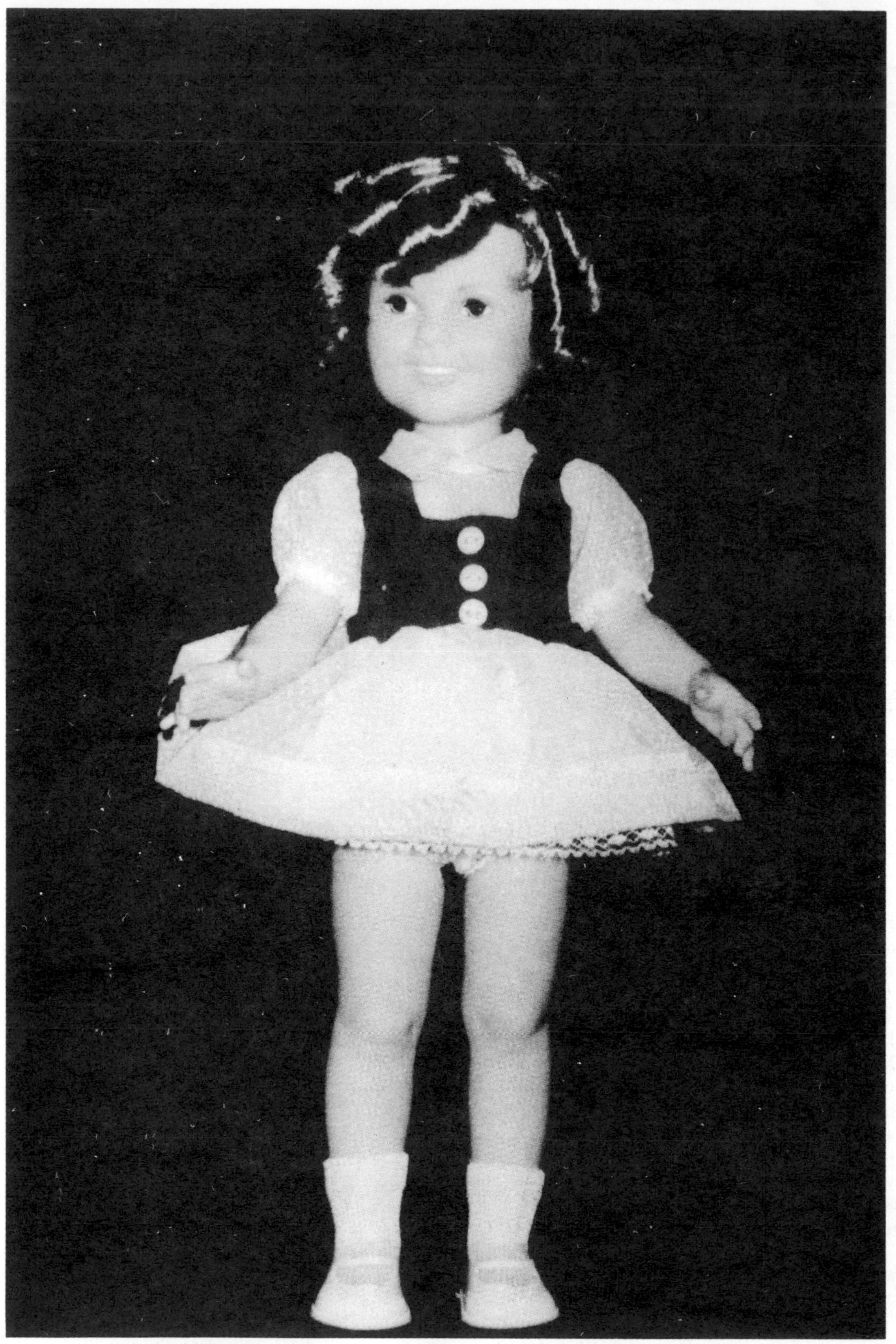

Limited edition "Shirley Temple," by Ideal is one of the most prized finds of collectors. Shirley Temple was the most popular of character dolls. Refer to the information beginning on page 179.

Modern Collector's Dolls

Collecting from garage sales, thrift shops and swap meets

To the antique collector, some of the dolls in this book are poor quality, but they are being collected. I have spent many hours talking to people at thrift shops, swap meets and flea markets. Some can only afford a more reasonably priced collection and others only have room for miniatures. I do, however, know this, they love their dolls just as much as the antique and the advanced collector loves their Brus and long faced Jumeaus.

This is not a book for antique collectors. It is designed and written for the new collector, the beginner who in the very act of "beginning" needs help and advice.

Most doll collectors start in a modest way by bringing home one doll. The modest start does not override what usually happens—a mania that makes little sense and is not based on logic. Some become so addicted that the house work lags behind, the car needs repair, and the children may do without new shoes.

Collecting antique dolls is a different story and requires thousands, not hundreds of dollars and most people cannot afford them. That is why this book is about modern dolls. The supply has to meet the demand, for awhile at least, and modern dolls are fairly numerous and in the realm of most pocketbooks.

Once we are caught up in the thrill of collecting, most of us have great hindsight and very little foresight. We remember dolls we should have gotten and see the ones we should have not gotten. We become hunters, detectives, as great as Sherlock Holmes. We sense the unexpected and cannot wait, to see, to grab, and to hope. More often than not, we are disappointed. Although every once in awhile we do come up with a beauty, a winner in the oasis of dolls. This does nothing but spur us on to more thrift shops, and to more garage sales.

The thrill of the hunt does not leave easily. Any collector can testify to this as she rolls up to park at a Goodwill store, does not take time to set the brakes or lock the car but just rushes inside this structure where "the find" is going to take place.

Do not be fooled. It is for certain the thrift shop is not. These people may have charitable backgrounds but they do know value. Do not expect to find a $100.00 doll for a $1.00. In fact, do not expect to find the doll at any price. It just does not happen anymore! But where we have an edge on them is we are looking for a modern doll which one day may have a $100.00 value. In this case our foresight extends beyond theirs.

Most of the charitable outlets have a "doll person" in a regional area. An expert on dolls. This person can either be male or female. They check dolls and have outlets, such as dealers in Chicago and New York. They also have friends to whom they sell the dolls. So do not expect to find very much at their stores. You will rarely find really good plastic and vinyl dolls unless it is bald and marked up so badly that even a poor child would not want it.

In the"olden" days, whatever was donated was placed out for the general public. But first one person, in the organization, started to collect glass, another had a friend who collected lead soldiers, still another had a aunt that collected dolls. The entire thing has evolved down to what it is now. The general public gets the leftovers of the leftovers and there is not much of a chance to happen onto anything that is very good. Most of us are aware of these facts and it does not stop us from going to look.

Since we see that the thrift shops are not a really good source, lets look at the garage sales. With garage sale "hopping", expect to spend time. By that I mean a lot of time! The percentage rate of finding dolls at a garage sale is very low because most people putting on the sale still have children at home and those children are playing with the very dolls that you may be searching for.

The best way to attack the garage sale (in most states) is on a Tuesday evening check the ads in the local paper. Most garage sales are on Wednesday, Thursday and Friday, some are on Saturday. Most "professionals" also run on Sunday. Have a city map and map out a route. This will save you some time. Get up early so you can leave home by 8:30 a.m. or 9:00 a.m. and do not expect to get back home before 3:00 p.m. When you get to a sale and you see anything that might interest you, pick it up and carry it with you. If you do not, it will be gone. You can find some very nice dolls and other items at a garage sale.

Let us look at the "swap meets". A majority of these are held at a drive-in theater during the summer months. Now this is where you may have a chance! People bring out their "junk" to sell at a low price. This is the stuff that used to go to the thrift shop or to the dump.

After one trip to a swap meet you will be able to tell the "pros" from the person who is just trying to get a little cash for their throw-aways. More and more professionals are showing up at the swap meets but there still are many opportunities to find reasonably priced dolls. Also more and more dolls are showing up at these meets because word gets around as to what is selling and they may be priced up a little but not so much that you can not afford them yet.

What about the indoor "flea markets"? These are professionals. They are in business. Expect to pay near to what the doll is worth; to the flea market dealer anyway. As anywhere else, you may know something that the dealer does not. Take a chance. It may surprise you to find a $25.00 doll for $5.00.

A word about friends or people that you meet where you can buy dolls from their home. There is more "boot-legging", that is selling without a tax stamp, going on in dolls, just as there is in ceramics or anything else where a person feels they can make a dollar. The problem with dolls is that most of these people mark them up 200 to 300%.

Let us say a little about prices. If you are buying dolls for pleasure only and if you feel that a certain doll is worth the price to you, then go ahead and buy it. You are the only one that can put the value on the doll in relation to the amount of personal pleasure and future enjoyment you will receive from it.

There are more and more modern dolls showing up in official "price listings". You will find these listings in doll publications, antique magazines, and hobby magazines. But just ask yourself who made the prices "official"? Well, someone made the prices up, thats how. A number of authors follow their books with a "price guide" and set their own prices, which are usually rather high and far above the actual marketing price. If you find a doll that you want and the price is way out of sight, ask the person selling where they got the price. If they state "its in the book", gently point out that the person who wrote the book or sold that doll first set the price.

If you are planning or re-selling dolls, make sure that you can market them at 40% over your cost. Do not be greedy and want 200 or 300% profit. You will find that you will sell more dolls and actually make more money if you are practical on your pricing.

After you settle down and stop buying a doll just because it is a doll and you define exactly what you want to collect, then get acquainted with the doll shops in you area. These people will in the long run, help you the most.

The doll shops business is to know dolls or at least to have the books for reference. Most of their business is with antiques but more and more modern dolls are showing up at the shops. Let them know what you are looking for. At a shop you will generally pay what the doll is worth on the market today. But what will this same doll be worth someday? By dealing with the dealer it will mean that you can not buy as many dolls for the same amount of money but it also means that you may be able to buy the dolls that you really want.

What about value? Value is relative to you, the buyer, pointed out a few paragraphs ago. There is a lady that paid an outragious price for one Dionne but she had four others at home. The set of four that should have been five did not mean much in terms of a collection, nor of value. The fifth Dionne completed that collection and meant the re-sale value was a whole lot greater. It was worth the high price to get the one doll.

Value is generally placed on an item because it is an antique. "Antique" means old. The world over an item must be 100 years old or it is not legally an antique. Most Americans are not that time conscious. After all, we have moved from the horse and buggy to landing on the moon in the space of fifty short years. Our European friends took hundreds of years to evolve to the means of mass production and innovation. To most Americans anything that is old or hard to find is considered an antique. Anything that someone else is collecting is considered old or antique. For example certain pieces of depression glass that were given away on Wednesday nights at the local movie or in a box of oats, will command more money than a beautiful piece of Haviland china. Why? because someone started to collect it. Or wrote a book about collecting it. It is as simple as that. The same thing happened to Avon bottles; someone started to collect them. Here with a little foresight, the doll collector can reason out the whole scene. Antiques are relative to the buyer just as value is. To be plainer, an antique becomes an antique when someone makes it one! This applies to the general buyer. There are some who really understand "antiques" appreciates the beauty of antiques but they are out numbered by the average collector. You see the mis-understanding of words comes with the difference between "antique" and "collectable". Antiques means that it is at least 100 years old. "Collectable" means anything from 100 years ago to now, this date.

We all know that bisque, china and some composition is "antique" and brings a higher price. But let us look at the period of this book: 1935 to 1971. That is 36 years and if you want a collection that spans this amount of time, you will have to locate dolls made of rubber, composition, magic skin, synthetic rubber, early plastic and vinyl, hard plastic, modern vinyl and plastic and finally dublon. These are now collectable and are the antique dolls of the future.

Logically let us look at each of them. We will take rubber first. Rubber is the milky sap of milkweed, the dandelion and the rubber tree. Anyone who has seen the pure rubber toys of the 30's and 40's and even into the early 50's has seen that they tend to "rot" and dissolve, just as the old tires did. Unless rubber is kept in a humid, cool place, it will collapse with time. This is due mainly because it is made up of living substances.

Next is compositon. Composition was the most commonly used material preceding World War II but was used up to 1950. It is made up of sawdust, starch and resin, mixed with water. Some companies claimed to have secret ingredients but as a general rule the above materials were used. The ingredients were pressed into a mold. There were good and there were bad mixtures. The best was hard and after painting with enamels looked very much like modern plastics. Composition dolls deteriorate. They must be kept in a dry area. Extreme cold and heat make them crack and break up. To best preserve them, keep them in a dry moderate area. They will all peel and crack with age. They usually begin with a bubbling under the eye, in the corner of the nose or under the lower lip and then the crack will open.

Magic skin is soft rubber (latex). The same thing that gloves for scrubbing are made of. It was filled with such things as cotton, wool "dust" from woolen mills and it felt like real live skin. Since it was a very thin material, it had a tendency to pull away from points of stress, such as the joints. The head of the doll usually pulled away first, due to the weight involved. Magic skin dolls in good condition are hard to find and it stands to reason that their value can only increase. Even if the bodies are completely "worn out", the heads number among the most beautiful and it may pay you to try and preserve them by building a cloth body around the old rubber one.

Next comes synthetic rubber. In May of 1942 all rubber had to go into the gigantic effort of winning World War II, so the synthetic rubber evolved. Out of this period, also, came the plastics. The synthetic rubber used by doll manufacturers was very much like the real rubber and had the same weakness.

Between 1936 and 1950 dolls were made up of all these materials, plus plastic, inter-mixed and in any combination. The reason was the doll makers were using up old stock, experimenting with the new ideas and some had serious shortages in stock. Therefore, do not be surprised at any combination you may find but try to determine if that certain combination is "for real" or just someones "put-together." (More about "put-togethers" in the next chapter).

Next in line are the hard plastics, a term used for a certain period of dolls. Most companies used hard plastic from 1946 to 1959. They are solid feeling dolls. Some were all hard plastic, others had composition arms and legs with hard plastic heads, still others had rubber arms and legs with a hard plastic head. Most of the dolls were of older children types or as adults. For example, the Toni doll. With a little practice you will be able to spot a hard plastic doll just by looking at it.

Hard plastic dolls are extremely durable. Very rarely will you find one that is marred or broken. The stringing has a tendency to go bad but then it is rubber encased in cloth and it will go bad. No one knows how long the hard plastics will endure. 50 or 500 years, but it is relatively certain they will outlast anything between bisque and themselves. At least, they will not crack, peel, melt, dissolve, break easily, or peel paint. What more does a collector need to convince himself that, logically this is the most outstanding collectables in the field of dolls? And that they are next in line to bring high prices? Their durability plus the fact that they are now 25 years old are two major selling points.

One point, the very early hard plastics do crack, just as composition. Not too many dolls were made at that time but the ones that were, look so very much like composition that it is necessary to look inside to know for certain.

What of modern plastics and vinyl? The really early plastics "wept". They became sticky and turned a very dark color. Some mistake this for synthetic rubber or for rubber itself. With the advent of plastics came the vinyl. Vinyl, introduced in 1951, is a formula of the univalent radical CH2;CH. It is derived from ethylene, compounds with undergo a polymerization, which forms a high molecular weight plastics and resins. Plastics include many groups of synthetic or natural materials, that can be shaped when soft and then hardened. These include many resins (vinyl being one) resinods, polymers, cellulose, derivatives, casein materials and proteins.

The word "plastic", meaning "moldable", has been used since the late 1800's. It did not mean the article was made of plastic but that the material it was made from was bendable or moldable.

Early vinyl was a strong and beautiful material. It has a strong, solid feel and has a tendency to turn orange with age. The darkening only seems to enhance its beauty and gives it a beautiful antique wax look.

Plastics are quite varied. Soft, rigid, and some in between. Plastic dolls are not painted. The plastic material itself is tinted to the flesh color. (Hard plastics were colored and "waxed" to a high polish and buffed.) No one knows how long plastics and vinyls will last but it is safe to believe that they will last for a long, long time.

The newest material introduced in 1970 is vinyl foam (one trademark is Dublon) used in some Mexico Mattel dolls and the new Softina line of Ideal. Soon will come the polyesters and from there anything can happen.

Here is a breakdown of the years of use on most materials. Remember most manufactures changed at different times but as a general rule it was within a year of each other.

My thanks to Horsman, Ideal and Effanbee for the following:

1940...Composition, rubber, magic skin
1942...Synthetic rubber, compositon
1943...Early plastics, composition, synthetic rubber
1946...Hard plastics, synthetic rubber, composition
1948...Hard plastic, magic skin, composition
1951...Vinyl, hard plastic, magic skin
1955...Vinyl skin, magic skin, hard plastic, soft plastic
1959...Hard plastic, rigid plastic, soft plastic, vinyl
1959 to 1970...Plastics and vinyl
1970...Vinyl foam, plastic and vinyl

Company Marks and Where to Look

When we discount the antiques, there are two categories that dolls fall into. One is the term Display Dolls. These are made for show and for collectors. Number two is Play Dolls. These are designed to be purchased for children.

The Display Dolls rarely, if ever, reach the thrift shop shelves and if they do, they are generally minus their clothes which was their identity.

Play Dolls are always on the market and they run in a three to five year cycle. That means the current dolls being sold over the retail counter right now, will reach the used market in three to five years, also minus their clothes and sometimes their identity.

Do not be afraid to look for a mark or date of the manufacture on the doll while in the shop or swap meet, or anyplace else. After all you wouldn't buy anything else without looking it over. You will save yourself a little cash and much disappointment if you do look. But first ask the price! Then start looking the doll over. The person selling is committed to the price so even if they do discover you checking over the doll and may get an idea that it may be worth more, they have already set the price and this should give you the go ahead to look for marks. There are only two things that can happen and they have both happened to me. One is for them to tell you that that was the doll they were going to save for someonelse. If you go back in a week chances are the doll will still be there and you can buy it then. Second it may stimulate the person's interest enough to start looking at dolls. Here again chances are that the interest will be short lived and you will still get the good dolls from this same source.

Identity in the shop: First turn the doll over and gently push the hair or wig so you can see the back of the neck. Gently because you may soon own that doll and you want it in good condition! If you need to wear glasses for close up, now is the time to have them on. Check to see if the manufacturer's name and date or anything else is on the back of the neck. Then check the area between the shoulders, then move on down to the area of the hips, check the bottom of the feet. After you have seen that the doll is marked somewhere and you have read these marks, then hold the doll out away from you and judge if it is a "put together." Does the head fit right? Do the arms look like they belong together? Does the entire doll look right? If so and you want the doll, go ahead and buy it.

Just a word here about "put togethers". People who work at the thrift shops or take things to a swap meet are interested in one thing only, to move the merchandise. So it stands to reason that if they have a broken doll and some parts that they will "put together" a doll so that it might sell. They are not there for the collector but for the general public. Do not hold these resources responsible. But if you purchase a doll from a known collector or someone who has been around dolls for a long time and apparently knows what they are doing and you get a "put together" and were not told about it at the time you bought it, then either take it back to them or do not buy any more dolls from that person.

Now that you have the doll at home and want to identify it, your best source is books and toy catalogs. If it is there, great, but remember just because it is not in a book does not mean that it is not a good collectable doll. It just means that whoever wrote the book did not have access to that particular doll at the time the book was written.

Because a doll is unmarked or has a number or group of letters on it does not discount it as being a collectable. American dollmakers have always been in a fiercely competitive market, therefore they will market dolls in many different areas outside the retail store. In many cases these dolls are numbered or lettered. Sometimes a store will ask a doll maker to make them a certain designed doll and these will be numbered or lettered. Most of the "name brand" dolls that are sold through catalog and discount stores are only lettered or numbered. Some parts are made by different manufacturers and are called "jobbers". For example the "AE" stamped on Deluxe Toy Creations "Rosemary" means that a jobber made the body for them, but it does not mean that all "AE"s are Deluxe Toy Creation's Dolls. It just boils down to doing a little detective work and checking in books, catalogs, and toy sheets until you locate that doll. Dolls have been manufactured by and for many people, such as Woolworth's "Marshmellow Baby" or Columbia Pictures' "Matt Helm's Slay Girls", neither of which I am aware of ever seeing. Yet, I may have and just did not know it.

Whatever you come up with on a doll, write a little note with the information on it, such as, the date that you bought it, the price that you paid for it, the place that you bought it, any information you have found about who the doll is and by whom make and the source of that information. Pin this under the clothing in the back of the doll. Then you will have the whole thing there in one place.

What to do with the doll after you bring it home is covered in the next chapter, so we will move onto what not to bring home. Yes, there are some that you should not buy. These four prints will show you what is a lost cause for collecting.

The picture captions explain why.

There are a few more things that you should be aware of as you try to identify your dolls. For one thing, the doll may have been packaged and sold with a number of identities. It could be "Liza," in a blue dress or "Paula" in a pink dress an all in the same year. Also it could be "Ruth" in 1964 and "Linda" in 1965. Do not be surprised nor dismayed at this. Remember that company is not in business for collectors but is striking at a varied market. Also you may find dolls that look alike but are made by different companies. This too is due to their marketing. If they see that one company has a success in a certain type of doll, then they, too, will try to capitalize on their competitor's success.

A word on buying mechanicals or as they should be called, "automations." Carry two double A, one C and two B batteries in your pocket or purse. Also a small two way screwdriver. Try the doll out before you buy it. You will find that in most thrift shops, that the battery covers seem to get lost somewhere between the child and the store shelf. Turn the doll so that it is lying flat. Put the batteries in the cavity, noting the manufacturer's marks for negative and positive. Put the battery cover on, if there is one, and see if the doll will work. If the battery cover is missing, then place the screwdriver across both batteries so a contact will be made. Hold the screwdriver tightly against the batteries and listen for the sound of a motor.

Even if you find an automation that does not work, you can always buy it and fix it up, then donate it to an old folks' home or the local firemen. The reason I say this is the automation seem to have less wear and tear, due, I guess, to the short lived interest of their former little owners.

There will be information on how each company marks their dolls included in the text of the company before each section of this book.

As with anything that is collectable, the wisest thing to do is keep improving your collection, so that one day you will have the finest that can be found.

Let us say that you have a "Chatty Cathy" which you picked up at a thrift shop for 50 cents. It does not work and has a stain on the leg that you cannot get off. You dressed it yourself. One day you run into a "Chatty Cathy" that is really clean but still does not work. It cost $2.00 but it does have on an original dress. Buy it and sell your other one. The first one cost you 50 cents plus, lets say $1.50 for clothes. Sell it for $2.75. Then one day you run across a "Chatty Cathy" that is clean and works and the price is $5.50 but it does not have original clothes. Buy it and change the dress from your second to the third. You now have an originally dressed, working "Chatty Cathy". Sell the second one for $2.75, with the dress from the third and the end result is that you have a good "Chatty Cathy" for a cost of $4.00. That amount is the difference between your sales and your buying. If you keep doing this throughout your collection you will find that you end up with a very fine collection.

You are the only one who can say what you want to collect, or how many. Some only want Alexanders, others only baby dolls, still some like them all and try to collect them all. I guess you can sum it up with whatever seems to "turn you on", to melt your heart or to bring back memories, that is what you should collect.

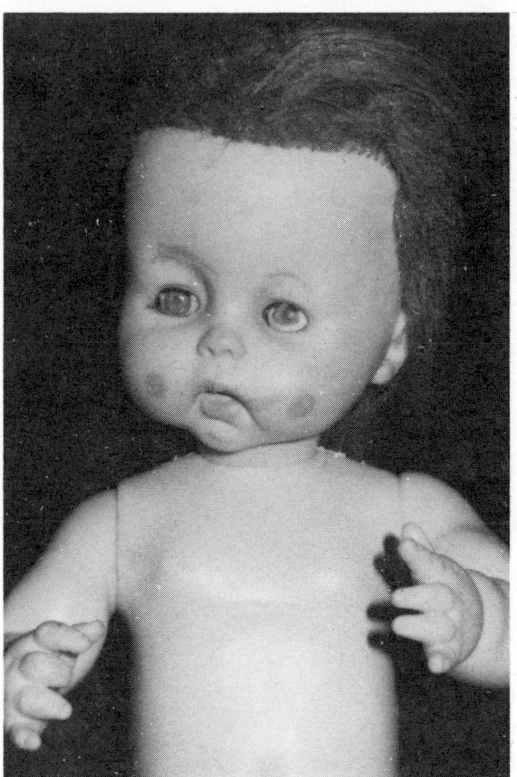

The eyes of this doll can be cleared up by using oil and the left eye can be re-set but the marks on this vinyl face cannot be removed easily as the vinyl has absorbed the marker pen ink. It is best not to bother with it.

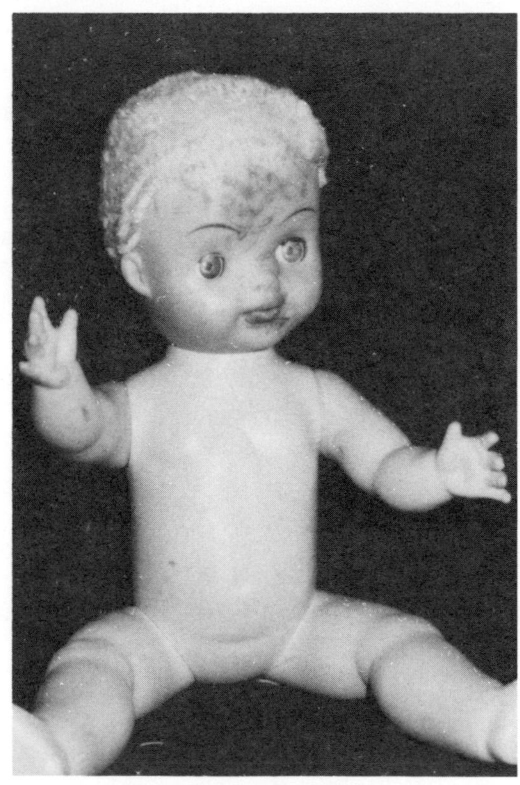

The dirt on this doll's face is just dust and dirt and will wash off but the hair has been cut to the roots and the doll is common enough not to warrant the cost of a replacement wig. Unless it is a rare doll you feel you may never find again, it is wisest not to bring it home.

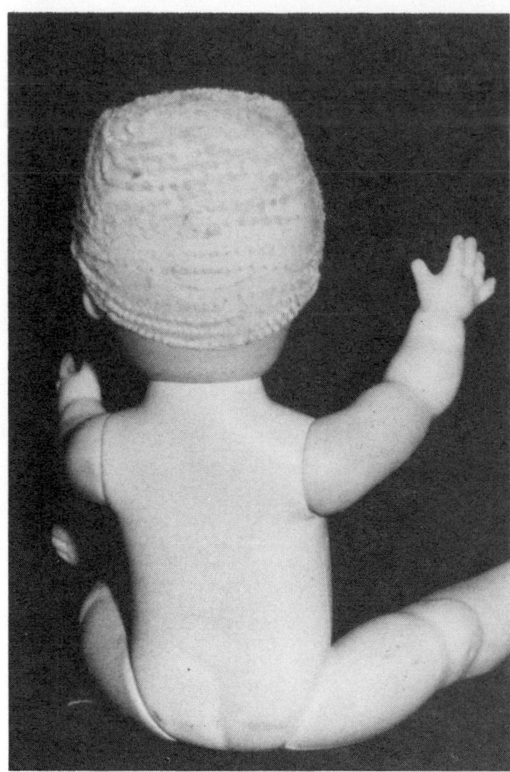

This is a back view of doll on Page 5, with hair cut too short to salvage.

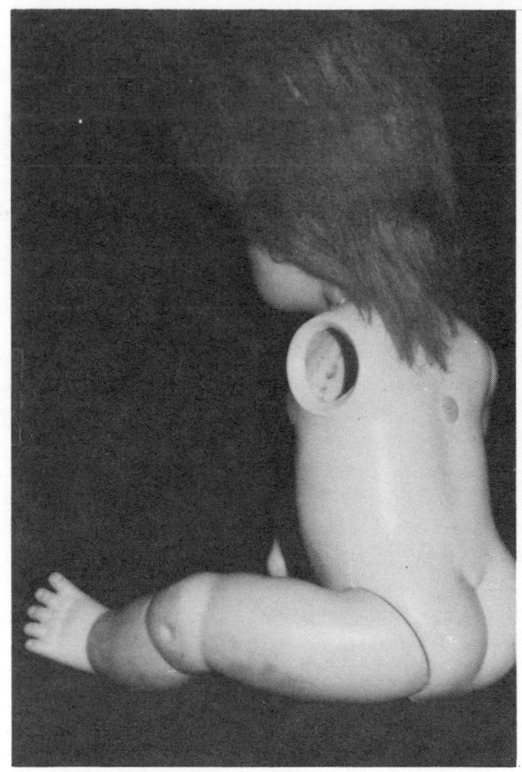

In replacing arms and legs, make certain that the replacement parts are from the very same type doll. By bringing home dolls that need replaced parts you create a storage problem and unless the doll warrants it, it is best to wait until you can find a complete one to buy.

Doll Restoration and Repair

Do not touch that composition! Take it to a doll hospital or to someone that you know is good at repair and clean-up of composition. But first check some of their work. Many good dolls have been ruined by amateurist work. Believe this: composition will melt. *Do not wash it.* If you must do it yourself use a baby oil and wipe it clean, followed by a soft cloth, to remove all the oil. More than likely the composition and some of the hard plastics will have mohair wigs. Mohair is the long silky hair of an Angora goat. *It is not washable.* It is difficult to comb and to clean and it has a tendency to mat. If the wig is in very bad condition it may be wiser to replace it. If you want to try and fix it, then use a baby's brush with very fine bristles and try to follow the natural waves. It can be curled but it is *not recommended* and if you do, use a warm (lukewarm) curling iron.

CARACUL HAIR: This is a type of hair used on some dolls, such as the Jerry Lee or the Mary Martin dolls. Caracul is the skin of a very young Asiatic or Russian sheep, Karakul, dressed like a fur. It resembles Astrakhan but has a much softer, flatter and looser curl.

ASTRAKHAN: This is the fur of young lambs. It has a lustrous, closely curled wool and is referred to as Lamb's wool. For example it was used on some of the Tiny Tears by Ideal.

Both of the above may be shampooed, using a good baby shampoo or a good quality hand soap.

HUMAN HAIR WIGS: Most of the time these wigs are glued on, so poses a problem with washing. If you do not want to remove the wig, then do not use a detergent soap as it can soften the glue and dry out the hair. A good toilet soap is best. One soaping. Rinse well and rinse again, making sure all the soap is out. *Do not wash it on a composition doll. Remove the wig and after cleaning, re-glue it to the doll.* Dry the wig on something round about the size of the dolls head, otherwise it will shrink and will not fit.

NYLON: The first plastics had nylon hair. It looks like human hair that can be combed, washed, brushed, and set, even put under a dryer. If cared for it will last for years.

DYNEL: Is softer and finer than nylon. It is very pretty and is generally used on the most expensive dolls. It can be combed, brushed, shampooed and set, just like nylon.

SARAN: Best for replacing mohair wigs. It is finer than nylon and less expensive than nylon or dynel. It can be combed, brushed and shampooed.

SARLON: Combination of saran and nylon. It can be combed, brushed and shampooed.

NYRAN: Is a mixture of nylon. It has all the advantages of nylon and is not as expensive.

Some dolls will smell. It is the glue that has "aged". Shampoo will help but the only way that you will get rid of it altogether is to remove the wig and clean off the glue and then re-glue the wig back into place.

TO WASH HAIR: Undress the doll. Use lukewarm water. Hold the doll over the sink with its head down. Be careful not to get water in the eyes and do not let water get into rooted hair openings in the scalp.

Put a small amount of wig shampoo, a good protein shampoo or a good quality toilet soap in your hand and work it up into a lather. Then rub the lather onto the hair. Rub it in gently. Rinse out all traces of the shampoo. Remember that plastic hair will become sticky if not rinsed well and will not comb out easily. Pat the rinsed hair with a towel. Then apply a hair softener or conditioner. Lacking that, use a fabric softener. Rinse again and pat dry. Always set hair when it is wet. Either brush or comb the hair gently to remove all tangles.

Before you set the hair, check the hairline to see how it was originally set. For example, if the hair is very closely rooted along the nape of the neck or at the ears, then it is wise to assume that the hair was up in these areas. A baby doll that has a great shock of hair on the top of its head with the remainder of the head with rather short hair, would indicate that there was either a top curl or braid tied with a ribbon.

Do not pincurl! Small soft rubber or metal curlers work fine. After the hair is dry, and just like a human wig, it takes longer to dry because there is no movement to circulate the air nor body heat to help dry the hair, comb it into style. If the ends are split and are frayed, trim it with a sharp pair of scissors. Never use a hot curling iron nor heated curlers. Just a reminder, most plastics, used for hair will melt. Do not wash wigs on composition. Remove the wig and then re-glue it.

After the hair has been combed into style, lightly spray it with a wig spray.

If you should want to give your Toni doll a "permanent wave" (or any other doll with nylon hair) use a wave setting gel or a solution of sugar and water.

Now let us look at the eyes. Composition and some hard plastics, at least the walkers, take to your local Doll Hospital. Most composition have rocker eyes and you will need an expert to repair them for you.

Plastic dolls have "Floating" eyes. This means that the eye is enclosed in a small container and the entire container forced into a socket. Each eye is separate. You will find that it is better to replace a damaged eye than to try and fix it.

To replace an eye container, first take the doll's head off. Some heads are stuffed, most are not. If there is any stuffing, remove it. Take a very sharp knife (the X-acto type) and cut half way around the eye socket. Push the eye container through the opening and insert the new eye container. Pull the socket back into position and cement the edges together with a vinyl cement. When dry put a coat of cement over the entire eye socket. Replace any stuffing and put the doll's head back onto the body. You can put the neck into hot water or hold it over steam for a few minutes to make it pliable enough for the pieces to go back together.

Some dolls you find lack eyelashes. Unless you can find some that are "stage girl" heavy and black, do not bother with the human kind of false eyelashes. Ask at a doll dealers for the name and address of a supply house where you can order doll eyelashes. You can buy them by the inch or by the yard. They are very low in price and you should keep a supply around. Cut the eyelashes to the size of the eye. Most lashes fit into a slot along the eyelid. Clean out this slot with a thin blade. Put the new lash in with glue. If you should want to get a lash onto a doll and haven't any lashes handy you can use a cheap paint brush. Stick the point of the brush into glue and push the brush into the slot of the eyelid. Hold your hand tight over the top of the bristles to fan them out. Let the glue dry before you cut off the brush.

For general cleaning of plastic and vinyl, use a mild soap such as soap used for washing dishes. *Do not bathe mechanical dolls. Wash off only.* On the ground in dirt around the arms and legs, you can use a powder cleanser. Scrub and rinse and dry with a soft cloth. *Do not get water into the doll's eyes.* Keep a toothbrush and scrub brush just for your dolls. The scrub brush for the bodies and the toothbrush for the fingernails, ears, nose, eyes, etc. You can dry brush the eyes with a toothbrush. If the dirt does not come off then wet the brush lightly, and repeat the brushing of the eyes. Sometimes you will find a doll that has eyes that look like they are "Blind". They will be rather filmy looking and a pale blue. This is because of water or moisture in the eye sockets. These bad eyes can be re-stored by putting a small amount of light sewing machine, gun, or watch oil into the eye. Rub the eye with your finger lightly. Add another drop and lay the doll on its stomach for about an hour. Wipe up any excess. Even if the eyes are good, it is a good idea to preserve them by putting a drop of oil into each eye and rubbing it in.

After the doll has been cleaned, take baby powder and rub it into the entire doll. *Not the eyes nor the hair.* This will help preserve the plastic and vinyl and give the doll that "just bought" look.

TO REPAIR CRACKS IN PLASTIC: All the glues that I have tried do not work very well. Fine line cracks can be filled with Elmer's glue but for larger ones, the best seems to be an electric soldering gun or a wood burning tool. Heat the area and either hold it or use an elastic band to hold it, or if it should require it, a vise, until it cools. Always use gloves. For small vinyl splits, glue joint, put a backing of cloth and sew it together with a transparent fish line. Any area that the vinyl may be pushed in or out of shape can be brought back into its former shape by heating the area (not too hot) push it into place and let cool.

REMOVING STAINS: Getting rid of pen and felt tip marks is the best kept secret in dolldom!! For some reason the people who know how to remove these marks feel that it is a trade secret! They sure will not tell anyone how they do it. Most of them have gone to or graduated from a "doll school". I do not understand why they want to be so secretive because people are not going to be taking marked up dolls to them for clean-up, they just are not going to buy them in the first place. Anyway, the following is the only things I can find out and only the first two worked for me and the last one I could not try because I could not find the ingredient.

Sunshine: It does work. *Never put rubber into the sun.* Put a narrow heavy strip of cloth around the eyes, in a blindfold manner. Rub a slice of lemon onto the marked up spot and lay it in the sunshine. It may take a couple of days but it does work.

OIL: If the doll is worth your time, start by applying a good amount of sewing machine oil on the spot and rub it in real good. Put the doll down for about eight hours. Cover the spot and the machine oil with a good coat of linseed oil. Wrap the area loosely with a white piece of cloth. Store the wrapped doll away from the light, in a drawer or a closet for a period of about six months. Now you see why I say If the doll is worth your time!

VINEGAR: Use the pepper sauce kind. Soak the stains in the vinegar until it is good and wet, then put it into the fresh air and sunshine. Wet it again and leave it in the sun. This will take several days but the stain should leave.

PLASTICGOOP: This is a Mattel product. In the flesh color, it was excellent for removing stains. Just rub into the stain with your finger, wipe it lightly with a soft cloth and if a faint hint of the stain is still there, buff it lightly with a fine steel wool. The only thing here is that Mattel does not market "Plasticgoop" any longer. At least I have been unable to find it. It was part of the "Creepy Crawler" set. The only reason that I mention it, is that some of you may have some around to try or maybe the stores in your area still sell it.

Waterless hand cleaner is great for removing deep soil and crayon marks. Alcohol will get stains out fast but you have to use it as soon as possible after the stain has been made. Deep rust and scorch spots cannot be removed.

A FEW WORDS OF CAUTION: Never mix ingredients. For example the mixture of bleach and vinegar is a deadly fume combination *Don't mix them together!* Do not use chlorine bleach as it will "set" the stain. Use lacquer thinner and nail polish remover (banana oil) with utmost care and never around the eyes, eyebrows, cheeks or lips.

If you should want to replace any limbs, first rub talcum powder onto the end of the limb and it will go in much easier. You can heat the limb to make it more pliable by putting it into rather hot water.

The finishing touches on the doll are clothes and make-up. The use of make-up is easier and takes a less skilled hand than painting. Since collector's dolls are for looking and not playing, the make-up works out fine.

If you have a composition that is in pretty good shape but has some hair lines running through it, then take some matte finish pancake type make-up near the same skin tone and rub a little over the enire composition area. Follow by rubbing rouge into the cheeks if it needs some.

Latex rubber or as it is sometimes called "Magic Skin" or "Live Skin" can be cleaned very gently. Here again use the talcum powder to help preserve it.

Synthetic rubber or "Magic Skin" can be washed gently. Dry well. Use the talcum powder sparingly. Use rouge and put lipstick on with a small brush.

Hard plastics may be passed up sometimes because they look "spotted". This is a finish of a wax type that the manufacturer put on the doll. Scrubbing will take it off and the doll will look fine. Use a cleaner with oil in it and go over the entire doll. About the only thing you will have to do, besides that, is to paint the lips. You may want to use a paint instead of lipstick here.

Early plastic vinyl "wept"or feels sticky. Do not try to clean them up. Just put as long of clothes on them that is necessary to hide everything but the hands and the head.

Rigid plastics are used mostly in the bodies and legs and sometimes the arms and about the only thing you can do is use a good soil remover or a powdered cleanser.

Rubber is hard to clean without damaging it. Use a little talcum powder and hope for the best. The best will only be a few short years.

Vinyl has the color already molded into it but if you have one that is faded, blend a permanent lipstick with petroleum jelly and rub it into the faded spot, using a cleansing tissue. Keep adding until you have the right color and no more will rub off. Do not over-do it. Add a little to the knees, cheeks, top of the hands and feet. Use a toothpick with a cotton tip, for applying lipstick. Do not go out of the lip-line.

Now to the clothes. If you are lucky enough to get any with the doll, look for tags stating the manufacturer's name and sometimes even the name of the doll. Most tags are sewn into the side seam but some are even found on the shoulder seam. If they did not come dressed, then dress it to suit yourself. Many collectors like to sew and make their own doll's clothes, others like to buy ready made clothes. It is what pleases you that counts. Of course, it is to your advantage to try and have an original outfit for the doll in case you ever want to sell it. It will bring a higher price dressed in an original outfit.

And a word on original. Modern dolls are not like some antique ones. They are marketed with many different outfits. You can see the same doll, in the same store, in many different outfits. So unless you know that the doll in put out with just one outfit and you go to sell it and you have her in original clothes then say that it is an original outfit.

To keep socks and booties on the doll, place rubber bands around them. Rubber will go bad with time and you may want to tie a ribbon around them instead.

With a baby doll that has had its hair pulled out or worn off, in the front, you can either pull the hair from the back over the top and put on a cap or if the hair remaining is not long enough to show, you can clip some ot the hair from the back and glue it to the head or the cap and when the glue dries put the cap on the doll's head.

A word on packing dolls away. Do not wrap them in newspaper as the vinyl will pick up the print. Most plastic and vinyl dolls are not stuffed and it will be to your advantage to remove the head and fill it either with paper towels or rags. This will help keep it from falling in or sinking in around the eyes and temples. Put the doll in a plastic bag and seal it with a string or wire. Place them in a box face down and try to see that the faces are not touching anything but are in an open space. You can put a number on the bottom of their shoe and the same number on the outside of the box and have the same number on a file card with the information of the doll written on it. Then if you should want to find a certain doll, all you have to do is find the box with the same number on it and not have to dig around in a lot of boxes. The very best way to store plastic dolls is to have a box tall enough to let them stand up, making sure the faces are not going to be crushed. *Store in a dry place where it is not too hot.*

Price Guide

The prices in this book are the retail prices of the dolls, if bought from a dealer. Prices change by demand and supply, but doll prices are fairly stable and only once in awhile do prices "shoot up" and generally this is due to a stimulated interest in a particular doll.

When I am asked "What is the value of my doll?", I always take two things into consideration. Number one is, how much sentimental value is placed on this particular doll, was it a childhood doll, a family heirloom? If so, this tends to impress the owner that the doll may be far more valuable than it really is and the truth of price may be upsetting. The second is condition.

The condition of the doll is uppermost in pricing! An all original and in excellent condition doll will bring top priced dollar where one that is damaged or without original clothes will bring less. The cost of doll repairs has soared and it is wise to judge the damage and estimate the cost repair before you buy or sell a damaged doll.

An all original means, original clothes and original wig hair. This type of doll is what the prices in this book are based on. The prices shown are top dollar prices for excellent and original dolls. If your doll is less than original, discount from the prices shown to allow for condition.

Another factor, in pricing, is size. For example, a 14" Princess Elizabeth will bring less money than 21" Princess Elizabeth, a 7½" Dionne Quint will be worth less than a 14" Dionne Quint.

No one knows your collection better than yourself and in the end you must ask yourself "Is the doll important enough, to me, to pay the asking price?" If so, you will buy it. If not, you will pass it by.

The prices shown are for dolls that are all original and in excellent condition.

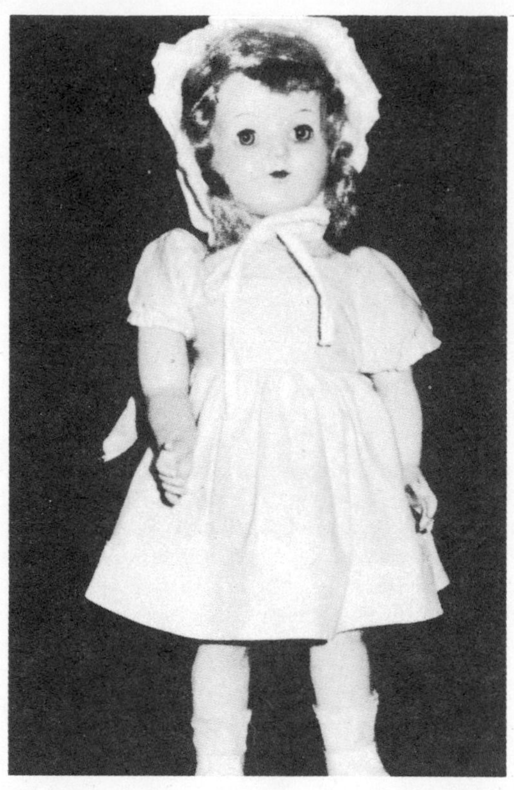

Advance Doll & Toy Co.--17½" "Wanda The Walking Wonder" All hard plastic with glued on mohair wig. Blue sleep eyes/lashes. Key wind on right side. Start and stop key on left side. Metal rollers set in metal plates on bottom of plastic shoes. As she walks head turns and arms swing back and forth. Marks: none. 1949. Original dress. This is the doll that is often called "Rita Hayworth" and was never meant to be a "star" doll by Advance Doll & Toy Co. $22.00

Alexander Doll Company

The Madame Alexander Doll Company began in 1923 with Bertha Alexander as president of the firm. Her late husband, Philip Behrman, was vice-president and treasurer. Now the vice-president is her grandson, William Birnbaum. Her daughter, Mildred Birnbaum, is research consultant.

Many Madame Alexander dolls have been "museum" pieces. The Americana Series are on permanent exhibit at the International Doll Museum in New Delhi, India and the Doll Museum of the Congressional Club, Washington D.C. Her dolls have been or are on display at the Brooklyn Childrens Museum, The Museum of Yesteryear, Florida and the Smithsonian Institution, Washington D.C.

Madame Alexander's creations specialize in characters that are not only works of art and things of beauty but also educate and create a spirit of understanding in children. Her characters have included many famous "little" people, such as Alice in Wonderland, The Little Colonel (often mistaken for Shirley Temple), Cinderella, Sleeping Beauty and so many others.

To a collector a Madame Alexander doll is a great find but I must be honest with you beginner collectors. Just because you find a doll marked "Alexander" does not mean that you will ever find out who it was meant to be. Unless the doll has original clothes or you can compare, not only the facial features but the hair style, with another doll or a picture, chances are you will never be certain. Of course, some are meant to carry on through the years, such as Elise or Cissy, who was dressed as a ballerina, a bride and had many separate wardrobes. In most cases the same doll was used for several different personalities. For example the same mold used for the Princess Elizabeth was also used for Kate Greenaway, a McGuffy Ana, Flora McFlimsy and Sleeping Beauty. Then the closed mouth, marked Princess Elizabeth is also Snow White. Another example would be the composition Margaret O'Brien, with reddish brown braids, the Ballerina, with blonde hair piled high on her head and the Alice in Wonderland, with a soft, loose hairdo. They are all from the same mold. Another one is a Scarlett O'Hara doll that was also used as Carmen Miranda and also as the Wedding Party doll, plus the Fairy Princess and the Fairy Queen. This use of the same face but with a different hairdo and clothes goes on and on, down through the years, and there is little else, in collecting dolls, that will get to you more than an Alexander doll stark naked, hair messed up and there you are trying to bring this inanimate object back to life with an identity of its own. It is then that we must realize that Madame Alexander survived and grew during a most difficult Depression and competitive period in the American industry history and that she was creating dolls for children first and collectors, second.

Alexander has made some "specials", some single personalities but not many. Sonja Henie was one, made in

1939 and came in 14", 18" and a 21" size. It was marked Madame Alexander/Sonja Henie, on the head or across the shoulders but many were unmarked with only the costume bearing a tag stating who she was. The so called "closed mouth Sonja Henie" came dressed as a bride, a WAC, etc.

There are many "famous" Alexanders, such as Jennie Walker, with puffed out cheeks, rosebud mouth and large sad looking sleep eyes. This doll had the only walker mechanism like it. There is a separate piece forming the crotch and screws joining the legs to the body. Another is Wendy Ann, in 1938, a sober wide eyed little girl with long, graceful arms and a jointed waist. She came with sleep and painted eyes, with wig and molded hair. The forerunner of the Alexander-kins was a Wendy Ann that is 9" and has the same leg design but with a slim waist that is unjointed. She came with painted eyes and dressed in round the world clothes. The most famous, to some, would have to be the Dionne Quints; Yvonne, Annette, Cecile, Emilie, and Marie Dionne born May 28, 1934 in Callender, Ontario. All the Dionne dolls are marked with the Alexander but not all of them are marked with the Dionne. The largest is a 20" cloth body baby and the smallest is a 7½" baby with painted eyes and molded hair. Toddlers came in 7½" size with painted eyes, with wigs and molded hair. The 10" baby had bent legs and molded hair. The 11" toddler came with molded hair, wigs, with sleep as well as painted eyes. The 14" toddler had sleep eyes and human hair wigs. All of these are marked Dionne/Alexander. Of the dolls released that were just marked "Alexander", there was a 14" and 15" toddler, a 17" with bent baby legs, a 19" toddler and a 13", 17" and 20" with cloth bodies. Some had wigs, others molded hair. The molded hair, on these "unmarked/marked" Dionnes, is a bit more curly than the ones marked Dionne/Alexander.

13" Little Betty, in 1935, was Alexander's "Patsy" type. She had blonde mohair over molded hair. Blue tin sleep eyes. A small "bow" mouth and a bent right arm.

There are a number of collectors that feel the dolls that are marked with an X, in a circle, are Madame Alexander dolls. I have compared and researched these dolls even to the point of finding one in the original Alexander box, I have talked to buyers for Catalog Order firms (where most X dolls are sold) and I was convinced that they ARE Alexander dolls but the Madame Alexander Doll Company does not claim these dolls and unless they do we cannot say that they are Alexanders.

Dolls are marked Mme Alexander, Alexander or Alex. Many dolls are unmarked and their original clothes will have a tag stating the name of the doll. Although I do have originally dressed dolls on which tag only says "Madame Alexander" and not the name of the doll.

The following are not all the dolls made by this company:

1935 to 1939: Dionne Quints (Also known as The Five Little Peppers, The Quints, The Five Babies 90.00 to 250.00 set), Snow White (35.00) Scarlet O'Hara (65.00), Sleeping Beauty (45.00), Kate Greenaway (50.00), Flora McFlimsey (42.00), Princess Elizabeth (35.00), McGuffey Ana (35.00), Jane Withers (90.00), Susie Q (32.00), Bobby Q (32.00), Pitty Pat (32.00), Tippie Toe (Country Cousins 32.00), Wendy Ann (16.00), Alice In Wonderland (35.00), Ballerina (35.00), Princess Alexandria (50.00), Lucy Bride (50.00), Jennie Walker (75.00), Little Colonel (75.00), Dickens Character Dolls Tiny Tim (20.00), David Copperfield (20.00), Little Nell (20.00), 9" Fairytale and Nursery Rhyme Series (16.00), The Little Genuis (16.00), Margaret O'Brien (65.00), Little Lord Fauntleroy (70.00), Doris Keane (35.00), Carmen (32.00), Mother & Me (45.00),Sonja Henie (45.00 to 60.00), Madelaine Du Bain (made exclusively for F.A.O. Schwartz Co.100.00), Neva Wet (18.00), Tweeny Twinkle (16.00), Anne Laurie (18.00), Little Shaver (20.00), Baby McGuffey (32.00)

1940: Butch McGuffey (30.00), Madelaine (Different from the Schwartz Madelaine 60.00), Little Angel (25.00), Mother & Me (45.00), Southern Belle (45.00)

1941: Sonja Henie (45.00 to 60.00), Jennie Walker (75.00), Lollie (made with LOV-LE-TEX-35.00), Baby McGuffey (Arms and legs of Lov-le-tex-35.00),

1942: Carmen Miranda (32.00), Scarlett O'Hara (65.00), McGuffey Ana (35.00), WAAC (55.00), WAVE (55.00), WAAF (65.00), Sonja Henie (45.00 to 60.00), Mother & Me (45.00), Jennie Walker (75.00), Butch McGuffey (30.00), Baby McGuffey (35.00), Country Cousins (32.00), Fairy Princess (45.00), Southern Girl (45.00), Kate Greenaway (50.00), Bride (45.00), Baby Genuis (16.00), So-Lite Dolls (16.00), Special Girl (45.00), Sleeping Baby (50.00)

1943: Jennie Walker (75.00), Fairy Princess (45.00), Southern Girl (45.00), Kate Greenaway (50.00), Carmen Miranda (32.00), Bride (45.00), Baby Genuis (16.00), So-Lite Dolls (16.00), Special Girl (45.00), Sonja Henie (45.00 to 60.00), Mother & Me (45.00), Butch McGuffey (30.00), Baby McGuffey (35.00), Country Cousins (32.00), McGuffey Ana (35.00)

1945: The Wedding Party (40.00 each), Judy (60.00)

1946: Bride (45.00), Margaret O'Brien (65.00), Bridesmaid (40.00), Ballerina (45.00), Alice In Wonderland (30.00)

1947: Fairy Queen (40.00), Little Women (First in hard plastic-25.00 each),

1948: Babs (The ice skating girl-30.00),

1949: Nina Ballerina (20.00), Polly Pigtails (25.00), Sleeping Beauty (30.00), Mary Martin (50.00)

1950: Cinderella (18.00), Wendy Ann (16.00), Baby Genuis (16.00), Mary Martin (50.00), Barbara Jane (40.00)

1951: Slumbermate (32.00), Bunny Soft (32.00), Clarabelle (The Clown-18.00), Alice (45.00), Maggie (35.00), Portrait Group (115.00 each), Violet (30.00), Little Women (18.00 each), Sonja Henie (Hard plastic-40.00), Penny (22.00), Christening Baby (18.00), Sunbeam (32.00), Bonnie (32.00), Bitsy (32.00), Honeybun (18.00), Kathy (38.00), Nina Ballerina (22.00), Wendy Bride (30.00), Rosamund-Bridesmaid(36.00)

1952: Rosebud (32.00), McGuffey Ana (18.00), Baby Genuis (16.00), Winnie Walker (30.00), Tommy Bangs and Stuffy (32.00), Re-issued Flora McFlimsey (25.00), Maggie (25.00), Violet (Plastic 25.00), Annabelle (35.00 to 50.00)

1953: Coronation Elizabeth (40.00), Prince Philip (45.00), Ruffles (The clown-32.00), Alexander-kin Line (15.00 each), Rosebud (32.00), Cry Dolly (18.00), Bud (30.00), McGuffey Ana (18.00), Binnie Walker (20.00), Quiz Kids (40.00), Bride (18.00), Story Princess (25.00), Lady Churchill (60.00), Kathy (16.00), Bible Character (20.00 each), Flower Girl (18.00), Snow Baby (45.00), Christening Baby (20.00), Mary Ellen (25.00), Bonnie (20.00), Cry Dolly (18.00), Rosebud (32.00), Violet (25.00), Glamour Dolls: Queen Elizabeth, Edwardian Period, Blue Danube, Garden Party, Dressed For The Opera, Godey Period, Victorian Period (110.00 each), Ballerina (32.00)
1954: Sweet Violet (28.00), Guardian Angel (18.00), Active Miss (28.00), 100 Years Of Fashion Series (110.00 each), Mary Ellen (25.00), Bonnie (20.00),
1955: Dumplin' (18.00), Nickey (30.00), Cissy (15.00), Cynthia (60.00), Romeo & Juliet (60.00 set), Cissette (12.00), Kathy (16.00), Binnie Walker (25.00), Story Princess (35.00), McGuffey Ane (28.00), Little Women (15.00 each)
1956: Melinda (35.00), Alexandria (45.00)
1957: Kathy (16.00), Lissey (15.00), Robin (25.00), Elise (20.00), Princess Anne (18.00), Bonnie Prince Charles (20.00), Hansel (16.00), Gretel (16.00), Kathy Cry Dolly (18.00), A Little Women Group of 11" size (20.00 each)
1958: Cuddles (12.00), Marybel (15.00), Edith (The Lonely Doll-25.00), Shari Lewis (50.00), New Little Genuis :(16.00), Kathy (16.00), Kelly (18.00)
1959: Kathleen (18.00), Sleeping Beauty (15.00), Kathy Tears (18.00), Little Women (15.00 each)
1960: Jacqueline (also known as Judy-30.00), Baby Dimples (12.00), Queen (20.00), Timmie Toddler (18.00), Joanie (15.00), Little Cherub (10.00), Genuis Baby (10.00), Maggie Mixup (35.00), Kathy Tears (18.00)
1961: Bobby (30.00), Lamkin (16.00), Mimi (45.00), Margot (35.00), Kitten (12.00), Chatterbox (48.00), Margot Ballerina (28.00), Caroline (28.00), Portrait Doll: Scarlett, Melanie, Renoir, Bride, Jenny Lind, Godey (105.00 each), Pollyanna (25.00), Mary Sunshine (25.00), Madelaine (30.00),
1962: Sweetie (16.00), Hello Baby (18.00), Smarty (22.00), Queen Of The May (25.00), Bunny (22.00), Melinda (30.00), Kathy (16.00), Kathy Tears (18.00), Dearest (22.00), Lively Kitten (18.00), Sweetie Baby (16.00), Sweetie Walker (32.00), Portrait Of Queen Elizabeth II (105.00), Bo Peep (15.00), Red Riding Hood (15.00), Little Women (15.00), International Series (15.00), Pamela (15.00), Little Genuis (10.00), Cissette (12.00)
1963: Little Shaver (10.00), Huggums (10.00), Quintie (20.00), Big Huggums (18.00), Laurie (Little Men 30.00), Wendy (12.00)
1964: Sugar Darlin' (Cloth body 16.00), Petti Toots (10.00), Alexander Rag Time Dolls (30.00 each), Funny (10.00), Jama Baby (15.00), Brenda Starr (20.00), Janie (16.00)
1965: Pussy Cat (12.00), Scarlet O'Hara (32.00), Orphan Annie (34.00), Baby Ellen (15.00), Leslie (25.00), Puddin' (12.00), Alice In Wonderland (18.00), Polly (15.00), Sugar Darlin' (All vinyl-16.00), Fairyland Dolls (15.00 each), Sweet Tears (16.00)
1966: Sound of Music Dolls (20.00 each), International Series (15.00 each), Leslie (25.00), Polly (15.00), Alice in Wonderland (18.00), Sweet Tears (16.00), Formal Elise (40.00), Muffin (10.00), Patchity Pam (10.00), Patchity Pepper (10.00), Portrait Series: Madame Doll, Godey, Melanie, Lissy, Scarlett, Renoir (90.00 each), Good Little Girl (15.00), Bad Little Girl (15.00), Butch (15.00), Bitsy (15.00), Janie (20.00), Gidget (35.00), Little Granny (30.00), Coco (45.00)
1967: Kitten (10.00), Kitten Kries (12.00), Rusty (15.00), Marlo Thomas (40.00), Carrot Top (18.00), Portrait Series: Scarlett, Renoir, Southern Belle, Godey, Melanie, Agatha (90.00 each), Portrait Children (25.00 each), Little Women (15.00), Laurie (30.00), Sweet Tears (16.00), Nancy Drew (40.00), Pumpkin (12.00), Riley's Little Annie (25.00)
1968: Americana Dolls (15.00 each), Gone With The Wind (Scarlett O'Hara-35.00), Cinderella (20.00), So Big (16.00), Portrettes (20.00 each), Rebecca (20.00)
1969: Puddin' (12.00), Mary Cassett Baby (15.00), Victoria (15.00), Heidi (20.00), Rozy (10.00), Peter Pan Group (18.00 each)
1970 Suzy (18.00), Heidi (20.00), Pumpkin (12.00), Happy (20.00), Lucinda (35.00), Grandma Jane (35.00), Jenny Lind and Her Listening Cat (25.00), Degas Portrait Child (20.00)
1971: Sleeping Beauty (15.00), Snow White (15.00), Formal Cinderella (18.00), Poor Cinderella (15.00), Baby McGuffey (12.00), Smiley (16.00), Red Boy (15.00), Blue Boy (18.00)

INTERNATIONAL DOLLS (15.00 each)

German	India
English Guard	Hungarian
African	Tyrolean Boy
Thailand	Tyrolean Girl
China	Irish
Israeli	Spanish Boy
Greek	Spanish Girl
Peruvian Boy	Polish
Argentine Boy	Bolivia
Argentine Girl	Equador
Brazil	French
Russian	Dutch
Mexican	Swedish
Dutch Boy	Italian
Scottish	Swiss

AMERICANA DOLLS (15.00 each)

Hiawatha	Amish Girl
Scarlett	Amish Boy
Cowboy	Eskimo
Cowgirl	Priscilla
Miss USA	Indian Boy
Pocahantas	Indian Girl
Hawaiian	Bride
Betsy Ross	Ballerina

SOUND OF MUSIC (20.00 each)

Liesl	Marta
Frederich	Louisa
Brigitta	Maria
Gretl	

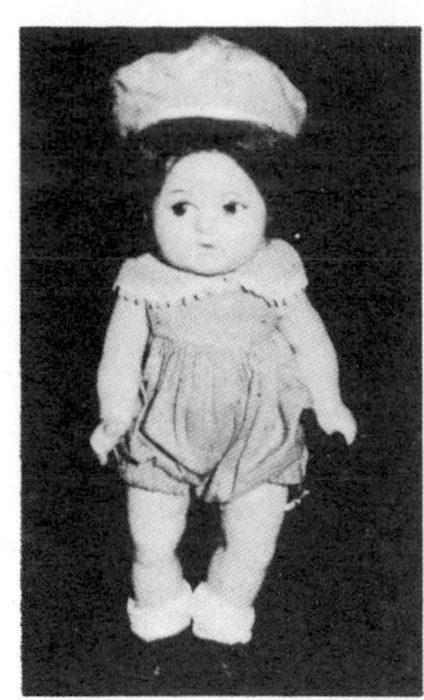

Alexander--7" "Dionne Quint" All composition with glued on human hair wig. Painted side glancing eyes. Toddler legs. Marks: Dionne/Alexander, on head. Tag: Dionne Quint. Alexander, on back. Original clothes. 1937. $22.00 (Courtesy Fye Collection)

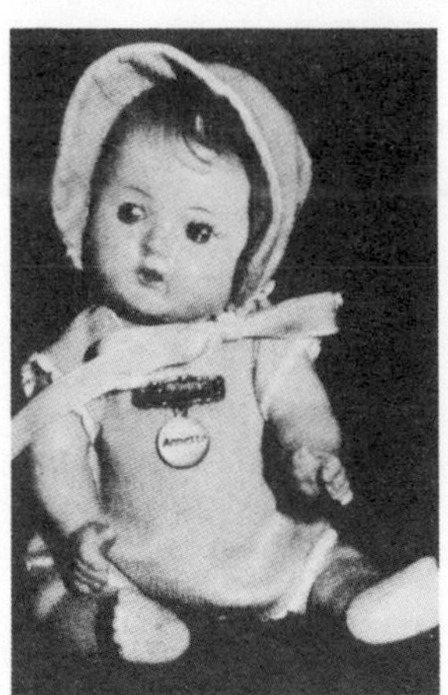

Alexander--7" "Dionne Quints" All composition with molded painted brown hair. Painted side glancing brown eyes. Marks: Alexander on head Tags: Dionne Quint Doll. Original clothes. 1936. $125.00 per set. (Courtesy Allin's Collection)

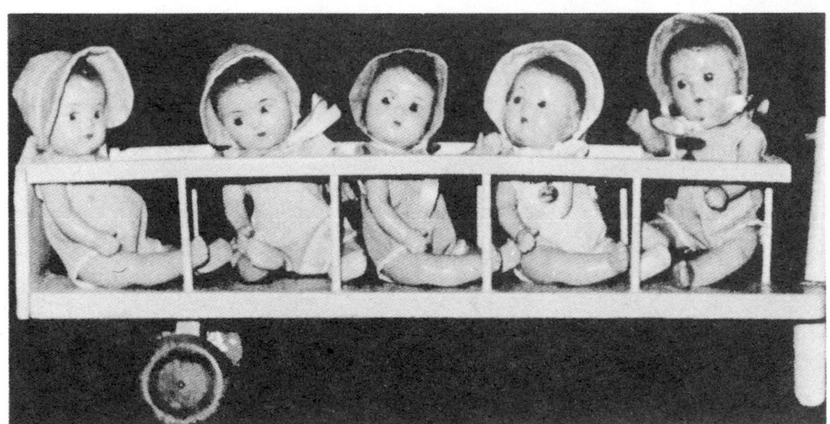

Dionne Quintuplets, left to right, Yvonne, Annette, Cecile, Emilie and Marie shown with their one childhood friend: Dr. Defoe.

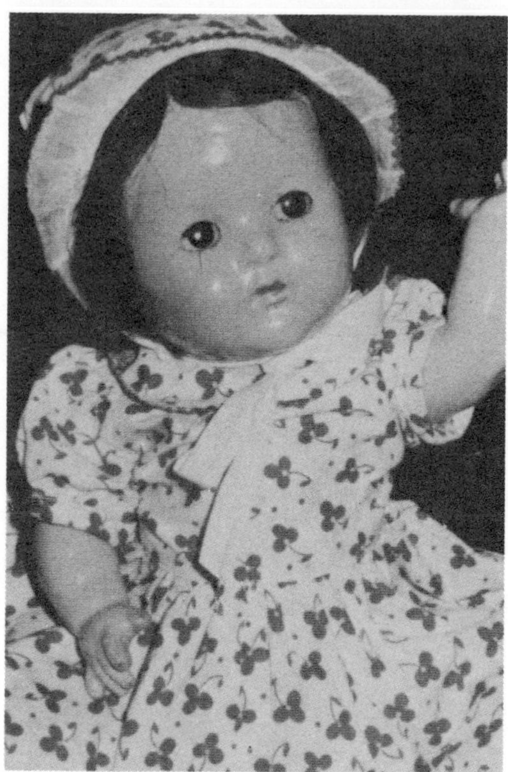

Alexander--14" "Dionne Quint Toddler" All composition with glued on brown human hair wig. Brown sleep eyes/lashes. Closed mouth. 2nd and 3rd fingers curled. Marks: Alexander on head and body. 1937. $35.00.

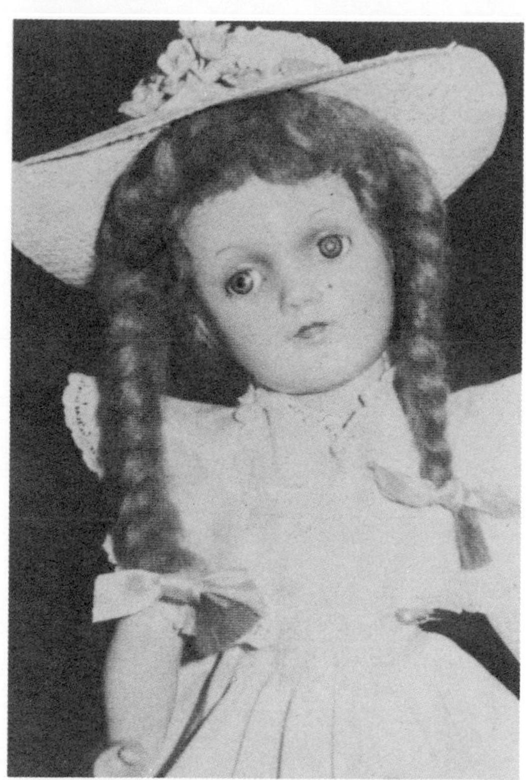

Alexander--14" "McGuffey Ana" All composition with red/brown glued on mohair wig. Brown tin sleep eyes/lashes. Black eye shadow. Very light cheek dimples. Marks: none. 1937. $35.00.

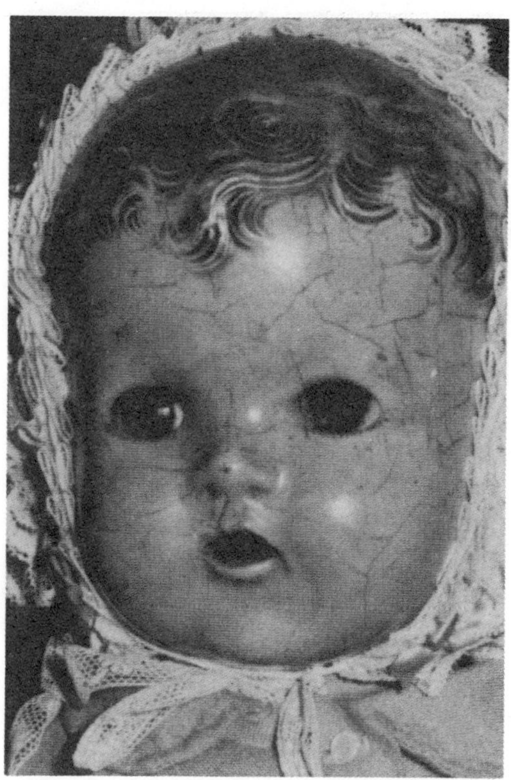

Alexander--24" "Princess Alexandria" Cloth body. Composition arms, legs and head. Molded hair. Brown sleep eyes/lashes. Open mouth with four teeth. Straight legs. Marks: none. 1938. $50.00. (Courtesy Earlene Johnston)

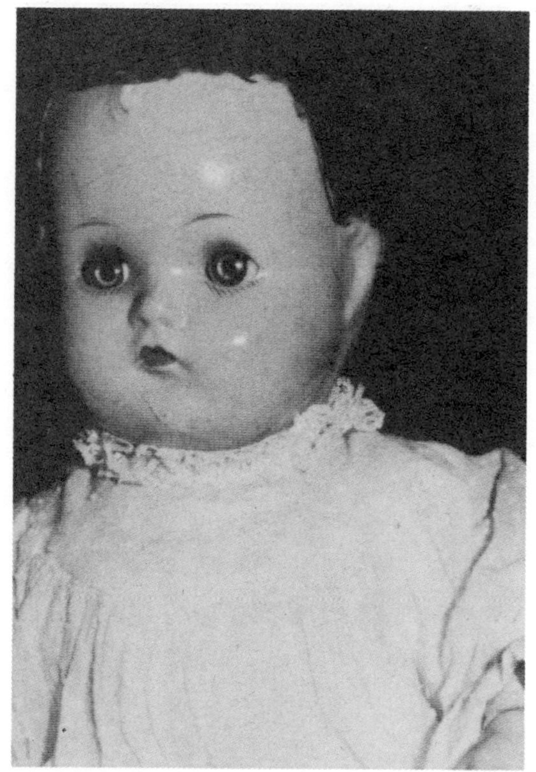

Alexander--15" "Butch" Cloth body with composition arms, legs and head. Blue sleep eyes/lashes. Eye shadow. Cloth upper arms with gauntlet hands. Marks: Alexander, on head. 1939. $30.00.

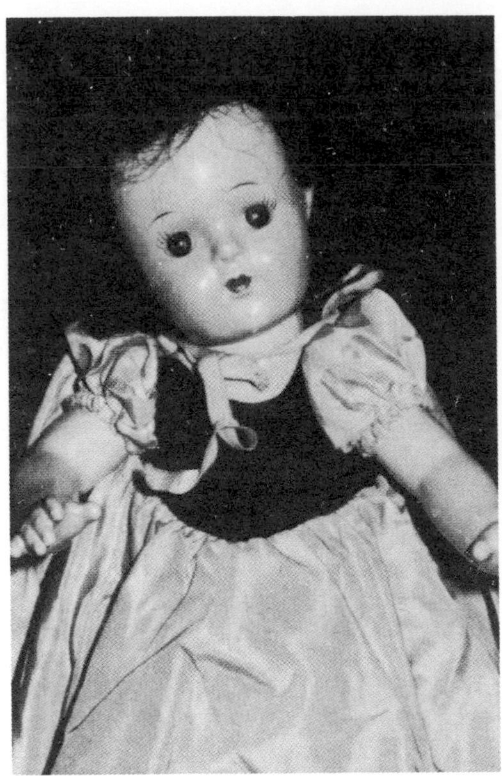

Alexander--16" "Snow White" All composition with glued on black human hair wig. Green sleep eyes. Closed mouth. Marks: Princess Elizabeth/ Alexander Doll Co., on head. 1939. $35.00 (Courtesy Allin's Collection)

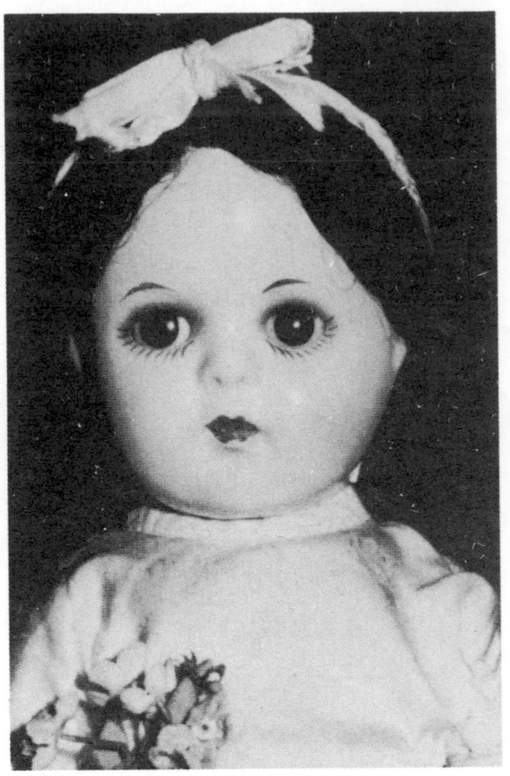

Alexander--13" "Snow White" All composition with glued on black mohair wig. Brown sleep eyes/lashes. Marks: Princess Elizabeth/Alexander, on head. 1939. $35.00.

Alexander--15" "Princess Elizabeth" All composition with glued on human hair wig. Blue sleep eyes/lashes. Open mouth with 4 teeth that are individually spaced. 2nd and 3rd fingers molded together. Hazy eye shadow. Marks: Princess Elizabeth/Alexander Doll Co., on head. 1939. $35.00

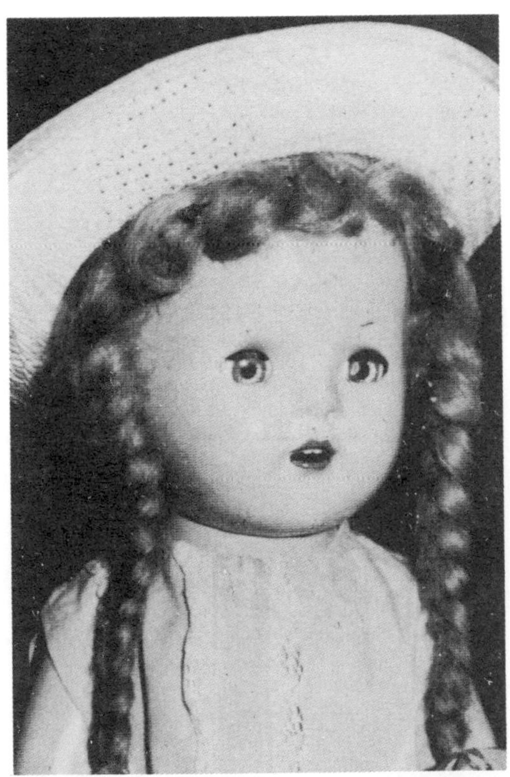

Alexander--15" "McGuffy Ana" All composition with glued on blonde human hair wig. Blue sleep eyes/lashes. Open mouth with four teeth. Marks: Princess Elizabeth /Madame Alexander Doll Co. 1939. $35.00.

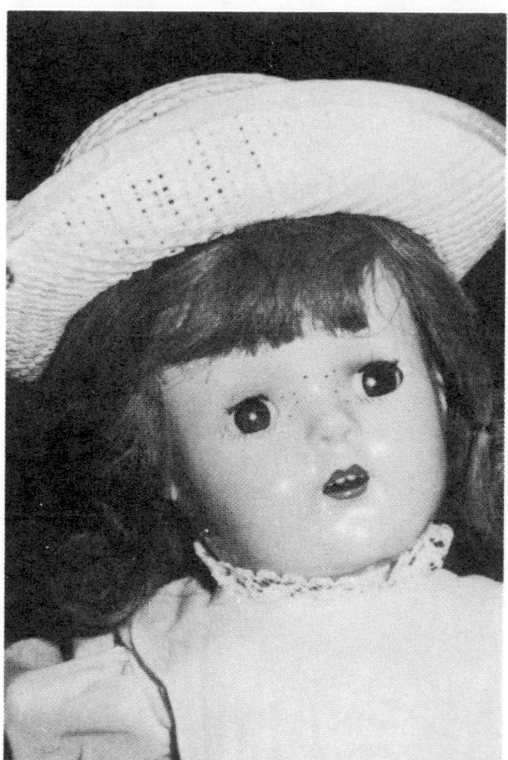

Alexander--16" "Flora McFlimsy" of Madison Square. All composition with glued on blonde human hair wig. Brown sleep eyes/lashes. Freckles across nose. Open mouth with four teeth. Marks: Princess Elizabeth/Alexander Doll Co., on head. 1939. $42.00.

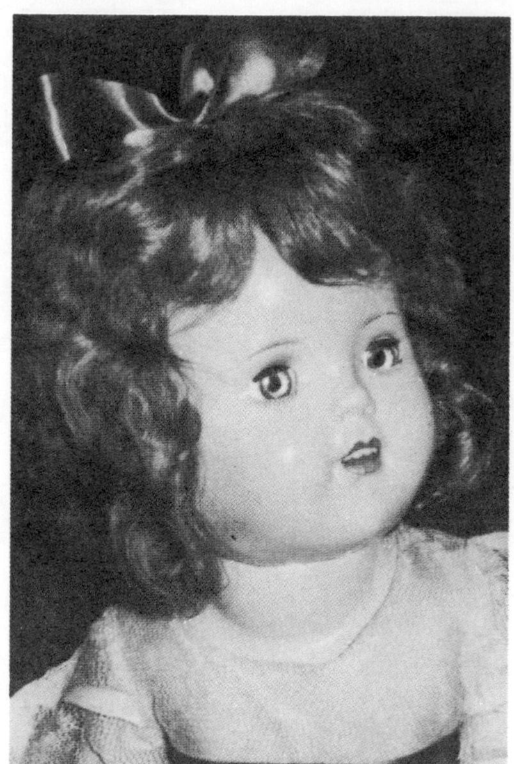

Alexander--24" "Kate Greenaway" All composition with golden red glued on mohair wig. Blue sleep eyes/lashes. Open mouth with four teeth. Original dress. Marks: Princess Elizabeth/ Alexander Doll Co., on head. Dress Tag: Madame Alexander. 1939. $50.00.

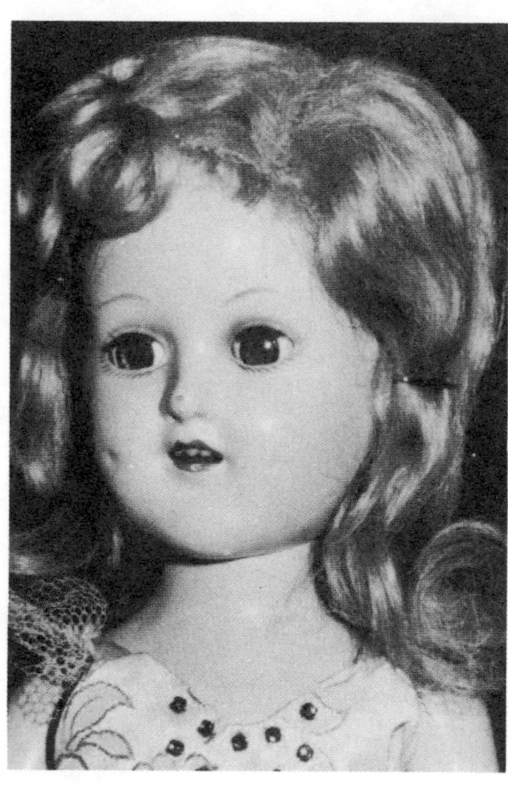

Alexander--14" "Sonja Henie" All composition with blonde mohair wig. Brown sleep eyes/lashes. Dimples. Open mouth with four teeth. Marks: Madame Alexander/Sonja/Henie on head. 1941. $45.00.

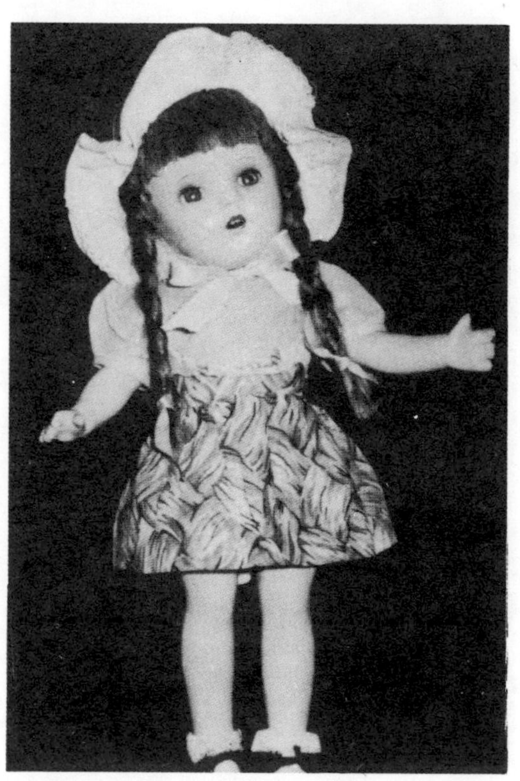

Alexander--13" "McGuffey Ana" All composition with glued on dark blonde wig. Blue sleep eyes/lashes. Open mouth with four teeth and felt tongue. Built on Ideal's Shirley Temple Body after molds were sold to Alexander Doll Company in 1941. Marks: A Circle/X, on head. A faint Shirley Temple over 13, on back. 1942. $35.

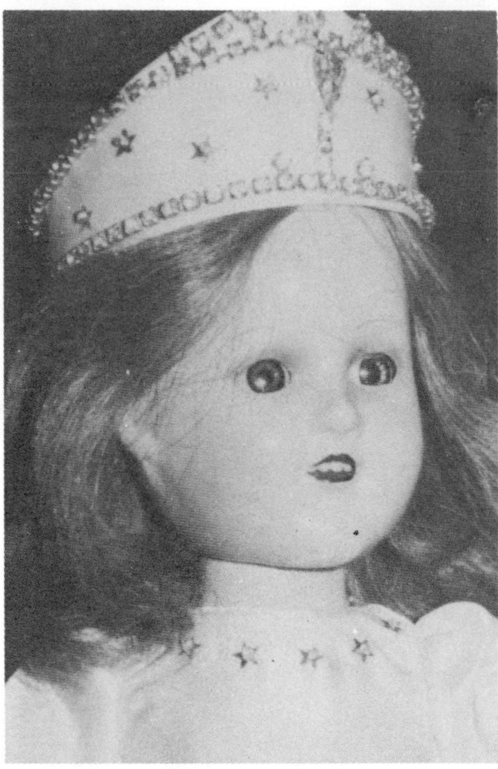

Alexander--14" "Sonja Henie" All composition with glued on human hair wig. Brown sleep eyes/lashes. Open mouth with four teeth.

Sonja Henie in one of her many, many beautiful skating costumes.

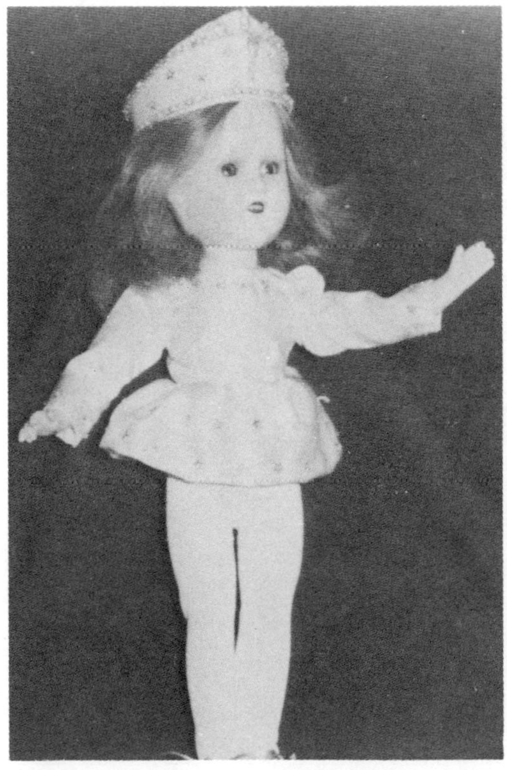

Dimples. Marks: Madame Alexander/Sonja/ Henie, on head. 1941. $45.00. (Courtesy Allin's Collection)

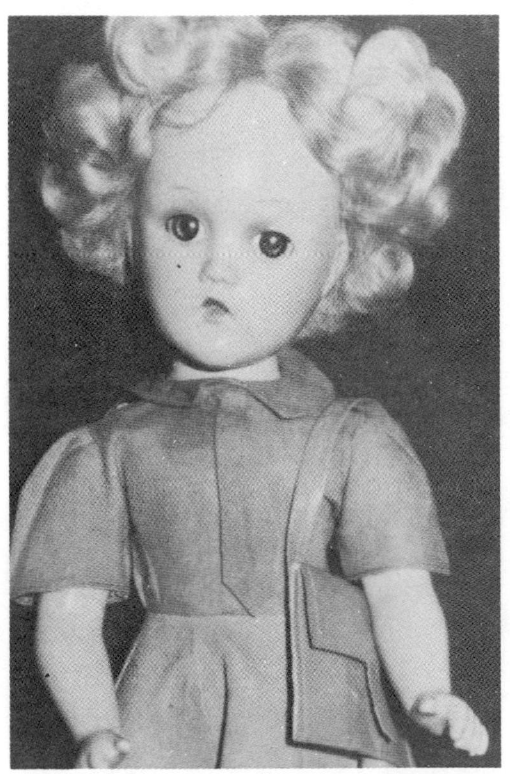

Alexander--14" "WAAC" All composition with glued on blonde mohair wig. Brown sleep eyes/lashes. Black eye shadow. Closed mouth. Marks: Mme. Alexander on head. Tag: WAAC/Madame Alexander/New York/All rights reserved. Original clothes. 1942. $55.00

Alexander--14" "Scarlett O'Hara" All composition with glued on black wig. Sleep eyes/lashes. Closed mouth. Original clothes. Marks: Mme Alexander on head. Dress Tag: Madame Alexander/New York USA. 1942. $65.00.

Alexander--14" "Margaret O'Brien" All composition with glued on replaced wig. Green eyes/lashes. Marks: Alexander, on head. 1946. $65.00. (Courtesy Allin's Collection)

Alexander--15" "Baby Genuis" Cloth body. Early vinyl arms and legs. Hard plastic head with molded hair. Big blue sleep eyes/lashes. Marks: Alexander, on head. 1950. $16.00

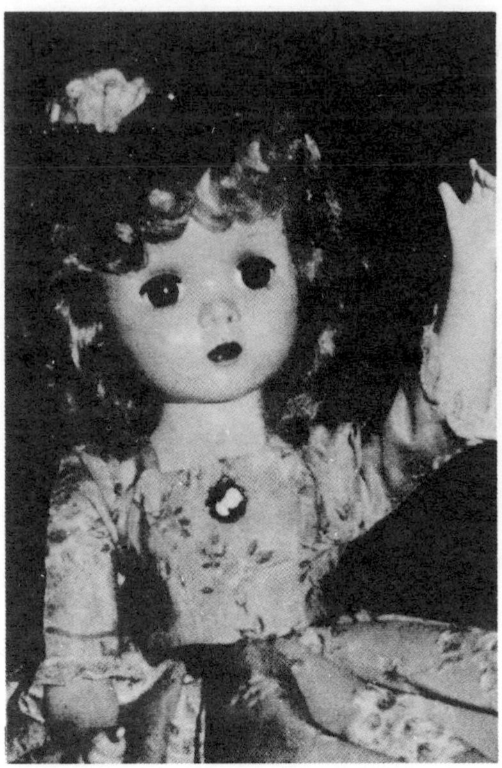

Alexander--17" "Kathy" All hard plastic with glued on blonde wig. Brown sleep eyes/lashes. Feathered eyelashes at lower corner of eyes. 2nd and 3rd fingers molded together. Marks: none. Dress Tag: Madame Alexander. 1951. $38.00.

Alexander--18" "Alice" All hard plastic with glued on red wig. Large blue sleep eyes/heavy lashes. 2nd and 3rd fingers molded together. Marks: None. 1951. $45.00. (Courtesy Dorothy Westbrook)

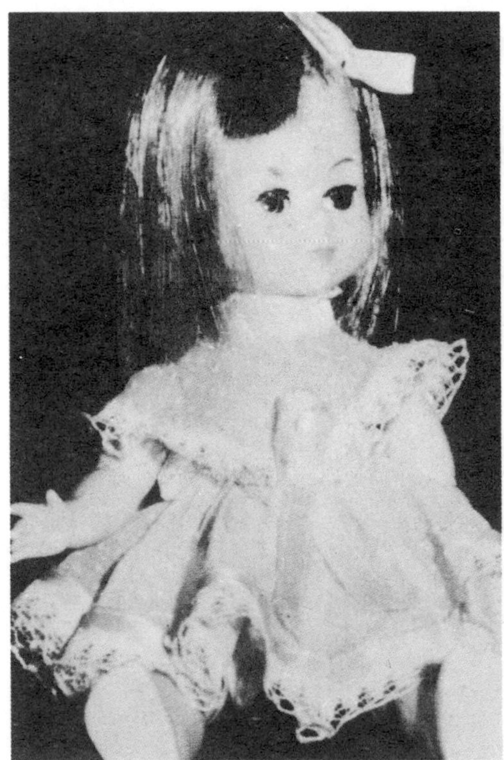

Alexander--7½" "Maggie Mixup" All hard plastic with jointed knees. Glued on red hair. Blue sleep eyes/molded lashes. Freckles. 2nd and 3rd fingers molded together. Marks: Alex., on back. 1952. $25.00.

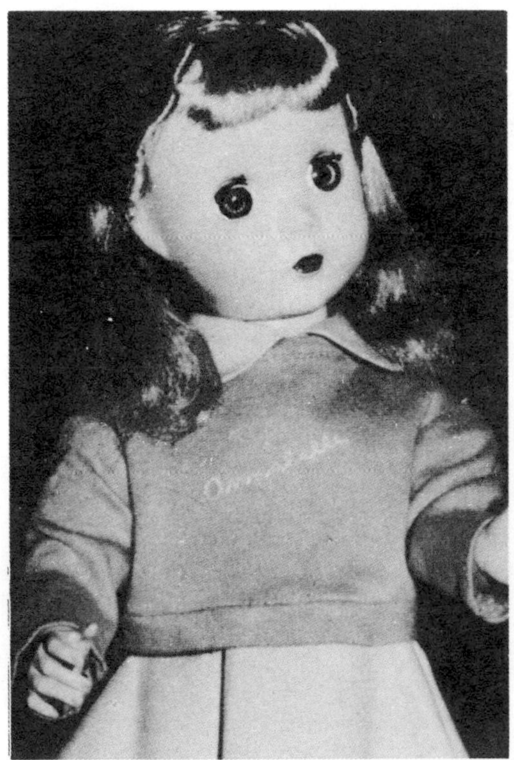

Alexander--20" "Kate Smith's Annabelle" All hard plastic with glued on blonde wig. Large round blue sleep eyes/lashes. Closed mouth. Right 2nd and 3rd fingers curled and molded together. Left 2nd and 3rd slightly curled and separated. Marks: none. (Some are marked "Alex".) Dress Tag; Kate Smith's Annabelle/By Madame Alexander. 1952. $50.00.

Alexander--14" & 20" "Annabelles" All hard plastic. Character taken from Storybook quarter hour of Storytime on TV show by Kate Smith. 1952. Doll was dressed in several different pastel color dresses, with sweaters of contrasting color such as a pink dress/blue sweater, a blue dress/Red sweater. Marks: Some Alex, on head. Others unmarked. (Photo and Information Courtesy Mrs. E. Goldsworthy)

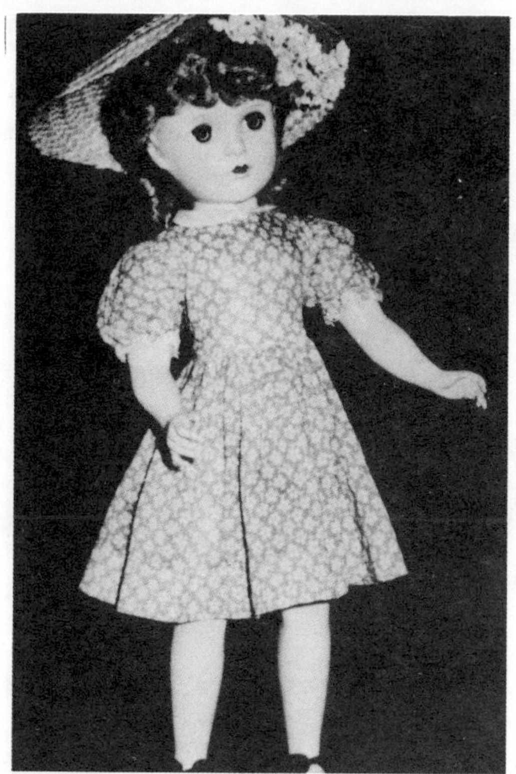

Alexander--17½" "McGuffey Ana" All hard plastic with blonde mohair wig in ponytails. Blue sleep eyes/lashes. Closed mouth. Ball jointed arms and legs. Both 2nd and 3rd fingers molded together. Marks: Alexander, on head. This dress belongs to the composition "McGuffey Ana". 1952. $18.00.

Alexander--9" "Cissette" All hard plastic with glued on red wig. Blue sleep eyes/molded lashes. Jointed knees. High heel feet. Marks: Mme. Alexander, on back. Tag: Cissette/Madame Alexander. 1955. Original clothes. $12.00. (Courtesy of Earlene Johnston Collection)

Alexander--22" "Dumplin Baby" Cloth body with vinyl arms and legs. Hard plastic head with glued on blonde mohair wig. Blue sleep eyes/lashes. Marks: Alexander, on head. 1955. (Replaced on composition and cloth body). $18.00.

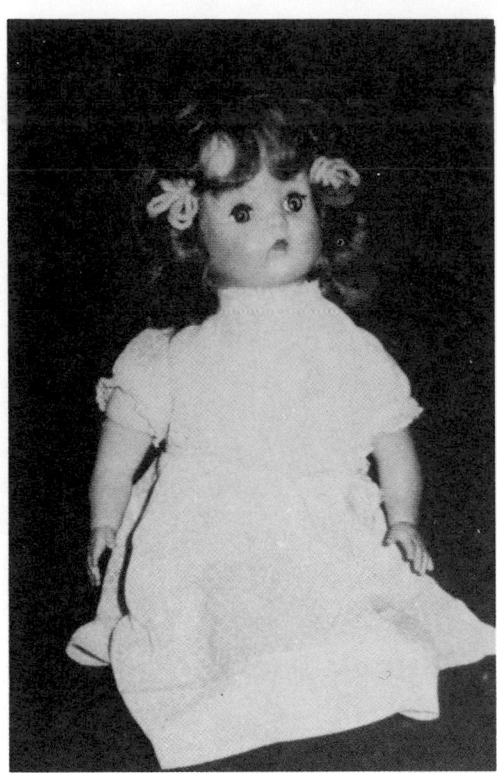

Alexander--17" "Rosebud" Cloth body. Vinyl arms, legs and head. Glued on red dynel wig. Blue sleep eyes/lashes. Closed mouth. Marks: Alexander, on head. 1953. $32.00. (Identity Courtesy Jane Thomas)

Alexander--16" "Cry Dolly" All vinyl with molded hair. Blue sleep eyes/lashes. Open mouth/nurser. Open hands facing body. Individual molded large toes. Marks: Alexander, on head. 1953. Same doll was Kathy in 1954, 1955 and 1956. Was Kathy Cry Dolly in 1957. $18.00. (Information Courtesy Jane Thomas)

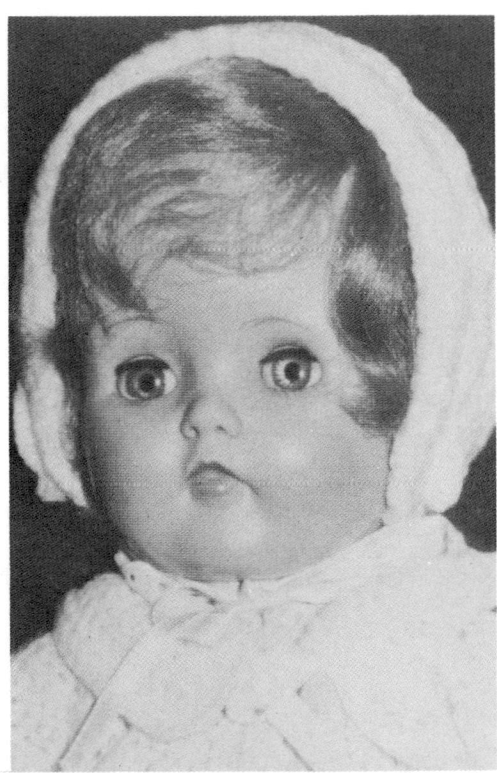

Alexander--19" "Bonnie" Stuffed one piece vinyl body and legs. Vinyl arms and head with rooted blonde hair. Blue sleep eyes/lashes. Open/closed mouth. Marks: Alexander, on head. 1954. $20.00. (Identity Courtesy Jane Thomas)

Alexander--19½" "Cissy" All hard plastic with vinyl covered arms. Jointed at neck, shoulders, elbows, hips and knees. Very high heel feet. Rooted blonde hair. Blue sleep eyes/lashes. Marks: Alexander, on head. 1955. $15.00.

Alexander--11" "Marme" All hard plastic with glued on brown hair. Blue sleep eyes/molded lashes. 2nd and 3rd fingers molded together. Dress Tag: Marme/By Madame Alexander. 1957. $20.00. (Courtesy Allin's Collection)

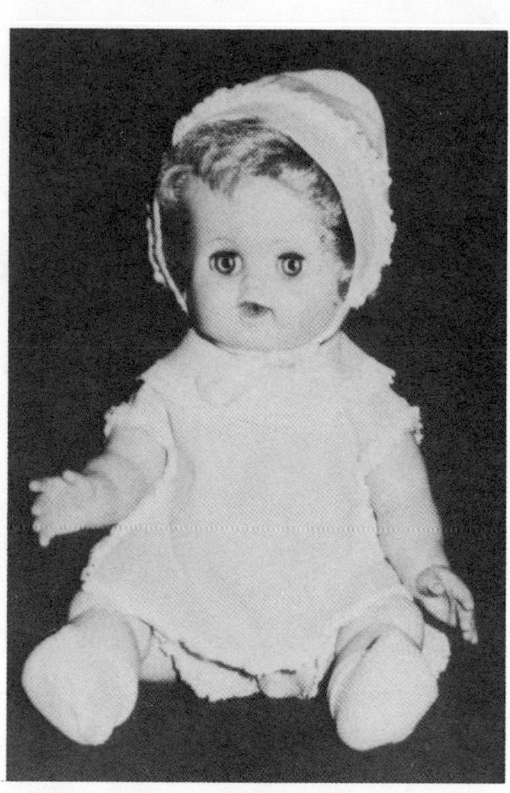

Alexander--14" "Kathy Cry Dolly" All vinyl with rooted dark blonde hair. Blue sleep eyes/lashes. Arms molded out. Seperate large toes. Open mouth/nurser with tube showing in mouth. Marks: Alexander, on head. 1957. $18.00.

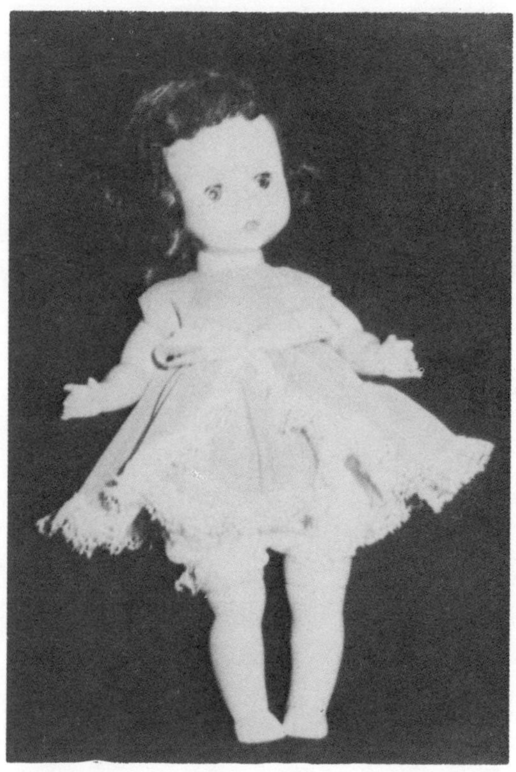

Alexander--8" "Princess Ann" All hard plastic with brown glued on wig. Blue sleep eyes. Jointed knees. Marks: Alex., on body 1957. $18.00.

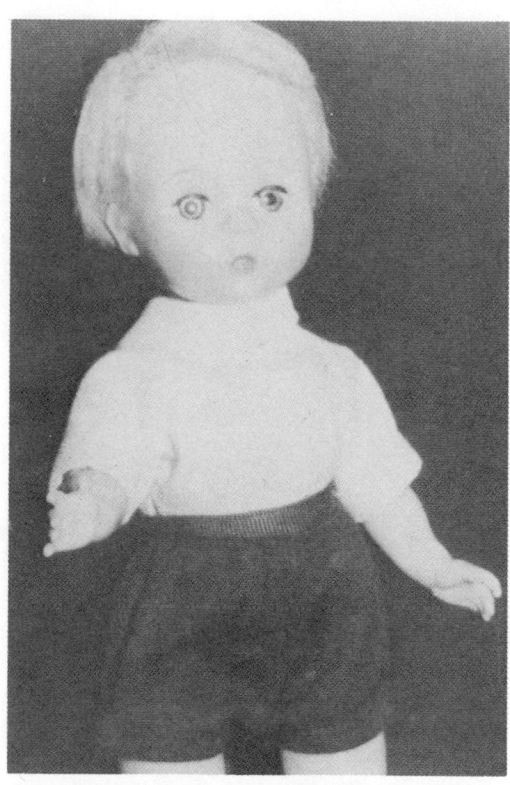

Alexander--8" "Bonnie Prince Charles" All hard plastic with glued on blonde hair. Blue sleep eyes/molded lashes. Jointed knees walker. Original clothes, minus jacket. Marks: Alex, on back Tag: Alexander-Kins/By Madame Alexander. 1957. $20.00

Alexander--15" "Elise" All hard plastic with vinyl over-sleeved arms. Glued on honey blonde hair. Blue sleep eyes/lashes. Jointed shoulders, elbows, hips, knees and ankles. Pierced ears. Marks: Alexander, on head. 1957. Original clothes. $20.00

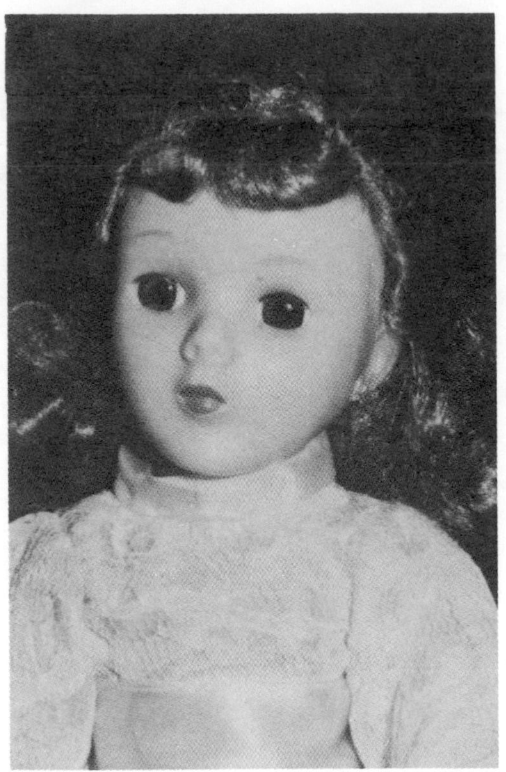

Alexander--13" "Shari Lewis" Rigid vinyl body and legs. Soft vinyl arms and head. Brown glued on wig. Green sleep eyes/lashes. Marks: 1958/Alexander, on head. $50.00. (Courtesy Allin's Collection)

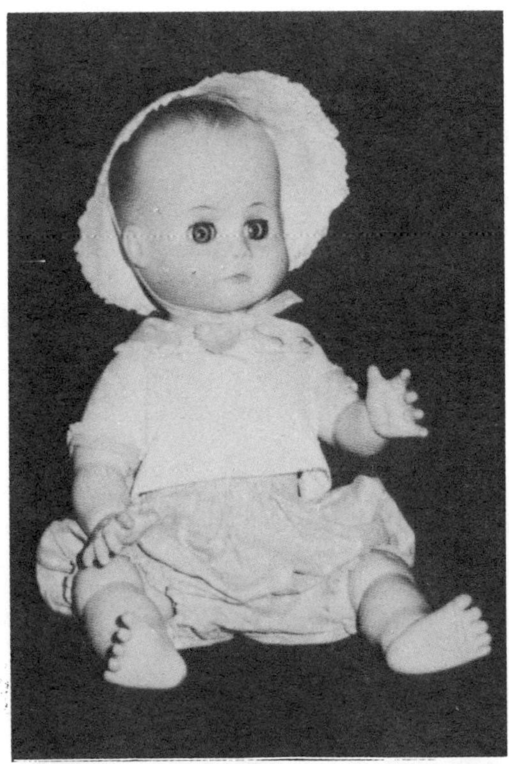

Alexander--16" "Kathy" All vinyl with molded and painted brown hair. Sleep aquamarine eyes/lashes. Open mouth/nurser. Individually molded toes. Marks: Mme (1958) Alexander, in circle on head. Tag On Clothes: Kathy Madame Alexander. Original clothes. $16.00.

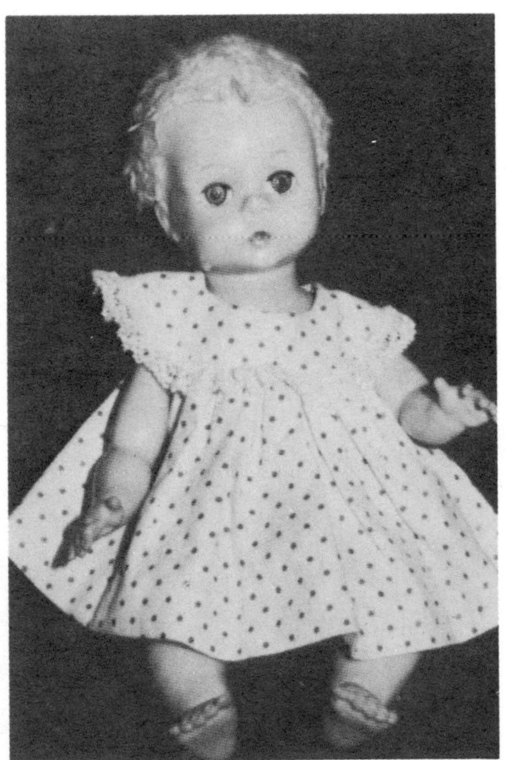

Alexander--7" "Little Genuis" Vinyl body, arms and legs. Hard plastic head. Yellow caracul hair glued on. Blue sleep eyes/molded lashes. Open mouth/dry nurser. Marks: none. Tag: Little Genuis/Madame Alexander. 1958. Original clothes. $16.00. (Courtesy Earlene Johnston Collection)

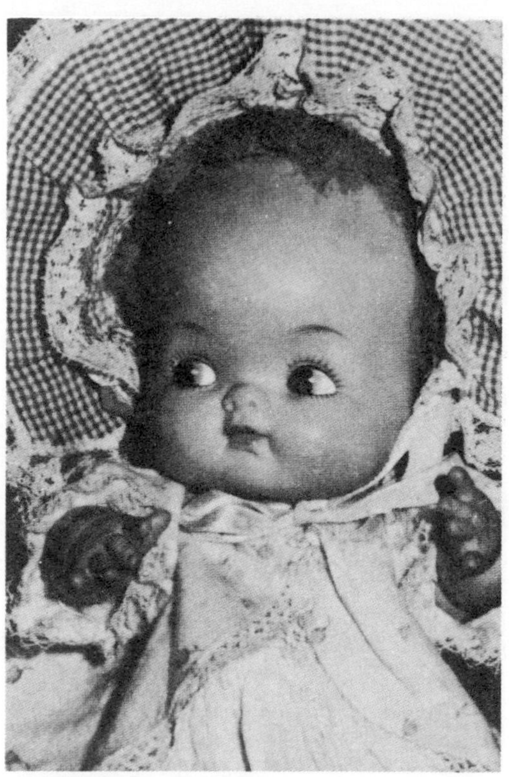

Alexander--10" "Little Shaver" All vinyl with rooted blonde hair. Painted side glancing eyes. Marks: Mme/Alexander, in circle on head and back. Doll is strung. 1963. $16.00. (Courtesy Allin's Collection)

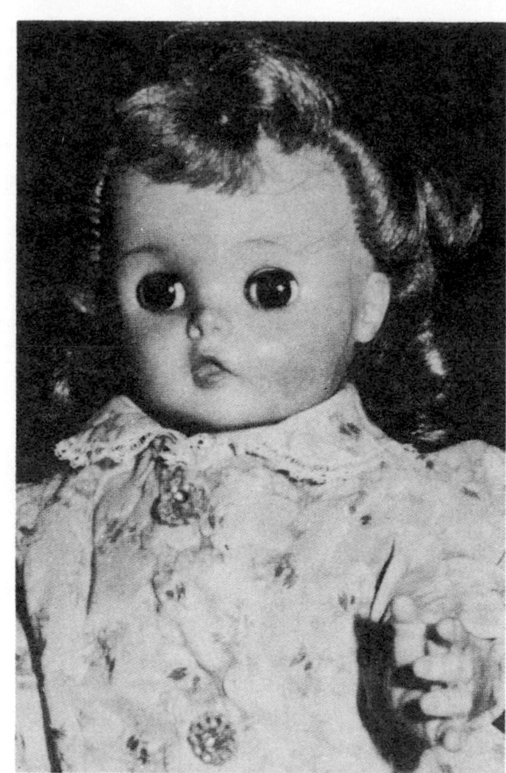

Alexander--15" "Marybel, The Doll That Gets Well" Rigid vinyl body, arms and legs. Vinyl head with rooted blonde hair. Brown sleep eyes/lashes. Open/closed mouth. Jointed waist. Marks: Mme Alexander, in a circle. 19 upside down 2-5 underneath. 1958. Also same doll used as Edith, Lonel Doll and Pollyanna. $15.00.

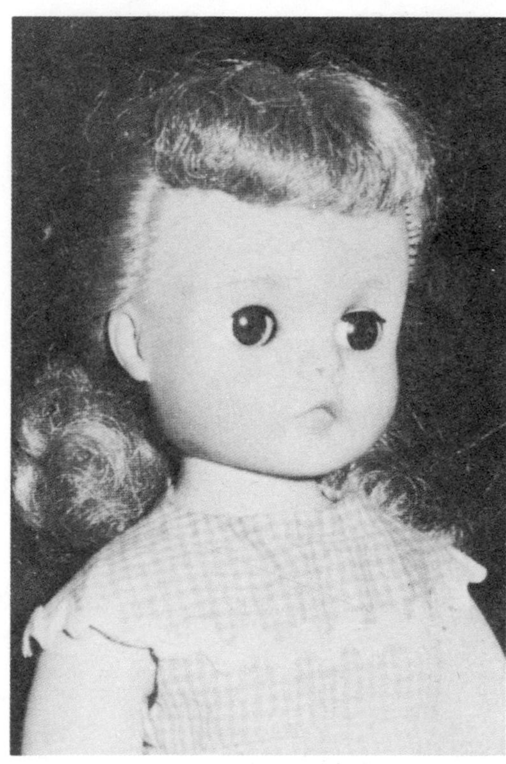

Alexander--15" "Edith, The Lonel Doll" All rigid vinyl with jointed waist. Came with brown and blue sleep eyes. Slightly open/closed mouth. Hair pulled into ponytail. Same doll as Marybel. Marks: Mme Alexander, in a circle, 1958 underneath. $25.00.

Alexander--15" "Kathy Tears" All vinyl. Rooted blonde hair. Blue sleep eyes/lashes. Marks: Alexander/1960, on head. Open mouth/nurser. Cries tears. $18.00.

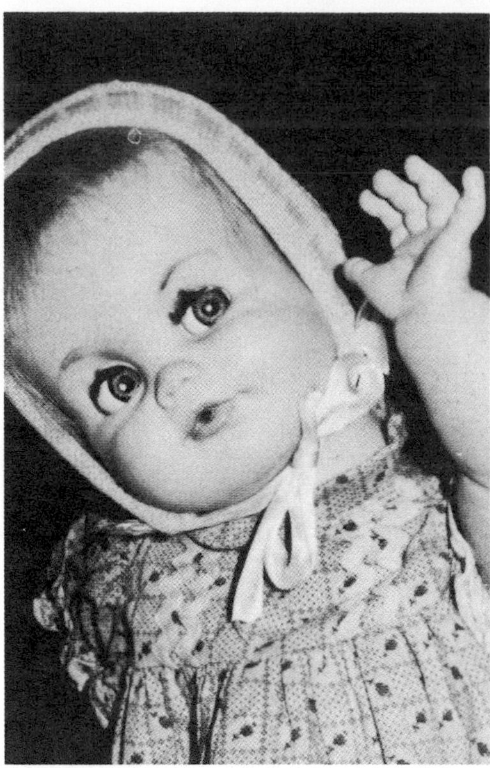

Alexander--19" "Genius Baby" Plastic body with vinyl, ball jointed arms, legs and head. Rooted blonde hair. Blue flirty sleep eyes/lashes. Open mouth nurser. Same head as used for Timmie Toddler. Marks: Alexander Doll/1960. $10.00.

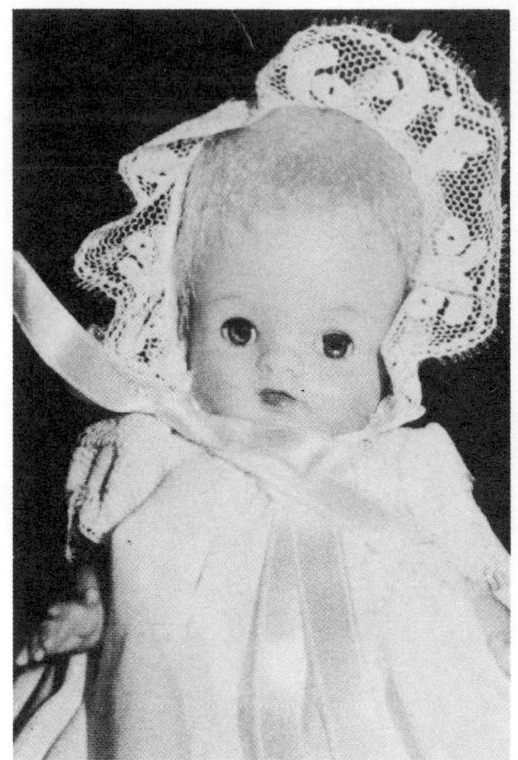

Alexander--7" "Little Cherub" All vinyl with rooted white hair. Blue sleep eyes/molded lashes. Closed mouth. Bent baby legs. Marks: Alexander, on head. 1960. Also came with molded hair. Original clothes. $10.00. (Courtesy Allin's Collection)

Alexander--9½" "Queen" All hard plastic with glued on dylon wig. Blue sleep eyes/molded lashes and eyelids painted blue. Closed mouth. Jointed knees. High heel feet. Marks: Mme. Alexander on back. Tag: Queen By/Madame Alexander. Original clothes. 1960. $20.00.

Alexander--21" "Melanie" Plastic body and legs. Vinyl head and arms. Rooted black hair. Blue sleep eyes/long lashes. Original clothes. Marks: Alexander/1961, on head. Tag: Melanie/Madame Alexander. $105.00

Alexander--21" "Godey" Plastic body and legs, Vinyl arms and head. Rooted blonde hair. Blue sleep eyes/long lashes. Original clothes. Marks: Alexander/1961, on head. Tag: Godey/Madame Alexander. $105.00.

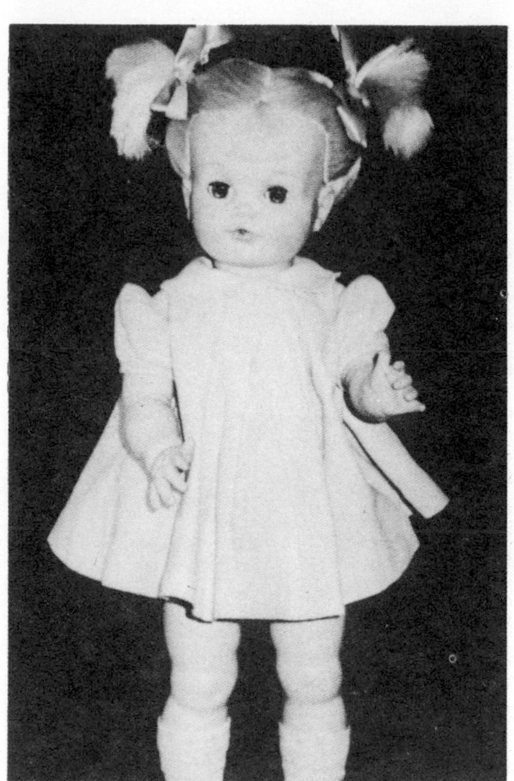

Alexander--23" "Chatterbox" Plastic body and legs. Vinyl arms and head. Rooted white hair. Blue sleep eyes/lashes. Open mouth/dry nurser. Open hands with thumbs up. Push button in center of stomach makes her talk. Battery operated with changeable records. Marks: Mme/1961/Alexander, on head. $48.00.

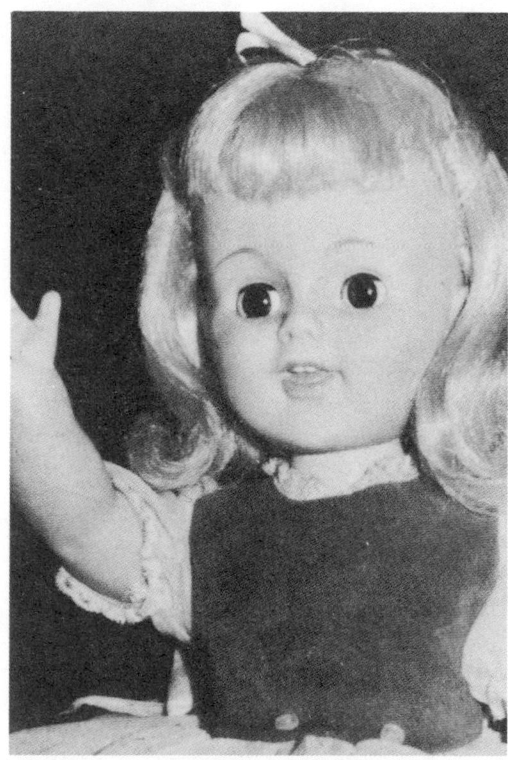

Alexander--16" "Melinda". Plastic body with ball jointed waist. Rigid vinyl arms and legs. Soft vinyl head with rooted blonde hair. Brown sleep eyes/lashes. Open/closed mouth with two painted upper teeth. Marks: Alexander/1962, on head. Original clothes. $30.00.

Alexander--11½" "Laurie". Plastic body, legs and arms. Vinyl head with rooted dark brown hair. Blue sleep eyes/molded lashes. Closed mouth. Open hands with 2nd and 3rd fingers molded together. Marks: Alexander 1963, on head. Tag: A Little Men/Laurie/ By Madame Alexander. Original clothes. $30.00.

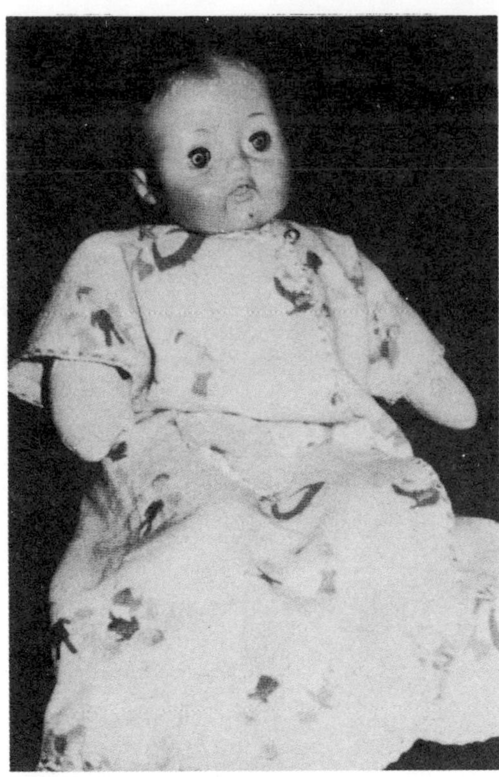

Alexander--12" "Little Huggums". All cloth with vinyl head. Molded painted light brown hair. Blue sleep eyes/molded lashes. Open/closed mouth. Marks: Alexander, on head. 1963. $10.00.

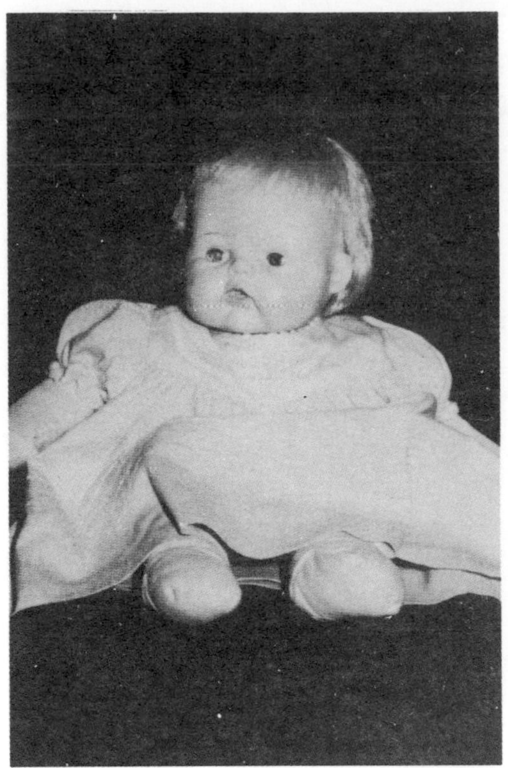

Alexander--12" "Little Huggums." Cloth body. Cloth arms and legs. Vinyl head with rooted blonde hair. Blue sleep eyes/molded lashes. Marks: Alexander/1963, on head. Tag on body: "Little Huggums"/By Madame Alexander. $10.00.

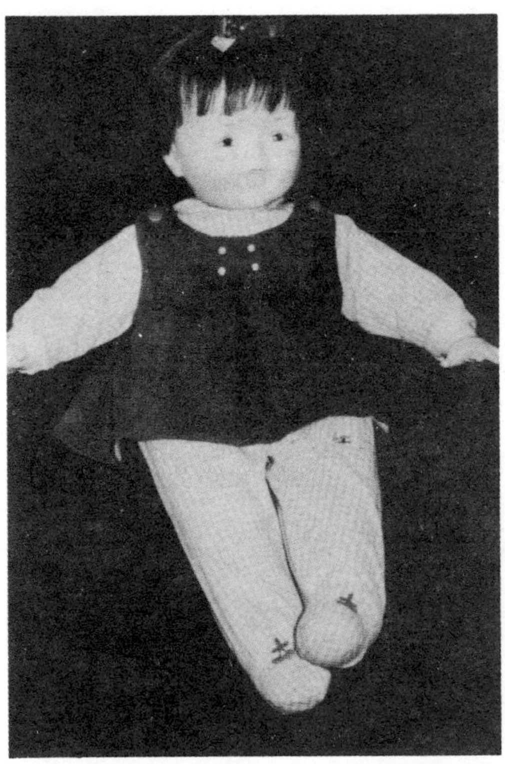

Alexander--25" "Big Huggums". Cloth body, arms and legs. Vinyl hands and head. Rooted dark brown hair. Painted blue eyes. Open/closed mouth with molded tongue and two lower teeth. Cryer. Marks: Alexander Doll Co., Inc, on head. 1963. $18.00.

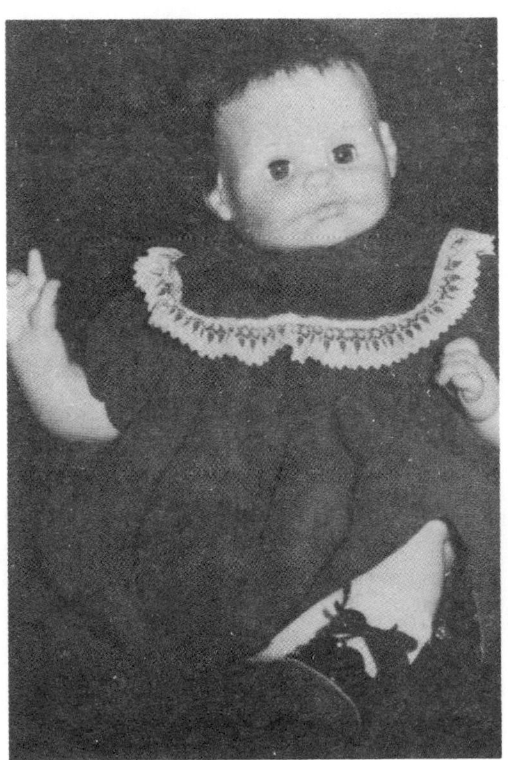

Alexander--14" "Sugar Darlin". Cloth body. Vinyl arms, legs and head. Rooted dark brown hair. Blue sleep eyes/lashes. Closed mouth. Marks: Alexander/1964, on head. Tag: Sugar Darlin'/By Madame Alexander. $16.00. (Courtesy Allin's Collection)

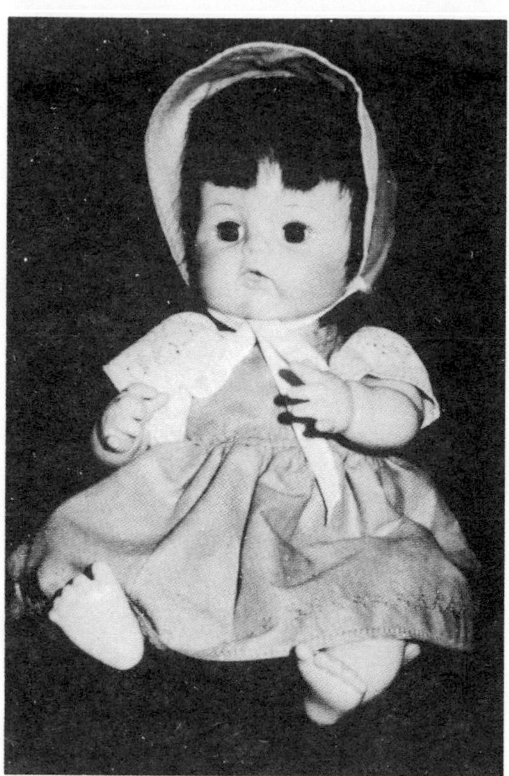

Alexander--13" "Sweet Tears". All vinyl with rooted black hair. Black sleep eyes/lashes. Open mouth/nurser. Left 2nd and 3rd fingers slightly curled. Right 2nd finger into palm, others slightly curled. Right toes curled under. Large toes molded separately. Marks: Alexander/ 1965, on head. $16.00.

Alexander--7½" "Bo Peep". All hard plastic with glued on yellow blonde wig. Blue sleep eyes/molded lashes. Closed mouth. 2nd and 3rd fingers molded together. Jointed knees. Marks: Alex. on back. Tag: Bo Peep/By Madame Alexander. Original clothes. 1965. $15.00.

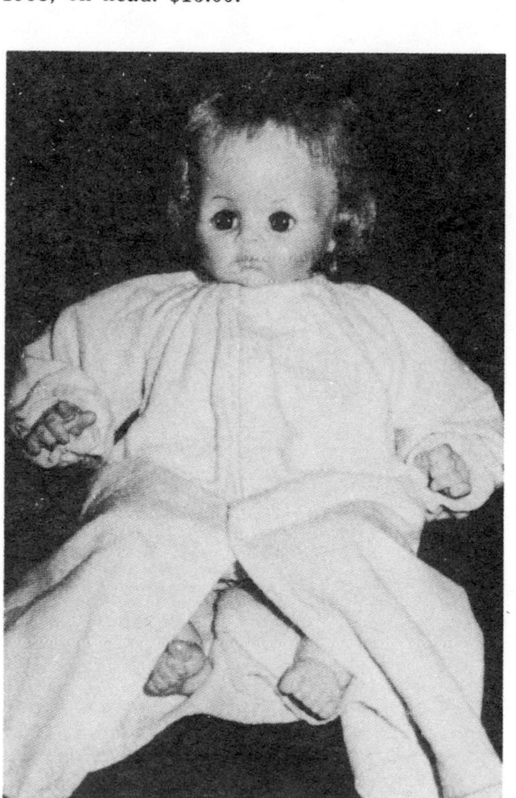

Alexander--15" "Pussy Cat". Cloth body. Vinyl arms, legs and head. Rooted blonde hair. Blue sleep eyes/lashes. Closed mouth. Cryer. Marks: Alexander/1965, on head. $12.00.

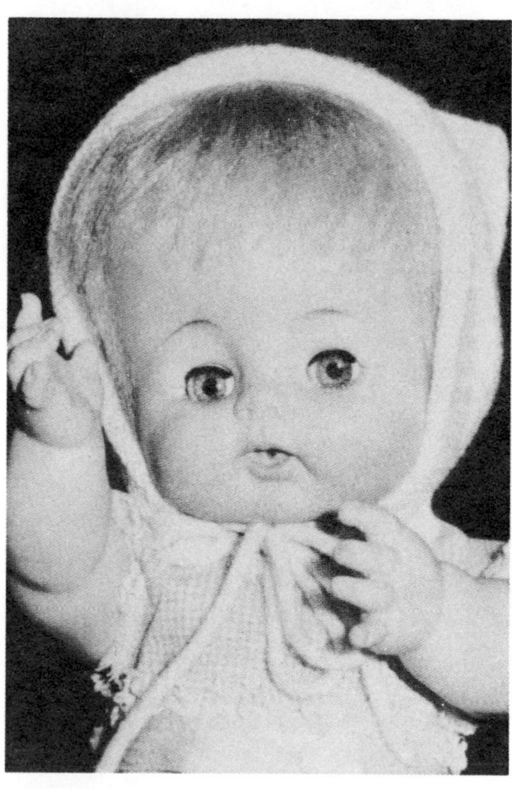

Alexander--15" "Sugar Darlin" All vinyl with rooted blonde hair. Blue sleep eyes/lashes. Open mouth/nurser. Crossed baby legs. Separate molded toes. Posable head. Marks: Alexander Doll Co/1965, on head. Also sold as Baby Genius. $16.00.

Alexander--13" "Alice In Wonderland" Plastic body and legs. Vinyl arms and head. Rooted blonde hair. Blue sleep eyes/lashes. Closed mouth. Open hands with left palm down. Right index finger pointing. Marks: Alexander 1965, on head. $18.00.

Alexander--17" "Leslie" Plastic body and legs. Vinyl arms and head. Rooted black hair. Brown sleep eyes. Marks: Alexander Doll Co Inc./1965, on head. $25.00. (Courtesy Earlene Johnston Collection)

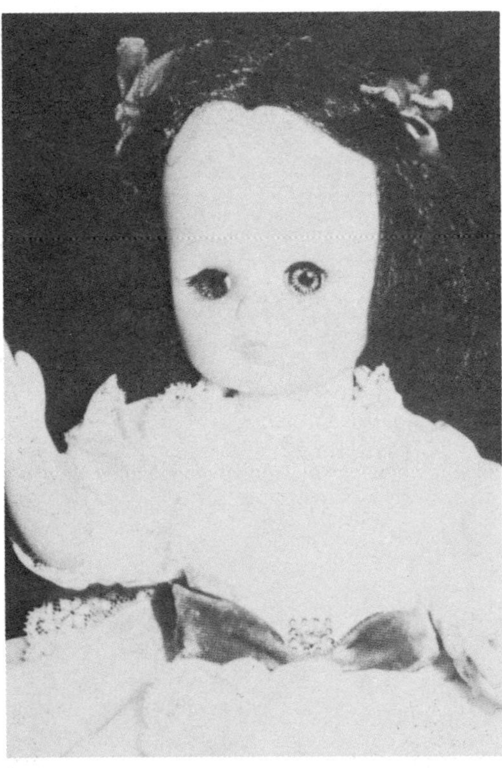

Alexander--13" "Scarlet O'Hara" Plastic body and legs. Vinyl head and arms. Rooted dark brown hair. Green sleep eyes/lashes. Closed mouth. All original. Marks: Unable To Make Out Marks On Head. Dress Tag: Scarlett By/Madame Alexander/New York USA. 1965. $32.00. (Courtesy Earlene Johnston Collection)

Alexander--7" "Storybook Doll". All composition with glued on yellow mohair wig. Painted side glancing blue eyes. Original clothes. Marks: Mme Alexander, on back. Dress Tag: Madame Alexander/New York. 1936. 1st storybook series. $16.00.

Alexander--7½" "Hansel & Gretel" All hard plastic with glued on orange/yellow wigs. Blue sleep eyes/molded lashes. Jointed knees. Marks: Alex., on backs. Tag On Clothes: Hansel By Madame Alexander. Gretel By Madame Alexander. 1965. $15.00. (Courtesy Fye Collection)

Alexander--8" "Hungarian" All hard plastic with blonde glued on wig. Blue sleep eyes/lashes molded. Jointed knee walker. Head turns. Original clothes. Marks: Alex., on back. Tag: Hungarian/Madame Alexander. 1966. $15.00.

Alexander--7½" "India" All hard plastic with glued on black wig. Black sleep eyes/molded lashes. Jointed knees. Original clothes. Marks: Alex., on back. Tag: India/Madame Alexander. 1966. 15.00.

Alexander--8" "Spanish Friend" Plastic body and legs. Vinyl arms and head with glued on black wig. Brown sleep eyes/molded lashes. Closed mouth. Pierced ears. Marks: Alex., on back. Tag: Spanish/Madame Alexander/New York USA. Original clothes. 1966. $15.00.

Alexander--17" "Elise" Plastic body and legs. Vinyl arms and head. Rooted blonde hair. Blue sleep eyes/lashes. Pierced ears. Original dress. Wears ring on finger. Marks: Alexander/1966 on head. Dress Tag: Madame Alexander/All Rights Reserved/New York USA. $40.00. (Courtesy Earlene Johnston Collection)

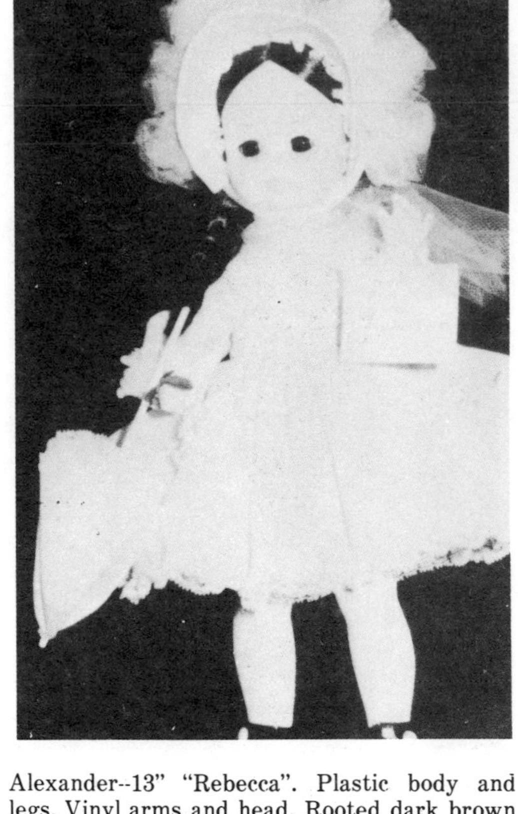

Alexander--13" "Rebecca". Plastic body and legs. Vinyl arms and head. Rooted dark brown hair in braids. Black pupiless sleep eyes. Original clothes. Marks: none. Dress Tag: Rebecca/Madame Alexander. 1968. $20.00.

Alexander--8" "Betsy Ross" All hard plastic with glued on dark blonde wig. Blue sleep eyes/molded lashes. Jointed knees. Original clothes. Marks: Alex. on back. Tag: Betsy Ross/Madame Alexander. 1968. $15.00.

Alexander--13" "Degas Portrait Child". Plastic body, arms and legs. Vinyl head with rooted brown hair. Blue sleep eyes/lashes. Closed mouth. Right index finger pointing. Marks: Alexander on head. Tag: Degas Girl By/Madame Alexander/New York USA. Original clothes. 1970. $20.00.

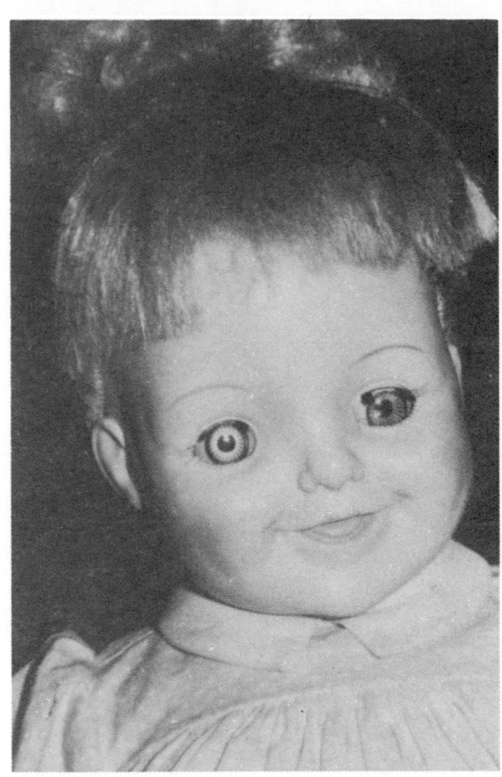

Alexander--20" "Happy" Cloth body with vinyl arms, legs and head. Rooted blonde hair. Blue sleep eyes/lashes. Open/closed mouth with molded tongue. Marks: Alexander/1970, on head. $20.00. (Courtesy Allin's Collection)

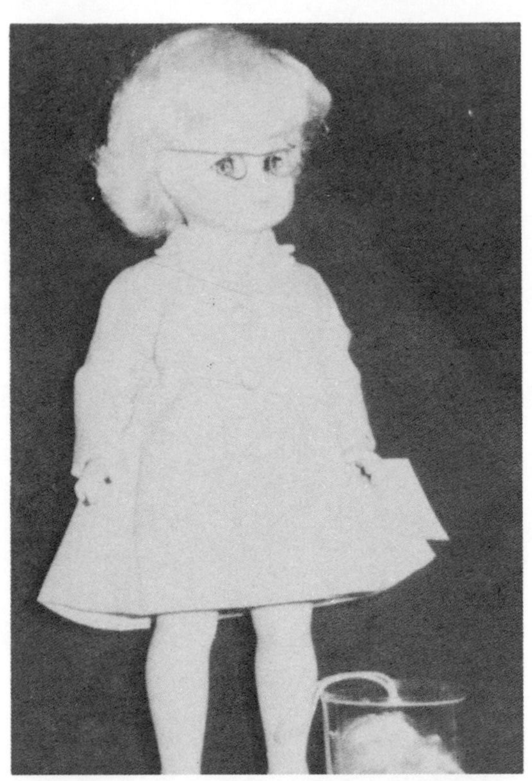

Alexander--13" "Grandma Jane" Plastic body and legs. Vinyl arms and head. Rooted grey hair. Blue sleep eyes. Wire glasses. Hatbox with hair piece and curlers. Original clothes. Marks: Alexander/1966. Tag: Grandma Jane/Madame Alexander. Doll marked 1966 but issued in 1970. $35.00.

Alexander--11½" "Blue Boy" Plastic body, arms and legs. Vinyl head with rooted dark brown hair. Blue sleep eyes/molded lashes. Closed mouth. 2nd and 3rd fingers molded together. Marks: Alexander/1968, on head. Jacket Tag: Blue Boy/By Madame Alexander. Original clothes. Doll marked 1968 but issued as Blue Boy in 1970. $18.00 (Courtesy Fye Collection).

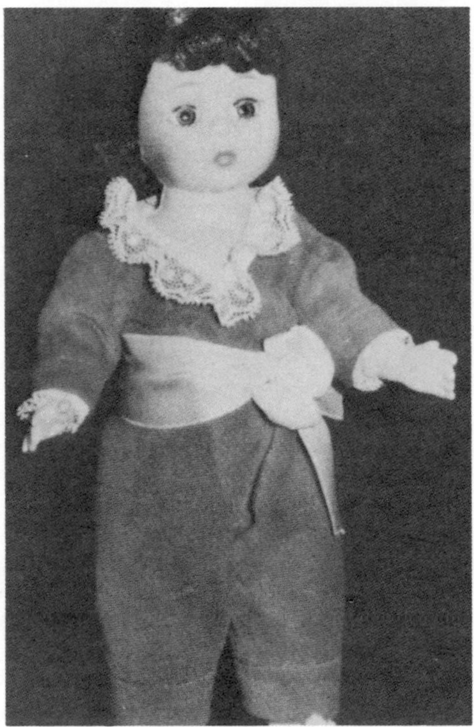

Alexander--7½ "Red Boy" All hard plastic with glued on brown hair. Brown sleep eyes/molded lashes. Jointed knees walker. Head turns. Marks: Alex., on back. Tag: Red Boy/Madame Alexander. Original clothes. 1971. $15.00.

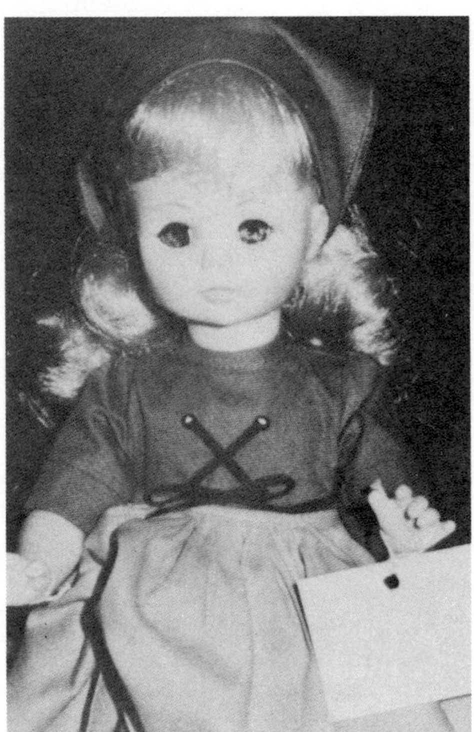

Alexander--13" "Cinderella" Plastic body and legs. Vinyl arms and head. Blonde rooted hair. Blue sleep eyes/lashes. Closed mouth. Right index pointing. Left 2nd and 3rd fingers molded together. Marks: Dress Tag: Cinderella By Madame Alexander. 1971. $15.00.

American Character Doll Company

The American Character Doll Company dates from 1918. It is now out of business. Molds, copyrights and equipment have been liquidated. The Ideal Toy Corporation has purchased molds and other equipment from American Character. For example, notice how the American Character's 1963 "Talking Marie" compares with the Ideal "Kissy" series.

Of course, American Character's "character" was Toodles but they have also supplied little girls and collectors with some of the finest quality dolls made. The dolls have personality and a beauty all their own. Any American Character doll is collectable not only for the quality but because the company is no longer operating.

For General Information: American Character's Patsy type was called Sally. Also American Doll and Toy Corporation is the same company.

After Mattel issued the Barbie doll, American Character introduced Tressy and concentrated on hair and hair styling.

This company has imported, through it's International Division, dolls that are collectors items. From Italy; Italo-Cremona, with wistful child faces and excellent skin tones, Ratti and Valenzasca, selling under the firm name of Ratti, with dark olive tones and made of paper weight thin plastic. Luigi Furga and Company, under the trade name of Furga, known for beautiful skin tones and great costuming. From France; Poupee's Bella of Terignan, France. From Germany; Rheinische Gummi Und Celuloid Fabrik of Mannheim, Germany, most of which are modern but there are a few character types, such as Hansel and Gretel. From England: Dolls from the Casseloid Company of Leicester, England.

Since American Character sold, in 1968, these companies have still imported dolls with the exception of Ratti, which was purchased by Mattel, Inc. in 1968.

American Character (and American Doll & Toy Corp.) marked dolls with the full company name or just Amer. Char., straight and later in a circle. Earlier composition dolls were marked Petite.

The following are not all the dolls made by this company

1942: Little Love (32.00), Dandy (10.00)
1945: Junior Miss (32.00)
1948: Miss Chickadee (18.00)
1950: Tiny Tears (8.00 to 18.00), Baby Tears (16.00), Chuckles (14.00), Baby Lu (5.00)
1951: Sunny Boy (20.00), Baby Sue (9.00)
1953: Sweet Suzanne (25.00), Little Rickey (40.00)
1955: Tiny Tears-vinyl (12.00), Sweet Sue Walker-Sweet Sue series 1955-1959 (30.00), Bride (35.00), American Beauty (40.00)

1956: Peek-a-Boo Toodles (16.00), Pretty Baby (9.00), Toodles Action Baby (22.00)
1957: Teenie Weenie (8.00), New Sweet Sue (18.00)
1958: Toni (10.00), New Born Baby (32.00), Teeny Betsy McCall (15.00)
1959: 36" Betsy McCall (45.00), Sandy McCall-36" Boy, molded hair, grin and freckles (50.00)
1960: Baby Dimples (10.00), Whimsies (25.00), Hedda Get Betta (27.00)
1961: Baby Marie (20.00), Little Baby Marie (16.00), Little Miss Marie (18.00), Tina Marie (16.00), Miss Marie (20.00), Butterball (32.00), Betsy McCall (12.00), Toodle Loo (32.00)
1962: Baby K (35.00), Eloise (16.00)
1963: Marshmellow Baby (35.00), Teeny Tiny Tears (5.00), Talking Marie (40.00), Teeny Weeny Tiny Tears (6.00), Chubby Tiny Tears (15.00), Tressy (6.00), Penny (4.00)
1964: New Tiny Tears (5.00), Little Love (6.00)
1965: Mary Make Up (8.00), Darlin' Dollface (8.00), Cricket (5.00), Margie Make Up (8.00), Pretty Penny (10.00), Deena Dollface (8.00) Mimsy (10.00)
1966: Snip N' Tuck (5.00), The Magic Make Up Face (8.00), Toodles Toddles (15.00), Moonbeams (15.00), Bonanza Characters (3.00 each)
1967: Sleep Weepy (8.00), Mendy (18.00), Turn and Learn (8.00)

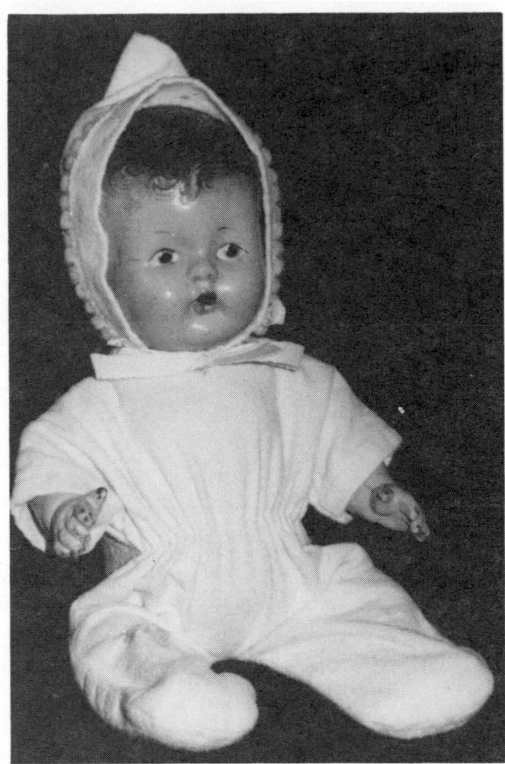

American Character--12" "Dandy" All composition with molded curly hair, painted black. Painted blue eyes. Closed mouth. Baby legs. One piece body and head. Marks: Ac, on head 1942. $10.00.

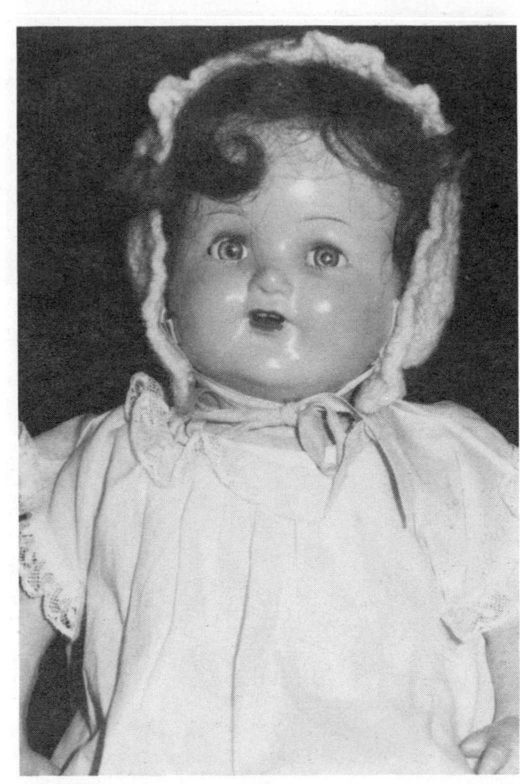

American Character--18" "Little Love" Cloth body. Composition arms, legs and head. Glued on brown human hair wig. Blue sleep eyes/lashes. Open mouth with two teeth and felt tongue. Black eye shadow. Marks: Amer. Char. Doll, on head. 1942. $32.00

American Character--8" "Miss Chicadee" All hard plastic, molded in one piece body and head. Molded brown hair. Painted blue eyes. Closed mouth. 2nd and 3rd fingers molded together and curled. Crossed baby legs. Rocker of wood and pressed paper. Marks: none. 1948. Original clothes and rocker. $18.00.

American Character--13½" "Baby Tiny Tears" Hard plastic head. Rubber body arms and legs. Molded hair. Hands open and in a down position. Blue sleep eyes/lashes. Open mouth/nurser. Pierced nostrils. Tear ducts inside edge of eyes. Marks: Pat. No. 2675644/American Character. 1950. Original Clothes. $8.00-$12.00.

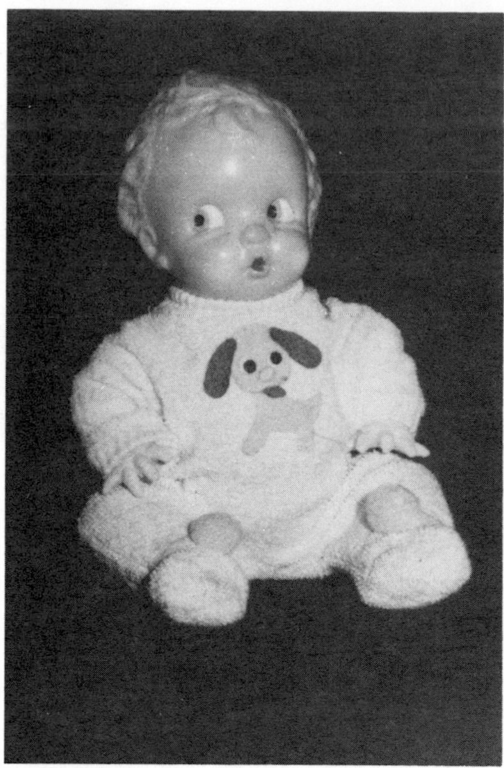

American Character--8" "Baby Lou" All early plastic. One piece head and body. Molded hair. Side glancing blue eyes. Open mouth/nurser. Bent baby legs. Open hands with palms down. Marks: Amer. Char., in a circle. 1950. $5.00.

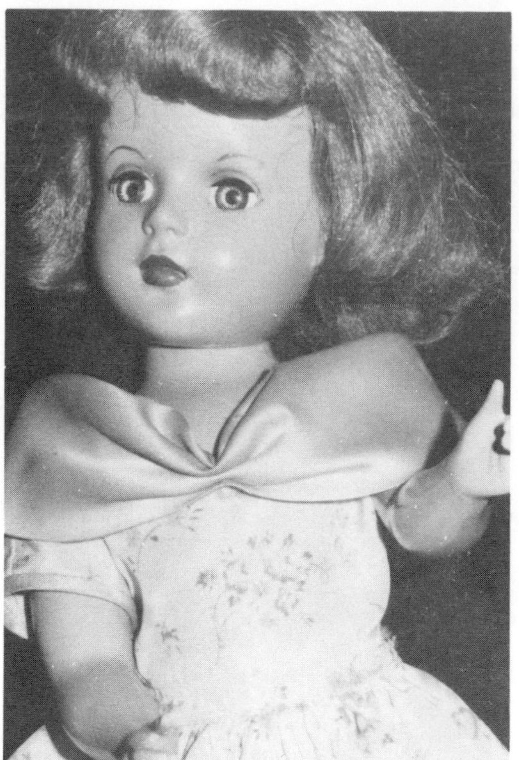

American Character--17" "Sweet Susanne" All hard plastic with glued on dark blonde wig. Blue sleep eyes/lashes. Closed mouth. Marks: none. 1953. $25.00. (Courtesy Allin's Collection)

American Character--19" "Sweet Sue" Hard plastic with vinyl head. Rooted brown hair. Blue sleep eyes/lashes. Closed mouth. Pale nail polish. Jointed waist and ankles. Pierced ears. Marks: none. Original dress. 1955. $30.00.

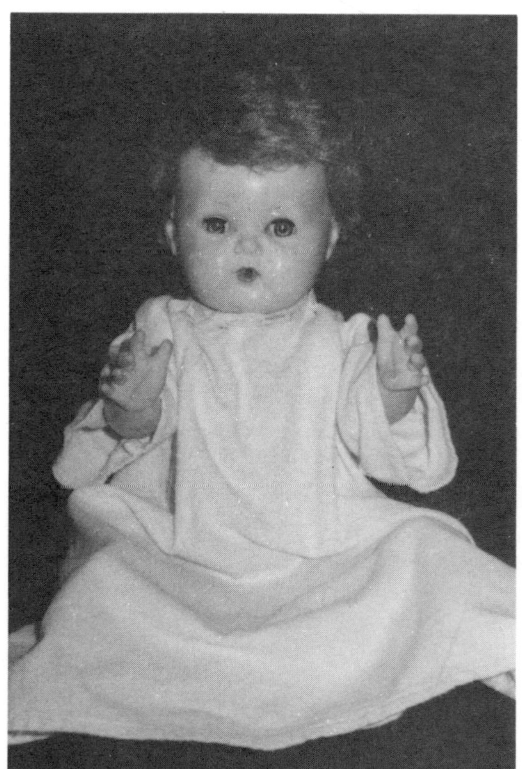

American Character--16" "Tiny Tears" Hard plastic head. Vinyl arms, legs and body. Rooted brown hair in skull cap. Blue sleep eyes/lashes. Left hand turned toward body. Right hand halfway between body and palm down. Individually molded toes. Open mouth/nurser. Marks: American Character Doll/Pat. $12.00.

American Character--18" "Bride" All hard plastic with vinyl covered arms. Dark blonde inset and rooted skull cap wig. Green sleep eyes/lashes. Closed mouth. Jointed elbow and knees. Marks: Amer. Char. Doll, on head. 1955. $35.00

American Character--22" "American Beauty" All hard plastic with inset skull cap rooted dark blonde saran hair. Blue sleep eyes/lashes. Left 2nd and 3rd fingers molded together. Flat feet. Painted fingernails. Marks: none. 1955. Original clothes. $40.00.

American Character--24" "Sweet Sue" All hard plastic with vinyl sleeve arms. Jointed elbows and knees. Walker, head turns. Blonde inset skull cap with rooted hair. Blue sleep eyes/lashes.Marks: Amer. Char. Doll on head. 1955. $35.00.

American Character--17" "Sweet Susanne" All hard plastic. Replaced human hair wig. Blue sleep eyes/lashes. Closed mouth. Walker, head turns. Marks: none. 1956. $22.00.

American Character--23" "Peek-A-Boo Toodles" All vinyl with rooted brown hair. Very large blue sleep eyes/long lashes. Deep set pupils make eyes "follow" without being "flirty". Marks: American Char. Doll/ A series of numbers I cannot read. 1956. The vinyl used was called "Lastic-Plastic". $16.00.

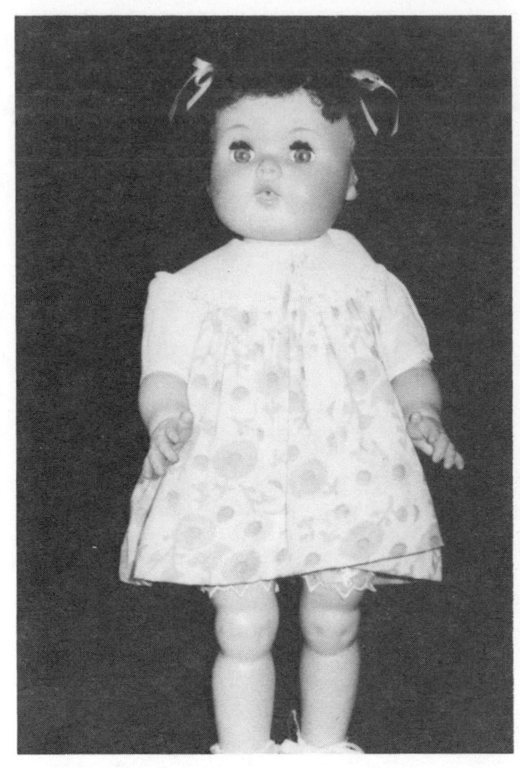

American Character--22""Toodles" This is a colored Toodles. All vinyl with dark brown tightly curled hair. Brown sleep eyes/heavy lashes. Flirty eyes. Open mouth/nurser. Marks: Amer. Char. Dolls Inc., on head. 1956. $22.00.

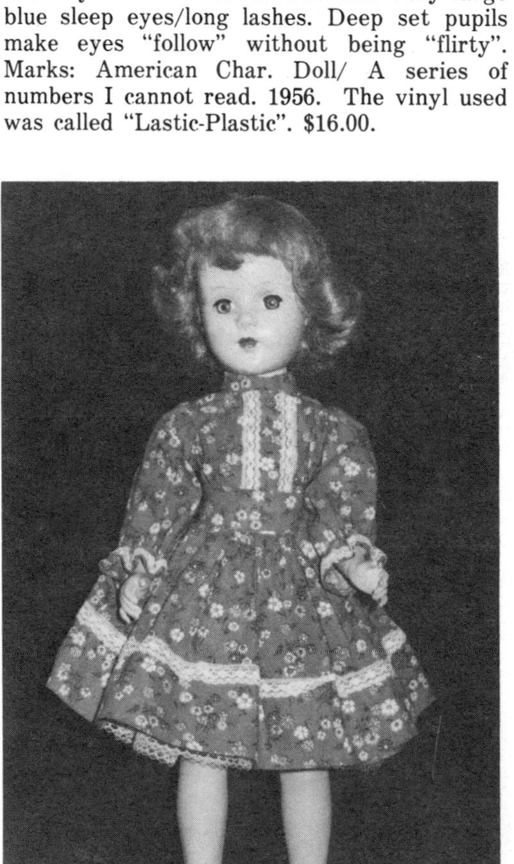

American Character--17½" "Sweet Sue" All hard plastic with glued on dark blonde wig. Blue sleep eyes/lashes. Closed mouth. 2nd and 3rd fingers molded together. Head turns as she walks. Marks: none. 1957. $18.00.

American Character--8" "Teeny Betsy McCall" All hard plastic with a creamy bisque finish. Rooted dark brown hair set in a skull cap and cap glued to head. Blue sleep eyes/molded lashes. Closed mouth. Mark: Center of back, in a circle: McCall Corp. 1958. Original dress. $15.00.

American Character--15" "New Born Baby" All vinyl with rooted dark blonde hair over molded hair. Small blue sleep eyes/lashes. Closed mouth. Individual molded toes. Marks: American Character/1958 on head. $32.00.

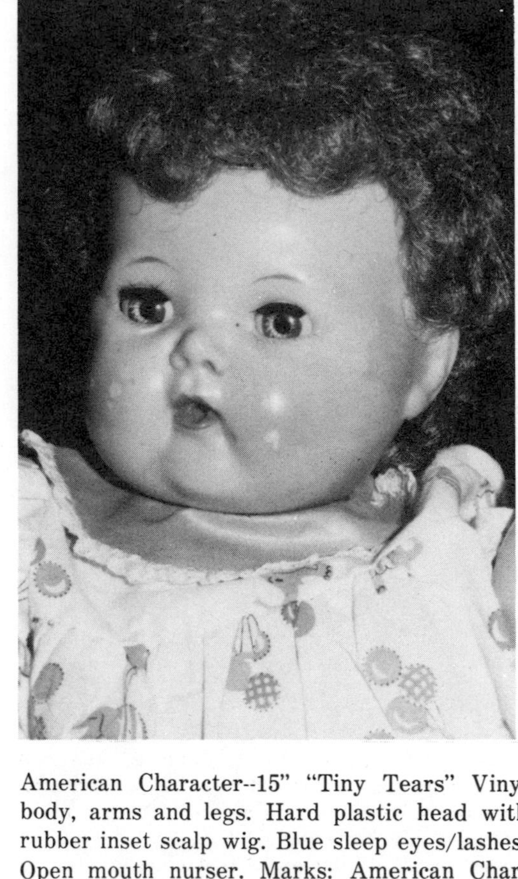

American Character--15" "Tiny Tears" Vinyl body, arms and legs. Hard plastic head with rubber inset scalp wig. Blue sleep eyes/lashes. Open mouth nurser. Marks: American Character Doll/Pat No. 2675644 on head. AC/6 on back. 1959. $12.00.

American Character-- 19" "Astronut" One piece vinyl body, arms and legs. Vinyl head with rooted green hair. Large painted green eyes. Blue painted gloves and feet. Marks: Amer. Doll & Toy Co./1960, on lower back. Whimsies/1960/ American Doll & Toy, in a circle on head. Original clothes. $25.00.

American Character--21" "Graduate" One piece vinyl body, arms and legs. Vinyl head with rooted tuffs of hair at sides. Painted eyes with molded lashes. Marks: Amer. Doll & Toy Co/1960/American Doll & Toy, in a circle on head. Original clothes. $25.00. (Courtesy Allin's Collection)

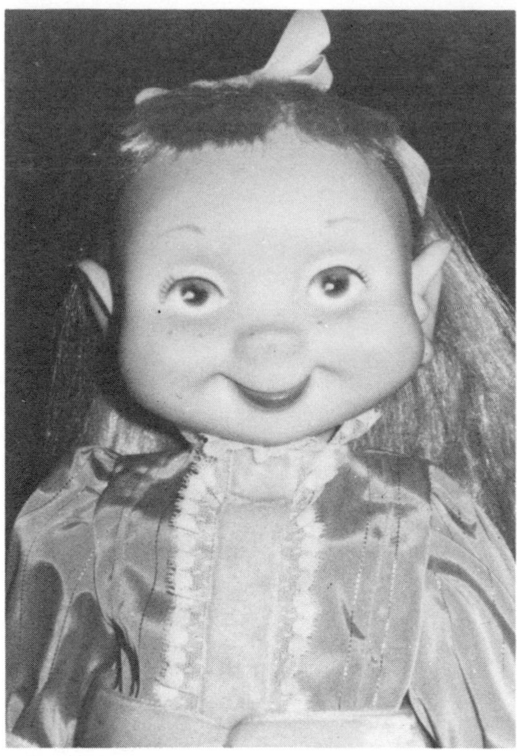

American Character--21" "Whimsie" All one piece vinyl body, arms and legs. Vinyl head with rooted blonde hair. Painted brown eyes. Freckles. Marks: Amer. Doll & Toy Co/1960, on lower back. Whimsies/1960/American Doll & Toy, in a circle on head. Original clothes. $25.00. (Courtesy Allin's Collection)

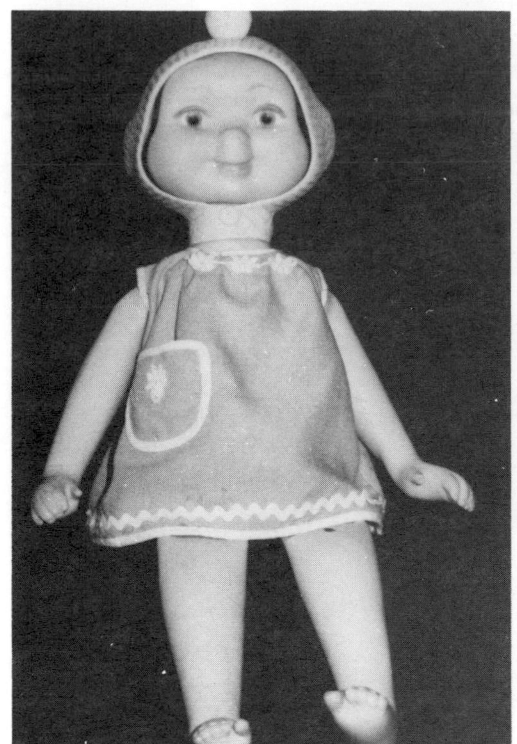

American Character--21" "Hedda Get Betta" Stuffed one piece vinyl, unjointed body. Hard plastic bonnet with three sided vinyl head. Knob on top turns face. Marks: American Doll & Toy Corp. 1961, in a circle on head. Whimsie/Amer. Doll & Toy Corp/1960, on back. $27.00. (Courtesy Earlene Johnston Collection)

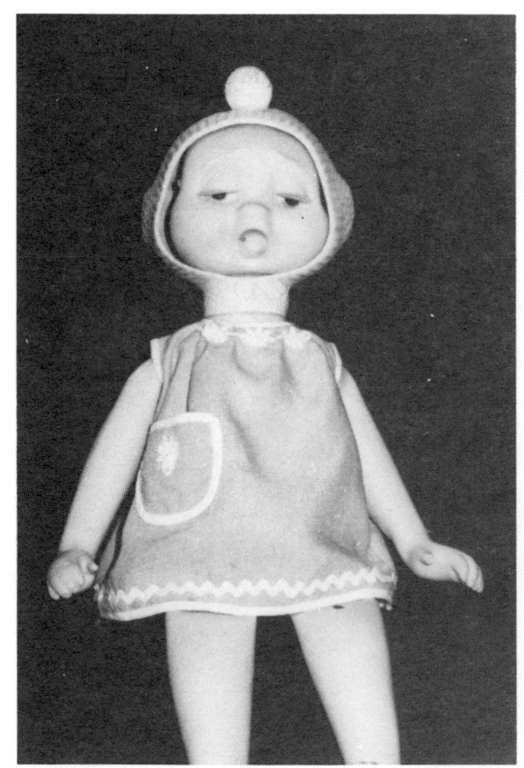

American Character--14" "Betsy McCall" Rigid vinyl body and legs. Vinyl arms and head. Rooted black hair. Blue sleep eyes/lashes. 2nd and 3rd fingers molded together. Medium high heel feet. 1961. $12.00.

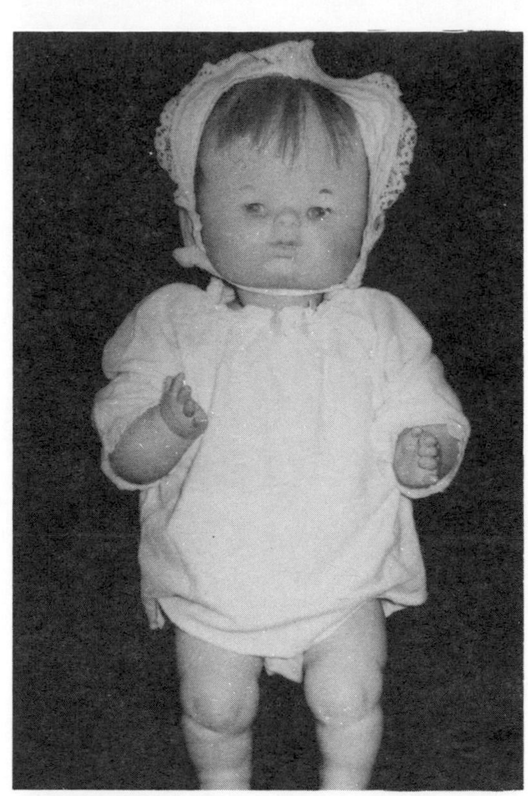

American Character--18" "Toodle-Loo" All vinyl with rooted ash blonde hair. Brown painted eyes. Open/closed mouth. Short chubby arms. Short chubby legs on a long body. Mark: 1961/American Doll & Toy Co, in a circle on head. $32.00.

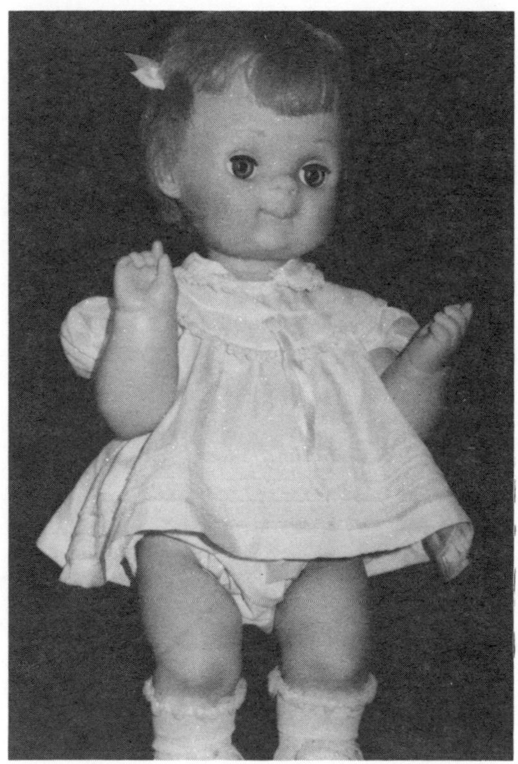

American Doll & Toy Co.--19" "Butterball" All vinyl with rooted ash blonde hair. Blue sleep eyes/lashes. Upper lip protruded. 2nd, 3rd and little fingers curled. Short stubby legs. Marks: in a circle, 1961 American Doll & Toy Co. Original clothes. $32.00.

American Character--18" "Talking Marie" Plastic body and legs. Vinyl arms and head. Rooted dark blonde hair. Blue sleep eyes/lashes. Closed mouth. Both hands wide open with palms down. Button in stomach starts record player. Speaker grill in chest. Battery operated. Marks: Amer. Char. Doll/1963, on head. $40.00.

American Doll & Toy Corp.--12" "Tressy" Plastic body and legs. Vinyl arms and head. Rooted dark blonde hair. Painted side glancing blue eyes. Hands open with all fingers molded together. High heel feet. "Growing hair" with turn knob in lower center back. Marks: American Doll & Toy Corp/1963 in a circle. Original clothes. $6.00.

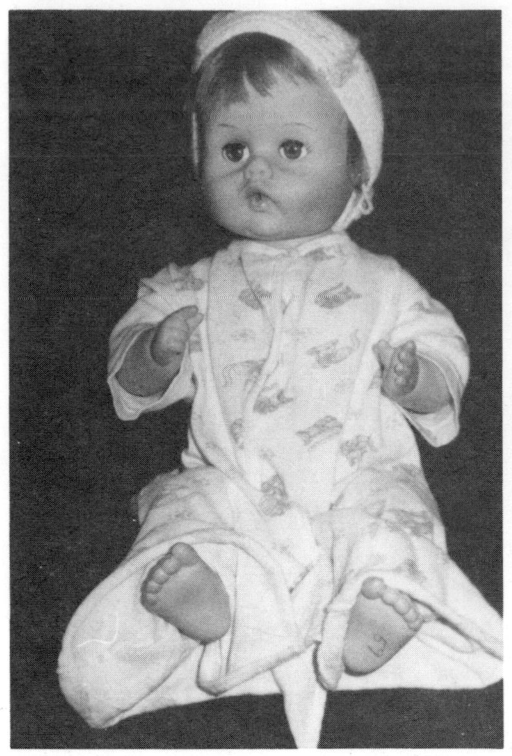

American Character--17" "New Tiny Tears" All vinyl with rooted red hair. Blue sleep eyes/lashes. Open mouth/nurser. Right hand with thumb and index finger extended. Left hand open and facing body. Marks: Amer. Char. Inc./1964 on head. $5.00.

Arranbee Doll Company

Arranbee is another doll company that did not survive. Founded in 1922 and purchased by Vogue Dolls Inc. in 1959. The use of the name Arranbee or the initials R & B was discontinued in 1961.

Some of the finest quality dolls came from the Arranbee factory. The hard plastics made by this company rate high for beauty and quality. The use of Nanette, one hard plastic character, ran from 1953 through 1958. The doll was made in many sizes and molds and was issued, as a great many dolls of that time, as many personalities with just costume and hair style changes to denote each one.

The best known "little ones" of this company are Nancy and Dream Baby, both made in the 20's and 30's. Although Dream Baby was made in composition with brown eyes and in 1940 and in 1944. In the 40's it was issued with a cloth body, with composition head, arms and legs and had molded ringlet hair.

The composition from this company was mainly marked with the full name Arranbee. The hard plastics were mostly marked with just the R & B or just Made In USA on the back or the mold number 210. A majority of the vinyls were marked with the full name of Arranbee.

The following are not all the dolls made by this company.
1940: Little Angel (20.00), Debu-teen (30.00), Nancy (18.00), Sonja Henie (35.00), Dream Baby (18.00)
1941: Snuggle Doll (35.00)
1942: Snuggle Muff (12.00)
1950: My Dream Baby (18.00), Peachy (7.00)
1951: Judy (46.00)
1952: Angline (35.00)
1953: Patty Ruth (16.00), Nanette (35.00)
1954: Taffy (40.00), Littlest Angel (8.00), Rock Me Baby (16.00), Dream Bride (30.00)
1955: Francine (35.00), New Happytot (16.00), Sally (18.00)
1956: Littlest Angel (8.00), Sweet Pea (8.00)
1957: April Showers (10.00), Prom Queen (32.00)
1959: My Angel (32.00), Nancy (8.00)
1960: Angel Face (18.00), Angel Bride (20.00), Angel Baby (20.00)

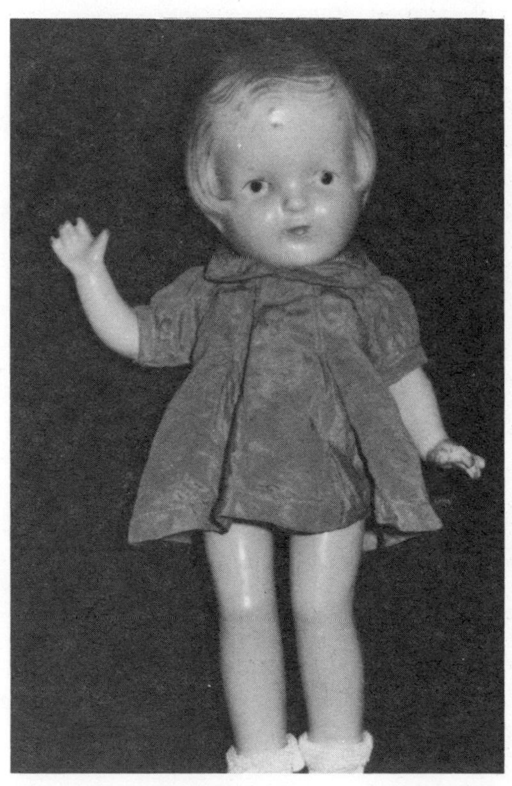

Arranbee--12" "Nancy" All composition with molded painted hair. Painted blue eyes. Closed mouth. Right arm molded bent at elbow. Marks: Nancy on back. This doll was made up to 1940. Original dress. $18.00.

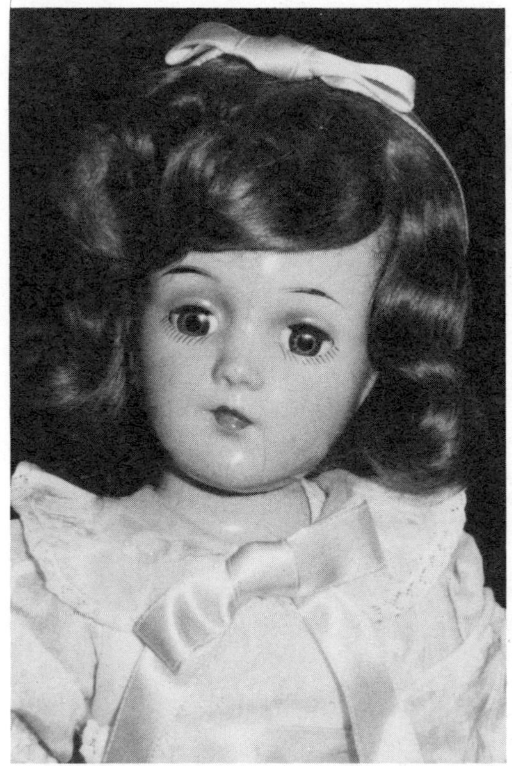

Arranbee--18" "Debu-Teen" Cloth body with composition arms, legs, head. Head is swivel shoulder plate. Glued on brown wig. Green sleep eyes/lashes. Closed mouth. Marks: R & B on head. R & B under arms. 3 R & B on left leg. 5 R & B on right leg. 1940. $30.00.

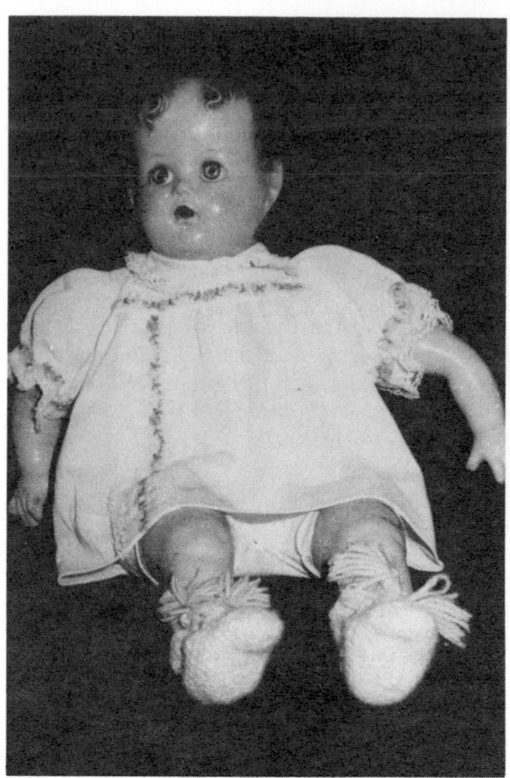

Arranbee--16" "Little Angel" Composition head, arms and legs. Stuffed cloth body. Molded and painted dark brown hair. Open mouth with two teeth. Blue sleep eyes/lashes. Black eye shadow. Marks: none. 1940. $20.00.

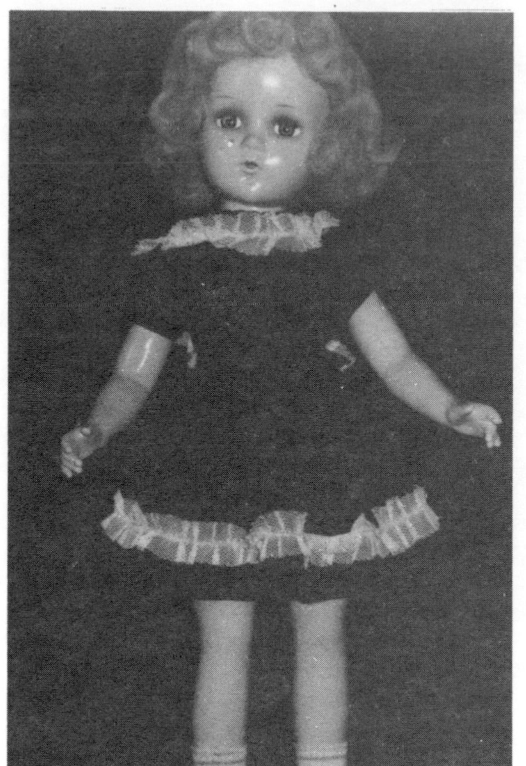

Arranbee--21" "Sonja Henie" All composition with glued on blonde mohair wig. Brown sleep eyes/lashes. Black eye shadow. Closed mouth. 2nd and 3rd fingers molded together. Marks: R & B on head. Original clothes. 1945. $35.00.

21" "Sonja Henie"

Arranbee--17" "Snuggle Doll" Stuffed cord filled body, arms and legs. Composition head with glued on dark blonde mohair wig. Inset stationary blue eyes. Closed mouth. Marks: none. 1941. Original. $35.00.

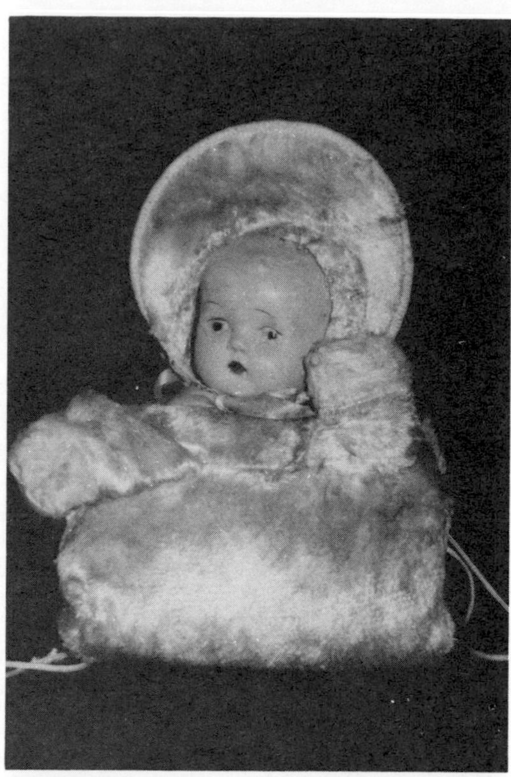

Arranbee--Childs "Snuggle Muff" Covered with pink plush with composition head. Painted features. Marks: R & B, on front neck. 1942. $12.00.

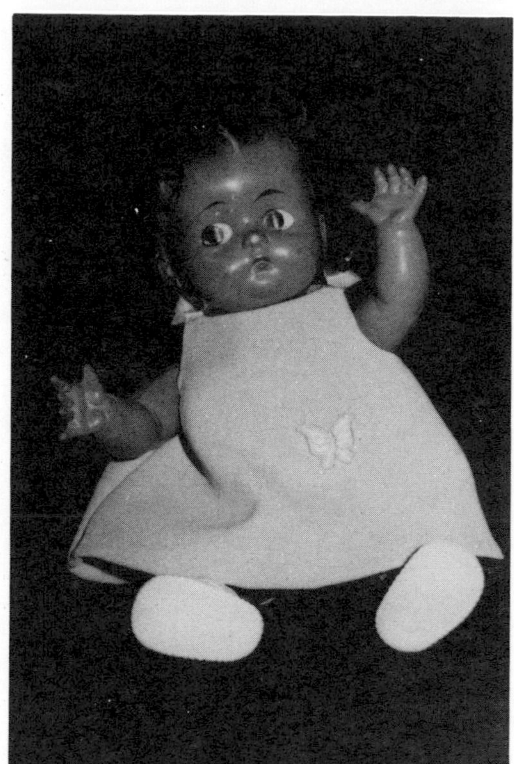

Arranbee--10" "Peachy" All hard plastic with molded hair. Side glancing brown eyes. Closed mouth. Open hands with palms down. One piece head and body. Baby legs. Hole in left side of head for ribbon/braids. Marks: none. 1950. $7.00.

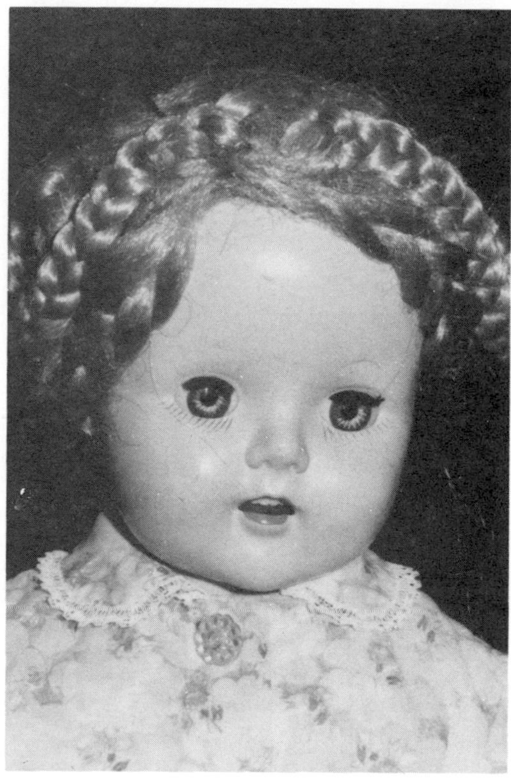

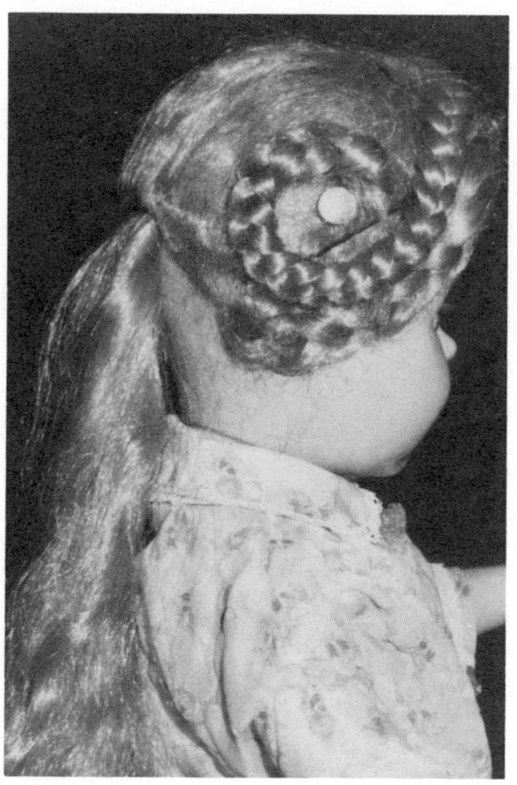

Arranbee--19" "Judy" All hard plastic with glued on nylon blonde wig in braids with a metal knob on the right side of head to wind hair back into slot molded in back of head. Blue sleep eyes/lashes. Open mouth with 4 teeth. Marks: 210 on head and 210 on body. Pat 2,537,598/other Pat. Pend. on head and on right side of underarm. Armiture on base of neck. 1951. $46.00.

Arranbee--18" "Angeline" All hard plastic with glued on mohair wig. Dark blue sleep eyes/lashes. Closed mouth. Walker, head turns. Marks: R & B on head. 1952. $35.00

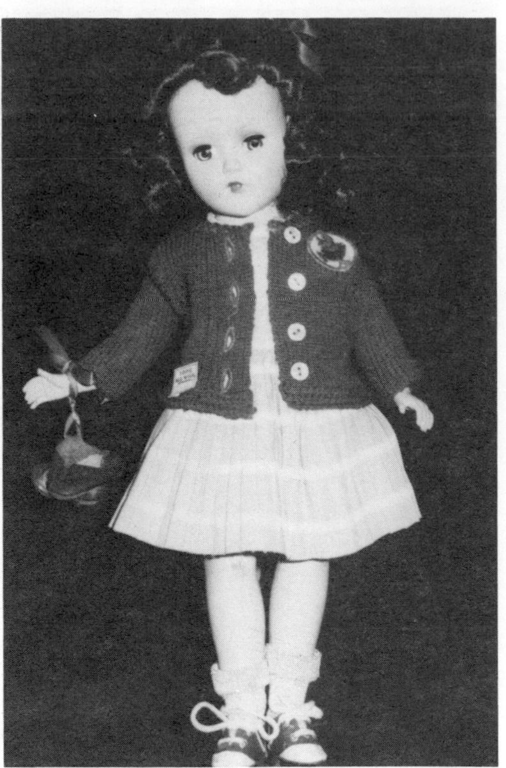

Arranbee--14" "Nanette" All hard plastic. Glued on dark brown dynel wig. Blue sleep eyes/lashes. Closed mouth. All left fingers molded together and slightly curled. Right little finger extended away from others. Marks: R & B, on head. Original clothes. 1953. $35.00.

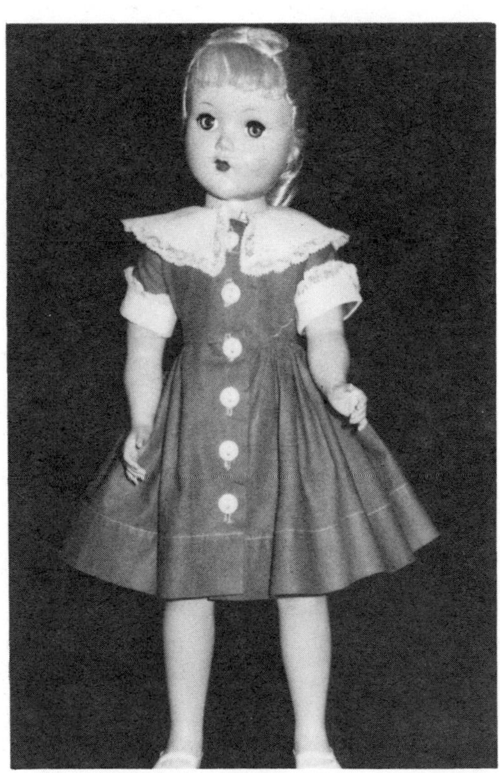

Arranbee--17" "Nanette" All hard plastic. Glued on blonde wig. Blue sleep eyes/lashes. Closed mouth. 2nd and 3rd fingers molded together and slightly curled. Marks: R & B, on head. 1954. $35.00.

Arranbee--21" "Dream Bride" All hard plastic with glued on wig. Blue sleep eyes/lashes. Closed mouth. Walker. Marks: R & B on head. 210 on body. Original clothes. 1954. $30.00. (Courtesy Allin's Collection)

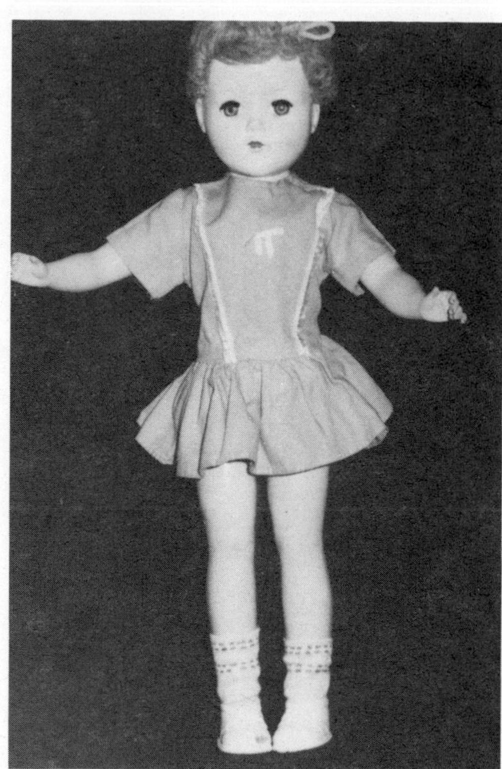

Arranbee--17" "Taffy" All hard plastic with red caricul fur hair set in scull cap. Green sleep eyes/lashes. Closed mouth. 2nd and 3rd fingers molded together. Marks; R & B on head. 1954. $40.00.

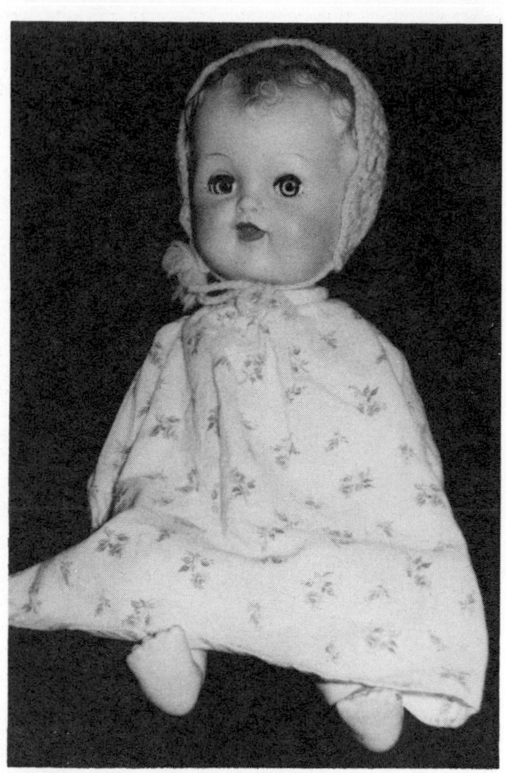

Arranbee--16" "New Happytot" One piece stuffed vinyl body arms and legs. Vinyl head with molded very curly, painted brown hair. Blue sleep eyes/lashes. Open/closed mouth. Marks: Arranbee on head. 1955. $16.00.

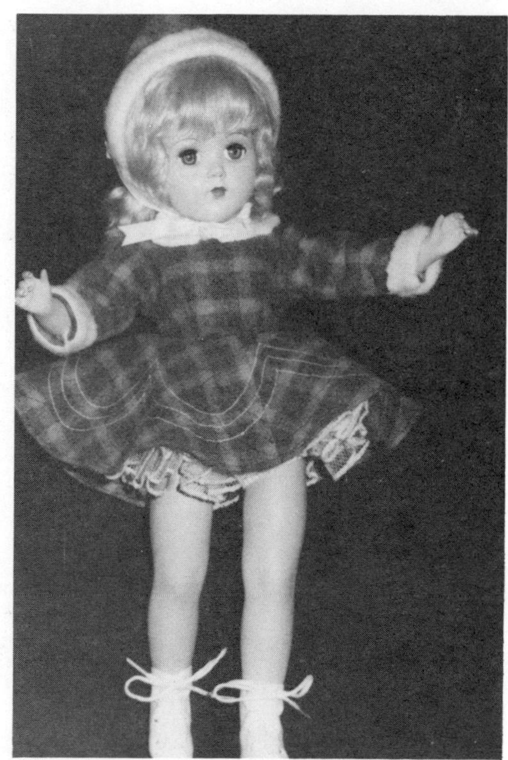

Arranbee--17" "Nanette" All hard plastic with glued on blonde mohair wig. Blue sleep eyes/lashes. Closed mouth. 2nd and 3rd fingers molded together and slightly curled. Marks: none. All original except skates. 1955. $35.00.

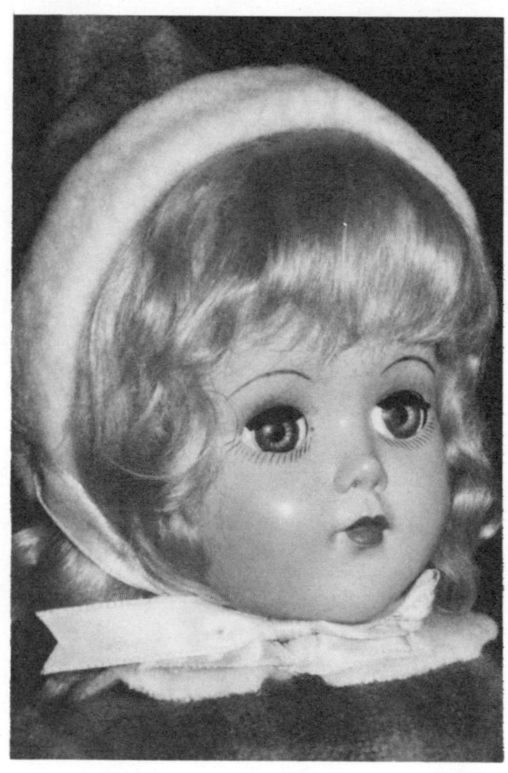

Arranbee--17" "Francine" All hard plastic with glued on, long blonde mohair wig. Blue sleep eyes/lashes. 2nd and 3rd fingers molded together. Marks: R & B on head. 1955. Original clothes. $35.00.

Arranbee--10" "Littlest Angel" All hard plastic with glued on dark brown wig. Blue sleep eyes/molded lashes. Closed mouth. Ball, pin socket walker. Head turns. Jointed knees. Marks: R & B on head. R & B on back. 1956. $8.00.

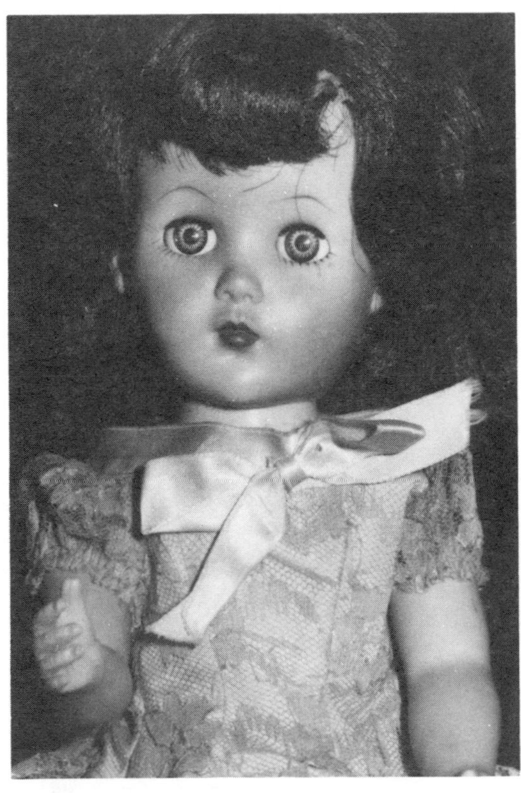

Arranbee--17½" "Prom Queen" Hard plastic body, arms and legs. Vinyl head with rooted dark brown hair. Blue sleep eyes/lashes. Closed mouth. Jointed knees. Walker. Marks: R & B, on head. 1957. Original clothes. $32.00. (Courtesy Allin's Collection)

Arranbee--11" "A Littlest Angel Doll" Hard plastic body with jointed shoulders, hips and knees. Vinyl head with rooted dark brown hair. Blue sleep eyes, lashes. Open mouth with molded tongue. Marks: R & B/49, on head. R & B Doll Co., on back. 1959. $6.00.

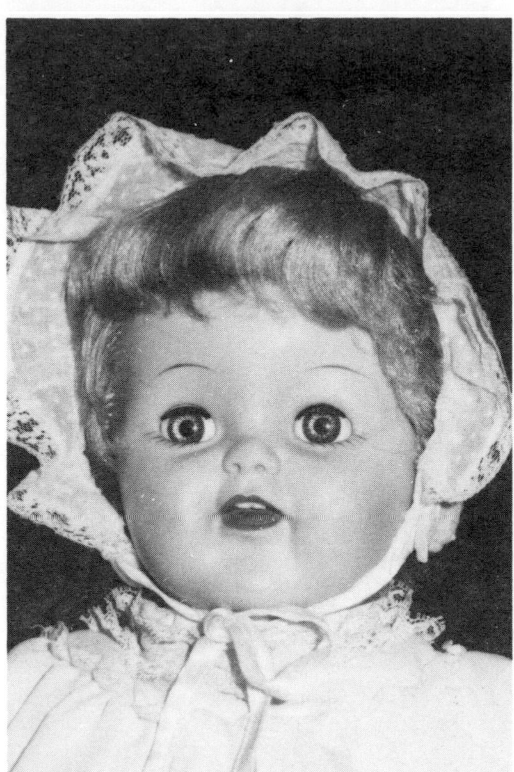

Arranbee--22" "My Angel" Oil cloth body with vinyl arms, legs and head. Rooted yellow hair. Blue sleep eyes/lashes. Open/closed mouth with two teeth and molded tongue. Marks: Arranbee on head. 1959. $32.00.

Arranbee--10½" "Littlest Angel" All hard plastic. Vinyl head with rooted orange hair. Green sleep eyes/lashes. Freckles. Open/closed mouth. Open hands with palms facing body. Jointed knees. Marks: R & B Doll Co., on back. 1960. $8.00.

Arrow Novelty--21" "Skookum" Portrait type face of plastic. Bronze in color. Horse hair wig. Marks: Paper Sticker On bottom Of Foot: Trademark Registered/Skookum/(Bully Good) Indian/USA/Patented. 1950. Original clothes and beads. Also sold through H.H. Tammen Co. Made since 1913. $42.00.

Arrow Novelty Co.--14" "Skookum" Cloth body with wooden legs. Paper arms. Plastic head with glued on horse hair wig. Painted features. Marks: Trademark Registered/Skookum/(Bully Good)/Indian/USA/Patented. 1950's. Original clothes and beads. $32.00. (Courtesy Earlene Johnston Collection)

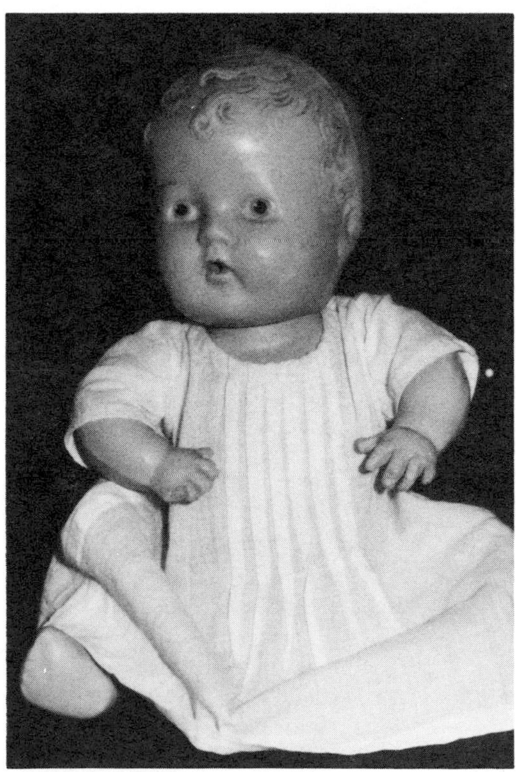

Arrow Plastics--11" "Playful" All rubber with molded hair and painted features.Open mouth/nurser. Molded bent elbows. Marks: Backward 42. 1941. $15.00.

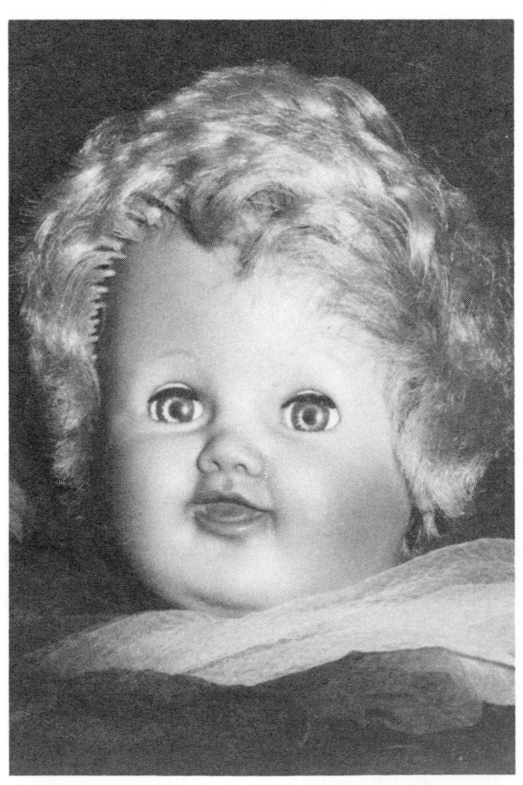

Arrow Plastics--17" "Bye-Bye Baby" Early vinyl head with rooted yellow hair. Sleep blue eyes/lashes. Open/closed/mouth with molded tongue. Latex body, arms and legs. Marks: Arrow Plastics /18 on head. 1957. $18.00. (Courtesy Earlene Johnston Collection)

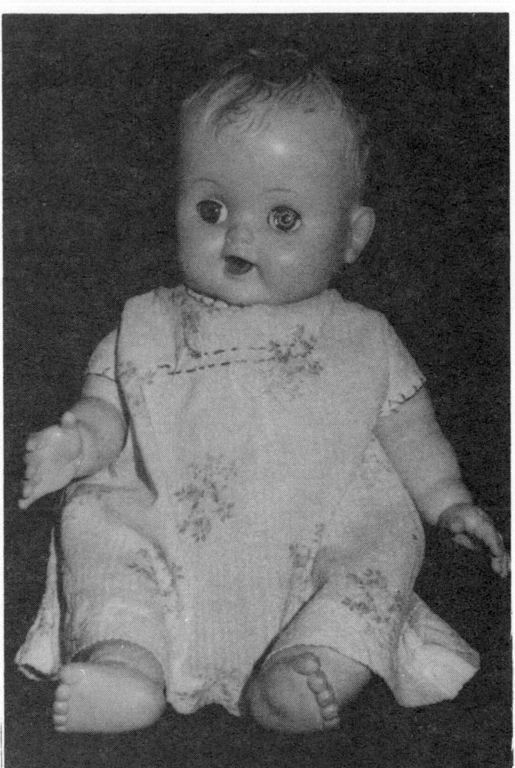

Arrow Plastics--9" "Baby Doo" All vinyl with molded hair. Blue sleep eyes/molded lashes. Open mouth/nurser. Marks: A diamond with an arrow in center, on head. 1957. $4.00.

Arrow Plastics--8" "Candy" All vinyl with molded clothes and doll. Molded hair. Painted blue side glancing eyes. Closed mouth. Marks: The Edward Moberly Co. 1958/Mfg by/Arrow Rubber & Plastic Corp, on right foot. $2.00.

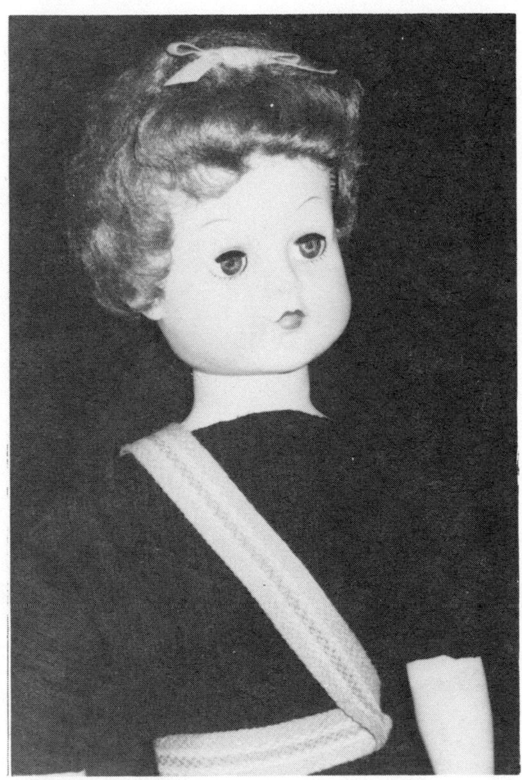

Arrow Plastics--31" "Pretty Lady" All stuffed vinyl. One piece body with unjointed arms and legs. Jointed vinyl head with rooted dark blonde hair. Blue sleep eyes/lashes. Closed mouth. Polished fingernails. High heel feet. Marks: High on neck: An arrow in a diamond. 52, on head. 1958. $16.00.

Arrow--13" "Pouty" All vinyl with molded, painted light brown hair. Blue sleep eyes/molded lashes. Open/closed mouth. Puckered expression. Dimple low on right cheek. Marks: Arrow Rubber, on head. 1959. $16.00.

Arrow Plastics--8" "Cindy" All vinyl with painted features. Jointed at neck only. Marks: 22/The Edward Moberly Co on head. The Edward Moberly Co. Mfg. By Arrow Rubber And Plastic Corp/27/1962 on back. $4.00.

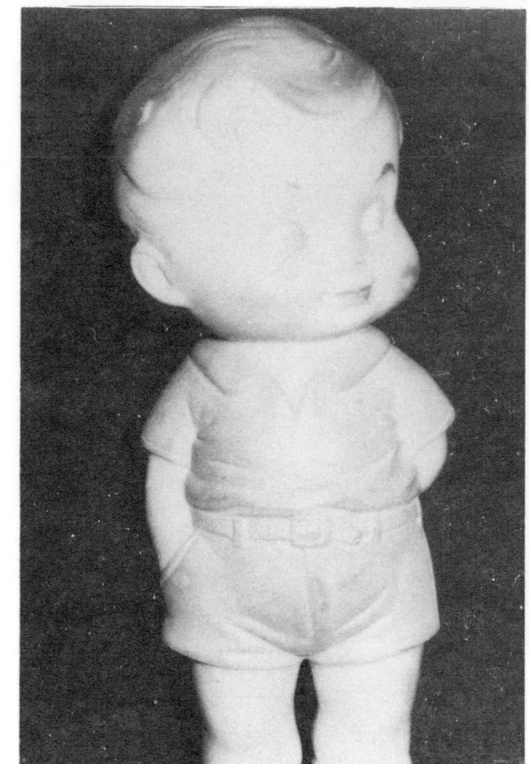

Arrow Rubber Co--8" "Master & His Frog". All vinyl with molded hair, clothes and holding frog in back of him. Jointed at neck. Painted side glancing eyes. Marks: The Edward Moberly Co. 1962/LS/Mfg By/The Arrow Rubber And Plastic Corp. $2.00. (Courtesy Allin's Collection)

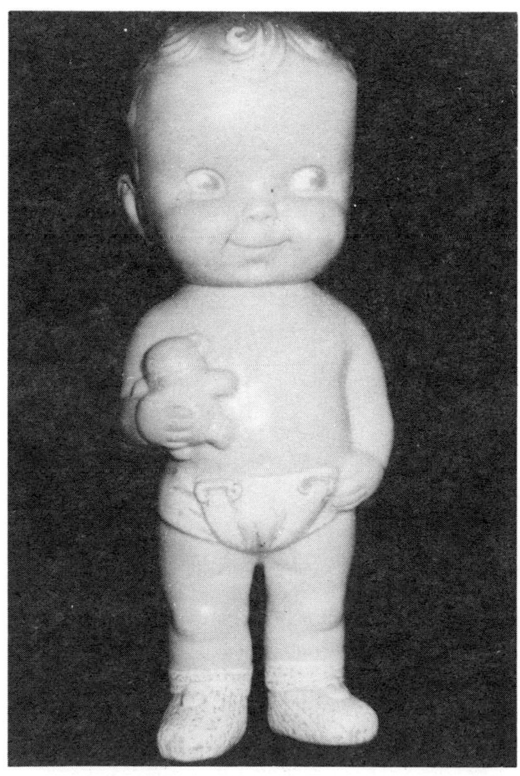

Arrow--8" "My Friend" All early vinyl with painted features and molded painted hair. Molded Teddy Bear, diaper and booties. Marks: 14, on head. The Edward Moberly Co/1964/Mfg. By/Arrow Industries, Inc. on back. $2.00.

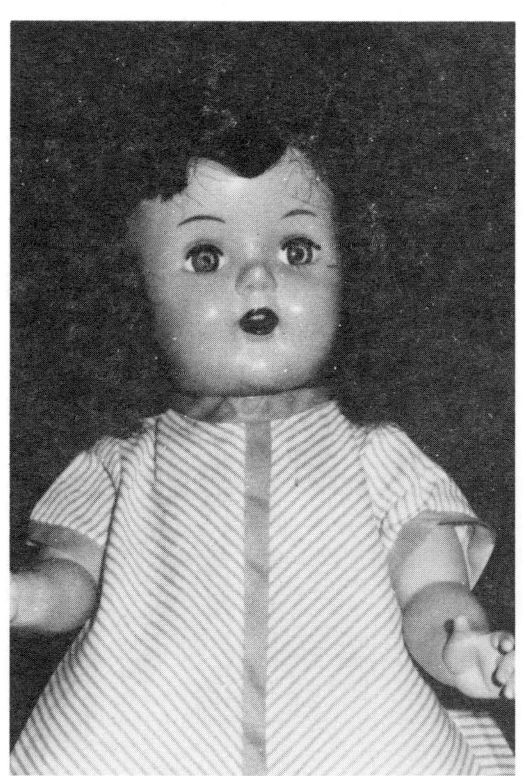

Artisan Novelty Co--18" "Little Miss Gadabout" All hard plastic with glued on black mohair wig. Blue sleep eyes/lashes. Open mouth with four teeth and felt tongue. Walker. Marks: none. This is same doll as "Raving Beauty" only made into a walker. Made for three years by the Artisan Novelty Co. Gardena Calif. 1950. $22.00.

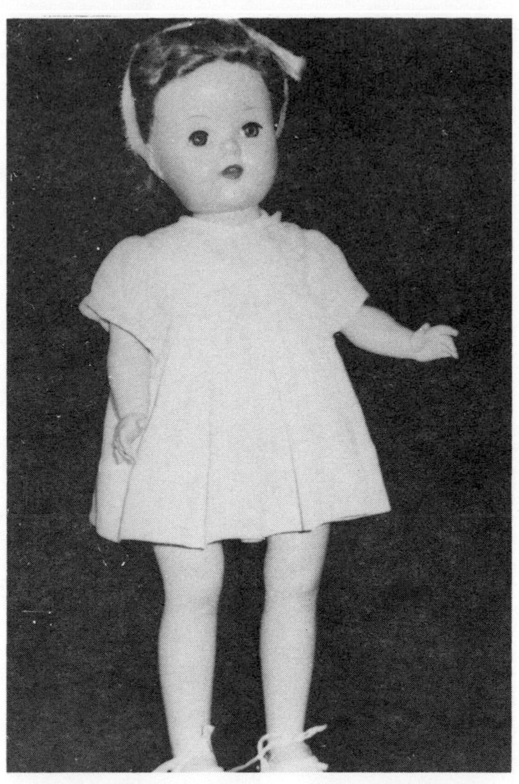

Artisan Novelty Co--19" "Raving Beauty" All hard plastic with glued on red wig. Brown sleep eyes/lashes. Open mouth with four teeth and felt tongue. 2nd and 3rd fingers slightly curled. Wide spread legs. 1953. Marks: none. $32.00.

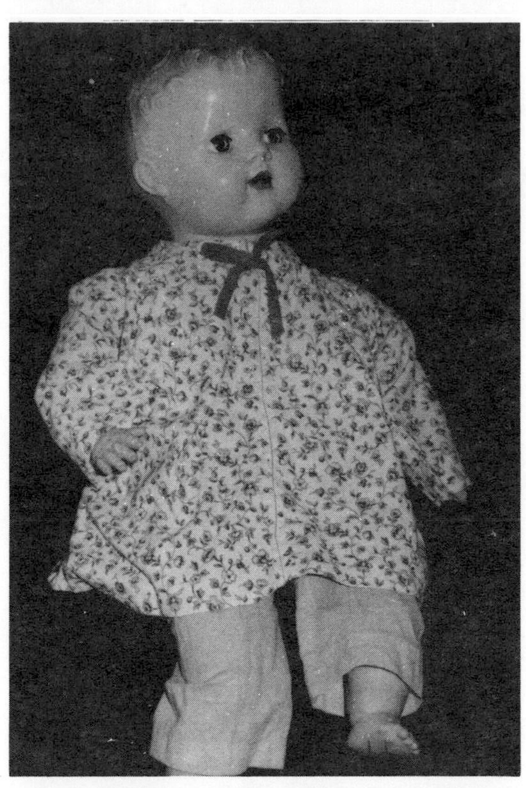

Artisan Novelty--22""Lov You". Cloth body with "voice" in center of chest. Vinyl arms and legs. Open mouth with two teeth and felt tongue. Marks: none. 1951. $22.00.

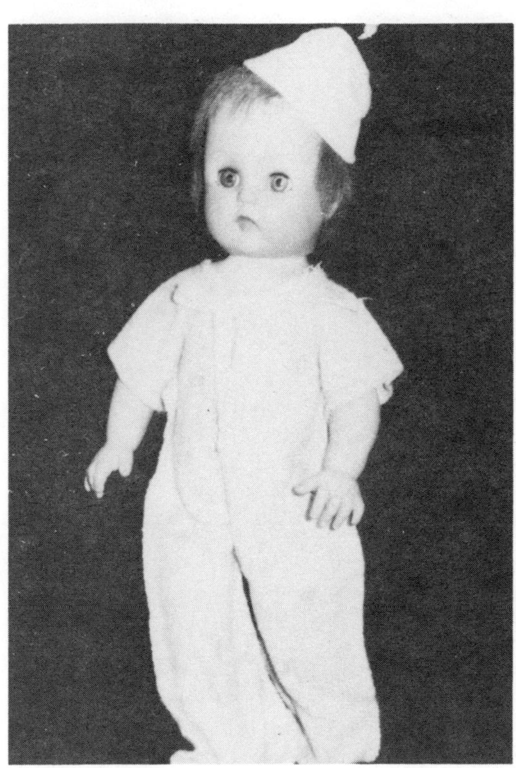

Belle--12" "Miss B One piece vinyl body, arms and legs. Vinyl head with rooted brown hair. Blue sleep eyes/lashes. Closed mouth. Marks: none. 1954. $3.00.

Belle--18" "Ballerina Belle" Hard plastic body and legs. Vinyl arms and head. Rooted dark brown hair. Blue sleep eyes/lashes. Closed mouth. Bent arms and molded ballerina feet. Legs lock in two positions. Marks: 16-VW, on head. 1956. $5.00.

Belle--10" "Belle-Lee" All vinyl with rooted blonde hair. Blue sleep eyes/lashes. Open mouth/nurser. Marks: none. 1958. $2.00.

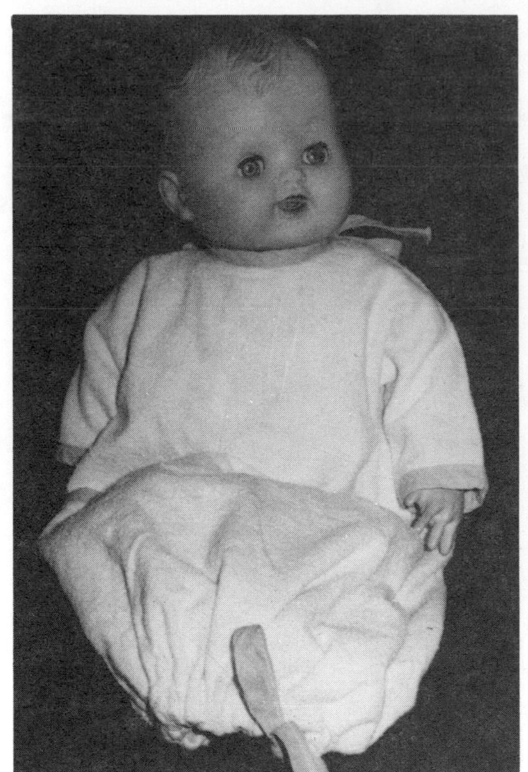

Blumberg--16" "Jimmy" Unjointed one piece latex, stuffed body. Vinyl head with molded hair and blue sleep eyes/lashes. Open/closed mouth with molded tongue. Marks: None. 1955. $4.00.

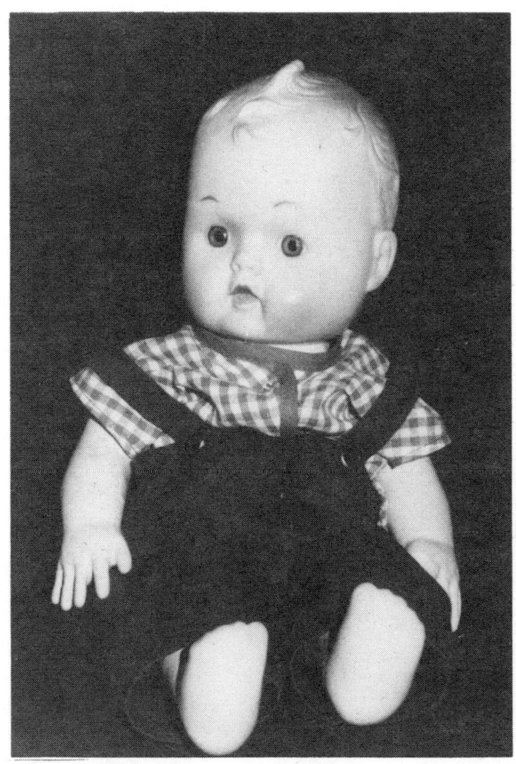

Blumberg--15" "Timmy" Stuffed latex one piece body, arms and legs. Vinyl head with molded light brown hair. Blue inset stationary eyes. Open/closed mouth. Marks: none. 1954. $3.00.

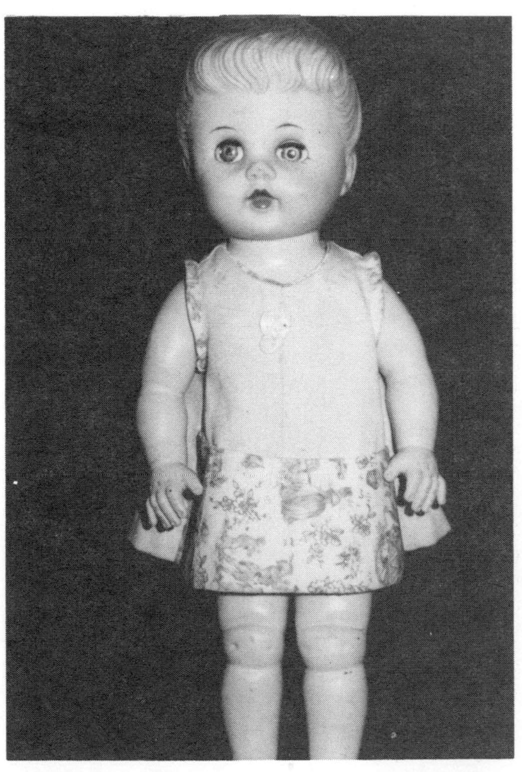

Blumberg--13" "Babies First Doll" One piece vinyl body, arms and legs. Vinyl head with molded hair. Blue sleep eyes/lashes. Open/closed mouth. Marks: 2/F-3 on head. A on lower back. 1960. $3.00.

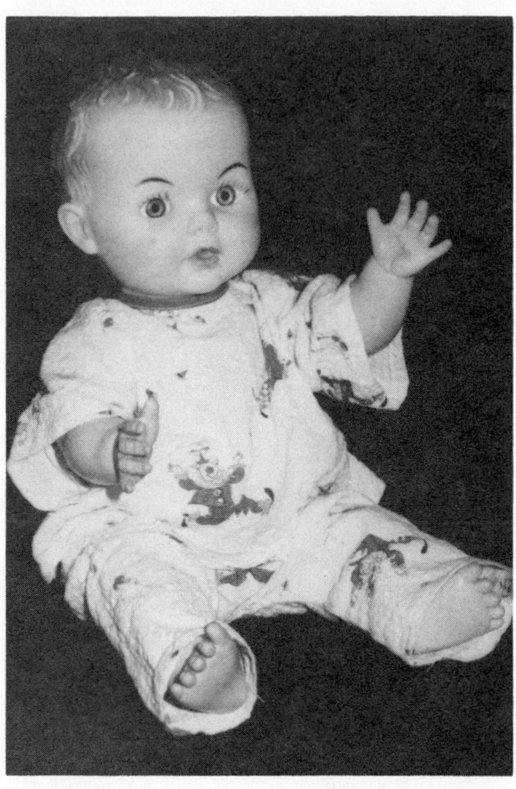

Blumberg--14" "Rock A Bye Baby" All vinyl one piece body and head. Molded hair. Inset stationary eyes. Open mouth/nurser. Individual toes. Marks: none. 1963. $4.00.

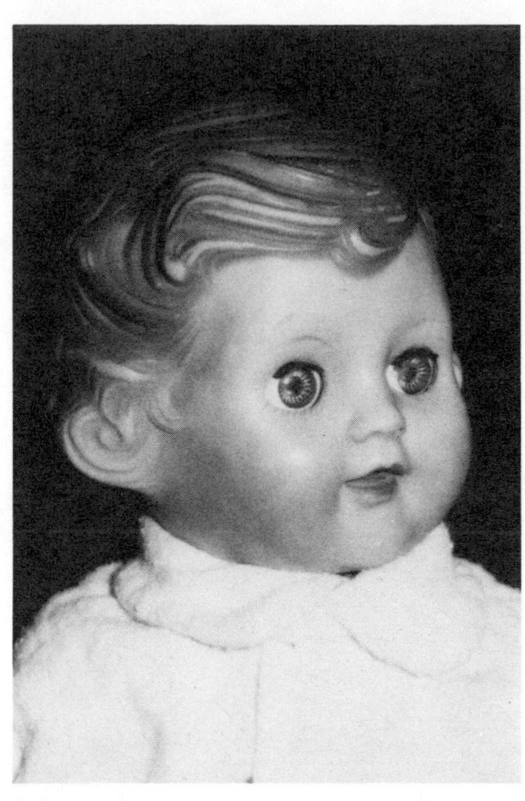

Blumberg--12" "Perky Bright" One piece vinyl body, arms and legs. Vinyl head with molded hair. Sleep blue eyes/molded lashes. Open/closed mouth. Marks: none. 1952. $7.00.

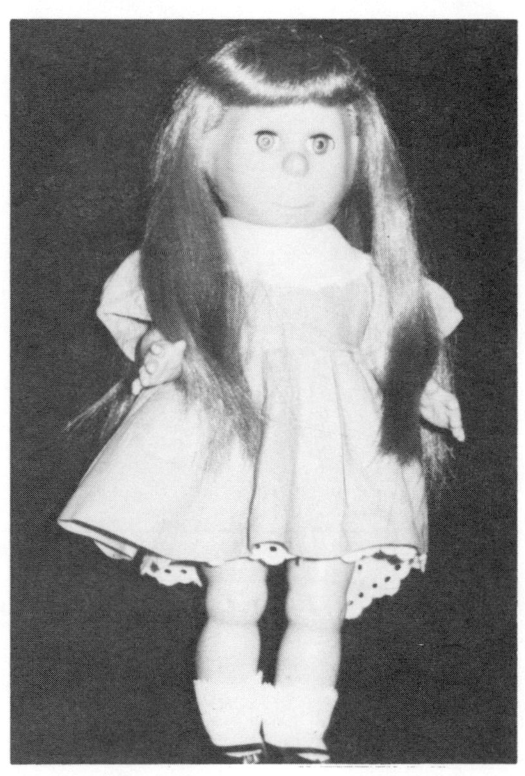

Brookglad--13" "Poor Pitiful Pearl" All vinyl with rooted blonde hair. Blue sleep eyes. Marks: A Brookglad Creation on head. 1957. $18.00.

Brookglad--16" "Rusty" All vinyl with one piece body, arms and legs. Molded red hair. Freckles. Open/closed mouth. Inset stationary blue eyes. Marks: Rusty on head. Large A on lower back. 1958. $16.00. (Courtesy Dorothy Bell Collection)

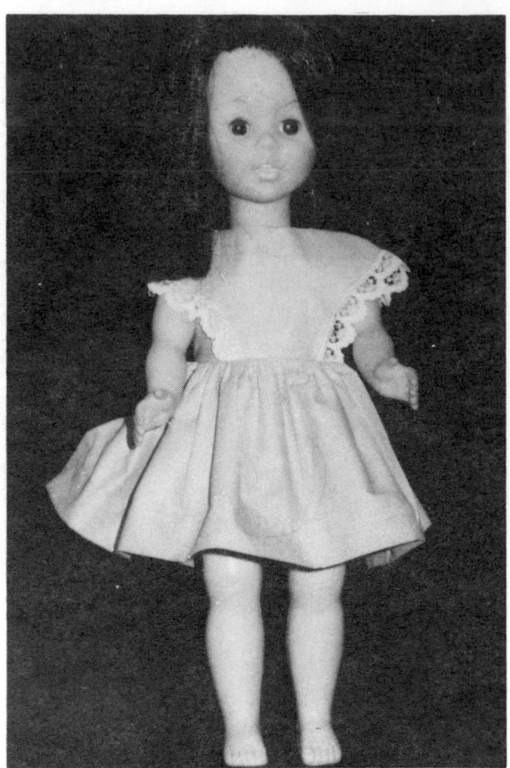

Camay--14" "Liza" Plastic body, legs and arms. Vinyl head with rooted black hair. Brown sleep eyes/lashes. Open/closed mouth. All fingers molded together. Marks: Made In Hong Kong on back. 1969. Original dress. $4.00.

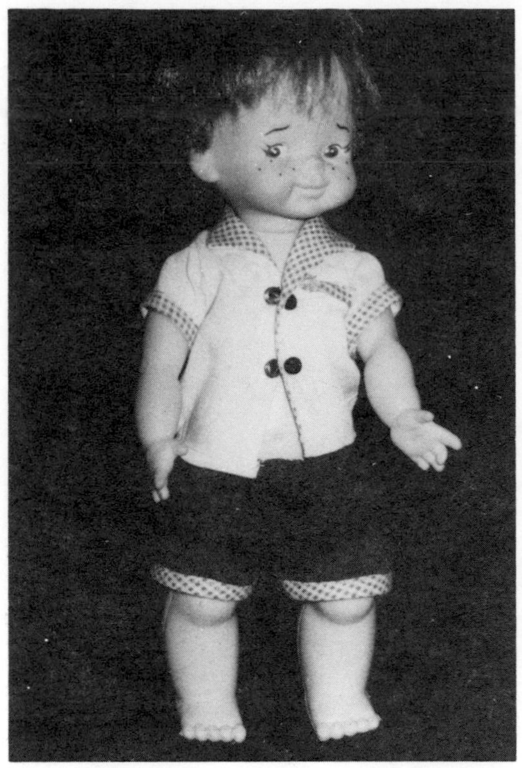

Camay--10" "Tim" Plastic body and legs. Vinyl arms and head. Rooted brown hair.Painted side glancing, eyes. Freckles. Closed mouth. Marks: Camay in a diamond. Made In Hong Kong/No. 7011, on back. Original clothes. 1969. $3.00.

Cameo Doll Products Company

Founded in 1922...sold in 1970 to Strombecker Corporation. What can be said about Cameo? One word Kewpie! They are Cameo's hallmark to fame. Information about this company and it's founders and designers has been written many times, so just a few words on what is happening now.

Kewpies are being reproduced in original molds by Strombecker. Mr. Joseph L. Kallus, the original owner of Cameo, retained some of the companies molds and he is re-issuing them under the name Cameo Exclusive Products. Some are being issued in a limited edition, for example a Kewpie head on a Miss Peep body.

One well loved character from Cameo was and still is Miss Peep and since the change over the new baby doll is called Baby Wendy.

All Cameo dolls are well marked with the trademark and company name. The Strombecker Kewpies, generally, have an "S71" along with the rest of the mold number, name information on the neck of the doll.

The following are not all the dolls made by this company.

1940: Ho Ho (18.00)
1946: Saucy Scottles (40.00), Impish Kewpie (30.00), Baby Blossom (40.00)
1952: Plum (40.00)
1954: Champ (18.00), Dyp a Babe (16.00)
1956: Miss Peep (16.00)
1958: Peanut (16.00), Margie (30.00)
1962: Baby Mine (45.00), New Born Miss Peep (20.00)
1964: Ragsy (3.00), Scootles (25.00)
1966: Joy (18.00)
1967: Giggles (18.00)
1971: Kewpie Gal (3.00)
1972: Kewpie (100th Anniversary of Montgomery Ward Co. 18.00), Baby Wendy (8.00)

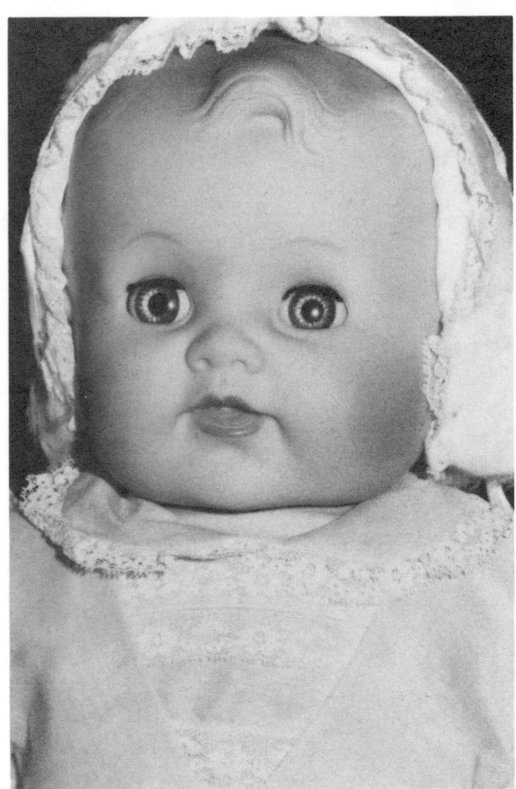

Cameo--24" "Plum" One piece latex body, arms and legs. Vinyl head with molded hair. Blue sleep eyes/lashes. Open/closed mouth. Two squeekers, one in bottom for spanking and one in center for hugging. Marks: Cameo, on neck. Plum/Designed and copywrited By/JLK, on box. 1952. This head was used as "Dyp-A-Babe", in 1956 and as "Affectionately Peanut", in 1958. $40.00.

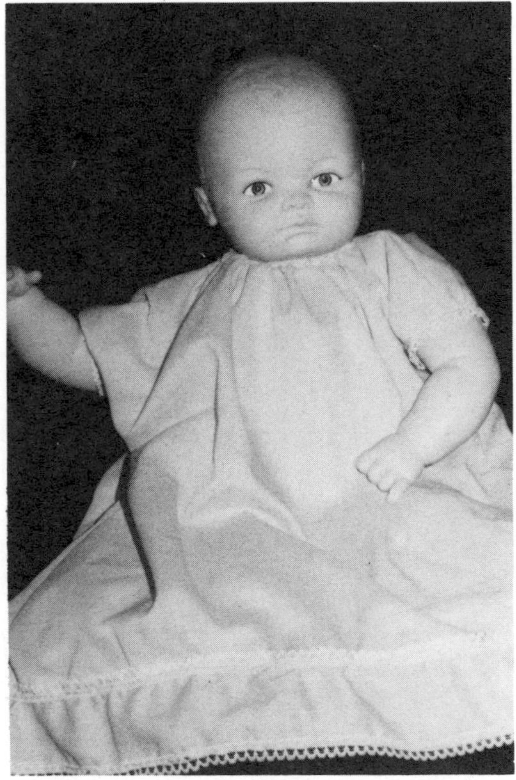

Cameo--18" "Miss Peep" All vinyl with pin hinged hips and shoulders. Hands face to back. Right hand 2nd and 3rd fingers curled. Left index curled and touching thumb, 2nd and 3rd curled. Vinyl head with molded hair. Stationary blue eyes. Closed mouth. Cryer in arms. Marks: Cameo, on head and body. 1957. $16.00.

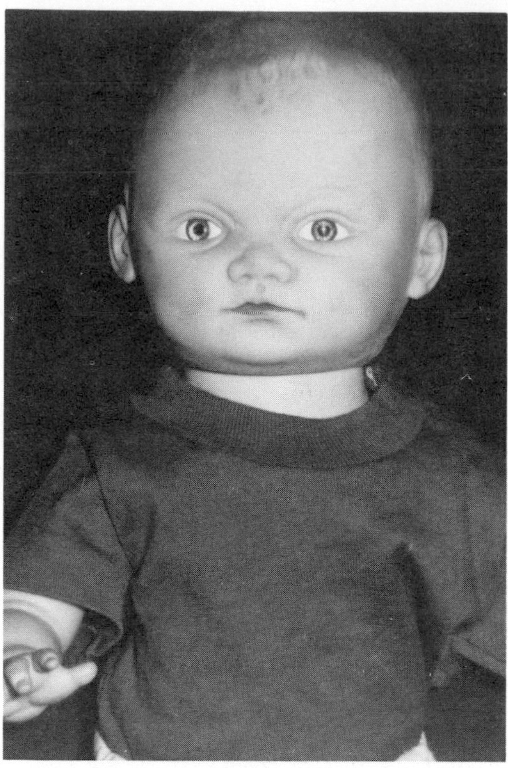

Cameo--20" "New Born Miss Peep" Vinyl one piece body and legs. Molded hair. Inset stationary eyes. Palms down. Marks: Cameo, on head. 12, on body. 1962. $20.00. (Courtesy Earlene Johnston Collection)

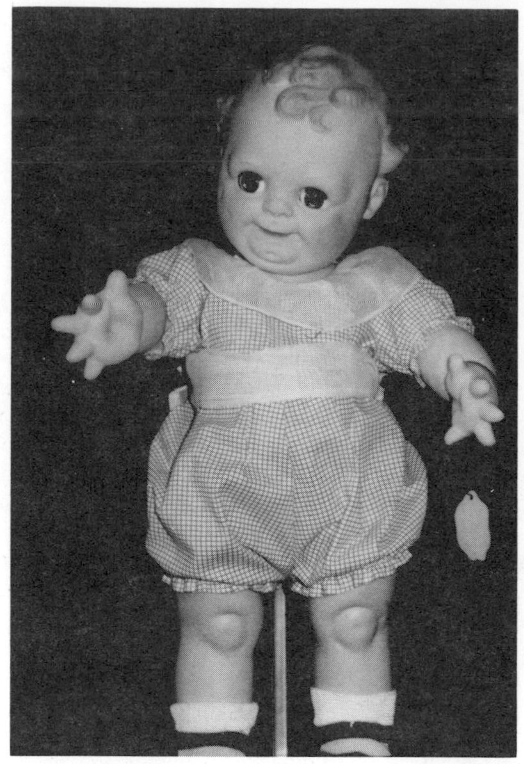

Cameo--19" "Scootles". All vinyl. Molded hair. Blue sleep eyes/lashes. Closed mouth. Dimpled cheeks. Marks: Tag: Designed & Copyright/ Rose O'Neill/A Cameo Doll. On head: Cameo. Cameo, on back. Original clothes. 1964. $25.00. (Courtesy Fye Collection)

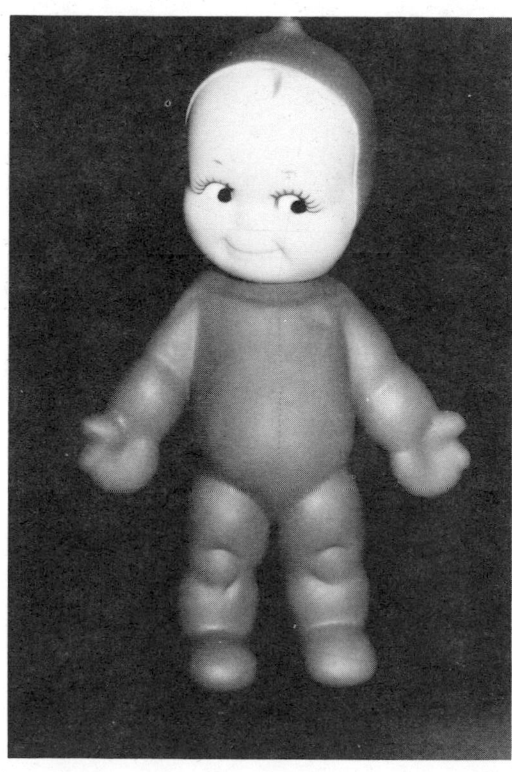

Cameo--8" "Ragsy Kewpie-Re-Issue" All vinyl with jointed neck. Painted features. Marks: Cameo 065 JLK on head. Cameo 65 on body. 1971. The 1964 issue has a heart in the center of chest. $3.00.

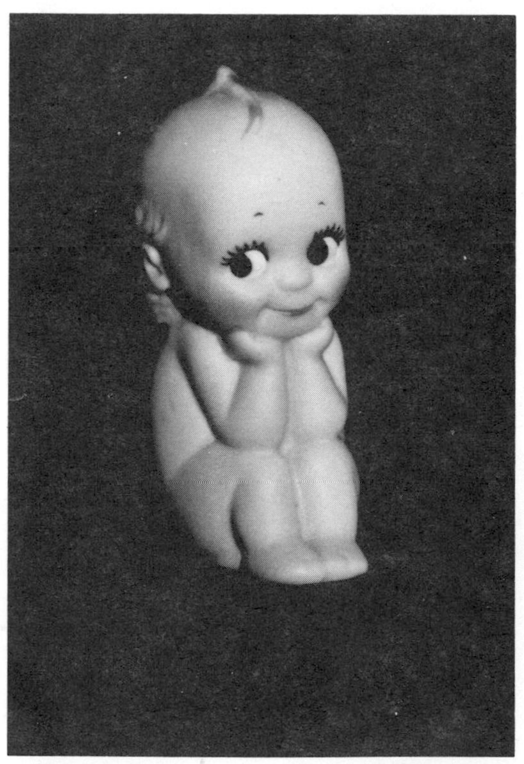

Cameo--3½" "Kewpie" All vinyl with painted features. Marks: Kewpie/Rose O'Neill/Cameo. 1971. $2.00.

Cameo--9" "Kewpie Gal" All vinyl with molded hair and glued on ribbon. Jointed neck, shoulders and hip. Marks: Cameo JLK on head. Cameo on back. There is an "S71" on upper right side of neck, this is Strombeckers mold number. These molds were sold by Cameo and are being reproduced by Strombecker. 1971. $3.00.

Cameo--8" "Kewpi" All vinyl with molded hair and painted features. Jointed head, shoulders and hip. Reproduced from original mold for Montgomery Wards 100th anniversary in 1972. Marks: '18 Cameo, on head. Cameo on body. Original clothes. $18.00.

Chadwick-Miller--8" "Sad Eyes" Plastic body, arms and legs. Vinyl head with rooted yellow blonde hair. Very large brown painted eyes. Marks: Made In Hong Kong, on back. Dress Tag: Made In Hong Kong. Box: Chadwick-Miller Made In Hong Kong. 1965. Original clothes. $2.00.

Confetti Doll--6½" "Cleaning Day" All composition with glued on blonde mohair wig. Brown painted, side glancing eyes. Closed mouth. Painted black shoes. Marks: Confetti/Doll, on back. 1945. $4.00.

Confetti--11" "Bribe" All composition with dark red mohair wig glued on. Blue painted side glancing eyes. Original gown and flowers. Marks: Dress Tag: Confetti Doll. 1947. $5.00.

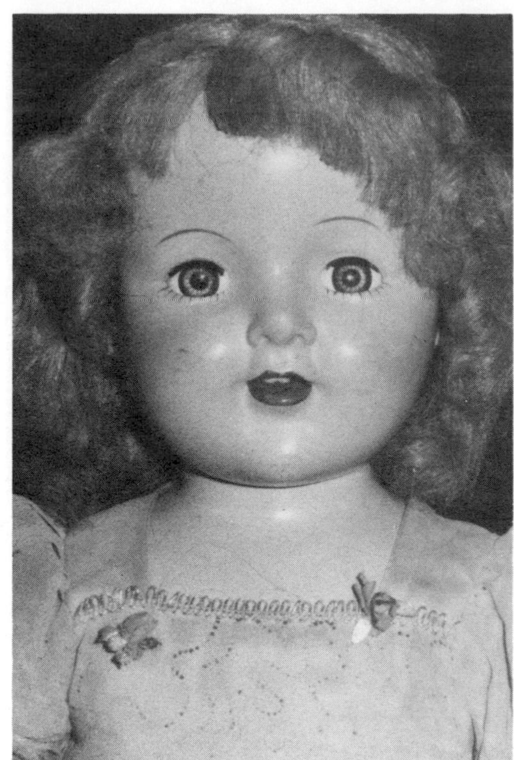

Cosmopolition Doll Company--29" "Gloria" Cloth body with latex arms and legs. Hard plastic shoulder plate, swivel head. Glued on dark blonde saran wig. Blue sleep eyes/lashes. Open mouth with 4 teeth. Original dress. Marks: none. 1948. $25.00.

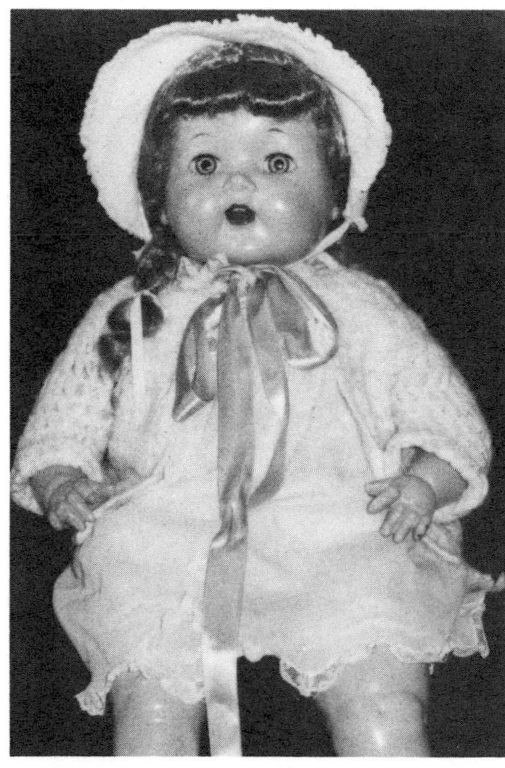

Cosmopolitan Doll Company--25" "Emily" Hard plastic jointed shoulder plate and head. Glued on blonde wig. Blue sleep eyes/lashes. Open mouth with two teeth. Cloth body. Composition arms and legs. Marks: none. 1949. $40.00. (Courtesy Allin's Collection)

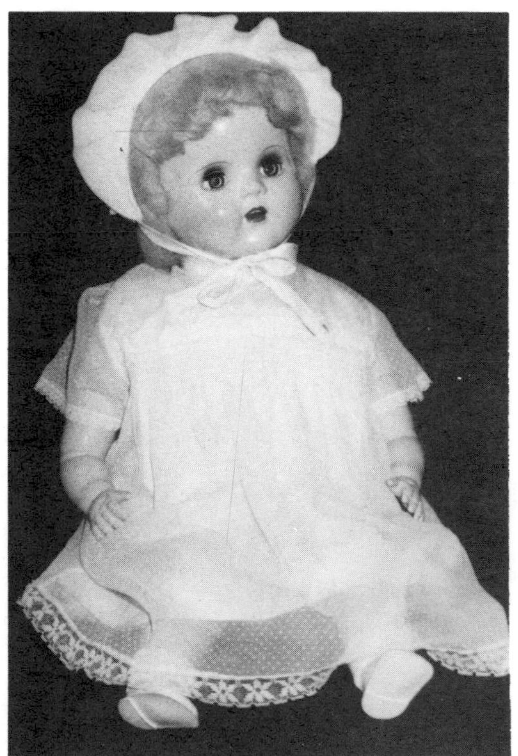

Cosmopolition Doll Company--22" "Pam" Cloth body. Vinyl arms, legs with hard plastic head. Glued on mohair wig. Blue sleep eyes/lashes. Black eye shadow. Open mouth with two teeth and a felt tongue. Marks: CDC on head. 1955. $20.00.

Deluxe Toys Company

Deluxe Reading, Deluxe Topper, Topper Corp, Topper Toys, Deluxe Toy Creations.

Yes, all the above listed are one company. The "parent" company is Deluxe Toys.

This company specializes in dolls that Do Things. Do not pass them up just because you do not know how or if they work. Check Chapter Two where I go into detail on the Automation Doll.

The quality of Deluxe Toys has always been good and they last and last. The Doll, that is, not the Mechanisms. One of their most delightful and enduring is Baby Tickle Tears or perhaps Lil Miss Fussy, who kicks and seems to stay in a pouty mood.

The Deluxe Toy group, as a general rule, have well marked dolls with the name of the company and the date. Once in awhile you will run into an unmarked doll made by them. For example Sweet Rosemary by Deluxe Toy Creations or Paula Mae by Topper Toys. There is only an AE series on it (251/AE 75). The AE number is the code for a jobber who made the bodies and as far as the doll goes, the Deluxe name was found only on the wrist tag attached to the doll. Both these dolls were made prior to the automation period of this company.

The following are not all the dolls made by this company.

1957: Sweet Rosemary (20.00)

1959: Paula Mae (16.00)

1960: Cuddly Cathy (16.00), Little Miss Fashion(20.00)

1963: Nancy Nurse (10.00), Baby Brite (8.00), Penny Brite (4.00)

1964: Susy Cute (4.00), Bonnie Bride (4.00)

1965: Bonnie Fashion (8.00), Baby Boo (8.00), Bride (8.00), The Go Go's (Brenda Brush, Private Ida, Hot Canary, Slick Chick, The Swinger-3.00 each)

1966: Baby Magic (10.00), Pretty Boy (12.00), Big Ears (8.00), Machine Gun Mike (4.00), Silly Safari (3.00), Combat Kid (3.00), Bugle Ben (4.00), Tex (4.00), Baby Tickle Tears (15.00), Glori Glamour (7.00), Mike (3.00), Susy Homemaker (18.00)

1967: Lil Miss Fussy (10.00), Party Time (10.00)

1968: Bikey (7.00), Tickles (10.00)

1969: Baby Catch a Ball (18.00), Baby Peek N Play (16.00), Baby Walker (9.00), Baby Party (10.00), Baby Fussy (10.00), Baby Bunny (10.00)

1970: Dawn (3.00), Glori (3.00), Angie (3.00)

1971: Smarty Pants (10.00), Jessica (3.00)

Deluxe Toy Creations--24" "Paula Marie" One piece vinyl (stuffed) body, arms and legs. Vinyl head with rooted blonde hair. Blue sleep eyes/lashes. Painted finger and toe nails. Marks: VH-25, between shoulders. Large A, on lower center back. VH-25-2, on bottom of right foot. 1959. $16.00.

Deluxe Reading--14" "Baby Brite" Plastic body. Vinyl head with rooted blonde hair. Blue sleep eyes/lashes. Open/closed mouth. Two buttons in stomach. Lower one flips head to the left. Top one makes arms fly up. Both arms and head are returned to natural position by pushing them. Marks: 28 Deluxe Reading Corp/1963/15 Me-H, on head. $8.00.

Deluxe Reading--8" "Penny Brite" All vinyl with blonde rooted hair. Painted side glancing black eyes. Dimples. Open/closed mouth with four teeth. Marks: A9/Deluxe Reading Corp/1963, on head. Deluxe Reading Corp/Elizabeth NJ/Pat. Pending, on back. Original clothes. $4.00.

Deluxe Reading--22" "Bonnie Bride" Plastic body, arms and legs. Vinyl head with rooted brown hair. Blue sleep eyes/lashes. Right hand cupped to hold bouquet. Button on right shoulder makes her walk and toss bouquet. Marks: 21HH/K50 on head. Deluxe Reading/ Elizabeth NJ/Pat. Pending on body. 1964. $4.00.

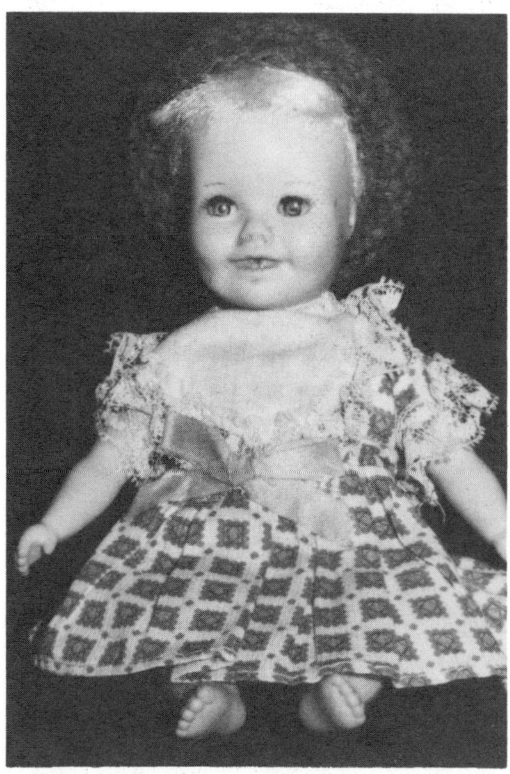

Deluxe Reading--7" "Susie Cute" All vinyl with rooted blonde hair. Stationary blue eyes/molded lashes. Open mouth/nurser. Mechanism in body operates arms. Push arms down; press chest and arms go up. Marks: Deluxe Reading/1964/ GX on head. Pat. Pend/1 on back. $4.00.

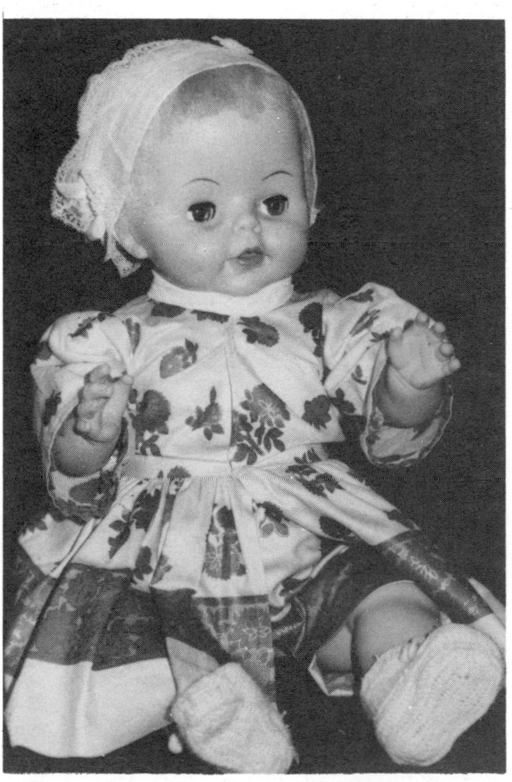

Deluxe Reading--21" "Baby Boo" Plastic body. Vinyl foam arms and legs. Vinyl head with rooted blonde hair. Blue sleep eyes/lashes.Open mouth/nurser. Dimple in right cheek. Battery operated. Marks: Deluxe Reading/1965/68 on head. Cries for pacifier, stops when put in mouth. $8.00.

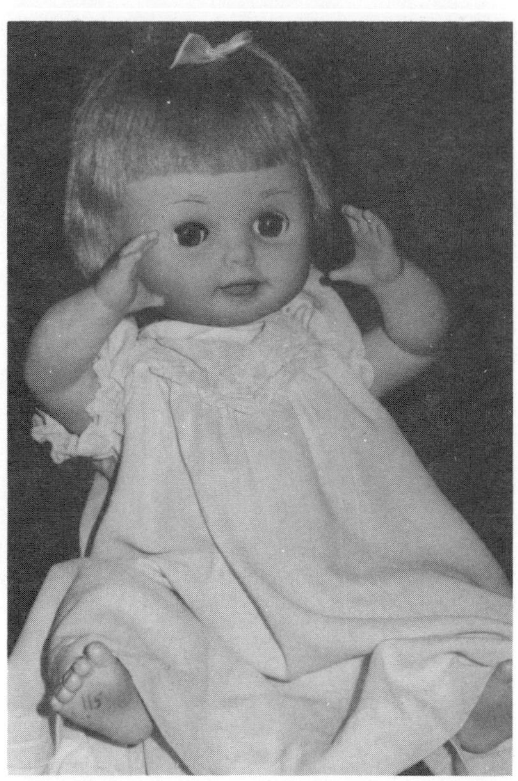

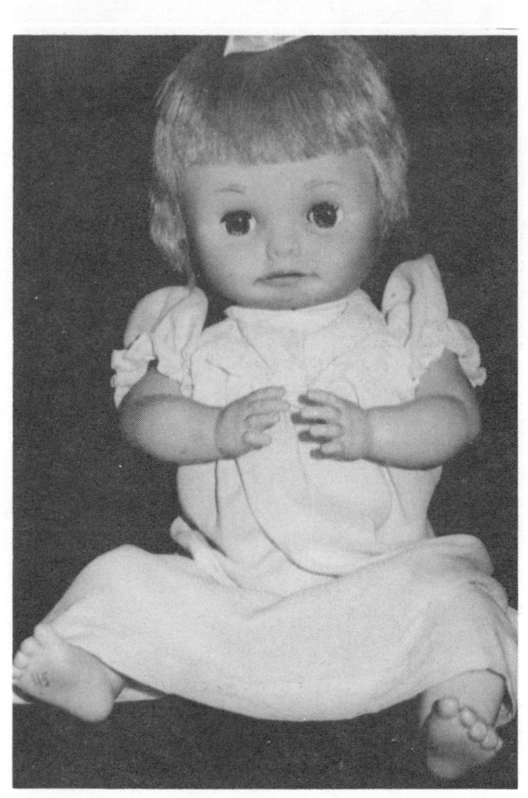

Deluxe Reading--18" "Baby Magic" Plastic with vinyl head. Rooted dark blonde hair. Blue sleep eyes/lashes. When arms are pulled down, she pouts. When hands go up, she smiles. Button in center of stomach. Open mouth/nurser. Marks: EK 43/Deluxe Reading/1966 on head. $10.00.

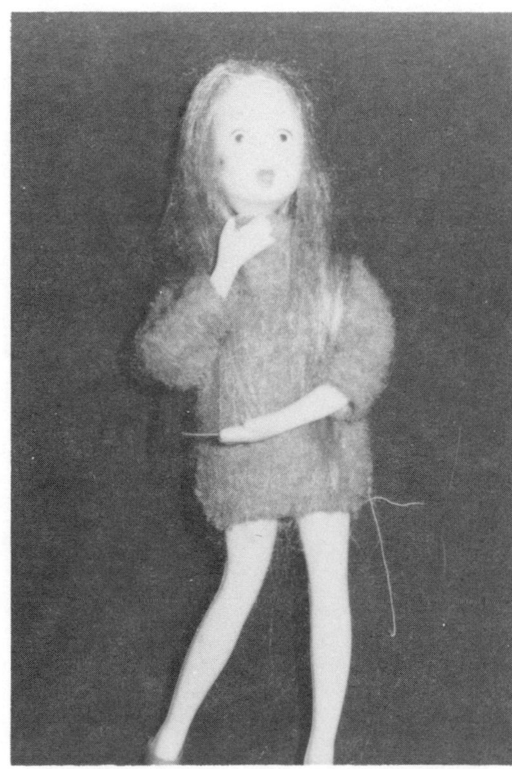

Deluxe Reading--6½" "Cool Cat, Of The Go Go's" All bendable vinyl with glued on hair. Painted features. Open/closed mouth. Held guitar. There are eight "Go-Go's" in a set. The others are: Slick Chick, Brenda Brush, Hot Canary, Tomboy, Yeah, Yeah, Swinger, Private Ida. Marks: Deluxe Reading Corp/1965. $3.00.

Deluxe Reading--14" "Baby Tickle Tears" Plastic body and legs. Vinyl arms and head. Rooted blonde hair. Painted black eyes with tear ducts in lower center of eyes. Open mouth/nurser. Bring arms down and she pouts. Other view on Page 64

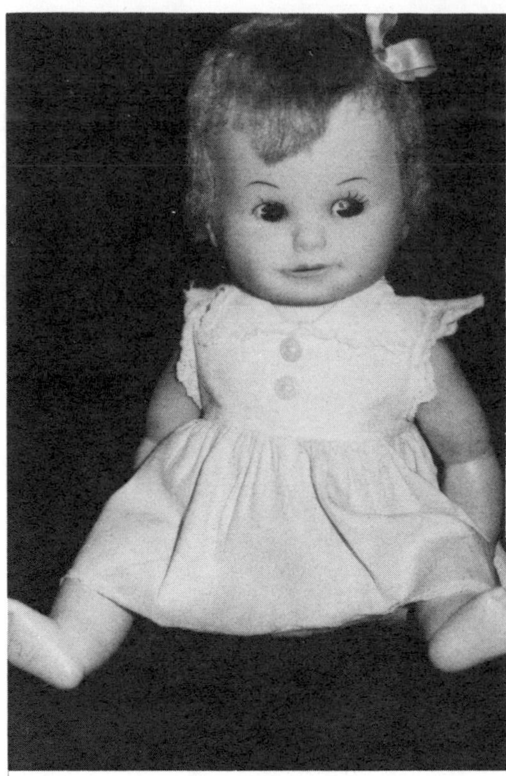

and cries. Push button in center of stomach and arms fly up and she smiles. Operates without a battery. Marks: Deluxe Reading Corp/1966, on head. $15.00.

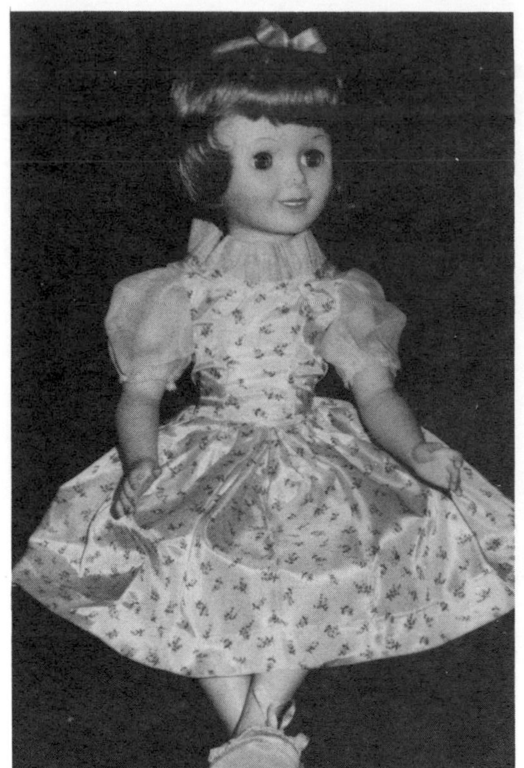

Deluxe Reading--21" "Susie Homemaker" Plastic body and legs. Jointed hips and knees. Vinyl head and arms. Rooted dark blonde hair. Blue sleep eyes/molded lashes. Open mouth with five painted teeth. Dimples far out on cheeks. Marks: 2/K26/Deluxe Reading/1966. $18.00.

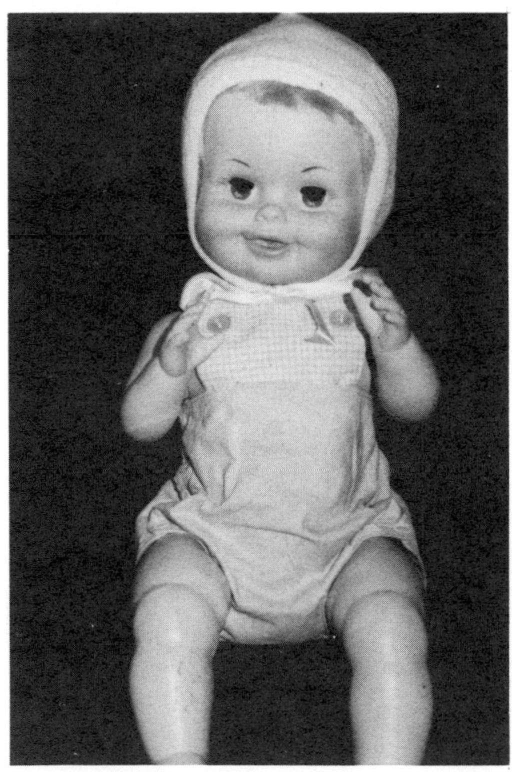

Deluxe Topper--18" "Party Time" Plastic body and legs. Vinyl arms and head. Stationary blue eyes. Open mouth/nurser. Open hands facing body sits on edge of table. Blows up balloons and blows noise makers. Battery operated. Marks: K-39/Deluxe Topper/1967. $10.00.

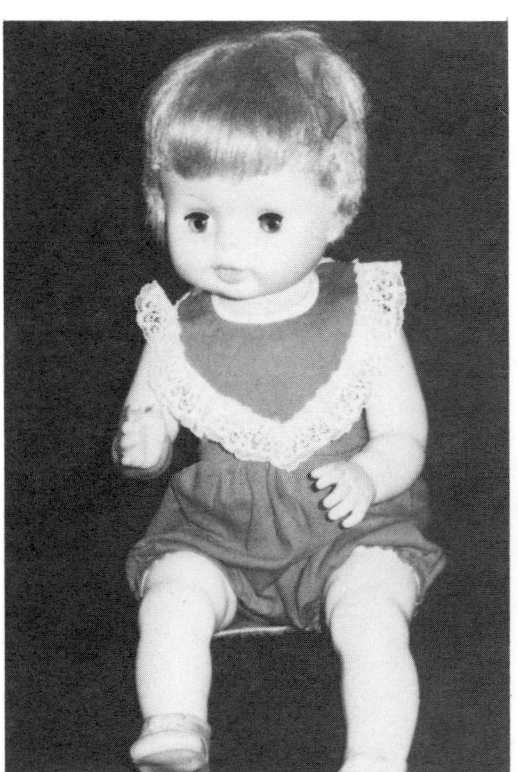

Deluxe Topper--18" "Lil Miss Fussy" Plastic body and legs. Vinyl arms and head. Rooted ash blonde hair. Blue inset stationary eyes. Open mouth/nurser. Molded, bent legs. After bottle she wets diaper, then cries and kicks her legs until diaper is changed. Battery operated. Marks: K-39/Deluxe Topper/1967 on head. $10.00.

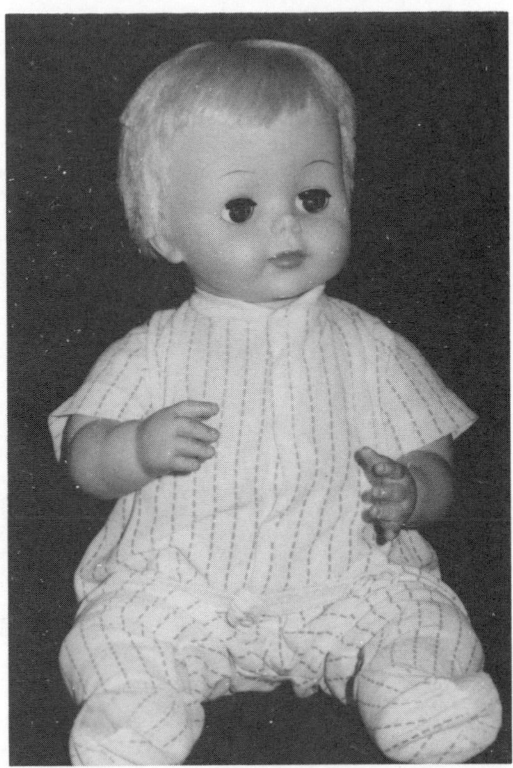

Deluxe Topper--20" "Tickles" Plastic body, arms and legs. Vinyl head with rooted blonde hair. Large blue sleep eyes/lashes. Closed mouth. Battery operated. Marks: 1963 Deluxe Reading/38, on head. Talker. $10.00.

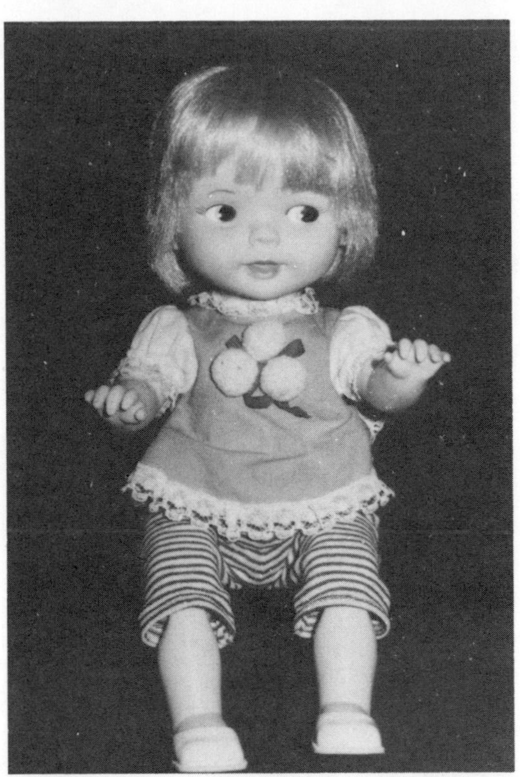

Deluxe Topper--11" "Bikey" Plastic body and legs. Vinyl arms and head. Rooted blonde hair. Painted side glancing blue eyes. Open/closed mouth. Hands molded to fit handlebars. Jointed knees. Legs wide spread. Battery operated. Marks: Bikey/Deluxe Topper/1968/Hong Kong on head. Original clothes. $7.00.

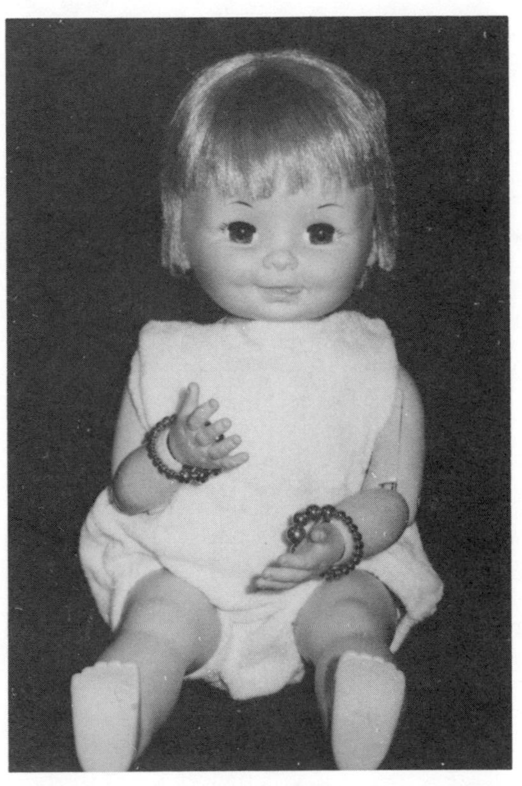

Deluxe Topper--18" "Baby Catch A Ball" Plastic body, arms and legs. Vinyl head with rooted blonde hair. Stationary blue eyes/lashes. Jointed wrists. Mechanical arms work with batteries. Throws ball when ball makes contact with bracelets around wrists. Marks: PB2/28/ Deluxe Topper/1969, on head. $18.00.

Deluxe Topper--18" "Baby Peek 'n Play" Plastic body and legs. Vinyl arms and head. Stationary blue eyes. Battery operated. With use of a "cricket" or slap of hands, her arms and hands come up. Marks: 17EYE/New/M.94/Deluxe Topper/1969, on head. Original clothes. $16.00.

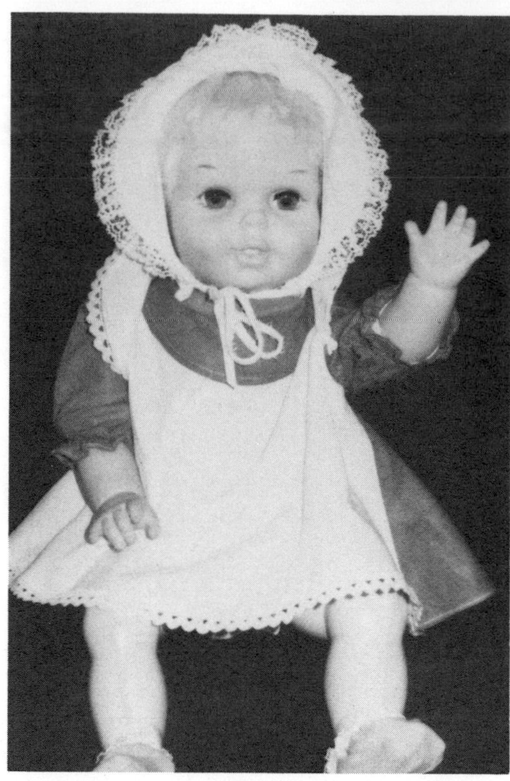

Deluxe Topper--20" "Baby Bunny" Plastic body and legs. Vinyl arms and head. Rooted white hair. Stationary blue eyes/lashes. Open/closed mouth. Sits on side of table. Marks: 51/Deluxe Topper/1969, on head. Waves her arms and legs and rocks from side to side. $10.00.

Topper Corp.--6" "Dawn" All vinyl with rooted blonde hair. Painted blue side glancing eyes. Closed mouth. Adult body. Jointed waist. Medium high heel feet. Bendable knees. Marks: 11A on head. 1970/Topper Corp/Hong Kong on lower back. Original clothes. $3.00.

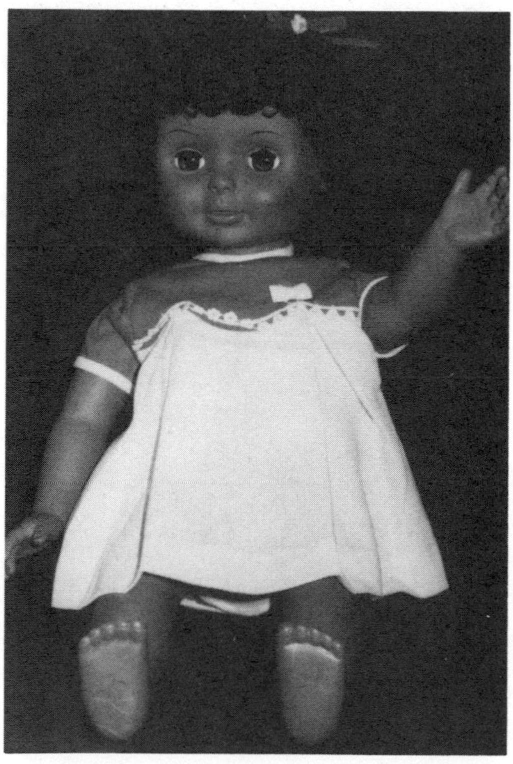

Topper--19" "Smarty Pants" Plastic body and legs. Vinyl arms and head. Rooted black hair. Brown sleep eyes/lashes. Battery operated. Push head or legs back or arms up and she will talk. Marks: Topper Co/1971, on head. Original clothes. $10.00.

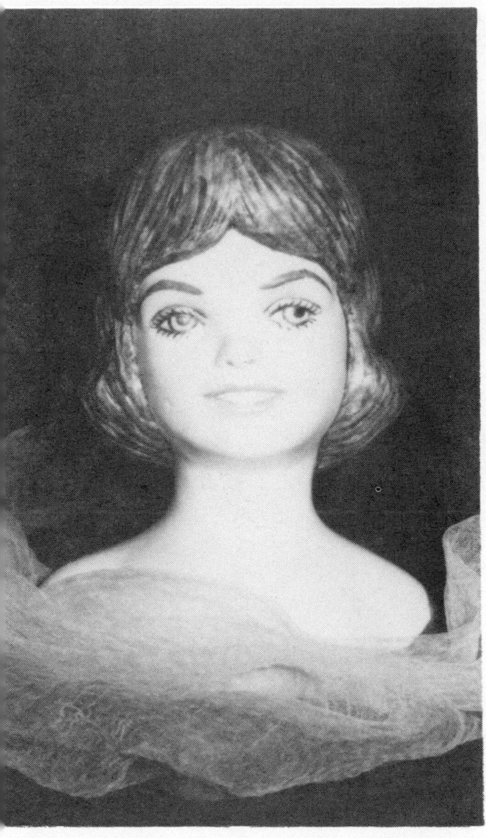

Doll Artist--14" "Sunny" By Lita Wilson. Bisque head, arms and legs. Cloth body. Molded painted hair and featuers. Open/closed mouth with painted teeth. Marks: Petite Portrait, on front of shoulder plate. Sunny/LW 1970, on back. $75.

Doll Artist--16" "Prince Ranier" By Lita Wilson. Bisque head, arms and legs. Cloth body. Painted and molded hair. Painted features. Marks: Petite Portraits on front of neck plate. Prince Ranier on back. LW on left side of back and 1971 on right. $95.00.

Doll Artist--15" "Liz Taylor" By Lita Wilson. Bisque head, arms and legs. Cloth body. Glued on black wig. Painted features. Ring on left hand. Marks: Petite Portraits, on front of neck plate. Liz Taylor, on back with LW in corner. $105.00.

Elizabeth Taylor shown with Richard Burton, from a scene in Cleopatra.

Doll Artist--22" "Nursing Gypsy Mother And Child" Cloth body, arms and legs. Gauntlet composition feet and hands. Composition head and shoulder plate. Painted features. Pierced ears. Baby all composition with open round mouth. Original clothes. $140.00. (Courtesy Allin's Collection)

Doll Artist--12" "Uncle Sam" Reproduction by Ida May Staples. Bisque head with blue glass stationary eyes. Grey hair and beard. On new ball jointed body. All original clothes. Marks: IMS on back of head. $60.00 (Courtesy Earlene Johnston Collection)

Doll Artist--9" "Little Women" By Aileen Harris. 1963. $65.00. (Courtesy Allin's Collection)

Doll Artist--9" "Little Women" By Aileen Harris. 1963. $65.00. (Courtesy Allin's Collection).

"Little Women" by Aileen Harris

"Little Women" by Aileen Harris

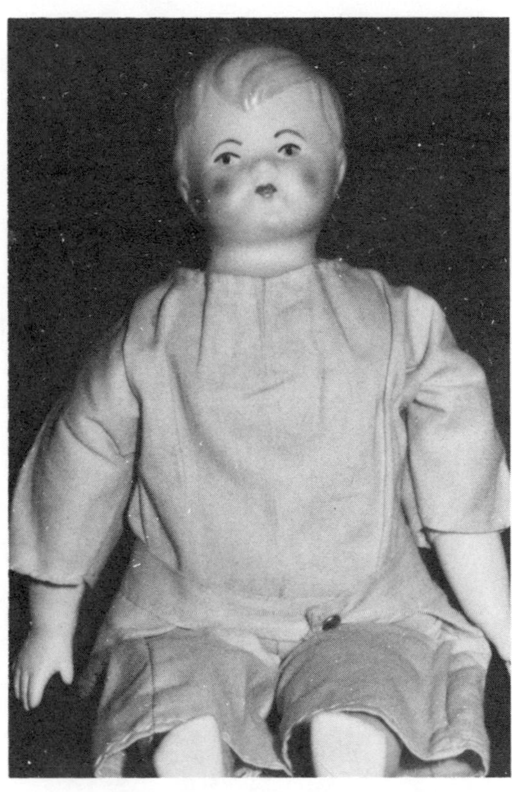

Doll Artist--13" "Boy" Cloth stuffed body. Bisque shoulder head, arms and legs. Original clothes. Marks: Mark Farmer on back of shoulders. $35.00 (Courtesy Earlene Johnston Collection)

Doll Artist--14½" "John F. Kennedy" A reproduction made by Mrs. Lucille Kimsey. Cloth and bisque. 1971. $35.00. (Courtesy Fye Collection)

Dam Things Originals--3" "Good Luck Troll Graduate" All vinyl with inset recessed skull grey and black hair. Inset, stationary brown eyes. Original clothes. Made in Vadue, Liechtenstein and sold by Royalty Design of Florida, Inc. Marks: Can't make out top line, except N./DAM, on back. 1965. $2.00.

Duchess Doll--7" "May" All hard plastic with white glued on mohair wig. Painted side glancing blue eyes. Painted shoes. Marks: None. 1947. Original clothes. $2.00.

Duchess Doll--7½" "Cinderella" All hard plastic with glued on blonde mohair wig. Blue sleep eyes/molded lashes. Painted on shoes. Marks: Duchess Doll Co/Design Copyright/1948. Original clothes. $2.00.

Duchess Doll--7½" "Scotch Miss" All hard plastic with glued on blonde mohair wig. Blue sleep eyes. Marks: Duchess Doll Corp/Design Copyright/1948. Original clothes. $2.00.

Duchess Doll--7½" "Martha Washington" All hard plastic with glued on white mohair wig. Blue sleep eyes. Marks: Duchess Doll Corp/Design /Copyright/1948. Original clothes. $2.00.

Duchess Doll--7" "Scarlet" All hard plastic with brown glued on mohair wig. Painted blue side glancing eyes. Open mouth with four painted teeth. Painted on shoes. Marks: Duchess Doll Corp/Design Copyright/1948. Original clothes. $4.00.

Duchess Doll--7¼" "Carmen" All hard plastic with painted side glancing eyes. Jointed shoulders and neck. Painted on shoes. Marks: Duchess Doll Co/Design copyright. 1948. Original clothes. $3.00.

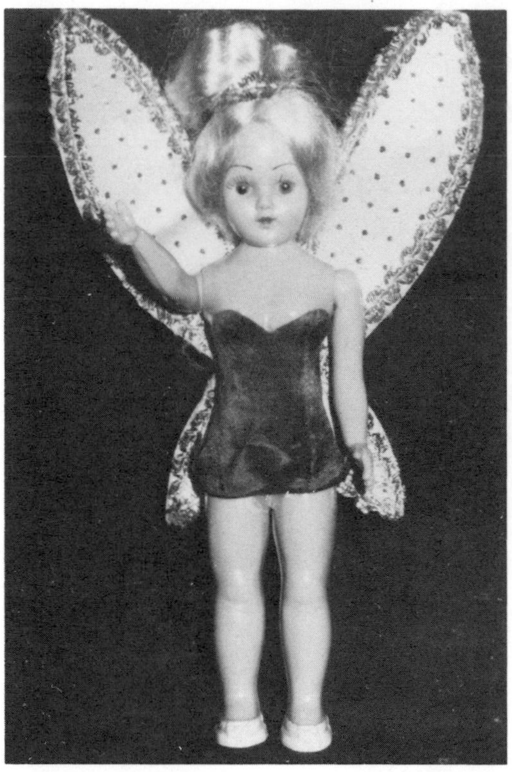

Duchess Doll--7" "Tinker Bell" All hard plastic with glued on blonde wig. Blue sleep eyes. Molded and painted on shoes. Marks: Duchess Doll Corp/Design Copyright/1948. Original clothes. $4.00.

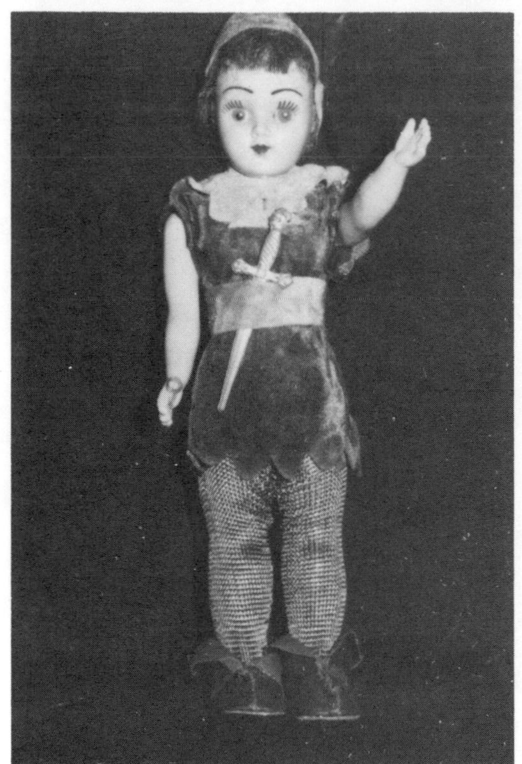

Duchess Doll--7" "Peter Pan" All hard plastic with glued on brown wig. Blue sleep eyes/painted lashes. Marks: Duchess Doll Corp/Design Copyright/1948. Original clothes. $4.00.

Duchess Doll--7" "Miss Hollywood 1949" All hard plastic with glued on brown mohair wig. Blue sleep eyes. Painted on shoes. Marks: Duchess Doll Corp/Design Copyright/1949. Original clothes. $2.00.

Duchess Doll--7" "Danny The Groom" All hard plastic with painted black hair. Painted blue side glancing eyes. Molded and painted shoes. Marks: none. Original clothes. 1949. Brides name was Irene. $4.00.

Duchess Doll--7" "Miss Tastee Freez-America's Sweetheart" All hard plastic with glued on brown mohair wig. Blue sleep eyes/molded lashes. One piece body and legs. Painted and molded on shoes. Marks: Duchess Doll Corp/Design Copyright/1948, on back. 1953. Original clothes. \$3.00.

Duchess Doll--8½" "Miss North American" All hard plastic with glued on blonde mohair wig. Sleep blue eyes/molded lashes. High heel feet. Head turns as she walks. Marks: none. 1959. \$3.00.

Eegee Doll Mfg. Company

The name of this company is made up from the name of the owner and founder, E.G. Goldberger. The company was founded in 1917 and the early dolls were marked E.G., then later E. Goldberger and now Eegee.

Eegee may not be the largest doll company but they have dolls that are above average in quality. They made one of the finest boy dolls to date (Bobby).

The following are not all the dolls made by this company.

1937: Miss Charming (35.00)
1951: GIGI Perreaux (35.00)
1955: Susan Stroller (18.00), Bobby (25.00)
1956: Miss Flexie (16.00), Lovable Baby (5.00), Janie (8.00), Little Susan (5.00), Robert (32.00)
1957: Snowbaby (20.00), Pretty Baby (8.00), Betsy McCall (10.00), Baby Susan (6.00), My Fair Lady (8.00), Kay (16.00), Grace (18.00)
1958: Lovable Skin Doll (8.00), Little Debutante (20.00), Baby Susan (6.00)
1959: Tina (5.00)
1960: Sun Bonnet Sue (20.00), Baby Susan (3.00)
1961: Tandy Talks (25.00), Babette (8.00), Annette (8.00), Miss Babette-11½" (5.00), Andy (5.00)
1962: Little Miss (5.00)
1963: Puppetrina (35.00), Puppetina (30.00), Bundle of Joy (6.00), Gemette (4.00), Sandy (7.00), Flowerkins-Blue Bell, Daisy Darlin', Rosie Red, Shammy Shamrock, Sweet Violet, Blackeyed Susan (10.00 each)
1964: Lil Sister (8.00), Bundle of Joy (5.00)
1965: Baby Waddles (10.00)
1966: Itsy Bitsy (4.00), Annette (8.00), Pix-i-Posie (8.00)
1967: Sugar Kandi (8.00), Softina (5.00), Sandi (7.00), Susan (7.00), Musical Baby (6.00), Baby Sniffles (6.00), Adorable (8.00), Sleepy (16.00), Bundle of Joy (4.00)
1969: Baby Care (8.00), Posi Playmate (6.00), Posi Ballerina (6.00), Annette Walker (9.00), Kandi (8.00)
1970: Baby Carrie (6.00), Camilla (6.00), A Posi Playmate Doll (6.00), Carol (6.00), Babette (4.00), Cuddlekins (3.00), Softina Line (4.00)

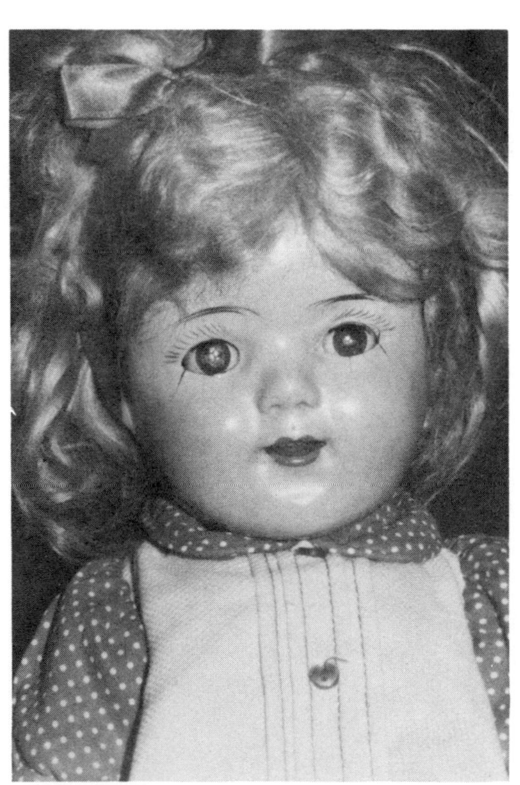

Eegee--19" "Miss Charming" All composition with glued on blonde wig. Blue sleep tin eyes/lashes. Open mouth with six teeth. A Shirley Temple look-a-like. 1936. Marks: E.G., on head. $35.00. (Courtesy Earlene Johnston Collection)

Eegee--17" "Gigi Perreaux" Hard plastic body, arms and legs. Early vinyl head with glued on dark brown hair. Brown sleep eyes/lashes. Open mouth with painted teeth. Feathered eyebrows. Marks: E.G., on head. 1951. Child Actress, licensed to Goldberger to make doll. $35.00.

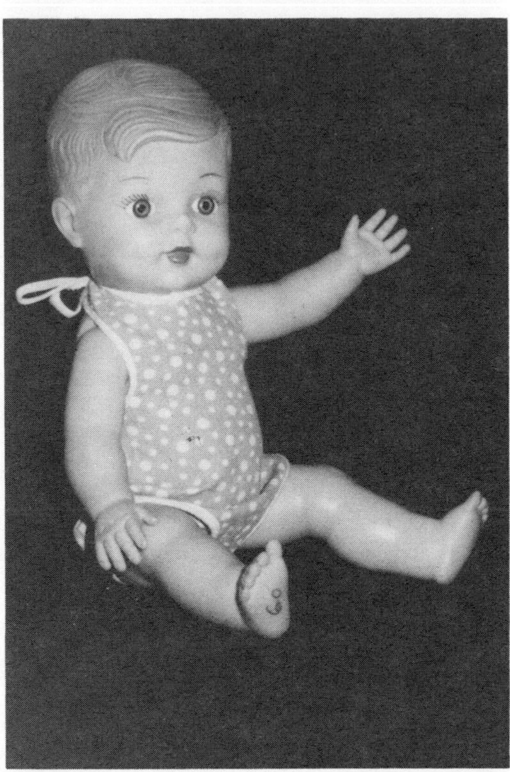

Eegee--13" "Bobby" All vinyl with deeply molded hair. Stationary blue eyes. Open/closed mouth. Dimpled cheeks. Marks: Eegee, on head. 1955. $25.00.

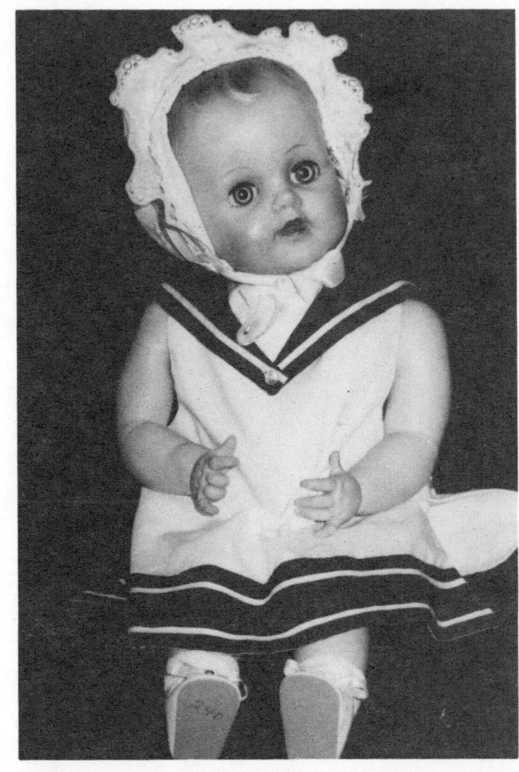

Eegee--21" "Robert" One piece latex body and legs. Vinyl arms and head. Molded and painted hair. Large blue sleep eyes/lashes. Open/closed mouth with molded tongue. Arms jointed by metal disc. Molded bent arms. Left 2nd and 3rd fingers molded into palm. Marks: Eegee on head. 1956. $32.00.

Eegee--10½" "Lil Susan" Hard plastic body, arms and legs. Vinyl head with rooted black hair. Blue sleep eyes/lashes. Closed mouth. Jointed knees. Open hands with palms facing body. Marks: Eegee, on head. 1956. $5.00.

Eegee--17" "Grace" One piece, unjointed heavy latex body, arms and legs. Vinyl head with rooted ash blonde hair. Blue sleep eyes/lashes and blue eyeshadow. Closed mouth. Pierced ears. High heel feet. Adult hands. 1957. Marks: 2(could be 3)-H/Eegee, on head. Eegee/H-18, on body. Original clothes. $18.00.

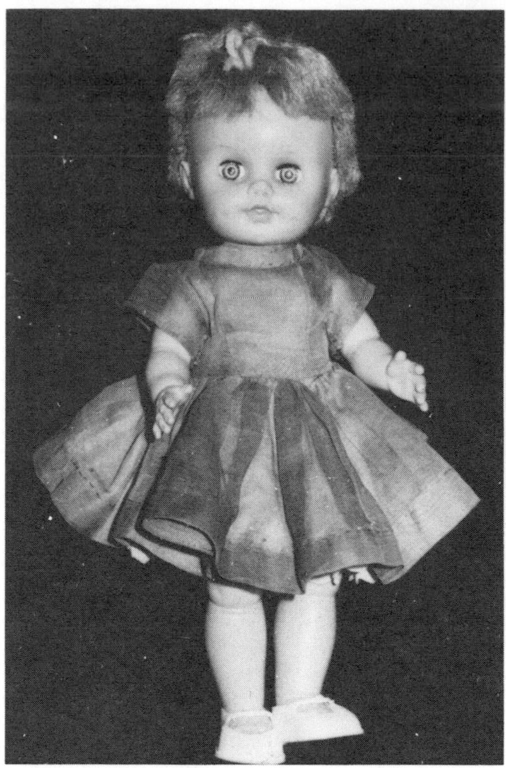

Eegee--12½" "Luvable Skin Doll" All vinyl. Rooted ash blonde hair. Blue sleep eyes/lashes. Open/closed mouth. Two deep cheek dimples. Open hands facing body. Toddler legs with dimpled knees. Marks: Eegee/1½-9, on head. 1958. $8.00.

Eegee--28" "Little Debutante" Hard plastic body and legs. Jointed knees. Vinyl arms, jointed at elbows. Vinyl head with rooted dark blonde hair. Blue sleep eyes/lashes and blue eyeshadow. Pierced ears. High heel feet. Head turns as she walks. Marks: 20-HH/Eegee, on head. Original clothes. 1958. $20.00.

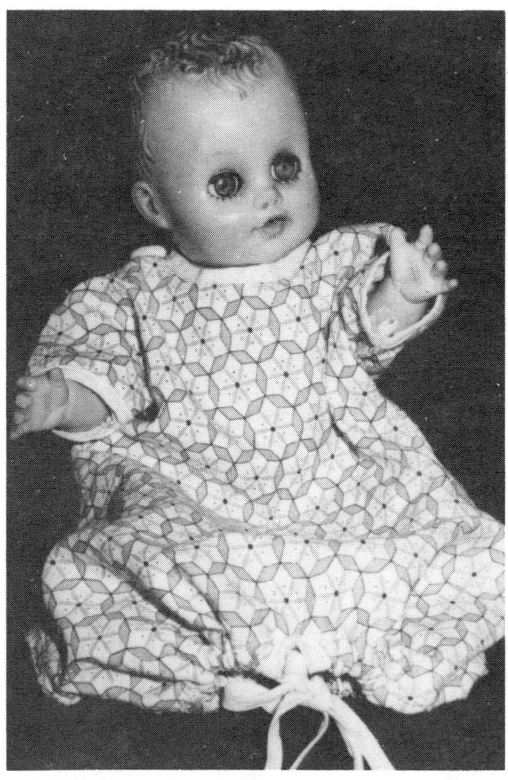

Eegee--10½" "Baby Susan" All vinyl with molded hair and large blue sleep eyes. Open mouth/nurser. Individual molded toes. Marks: Eegee, on head. 1958. $6.00.

Eegee--11" "Tina" Hard plastic body and legs. Vinyl head with rooted blonde hair. Blue sleep eyes/molded lashes. Closed mouth. Jointed knees. Walker, head turns as she walks. Marks: S, on head. 1959. $5.00.

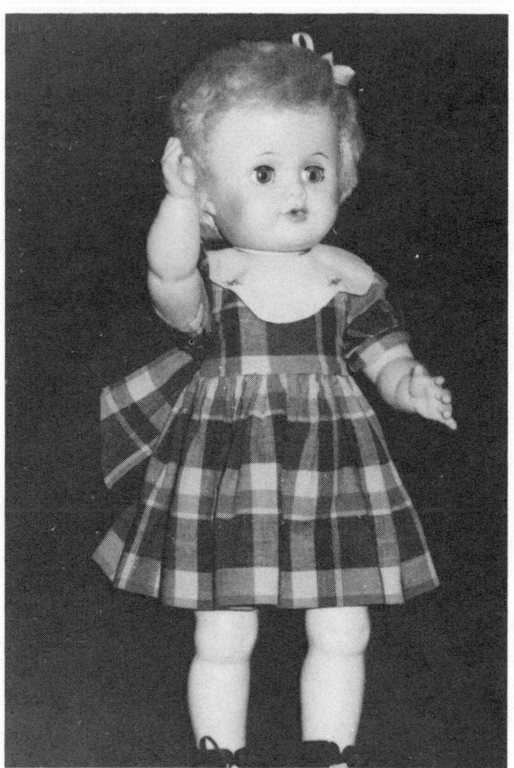

Eegee--16" "Lil Susan" Plastic body and legs. Vinyl arms and head. Rooted blonde hair. Blue eyes/lashes. Open mouth/nurser. Wide spread fingers. Marks: 14K/Eegee/22, on head. 1960. $3.00.

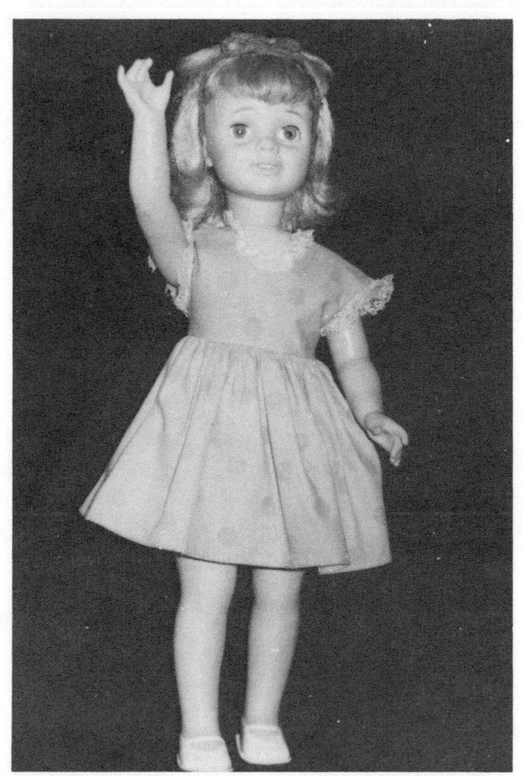

Eegee--21" "Tandy Talks" Plastic body and legs. Vinyl arms and head. Rooted blonde hair. Blue eyes/lashes. Pull string talker. Open mouth with four molded teeth. Freckles. Marks: 15P/Eegee, on head. 1961. $25.00.

Eegee--12" "Andy" Plastic body and legs. Vinyl arms and head. Molded blonde hair. Painted side glancing eyes. Marks: EG-1961, on head. EG-1961, on lower back. $5.00.

Eegee--16" "Little Miss" Plastic body and legs. Vinyl arms and head. Rooted blonde hair. Sleep blue eyes/lashes. Open/closed mouth. Marks: 15US/Eegee Co on head. Goldberger Doll/Mfg Co Inc/Pat Pend on back. 1962. $5.00. (Courtesy Allin's Collection)

Eegee--15" "Gemette" Plastic body and legs. Vinyl arms and head. Rooted brown hair. Blue eyes/lashes molded. Beautifully molded adult hands. Closed mouth. Marks: Eegee 1963/11 on head. 1963/Eegee Co on back. Original clothes. $4.00.

Eegee--16" "Daisy Darlin' / Flowerkin" Plastic body and legs. Vinyl arms and head. Blue sleep eyes/lashes. Closed mouth Palms down. Marks: F2/Eegee Co, on head. 1963. $10.00.

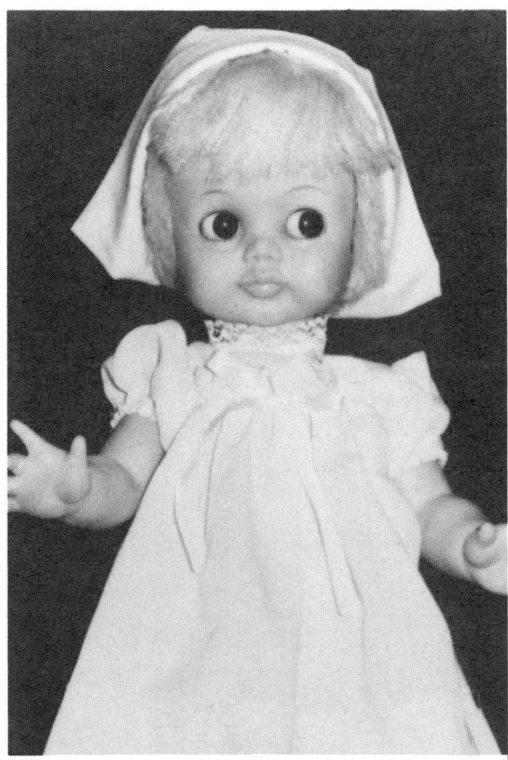

Eegee--16" "Flowerkin-Rosie Red" Plastic body and legs. Vinyl arms and head. Rooted white hair. Large black gooly eyes/lashes. Closed mouth. Open hands palms down with 2nd and 3rd fingers curled. Marks: F2/Eegee on head. Goldberger Doll/Mfg Co Inc/Pat Pend. on back. 1963. $10.00.

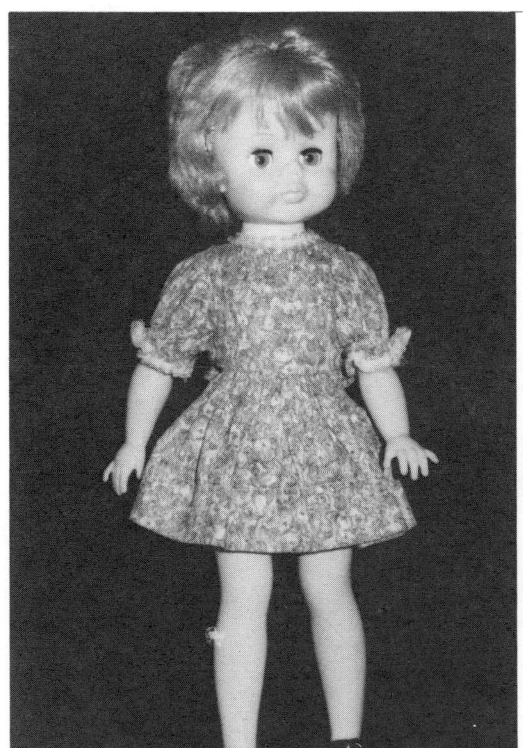

Eegee--15" "Sandi" Plastic body and legs. Vinyl arms and head. Rooted blonde hair. Dark blue sleep eyes/lashes. Closed mouth. Marks: 12/5/Eegee Co/F2-13. An original dress. 1963. $7.00.

Eegee--19" "Bundle Of Joy" Stuffed cloth body. Plastic legs. Vinyl arms and head. Light brown rooted hair. Dark blue sleep eyes. Open mouth with large overhanging upper lip/closed. Left hand with 2nd and 3rd fingers curled. Right hand with index finger over thumb. Marks: 19-4/Eegee Co on head. 1964. $5.00.

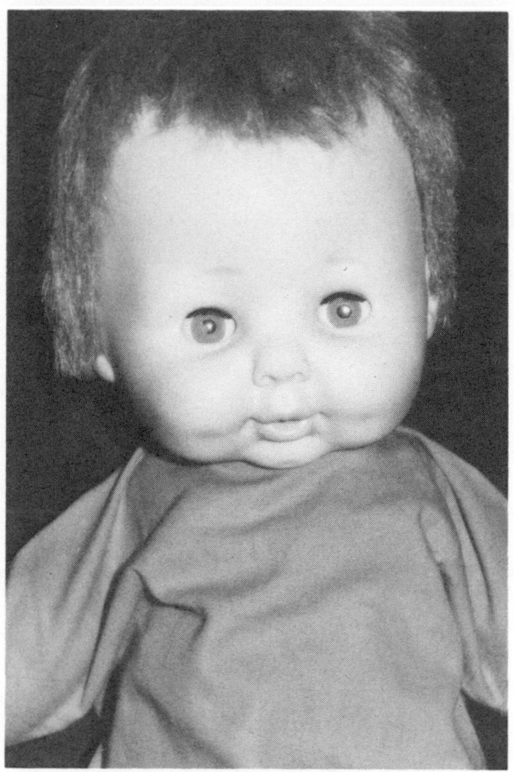

Eegee--18" "Pix-I-Posie" All dublon body, arms and legs. Vinyl head. Rooted ash blonde hair. Blue sleep eyes/lashes. Open/closed mouth. Marks: Eegee Co/1966/18½, on head. Pat. No./3,319,370/24/Eegee Co/1966 Dublon /Pat. Pend, on back. One of the Posi Pixie series. $8.00.

Eegee--25" "Annette". Plastic body and legs. Vinyl arms and head. Rooted blonde hair. Dark blue sleep eyes/lashes. Closed mouth. Marks: Eegee 20/25M/13 on head. 1966. Original dress. Later called Carol. $8.00.

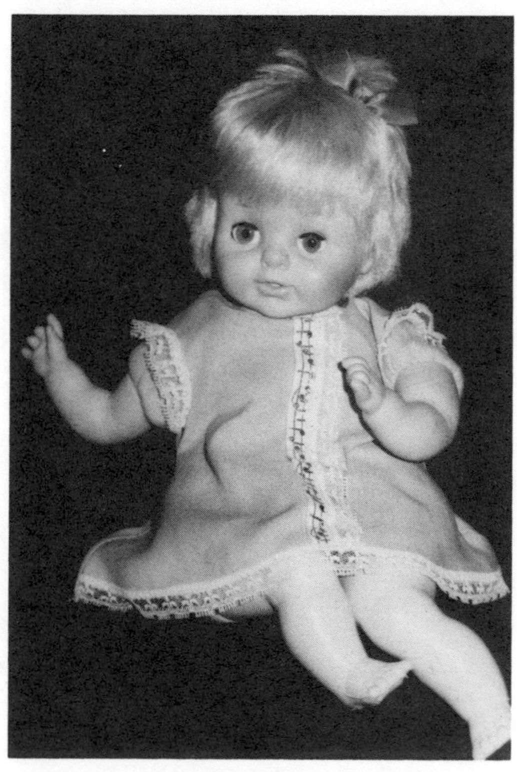

Eegee--17" "Musical Baby" Cloth body. Plastic legs. Vinyl arms and head. Rooted blonde hair. Dark blue eyes/lashes. Open/closed mouth. Key wind music box plays lullabye. Marks: 15/ Eegee Co/16W, on head. Tag:Goldberger Doll/ Mfg Co/Brooklyn NY. 1967. Original clothes. $6.00.

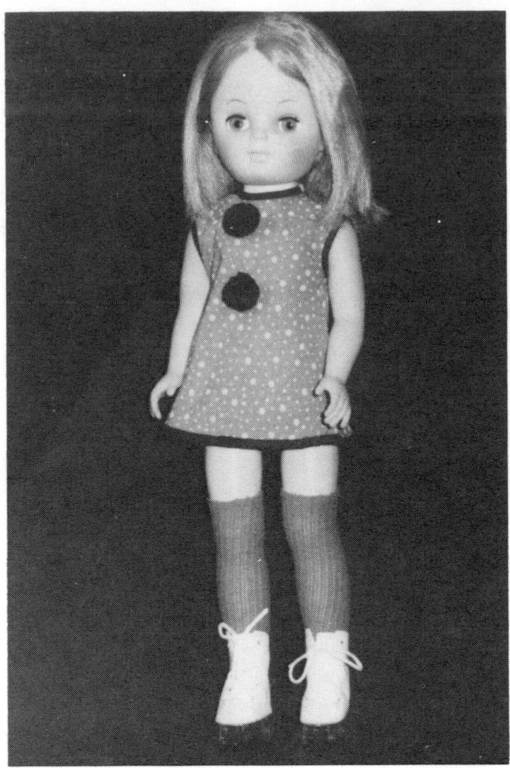

Eegee--17" "Susan" Plastic legs and body. Vinyl arms and head. Rooted blonde hair. Large dark blue sleep eyes/lashes. All fingers slightly curled. Marks: Eegee/1967, on head. $8.00.

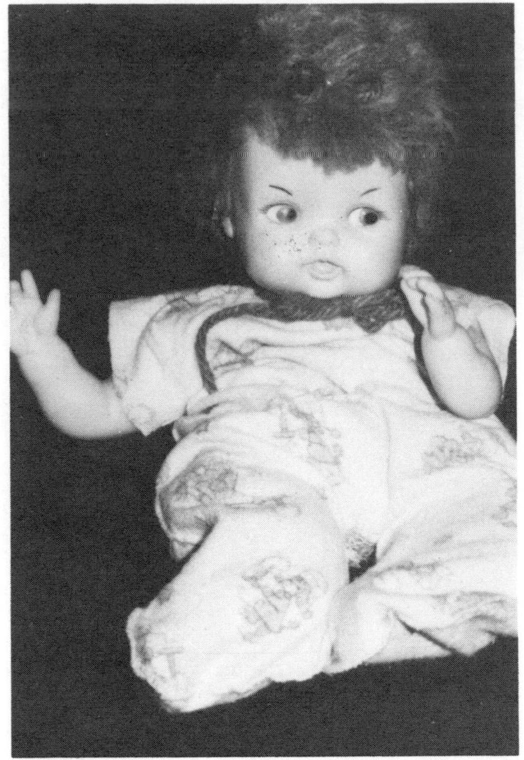

Eegee--14" "Bundle Of Joy" Cloth body. Plastic legs. Vinyl arms and head. Rooted light brown hair. Painted blue side glancing eyes. Open/closed mouth with molded tongue. Right 3rd finger molded into palm. Left thumb, index and 2nd fingers molded together. Marks: Eegee Co/1967/12LTPE, Tag: Goldberger Mfg, $4.00.

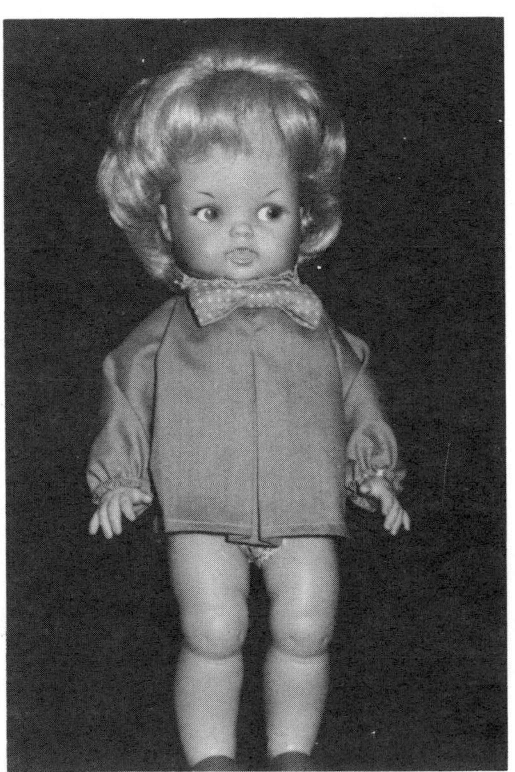

Eegee--13" "Adorable" Softina one piece body, unjointed. Vinyl head with rooted blonde hair. Painted side glancing blue eyes. Open mouth/nurser. Molded tongue. Dimpled knees. Marks: 35/Eegee Co/1967/12LTPE, on head. $8.00.

Eegee--12" "Baby Sniffles" Plastic body, arms and legs. Vinyl head with rooted red hair. Blue sleep eyes/molded lashes. Open mouth/nurser. Marks: 14J/Eegee Co/1967, on head. Original clothes. $6.00.

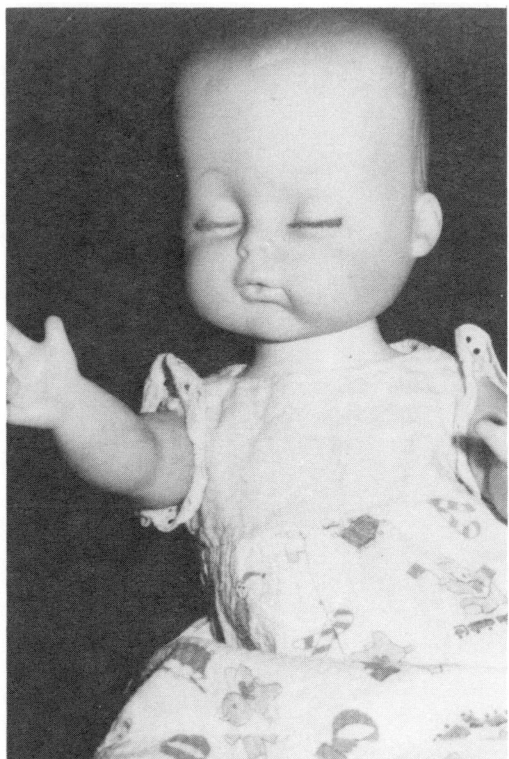

Eegee--14" "Sleepy" Plastic body. Vinyl arms, legs and head. Molded, painted hair. Asleep eyes/heavy lashes. Closed mouth. Marks: Eegee/1967 on head. $16.00. (Courtesy Allin's Collection)

Eegee--18" "Posi-Playmate" All foam body, arms and legs. Vinyl glove hands and head. Rooted white hair. Black side glancing eyes/lashes. Open/closed mouth. Marks: 18LT 1/Eegee Co, on head. Original clothes. 1969. $6.00. (Courtesy Dorothy Westbrook)

Eegee--13" "Softina" One piece, unjointed dublon body. Vinyl head with rooted blonde hair. Blue/black painted eyes. Open mouth/nurser. Marks: Eegee Co/14P, on head. Dublon (in oval)/Pat. No. 3,432,581/3,466,0646/ Other Pats Pend., on back. Eegee, on lower back. 1970. Original dress. $4.00.

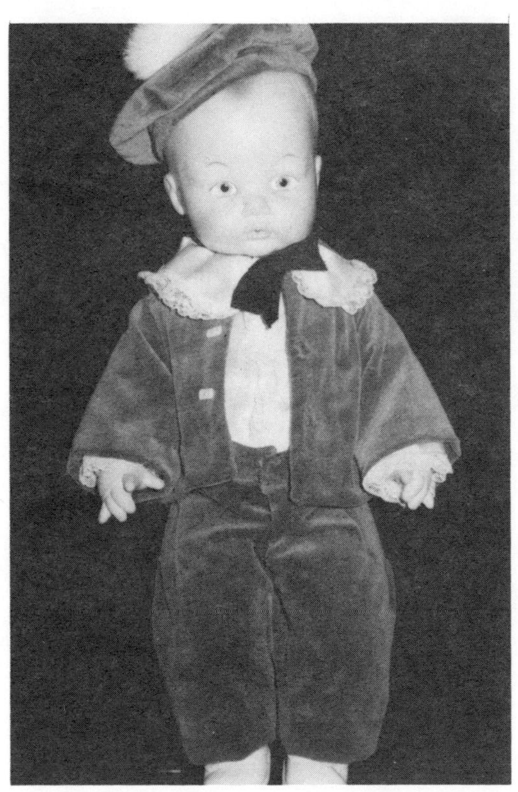

Eegee--16" "Baby Softina" One piece, unjointed dublon body. Both hands have 2nd and 3rd fingers curled. Vinyl head. Lightly molded and painted brown hair. Inset, stationary blue eyes/no lashes. Open mouth/nurser. 1970. Marks: 3/Eegee Co/16V3, on head. 18 Dublon, on body. $4.00. (Courtesy Allin's Collection)

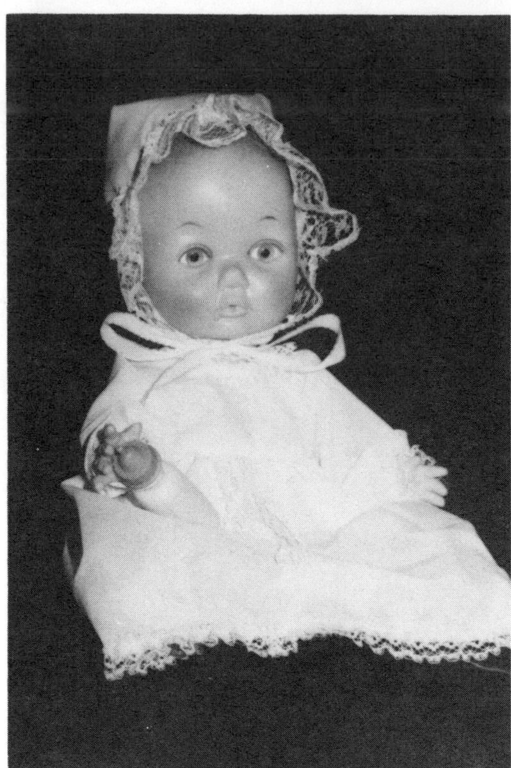

Eegee--10" "Cuddlekins" Plastic body and legs. Vinyl arms and head. Molded hair. Inset stationary blue eyes. Open mouth/nurser. Marks: Eegee Co/13-VS. 1970. Original clothes. $3.00.

Effanbee Doll Company

Effanbee is the original company started by Bernard E. Fleischaker and Hugo Baum. The company was founded in 1910. Effanbee was bought by the Christmas decorations company of Noma in 1947 but sold back to the son of one of the founders, Walter Fleischaker and two partners, who ran the business until 1971 when the company was sold once more. Records, catalogs, office information is quite sketchy before 1957.

The dolls are marked F & B but generally with the full name of Effanbee. The most common marks used in the early years was the full company name plus the name of the doll. Some unmarked dolls and ones marked only with the Made In USA are Effanbees but remember that R & B, Ideal, Imperial Crown and Irwin also marked dolls this way. If you happen to run across an older doll marked Effandbee, it is not misspelled. A few dolls were marked with And between the Eff and the Bee.

Almost all Effanbee babies number among the most beautiful in the world and the most famous children, of this parent company, are Patsy and her family. Patsy was made as a baby, Patsyette (9"), Patsy (13"), Patricia (14"), Patsy Joan (16"), Patsy Ann (18"), and the rarest of her family is the Patsy Lou (22") and Patsy Mae (30"). Patsy Mae had a cloth body. But the rarest of all is the colored Patsyette. Patsy and Patsy Joan were made through 1949. With the post World War II materials being scarce, there are genuine unmarked Patsys. They are hard polished composition and 13½" tall.

Bernard Lipfert designed the Patsy and Family as well as the original Dy Dee Baby, Bubbles and many more that include Ideal's Shirley Temple, The Dionne Quints for Alexander and Baby Dimples for Horsman (Effanbee sued Horsman at this point and won their case).

Patsy and Patsy Joan were first introduced in 1936 with celluloid fingernails that could be polished. Also the Patsy body was used on the Patsy Baby and for Skippy (14"), as well as the Patsy head on a body that is marked Patricia.

From 1936 to 1939 Effanbee used Dee Wees Cochran's master molds for her American Children Series (Four of her first six "look alike"). All are excellent quality and came in two age size bodies, one six years old and the other as a ten year old. Dee Wees Cochran is one of the most talented and creative American Doll artist to date. She designed another doll for Effanbee and it is wrongly referred to as an "open mouth" Ann Shirley.

Effanbee issued several sets of Historical Dolls in 1939. These sets were displayed in store toy sections across the nation. The advertising stated "Learn American history with the Effanbee Historical Dolls". These dolls were 20", all composition with hand painted features. They had human hair wigs and clothes of silk, wools and velvets. They were marked American Children and the original models were by Dee Wees Cochran. The bodies are marked Effanbee/Anne Shirley. These dolls were the first in composition to have fingers that could wear gloves. The dolls were sold after the promotional tour was ended.

Effanbee then issued the "copies" of these historical dolls. The copies were all composition with painted features but 14" tall, had mohair wigs and cotton fabrics in the clothes. A new head was used and it was the same used for the Little Lady line (the Little Lady line had sleep eyes) and the doll is now being sold as the "painted eyed" Anne Shirley, because the heads are unmarked but the bodies are marked Effanbee/Anne Shirley. The boxes used for the Original and the Copies are the same: an overall pattern of red and white stripes with blue stars.

The dolls marked Effanbee on the head and Effanbee/Anne Shirley on the back, all composition with sleep eyes, an open mouth with four upper teeth were sold as Skating Queen and Ice Queen. This doll's face is shorter and wider than the Historical Dolls.

The first Anne Shirley came in 9", 12" and 15", was all composition, with brown or green sleep eyes, with human hair wigs and looked like the Patricia Doll. She was first introduced in 1936 as Anne Of Green Gables. Then, in 1938 Anne Shirley came out in a 14" size, all composition, with saran wig, blue eyes and dark eyeshadow. This Anne had a wider mouth than the Patricia used as Anne Shirley in 1936. By 1939 many different heads were sold on the Anne Shirley body (14" to 22"). All had large hands and seperate fingers. These same bodies were used for: Dee Wees Cochran's Portraits, the Historical series, American Children, Ice Queen, Skating Queen, and the Little Lady series (the Little Lady line was made from renewed molds in 1941 and from that point on were marked only with the Effanbee/Made In USA). The Anne Shirley was reissued in 1952, in hard plastic, but without the metal heart bracelet. The bracelet was discontinued in 1945, although the stock was used up on some later dolls.

The famous Magnetic Hand Dolls were not all Effanbees. The idea was sold to the F.A.O. Schwartz Company and they re-worked the dolls at the store by imbedding a small magnet in the palm of the hands and repainted them. The Effanbee dolls used were 1936: Suzanne (holding an American Flag), Skippy, Patricia, 1937: Patsy Joan, Babykin Patsy, Sugar Baby and Little Lady.

The following do not include all dolls by this company.

1935: Judy Doll (45.00), Mary Lee (50.00)

1936: Patsy (30.00), Patsy Joan (32.00), Patsy Ann (34.00), Patsy Ruth (36.00), Anne of Green Gables (45.00), Anne Shirley-(1st-40.00), Colored Anne Shirley (65.00), Sugar Baby (35.00), Babyette (1931 to 1951-10.00 to 35.00), Patricia (45.00)

1937: Emily Ann (45.00), Clippo Clown (45.00)

1937 to 1970: Charley McCarthy (16.00 to 45.00)

1939: Historical Dolls (1st series 95.00-2nd series 65.00), Sweetie Pie (32.00), Patricia (45.00), Mickey Baby (32.00), Pat O Pat (36.00), Boo Hoo (12.00), Ha Ha (18.00), Little Lady Line with hard rubber arms (32.00)

1940: Bitsy & Butch (45.00), Baby Bright Eyes (20.00), Tommy Tucker (18.00), Historical copies (65.00), Magnetic Dolls (65.00), Rubber eared Dy Dee Baby (First introduced

in 1933 but the first were without ears-8.00 to 30.00), Dy Dee Ellen (25.00),(Dy Dee Jane (25.00), Dy Dee Louise (25.00), Dy Dee Kins (25.00), Dy Deette (25.00), Suzette (32.00), Portrait Series (90.00), Babykin (1940 to 1950-8.00 to 16.00), Jambo (16.00), Kilroy (16.00), Toonga (16.00), Pimbo (16.00)
1942: Suzanne (35.00), DyDee (10.00), Miss Glamour Girl (25.00), Baby Heart Beat (36.00), Bright Eyes (Boy and girl-45.00 set), Little Lady (with cotton yarn hair-50.00), Sister & Brother (45.00 set)
1943: Sleeping Baby (Babyette-16.00),(Babyet-16.00)
1944: Beautee Skin Babies (16.00)
1946: Candy Kid (35.00), Re-issue Patsy (30.00), Re-issue Patsy Joan (32.00)
1947: Patricia (30.00), 18" Musical Girl (45.00), Howdy Doody (15.00), Lil Darlin' (15.00)
1948: Special issue Patsy Joan (45.00)
1949: Honey (20.00)
1950: Honey Walker (22.00), Little Lady (22.00), Patricia (30.00), Dy Dee Baby (10.00)
1951: Lil Darlin' (15.00), Twins & Quads (10.00), Tintair Doll (40.00)
1952: Baby Twinkie (8.00), Mommy's Baby (20.00), Patsy Babyette (8.00), Babykins (8.00), Honey Girl (22.00), Prince Charming (28.00), First New Mickey (6.00), Portrait Series (90.00 each), TV Puppets-Toonga (6.00), Pimbo (6.00), Jambo (6.00), Kilroy (6.00), Large Baby Mickey (22.00), Honey Formal (35.00), Re-issue Anne Shirley in hard plastic (35.00)
1953: Melodie (45.00), Cuddle Up (20.00), Noma Talker (30.00), 18" Honey Walker in 14 outfits by Schiaparelli (45.00 each, Honey Ballerina (jointed knees & ankles-45.00), Honey Ice Skater (Jointed knees & ankles-45.00)
1954: Bubbles (16.00), Candy Kid Twins (45.00 set), Candy Ann (16.00), Patricia Walker (30.00), Little Lady (all vinyl-25.00), Fluffy Series (6.00), Rootie Kazootie (40.00), Polka Dottie (40.00), Honeykins (8.00)
1955: Tiny Tubber (8.00), Mary Jane (10.00), Christening Baby (10.00), Rusty (18.00), Sherry (18.00)
1956: Mickey (in baseball & football outfits-5.00), Baby Twinkie (8.00), Dy Dee Baby (8.00)
1957: Dy Dee Ellen (9.00), Dy Dee Jane (9.00), Dy Dee Lu (9.00), Katie (Fluffy with molded hair-16.00), Mother (16.00)
1958: My Fair Baby (16.00), My Precious Baby (fully jointed-20.00), Bubbles (vinyl-18.00), Toddle Tot (10.00), Little Lady (20.00), Alice (30.00), Junior Miss (15.00), Happy Family (mother & three children-50.00 set)
1959: Patsy (vinyl-16.00), Patsy Ann (vinyl-18.00), Sugar Baby (9.00), Suzette (8.00), Alyssa (25.00), Boudoir Doll (20.00), Sweetie Pie (8.00), Mary Jane (16.00), Lil Darlin' (10.00), Babykin (8.00), Tiny Tubber (6.00), Mickey (Boy Scout-5.00)
1960: My Fair Baby (8.00), My Precious Baby (10.00), Mickey (Sailor, Boxer, Aviator, Soldier, Fireman & Policeman-5.00), Alyssa & Boy Friend, Bud (45.00 set), Bettina (20.00), Bubbles (18.00), Happy Boy (9.00)
1961: Susie Sunshine (8.00)
1962: Belle Telle (15.00), Gumdrop (8.00), Little Gumdrop (10.00), Precious New Born (18.00)
1963: Baby Butterball (5.00), Baby Twinkie (4.00), Baby Sweetie Pie (6.00)
1964: Babykin (4.00), My Fair Baby (6.00)
1965: Miss Chips (15.00), Chipper (15.00), Thumkin (8.00), Peaches (16.00)
1966: Pumkin (7.00), Baby Twinkie (4.00), Charlee (18.00), Half Pint (6.00), Chipper (15.00), Peaches (16.00)
1967: Honey Bun (10.00), Dy Dee Darlin (7.00), Lil Sweetie (10.00), Button Nose (16.00), Baby Cuddles (10.00), Baby Face (8.00)
1968: New Dy Dee (1967 as Lil Sweetie-7.00), Toddletot (8.00), Tiny Tubber (7.00), Button Nose (10.00), Cookie (10.00), Sweetie Pie (8.00)
1969: Baby Butterball (8.00), Sugar Plum (16.00), Fair Baby (8.00), Babykin (4.00), Baby Button Nose (8.00), Baby Face (8.00)
1971: Little Luv (18.00)
1972: Dy Dee Educational Baby (50.00)

Effanbee--14" "Patricia" All composition with glued on red wig. Brown sleep eyes/lashes. Closed mouth. 2nd & 3rd fingers curled and molded together. Marks: Effanbee/Patricia, on back. 1932 to 1936. $45.00.

Effanbee--14" "Anne Of Green Gables" All composition with glued on dark reddish blonde saran wig in pigtails. Blue sleep eyes/lashes. Eyeshadow. Marks: F & B, on head. 1937. Two dolls were made for F O A Swartz Co. First in 1936 (Patricia doll). $40.00.

Effanbee--20" "Anne Shirley/Little Lady" Composition body, legs and head. Hard rubber arms. Glued on blonde human hair wig. Marks: Effanbee/USA, on head. Effanbee/Anne Shirley, on back. Effanbee Durable Doll, on wrist tag. 1939. Original clothes. $25.00.

Anne Shirley, one of the top stars of the 1930's.

Effanbee--13½" "Suzanne" All composition with glued on ash blonde human hair wig. Brown sleep eyes/lashes. Closed mouth. Marks: Suzanne/Effanbee, on head. Suzanne/Effanbee/ Made In USA, on back. 1940. $35.00.

Effanbee--18" "Little Lady" All composition with glued on red human hair wig. Green sleep eyes/lashes. Closed mouth. Open hands with painted fingernails. Marks: Effanbee/USA, on head and back. 1941. $25.00.

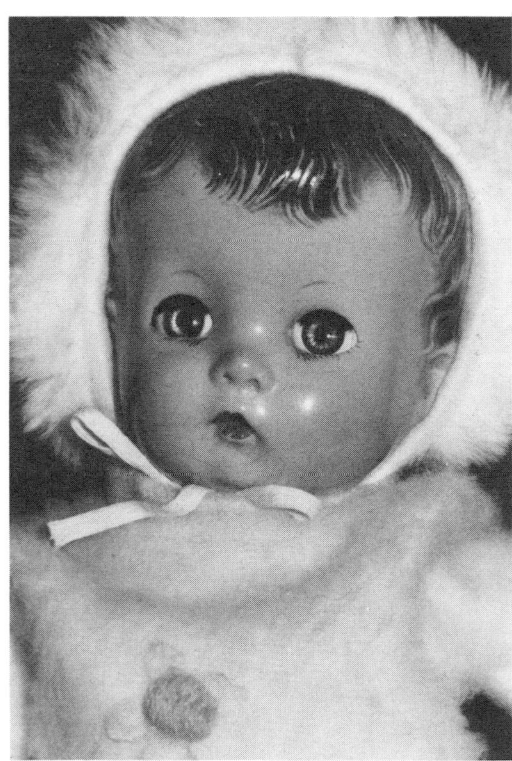

Effanbee--12½" "Candy Kid" All composition with molded dark brown hair. Sleep blue eyes/lashes. Closed mouth. Marks: Effanbee, on head. 1946. $35.00. (Courtesy Earlene Johnston Collection)

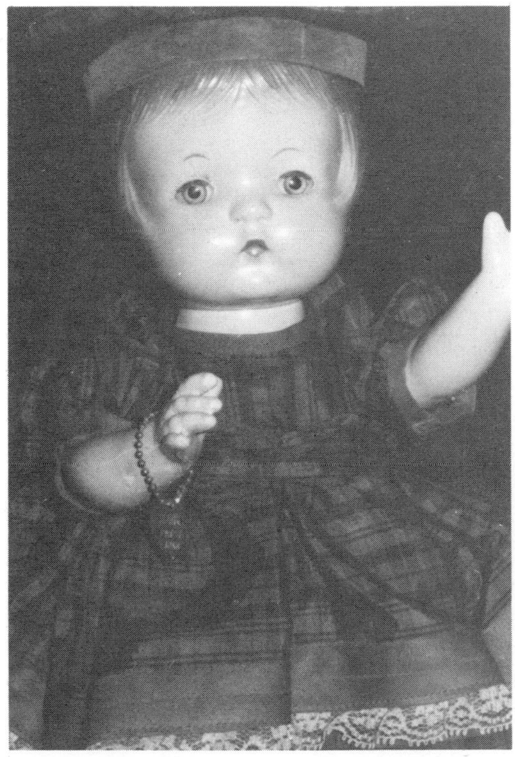

Effanbee--16" "Patsy Joan" All composition with molded blonde hair. Green sleep eyes/lashes. Marks: Effanbee/Patsy Joan, on back. Wrist Tag: Effanbee/Patsy Joan. Made in 1927-28. Re-issues in 1946-49. $32.00. (Courtesy Allin's Collection)

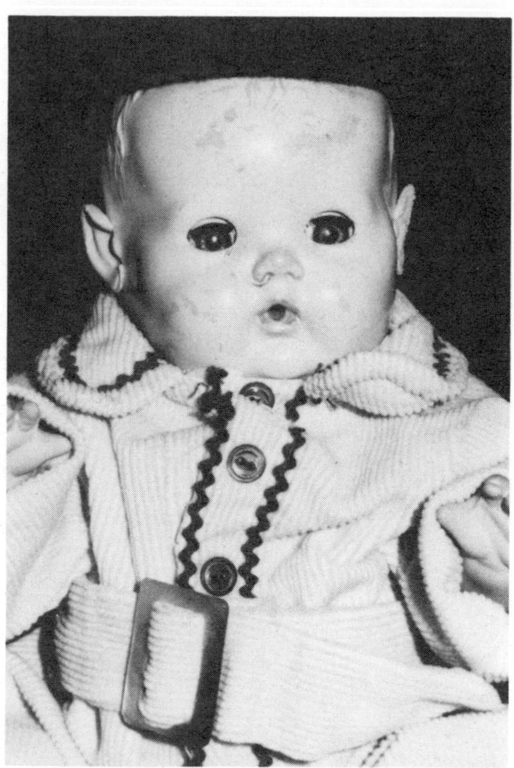

Effanbee--11" "Dy Dee Baby" Rubber body (bodies made by the Miller Rubber Company) Hard plastic head with applied rubber ears. Molded hair. Open mouth/nurser. Blue sleep eyes. Marks: Effanbee, on head. 1950. Dy Dee has been made since 1933. The first ones were made without ears. $10.00.

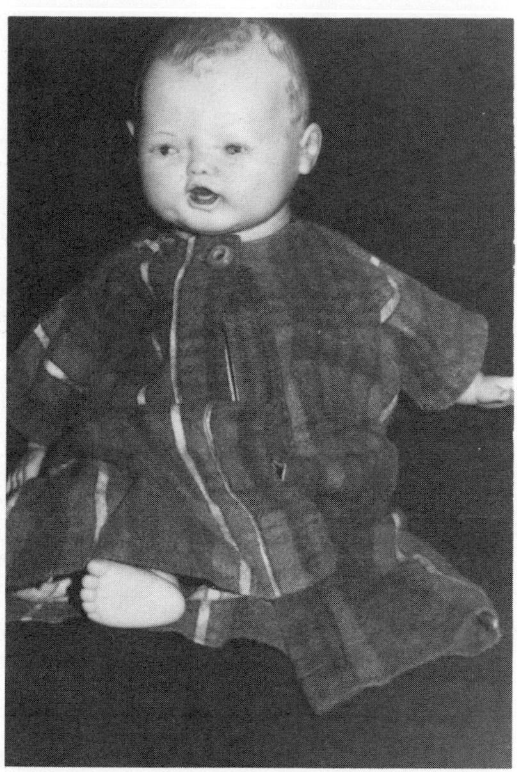

Effanbee--13" "Lil Darlin" Cloth body. Early vinyl arms, legs and head. Molded and painted light brown hair. Blue painted eyes. Open/closed mouth with molded tongue. Palms down. Cryer in center of stomach. Marks: Effanbee, on head. 1951. Lil Darlin was first issued in 1947. $15.00.

Effanbee--13½" "Honey Girl" All hard plastic. Glued on blonde wig. Sleep blue eyes/lashes. Closed mouth. Open hands with all fingers extended. Marks: Effanbee, on head. Effanbee, on body. The Honey line ran from 1949 through 1955. $20.00.

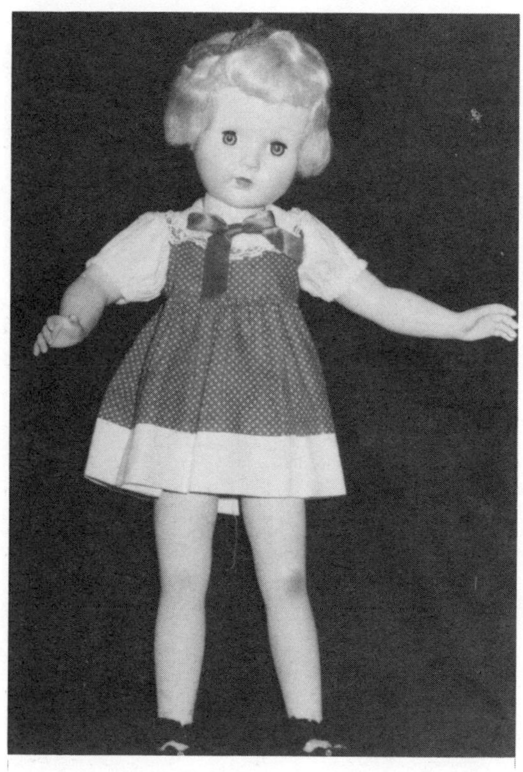

Effanbee--18" "Tintair" All hard plastic. White glued on dynel wig. Blue sleep eyes/lashes. Open/closed mouth. Open hands all fingers curled. Marks: Effanbee, on head. Effanbee, on back. 1951. (Courtesy Montgomery Ward 1951 Catalog) Also sold as Honey and Honey Walker for a number of years. $40.00.

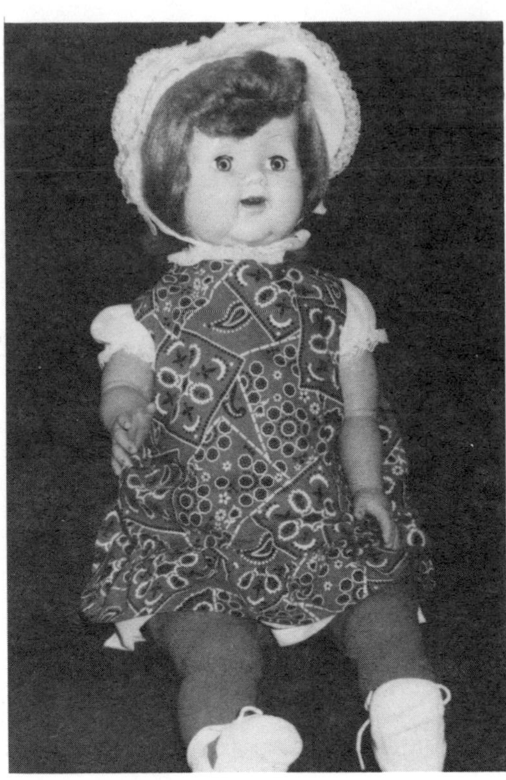

Effanbee--27" "Mommy's Baby" Cloth body. Large cryer in lower right back. Early plastic arms and legs. Limbs attached by tin lid discs. Blue sleep eyes/lashes. Hard plastic shoulder plate with swivel hard plastic head. Open mouth with two upper teeth and felt tongue. Dimpled chin. Marks: Effanbee, on head. 1952. $20.00.

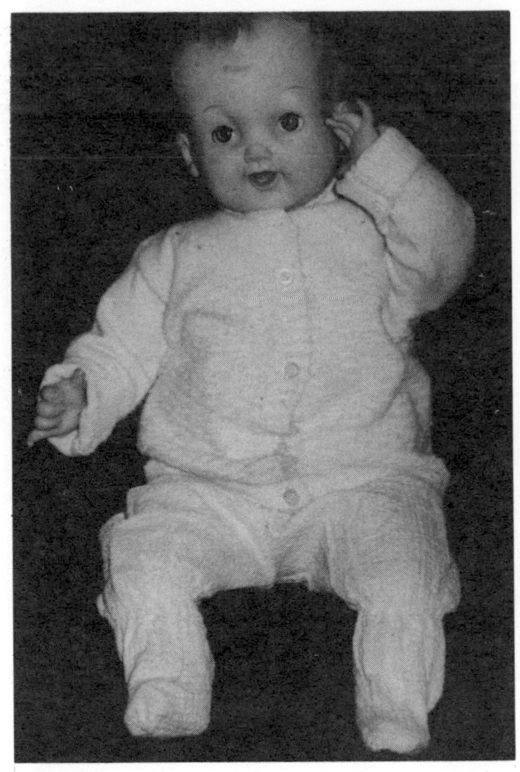

Effanbee--23" "Baby Cuddle-Up" Vinyl cloth body. Vinyl arms, legs and head. Molded painted brown hair. Blue sleep eyes/lashes. Open mouth with two lower teeth. Right 2nd and 3rd fingers molded into palm. Marks: Effanbee, on head. 1953. $20.00.

Effanbee--10" "Fluffy" All early vinyl. Yellow rooted hair. Blue sleep eyes/molded lashes. Closed mouth. Toddler legs with dimpled knees. Marks: P-U, on head. Effanbee, on body. 1954. $6.00.

Effanbee--19" "Polka Dotty" Vinyl coated cloth body, arms and legs. Early vinyl gauntlet hands and head. Molded painted red hair. Side glancing blue painted eyes. Open/closed mouth with molded tongue. Deep dimples. Marks: Polka Dotty/Rootie Kazootie/Effanbee. 1954. $40.00.

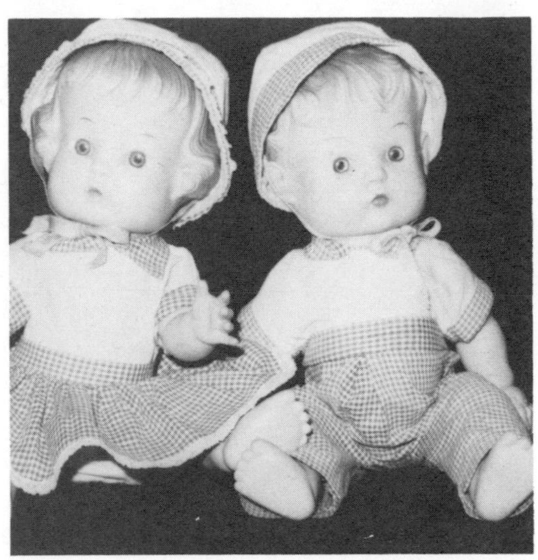

Effanbee--11" "Candy Twins" All early vinyl with molded and painted hair. Blue inset, stationary eyes. Closed mouths. Baby legs. Marks: Effanbee, on heads. Original clothes. 1954. $45.00 set.

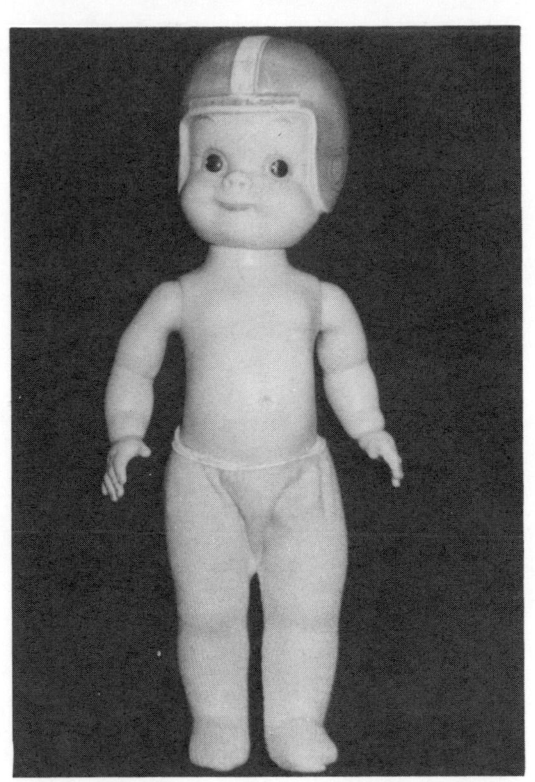

Effanbee--11" "Mickey". All vinyl. Molded on football helmet. Painted features. Marks: Effanbee/10 on head. Effanbee/8 on back. 1956. $5.00.

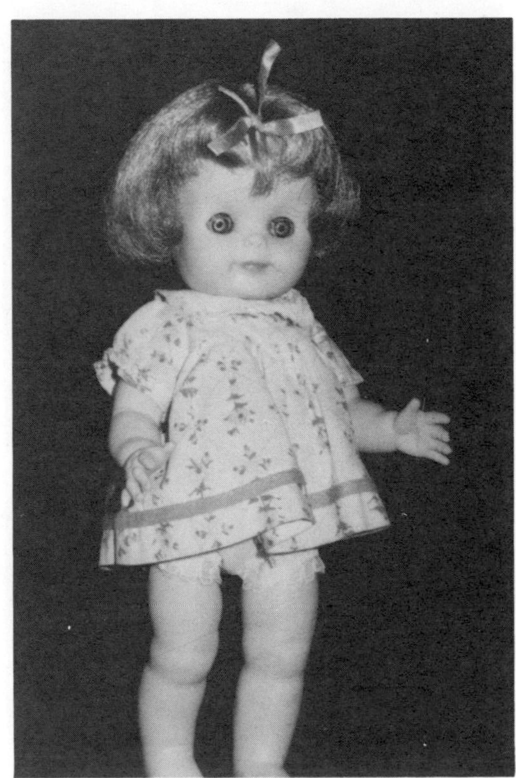

Effanbee--10½" "Fluffy" All vinyl with rooted dark blonde hair. Blue sleep eyes/lashes, molded. Closed mouth. Marks: Fluffy/Effanbee, on head. 10/Effanbee/8, on back. 1956. $6.00.

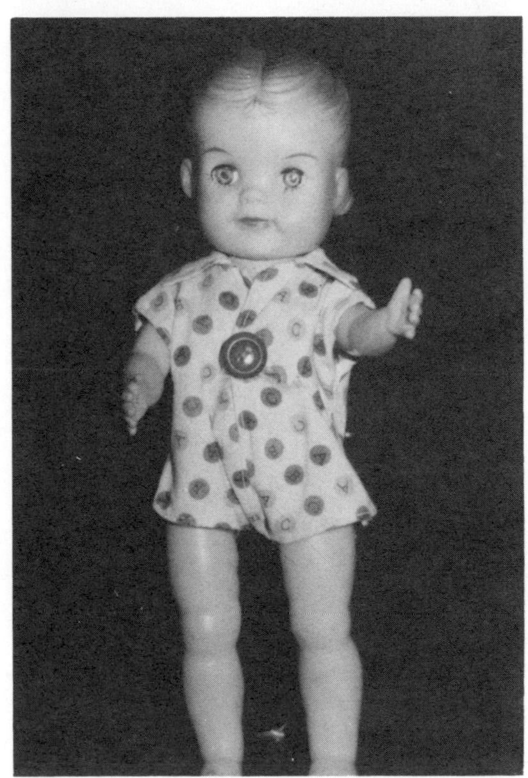

Effanbee--8½" "Katie" All vinyl with molded and painted light brown hair. Blue sleep eyes/molded lashes. Closed mouth. Straight legs with dimpled knees. Marks: Fluffy/Effanbee, on head. 1957. $16.00. Photo of back on Page 90.

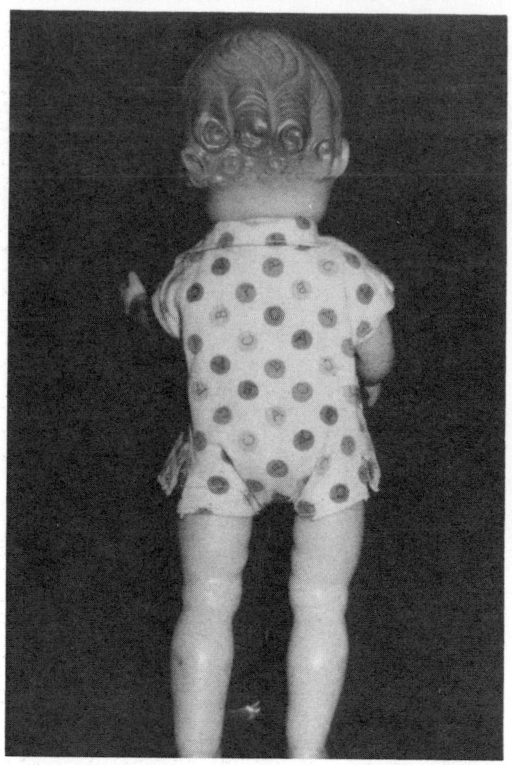

Effanbee--8½" "Katie"1957. Photo of face on Page 89.

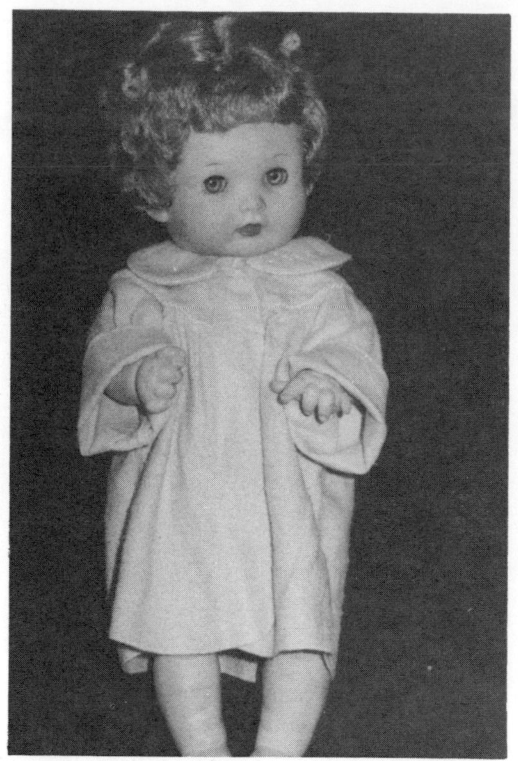

Effanbee--18" "My Fair Baby" All vinyl with rooted dark blonde hair. Blue sleep eyes/lashes. Right index over thumb. Left index and little finger extended. All toes spread out. Open mouth/nurser. Marks: Effanbee, on head. Effanbee, on back. 1958. $16.00.

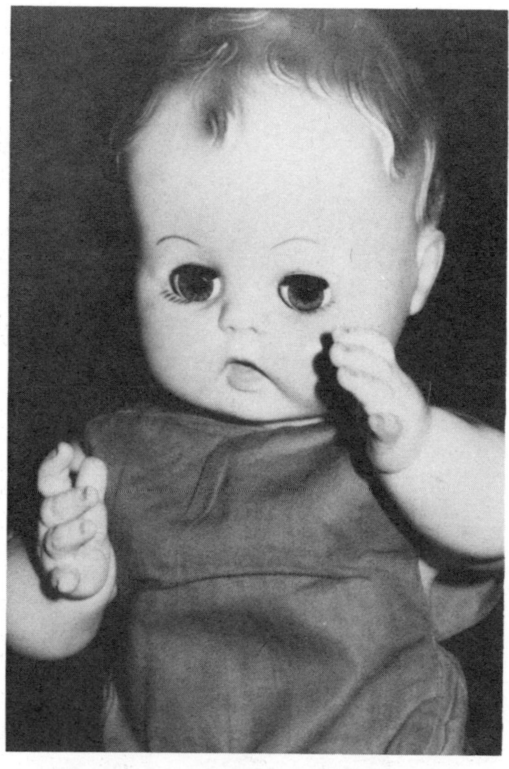

Effanbee--15" "Twinkie" All vinyl with molded hair. Blue sleep eyes/lashes. Open mouth/nurser. Marks: Effanbee/1959, on head. $8.00. (Courtesy Earlene Johnston Collection)

Effanbee--15" "Patsy Ann" Rigid vinyl arms, legs and body. Vinyl head with rooted dark blonde hair. Blue sleep eyes/lashes. Closed mouth. Freckles. Jointed waist. Marks: Effanbee/Patsy Ann/1959, on head. $18.00.

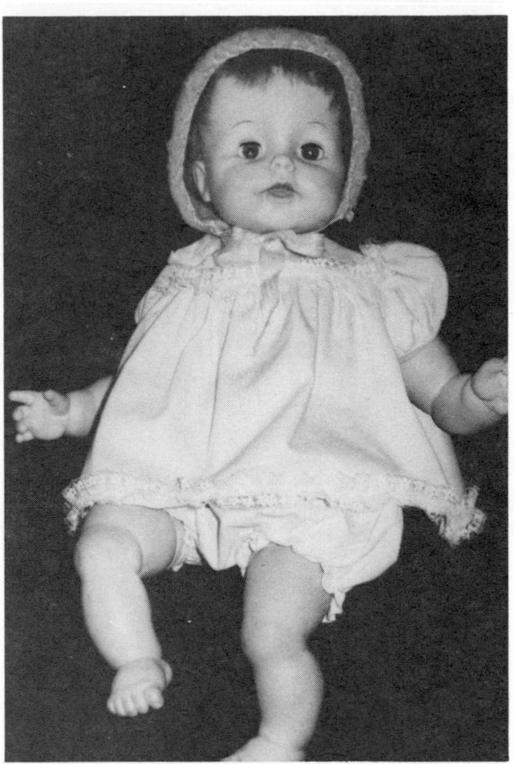

Effanbee--20" "My Precious Baby" Cloth body. Vinyl arms, legs and head. Rooted dark blonde hair. Sleep blue eyes/lashes. Open/closed mouth. Left fingers all curled. Right index and thumb extended. Right toes curled under. Cryer. Marks: 1960/Effanbee. $10.00.

Effanbee--17" "Suzie Sunshine" Plastic body and legs. Vinyl arms and head. Rooted blonde hair. Blue sleep eyes/lashes. Freckles. Closed mouth with overhanging upper lip. Marks: Effanbee/1961, on head. $8.00.

Effanbee--16" "Gumdrop" Plastic body and legs. Vinyl arms and head. Rooted blonde hair. Blue sleep eyes/lashes. Marks: 1962/Effanbee, on head. $8.00.

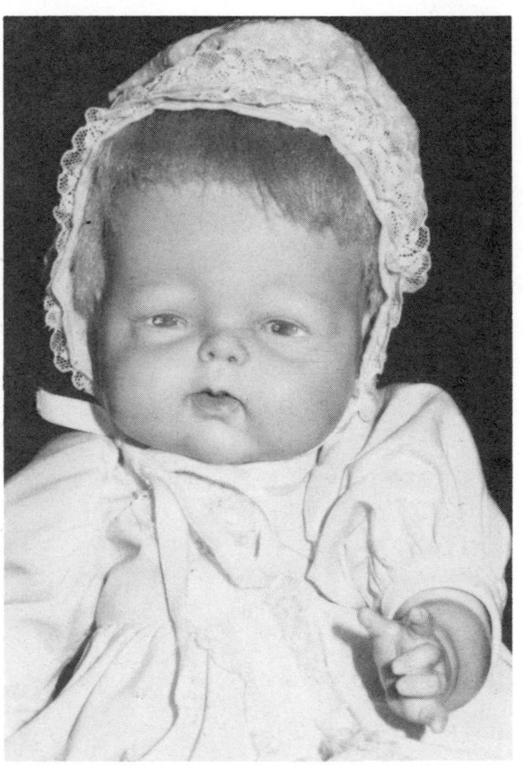

Effanbee--14" "Precious New Born" Cloth body with vinyl arms, legs and head. Rooted white hair. Painted blue eyes. Deeply molded open/closed mouth. Marks: Effanbee/1962, on head. $18.00.

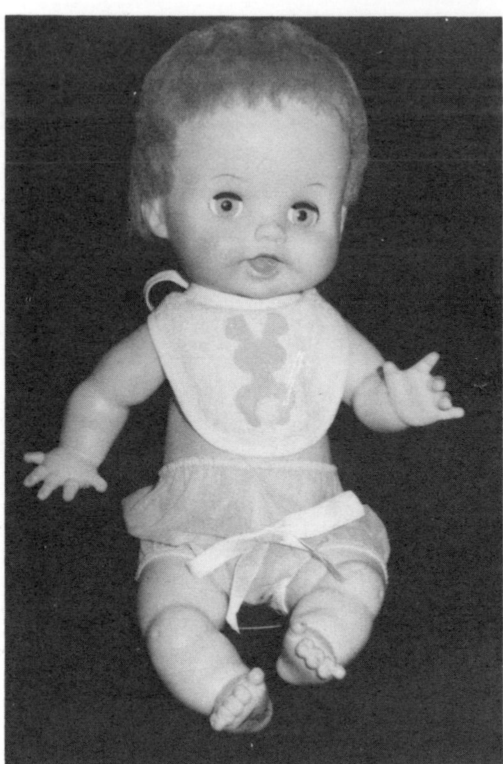

Effanbee--12" "Baby Butterball" All vinyl with rooted ash blonde hair. Blue sleep eyes/lashes. Open mouth/nurser. Both index fingers pointing out and both large toes spread out. Marks: Effanbee-1963, on head. Effanbee-1963 on body. $5.00.

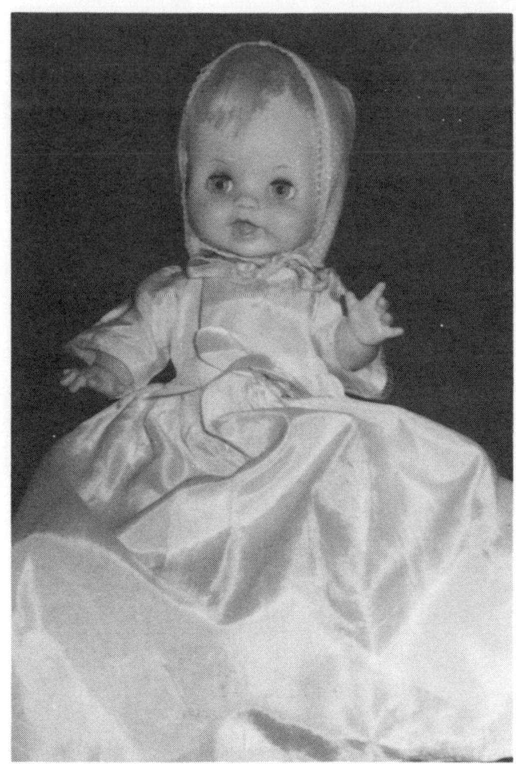

Effanbee--12" "Baby Sweetie Pie" All vinyl. Rooted white hair. Blue sleep eyes/lashes. Open/closed mouth. Wide open hands with 2nd and 3rd fingers slightly curled. Baby crossed legs. Large toes individually molded. Marks: Effanbee/1963 on head. $6.00.

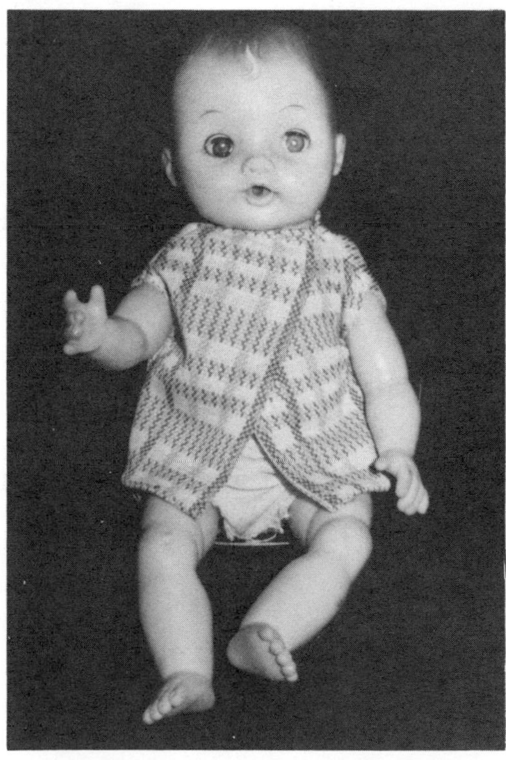

Effanbee--8½" "Babykin" All vinyl with molded and painted brown hair. Blue sleep eyes/molded lashes. Open mouth/nurser. Open hands with 2nd and 3rd fingers molded together. Thin baby legs. Marks: Effanbee/1964. $4.00.

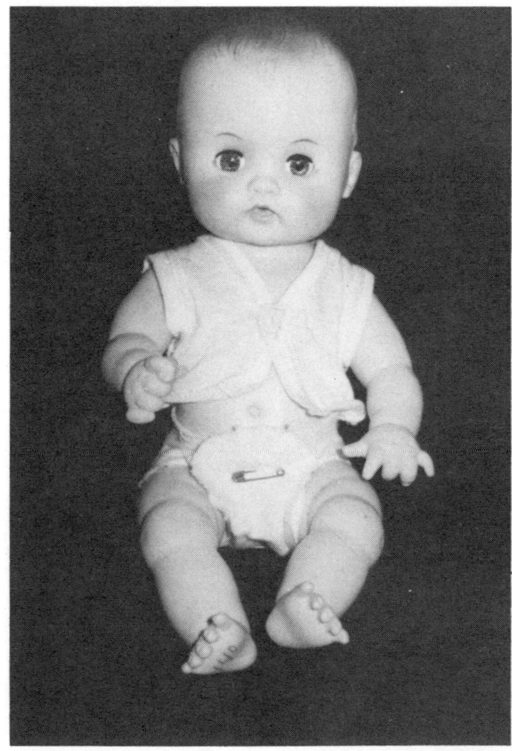

Effanbee--12" "My Fair Baby" All vinyl with molded hair. Blue sleep eyes/lashes. Open mouth/nurser. Right index crosses thumb. Marks: Effanbee 1964, on head. $6.00.

Effanbee--18" "Miss Chips" Plastic body and legs. Vinyl arms and head. Rooted black hair. Brown sleep eyes/lashes. Marks: Effanbee/1965 1700, on head. Original clothes. $15.00. (Courtesy Allin's Collection)

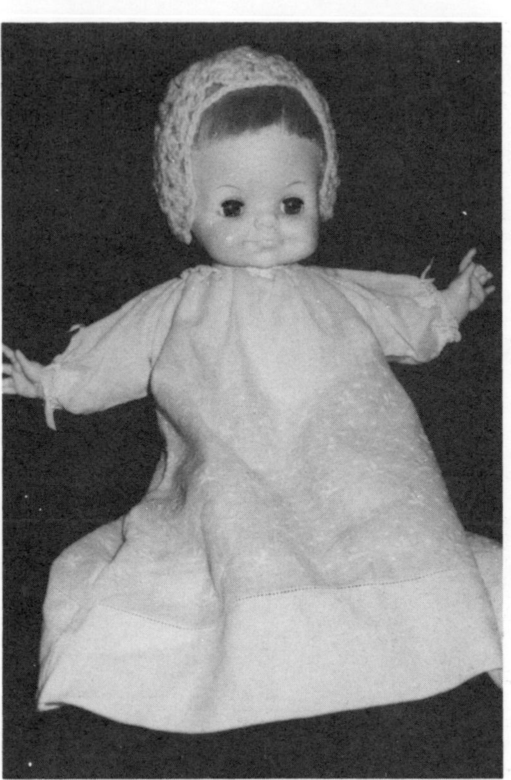

Effanbee--15" "Peaches" Cloth body. Vinyl arms, legs and head. Rooted blonde hair. Blue sleep eyes/lashes. Dimples. Marks: Effanbee 1965, on head. $16.00.

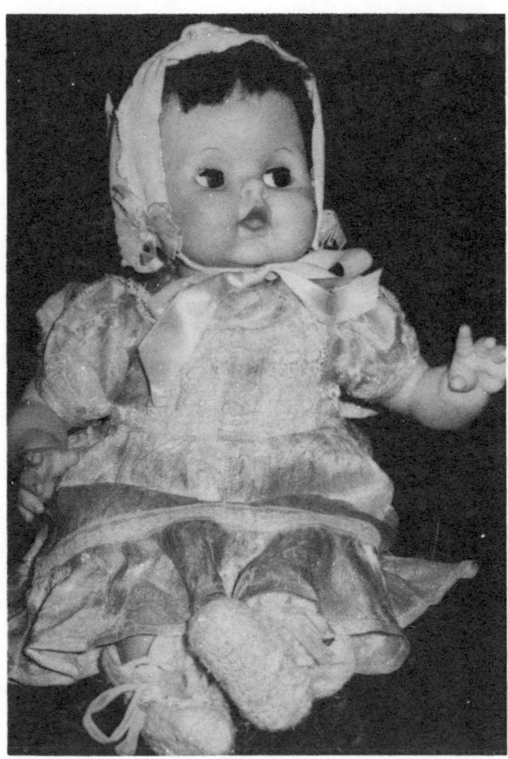

Effanbee--18" "Thumkin" Cloth body. Vinyl arms, legs and head. Rooted dark brown hair. Black side glancing sleep eyes. Both large toes up and all small toes curled. Marks: Effanbee/1965/9500U1 on head. $8.00.

Effanbee--14" "Chipper" Plastic body and legs. Vinyl arms and head. Rooted brown hair. Blue sleep eyes/lashes. Original clothes. Marks: Effanbee/1966 on head. Tag: This Is /Chipper/An Effanbee/Durable Doll. $15.00.

Effanbee--10½" "Pum'kin" All vinyl. Rooted medium blonde hair. Blue sleep, side glancing eyes/molded lashes. Closed mouth. Marks: Effanbee/1966, on head. F-B, on back. Original dress. $7.00.

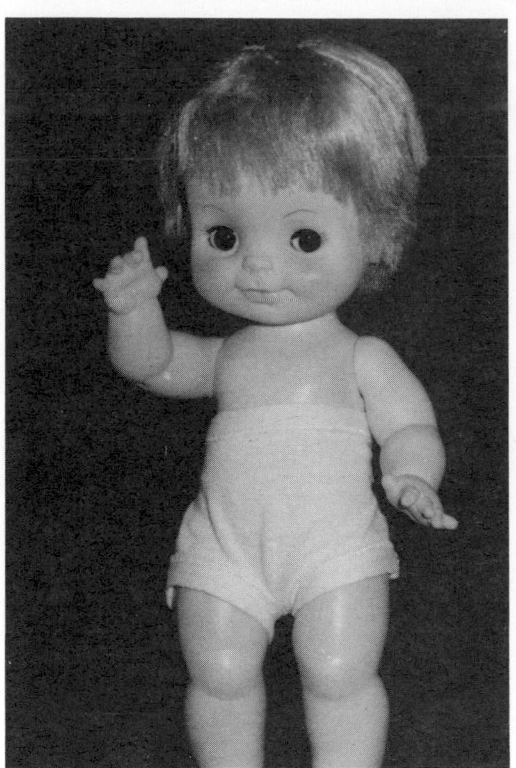

Effanbee--10" "Half-Pint" Plastic body and legs. Vinyl arms and head. Rooted blonde hair. Black pupiless eyes glancing to the side. Posable head. Open hands with stubby fingers. Individual toes. Marks: Effanbee 1966, on head. $6.00.

Effanbee--17" "New Dy Dee Baby" All vinyl with blonde rooted hair. Blue sleep eyes/lashes. Open mouth/nurser. Right index over thumb, others curled into palm. Left 2nd and 3rd fingers curled. Individual toes. Marks: Effanbee/1969, on head. Effanbee/1967, on body. $7.00.

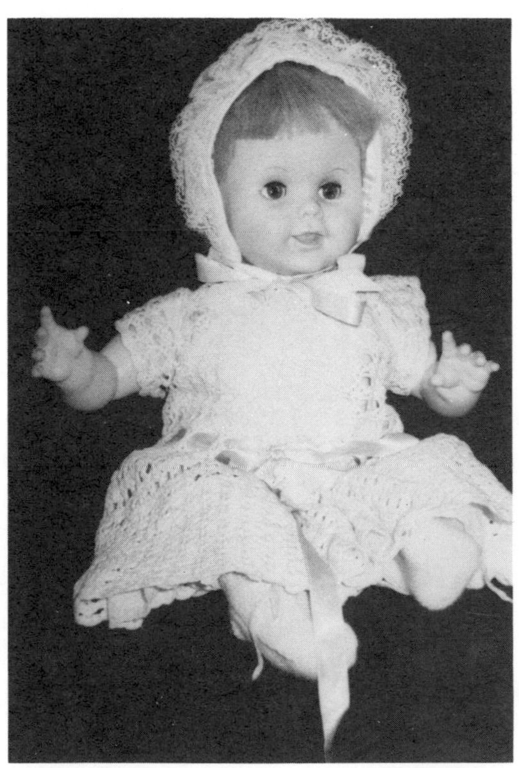

Effanbee--17" "Honey Bun" Cloth body. Vinyl arms, legs and head. Rooted blonde hair. Blue sleep eyes/lashes. Open closed mouth. All fingers extended. Marks: 9567J/Effanbee/1967 on head. $10.00.

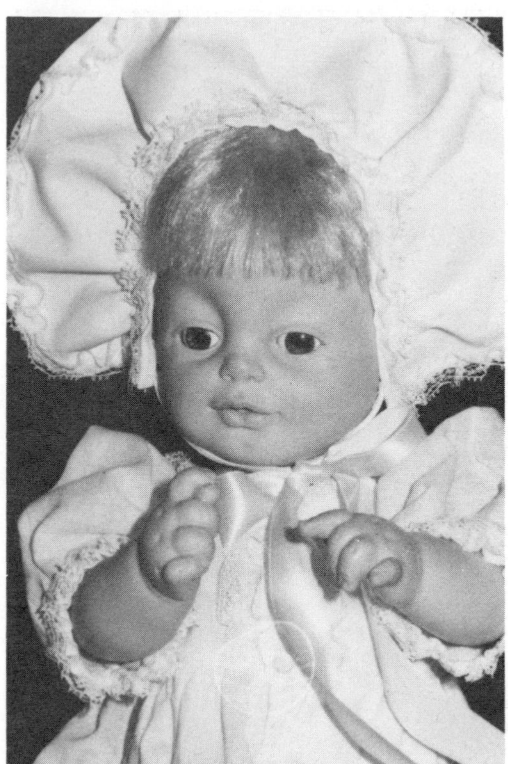

Effanbee--16" "Lil Sweetie" All vinyl with rooted blonde hair. Blue sleep eyes/no lashes or brows. Open mouth/nurser. Marks: 5667/Effanbee/1967, on head. Effanbee/1967, on back. Also Dy Dee Darlin' in 1968. $10.00

Effanbee--10" "Tiny Tubber" All vinyl with rooted light blonde hair. Blue sleep eyes/molded lashes. Open mouth/nurser. Open hands palms toward body. Marks: Effanbee 19-can't make out the rest. 1968. $7.00.

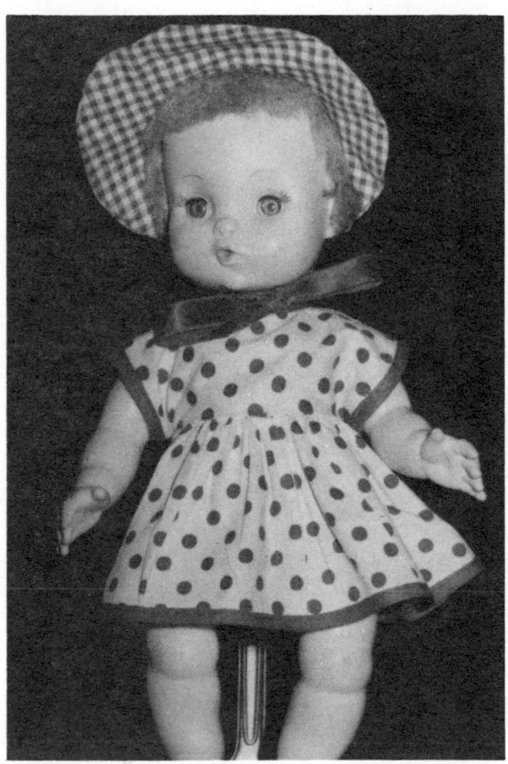

Effanbee--15" "Baby Face" Plastic body and legs. Vinyl arms and head. Rooted dark brown hair. Blue sleep eyes, side glancing/lashes. Closed mouth. Dimpled chin. Left palm down. Right 2nd and 3rd fingers curled. Marks: Effanbee/1967/2600 on head. $8.00.

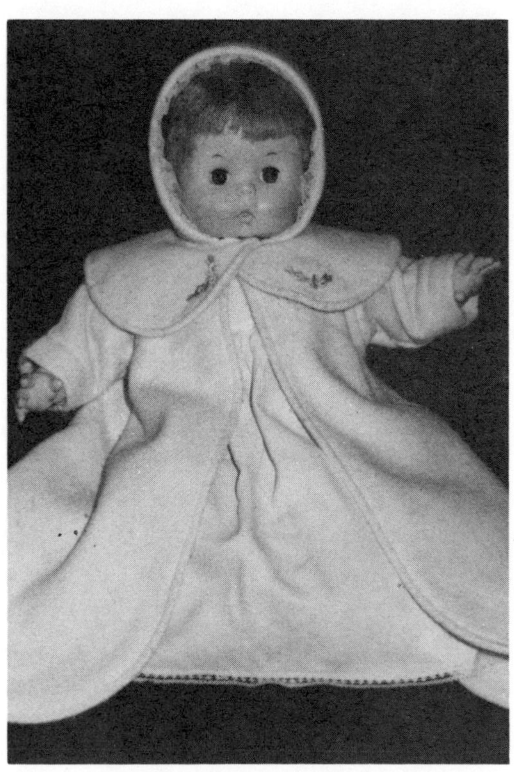

Effanbee--17" "Button Nose" Cloth body. Vinyl arms, legs and head. Rooted blonde hair. Blue sleep eyes/lashes. Open/closed mouth. Open chubby hands. Deeply dimpled knees. Cryer. Marks: 15/Effanbee/1968/9508 on head. Original clothes. $16.00.

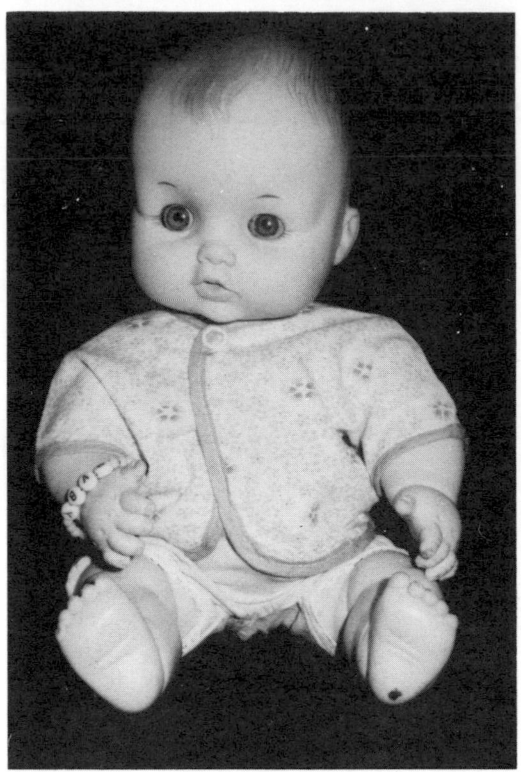

Effanbee--12" "Butterball" All vinyl with molded, painted light brown hair. Blue sleep eyes/lashes. Open mouth/nurser. All fingers slightly curled. Marks: Effanbee/1969/6569, on head and back. Original ID braclet. $8.00.

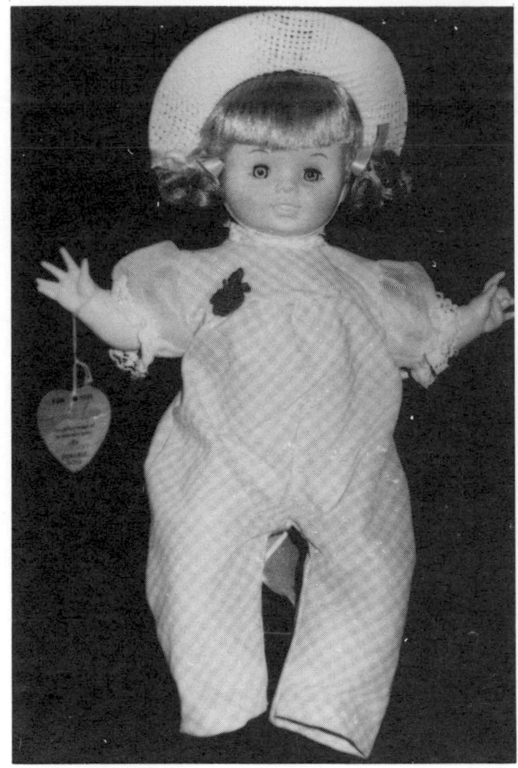

Effanbee--14" "Little Luv" Cloth body. Vinyl arms, legs and head. Rooted ash blonde hair. Blue sleep eyes/lashes. Open/closed mouth. Dimpled cheeks. Right 3rd and little fingers molded together. Left 2nd and 3rd fingers curled. Marks: Effanbee/1970/9370, on head. Original clothes. $18.00.

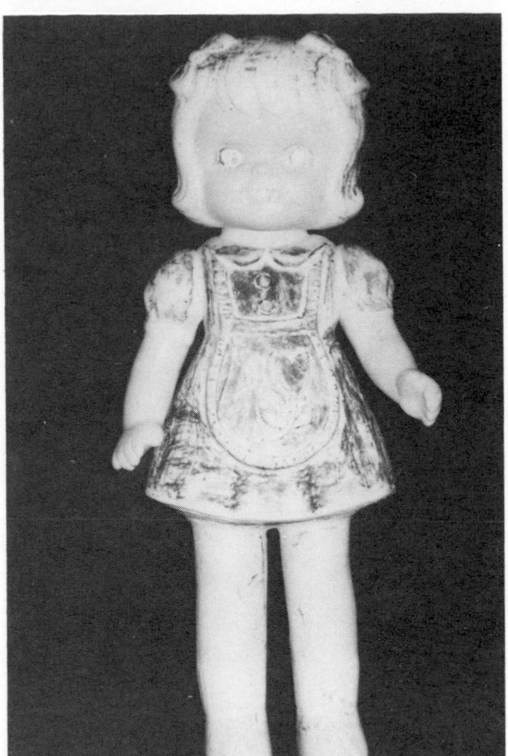

Eppy--12" "Color Me" All plastic. One piece body and legs. Jointed shoulders and neck. Molded on hair and clothes. Put out with washable crayons so that it can be recolored. Marks: Eppy 1964/Pat Pending. $4.00.

Eugenia--17½" "Personality Playmate" All hard plastic with glued on dark brown mohair wig. Brown sleep eyes/lashes. Closed mouth. Feathered eyebrows. 2nd and 3rd fingers molded together. Marks: none. 1948, was in composition. Hard plastic made in 1950. $25.00.

Eugenia--15" "Sandra" All hard plastic with glued on blonde mohair wig. Blue sleep eyes/lashes. Closed mouth. Marks: none. 1950. One of the Personality Playmates made for Eugenia by Ideal Toy Corp. Made in composition in 1948. $25.00. (Information Courtesy Pat Schoonmaker)

Famous Plaything--24" "Precious" Cloth body with rubber arms and legs. Composition head with stapled on blonde mohair wig. Blue sleep eyes/lashes. Open mouth with two teeth. Marks: Plaything, on head. Original clothes. 1937. $18.00.

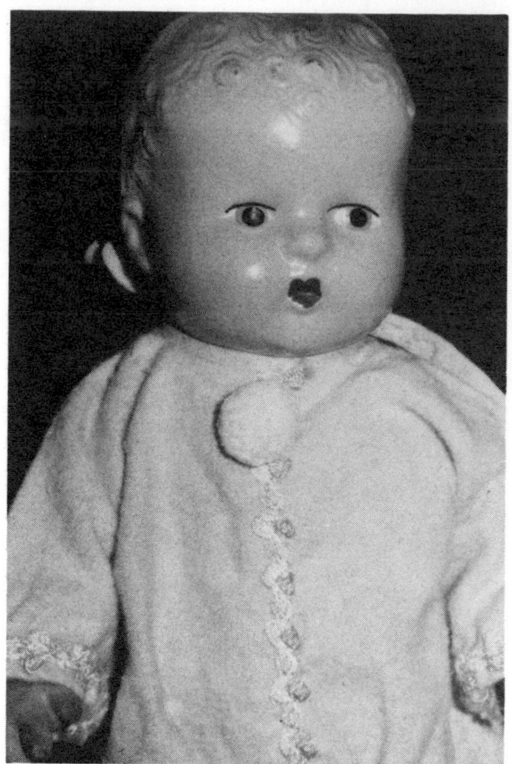

Famous Plaything--12" "Curly" Composition head strung on wooden block. Molded hair. Painted eyes. Magic skin, one piece body, arms and legs. Mark: Plaything, on head. 1947. $8.00.

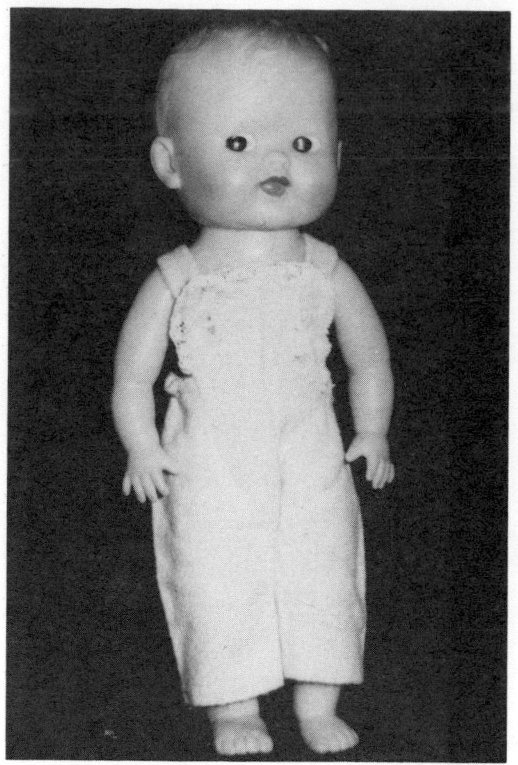

F.D. Company--8½" "Winkin" One piece vinyl unjointed body, arms and legs. Vinyl head with molded hair. Painted side glancing black eyes. Open/closed mouth. Molded tongue. Open hands with palms down. Marks: F.D., on head. 1956. $4.00.

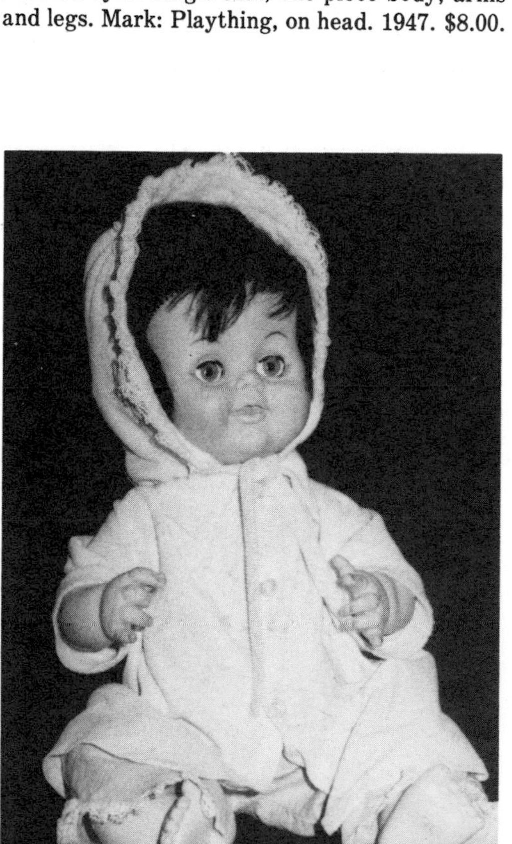

F.D. Company--18" "Sissy" Plastic body and legs. Vinyl arms and head. Rooted dark brown hair. Dark blue sleep eyes/lashes. Open mouth/nurser. Marks: F.D., on head. 1963. $6.00.

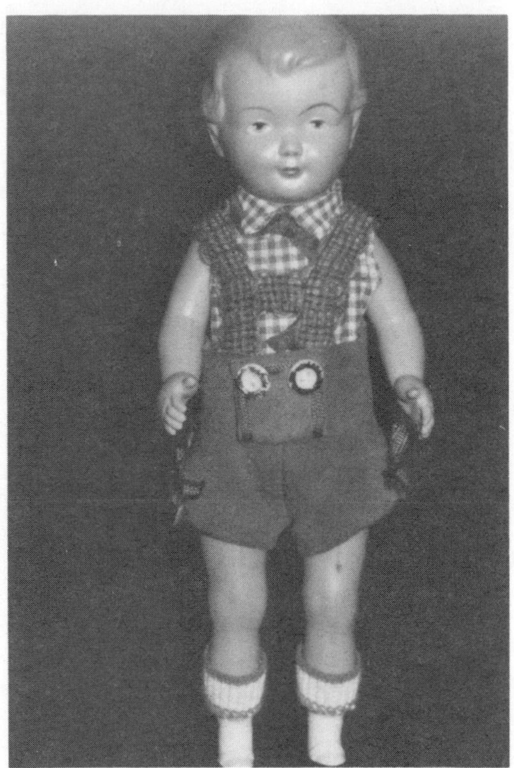

Austria--8½" "Friedel" All celluloid with one piece body and head. Jointed at shoulders and hips. Glued on dark brown mohair wig. Painted features. Marks: Animal with spread wings and a fish tail, in a square on back. 1937. Adelheid Nogler Innsbruck Doll Co. $20.00.

Austria--8½" "Trudila" All celluloid one piece body and head. Jointed at shoulders and hips. Glued on blonde mohair wig. Painted features. Marks: Animal with spread wings and a fish tail, in a square, on the back. 1937. Adelheid Nogler Innsbruck Doll Co. $20.00.

Austria--8½" "Bettina" All celluloid with hair. Jointed hips and shoulders. Painted features and socks and shoes. Marks: Animal with spread wings and a fish tail, in a square. 1937. Adelheid Nogler Innsbruck Doll Co. $20.00.

Reliable Canada--12" "Jamie" All composition with glued on hat over molded/ringlet, painted reddish brown hair. Dimpled chin and knees. Open hands, facing body. Painted blue eyes. Marks: Reliable/Made In Canada on head. Original clothes. 1937. $22.00.

Dee Cee-Canada--14" "Dee Dee" Plastic body. Vinyl arms legs and head. Rooted blonde hair. Blue sleep eyes/lashes. Open mouth/nurser. Open hands with fingers slightly curled. Individually molded toes. This company was purchased by Mattel in 1962. Marks: Dee Cee on head. Dee And Cee on lower back. 1961. $16.00.

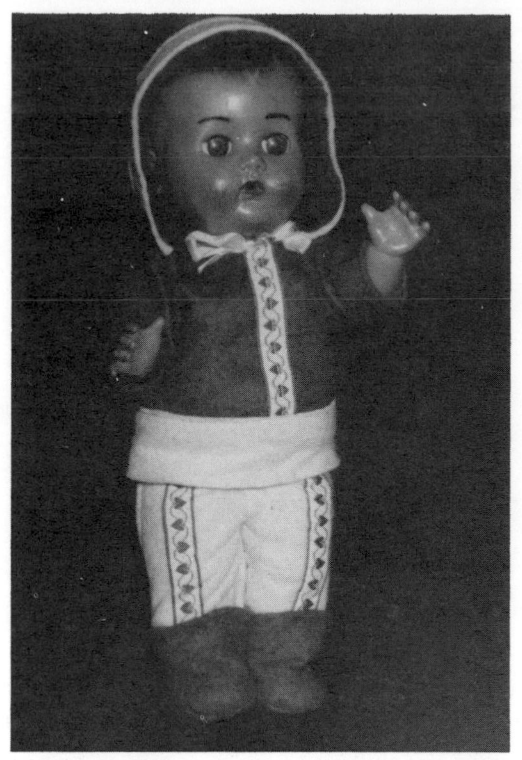

Canada--11" "Nantoc" All plastic with molded, painted black hair. Amber sleep eyes/molded lashes. Open mouth/nurser. One piece body and head. Jointed shoulders and hips. Marks: Reliable/Made In Canada, on back. Original clothes. 1963. $16.00.

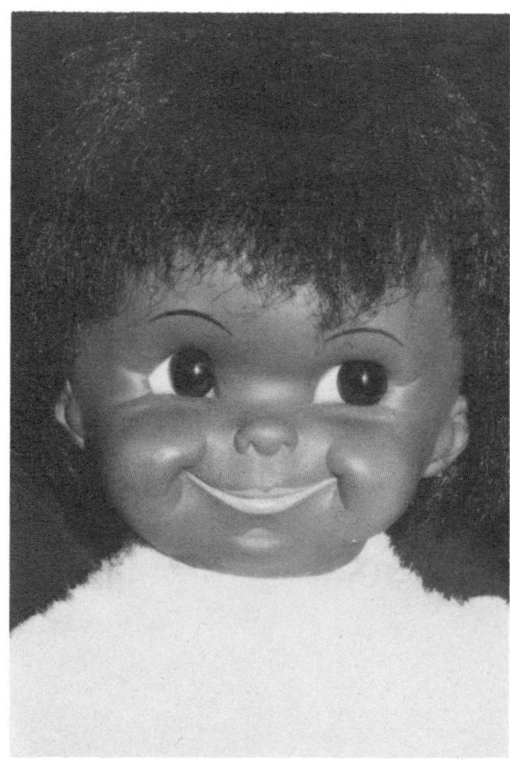

Canada--16" "Eskimo" Plush body, arms and legs. Excellsier filled. Vinyl head with rooted black hair. Inset, stationary eyes. Marks: Regal/Made In Canada. 1965. $16.00. (Courtesy Allin's Collection)

Canada--12½" "Col. Harland Sanders" All plastic. Painted features, hands and shoes. Side of base reads: Col. Harland Sanders/Kentucky Fried Chicken. Marks: Ron Starling Plastics LTD/London Canada/Made In Canada, on bottom. 1965. $7.00. (Courtesy Allins Collection)

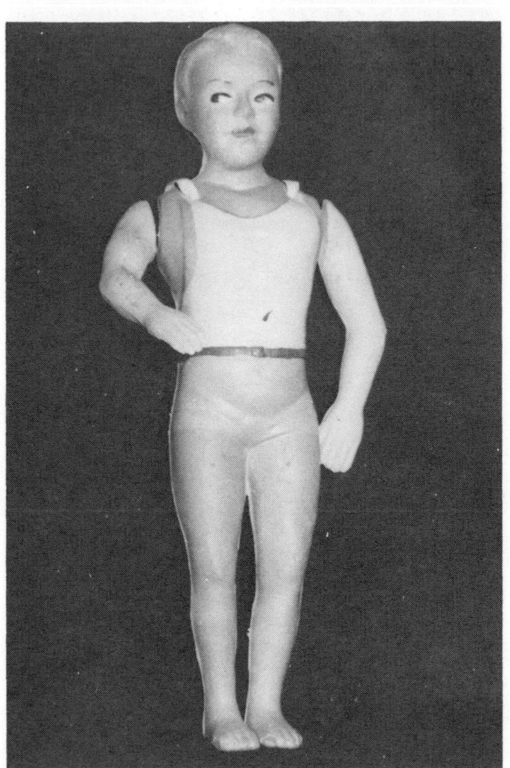

England Rosebud Doll Co.--11" "Channel Swimmer" Rubber coated, heavy painted composition arms. Molded rubber body, legs and head. Painted side glancing eyes. Painted on swimsuit. Brass holder for heavy rubber band in back. Snaps hold top on. Marks: none. 1940. $40.00.

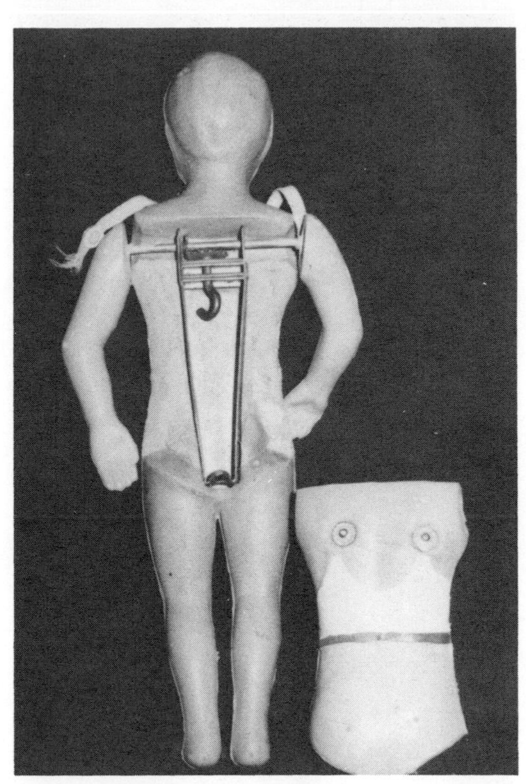

England--Back view of "Channel Swimmer"

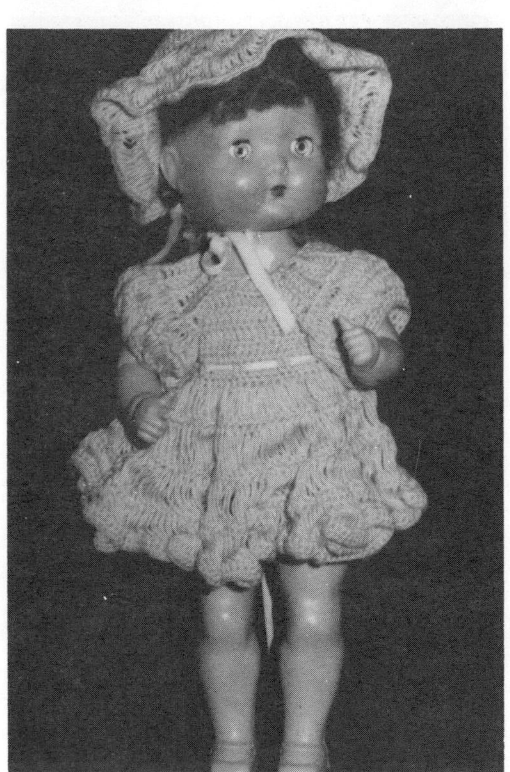

England--12" "Janie" All plastic. Glued on wig. Blue sleep eyes/lashes. Both thumbs up with index finger of right hand pointing. Walker. Head turns as she walks. Non-mechanical head action. Marks: Roddy/Made In England on back. 1951. $18.00.

Rosebud LTD.--14" "Rosette" Plastic body and legs. Vinyl arms and head. Rooted white hair. Blue sleep eyes/lashes. Blue eye shadow. Closed mouth. Nailpolish. High heel feet. Marks: Rosebud, in a key shaped square with a rose. Made in England. 1958. Original clothes. $32.00.

England--19" "Mariann" Plastic body and legs. Vinyl arms and head. Brown rooted hair. Blue sleep eyes/lashes. High heel feet. Marks: Rosebud on center top scalp under hair. 1959. $9.00 (Courtesy Earlene Johnston's Collection)

England--12" "Flirty" Plastic body arms and legs. Vinyl head with rooted hair. Blue sleep eyes/lashes. Closed mouth. Marks: Made In England on head. 1960. $9.00

England--13" "Cindy" All vinyl with rooted dark brown hair. Pale blue sleep eyes. Open/closed mouth. Molded bent arms. Left hand 2nd and 3rd fingers molded together. Baby legs with large toes extended and 3rd and 4th toes molded together. Marks: Made in England on head and body. 1962. Roddy Doll Co. $16.00

England-Rosebud--14" "Rose Of 1963" Plastic body and legs. Vinyl arms and head. Rooted dark auburn hair. Blue sleep eyes. Closed mouth. Marks: Rosebud on head. Made In England on back. $18.00

England--5" "Beatles" Paul and George are all vinyl. Ringo and John are all hard plastic. Marks: The Beatles on back. NEMS/ENT. Ltd/1964 on one foot. Lic. By Seltaeb, Inc. on the other foot. $35.00 per set. (Courtesy Earlene Johnston)

Peggy Nesbit--7" "Sonja-The Skating Girl" All plastic one piece body, legs and head. Jointed shoulders. Painted brown hair. Painted blue eyes. Closed mouth. Glued on cap. Removable clothes and muff. Painted shoes/glued on skates. Marks: none. Attached Tag; Costume Doll By Peggy Nesbit/Made in England. 1969. $5.00

Jumeau

The makers of Jumeau dolls were mentioned as early as the Universal Exposition, in Paris, in 1844. The manufacture of dolls was continued until the end of the 19th century by the Jumeau family.

The Jumeau House was absorbed in March 1899 by the formation of the Societe Francaise De Fabrication De Bebe Et Jouets, Paris, France (S.F.B.J.). They continued to make Bebe Jumeaus, and Bebe Jumeaus were still being made in 1954.

Jumeaus of the late 40's and early 50's moved, had sleeping eyes and some talked. The first post-war Jumeau heads were of porcelain, made in Montreuil S Bois, Seine and had human hair. They were dressed in designer clothes made at 160 Rue de Picpus, Paris. The Societe made, under the name Jumeau, special dolls such as reproductions and exact copies of the 1938 doll made especially to offer to the English Princess. Also Jumeau dolls costumed in the traditional dress of all the French provinces.

The Societe began to reproduce dolls from the old Jumeau molds in 1949. New dolls being imported must bear the name of the maker and the mark S.F.B.J. (this would date them 1899 or later as the U.S. passed a law in 1890 which required all imports to bear the name of the maker and country). A number of these dolls have found their way into the U.S. that was meant for sales in France and they are marked only Jumeau on the heads.

The Societe started using a composition plastic in 1949 and 1950. The skin tones are dark red and coloring is exquisite. The dolls came with open and closed mouths, sleep and stationary eyes and painted features. They had paper tags attached to the left arm stating they were Jumeaus. The use of the old style ball jointed body jointed at elbow, wrist and knees was used through 1953. All were the older girl type and one little girl line was Promentte, a character doll line with sleep eyes.

France--8" "Andra" Cloth body, arms and legs. Glued on caracul hair. Blue painted eyes. Closed mouth. Removable clothes. Marks: Tag: English and French: My Name is Andra. The Handmade Dress I Wear Is An Exact Copy Of An Original National Costume Worn In My Country, Czechoslovakia. 1940. $16.00.

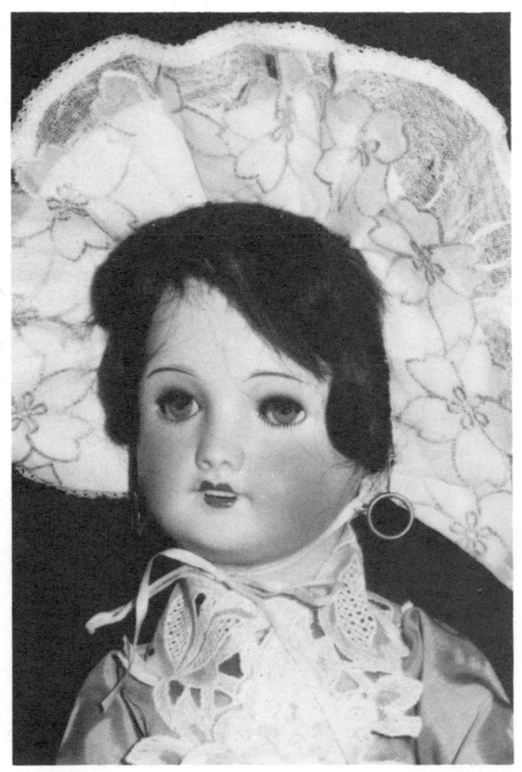

France--20" "Province of Boulonnaise" Bisque head. Tag: Fabrication/Jumeau/Paris. Made in France, stamped on back and on dress tag. Head marked: Paris/France, in an oval, 71 and 149 with 301, an R, in a circle, with a B beneath. Original clothes. 1949. $125.00.

France--14" "Province of Lorraine" Composition plastic (resembles celluloid) with red/brown mohair wig. Stationary brown eyes/lashes. Closed mouth. Ball jointed boyd. Jointed elbows and wrist. Marks:Jumeau, on head. 1951. $80.

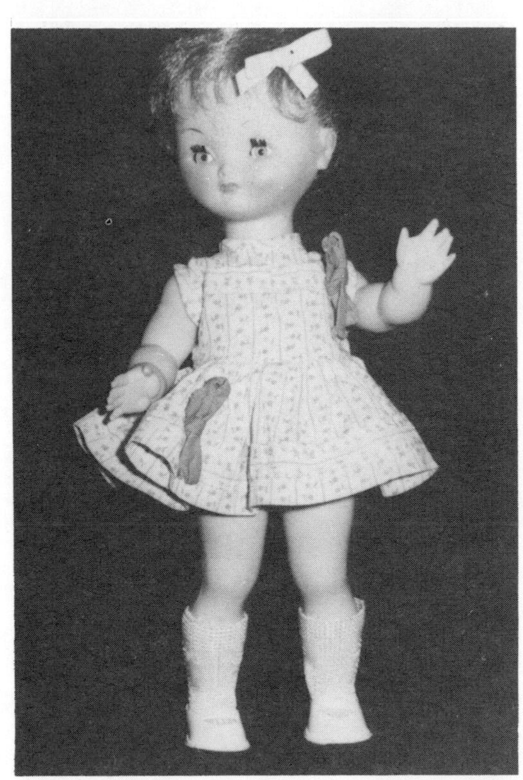

France--11" "Bella-Bee" Plastic body, arms and legs. Vinyl head. Rooted blonde hair. Small blue sleep eyes/lashes. Long neck. Marks: Bella/Made In France/MM-something- 1960. Original dress. $25.00.

France--14" "Lynette" Soft plastic body and legs. Vinyl arms and head. Rooted blonde hair. Blue sleep eyes/lashes. Closed mouth. Marks: CD7 on head./Made In France/CD7 on body. 1962. $16.00 (Courtesy Allin's Collection)

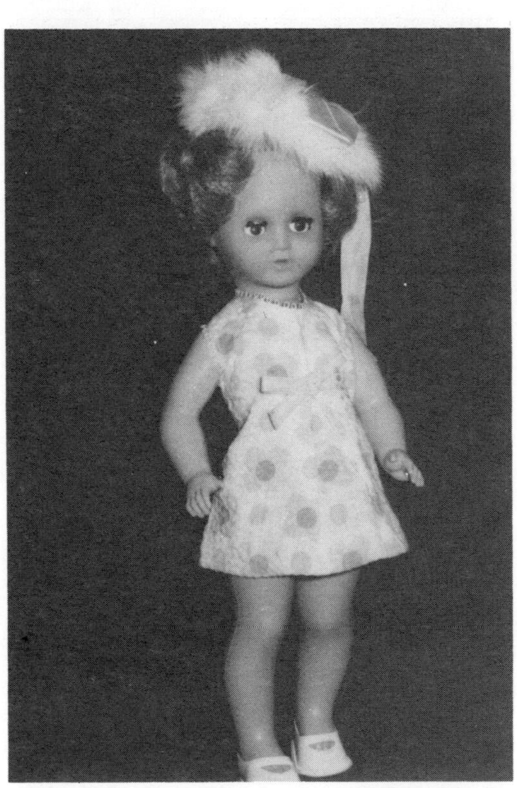

France--11" "Ge-Ge" Plastic body, arms and legs with vinyl head. Rooted dark blonde hair. Brown sleep eyes/long lashes. Closed mouth. Posable head. Marks: Ge-Ge-/9N on head. 1962. Ge-Ge is the trademark for G Giroud & Cie, Montribson, France. $35.00

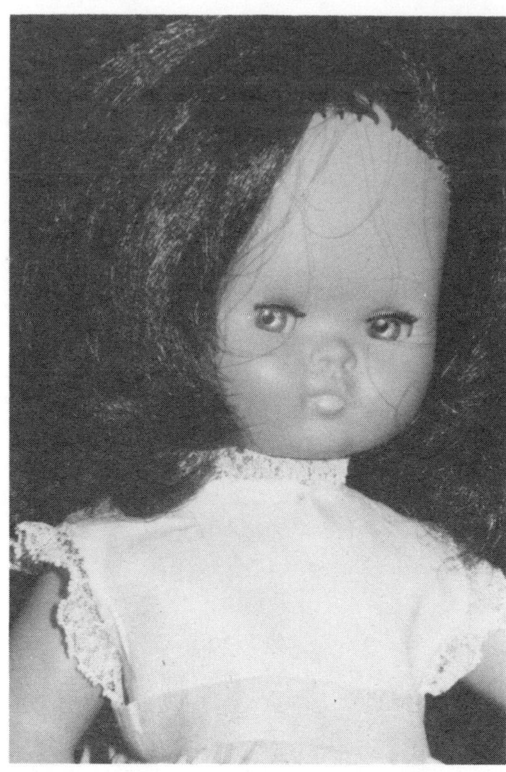

France--13½""Polly" polyfex plastic body, arms and legs. Vinyl head with rooted black hair. Blue sleep eyes/lashes. Closed mouth. Marks: Polyfex over circle with a stork, sheath of wheat and a bird in a nest/Made In France. 1963. $16.00 (Courtesy Allin's Collection).

France--12½" "Soupee" Plastic body, arms and legs. Vinyl head with floor length brown rooted hair. Blue sleep eyes/lashes. Closed mouth. Open hands with palms down. 2nd and 3rd fingers molded together. Marks: Bella/Made In France/Orenete 1000 on back. 1963. $18.00.

France--13" "El Poupee Toddler" Plastic body, arms and legs. Vinyl head with rooted light brown hair. Blue sleep eyes/lashes. Open mouth/nurser. Palms down. Marks: Bella/Made In France/Orevete-1000 on back. 1964. $16.00.

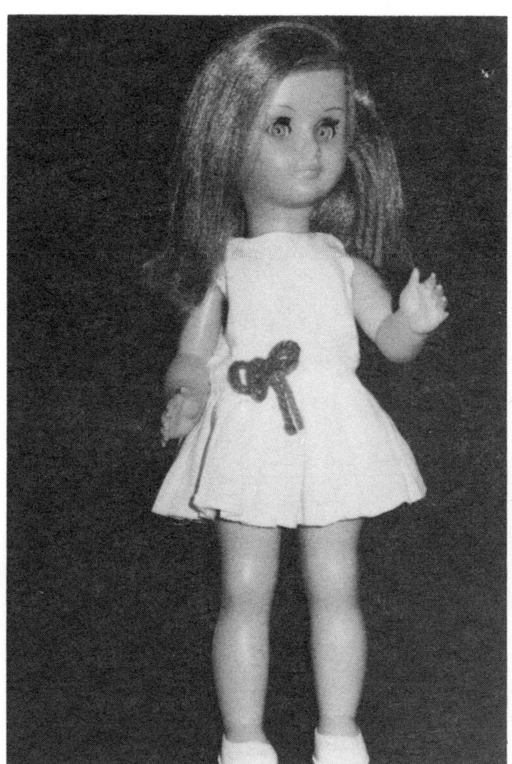

France--13½" "Soupee Bella" Dark toned plastic with vinyl head. Rooted brown hair. Pale blue sleep eyes/long lashes. Marks: Bella/Made In France/Baevete 6000 on back. Dress Tag: Soupe/Bella. 1965. $20.00.

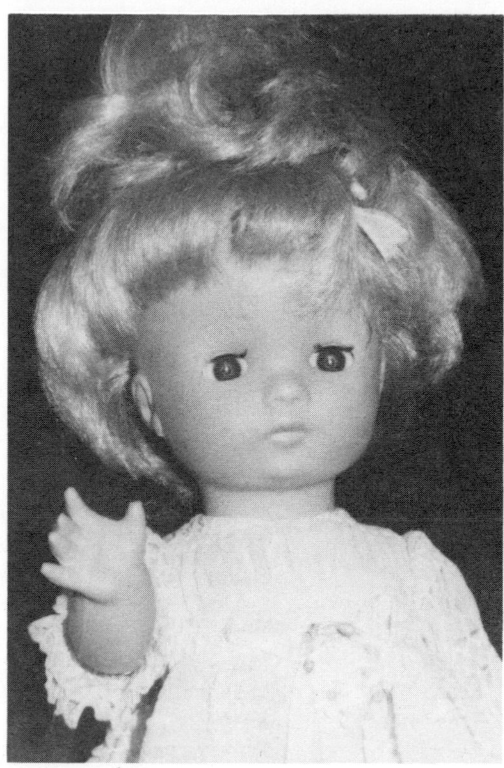

France--14" "Rosemund" All plastic with inset skull cap rooted blonde hair. Pale brown sleep eyes/lashes. Posable head. Original clothes. Marks: Clodrey/Made In France, on back. 1965. $30.00.

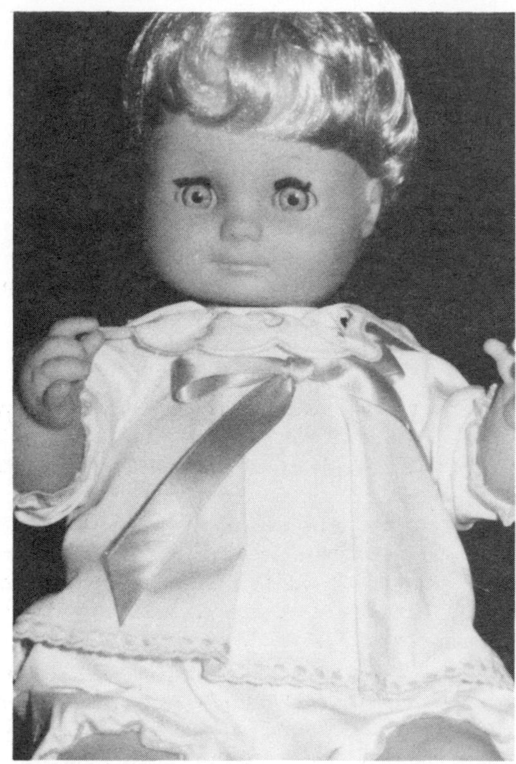

France--15" "Michelle" Foam and cloth body. Vinyl arms, legs and head. Rooted blonde hair. Blue sleep eyes/lashes. Dimples. Marks: Clodrey/Made In France on head. Original clothes. 1969. $16.00 (Courtesy Allin's Collection).

France--18" "Claudette" Polyfoam covered with cloth body. Vinyl arms, legs and head. Rooted blonde hair. Blue sleep eyes/lashes. Marks: Clodrey/2-18-2926, on head. 1969. $32.00 (Courtesy Allin's Collection).

France--11" "Pretty" Plastic body and legs. Vinyl arms and head. Rooted orange/red hair. Sleep blue eyes/lashes. Closed mouth. Both hands spread wide open. Marks: Made In France/MO6/2012 on head. 1970. $15.00. (Courtesy of Dorothy Westbrook Collection).

Kathe Kruse Dolls, Germany

Founded in 1910 by Kathe Kruse, the wife of a well known Berlin sculpter. Her first dolls were copies of a baby of the Renaissance period and of her own children. The heads were hand painted in oils.

In 1916 she obtained a patent for a wire coil doll. They were Kathrinchen, a Dutch doll, Lutt Martin, Fritz, Christincen, and Michel. In 1923 she registered, as a trademark, in Germany, a double K with the first one reversed and the name Kathe Kruse.

After World War II Kathe Kruse dolls were made of plastics by the Rheinische Gummi Celuloid Fabrik Company of Germany. These plastics were first shown at the Toy Fair in Nuremberg, in 1955. They are still being made.

The following are some of the names given to the Kathe Kruse dolls.

Kathel	Lisel	Rudi
Willi	Hans	Babu
Ullrich	Karlchen	Erika
Peter	Pauline	Bettina
Robert	Louise	Ursel
Trudila	Wera	Olga
Hilde	Fanny	Pumpernella
Beate	Wilhelminchen	Erna
Henriette	Emmy	Pepi
Conrad	Rumpumpel	Linda
Hermann	Manne	Friedel
Max	Barbel	

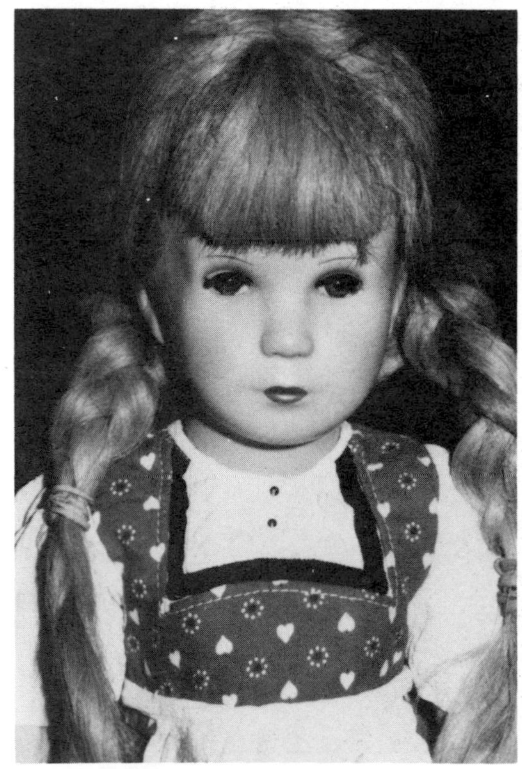

Germany- Kruse--16" "Pauline" All plastic with glued on blonde human hair wig. Rocker blue sleep eyes/lashes. Closed mouth. Marks: Turtle In A Diamond/T 40 on head. Turtle Mark/ Modell/Kathe Kruse/T40 on back. 1949. $45.00. (Courtesy Earlene Johnston Collection)

Germany--5" Tall/3½" long "Crawler" All plastic with white mohair over molded hair. Painted blue eyes. Closed mouth. Marks: Picture of monkey in a circle. M-32/West Germany/Original. 1956. Original clothes. $16.00.

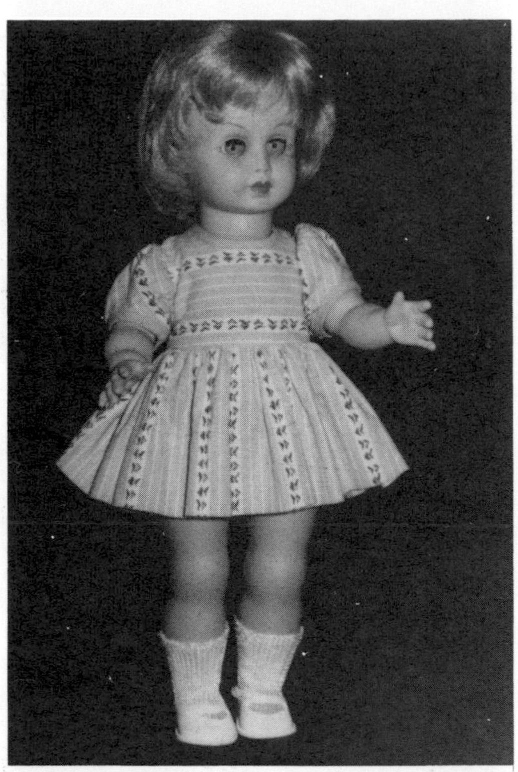

Germany--12" "Katinka" Plastic body and legs. Vinyl arms and head with rooted dark frosted blonde hair. Blue sleep eyes/lashes. Closed mouth. Marks: three M's running vertically, on head. Three M's/30 on back. 1957. Maar-Sohn Doll Co. $32.00.

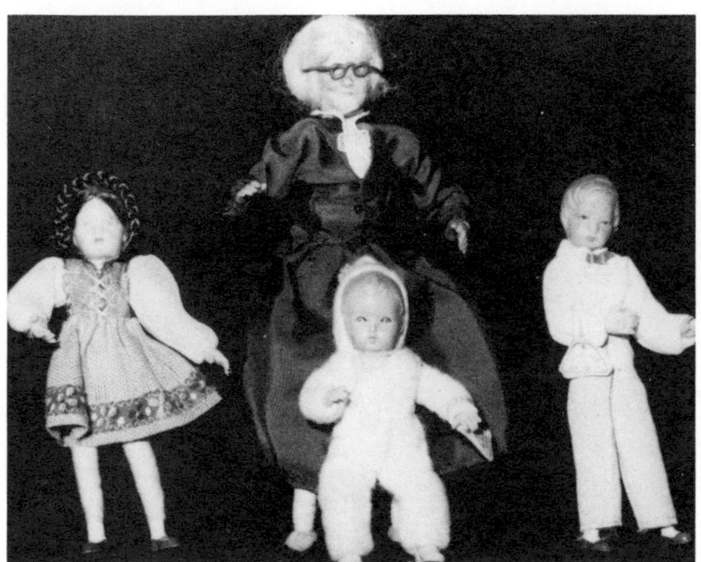

Germany Shackman--"Peasant Family" Granny has composition head with hard plastic hands. Little girl has composition head and hard plastic hands. Baby has hard plastic head and hands. Little boy has hard plastic head and hands. All have wire, covered with string, body and legs. All have lead shoes. Original clothes. 1958. Shackman, Germany. $5.00 each. (Courtesy Earlene Johnston collection)

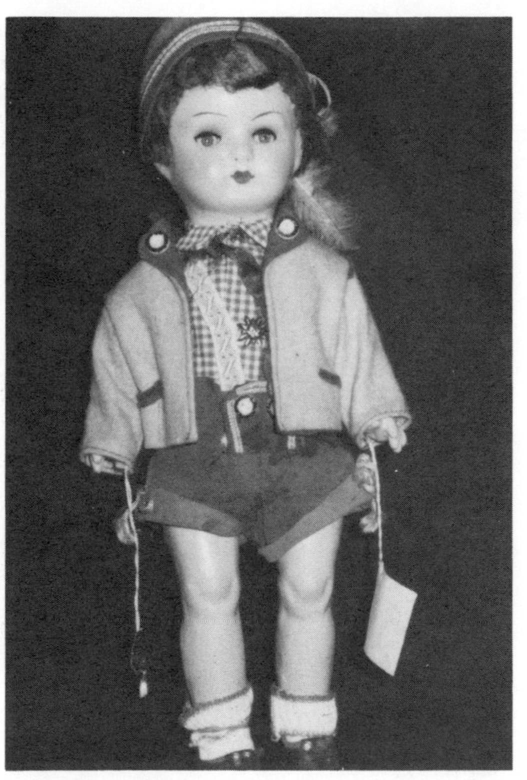

Germany--12½" "Gura" All paper mache. Glued on brown mohair wig. Blue sleep rocker eyes/lashes. Closed mouth. Marks: Tag: Gura. This is an original costume doll as worn in the region of Bavarian Boy. H.J. on head. 1958. Original clothes. (Courtesy Vicky Johnston Collection)

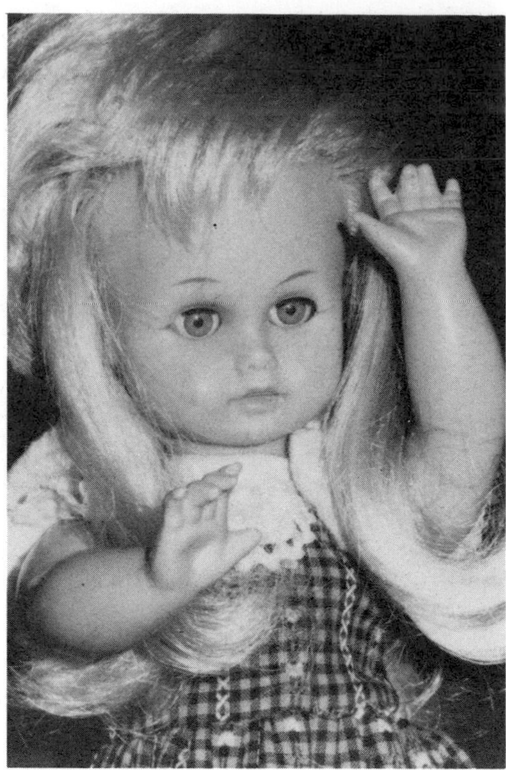

Germany--13" "Gretchen" Rigid vinyl body. Ball jointed at shoulders and hips. (Joints of hard plastic) Rooted blonde hair. Blue sleep eyes/lashes. Closed mouth. Original dress. Marks: Geo. Gesch, on head. 1960. $16.00.

Germany--8" "Black Forest Barbel" All plastic with glued on brown wig. Painted features. Painted on long socks and shoes. Posable head. Marks: Tag: Original Schmider Trachten. 1965. $7.00. (Courtesy Vickie Johnston Collection)

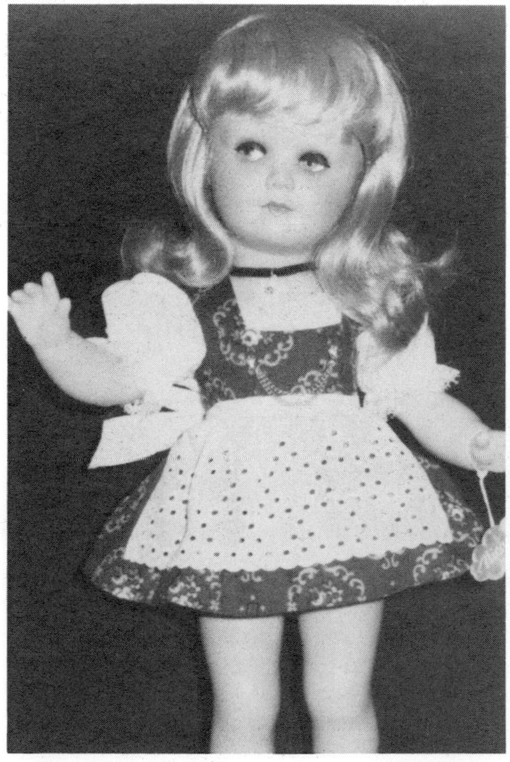

Germany--17" "Pride" Plastic body, legs and head. Vinyl arms. Combination of woven and rooted hair (human) set in vinyl skull cap. Cryer in center back. Palms down. Blue flirty sleep eyes/heavy lashes. Closed mouth. Arms and legs are strung. Posable head. Original clothes. Marks: K & W/151/45, on head. 44/Made In/W. Germany, on body. Tag: Nicaput/Wernicke. 1968. $80.00.

Hawaii--10½" "Lonee" All hard plastic with glued on black wig. Brown sleep eyes/molded lashes. One piece body and legs. Jointed neck and shoulders. Marks: Made In Hawaii/Elsie Denney. 1951. $4.00.

Hong Kong--10" "Freckles" All hard plastic with glued on cap with front curl attached. Blue sleep eyes/molded lashes. Freckles. Closed mouth. Marks: Made In Hong Kong, on head. Original clothes. 1950. $3.00.

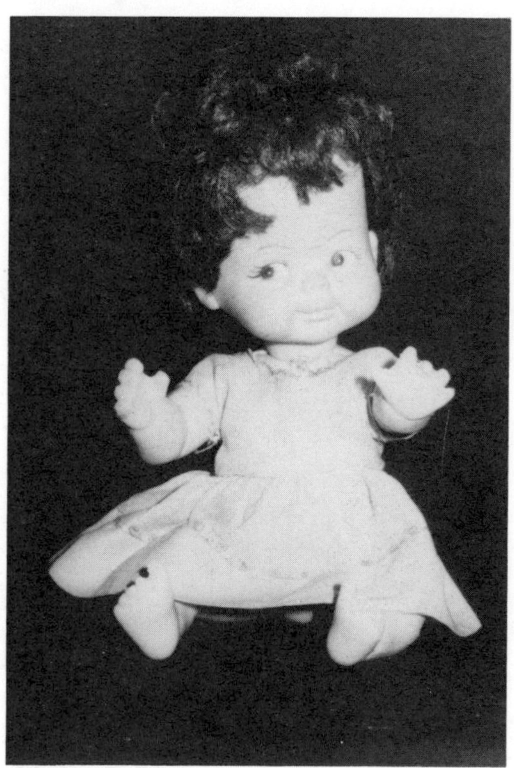

Hong Kong--8" "Bee Bee" Plastic body, arms and legs. Vinyl head with rooted brown hair. Painted side glancing eyes. Closed mouth. Posable head. Baby legs. Marks: Made In Hong Kong, on back. 1965.

Hong Kong--12" "Lovely" Plastic body, arms and legs. Vinyl head with rooted curly dark brown hair. Painted blue/black eyes. Open mouth/nurser. Marks: Made In Hong Kong, on head. 1965. $3.00.

Hong Kong--9" Eggie" All plastic with painted features. All fingers curled on right hand. Marks: Perfekta/Made In Hong Kong on head. Hong Kong, on back. 1966. $4.00.

Hong Kong--5" "Jane" All vinyl with rooted blonde hair. Blue painted eyes. Closed mouth. Marks: Made In Hong Kong, on back. Original clothes. 1966. $2.00

Hong Kong--11½" "Lily" Plastic body, arms and legs. Vinyl head with rooted dark brown hair. Side glancing black eyes. Closed mouth. Jointed waist. Very small high heel feet. Marks: Made In Hong Kong, on body. 1967. Original clothes.

Hong Kong--8" "Clown" Plastic body, arms and legs. Vinyl head. Rooted orange hair. Stationary inset black eyes/lashes. Marks: Made In Hong Kong, on back. Original clothes. 1967. $3.00.

Hong Kong--13" "Junie" Plastic body, legs. Vinyl arms and head. Rooted yellow blonde hair. Painted brown eyes. Closed mouth. Jointed waist Marks: Made In Hong Kong, on back. 1968. $8.00.

Hong Kong--8" "My Little Girl" Plastic and vinyl with rooted blonde hair. Painted side glancing blue eyes/long lashes. Open/closed mouth. Made in Hong Kong, on back. 1968. $8.00.

Hong Kong--11" "Mod" Plastic body. Vinyl arms, legs and head. Rooted long yellow hair. Painted brown eyes/lashes. Open/closed mouth with painted teeth. Deep cheek dimples. Posable head. Jointed waist. Small high heel feet. Marks: Made In Hong Kong, on back. 1969. $3.00.

Hong Kong--10½" "Lil' Bit" Plastic body, arms and legs. Vinyl head with rooted white hair. Painted side glancing blue eyes. Closed mouth. Freckles. Marks: Made In Hong Kong, on head. Made In Hong Kong, on back. Original clothes. 1969. $2.00.

Hong Kong--7½" "Little Guy" Plastic with vinyl head. Rooted blonde hair. Painted blue eyes, side glancing. Closed mouth. Marks: Made In Hong Kong/CPC, in a diamond. Original clothes. 1969. $2.00.

Hong Kong--8" "Baby Jane" Plastic body, arms and legs. Vinyl head. Painted side glancing eyes. Open mouth/nurser. Marks: Made In Hong Kong, on head. 1970. $2.00.

Hong Kong--8" "Liza" Plastic body. Vinyl arms, legs and head. Rooted blonde hair. Blue sleep eyes/molded lashes. Closed mouth. Marks: Made In Hong Kong., on back. 1970. Original clothes. $4.00.

CPC Hong Kong--7½" "Picture This" Plastic body and legs. Vinyl arms and head. Rooted dark blonde hair. Blue painted side glancing eyes. Closed mouth. Marks: Made In Hong Kong. CPC, in a diamond beneath, on body. Original clothes and frame. 1971. $4.00.

India--10½" Miss India" One piece unjointed head, body, arms and legs, cloth filled. Molded face mask. Glued on mohair wig. Painted features. Marks: Tag: Made by poor widows at Nagpada Neighborhood House. Byculla, Bombay, India. All original. 1947. $18.00.

Italy--5½" "Red Riding Hood" All plastic with glued on light brown wig. Blue sleep eyes. Closed mouth. Open hands with all fingers slightly curled. Marks: Made In Italy, on back. 1956. Original clothes. $8.00.

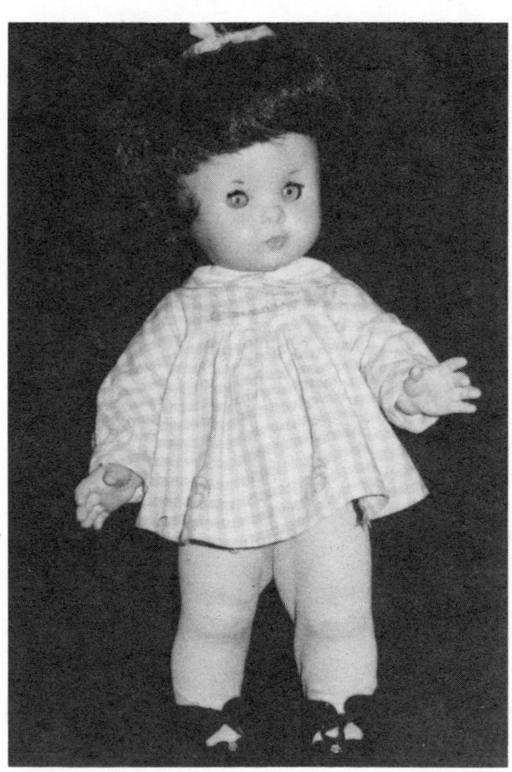

Furga--13" "Carolina" All vinyl foam with vinyl head. Rooted black hair. Blue sleep eyes/lashes. Closed mouth. Open hands with left 2nd finger slightly curled. Toddler legs with dimpled knees. Marks: Furga Italy, on head. 1961. Original dress only $18.00.

Furga--10½" "Angelica" All vinyl with rooted red hair. Pale blue stationary eyes/lashes. Open mouth with two painted teeth. Dimples. Marks: Furga-Italy on head. Furga/Italy, on back. 1964. $18.00

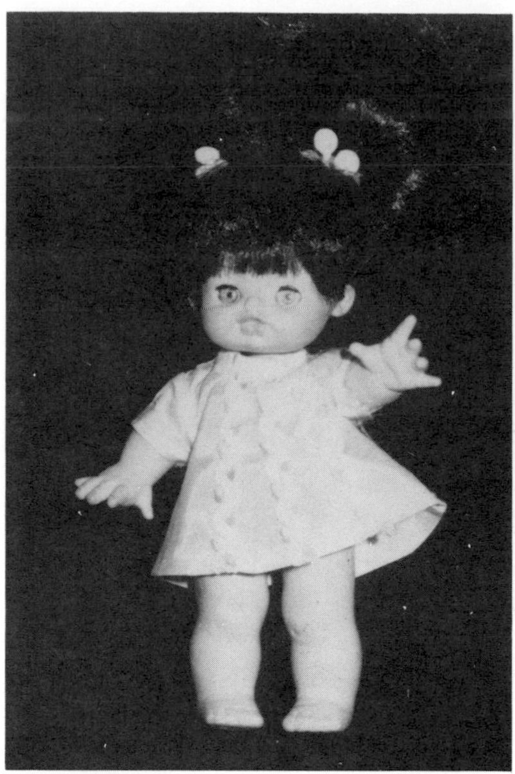

Furga--6" "Betta" All vinyl with rooted dark brown hair/long lashes. Open/closed mouth. Marks: Furga/Italy. Original clothes. 1967. $4.00.

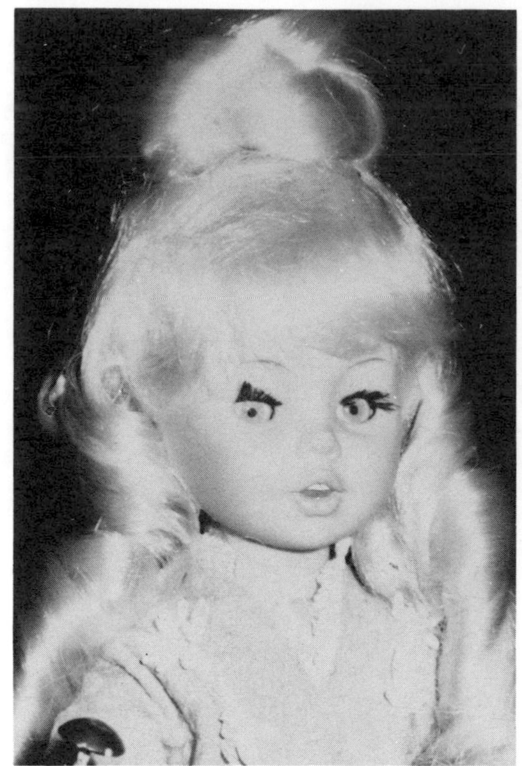

Furga--14" "Sweet Adriana" Plastic body and legs. Vinyl arms and head. Rooted blonde hair. Aqua sleep eyes/lashes. Open/closed mouth with two painted upper teeth. Original with pantaloons and large brimmed hat. Cry voice. Marked: Furga Italy, on head. 1967. $35.00. (Courtesy of Earlene Johnston)

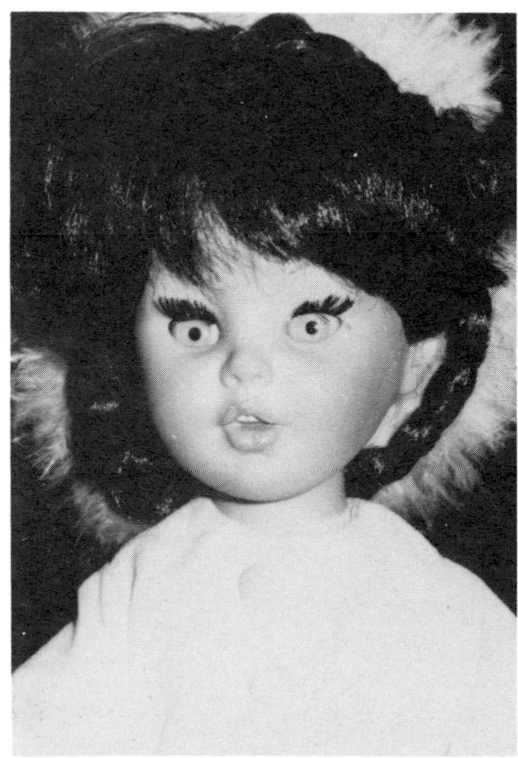

Furga Italy--16" "Bride" All vinyl with a combination of glued and rooted black hair. Vivid blue sleep eyes/lashes. Open/closed mouth with two painted teeth. Original. Dressed in long brides gown, knit gloves. Marks: Furga Italy, on head. 1968. $35.00. (Courtesy Vickie Johnston)

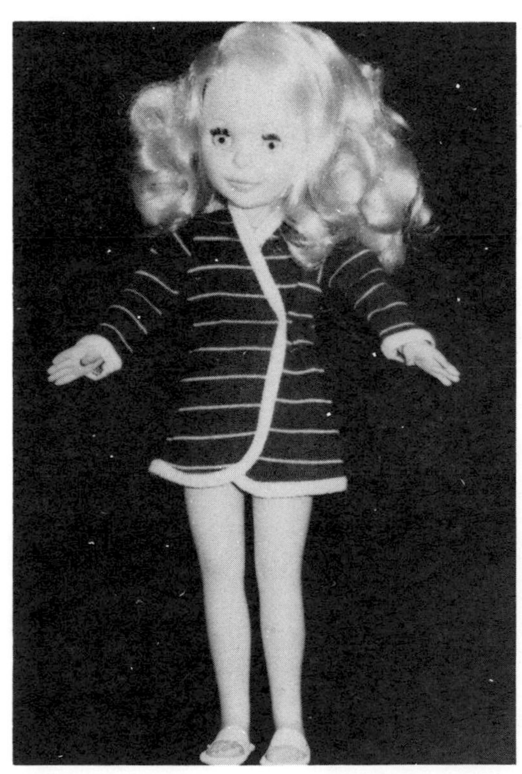

Furga--15" "Valentina" All vinyl with rooted white hair. Blue sleep eyes/long lashes. Toe and nail polish. Jointed waist. Can pose in 15 different positions. Marks: Furga/Italy, on head. Same on back. 1969. Original clothes. $10.00.

Furga--14" "Anita" Plastic body and legs. Vinyl arms and head. Rooted white hair. Blue sleep eyes/lashes. Open closed mouth. Open hands with all fingers extended. Marks: figure of doll and Furga in square, on head. Unreadable mold marks, on back. 1969. Original clothes. $35.00.

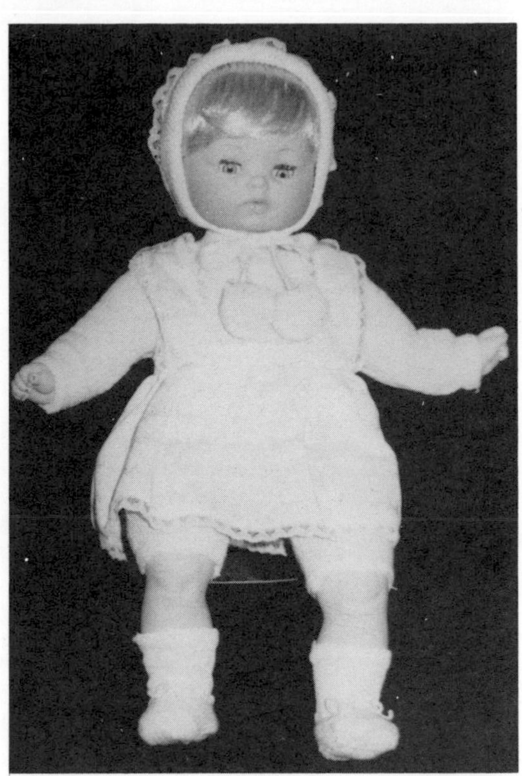

Foreign Furga, Italy--16" "Guilietta" Cloth body with vinyl arms, legs and head. Rooted white hair. Blue sleep eyes/lashes. Open/closed mouth. All fingers curled into palms. Marks: Furga, on head. 1970. An original outfit. 1970. $20.00.

Italy--20" "Alicia" All vinyl with rooted brown hair. Blue sleep eyes/lashes. Open/closed mouth. Marks: Furga/Italy, on head and body. Original clothes. 1970. $38.00. (Courtesy Allin's Collection)

Italy--16" "Georgeous Gabriella" All vinyl with rooted blonde hair. Blue sleep eyes/lashes. Open closed mouth with two painted teeth. Marks: Furga Italy, on back of head. Original clothes. 1971. $35.00. (Courtesy Allin's Collection)

Italy--16" "Georgeous Gabriella."

Italy--14" "Florenza" All vinyl with rooted white hair. Blue sleep eyes/lashes. Open/closed mouth with two painted teeth. Marks: Furga Italy, on head. Furga Italy, on body. Original clothes. 1969. $35.00. (Courtesy Allin's Collection)

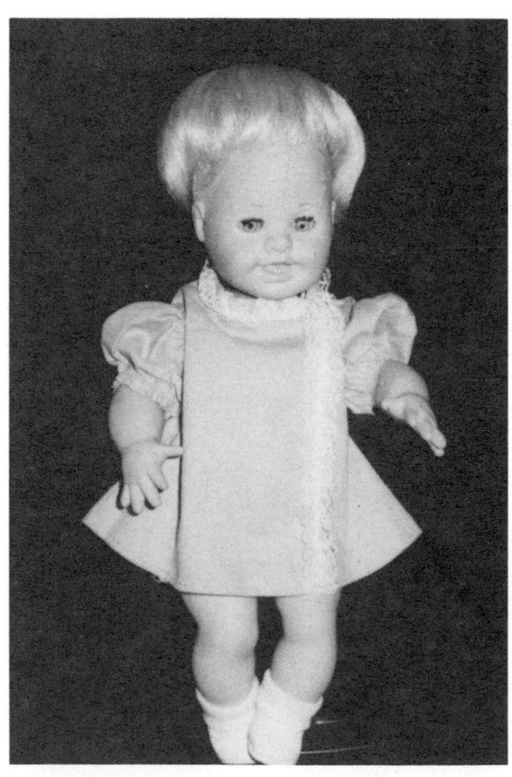

Italy--12" "Bonomi Baby Girl" Plastic & vinyl. Rooted white hair. Pale blue sleep eyes/heavy lashes. Open mouth. Painted two lower teeth. Open hands with palms down. Dimple in chin. Marks: 1964/IC (in square) on head. 445/Made In Italy, on body. $16.00.

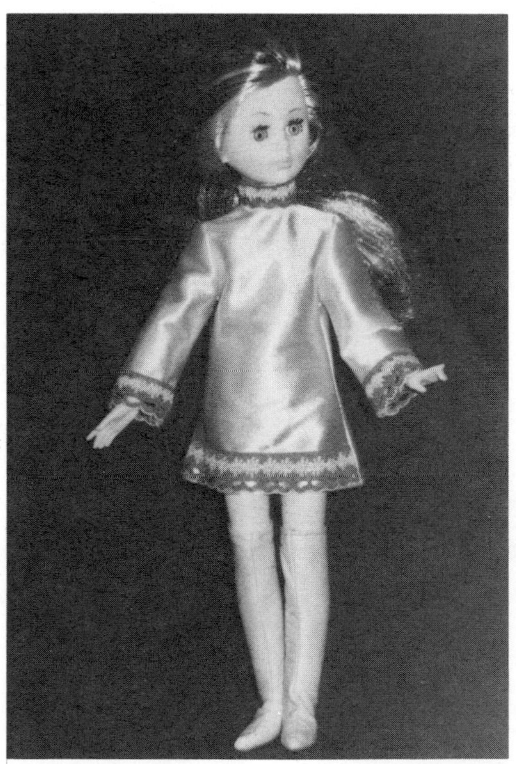

Italocremona--15" "Vanessa" Plastic body and legs. Vinyl arms and head. Rooted frosted brown/blonde hair. Blue sleep eyes/long lashes. Closed mouth. Marks: IC in a square/1965, on head. 736/Made In Italy, on back. Original clothes. $18.00.

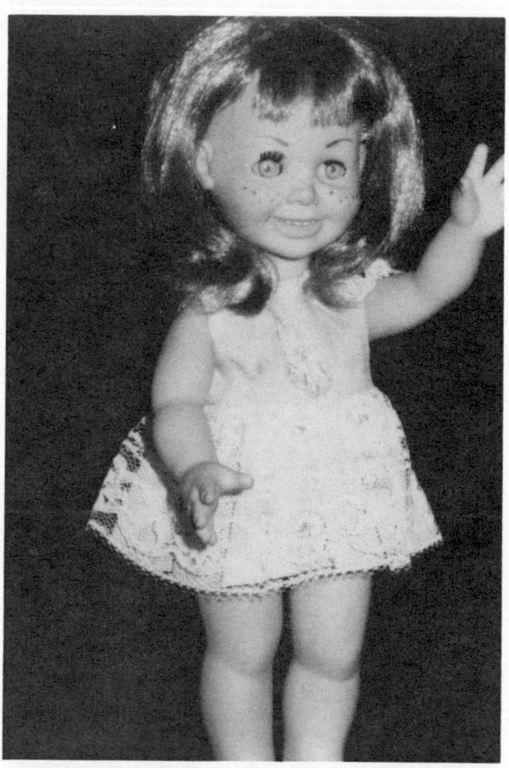

Italocremona--11" "Nina" Plastic body and legs. Vinyl arms and head. Rooted dark blonde hair. Blue sleep eyes/lashes. Open mouth with four painted teeth. Freckles on cheeks. Marks: IC in circle/1965, on head. 900/Made In Italy, on back. $32.00.

Italocremona--11½" "Lizza" Plastic and vinyl with rooted white blonde hair. Pale blue sleep eyes/lashes. Puckered closed mouth. Open hands with palms down. Long neck. Marks: IC, in a square/1965, on head. 751/Made In Italy on body. $18.00.

Italocremona--12" "Mariella" Plastic and vinyl. Light brown rooted hair. Pale blue sleep eyes/lashes. Open hands with palms down. Closed mouth. Marks: IC, in a square/1967, on 751/Made In Italy, on body. $16.00.

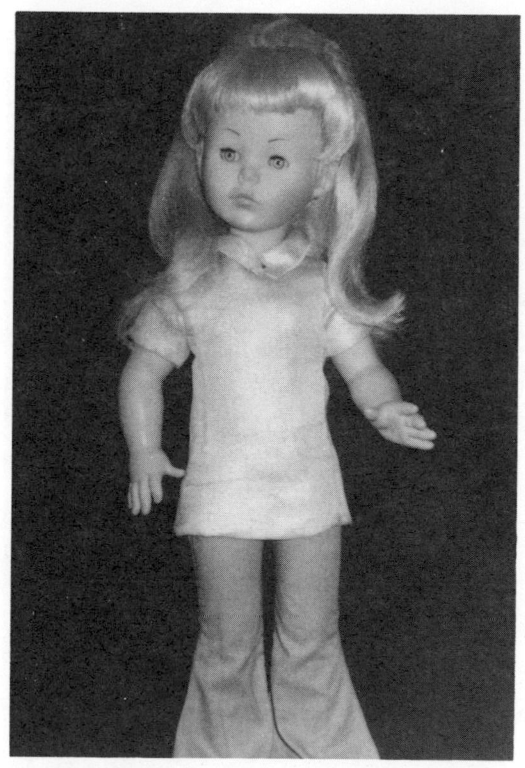

Italocremona--18" "Christina" Plastic body and legs. Vinyl arms and head. Rooted white hair. Pale blue sleep eyes/long lashes. Closed mouth. Marks: IC in a square/1967, on head. 638/Made In Italy, on body. $20.00.

Italy--11" "Dama" All vinyl with rooted brown hair. Blue sleep eyes/lashes. Closed mouth. Marks: 1968/Made In Italy, on back. Wrist Tag: IC/Italocremona. $30.00. (Courtesy Allin's Collection)

Migliorati--10" "Mia" All vinyl with rooted ash blonde hair. Painted, side glancing blue eyes. Open/closed mouth. Wide open hands. Molded, painted eyebrows. Chubby short legs. Marks: Little girl holding up an M, in an oval/Italy, beneath with Migliorati, in a square beneath that. 1960. $20.00.

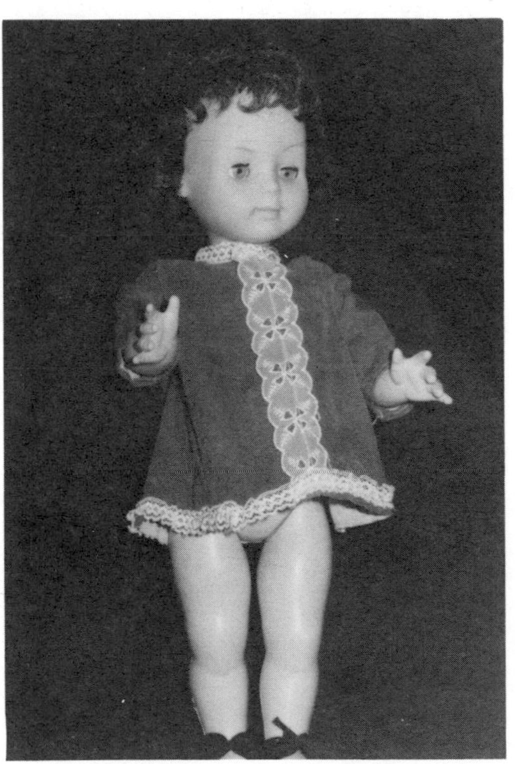

Migliorati--14" "Kitten" Plastic body, arms and legs. Vinyl head with rooted black hair. Blue sleep eyes/lashes. Closed mouth. Marks: Oval with girl with braids, holding up an M, with Italy beneath. /Migliorati, on head. Migliorati in square/40/Italy. 1964. $16.00.

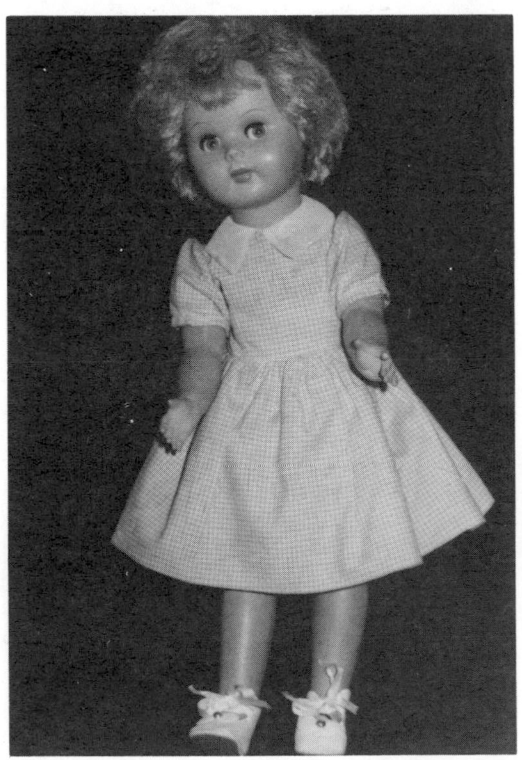

Ratti--16" "Flirty Cristina" All painted plastic with woven blonde wig set in a skull cap and glued to head. Flirty, sleep blue eyes/lashes. Closed mouth. Mold lines around wrists. Left hand 2nd and 3rd fingers molded together. Posable head. Marks: A circle with Ratti and two rats sitting up. 1958. $35.00.

Ratti Italy--27" "Bed Doll" All extremely light plastic. Glued on black mohair wig. Rocker, brown sleep eyes/lashes. Cryer. Marks: none. All original. 1961. $30.00.

Japan--3" "Kewpie" All celluloid with painted features. Jointed shoulders. Green wings on back. Red tufts of painted hair. Marks: Japan, on back. 1936. $8.00.

Japan--5" "Playmate" All bisque made in one piece body, head and legs. Jointed shoulders. Curled hands. Molded painted hair and bow. Blue painted eyes. Molded and painted on shoes and socks. Original clothes. 1936. Marks: Japan on back of clothes. $5.00.

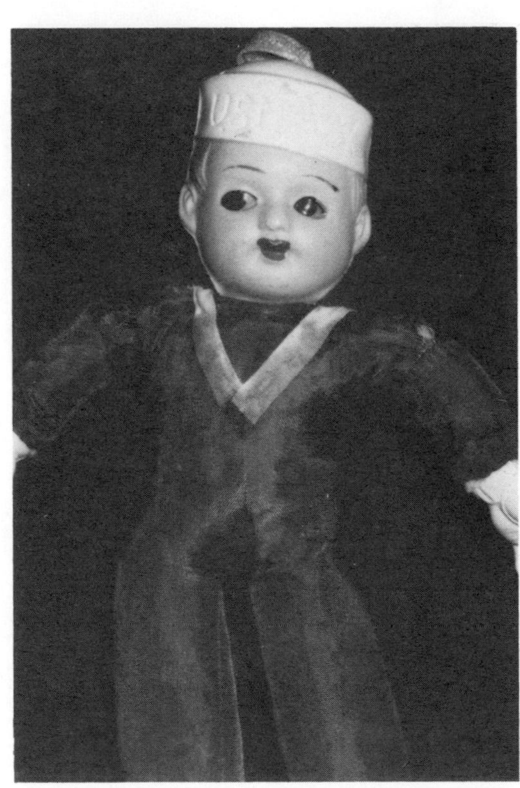

Japan--8" "Sailor" Cloth over excelsior Celluloid head, hands and feet. Painted features. Marks: Japan, on base of hat. 1939. $16.00.

Japan--8" "Monkey" Cloth over excelsior. Celluloid head, hands and feet. Painted features. 1939. Marks: Japan, on base of hat. $16.00.

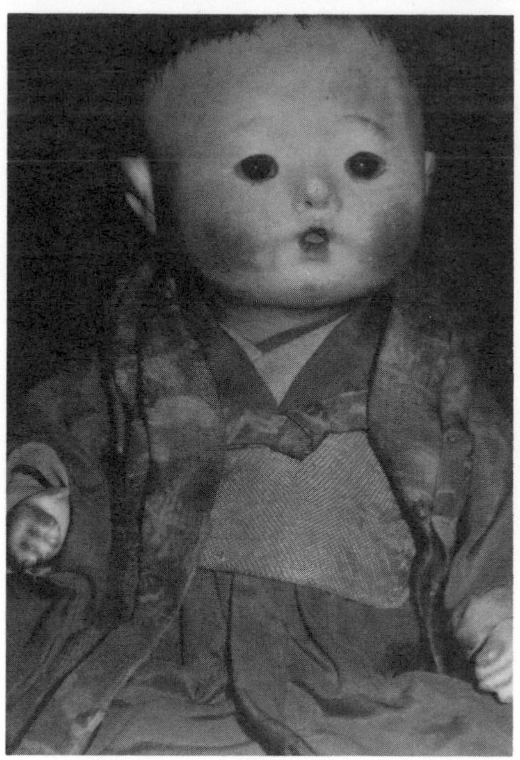

Japan--9" "Baby" Paper mache body, arms legs and head. Glass inset eyes. Pierced nostrils. Open/closed mouth with tongue. Human hair wig. All original. Sent to the collector by her cousin in the service, in 1945. $7.00. (Courtesy Earlene Johnston)

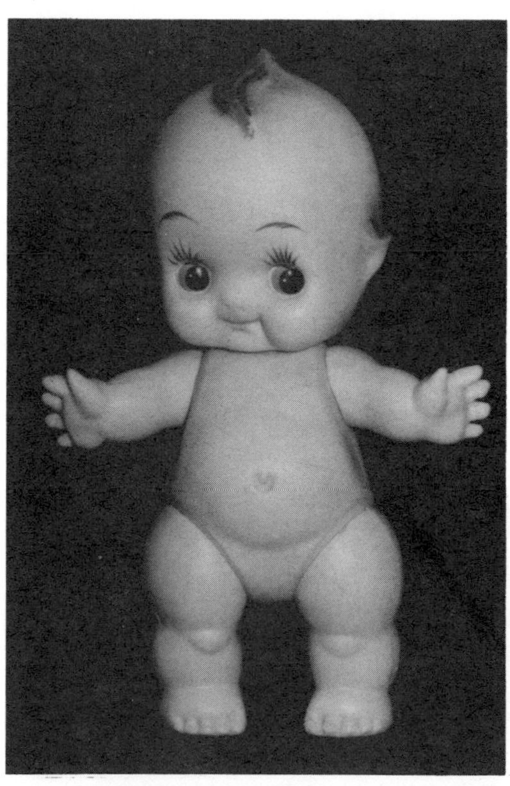

Japan--9" "Kewpie Type" All vinyl with painted features. Marks: Made In Japan, on back. 1954. Heart shape, molded naval. $18.00.

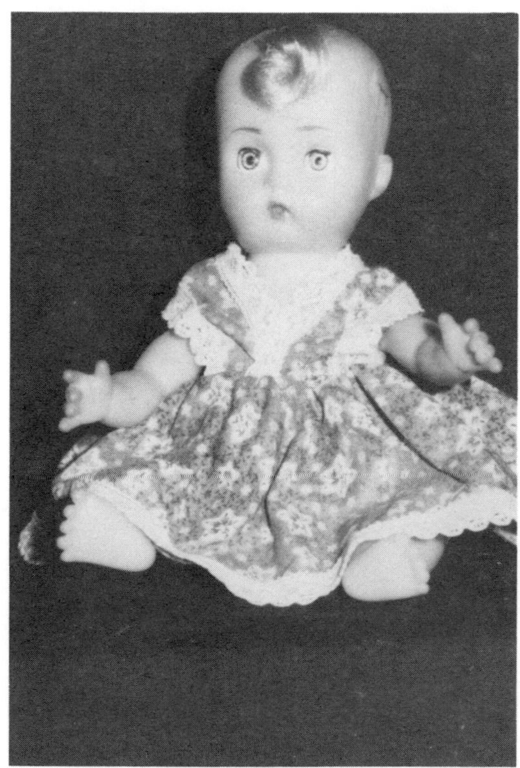

Japan--8" "Indy" All vinyl with one rooted curl with molded and painted hair. Blue sleep eyes/lashes. Open mouth/nurser. 2nd and 3rd fingers molded together. Marks: ATC/Made In Japan. Original clothes. 1961. $2.00.

Japan--15" "Santa Claus" Foam body, arms and legs. Wire in arms for posing. Plastic face mask with painted features. Put out in 1962 by 7 Up Bottling Co. Marks: Box: Made In Japan. $6.00. (Courtesy Earlene Johnston Collection)

real fur cap, plastic arms and is marked: A Pick-The Eskimo Doll. Other has rooted blonde hair, vinyl arms and head and is jointed at the neck and shoulders. Eskimo was made in 1948. Other is called "Patti" and made in 1960. $2.00 each.

Japan--8" "Kutie" All vinyl with rooted blonde hair, fixed in very long pony tail. Painted blue eyes. Closed smiling mouth. Marks: Japan on head and back. 1963. $18.00.

Japan--5½" "Edy" Cloth, excelsor filled body. Wire bendable legs. Sewn together paper filled arms. Plastic head with inset stationary blue eyes, side glancing. Rooted white hair. Yellow bunny ears and tail, glued on. Marks: Tag: 1966 Kamar/Made In Japan. $2.00.

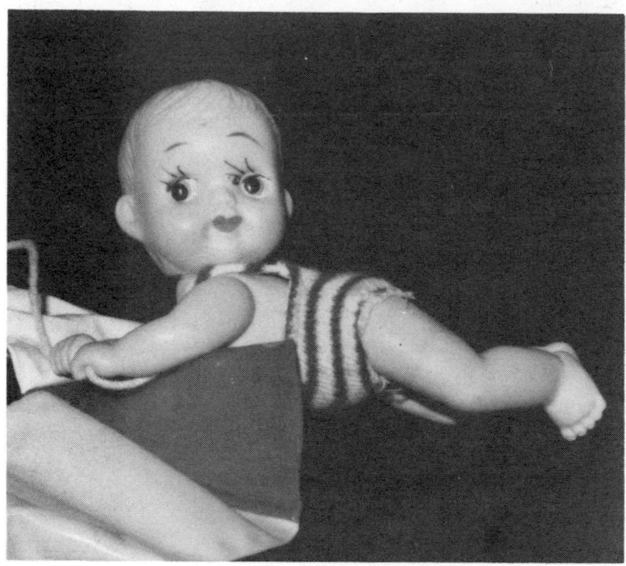

Japan--4" "Swimmer" All vinyl with molded hair and painted features. Hands molded around rope of buoy ring. With air in ring doll floats. Marks: none. 1962. $3.00. (Courtesy Allin's Collection)

Japan--7½" "Doris" Plastic molded and painted slack suit. Painted shoes and hands. Vinyl head with rooted blonde hair. Large black with white/yellow/blue dotted eyes. Freckles. Marks: Made In Japan on bottom of right foot. 1967. $4.00.

Japan--7" "Mary, Mary" All vinyl with rooted black hair. Side glancing brown eyes. Closed mouth. Open hands with palms down. Marks: Japan, on bottom of foot. 1968. $2.00.

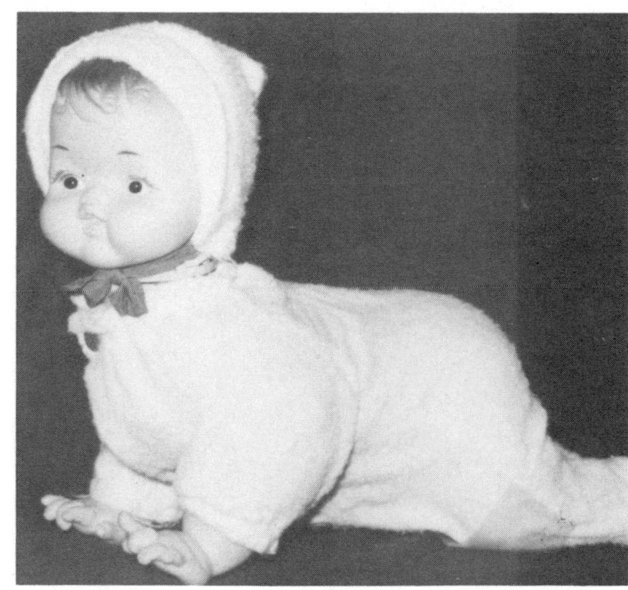

Japan--13" "Crawler" Plastic and metal body. Vinyl head with painted features. Battery operated. Marks: none. 1967. Original clothes. $16.00. (Courtesy Allin's Collection)

Japan--8½" "Tiny" All vinyl with rooted dark blonde hair. Large side glancing green/black eyes. Closed smiling mouth. Freckles. Knock kneed. Right hand fisted. Marks: Japan on back. 1968. $2.00.

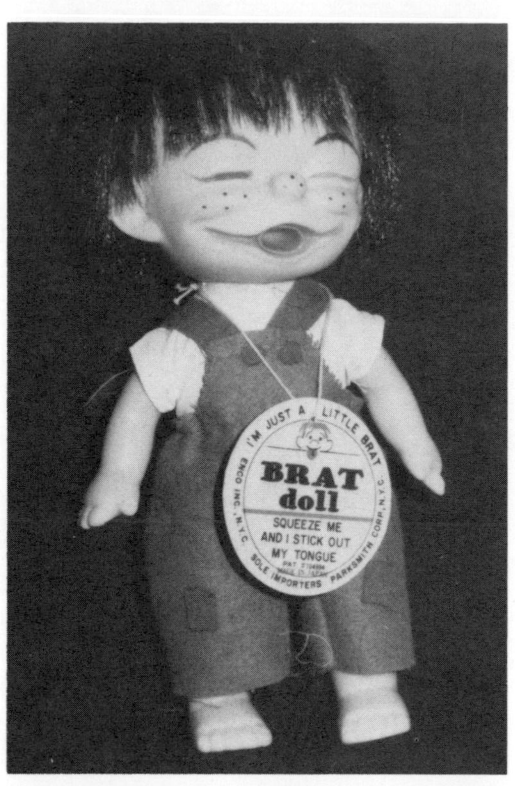

Japan--7" "Brat" All vinyl with rooted black hair. Closed eyes. Freckles. Open mouth. Squeeze and he sticks out his tongue. Marks: Pat. 104994 on head. Made In Japan on bottom of left foot. 1968. $3.00.

Korean--19" "Charleen" One piece silk covered body and silk clothes. Satin covered head with painted features. Glued on blonde wig. Earrings. Mounted on plastic base. Marks: So-Yea Doll Institute/Seoul Korea. 1969. $48.00.

Korean--19" "Wind Song" One piece silk covered body. Silk clothes with satin covered head with glued on black wig. Painted features. Earrings. Mounted on plastic base. Marks: So Yea Doll Institute/Seoul Korea, on base. 1969. $48.00.

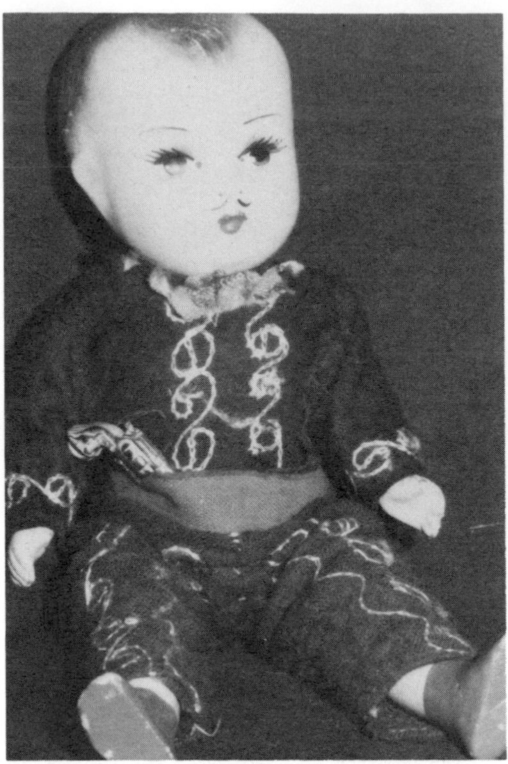

Mexico--9" "Cisco Kid" All composition with molded hair. Painted features. One piece body and head. Jointed shoulders and hips. Painted on red shoes and socks. Original clothes, minus hat. Marks: PAT, base of neck. 1939. $9.00.

Mexico--9" "Romona" Cisco's girlfriend by Perez Doll Co. All composition. One piece body and head. Black mohair wig glued on. Painted features. Black eye shadow. Jointed shoulders and hips. Original clothes. Marks: PAT base of neck. 1939. $9.00.

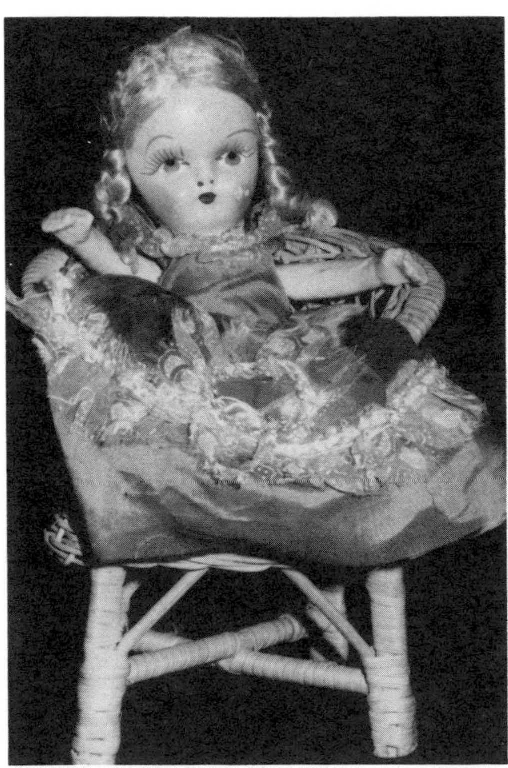

Perez Mexico--9" "Americana" All composition. Glued on blonde mohair wig. Painted features. Painted on socks and shoes. Marks: none. 1940. Original ball gown. $7.00.

Perez Mexico--9" "Juanita" All composition with silk thread hair glued on. Painted features. Painted shoes and socks. Earrings sewn to hair. Stamped "Made In Mexico" up the front of both legs. 1945. Original. $7.00.

Fortune Toys--7½" "Pam" All hard plastic with glued on blonde hair. Blue sleep eyes/molded lashes. Closed mouth. Walker and head turns. Marks: none. 1956. Pam's outfits were designed by Michele Cartier. $8.00.

Fortune Toys--7½" "Cowgirl Pam" All hard plastic with glued on brown wig. Blue sleep eyes/molded lashes. Walker, head turns. Original clothes. Marks: none. 1953. Made from 1952 through 1956. Extensive wardrobe designed by Michele Cartier. Dynel hair and not jointed at the knees. $10.00.

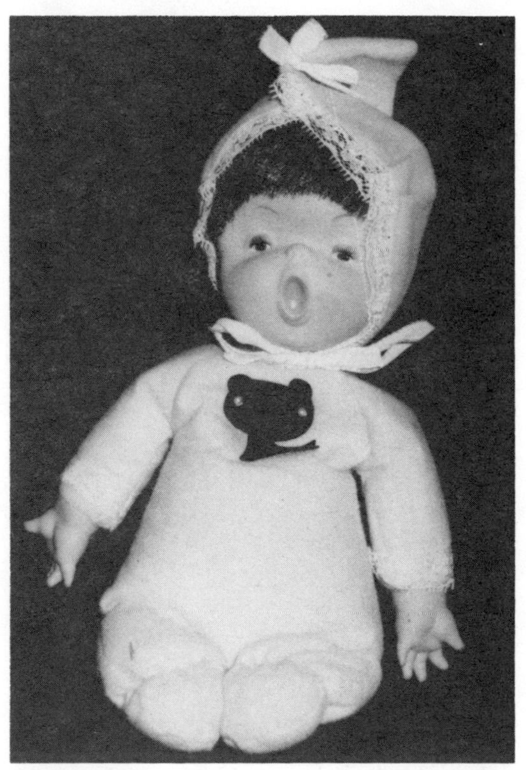

Fun World Inc.--11" "Sleepy Head" Bean bag body and upper arms and legs. Vinyl hands and head. One row of rooted dark brown hair. Painted half closed eyes. Wide open/closed mouth. Marks: Fun World, on head. Arm Band: Sleepy Head By Fun World. 1971. $4.00.

Fun World Inc.--8" "Soul Sister" Plastic and vinyl with rooted black hair. Large painted brown eyes with green eyeshadow under eyes, black over eyes. Open hands with palms down. Marks: A picture of a Bell-8/Reg Design No./ 915/664/Made In Hong Kong on head. Made In Hong Kong on body. 1971. Orig clothes. $4.00.

FUNWORLD

GEM

GIRL'S WORLD

GRANT

Fun World Inc.--9" "Huggles" Soft body, arms and legs. Vinyl gauntlet hands. Vinyl head with rooted orange hair. Painted blue eyes. Upper lip over bottom one. Clothes are not removable. Original. Marks: Tag: Huggles By Fun World. 1971. $3.00.

Gem Toy Co.--12" "Chubby Kid" All composition with painted features and jointed shoulders. Painted on shoes. Gem made this doll for Sears, Roebuck Company. Often mistaken for a Buddy Lee doll, especially when dressed in Lee type clothes. Marks: none. 1922. $48.00 (Courtesy Allin's Collection)

Girl's World--7" "Emerald, The Enchanting Witch" Plastic body with vinyl arms, legs and head. Rooted green hair. Inset clear green eyes. Lilac skin on all body parts. Green and gold eyeshadow. Battery operated. Marks: 1971/Girls World/Pat Pend/Made In Japan. Dress Tag: Emerald Witch Costumes. Girls World Inc. $20

Grant--11½" "Dress Me Doll" Plastic body, arms and legs. Vinyl head. Blue painted, side glancing, eyes. Closed mouth. Flat feet. Glued on mohair yellow wig. Marks: 1963/Grant Plastics Co. Used for promotional programs. $4.00.

H.D. Lee--13" "Buddy Lee" All hard plastic made in one piece body, legs and head. Molded painted hair. Painted black eyes side glancing. Painted on cowboy boots. Trademark doll for

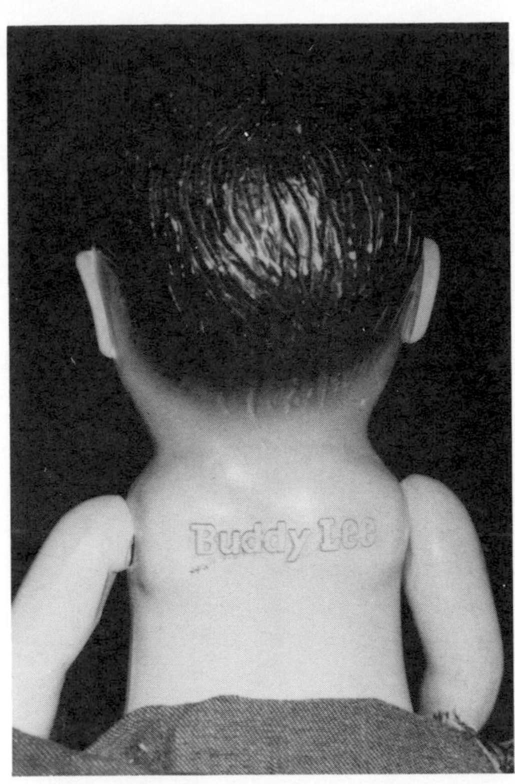

H.D. Lee Co. Clothes were made in Lee Plant. Hats were made by outside source. Marks: Buddy Lee on back. 1949. $35.00.

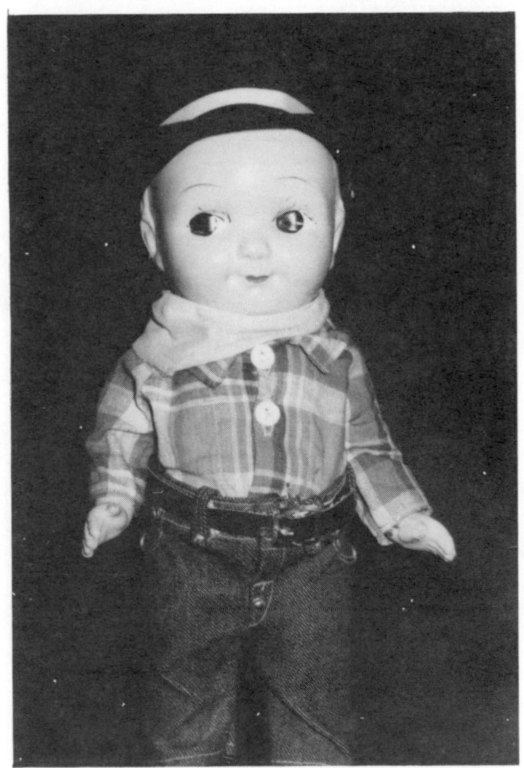

Buddy Lee--12" "Buddy Lee" All composition with painted features. Painted on boots. One piece body, legs and head. Jointed shoulders.

$48.00. (Cowboy courtesy Johnston Collection, Coke courtesy Allin's Collection)

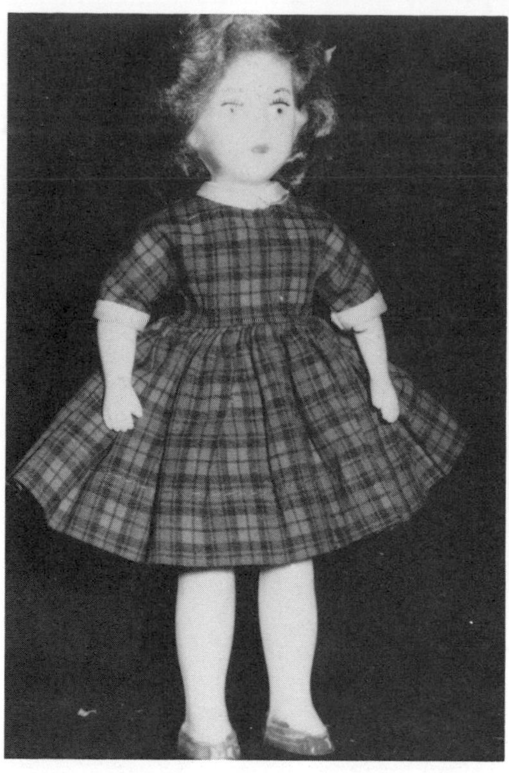

Hasbro--7" "Doll House Mother" All early plastic with glued on mohair wig over molded hair. Large painted "stare" eyes. Painted on red shoes with bows. Marks: Hasbro/USA, on head. 1957. $3.00.

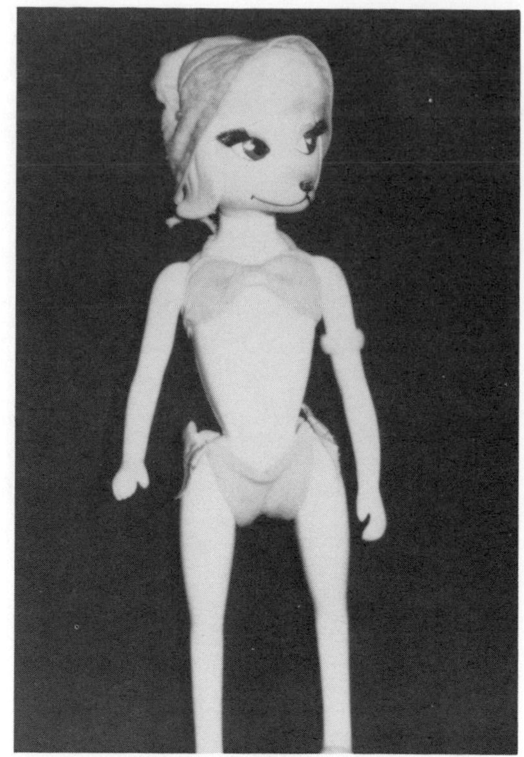

Hasbro--9½" "Poodle-oodle" Plastic body. Vinyl arms, legs and head. Cotton, glued on hair. Painted brown eyes/lashes. Original clothes. Marks: 1966/Hasbro/Japan/Patent Pending. The set included an entire family of poodles along with poodle house. $4.00.

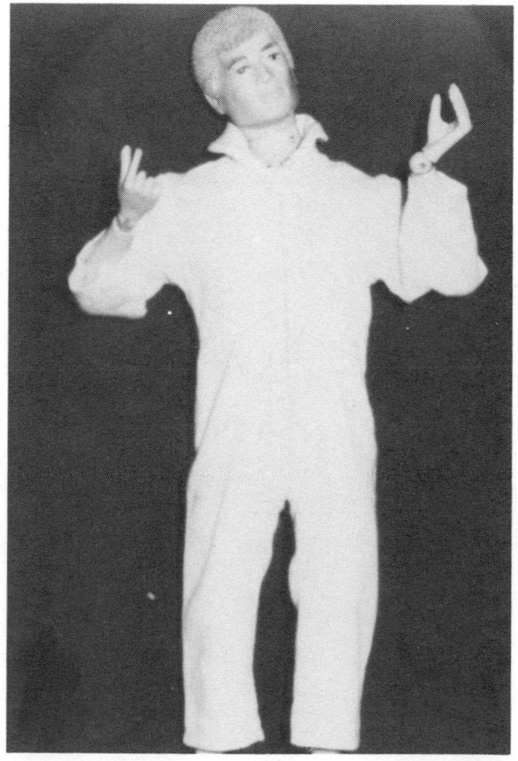

Hasbro--12" "G.I.Joes" All plastic with molded or flocked hair. Painted features. Jointed at neck, shoulders, elbows, wrists, waist, hips, knee, and ankles. Marks: G.I.Joe/ Copyright 1964/By Hasbro/Pat. No. 3277602/Made In USA. on body. $4.00.

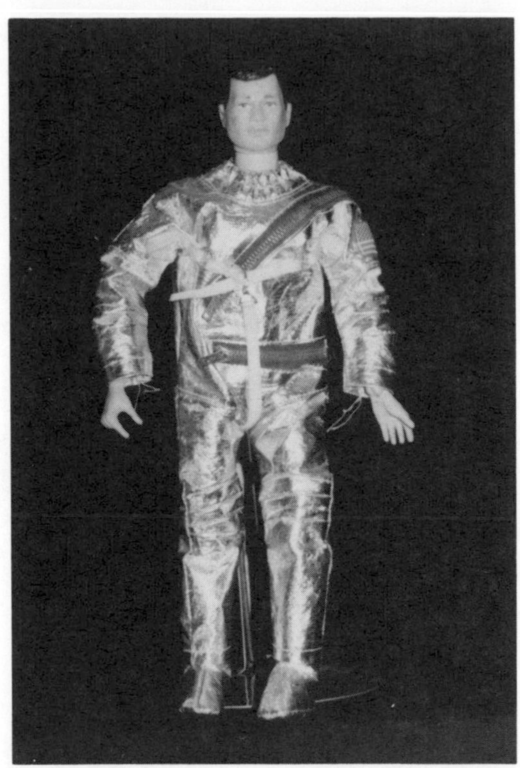

Hasbro--11½" "G.I.Joe" All plastic with vinyl head. Painted features. Ball and pin jointed at neck, shoulders, mid biceps, elbow, wrist, waist, hip, knees, and ankles. Marks: G I Joe TM/Copyright 1964/Hasbro/Patent Pending/ Made In USA. $4.00. (Courtesy of Ricky Johnston Collection)

Hasbro--4" "Sunday" Soft vinyl body, arms and legs. Painted on socks, shoes and gloves. Rigid vinyl head with molded blonde hair and ribbon. Painted side glancing blue eyes. Open/closed mouth with one painted upper tooth. Marks: 1965/Hasbro/Japan, on head. $3.00.

Hasbro--15" "Little Miss No Name" Plastic body, arms and legs. Vinyl head with rooted blonde hair. Large brown eyes. Tear on left cheek. Outstretched right hand. Marks: 1965 Hasbro on head. Original clothes. $16.00.

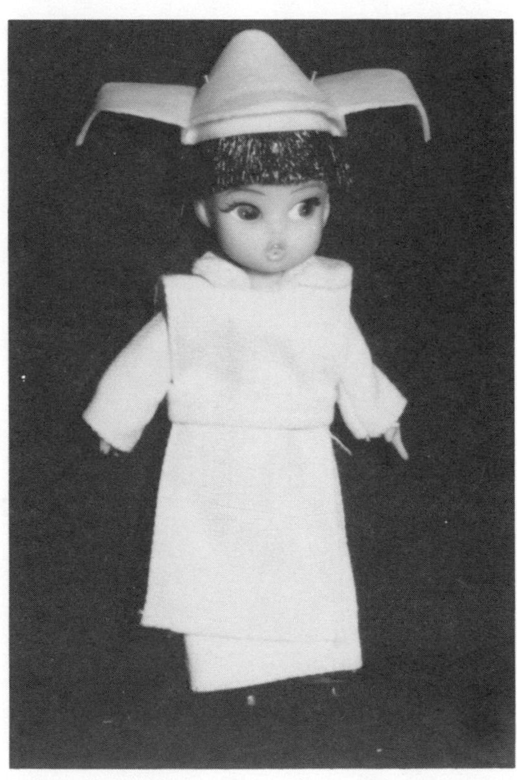

Hasbro--5" "Flying Nun" All vinyl with rooted hair and painted features. Title role on T.V. was played by Sally Fields. Marks: 1967/Hasbro/ Hong Kong. Original $7.00.

Hasbro--3" "Sleeping Beauty" All vinyl with rooted black hair. Painted features. Original. 1967. $4.00. (Courtesy Earlene Johnston Collection)

Hasbro--3" "Rumpelstilskin" All vinyl. Rooted hair and beard. Painted features. Original. Marks: Hasbro. 1967. $4.00. (Courtesy Earlene Johnston Collection)

Hasbro--3" "Goldilocks And Three Bears" All vinyl with rooted hair. Jointed at neck with one piece bendable body. Painted features. 1967. Original. $4.00. (Courtesy Earlene Johnston Collection)

Hasbro--3" and 1½" "Snow White And The Seven Dwarfs" All vinyl with rooted hair and painted features. 1967. Original. $6.00. (Courtesy Earlene Johnston Collection)

Hasbro--3" "Prince Charming" All vinyl with rooted hair and painted features. Jointed at neck with one piece bendable body. 1967. $4.00. (Courtesy Earlene Johnston Collection)

Hasbro--3" "Michelle" All vinyl with rooted hair. Painted features. One of the "Show Biz Babies" series. 1967. $6.00. (Courtesy Earlene Johnston Collection)

Hasbro--9" "The World Of Love" All vinyl with rooted black hair. Painted features. Jointed waist that can be tilted in any direction. Snapping knees, forward and back, one position forward and two positions back. Original clothes. Marks: Hasbro/U S Pat. Pend. on head. 1968. $3.00.

Hasbro--10½" "Baby Ruth" Bean bag body. Vinyl head with rooted blonde hair in three curls, cap glued on. Painted features. Vinyl hands. Marks: Tag: Baby Ruth/1971 Hasbro Industries Inc. Original. Was made for Curtis Candy Co. $3.00.

Hollywood Doll Mfg. Company

The founder of Hollywood Dolls was Domenick Ippolite and in a span of 15 years put onto the market more dolls than any other manufacturer of his time. Unfortunately this is also a series of dolls that, if undressed, will be next to impossible to figure out WHO they were. The dolls are well marked and are made in bisque, composition and hard plastics.

The following are not all the dolls made by this company.

All Hollywood Bisque Dolls sell for $8.00.

All Hollywood hard plastic dolls sell for $6.00.

1942: Mother Goose Story Dolls

1944: Garden Series, Hollywood Lucky Stars

1945: Nursery Rhymes Series, Toyland Series

1946: Annabella, Camellia, Dottie, Forget Me Not, Garden Lady, Lady Elaine, Lady Guinevier, Lady Isele, Lady Lynette, Lady of the Lake, Lady Slipper, Marie Helena, Mary Mary Quite Contrary, Masquerade, Miss Gingerbread, Miss Teeter Totter, Muffie with her spider, Pat a Cake, Queen Silver Bell, Sleepyhead, Star Dust, Sweet Spirit, Grandma's Dolls, Hollywood Book Dolls, Red Riding Hood

1947: Cowgirl, Beauty Rose, Bonnie Blue Bell, Little Nancy Etticoat, Little Rose, Lizabeth, Long Frock, Pretty Kitty, Princess Beauty, Sleeping Beauty, Tiny Tina, Little Girl Where Have You Been, A Wee Bonnie Lassie, American Beauty, Little Blue Apron, Little Miss Bunnie, Little Red, Little Shepherdess, Miss Hollywood, Nancy Lue, The Bride, Western Series, Little Friend

1950: The Wishing Doll, Everyday Series, Sweet Janice

1951: Wedens Baby Born on Wednesday, Thors Baby Born on Thursday, Freyas Baby Born on Friday, Saturn Baby Born on Saturday, Suns Baby Born on Sunday, Moons Baby Born on Monday, Tius Baby Born on Tuesday.

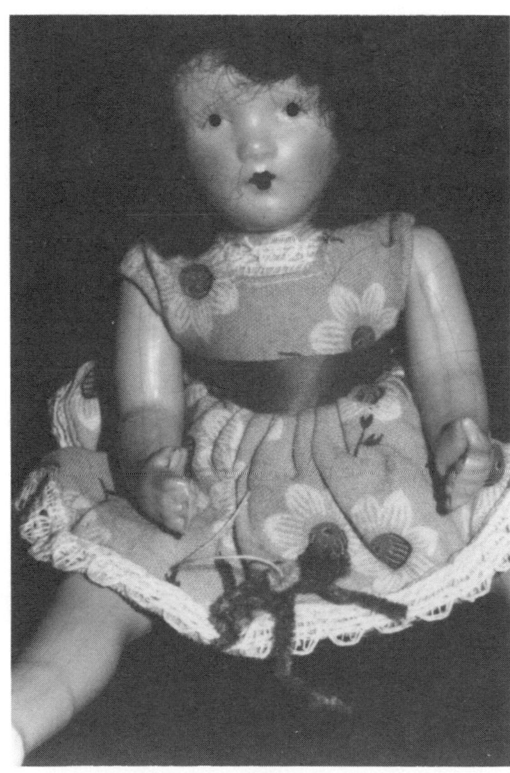

Hollywood Dolls--9" "Little Miss Muffet" All composition with painted features. Glued on black mohair wig. Painted on shoes and socks. Marks: Hollywood Doll on back. 1945. Original clothes. $6.00. (Courtesy Earlene Johnston Collection)

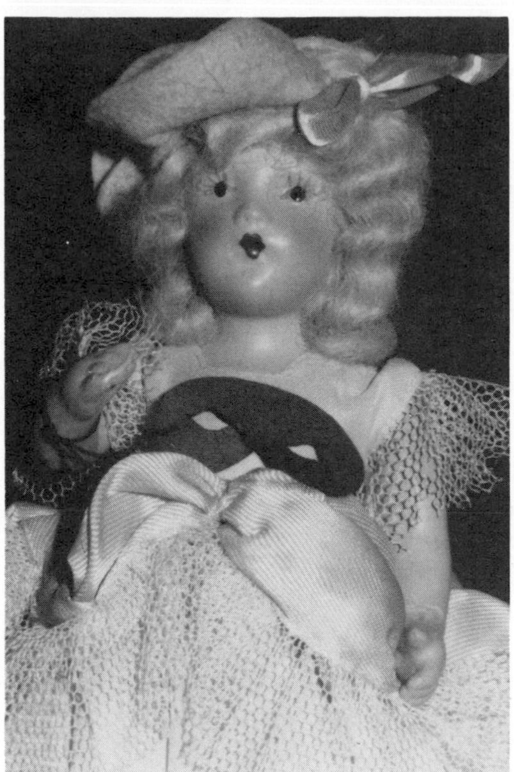

Hollywood Dolls--9" "Masquerade" All composition with painted features. Painted on shoes and socks. Glued on blonde mohair wig. Marks: Hollywood Doll, on back. Original clothes. $6.00. (Courtesy Earlene Johnston Collection)

Hollywood Dolls--9" "Bonnie Blue Bell" All composition with painted features. Glued on blonde mohair wig. Marks: Hollywood Doll between shoulders. 1945. Original clothes. $6.00. (Courtesy Earlene Johnston Collection)

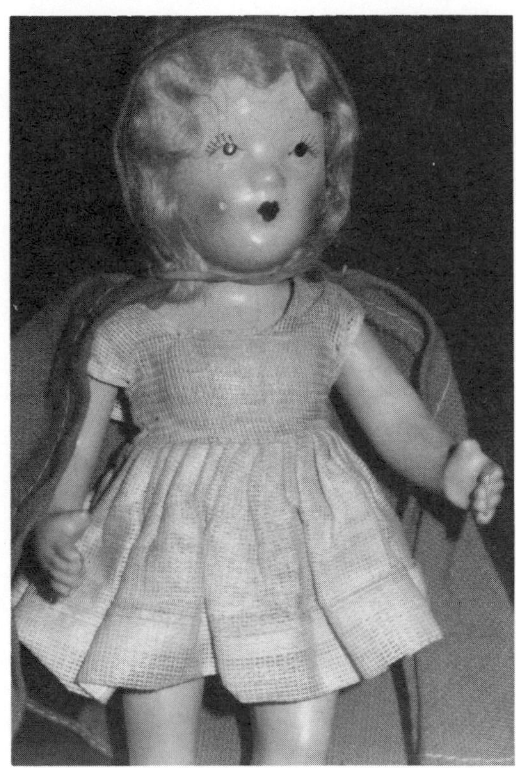

Hollywood Dolls--9" "Red Riding Hood" Composition with painted features. Molded and painted on shoes and socks. Glued on blonde mohair wig. Marks: none. 1946. Original clothes. $6.00. (Courtesy Earlene Johnston Collection)

Hollywood Dolls--5½" "Sweet Janice" All hard plastic with glued on blonde mohair wig. Blue sleep eyes/lashes, painted. Original clothes. Marks: Hollywood Doll in star on back. Wrist Tag: Sweet Janice/Hollywood Doll in star. 1950. $6.00.

Horsman Dolls Company Inc.

The first "all American" doll was made by the Goodyear Rubber company in 1856 and only a few others, such as the Joel Ellis wooden dolls in 1873, came between it and the company Mr. E. I. Horsman founded in New York, in 1865.

Mr. Horsman was a member of an old German toymaking family and he began by importing the finest European doll heads and bodies and putting them together here in the USA.

It wasn't long before Mr. Horsman began making dolls here in America and his first was "Baby Bisque" known for her beautiful complexion and human hair. Next famous was the Campbell kids, modeled like the famous children in the Campbell Soup advertisements, this was 1910, then came the HEbee-SHEbee's of 1925 and Ella Cinders, also 1925. Horsman also helped in design and making some Fulpher dolls and they are marked with both names.

This company has been, and we hope continues to be, one of the leaders of the doll industry. Not only have they offered variety but also quality. Most Horsman dolls look like members of a large family. After you become familiar with them, you can pick them out of a crowd.

Horsman invented "Fairy Skin" in 1946 and "Miracle Hair" in 1952 and in 1954 "Super Flex" bodies so the doll would bend, kneel, and sit alone. The Horsman process for synthetic rubber and early vinyl has defied the laws of disintergration and carried their beauty right to today. The Horsman latex bodies go by the wayside, or should I say neck, just as all the rest do but do not pass up the heads as they are generally works of art. Try to build another body around them.

Horsman is one of the few companies, in the doll field, that is thorough and business like. I have appreciated the help of their chief Engineer, W.W. Koliski.

Horsman's Patsy type was called Dorothy and Sally. Their Shirley Temple type was called Shirley and had blonde mohair wig, blue eyes, open mouth with teeth, dimples and dressed as the Little Colonel. She came with a pin stating her name Shirley. The hard plastic mold number 170 is theirs.

Two outstanding dolls from this company have been the Gold Medal Babies and the Mary Poppins, which was designed by Irene Szor (she also designed the Princess line) The following are not all the dolls made by this company

1936: Shirley (40.00)
1937: Jo Jo (32.00), Sister (35.00), Brother (35.00)
1940: Louisa (18.00), Baby Chubby (18.00)
1942: Chubby Baby (18.00)
1948: Campbell Kids (10.00)
1949: Flirty Sue (16.00)
1950: Cindy Kay (10.00), Magic Baby (9.00)
1951: Sleepy (8.00), Little Sister (9.00), Chubby Baby (8.00), Betty Anne (16.00), Shadow Wave Baby (35.00)
1953: Fair Skin Doll (8.00), Gold Medal Baby (55.00), Cindy Strutter (22.00), Dolly Dreamland (8.00), Pretty Baby (16.00)
1954: Betty Series (16.00), Love Me Doll (8.00), Chubby Baby (16.00), Draft Dodger (8.00), Tynie Baby (8.00), Pitter Patty (8.00), Pram Baby (8.00)
1955: Little Betty (4.00), Cindy Kay (25.00)
1956: Love Me Baby (8.00)
1957: Lullabye Baby (8.00), Cindy (16.00), Ruthie (8.00), Baby Precious (16.00), Peggy (40.00)
1958: Drinkie Walker (10.00)
1960: Ruthie's Sister (25.00), Peggy Ann (9.00), Sweetheart (18.00), Fair Skin Doll (10.00)
1961: Lil Happy Fella (also known as Perthy-20.00), Thirstie Baby (5.00), Spring Beauty (16.00), Softie (8.00), Nurse Ruth (35.00), Princess Peggy (20.00), Kindergarten Kathy (6.00), Vacation Gal (16.00), Flopsie (18.00)
1962: Grown Up Miss (8.00), Jo Anne (16.00), Betty Jo (16.00)
1963: Buttercup (5.00), Lullabye Baby (5.00), Wee Bonnie Baby (4.00), Gloria Jean (4.00), Poor Pitiful Pearl (18.00), Princess (30.00)
1964: Tynie Toddler (4.00), Baby Buttercup (3.00), Drinkie Tot (6.00), My Ruthie (5.00), Betty (4.00), Mary Poppins (18.00), Michael (8.00), Jane (8.00)
1965: Softskin (3.00), Softie Baby (4.00), Tynie (3.00), Sleepy Baby (18.00), Toddler Betty (4.00)
1966: Tuffie (18.00), Baby Grow Up (4.00), Pattie Duke (10.00), Baby First Tooth (8.00), Posing Flopsie (8.00), Pugie (8.00), Answer Doll (6.00), Christopher Robin (18.00), Winnie the Pooh (16.00), Baby Darling (4.00), Teensie Baby (8.00), Ruthie (16.00)
1967: Baby Tweaks (16.00), Cuddles Baby (8.00), Twistie (3.00), Ruthie's Baby (16.00), Athlete (3.00), Mommy's Darling (16.00), Walker Ruth (7.00), Songster (4.00), Ruthie (4.00), Lullabye Baby (6.00)
1968: Lil Softie (2.00), Softie Baby (2.00), My Baby (4.00)
1969: Love Me Baby (3.00), Pooty Tat (2.00), Bootsie (16.00)
1970: Peggy Pen Pal (10.00), Cindy (4.00), Buttercup (3.00)
1972: Bi Lo Baby (18.00)

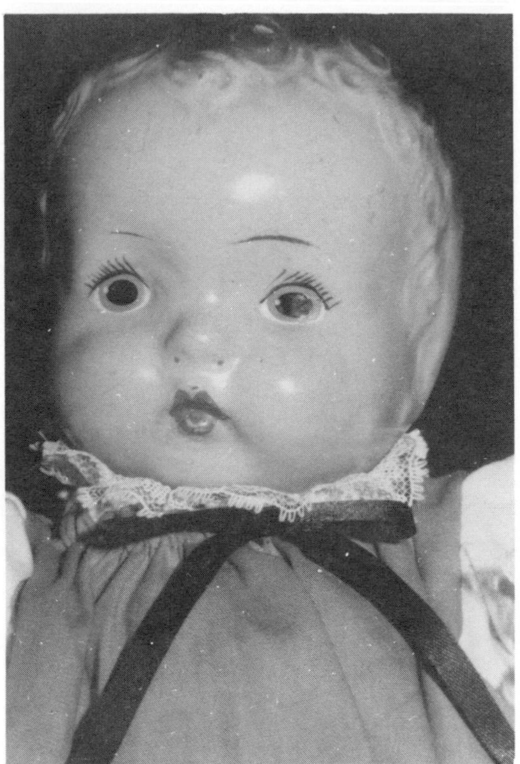

Horsman--12" "Jo Jo" All composition with molded, painted black hair. Painted blue eyes. Marks: Jo Jo/1937 Horsman on head. $32.00.

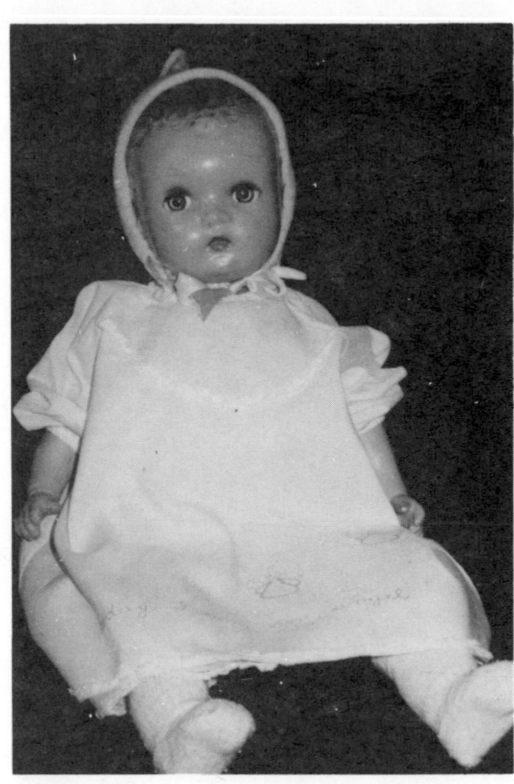

Horsman--23" "Baby Chubby" Cloth body with composition arms, legs and head. Molded hair. Blue sleep eyes/lashes. Eye shadow. Marks: A/Horsman, on head. 1940. $18.00.

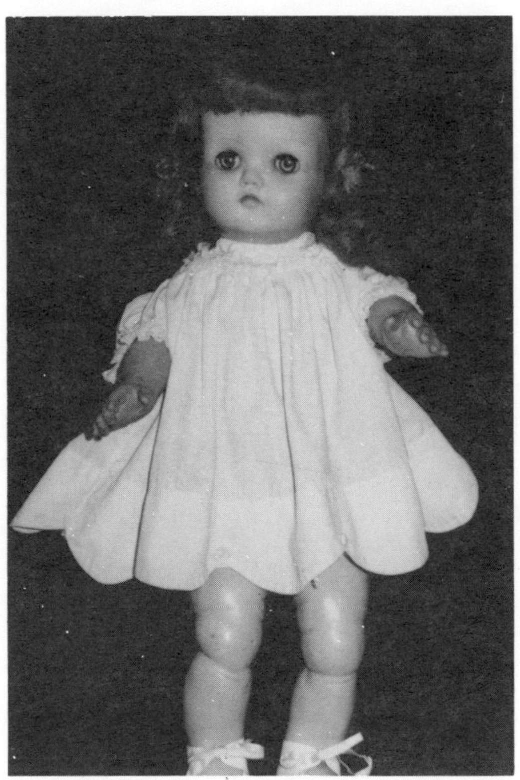

Horsman--19" "Shadow Wave Baby" Stuffed one piece body and legs. Disc jointed arms. All early vinyl. Large blue sleep eyes/lashes. Closed mouth. Open hands with palms down. Marks: Horsman/Several dots beneath. 1951. Sold with shadow wave kit. $35.00.

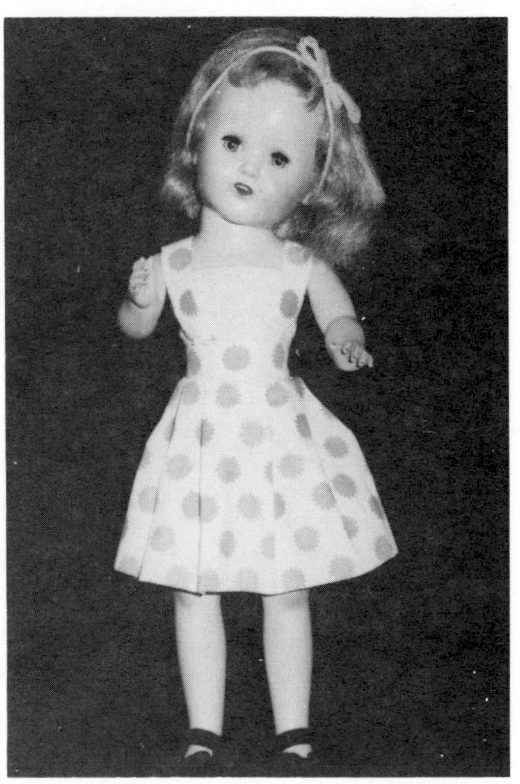

Horsman--15" "Cindy Kay" All hard plastic with glued on dark blonde wig. Blue sleep eyes/lashes. Open mouth with four teeth and felt tongue. Open hands with all fingers slightly curled. Marks: Horsman, on head. 1950. $18.00.

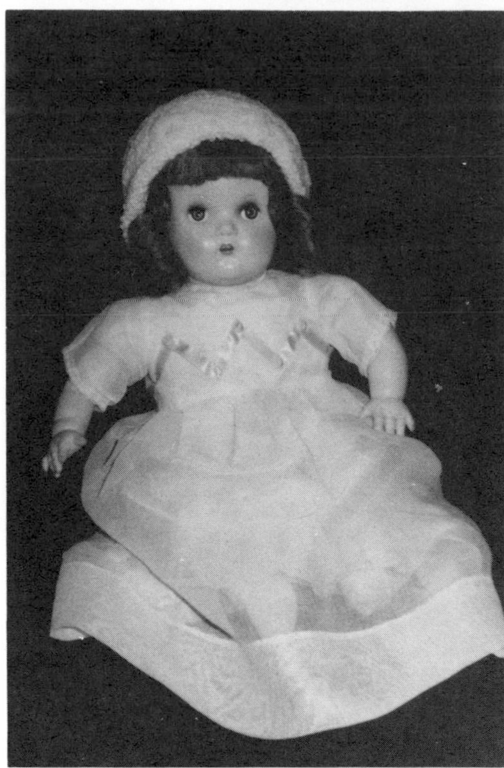

Horsman--19" "Betty Ann" Cloth body. Hard plastic head with dark red, stapled on, mohair wig. Vinyl hands with palms down. Vinyl legs. Sleep blue eyes/lashes. Open mouth with two teeth and felt tongue. Black eye shadow. Marks: Horsman/Doll, on head. 1951. $16.00.

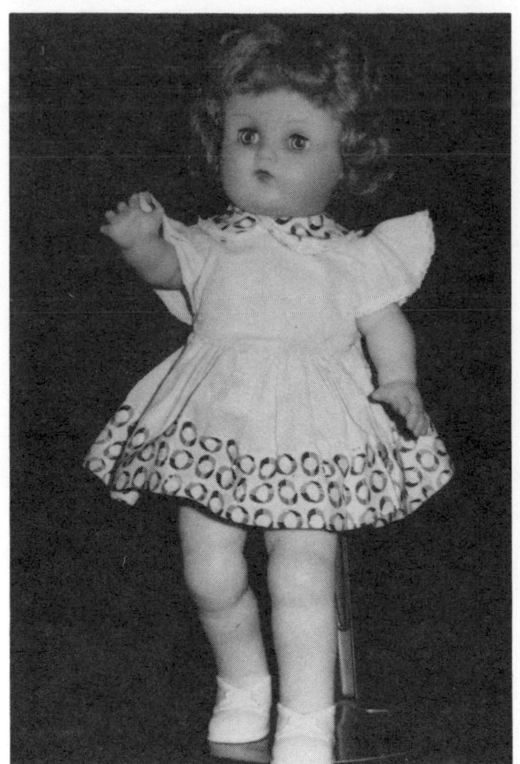

Horsman--16" "Little Sister" One piece body and legs in early vinyl. Medal disc jointed early vinyl arms. Vinyl head with rooted mohair wig. Blue sleep eyes/lashes. Open hanαs. Marks: Horsman on head. An original dress. 1951. $9.00.

Horsman--15" "Dolly Dreamland" All hard plastic with glued on red wig. Blue sleep eyes/lashes. Open mouth with four teeth and felt tongue. 2nd and 3rd fingers slightly curled. Marks: 170, on head. Made In USA/170, on body. Dress Tag: Dollie Dreamland. 1953. $20.00. (Courtesy Earlene Johnston Collection)

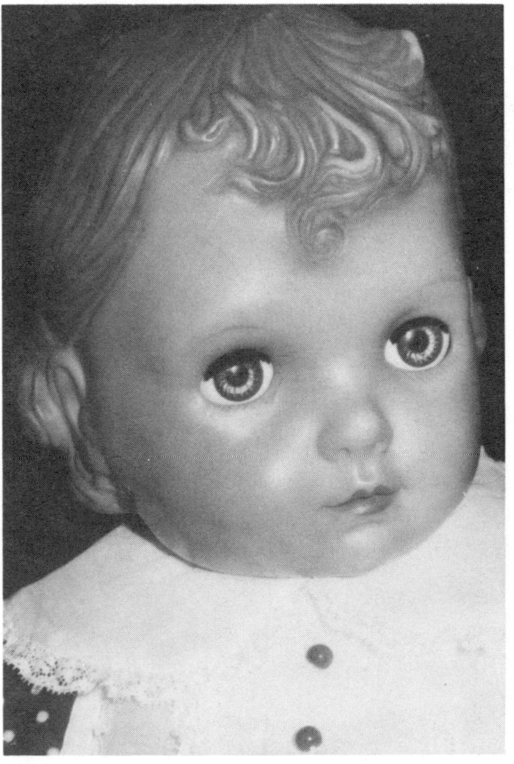

Horsman--26" "Gold Medal Doll" All early vinyl with one piece body and legs. Molded hair. Large blue sleep eyes/lashes. Closed mouth. Marks: Horsman with a series of six dots underneath. 1953. $55.00.

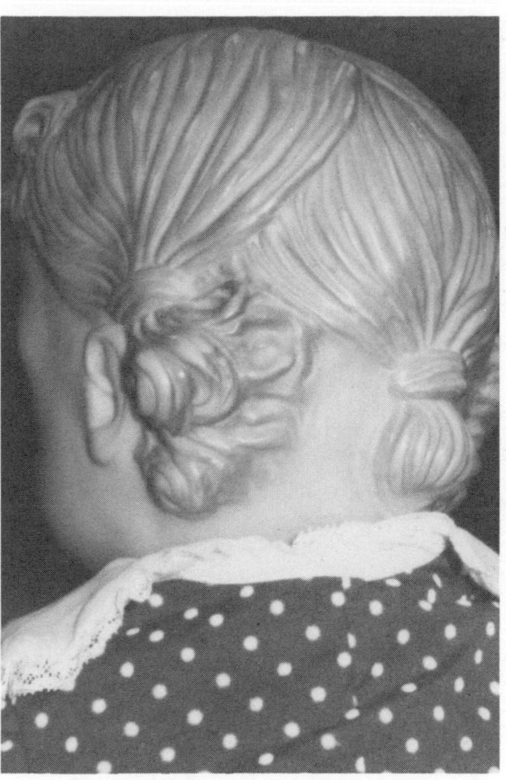

Horsman--26" "Gold Medal Doll"

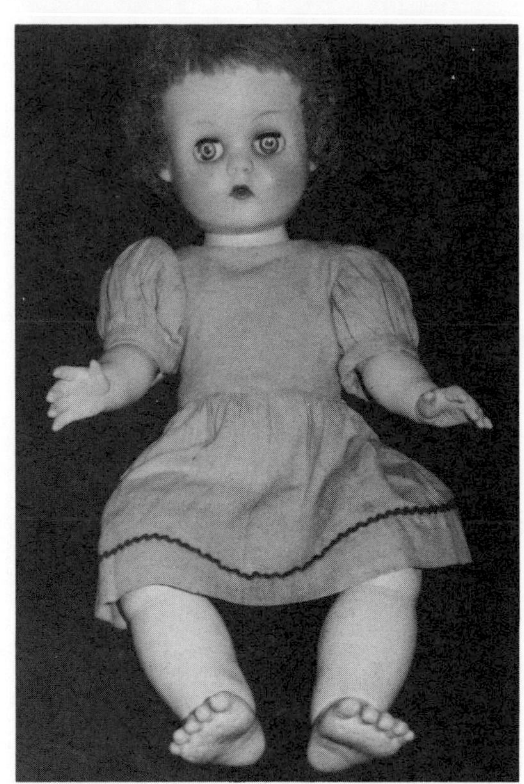

Horsman--16" "Pretty Betty" All vinyl. Light brown rooted hair. Blue sleep eyes/lashes. Open mouth/nurser. Stocky legs and large feet with individual toes. Marks: Horsman, on head. 1-S-5, on lower body. 1954. $16.00.

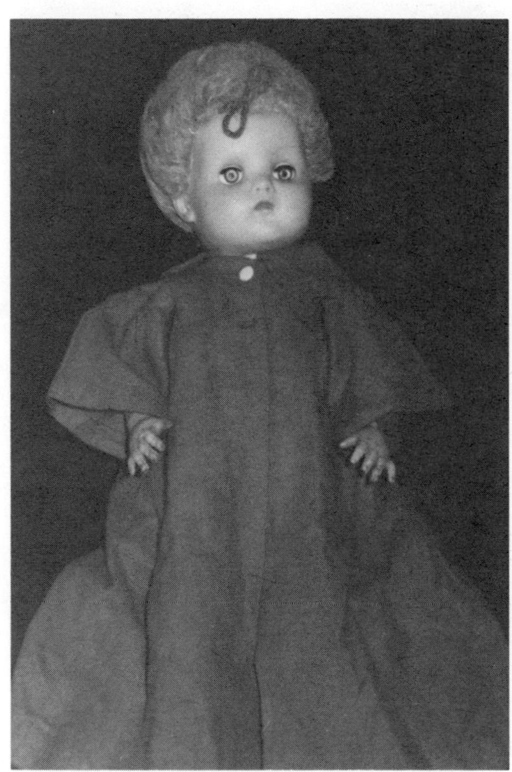

Horsman--20" "Chubby Baby" All early vinyl. One piece stuffed body, arms and legs. Metal disc jointed arms. Stuffed vinyl head with rooted blonde hair. Blue sleep eyes/lashes. Open hands, palms down. Marks: Horsman, on head. 1954. $16.00.

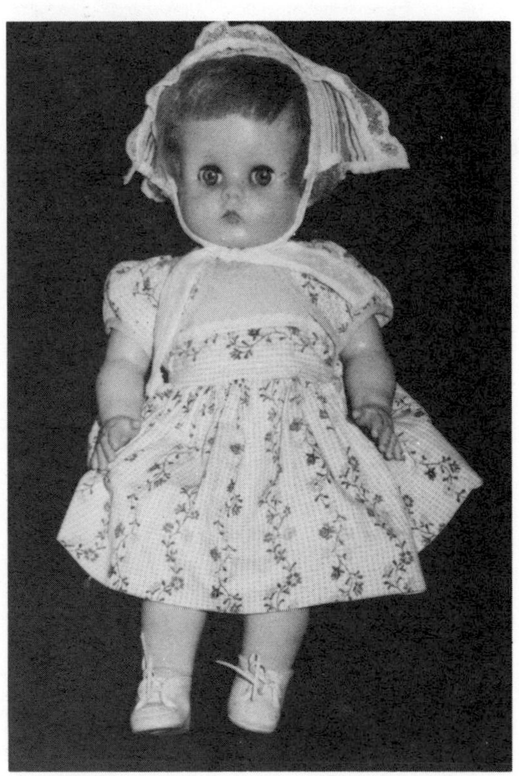

Horsman--14" "Betty" One piece stuffed vinyl body, arms and legs. Stuffed vinyl head with rooted blonde hair. Blue sleep eyes/lashes, molded. Wire runs through legs for posing. Marks: Horsman, with what looks like an 11 or 112 beneath. 1954. $16.00.

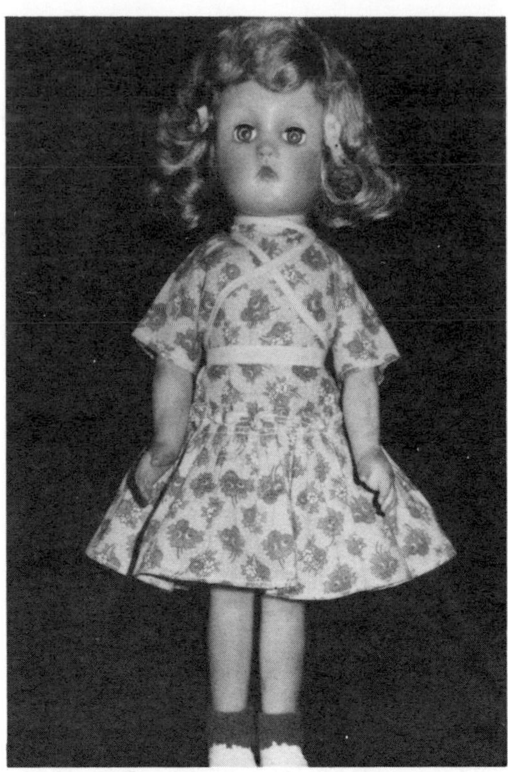

Horsman--15" "Cindy Kay" All very early vinyl. Medal disk joints at shoulders and hips. Glued on human hair wig. Blue sleep eyes/lashes. Open hand facing body. Very long arms. Marks: Horsman, on neck. 1955. $25.00.

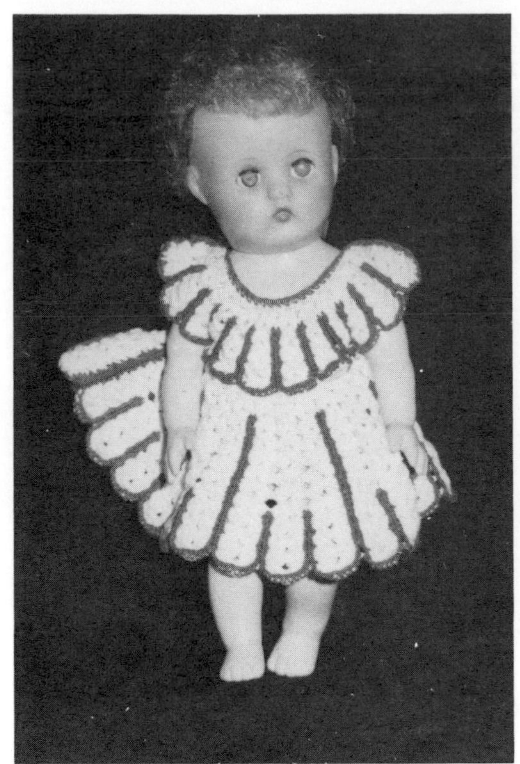

Horsman--8" "Little Miss Betty" One piece stuffed vinyl body, arms and legs. Vinyl head with rooted dark blonde hair. Blue sleep eyes/molded lashes. Marks: Horsman, on head. 1955. $4.00.

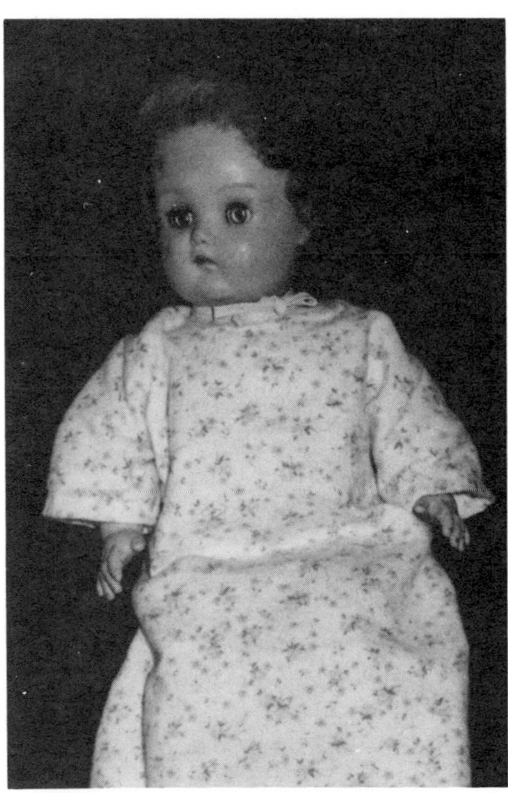

Horsman--14" "Baby Precious" All early vinyl. One piece unjointed body, arms and legs. Early vinyl head with rooted dark blonde hair. Blue sleep eyes/lashes. Closed mouth. Chubby body. Marks: Horsman, on head. 1957. $16.00.

Horsman--25" "Peggy" All early vinyl with one piece body and legs. Medal disc jointed arms. Rooted light brown hair. Blue sleep eyes/lashes. Straight legs. Palms in down position. Marks: Horsman, on head. 1957. $40.00.

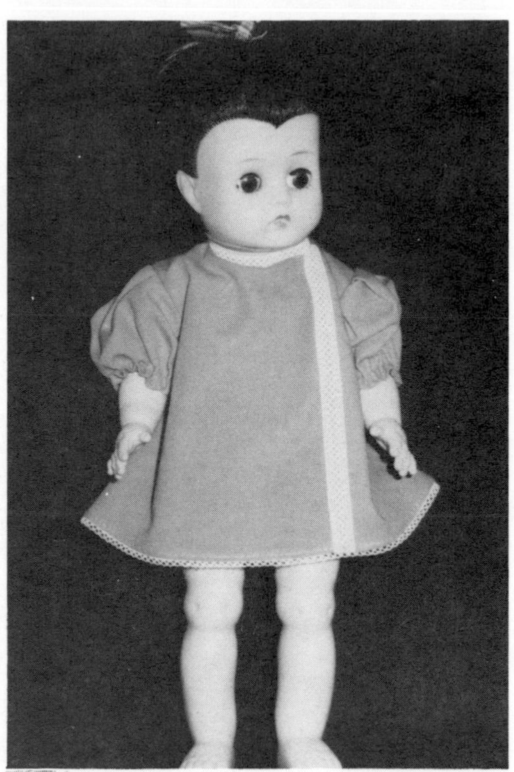

Horsman--12½" "Ruthie" All vinyl with rooted black hair, set in oriental style. Black sleep eyes/lashes. Long straight legs. Large dimpled knees. Marks: 12-6aa, on upper legs. B-1, on upper arms. 1958. $8.00.

Horsman--19" "Cindy" All vinyl with rooted deep red hair. Blue sleep eyes/lashes. Closed mouth. Jointed at waist. Open hands facing body. High heel feet. Pierced ears. Marks: Horsman/82 on head. Original clothes. 1959. $16.00.

Horsman--15" "Fair Skin Doll" All vinyl. Rooted long blonde hair. Sleep blue eyes/lashes. Closed mouth. Dimpled knees. Marks: Horsman/H-14 on head. S-16 on bottom of feet. 1960. $10.00.

Horsman--26" "Ruth's Sister" 1960. Plastic body and legs. Vinyl arms and head. Rooted dark blonde hair. Blue sleep eyes/lashes. Open/closed mouth. Posable head. Marks: Horsman/T-27 on head. $25.00.

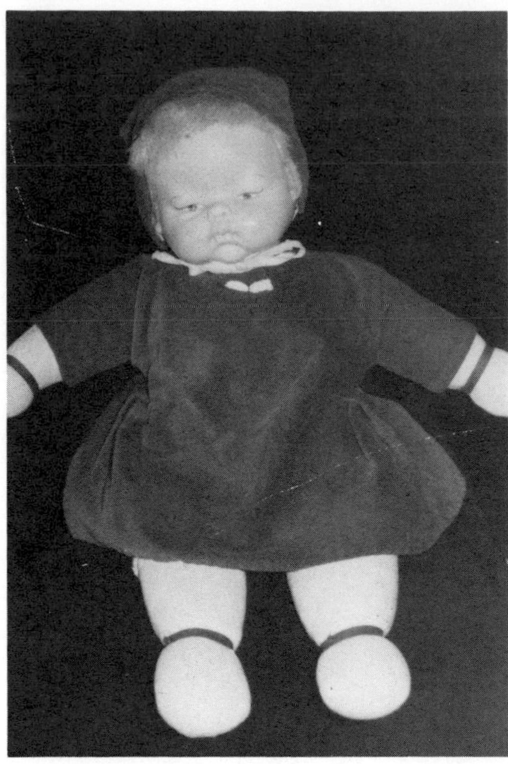

Horsman--17" "Flopsie" Cloth body, arms and legs. Vinyl head with rooted blonde hair. Painted blue eyes. Closed mouth. Marks: Horsman Doll Inc/1961/F-16 or 18. $18.00.

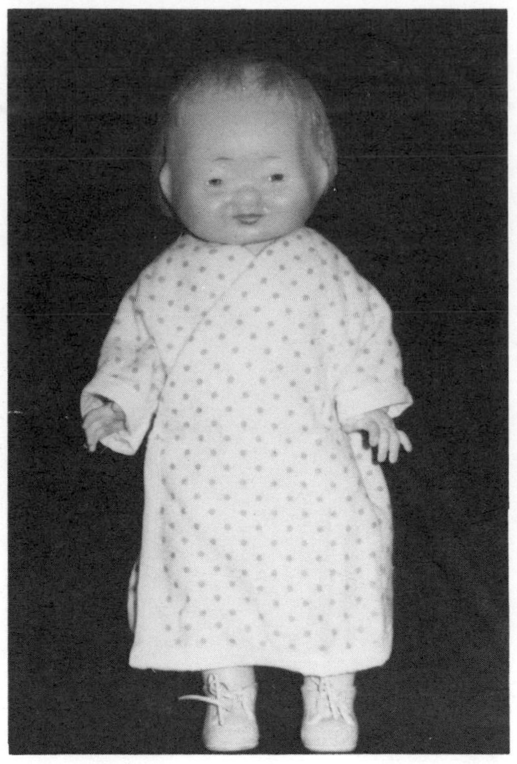

Horsman--13" "Little Happy Fella" All vinyl with rooted blonde hair. Small, squinting, blue inset stationary eyes. Open/closed mouth. Large hands and very flat feet. Toddler legs with dimpled knees. Marks: Something/Horsman Doll/1961 on head. 14, on body. S-14 on the soles of feet. $20.00.

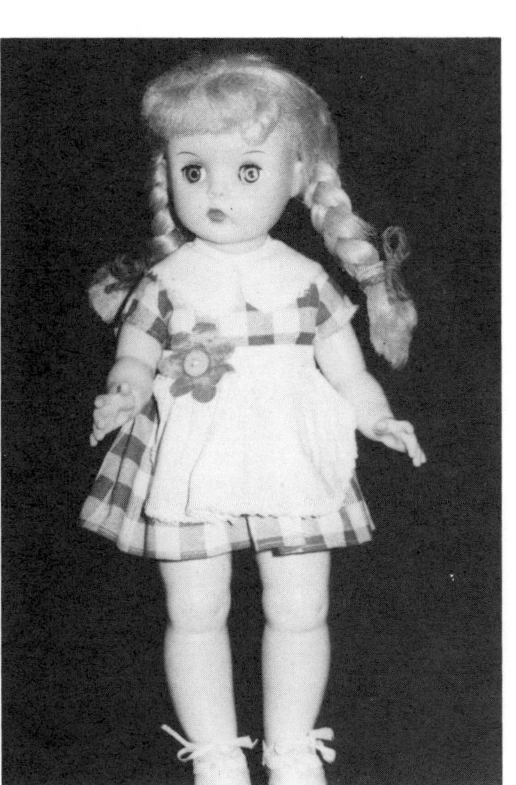

Horsman--15" "Kindergarten Kathy" Plastic body and legs. Vinyl arms and head. Rooted blonde hair. Blue sleep eyes/lashes. Open/closed mouth. Marks: Horsman/T14, on head. 1961. Original dress. $6.00.

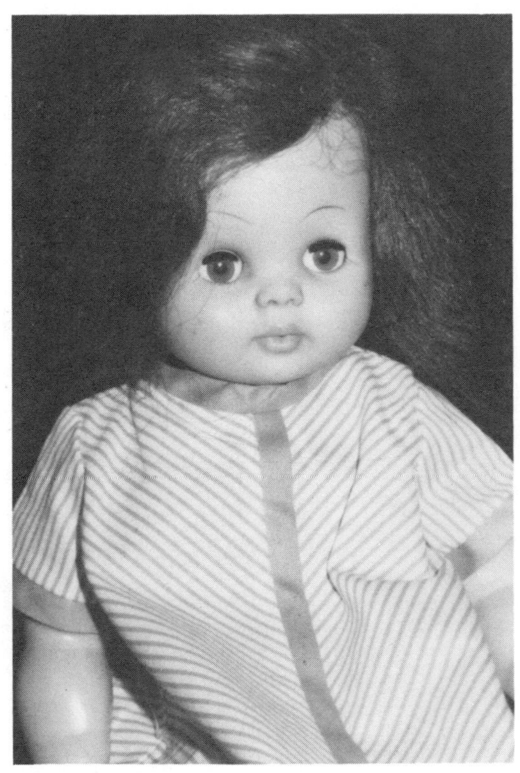

Horsman--16" "Betty Jo" Plastic body and legs. Vinyl arms and head. Rooted red hair. Blue sleep eyes/lashes. Open/closed mouth. Marks: Horsman Dolls Inc/06183/4, on head. 1962. $16.00.

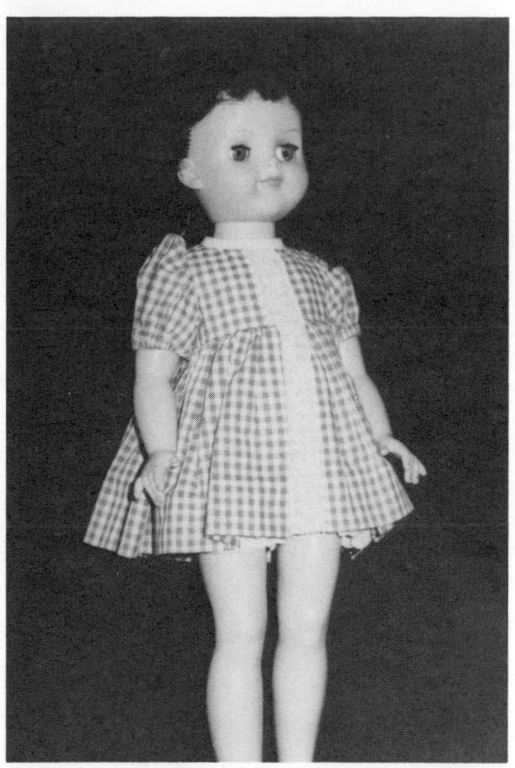

Horsman--18" "Grown Up Miss" All vinyl with rooted black hair. Blue sleep eyes/lashes. Left 2nd and 3rd fingers molded together. Marks: Horsman, on head. Horsman/19, on body. 1961. Called "Sub-teen Beauty" in 1962. $8.00.

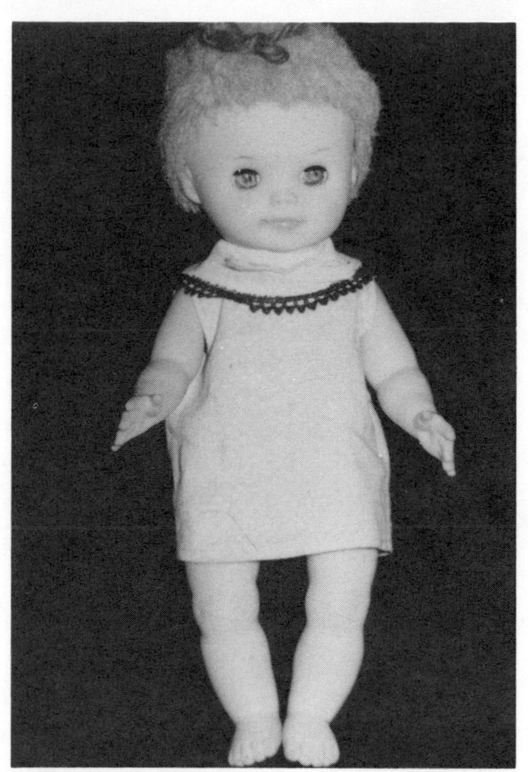

Horsman--10" "Gloria Jean" All vinyl with rooted blonde hair. Blue sleep eyes/lashes. Deep dimples at sides of mouth. Marks: Horsman, on lower part of back. 1963. $4.00.

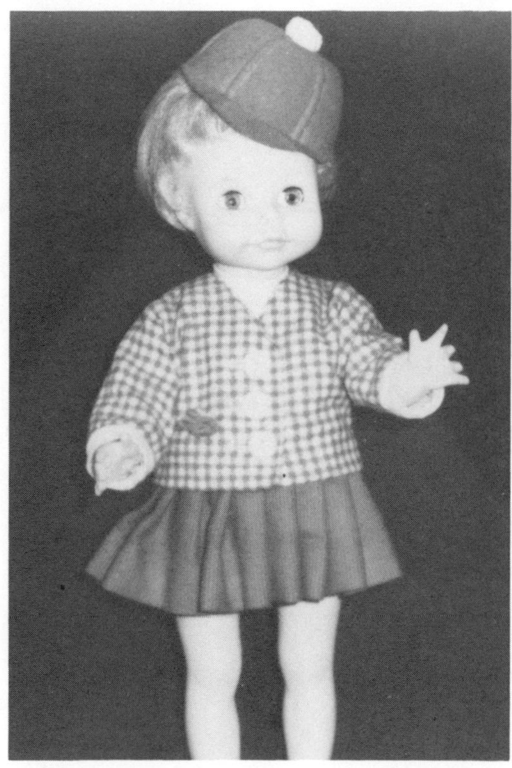

Horsman--15½" "Princess" Plastic body and legs. Vinyl arms and head. Rooted frosted blonde hair. Blue sleep eyes/lashes. Closed mouth with upper lip protruded. 2nd and 3rd fingers slightly curled. Marks: 1963 Irene Szor/Horsman Doll Inc. Original clothes. $30.00.

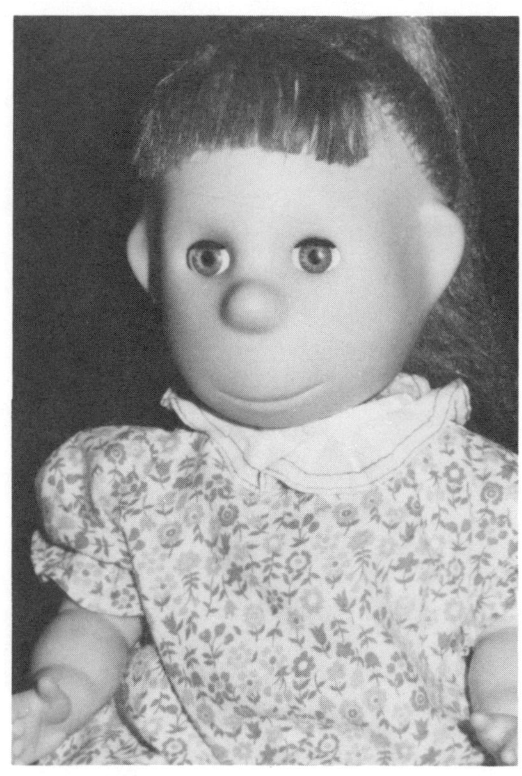

Horsman--17" "Poor Pitiful Pearl" Plastic body and legs. Vinyl arms and head. Rooted blonde hair. Blue sleep eyes/lashes. Marks: 1963/WM Steig/Horsman Dolls Inc., on head. $18.00. (Courtesy Allin's Collection)

Horsman--14" "Buttercup" Plastic body. Vinyl arms, legs and head. Rooted light brown hair. Blue sleep eyes/lashes. 2nd and 3rd fingers of both hands curled. Open mouth/nurser. Marks: 2316/13EYE/9/Horsman Doll Inc./07151 on head. Horsman/BC 15 on back. 1963. $5.00.

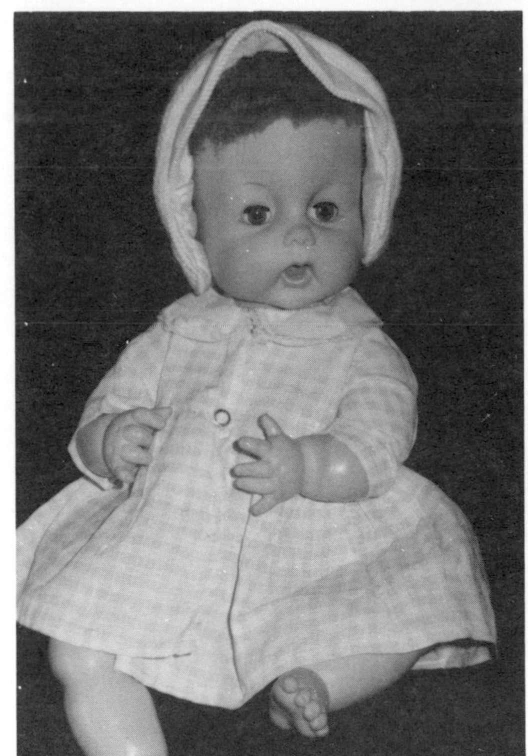

Horsman--18" "Thirstee Baby" Plastic body. Vinyl arms, legs and head. Rooted light brown hair. Blue sleep eyes/lashes. Large open mouth/nurser. Legs molded to bend at knees. Marks: Horsman on head. 1963. $5.00.

Horsman--15" "Tynie Toddler" Plastic body and legs. Vinyl arms and head. Rooted blonde hair. Blue sleep eyes/lashes. Open/closed mouth. Marks: Horsman Dolls Inc/67165, on head. 1964. $4.00.

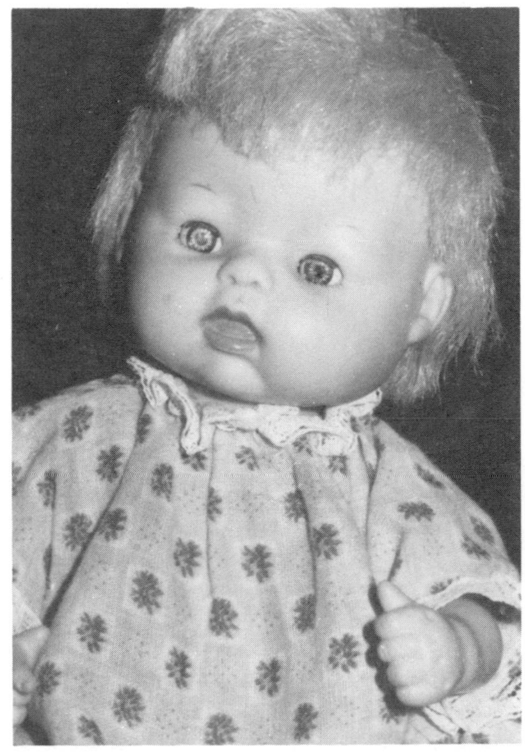

Horsman--12" "Lullabye Baby" All vinyl with rooted blonde hair. Blue sleep eyes/lashes. Open closed mouth. Key wind music box in center of back. Marks: M12/Horsman Doll, on head. 1964. $5.00. (Courtesy Allin's Collection)

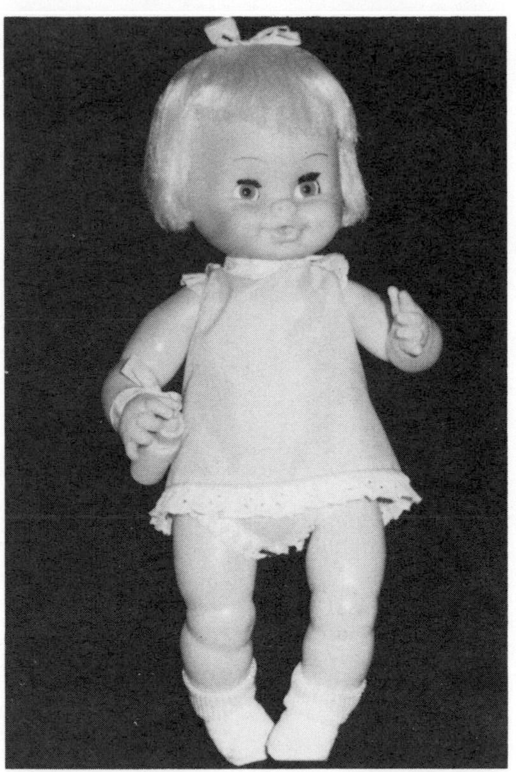

Horsman--13" "Baby Buttercup" Plastic body. Vinyl arms, legs and head. Rooted white hair. Dark blue sleep eyes/long lashes. Right hand with middle and 3rd fingers into palm. Individual molded toes. Marks: Horsman/1964/ B144/1, on head. Original clothes. $3.00.

Horsman--15" "Betty" Plastic body and legs. Vinyl arms and head. Rooted blonde hair. Blue sleep eyes/lashes. Closed mouth. Posable head. Marks: Horsman T-11 on head. 1965. $4.00.

Horsman--12" "Mary Poppins" Plastic body and legs. Vinyl arms and head. Rooted black hair. Side glancing blue eyes. Marks: H, on head. 1964. Mary Poppins was played by Julie Andrews in the 1964 movie of P.L. Traver's story. Walt Disney Productions. $18.00.

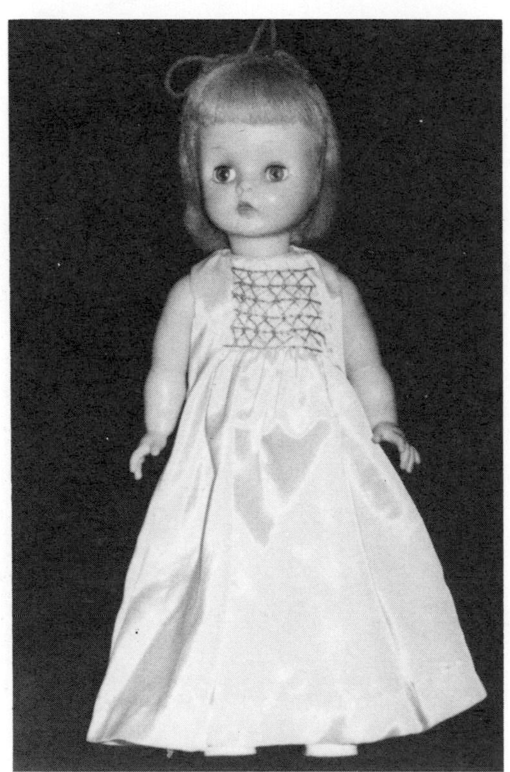

Horsman--15" "My Ruthie" Plastic body and legs. Vinyl arms and head. Rooted blonde hair. Blue sleep eyes/lashes. Wide open hands with 2nd and 3rd fingers curled. Marks: Horsman Dolls Inc/1964/216, on head. $5.00.

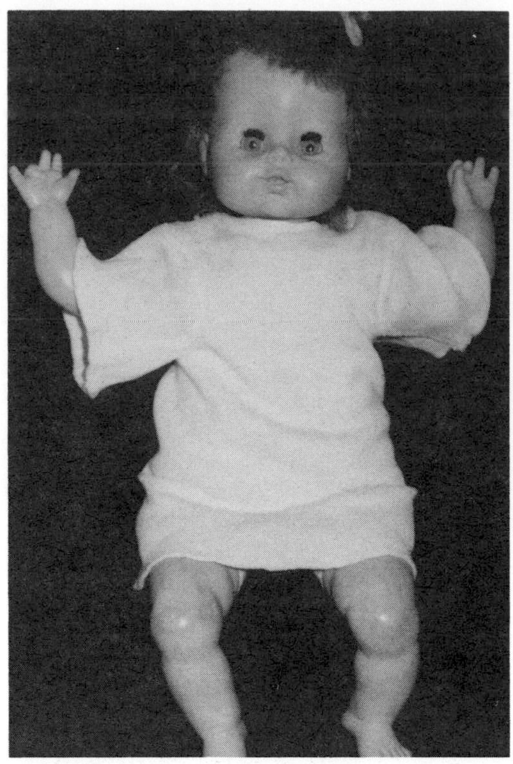

Horsman--14" "Softie Baby" Cloth body with vinyl arms, legs and head. Rooted light brown hair. Blue sleep eyes/lashes. Open/closed mouth with molded tongue. Marks: 2515/10 Eye/S14/2/Horsman Dolls Inc/070141, on head. 1965. $4.00.

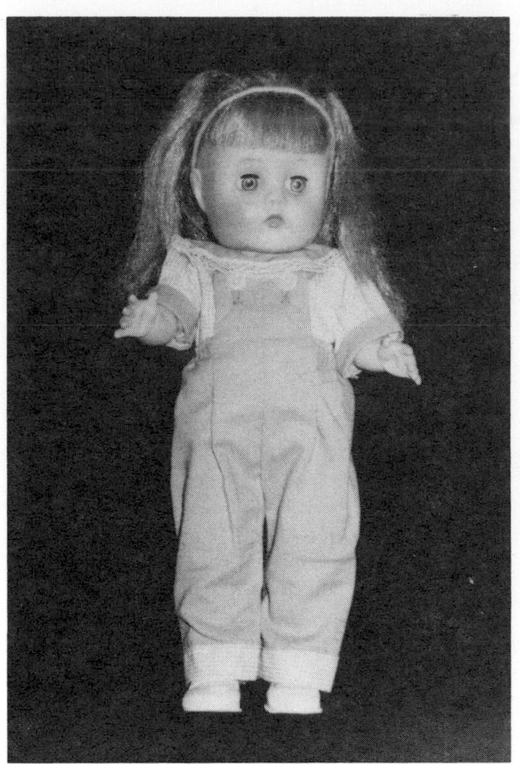

Horsman--11" "Toddler Betty" Plastic legs. Vinyl arms, body and head. Rooted blonde hair. Blue sleep eyes/lashes. Closed mouth. Marks: Horsman on head. 1965. $4.00.

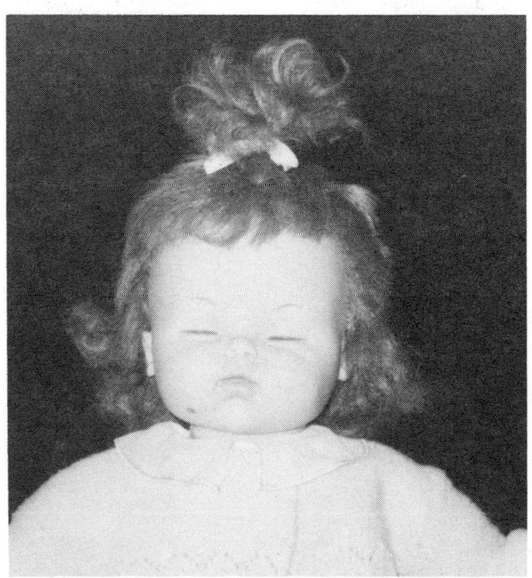

Horsman--24" "Sleepy Baby" Foam filled, cloth covered body. Vinyl arms, legs and head. Rooted dark blonde hair. Closed, sleeping eyes. Open/closed mouth. Right hand three fingers curled into palm. Left hand all fingers curled into palm. Marks: Horsman Dolls Inc/1965. Tag On Body: Mfgd By Horsman Dolls Inc. $18.00.

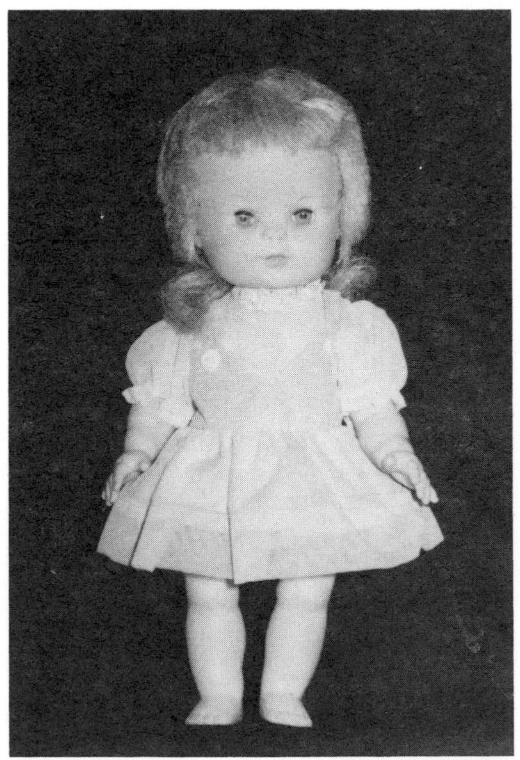

Horsman--10" "Answer Doll" Solid vinyl body, arms and legs. Vinyl head with rooted hair. Dark blue sleep eyes/molded lashes. Closed mouth. Button in back makes head nod yes. Button in front makes head shake no. Marks: 66-100/10/Horsman Dolls/1966. $6.00.

Horsman--14" "Baby Darling" Cloth body. Vinyl arms, legs and head. Rooted blonde hair. Blue sleep eyes/long lashes. Closed, puckered mouth. Right hand 3rd finger curled into palm. Marks: 2986 or 2966/13 EYE/64/Horsman Dolls Inc/1966 on head. Tag On Body: Horsman Dolls Inc. $4.00.

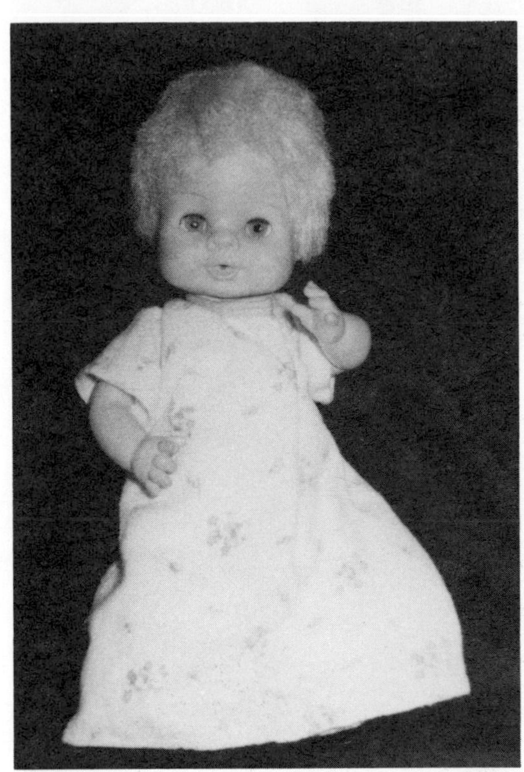

Horsman--9" 'Teensie Baby" Plastic body. Vinyl arms, legs and head with blonde rooted hair. Dark blue sleep eyes/lashes. Open mouth/nurser. Arms and hands molded to hold bottle. Molded crossed baby legs. Will suck thumb. Marks: 2481/3Eye/36/Horsman Dolls Inc/0791 on head. 1966. $3.00.

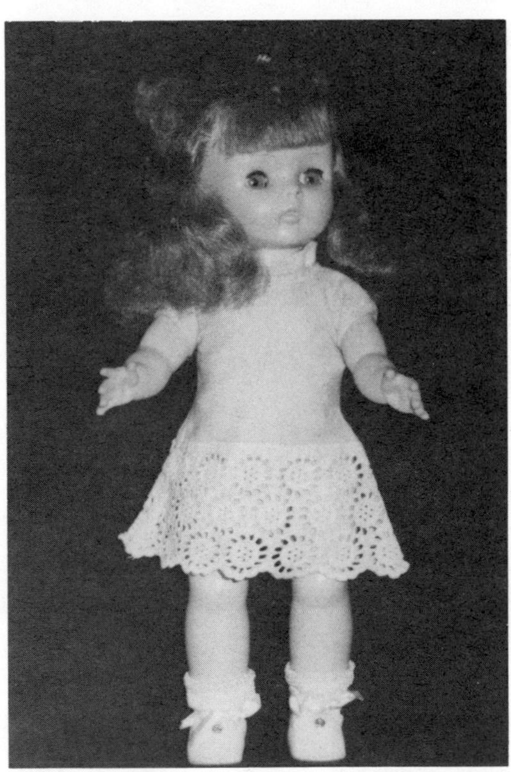

Horsman--13" "Ruthie" Plastic body and legs. Vinyl arms and head. Dark blue sleep eyes/lashes. Closed mouth. Marks: Horsman/T-13 on head. 1966. $16.00.

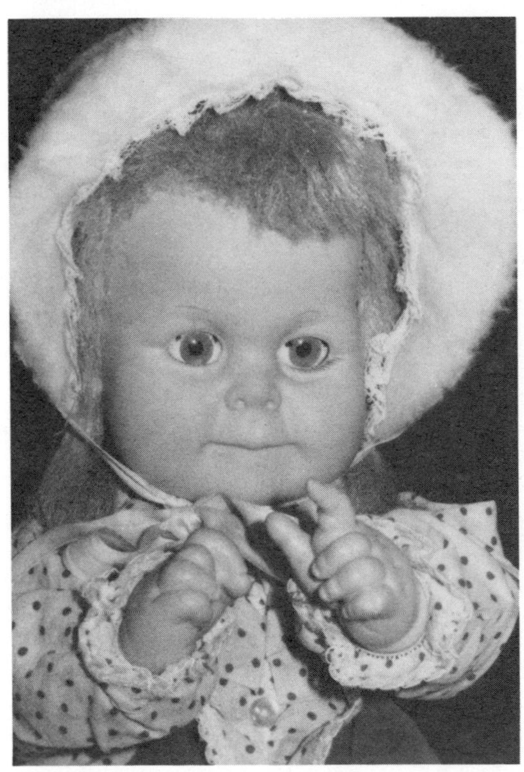

Horsman--16" "Tuffie" All vinyl with rooted blonde hair. Blue sleep eyes/lashes. Upper lip over lower. Marks: Horsman Doll Inc/B19 on head and body. 1966. $18.00.

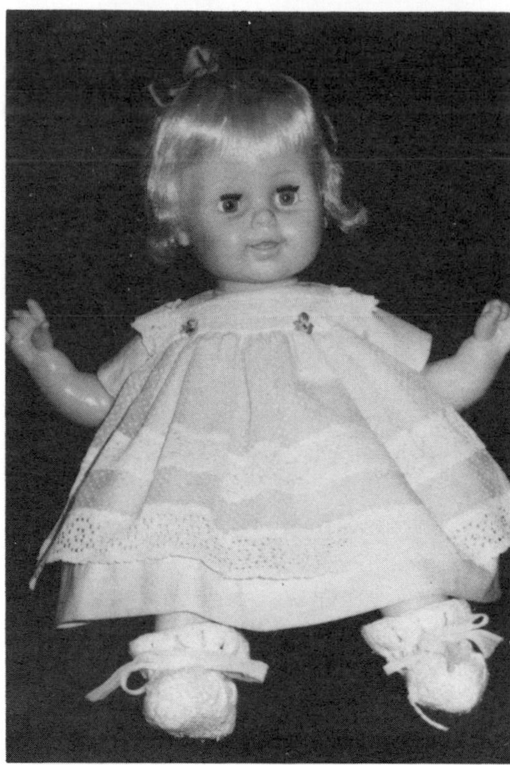

Horsman--18" "Mommy's Darling" Stuffed cloth body. Vinyl arms, legs and head. Rooted blonde hair. Blue sleep eyes/lashes. Open/closed mouth. Left thumb, index and 2nd fingers molded together. Right 3rd finger deeply curled into palm. Individually molded toes. Cryer. Marks: 2738/18Eye/14/Horsman Doll/67 $16.00.

Horsman--12½" "Ruthie" Plastic body and legs. Vinyl arms and head. Rooted ash blonde hair. Dark blue sleep eyes/long lashes. Closed mouth. Open hands with fingers pointing away from body. Marks: Horsman Dolls, Inc/1967 on head. Horsman Dolls Inc./Pat. Pend. on body. $6.00.

Horsman--11" "Ruthie Baby" Plastic body and legs. Vinyl arms and head. Rooted black hair. Brown sleep eyes/lashes. Closed mouth. Open hands with palms down. Original clothes. Marks: 2609/10Eye/39/07116/Horsman Dolls Inc/1967 on head. $16.00. (Courtesy Allin's Collection)

Horsman--20" "Walker Ruth" Plastic body and legs walk feature. Vinyl arms and head. Rooted light brown hair. Dark blue sleep eyes/lashes. Closed mouth. Index and 2nd fingers, of left hand, molded together. Marks: Horsman/T-21, on head. 1967. $7.00.

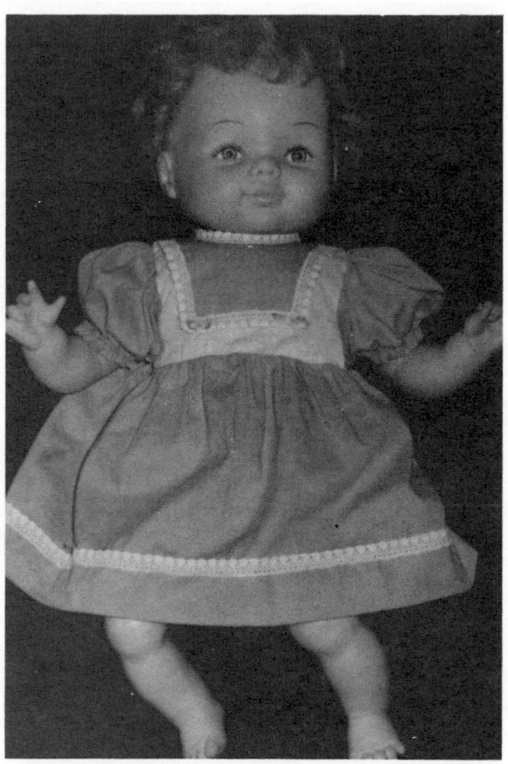

Horsman--20" "Baby Tweaks" Cloth body. Vinyl arms, legs and head. Rooted blonde hair. Inset stationary blue eyes. Right hand 3rd finger molded into palm. Individual molded toes. Squeekers in both legs. Marks: Horsman Dolls Inc/1967/07181 on head. Tag On Body: Horsman Dolls Inc. $16.00.

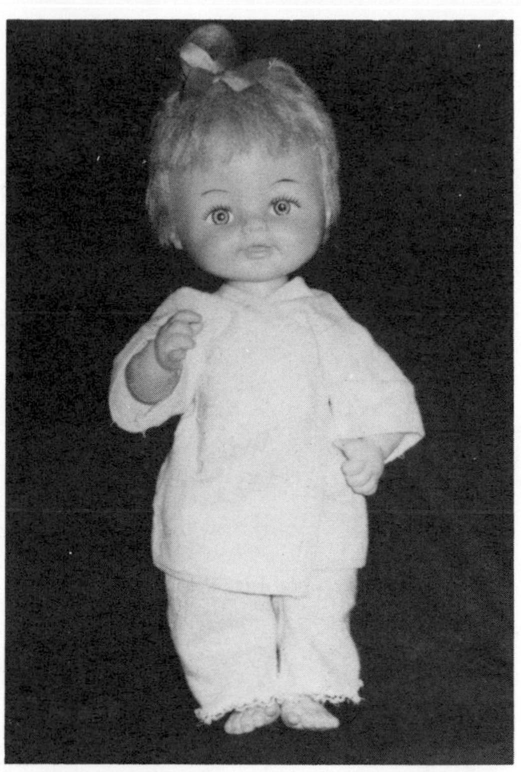

Horsman--12" "Lullabye Baby" All vinyl. Rooted blonde hair. Blue stationary eyes. Open mouth/nurser. Left hand all fingers curled into palm. Large toes individually molded. Pull string in center of back. Plays lullaby and makes body and head move. Marks: B1441/Horsman Dolls Inc/1967, on head. $6.00.

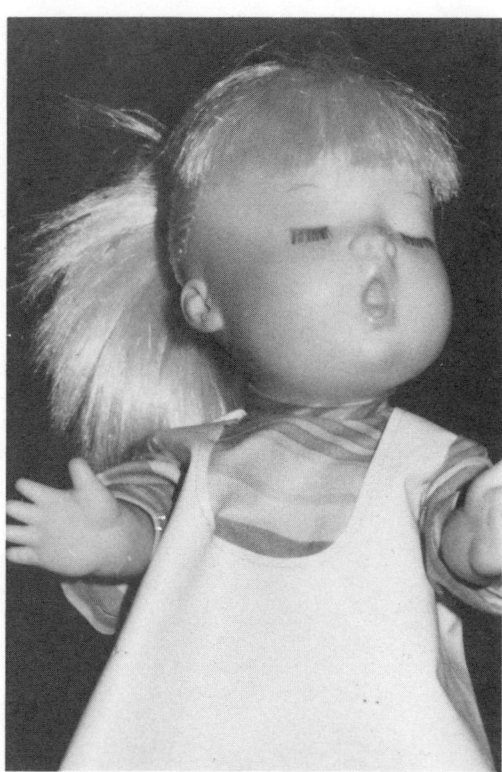

Horsman--12" "Songster" Plastic body and legs. Vinyl arms and head. Rooted white hair. Closed eyes/lashes. Open/closed mouth. Marks: Horsman Doll Inc/1967/0712, on head. Original clothes. $4.00. (Courtesy Allin's Collection.

Horsman--6" "Twistie" All vinyl with rooted ash blonde hair. Painted brown eyes. Closed mouth. Hands open with palms down. Shoes attached to stand. Key wind in center of back to make her twist. Marks: Horsman Dolls Inc./1967 on back. Original clothes. $3.00.

Horsman--5½" "Athelete" Plastic body and legs. Vinyl arms and head. Key wind. Slip on shoes. Shoes attached to a stand. Molded crew cut hair. Brown side glancing, painted eyes. Marks: Horsman Dolls Inc/1967. Original uniform with a #1 added to the 7 on front of shirt. $3.00.

Horsman--9" 'My Baby" All vinyl with rooted blonde hair. Sleep blue eyes/molded lashes. Closed mouth. 2nd and 3rd fingers molded together. Marks: Horsman/01, on head. 1968. $4.00.

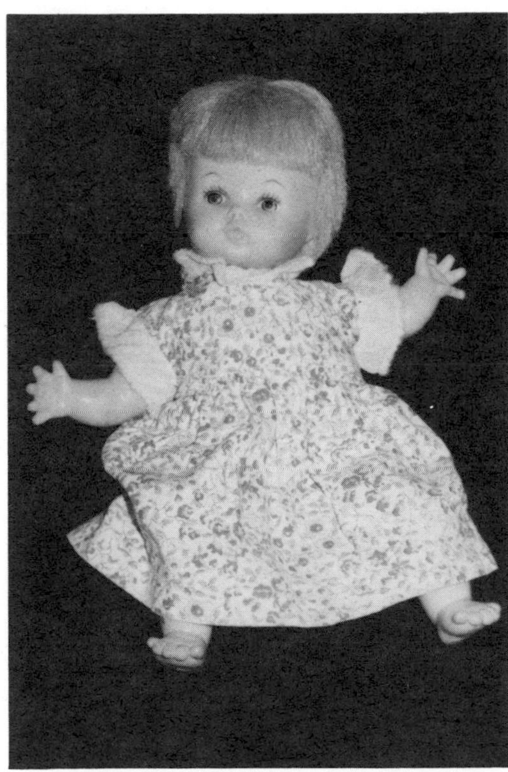

Horsman--11" "Lil Softee" Cloth body. Vinyl arms, legs and head. Rooted blonde hair. Blue painted eyes. Closed mouth. Left 2nd and 3rd fingers slightly curled. Both large toes slightly extended. Marks: 35/Horsman Dolls Inc/1968 on head. Tag On Body: Mfgd By Horsman Dolls Inc. $2.00.

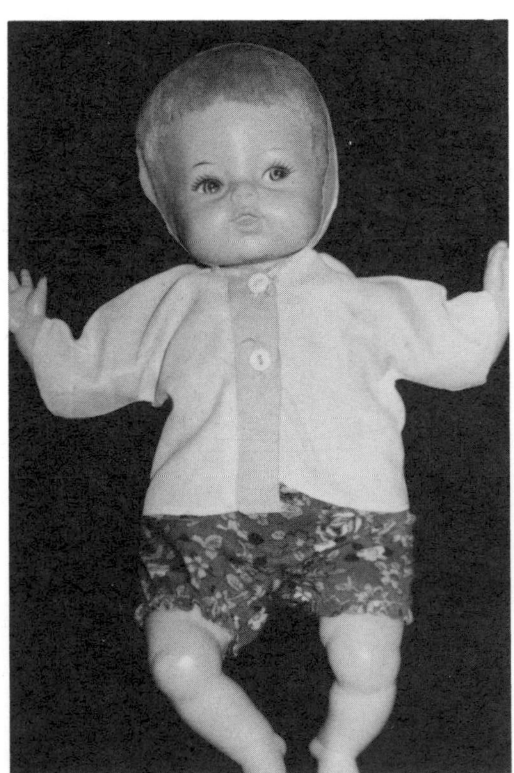

Horsman--14" "Softee Baby" Cloth body. Vinyl arms, legs and head. Rooted blonde hair. Painted blue eyes. Open/closed mouth. Right 3rd finger molded into palm. Left thumb, index and 2nd fingers molded together. Marks: 37/Horsman Dolls Inc./1968. Tag On Body: Mfgd By Horsman Dolls Inc. $2.00.

Horsman--16" "Love Me Baby" Plastic body. Vinyl arms, legs and head. Rooted white hair. Dark blue sleep eyes/long lashes. Open mouth/nurser. Large dimples in knees. Individually molded toes. Marks: 2954/14Eye/1/ Horsman Dolls Inc/1969 on head. Horsman Dolls Inc on body. $3.00.

Horsman--9" "Pooty Tat" All vinyl. Rooted orange hair. Brown sleep eyes/long lashes. Very short stocky legs. Marks: 20SA/D on bottom of feet. Hong Kong on head. Horsman Dolls Inc/Made in Hong Kong on back. 1969. $2.00.

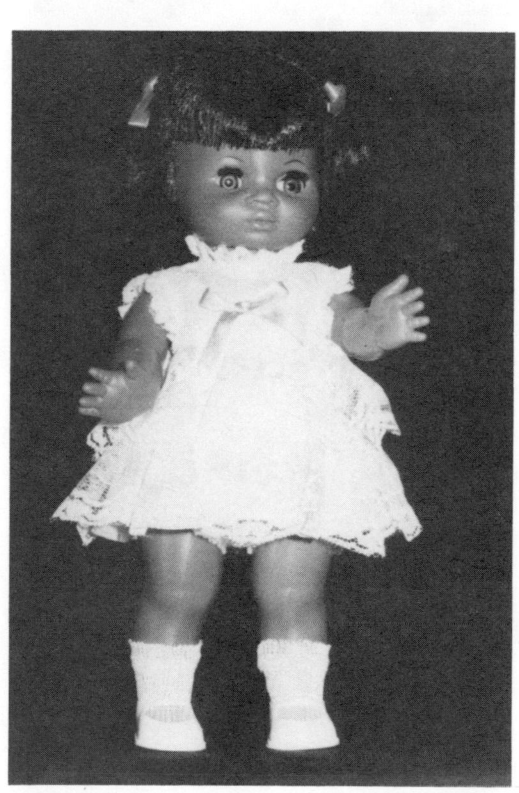

Horsman--12" "Bootsie" Plastic body and legs. Vinyl arms and head. Rooted black hair. Brown sleep eyes/long lashes. Marks: 1125/4/Horsman Dolls/1969 on head. An original outfit. $16.00.

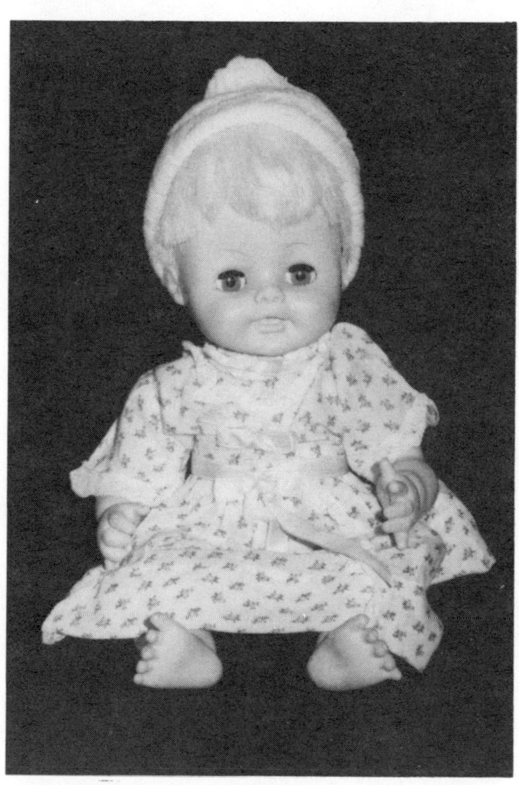

Horsman--13" "Cindy" Plastic body. Vinyl arms, legs and head. Rooted white hair. Blue sleep eyes/lashes. Open mouth/nurser. Right hand 2nd and 3rd fingers deeply curled. Left hand 2nd and 3rd finger slightly curled. Baby legs. Marks: Horsman Dolls Inc/1970 on head. Horsman Dolls Inc./BC15 on back. $4.00.

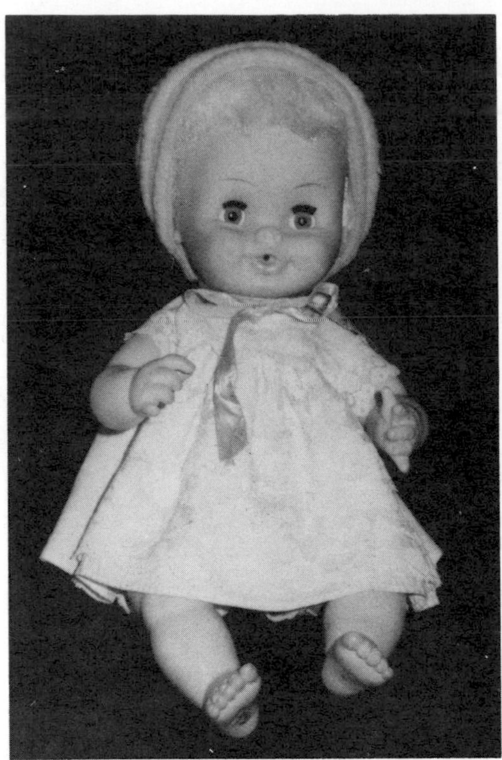

Horsman--14" "Buttercup" Plastic body. Vinyl arms, legs and head. Rooted white hair. Vivid blue sleep eyes/lashes. Dimpled cheeks and chin. Open mouth/nurser. 2nd and 3rd fingers curled. Dimpled knees. Marks: 3174/13EYE/11/ Horsman Dolls/1970 on head. Horsman Dolls Inc./BC15 on back. $3.00.

Horsman--14" "Bi Lo" Cloth body. Vinyl arms, legs and head. Molded straight hair. Painted blue eyes. Open/closed mouth. Left thumb, index and 2nd fingers molded together. Right 3rd finger molded into palm. This doll was issued for the 100th anniversary of Montgomery Wards. (1972). Marks: Horsman Doll/1972 on head. $18.00.

Ideal Toy Corporation

In 1902 the Ideal Toy Corporation was formed under the name Ideal Novelty and Toy Company, by Morris Michtom, for the express purpose to produce his TEDDY BEAR. By 1915 the company was going strong and led the industry by first introducing sleep eyes. The Shirley Temple doll in 1934, the Betsy Wetsy in 1937 and the Toni dolls in 1949 are only part of the great stable of stars created by this company. They still led the field by introducing new ideas and new materials. For example in 1939, Ideal developed a synthetic material which looked and felt like human skin and called it Magic Skin. Ideal was first to use plastics.

The company founder's son, Benjamin F. Michtom, has been active in the company since 1924. My correspondence with Ideal has been good, although they tell me that their records before 1950 are very sketchy.

A word here on the Shirley Temple doll. I have set aside an entire chapter on this doll and it follows this section.

Early Ideal's are marked with the company name in a diamond and later just with the name. They use numbers in series, along with the name of the company. Many are only marked "Made In USA" in the center of the back and some of these will have a number on the head or back. But remember that in the hard plastics, Arranbee, Horsman, Irwin and Imperial Crown also marked dolls this way.

The following are not all the dolls made by this company

1932 to 1938: Honeysuckle Line which includes: Ducky (35.00), Snoozie (35.00), Winnie (35.00), Cuddles (35.00)

1934: Shirley Temple (32.00 to 140.00)

1935: Curly Top (40.00), Our Little Girl (40.00), The Littlest Rebel (40.00)

1936: Sunbonnet Sue (25.00)

1937: Suck A Thumb (28.00), Composition Betsy Wetsy (37.00)

1938: Baby Snooks (39.00), Princess Sonja (40.00), Beatrix (35.00)

1939: Deanna Durbin (45.00 to 125.00), Judy Garland (Dorothy of Wizard Of Oz-45.00 to 90.00)

1940: Pinocchio (22.00), Jiminy Cricket (22.00), Poppa-Momma (16.00), Little Miss America (25.00), Judy Garland (Strike Up The Band-45.00 to 75.00), Fanny Brice (63.00), Magic Skin Baby (10.00)

1941: Judy Garland (Babes On Broadway-45.00 to 75.00), Gorgeous (16.00), Magic Squeezums (16.00), Nancy (16.00)

1942: Plassie (18.00), Flexy Soldier (32.00), Miss Deb (22.00)

1943: Lazy Bones (35.00)

1944: Pin Up Girl (18.00)

1945: Bit of Heaven (16.00), Continental (22.00), Baby Beautiful (16.00), Sleep Time Twins (35.00)

1946: Magic Skin Doll (16.00)

1947: Honeyfoam (9.00), Sparkle Plenty (22.00)

1948: Baby Coos (30.00), Baby Sox (20.00), Softee (3.00), Bobby Sox (30.00), Boopsie (10.00), Brother Coos (22.00), Plassie (18.00), Tickletoes (18.00)

1949: Toni Doll (20.00), Linda (10.00), Olive (10.00), Snoozie (10.00), Miss Curity (25.00), Also a 20" Miss Curity in Composition (45.00), Hopalong Cassity (40.00), Magic Skin Baby (10.00)

1950: Judy Splinters (22.00), Lovely Coos (18.00), Baby Gurgles (18.00), Talkytot (40.00), Blessed Event (20.00), Tummy (16.00), Itsy Bitsy (8.00), Snoozie (8.00), Baby Mine (18.00), Little Miss Mischief (30.00), Pete & Repete (6.00 each), Tony Walker (22.00), Howdy Doody (8.00), Tiny Girl (4.00)

1951: Catherine (15.00), Heart Beat Doll (15.00), Honey Bunch (12.00), Kiss Me (18.00), Tribly (15.00), Bonnie Braids (22.00), Saralee (30.00), Saucy Walker (16.00), Sister Coos (18.00)

1952: Baby Jeans (15.00), Baby Jo Anne (15.00), Betsy McCall (20.00), Mary Hartline (25.00), Miss Curity (25.00), Joan Polooka (22.00), Baby Ruth (10.00)

1953: Mysterious Yokum (10.00), Lollapalooza (10.00), Harriet Hubbard Ayers (25.00 to 45.00)

1954: Little Sister (15.00), Carol the Walking Doll (18.00), Posie (8.00), Baby Big Eyes (32.00), Super Walker (15.00), Princess Mary Line (22.00)

1955: Patti Prays (25.00), Magic Lips (40.00), Campbell Kids (8.00), Jackie Doll (15.00), Betsy Wetsy Series (4.00 to 30.00), Saucy Walker (reissued with vinyl head 25.00)

1956: Baby Coos (16.00), Miss Revlon (22.00), Ginger (15.00), Dream Doll (15.00), Baby June (45.00)

1957: Twinkle Eyes (15.00), Little Miss Revlon (14.00), Shirley Temple (8.00 to 30.00)

1958: Fashion Miss Revlons (7.00 to 22.00)

1959: Cream Puff (18.00), Penny Playpal (45.00)

1960: Bye Bye Baby (8.00), Mitzi (8.00)

1961: Miss Ideal (36.00), Dew Drop (7.00), Patti Playpal (18.00)

1962: Tiny Kissy (18.00), Thumbelina (12.00), The Kuinks (4.00), Tammy (4.00)

1963: Ruckus (5.00), Smoochie (4.00), Bam Bam (7.00), Pebbles (7.00), Glamour Misty (5.00), Baby Snoozie (5.00), Mom (4.00), Dad (4.00), Pepper (4.00), Ted (4.00)

1964: Misty (5.00), Tearie (7.00), Cuddly Kissy (30.00), Pete (8.00), Tearful Thumbelina (7.00)

1965: Honeymoon (18.00), Betsy Baby (8.00), Dodi (10.00), Goody Two Shoes (25.00), Miss Clairol (5.00), Patty Duke (8.00), Illya Kuryakin (30.00), James Bond (30.00), Baby Giggles (22.00), Snoozie (9.00)

1966: Captain Action (7.00), Tubbsy (18.00), Baby Lu (6.00), Giggles (15.00), Samantha The Witch (16.00), Baby Giggles (22.00), Honeyball (4.00), Tabatha (Samantha's baby-40.00), Tearful Thumbelina (18.00), Tiny Baby Kissy (16.00)

1967: Newborn Thumbelina (18.00), Giggles Toddler (25.00), Daisy (6.00), Pixie (7.00), Tearie Betsy (6.00)

1968: Beautiful Crissy (6.00), Little Lost Baby (22.00), Toddler Thumbelina (6.00), April Showers (22.00)

1969: Dianna Ross (15.00), Flatsy Series (3.00), Velvet (7.00), Kissin' Thumbelina (6.00)

1970: Crissy (6.00), Baby Belly Button (4.00), Patti Playful (35.00), Tiny Thumbelina (6.00), In A Minute Thumbelina (6.00)

1971: Lazy Dazy (5.00), Dina (25.00), Play N Jane (9.00)

1972: Shirley Temple (10.00 to 30.00)

Ideal--17" "Deanna Durbin" All composition with glued on dark brown wig. Brown sleep eyes/lashes. Dark grey eye shadow. Open mouth with felt tongue and five teeth. Dimples far out on cheeks. Marks: Deanna Durbin/Ideal Toy Co. on head. 1939. $75.00. (Courtesy Allin's Collection).

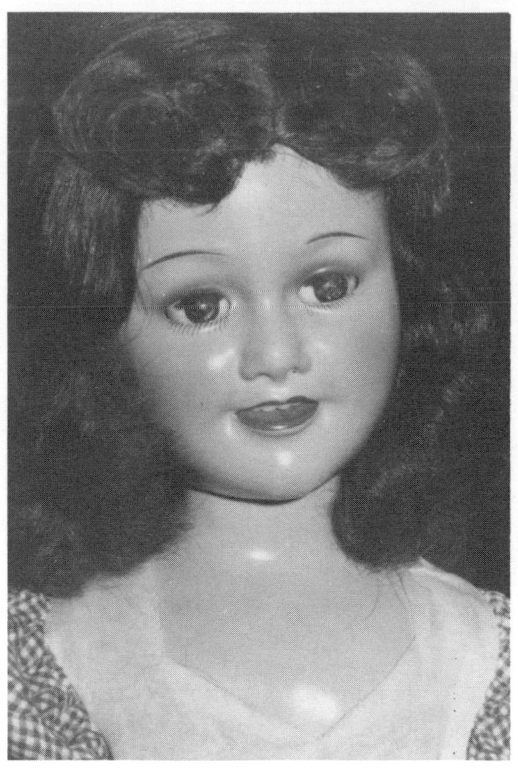

Ideal--21" "Deanna Durbin" All composition with glued on black human hair wig. Green sleep eyes/lashes. Open mouth with 6 teeth and felt tongue. 2nd and 3rd fingers curled. Long straight legs. Marks: Deanna Durbin/Ideal Doll

on head. Ideal Doll on body. Dress Tag; "21". 1940. Original dress. Was sold in 1941 as Judy Garland. $90.00.

A Closeup of the singing beauty, whose voice toppped all of the 1930's and 1940's.

Ideal--14" "Judy Garland Teen Doll" All composition with glued on dark auburn human hair wig. Blue sleep eyes/lashes. Open mouth with six teeth. Marks: Ideal Doll, on head. 1941. Original clothes. This is a different doll altogether, than the Dorothy, issued for the Wizard Of Oz in 1939. $45.00.

Judy Garland shown as Dorothy in The Wizard Of Oz, 1941.

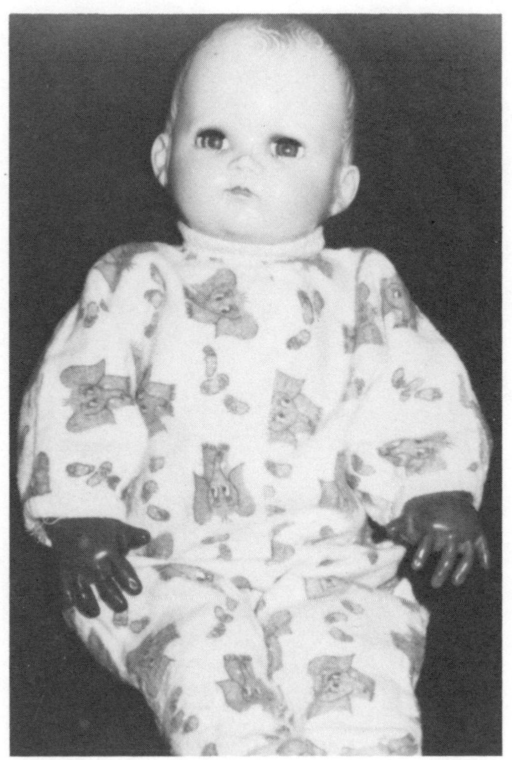

Ideal--17" "Magic Skin Baby" One piece latex body, arms and legs. Hard plastic head with molded, painted hair. Blue sleep eyes/lashes. Closed mouth. Posable head. Marks: Made In USA/Pat. No. 2252077, on head. 1940. $10.00.

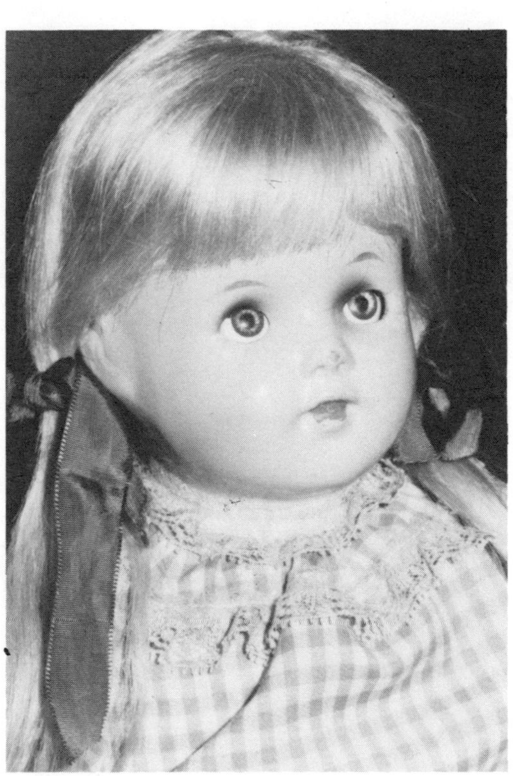

Ideal--17" "Georgous" Cloth body with composition shoulder plate head. Composition arms, legs and head with glued on blonde human hair wig. Blue sleep eyes with black eyeshadow. Closed mouth. Marks: Ideal on head. 1941. $16.00.

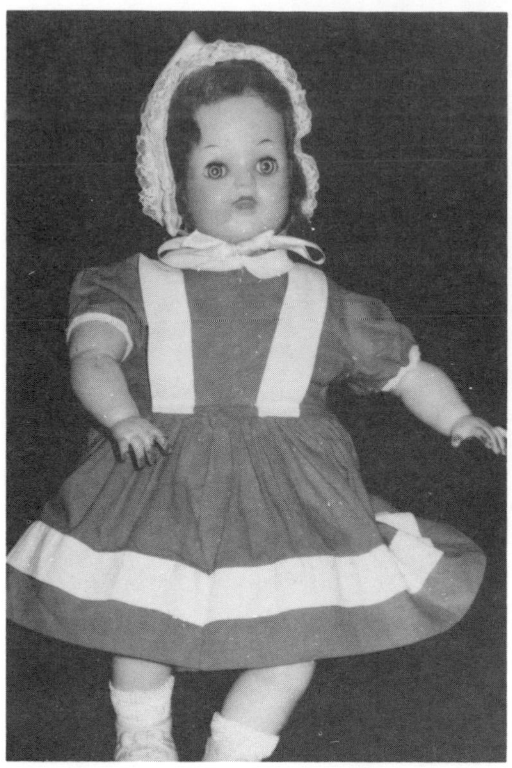

Ideal--16" "Magic Skin Doll" Oil cloth covered body. Early vinyl arms, legs and head. Glued on brown wig. Blue sleep eyes/lashes. Open/closed mouth with molded tongue. Very wide neck. Cryer. Marks: Something-B-14/Ideal Doll, on head. 1946. $16.00.

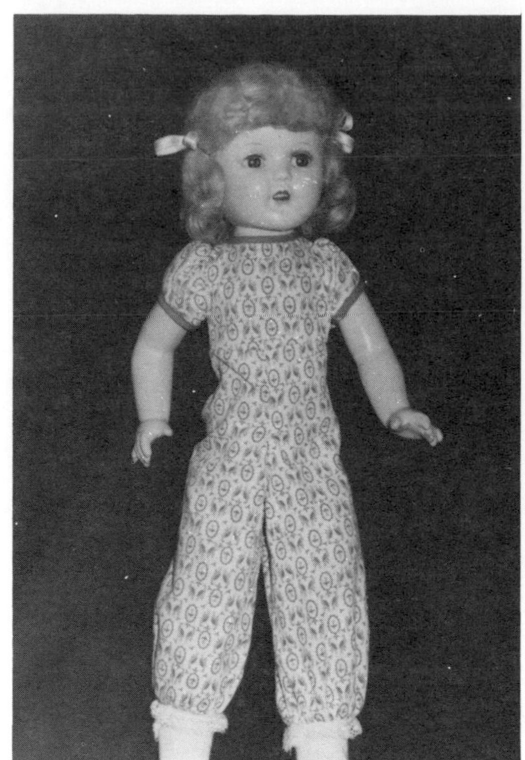

Ideal--18" "Miss Deb Of 1942" All composition. Glued on blonde mohair wig. Brown sleep eyes. Open mouth with 5 teeth. Marks: 18, on back. $22.00.

Ideal--12" "Flexy Soldier" Composition hands, feet and head. Molded hair and painted features. Flexable spring arms and legs. Wood body. Marks: Ideal Doll, on head. Original clothes. 1942. $32.00. (Courtesy Allin's Collection).

Ideal--15" "Sparkle Plenty" Latex one piece body and legs. Latex arms disc jointed at shoulders. Hard plastic head with glued on yellow yarn hair. Blue sleep eyes/lashes. Closed mouth. Marks: Made In USA/Pat. No. 2252077. (Ideal's patent # for hard plastic) 1947. $22.00.

Ideal--14" "Baby Coo's" Latex body with metal disc, jointed latex arms and legs. Glued on brown hair over brown painted and molded hair. Brown sleep eyes/lashes. Closed mouth. Chubby body. Coo voice. Marks: A Backward "S" or "2" on head. 1948. $30.00.

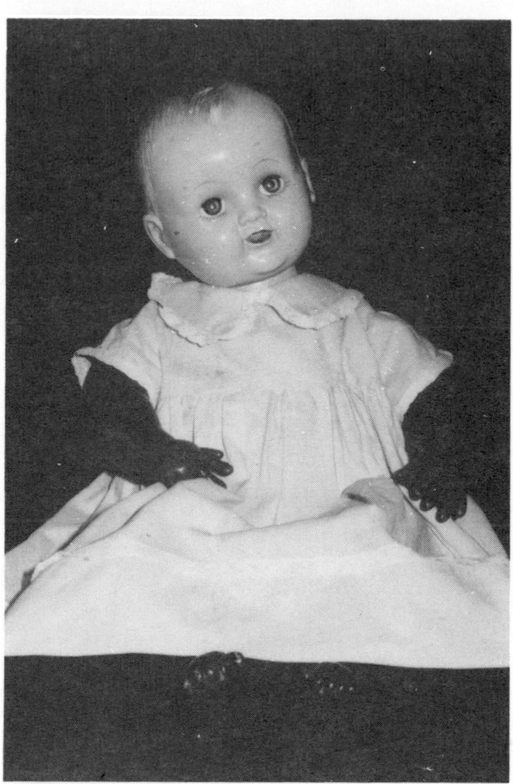

Ideal--17" "Tickletoes" Cloth body with cryer in center of stomach. Magic skin early vinyl plastic. The magic skin has turned very dark. Hard plastic shoulder plate, ball jointed head with molded/painted brown hair. Blue sleep eyes. Open/closed mouth. Marks: 16/Ideal Doll Made In USA, on head. 1948. $18.00.

Ideal--23" "Tickletoes" Hard plastic head. Latex arms and legs. Cloth body. Blue sleep eyes/lashes. Open mouth with two upper teeth and felt tongue. Glued on dark brown wig. "Mama" cry voice in center of stomach. Marks: P200/Ideal Doll on head. 1948. $18.00.

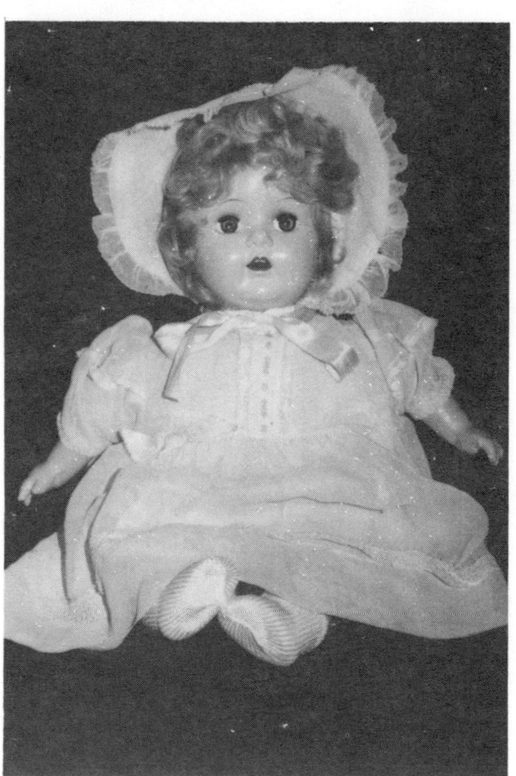

Ideal--17½" "Plasssie" Cloth body. Composition arms and legs. Hard plastic head with open mouth and two upper teeth. Felt tongue. Glued on blonde mohair wig. Blue sleep eyes. Marks: P-50/Ideal/Made In USA on head. 1948. $18.00.

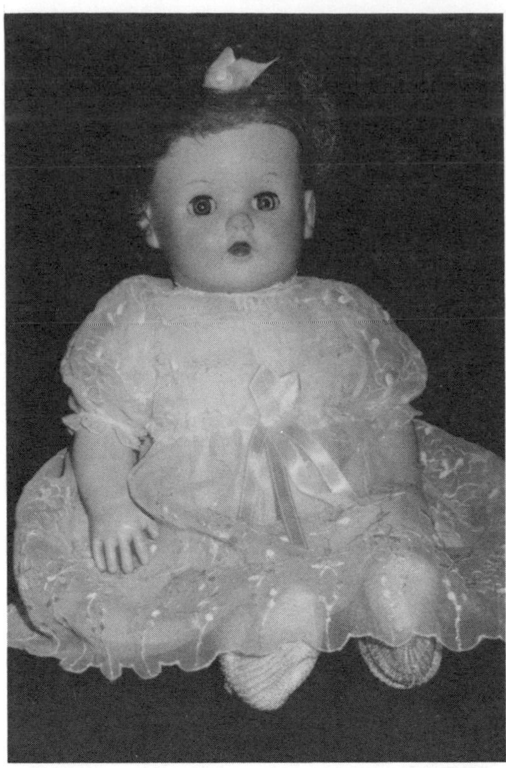

Ideal--15" "Magic Skin Baby" One piece latex body, arms and legs. Vinyl head with rooted brown hair. Blue sleep eyes/lashes. Marks: 72, on head. 1948. $10.00.

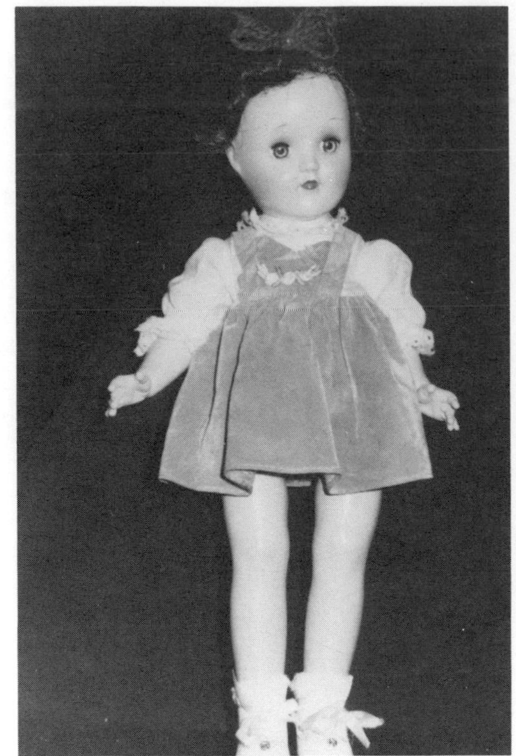

Ideal--14" "Tonie" All hard plastic with glued on black nylon wig. Blue sleep eyes/lashes. Closed mouth. Open hands with index and little fingers extended above other. Marks: Ideal Doll/Made In USA, on head. Ideal Doll P-90 on body. 1949. $20.00.

Ideal--14" "Toni" All hard plastic with glued on red nylon wig. Blue sleep eyes/lashes. Closed mouth. Open hands with index and little fingers extended above others. Marks: Ideal Doll/Made In USA on head. Ideal Doll/P-90 on body. Dress Tag: Genuine Toni Doll with nylon wig Made By Ideal Toy Corp. 1949. $20.00.

Ideal--15" "Toni" All hard plastic. Glued on blonde nylon wig. Blue sleep eyes/lashes. Closed mouth. Marks: Ideal Doll/Made In USA on head. Ideal Doll P-91 on back. 1949. $20.00.

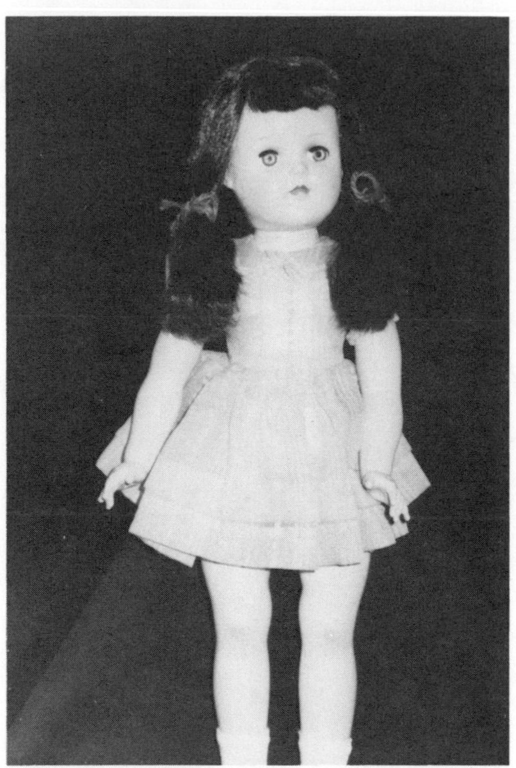

Ideal--21" "Toni Walker" All hard plastic with glued on black nylon wig. Green sleep eyes/lashes. Eye shadow. Marks: P-93 Ideal Doll Made In USA on head. Ideal Doll/P-93, on body. 1950. $22.00.

Ideal--9" "Tiny Girl" All hard plastic with molded hair. Blue sleep eyes/molded lashes. Closed mouth. Early type walker with ball jointed, in front, hip sockets. Marks: Ideal Doll/9, on body. 1950. $4.00.

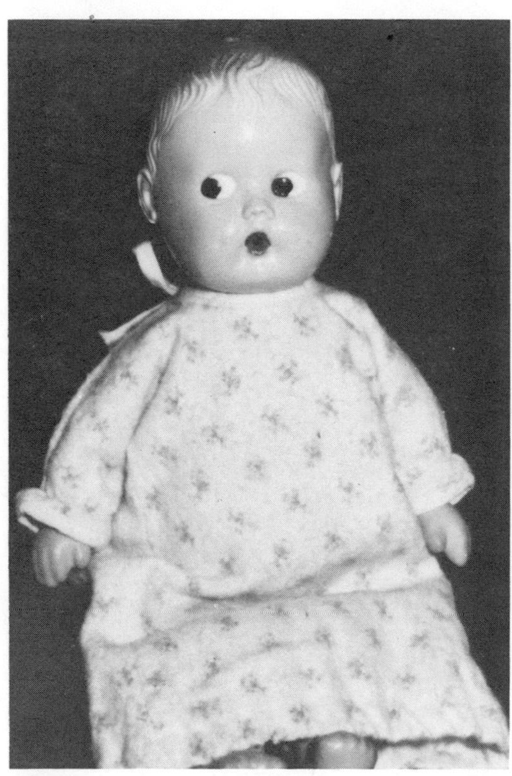

Ideal--8" "Pete" Stuffed latex one piece body, arms and legs. Hard plastic head with molded, painted hair. Painted side glancing eyes. Open mouth/dry nurser. Marks: none. 1950. One of twins: Pete and Repete. $6.00.

Ideal--22" "Saucy Walker" All hard plastic with glued on dark blonde wig. Blue flirty eyes/lashes. Open/closed mouth with two upper teeth. Head turns as she walks. Marks: Ideal Doll, on head and body. Original dress. 1951. $16.00 (Courtesy Earlene Johnston Collection).

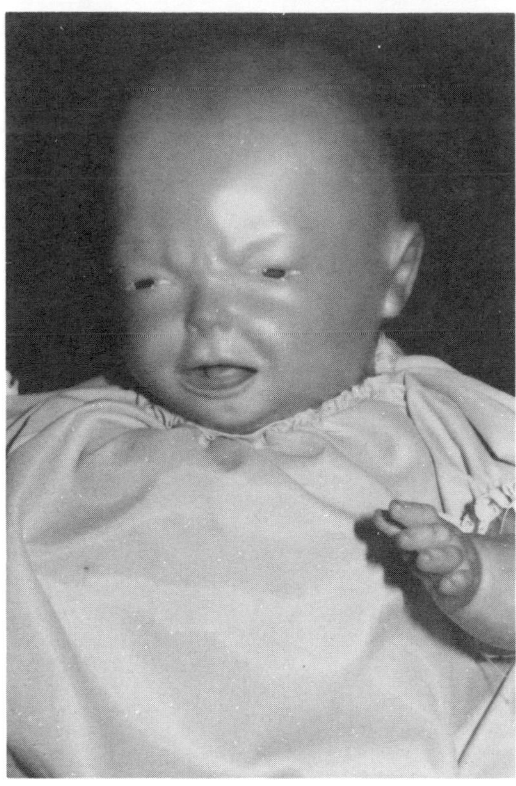

Ideal--18" "Kiss Me" Cloth body. Early vinyl arms, legs and head. Brown molded hair. Painted blue eyes. Wide open mouth with molded tongue. Mouth opens and closed by pressing back. Marks: S3/Ideal Doll/Pat. Pending, on head. 1951. $18.00. (Courtesy Allin's Collection).

Ideal--13" "Bonnie Braids" Hard plastic body. Vinyl head with one piece braided saran hair pulled through two holes in the sides of head. Blue sleep eyes/lashes. Open mouth with three painted teeth. Marks: 1951/Chicago Tribune/ Ideal Doll on head. $22.00.

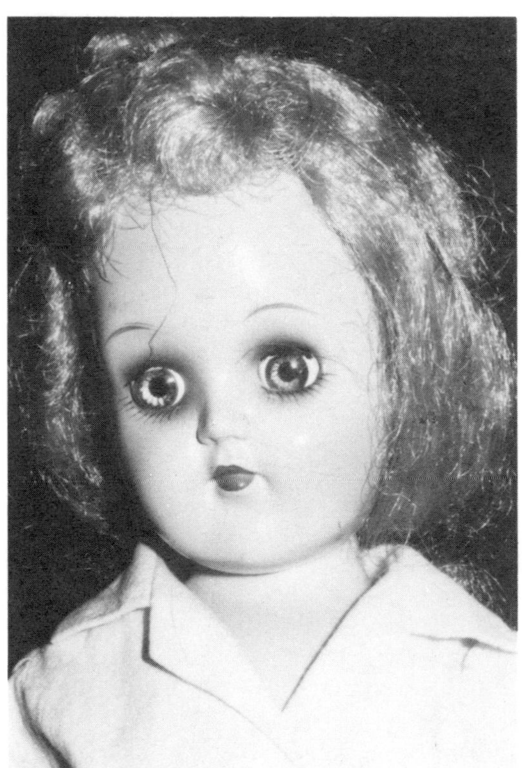

Ideal--14" "Miss Curity" All hard plastic with glued on yellow saran wig. Blue sleep eyes/lashes. Eye shadow over and under eyes. Posable legs and arms. Original uniform. Marks: Ideal Doll/Made In USA, on head. Ideal Doll/P-90, on body. This is same body and head used for the Toni Doll. 1952. $25.00.

Ideal--14" "Betsy McCall" Hard plastic body, arms and legs. Early vinyl head with glued on dark brown hair. Brown sleep eyes/lashes. Closed mouth. Marks: McCall Corp. on head. Ideal Doll/P-90 on body. 1952. $20.00.

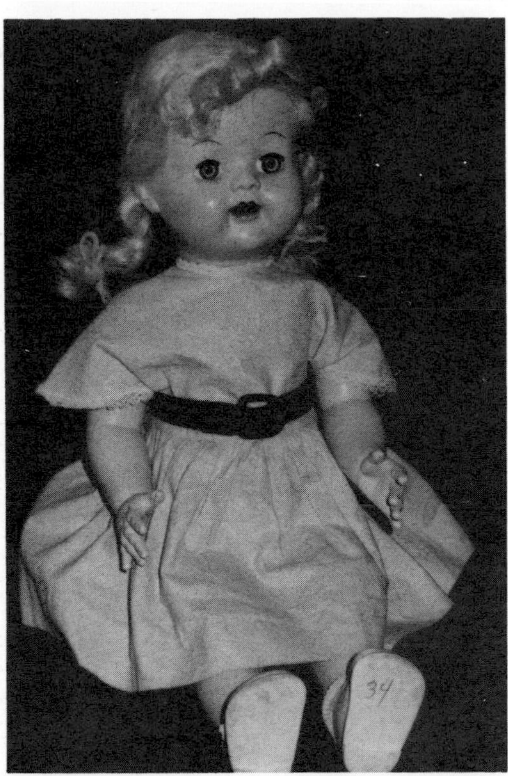

Ideal--22" "Saucy Walker" All hard plastic with yellow glued on mohair wig. Large blue sleep eyes/lashes. Open/closed mouth with two teeth and felt tongue. Open hands facing body. Mama crier. Series of holes in chest. Legs socketed in cut out ovals in hips. Backward push of legs make head turn. Marks: none. 1953. $16.00.

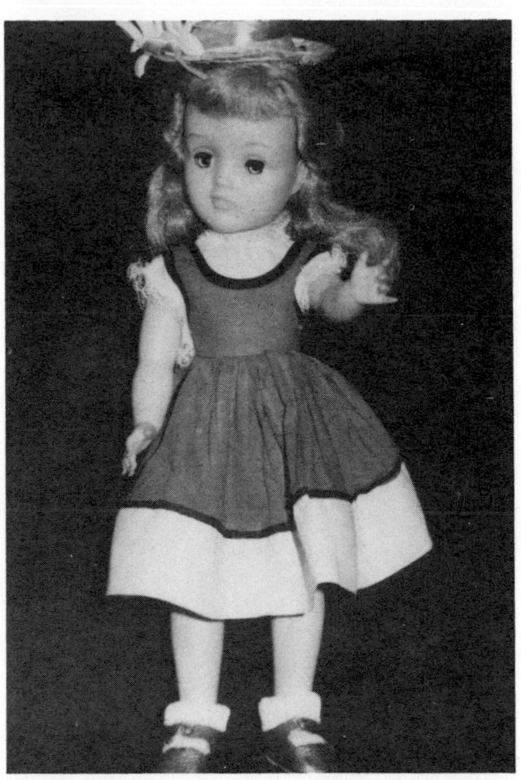

Ideal--14½" "Harriet Hubbard Ayers" Hard plastic body and legs. Early vinyl Magic Flesh arms and head. Blonde glued on wig. Marks: MK-14/Ideal Doll, on head. Ideal Doll/P-90, on body. 1953. This same body was used for the Toni, Miss Curity, Mary Hartline, Betsy McCall, etc. $25.00.

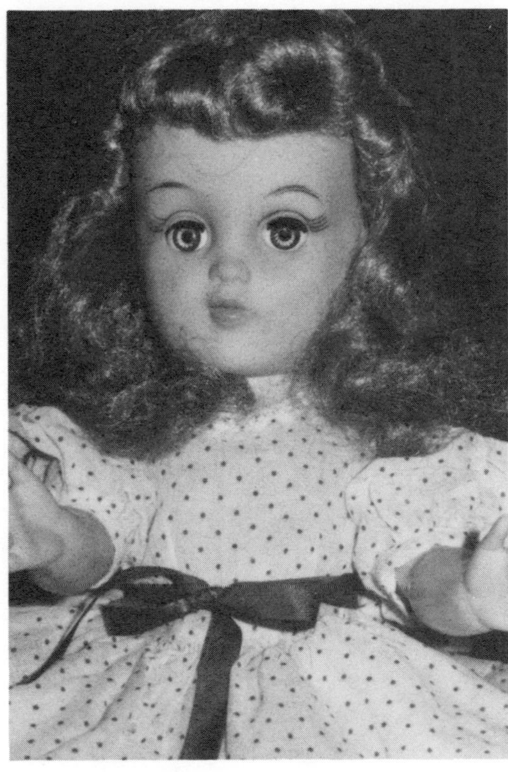

Ideal--18" "Harriet Hubbard Ayers" Hard plastic body and legs. Early vinyl "Magic Flesh" arms and head. Blonde glued on wig over hole in top of head that is stuffed. Blue sleep eyes/lashes. Marks: MK-18/Ideal Doll on head. Ideal Doll on body. 1953. $45.00.

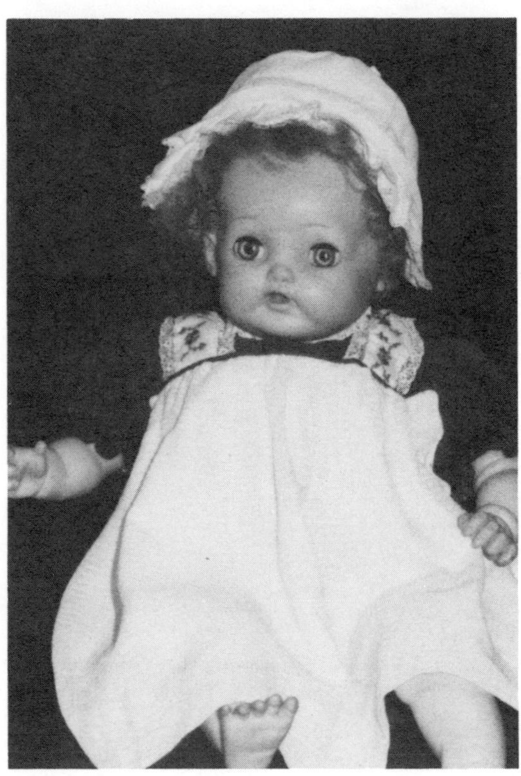

Ideal--21" "Baby Big Eyes" Vinyl coated cloth body. Early vinyl arms, legs and head. Rooted blonde hair. Large blue sleep eyes/lashes. Open/closed mouth. Left fingers curled. Right 2nd and 3rd and index curled. Individual toes. Can suck thumb. Marks: Ideal Doll, on head. 1954. $32.00.

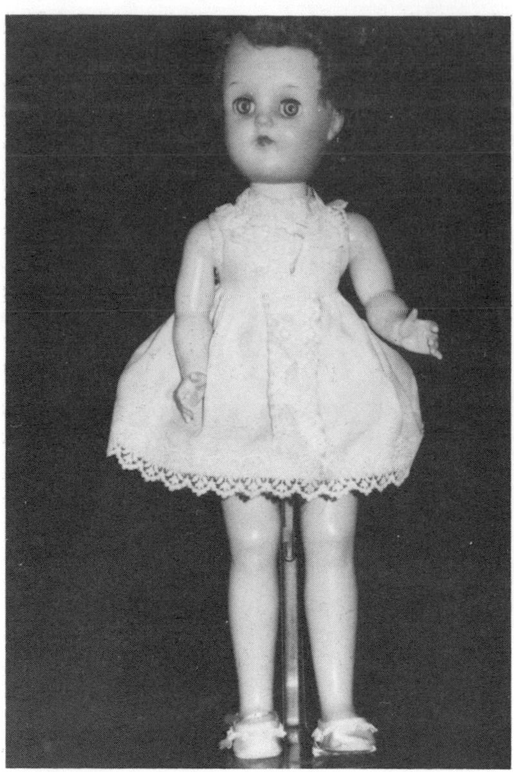

Ideal--17" "Princess Mary" Hard plastic body, arms and legs. Vinyl head with rooted dark blonde hair. Blue sleep eyes/lashes. Closed mouth. Cryer in center of stomach. Marks: Ideal Doll/VP 17, on head. Ideal Doll/W 18, on back. Original dress. 1954.

Ideal--19" "Saucy Walker" Hard plastic body, arms and legs. Vinyl head with rooted dark brown hair. Blue sleep eyes/lashes. Closed mouth. Open hands facing body. Ball jointed, pinned legs. Walker. Marks: Ideal Doll/3V-92, on head. Ideal Doll/19, on body. 1955. $25.00.

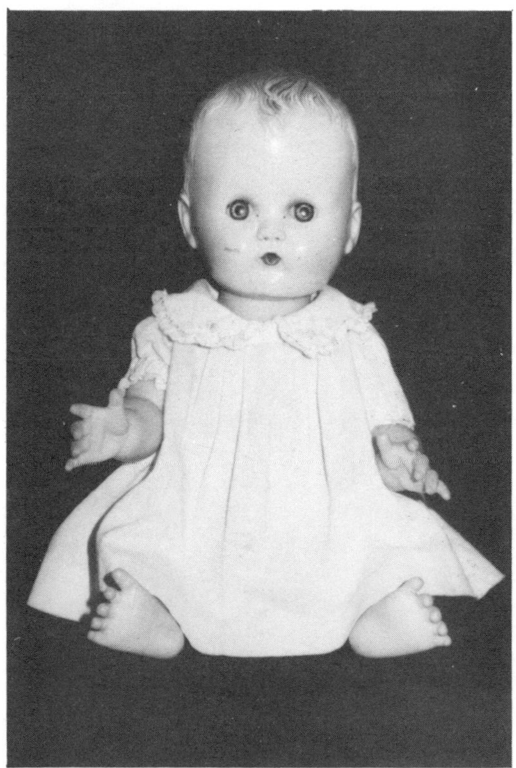

Ideal--13" "Betsy Wetsy" Hard plastic head with molded hair. Blue sleep eyes/lashes. Tear ducts, pierced nostrils. Coo/nurser mouth. Early vinyl body with disc jointed shoulder and hips. Open hands and individual toes. Marks: 14/Ideal Doll/Made In USA, on head. Ideal/14, on body. 1955. $30.00.

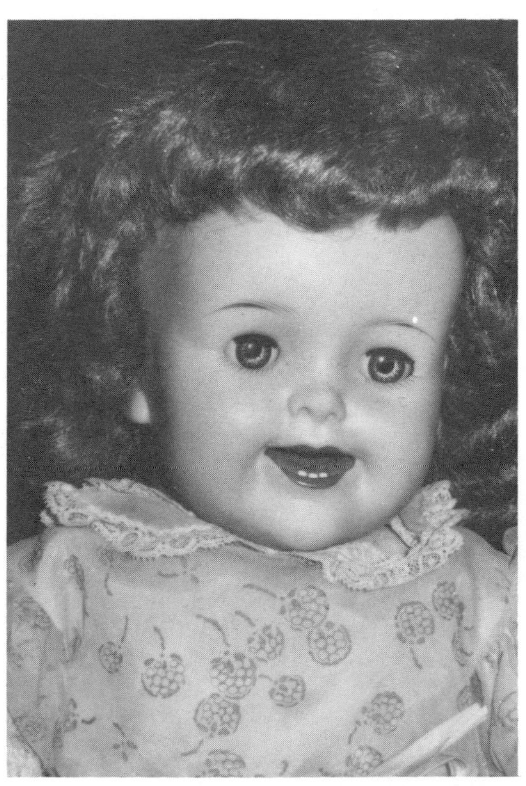

Ideal--24" "Magic Lips" Vinyl coated cloth body. Vinyl arms, legs and head. Rooted dark blonde hair. Blue sleep eyes/lashes. Open mouth with three lower teeth. Press her back and she closes her mouth. Release and mouth opens with a cooing sound. Marks: Ideal Doll/T25. 1955. $40.00.

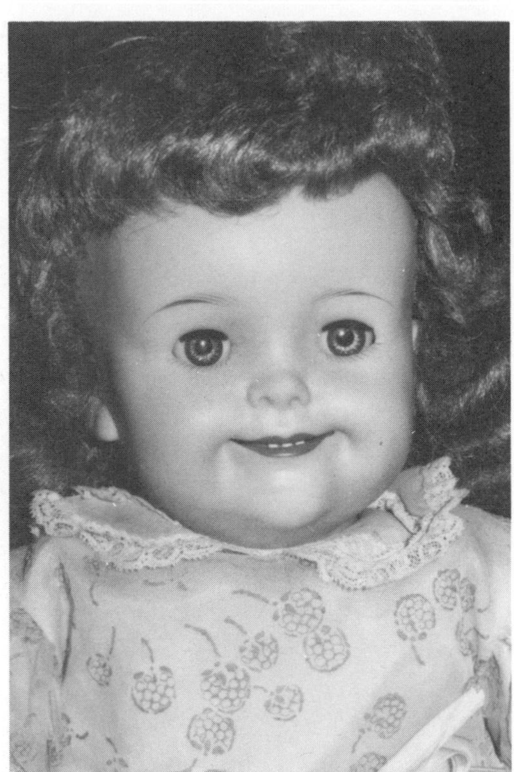

Ideal--24" "Magic Lips"

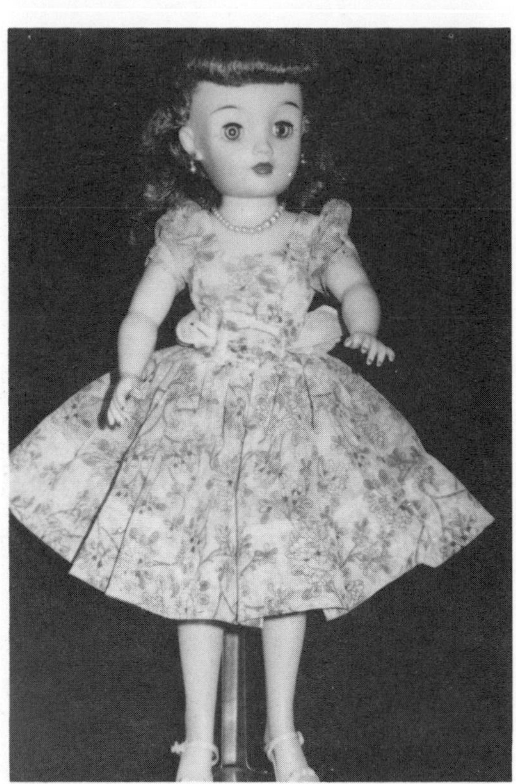

Ideal--17" "Miss Revlon" Solid vinyl body, arms and legs. Vinyl head with rooted brown hair. Blue sleep eyes/lashes. Closed mouth. Open hands with 2nd and 3rd fingers curled. Jointed waist. Polished fingers and toes. High heel feet. Marks: Ideal Doll/VT-18 on head. Ideal Doll/VT-18 on body. Orig. clothes. 1956. $22.00.

Ideal--15" "Baby June" Vinyl one piece unjointed body, arms and legs. Vinyl head with rooted dark brown hair. Blue sleep eyes/lashes. Closed mouth. Open hands with palms down. Marks: Ideal Doll/VS-15-2, on head. Ideal Doll VS-14, on back. 1956. $45.00.

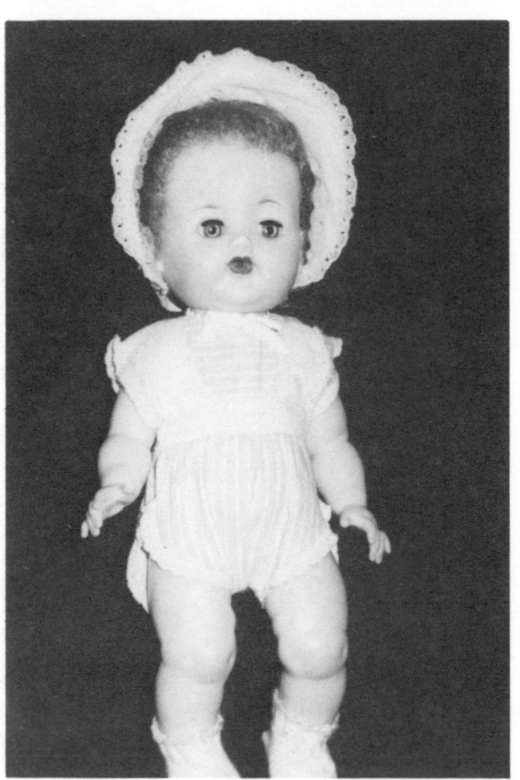

Ideal--13½" "Betsy Wetsy" All vinyl. Rooted light brown hair. Blue sleep eyes/lashes. Open mouth/nurser. Open hands, palms toward body. Dimpled knees. Individual molded toes. Marks: Ideal Doll/VW-2 on head. 1956. $5.00.

Ideal--10½" "Little Miss Revlon" Plastic and vinyl. Jointed waist. Blue sleep eyes/molded lashes. Rooted dark blonde hair. Pierced ears. Painted fingernails and toes. Marks: Ideal Toy Corp/VT-10½ on head. 1957. $14.00.

Ideal--17" "Miss Revlon" All vinyl with rooted pink hair. Large blue sleep eyes/lashes. Closed mouth. Jointed waist. Pierced ears. Marks: Ideal Doll/VT-18 on head. 1957. $18.00.

Ideal--19" "Miss Revlon" Solid vinyl body, arms and legs. Vinyl head with rooted blonde hair. Blue sleep eyes/lashes. Jointed waist. Pierced ears. High heel feet. Polished nails and toes. Marks: 14R, on head. 1958. Original dress. $18.00.

Ideal--18" "Mrs. Revlon" Mother of the Bride. Solid vinyl one piece body and legs. Vinyl arms and head. Rooted grey hair. Blue sleep eyes/lashes and purple eye shadow. Polished nails. High heel feet. Marks: 14R, on head. 1958. $22.00.

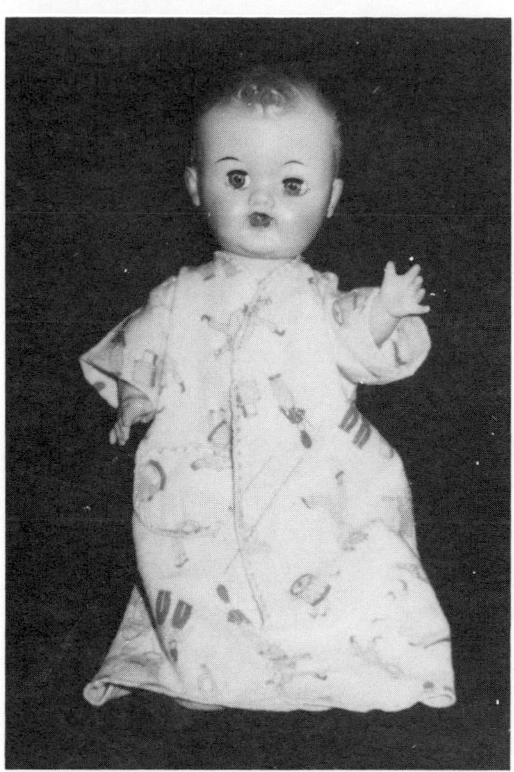

Ideal--12" "Betsy Wetsy" All vinyl with molded, painted brown hair. Big blue sleep eyes/lashes. Open mouth/nurser. Open hands. Baby legs. Individual molded toes. Cries with a coo voice when stomach is pressed and tears roll down Has holes in ears to allow air flow for coo voice. Marks: Ideal Doll/W-C-1-1 on head. 1959. $5.00.

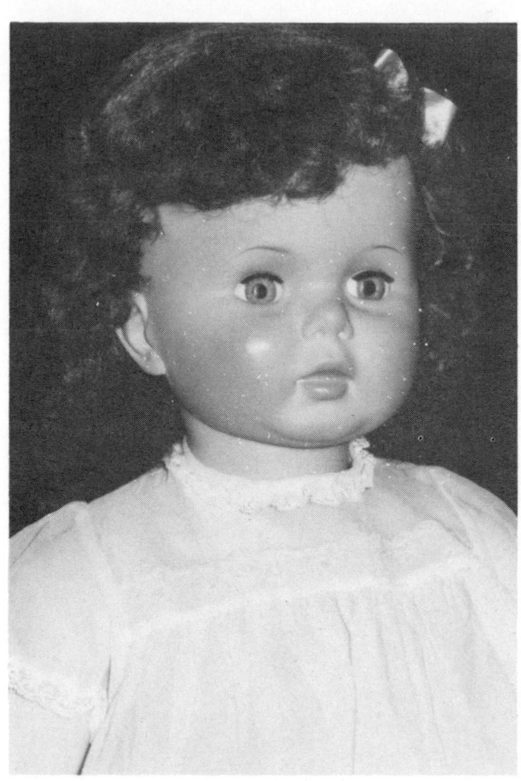

Ideal--32" "Penny Playpal" Plastic body and legs. Vinyl arms and head. Rooted red hair. Blue sleep eyes/lashes. Open/closed mouth. Posable head. Marks: Ideal Doll/B-32-B, on head. Ideal Toy Corp/B-32/Pat. Pend, on back. 1959. $45.00.

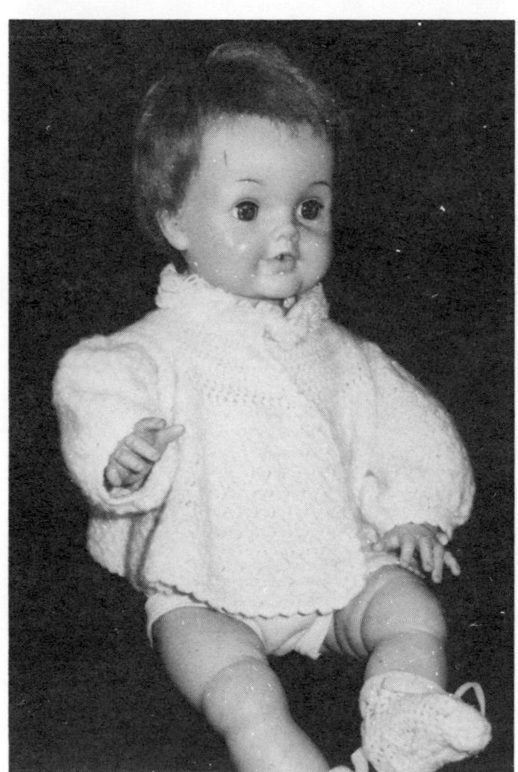

Ideal--23" "Betsy Wetsy" All vinyl with rooted light brown hair. Blue sleep eyes/lashes. Open mouth/nurser. Marks: Ideal Toy Corp/BW-20-F on head. Ideal Toy Corp/BW-20 on body. 1959. $20.00.

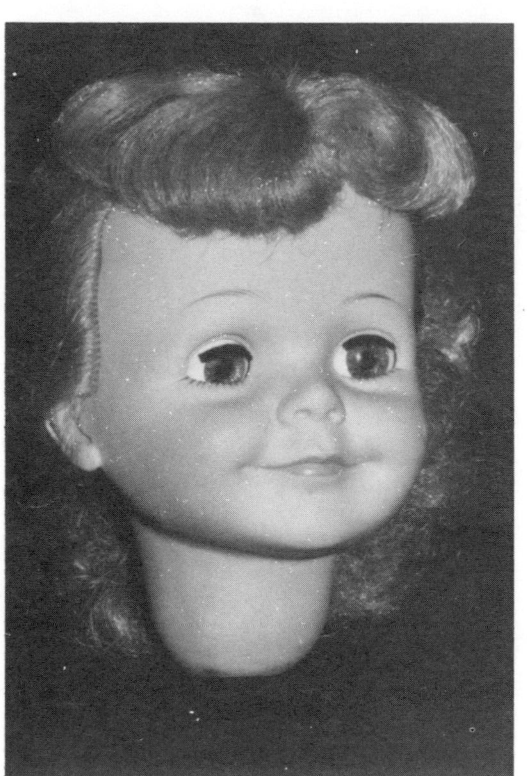

Ideal--25" "Miss Ideal" Plastic body and legs. Vinyl arms and head. Rooted ash blonde hair. Blue sleep eyes/lashes. Closed mouth. Jointed waist, wrists, shoulders, hips and ankles. Marks: Ideal Toy Corp/SP-25-S on head. 1961. This doll came "unstrung" just as camera was ready. We took her picture anyway. $36.00.

Ideal--30" "Pattie Playpal" Plastic body and legs. Vinyl arms and head. Rooted light brown hair. Blue sleep eyes/lashes. 2nd and 3rd fingers curled and molded together. Marks: none. 1961. Original dress. $18.00.

Ideal--18" "Cream Puff" All vinyl with rooted reddish brown hair. Blue sleep eyes/lashes. Closed mouth. Crossed baby legs. Dimpled knees. Individually molded toes. Marks: Ideal Doll/OB-19-2 on head. Ideal Toy Corp/B-19 on back. 1961. $18.00.

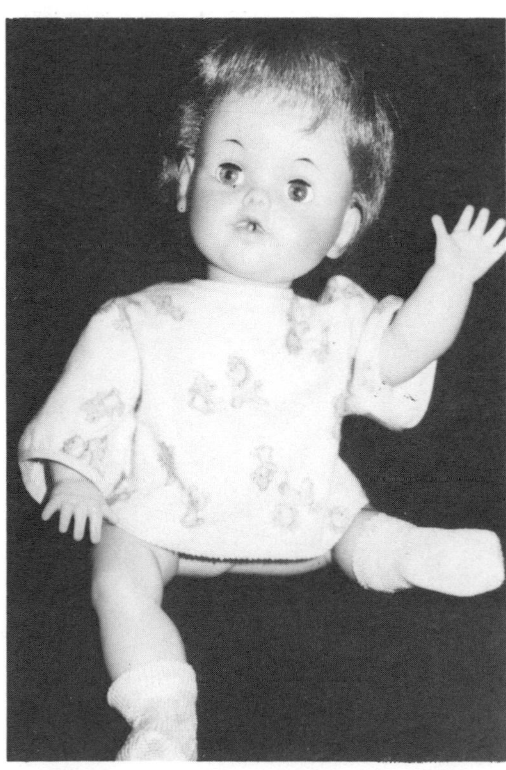

Ideal--13" "Betsy Wetsy" All vinyl with rooted brown hair. Blue sleep eyes/lashes. Open mouth/nurser. Open hands with palms down. Left index finger extended. Both large toes raised above others. Marks: Ideal Toy Corp/O-BW-13-L on head. Ideal Toy Corp/BW-13 on back. 1961. $16.00.

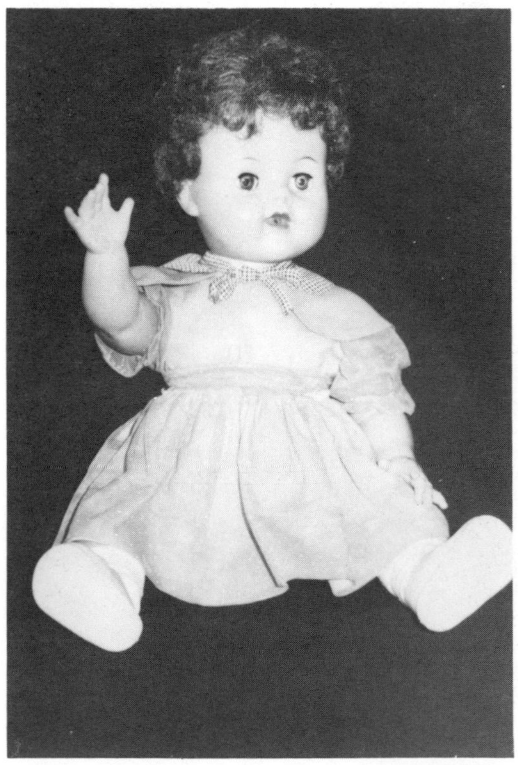

Ideal--20" "Dew Drop" Plastic and vinyl. Rooted brown hair. Deep blue sleep eyes. Open mouth/nurser. Individual toes. Cries tears. Marks: V-S-22/Ideal on head. 1961. $7.00.

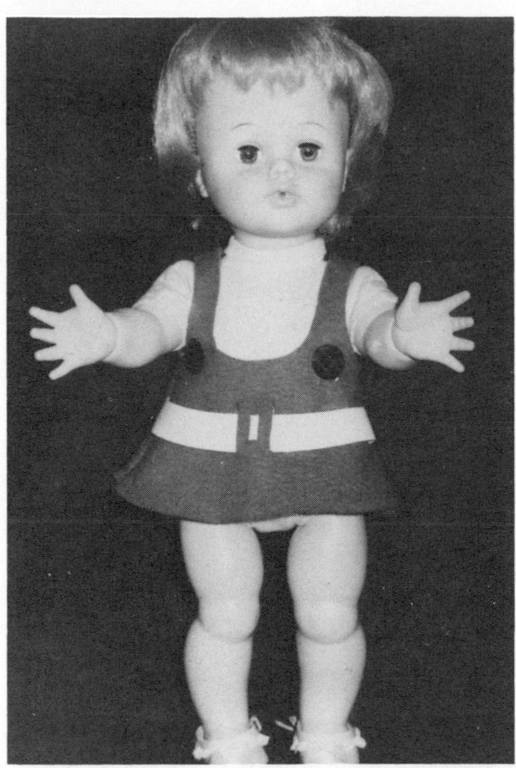

Ideal--16" "Tiny Kissey" Plastic body and legs. Vinyl arms and head. Rooted light blonde hair. Sleep blue eyes/lashes. Jointed wrists. Press arms together and head nods and mouth puckers with a kissing sound. Marks: Ideal Toy Corp/K-L6/3 on head. Original clothes. 1962. $18.00.

Ideal--20" "Thumbelina" Cloth body. Vinyl arms, legs and head. Rooted dark blonde hair. Painted blue eyes. Deep open/closed mouth. Right thumb and index extended. Left fingers curled. Mechanism in center back makes her wiggle. Crier. Marks: Ideal Toy Corp/0 or 9 TT-19, on head. 1962. $12.00.

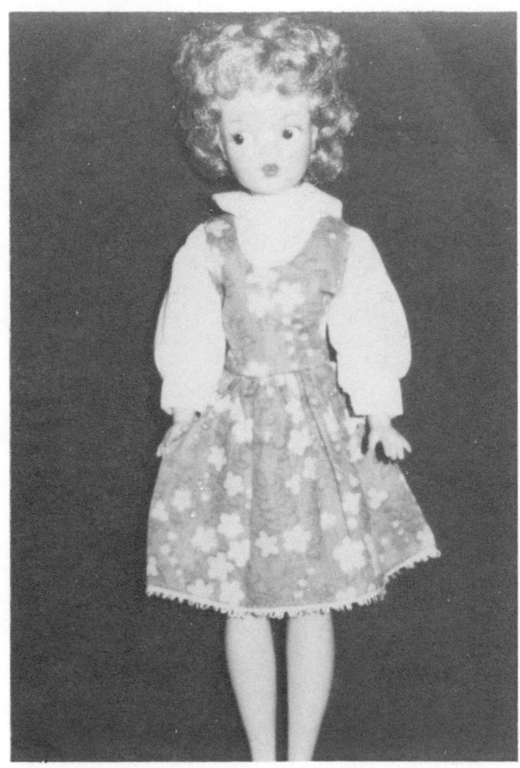

Ideal--12" "Tammy" Plastic and vinyl with rooted blonde hair. Painted blue side glancing eyes. Closed mouth. Medium high heel feet. Marks: Ideal Toy Corp/BS-12 on head. Ideal Toy Corp/BS-12 on back. 1962. $4.00.

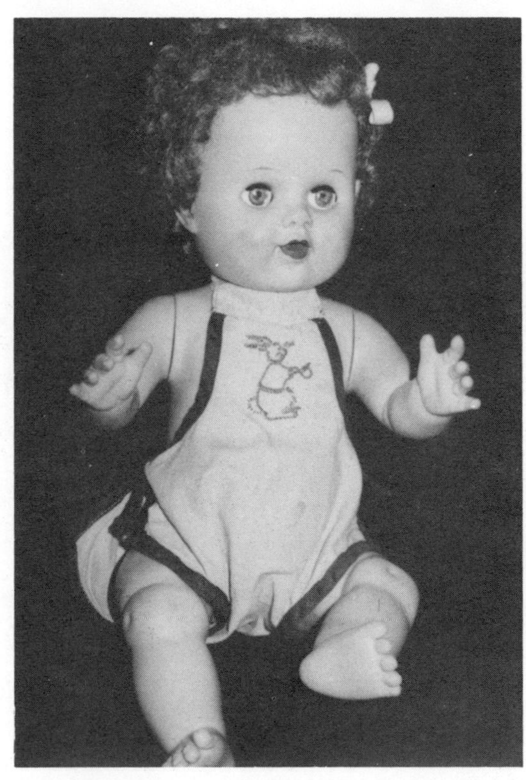

Ideal--16" "Betsy Wetsy" All vinyl with rooted, close curled, light brown hair. Blue sleep eyes/lashes. Open mouth nurser. Individually molded toes. Marks: 37P on head. 1962. Cries tears. $7.00.

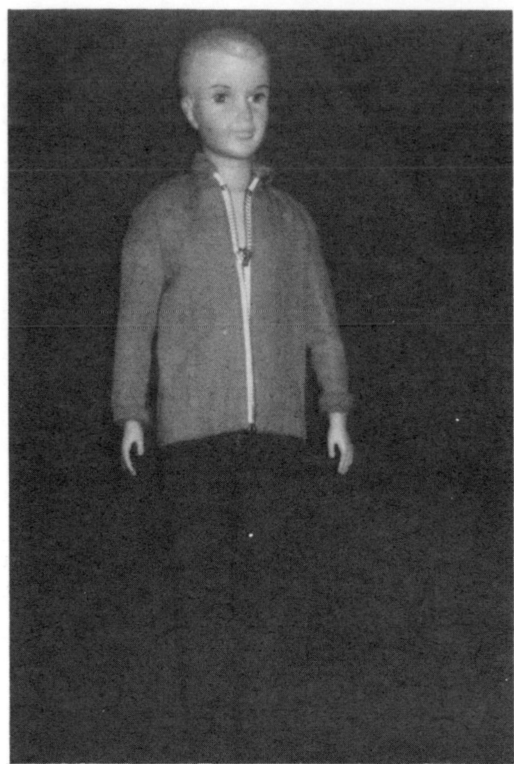

Ideal--12½" "Ted" Plastic body and legs. Vinyl head and arms. Molded and painted light brown hair. Painted brown eyes. Closed mouth. Marks: Ideal Toy Corp/B-12½-M-2. 1963. $4.00.

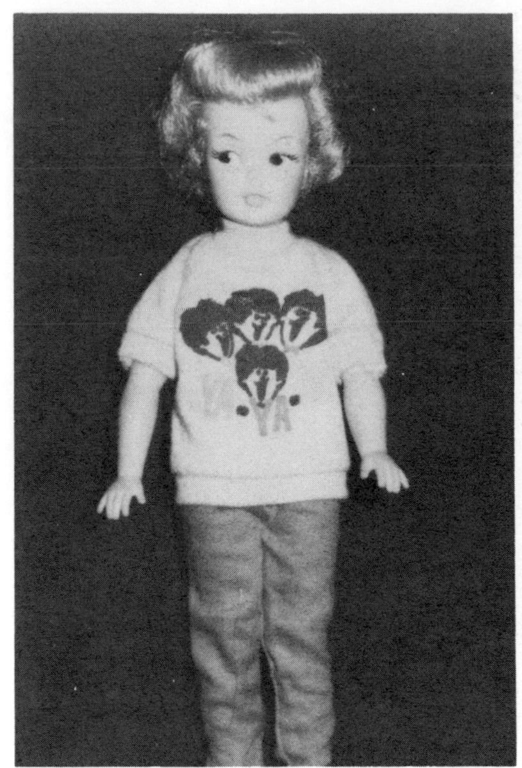

Ideal--9" "Pepper" Plastic body and legs. Vinyl arms and head. Rooted blonde hair. Painted side glancing eyes. Closed mouth. Open hands with palms down. Marks: Ideal Toy Corp/6-9-W/2 on back. Ideal Toy Corp/G9-E on head. 1963. Original clothes. $4.00.

Ideal--12" "Pebbles" Plastic body and legs. Vinyl arms and head. Rooted ash blonde hair. Painted eyes, side glancing. Marks: Hanna Barbera Products Inc/Ideal Toy Corp/F.S.-11-2 on neck. Hanna Barbera Products Inc/Ideal Toy Corp/F S-11½ on back. 1963. $7.00. (Courtesy of Vickie Johnston)

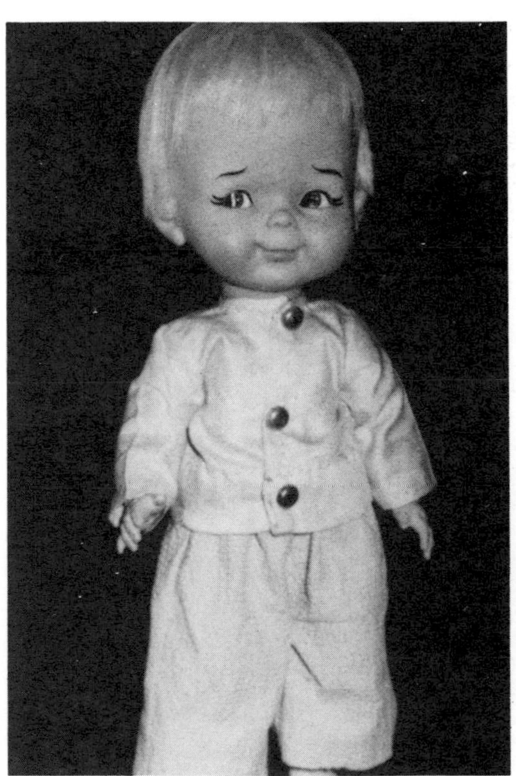

Ideal--16" "BamBam" All vinyl with rooted blonde hair. Painted, side glancing brown eyes. this doll may be on the wrong body as I have never seen another one that does not have the right hand molded to hold a club. Marks: Hanna Barbera Prods Inc/Ideal Toy Corp/BB-17, on head. 1963. $7.00.

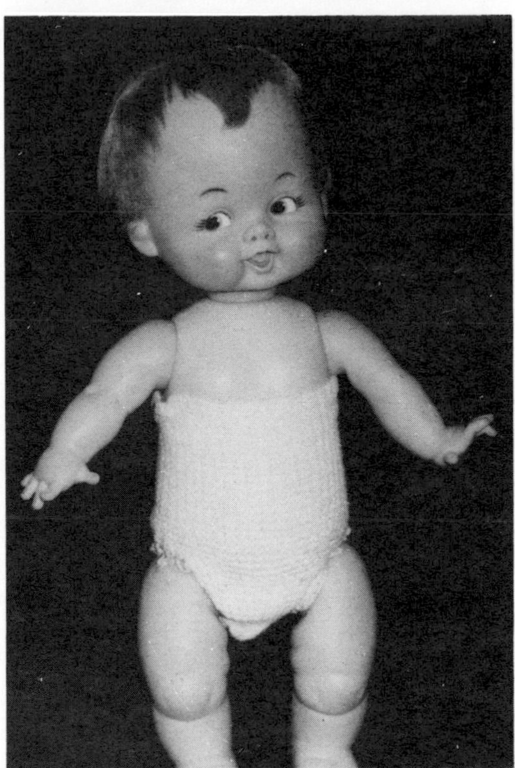

Ideal--15" "Pebbles" Plastic body. Vinyl arms, legs and head. Rooted blonde hair. Posable head. Painted, side glancing blue eyes. Open/closed mouth with molded tongue. Marks: Hanna Barbera Prods/Ideal Toy Corp/FS-16-J-1, on head. Hanna Barbera Prods/Ideal Toy Corp/FS-16-J, on body. 1963. $7.00.

Ideal--17" "Cuddly Kissy" Cloth body. Vinyl arms, legs and head. Press stomach and hands come together, head forward and lips pucker and she makes a kissing sound. Right 3rd finger curled into palm. Right toes curled under. Marks: Ideal Toy Corp/KB-17-E on head. 1964. $30.00.

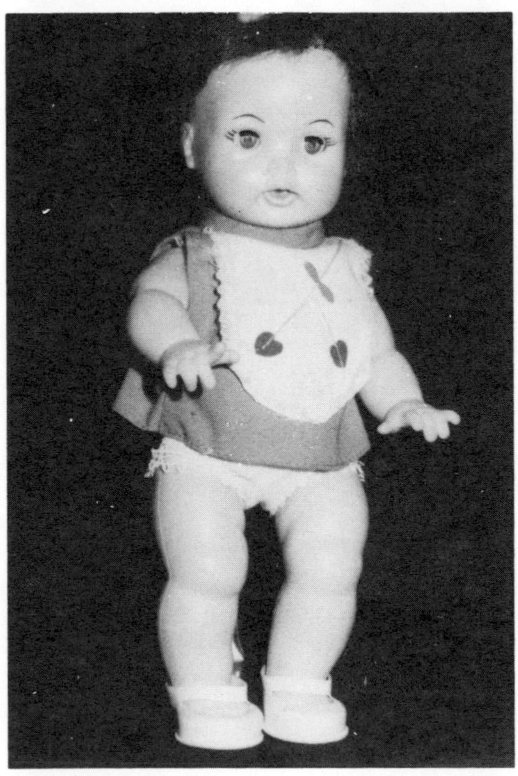

Ideal--9" "Baby Betsy Wetsy" All vinyl with rooted brown hair. Blue sleep eyes/molded lashes. Both index fingers extended. Open mouth/nurser. Marks: 1964/Ideal Toy Corp/B-W-9-4, on head. Ideal Toy Corp/1964/BW-9, on body. $4.00.

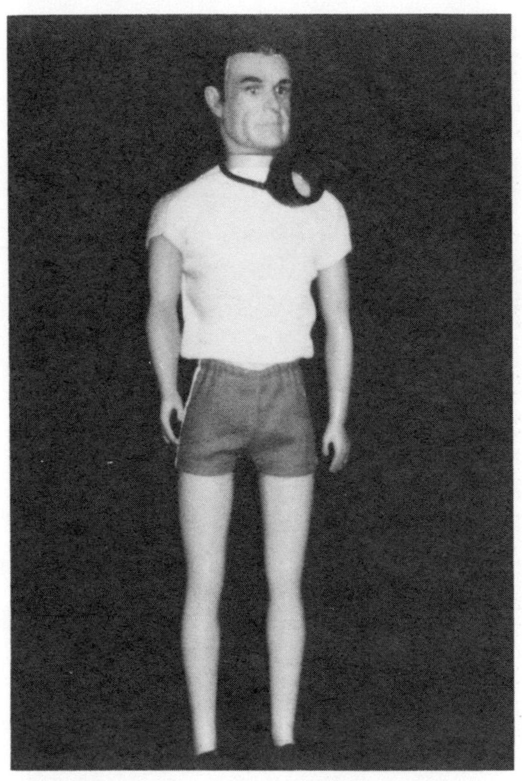

Ideal--12½" "007-James Bond" Plastic body and legs. Vinyl arms and head. Molded hair. Painted eyes. Open hands with right toward body (arms snap up) to hold gun and other accessories. Marks: Ideal Toy Corp/B-12½-2. 1965. Mfg'd for A.C. Gilbert Co. $30.00.

Ideal--12½" "Illya Kuryakin, #2 Man From U.N.C.L.E." Plastic body and legs. Vinyl arms and head. Molded blonde hair. Painted features. Marks: K-99 on head. Clothes Tag: Made In Spain. 1965. Illya Kuryakin was portrayed by David McCallum on the NBC-TV show "Man from U.N.C.L.E. 1965. $30.00.

Ideal--12" "Miss Clairol, Glamour Misty" Plastic and vinyl with rooted hair. Painted side glancing eyes. High heel feet. Marks: 1965/Ideal Toy Co/W-12-3 on head. 1/1965/Ideal, in an oval and M-12 on hip. $5.00.

Ideal--15" "Honeymoon" Stuffed cloth body. Vinyl arms, legs and head. Rooted white yarn hair. Painted side glancing black/yellow eyes. Open/closed mouth with molded tongue. Open hands. Left hand little finger extended. Marks: 1965 C.T.-NY NS/Ideal Toy Corp/HM 14-2-2H. $18.00.

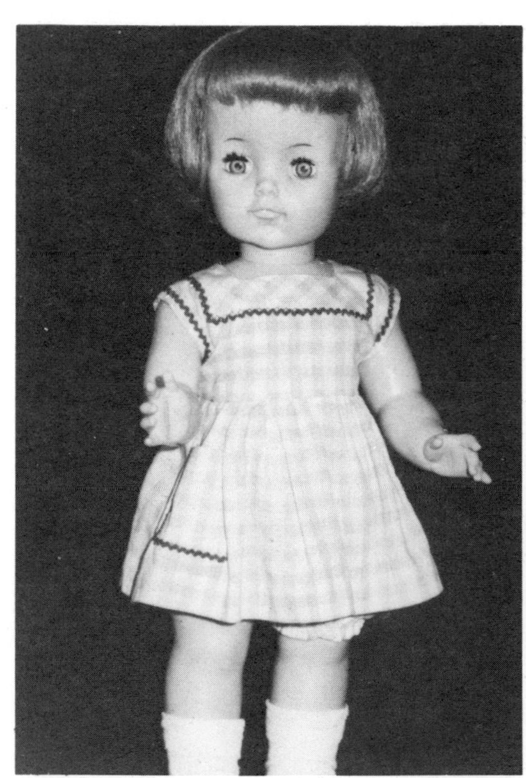

Ideal--18" "Goody Two Shoes" Plastic body and legs. Vinyl arms and head. Rooted dark blonde hair. Blue sleep eyes/long lashes. Closed mouth. Battery operated walker. On and off switch on back. Battery cover plate marked: 1965/Ideal Toy Corp/WT-18/Pat. Pending. Marks: 1965/Ideal Toy Corp/T-W-18-4-L-H4 on head. $25.00.

Ideal--18" "Betsy Wetsy" All vinyl with rooted blonde hair. Blue sleep eyes/lashes. Open mouth/nurser. Index of left hand curled. Index and little finger of right hand extended. Marks: 1965/Ideal Toy Corp/TD-1-E-W-2, on head. Ideal Toy Corp/Td-18, on body. $30.00.

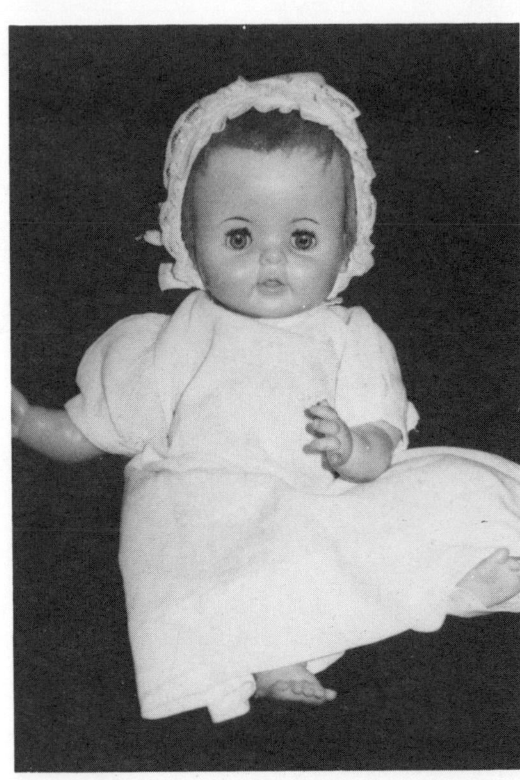

Ideal--14½" Baby Snoozie" Cloth body. Vinyl arms, legs and head. Rooted light brown hair. Knob in center of back makes her wiggle and open and close her eyes. Press back(bulb) and she cries. Marks: 1965/Ideal Toy Corp/YTT-14-E, on head. On Knob: Ideal Toy Corp/U S Pat No 3,029,552. $9.00.

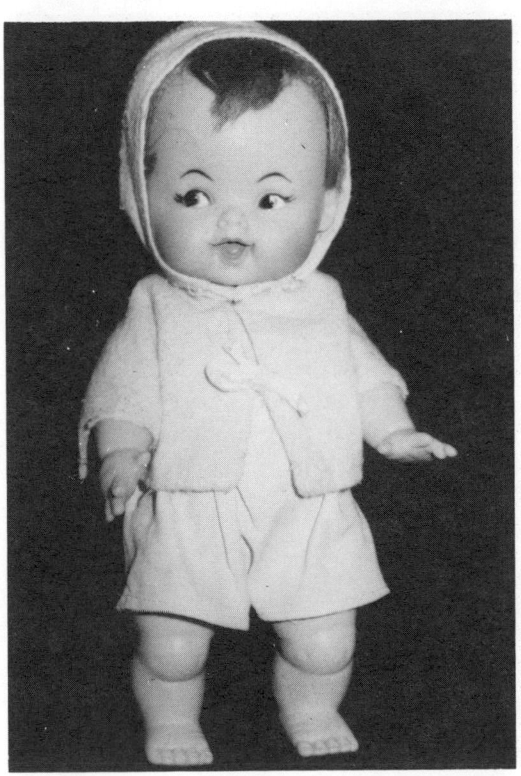

Ideal--8" "Pebbles" Plastic body and legs. Vinyl arms and head. Rooted dark blonde hair. Open mouth with molded tongue. Right hand wide open palm toward body. Left hand palm down and 2nd finger curled. Marks: Ideal Toy Corp/FS-8¼/1965, on head. Hanna Barbera/ Ideal Toy Corp/FS-9 on body. $7.00.

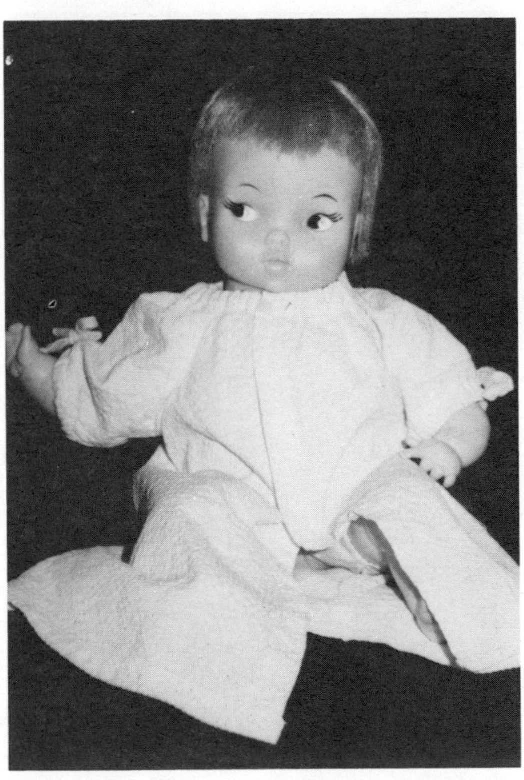

Ideal--15" "Tabatha" Cloth body. Vinyl arms, legs and head. Rooted dark blonde hair. Open/closed mouth. Right index, 2nd and 3rd fingers curled. Left thumb and index extended. Toes individually molded. Marks: 1966/Ideal Toy Corp/T A T-14-H-62 or 82. Samantha's Baby from TV "Bewitched". $40.00.

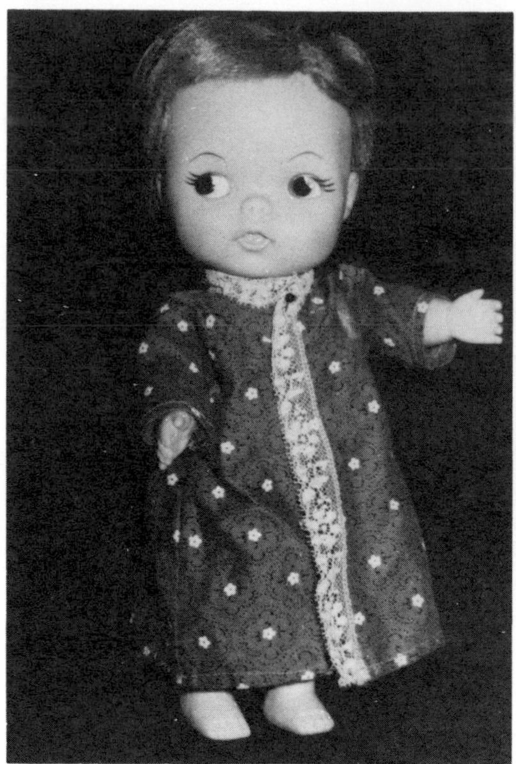

Ideal--9½" "Honeyball" All vinyl with oversized head. Rooted brown hair. Blue, side glancing eyes. Open/closed mouth with molded tongue. Arms move individually or together. Legs joints set deep into hips. Marks: 1966 Ideal Toy Corp/M-9-H-4, on head.$4.00.

Ideal--15" "Tearful Thumbelina" 1966. Stuffed vinyl coated body. Vinyl arms, legs and head. Rooted blonde hair. Blue sleep eyes/lashes. Press her stomach and she crys tears. Marks: Ideal Toy Corp/OTW-14-W, on head. Ideal Toy Corp/US Pat #3,029,552 on knob. $18.00.

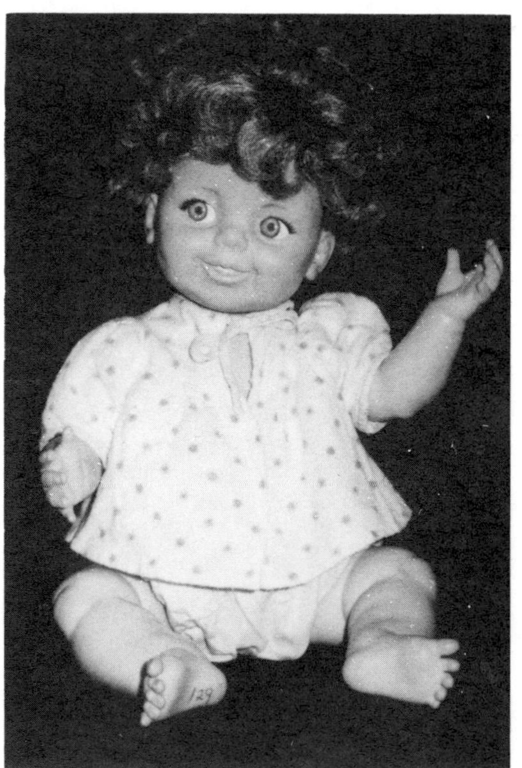

Ideal--16" "Baby Giggles" Plastic body. Vinyl arms, legs and head. Blue open eyes that move side to side. Open mouth. Open hands with all fingers slightly curled. Marks: 1966/Ideal Toy Corp/BG-18-H-118 on head. 1968/Ideal Toy Corp/BG-16 on right hip. $22.00.

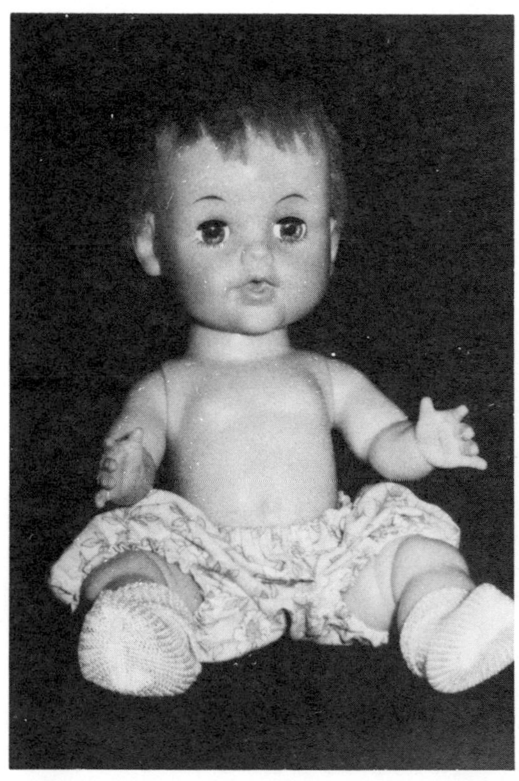

Ideal--12" "Tiny Baby Kissy" All vinyl with rooted light brown hair. Blue sleep eyes/lashes. Open mouth/nurser. Individual toes. Posable head. Pressure on stomach makes mouth pucker for a kiss. Marks: Ideal Doll Corp/K-12*W, on head. Ideal Doll/12, on body. 1966. $16.00.

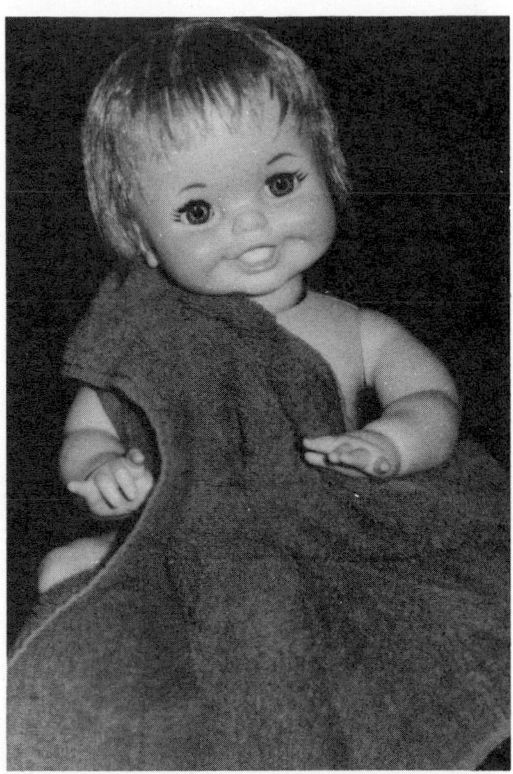

Ideal--18" "Tubbsy" Plastic body and legs. Vinyl arms and head. Open mouth with two lower teeth. Battery operated. Hands splash in water, head attached to mechanism and bobs side to side. Holes in feet for water to drain. Marks: 1966/Ideal Toy Corp/B-T-E-18-II79/ on head. 1967/Ideal Toy Corp/BT-18/2 on back. $18.00.

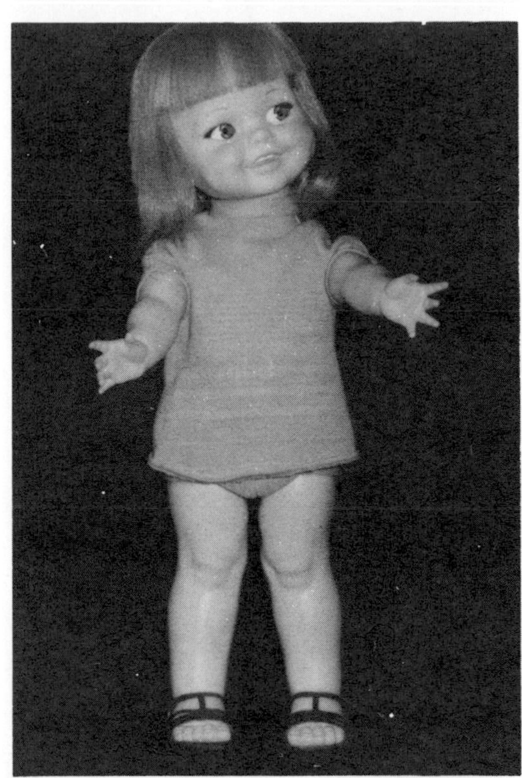

Ideal--18" "Giggles Toddler" Plastic and vinyl. Right hand index and little finger extended. Push arms out, her head tilts and she giggles. Pull arms back toward body and the head tilts in the opposite direction. Marks: Ideal Toy Corp/GG 18 H 77/1967 on head. Ideal Toy Corp/GG-18 on hip. Original clothes. $25.00.

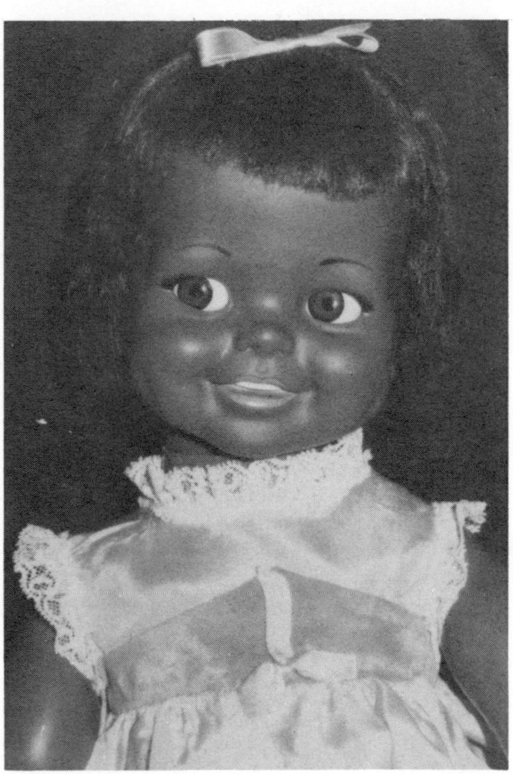

Ideal--17" "Giggles" Plastic and vinyl. Rooted black hair. Brown flirty eyes/lashes. Open/closed mouth with painted teeth. Push arms back and head tilts and she giggles. Marks: Ideal Toy Corp/GG-18-H-77/1967 on head. Ideal Toy Corp/GG-18 on hip. Original clothes. $30.00. (Courtesy Allin's Collection)

Ideal--17" "Daisy" All foam body. Vinyl head with rooted orange hair. Big vivid blue stationary eyes/heavy lashes. Open mouth with two molded teeth. Marks: 1967/Ideal Toy Corp/F-18-F-CM-891, on head. Replaced right hand. $6.00.

Ideal--16" "Pixie" One piece foam body, legs and arms. Vinyl gauntlet hands. Vinyl head with rooted red hair. Painted blue side glancing eyes/lashes. Open/closed mouth. Marks: 1967/Ideal Toy Corp/F-18-P-H-85 on head. $7.00. (Courtesy Allin's Collection)

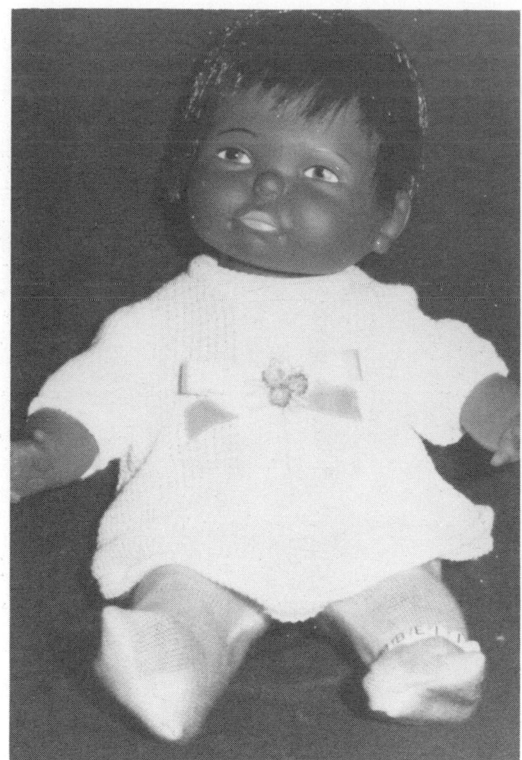

Ideal--9" "Newborn Thumbelina" Original clothes includes name band around leg. 1967. $7.00. (Courtesy Allin's Collection)

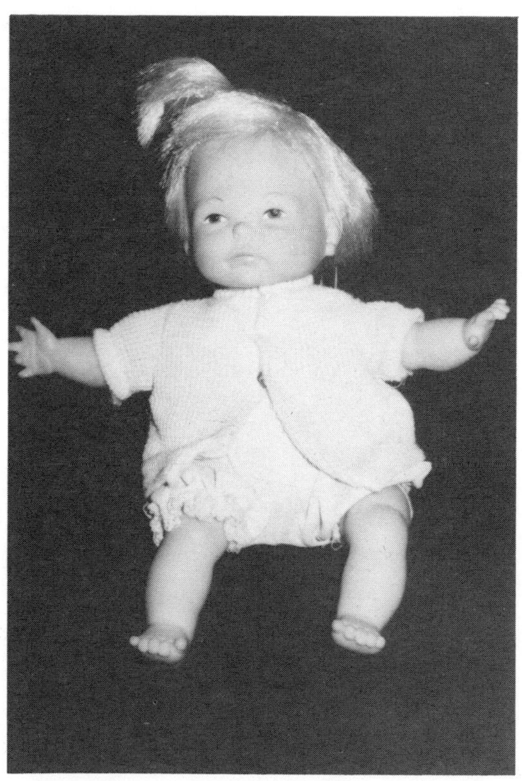

Ideal--10½" "Newborn Thumbelina" Foam filled cloth body. Vinyl arms, legs and head. Rooted blonde hair. Blue painted eyes. Closed mouth. Pull string located in center of back makes her squirm. Marks: 1967/Ideal in circle. TT-8-H-108 on head. Tag on body: Newborn Thumbelina/ Ideal. An original top. $5.00.

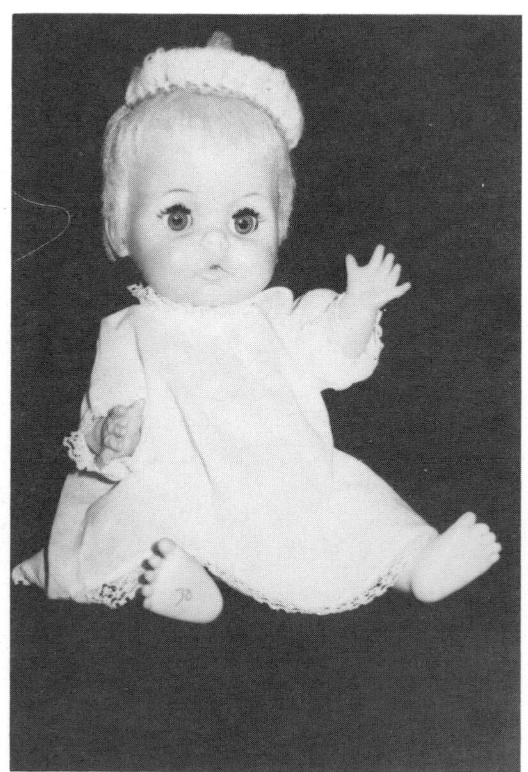

Ideal--11" "Tearie Betsy" All vinyl with rooted blonde hair. Blue sleep eyes/lashes. Open mouth nurser. Individual molded toes. Marks: 1967/Ideal Toy Corp/BW-12-H-86 on head. Ideal Doll, on back. $6.00.

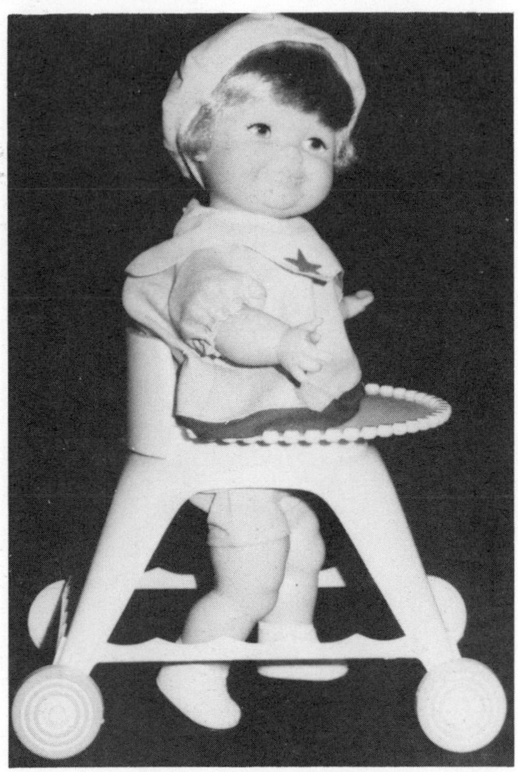

Ideal--10½" "Toddler Thumbelina" Cloth body. Vinyl arms, legs and head. Rooted blonde hair. Molded and painted shoes and socks. Pull string in center of back, makes legs move to walk and head move. Marks: 1968/Ideal Toy Corp/BTT9-H-124, on head. Tag: Toddler Thumbelina/Ideal, in an oval. Original clothes. $6.00.

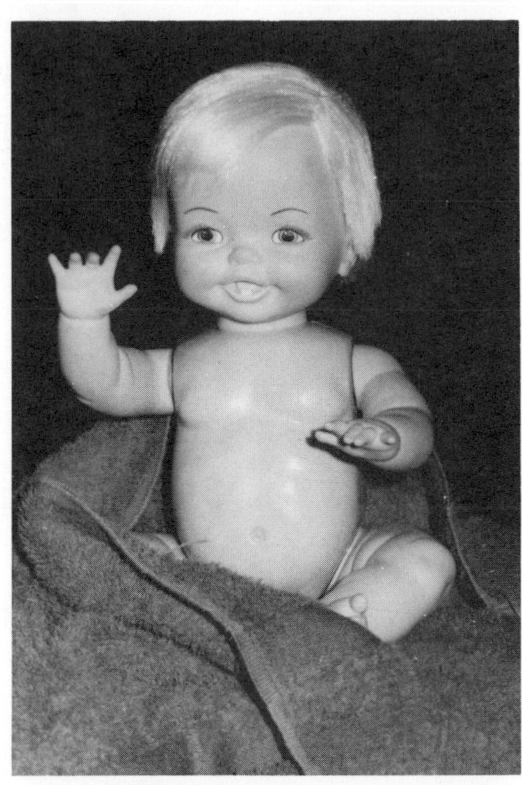

Ideal--14" "April Showers" Plastic body. Vinyl arms, legs and head. Rooted white hair. Painted blue eyes. Open mouth with two painted and molded lower teeth. Battery operated. Splashes in water and turns head. Holes in heels for water to drain. Marks: 1968/Ideal Toy Corp/Hong Kong/BT-11-H-12-S, on head. $22.00.

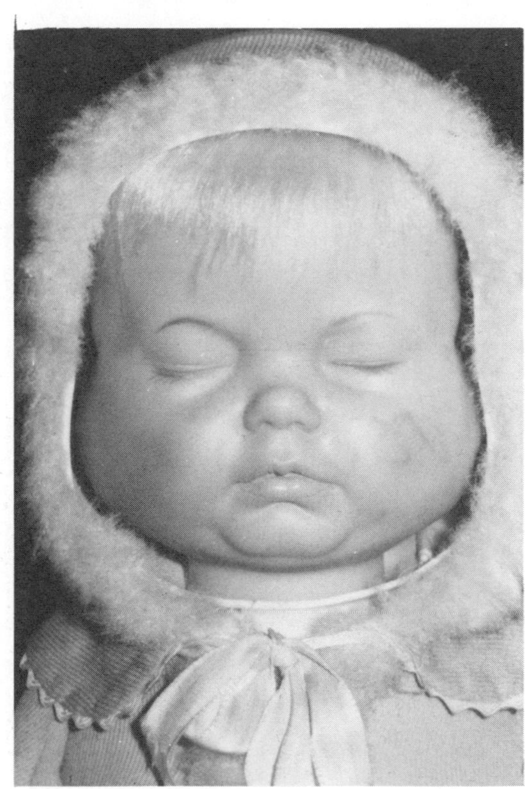

Ideal--22" "Little Lost Baby" Foam body. Encased plastic legs. Stuffed arms. Vinyl three sided head. Plastic head cover. Vinyl gauntlet hands. Lever at base of back neck controls turning head. Battery holder on lower back controls voice. Marks: Tag: Little Lost Baby/1968 Ideal Toy Corp. $22.00. 3rd face on Page 176.

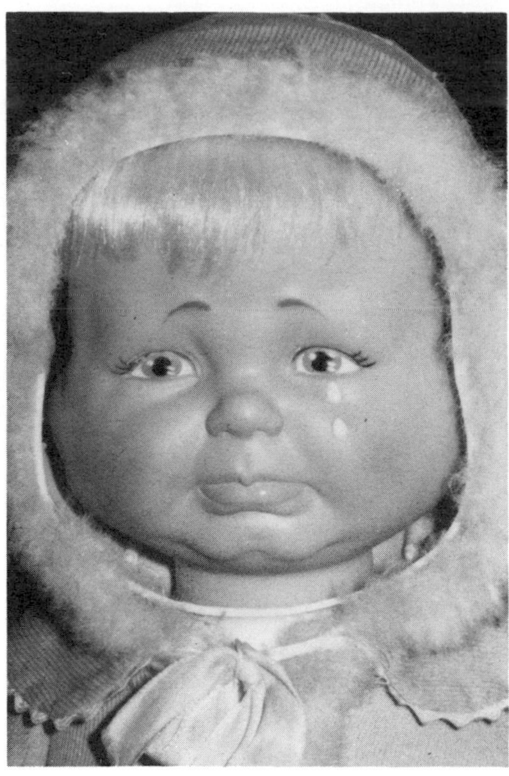

Ideal--22" " Little Lost Baby"

Ideal--18" "Beautiful Crissy" All vinyl with rooted black hair. Hair has grow feature with knob located in the center of the back. Brown sleep eyes/lashes. Open mouth with painted teeth. Marks: 1968/Ideal Toy Corp/GH-17-H-120 on head. 1969/Ideal Toy Corp/GH-18/US Pat #3,162,976 on back. Original clothes. $6.00.

Ideal--16" "Velvet" Plastic body and legs. Vinyl arms and head. Rooted blonde hair with "grow" feature. Knob in center of back makes hair grow. Button in center of stomach makes hair go back into head. Lavendar sleep eyes/lashes. 2nd and 3rd fingers molded together. Marks: 1969 Ideal Toy Corp/GH-15-H-157. Orig. dress. $7.00.

Ideal--8" "Fashion Flatsy Dale" All bendable flat vinyl. Rooted blue hair. Decal blue eyes/lashes. Molded high heel feet. Marks: Ideal in an oval/1969/US Patent/No 3,500,578/Hong Kong/ 4/4/ on back. Original clothes. $3.00.

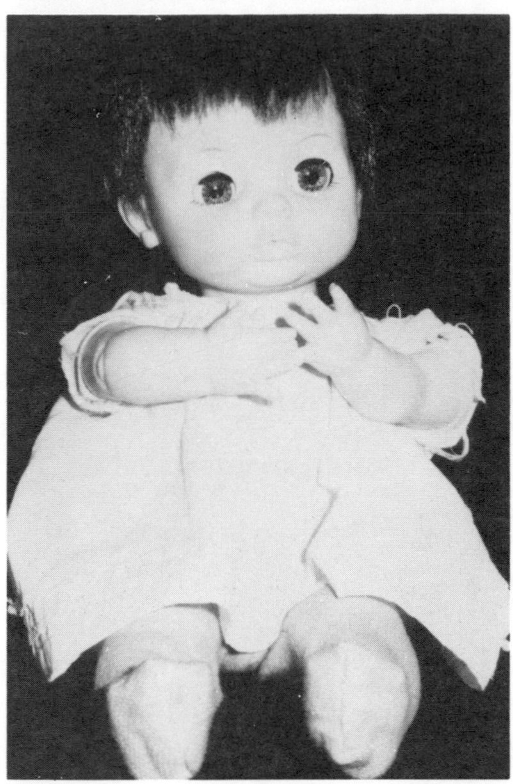

Ideal--10½" "Kissing Thumbelina" Foam, cloth covered body. Vinyl arms, legs and head. Pull arms forward. Release button in back, arms fly back with a kissing sound. Pull string makes her wiggle. Marks: 1969/Ideal Toy Corp/KT-9-H-154 /Hong Kong on head. Tag: Kissin' Thumbelina/Ideal. $6.00.

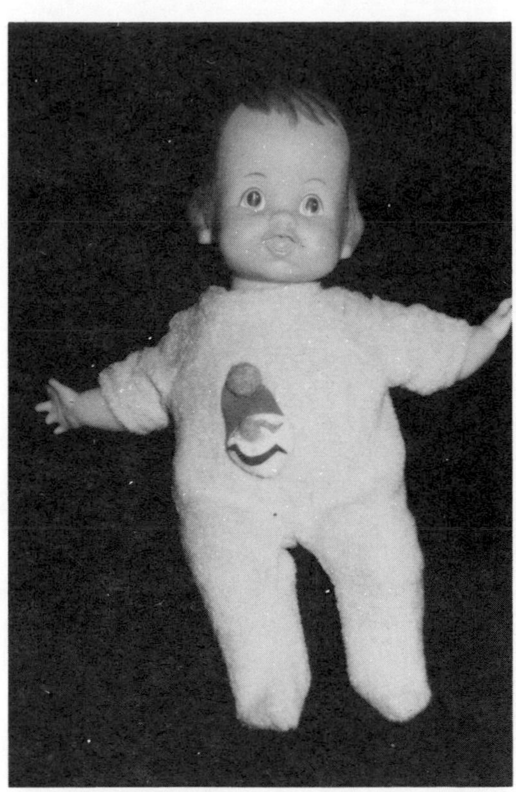

Ideal--10" "Tiny Thumbelina" Cloth body. Vinyl arms, legs and head. Painted eyes. Open/closed mouth. Pull string between shoulders makes doll squirm. Molded light brown hair. Marks: 1970/Ideal Toy Corp/STT-9-H-180/Hong (S2, in a square) Kong. Original clothes. $6.00.

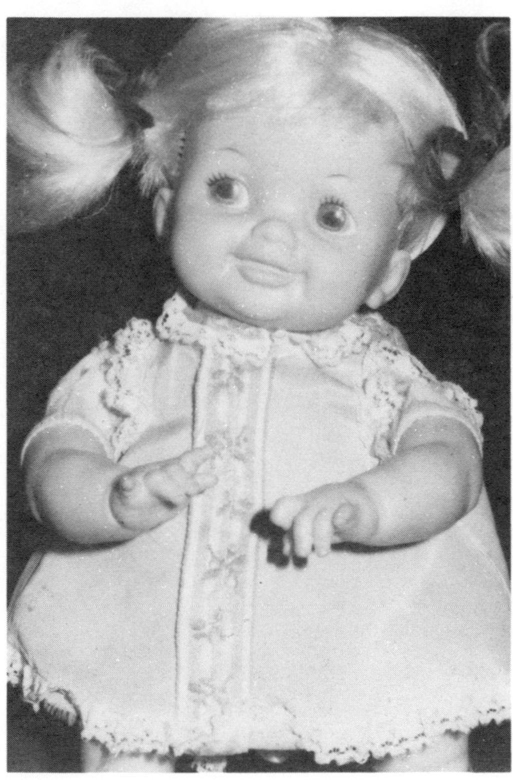

Ideal--10" "In A Minute Thumbelina" Cloth body. Vinyl hands and feet. Molded on shoes and socks. Vinyl head with rooted blonde hair. Painted blue eyes. Open/closed mouth. Pull string operated. Arms wave up and down and head rotates. Marks: 1970/Ideal Toy Corp/IT-9-H-175/Hong Kong. R 57 on foot. $6.00.

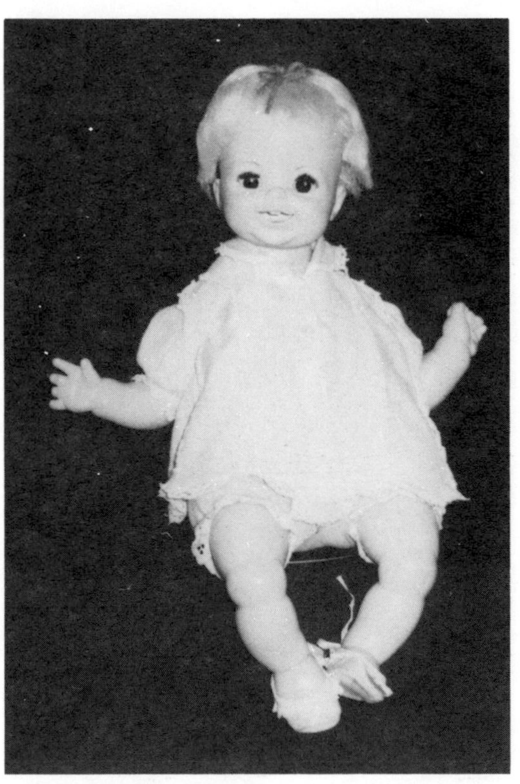

Ideal--16" "Patti Playful" Foam stuffed cloth body. Vinyl arms, legs and head. Rooted white hair. Black eyes/long lashes. Wide open mouth with two upper teeth. Works like a puppet. Yawns, claps, waves, sucks thumb, or pacifier, opens and closes mouth. Marks: 1970/Ideal Toy Corp/LL-16-H-162, on head. $35.00.

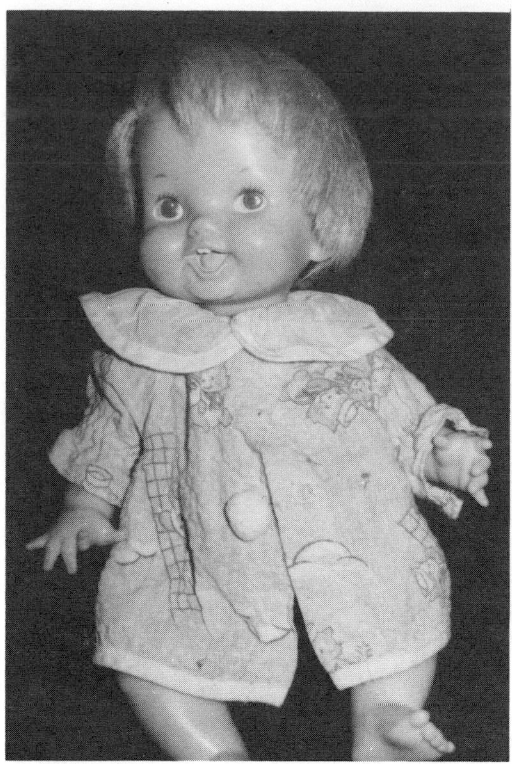

Ideal--9" "Baby Belly Button" Plastic body. Vinyl arms, legs and head. Rooted blonde hair. Marks: 1970/Ideal Toy Corp/E-9-1-H-164 /Hong Kong, on head. Ideal Toy Corp/Hong Kong/2A-0155 on body. $4.00.

Ideal--16" "Play N' Jane" Plastic body, arms and legs. Right arm molded in bent position. All fingers on right hand molded together. Rooted red nylon hair. Painted green eyes. Marks: 1971/Ideal Toy Corp/Tic-16-P-H-191, on head. 1971/Ideal Toy Corp/TIC-16, on body. $9.00.

Ideal--15" "Dina" Plastic body and legs. Vinyl arms and head. Rooted blonde hair with grow feature. Knob on center of back. Marks: Ideal Toy Corp/MG-15/US Pat 3162976/Other Pat. Pend./Hong Kong on back. 1971/Ideal Toy Corp/GHD-15-H-186/Hong Kong on head. $25.00. (Courtesy Allin's Collection)

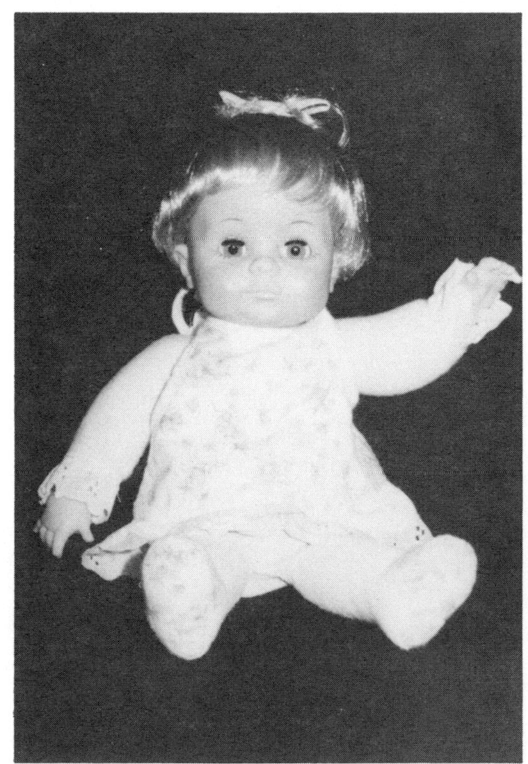

Ideal--12" "Lazy Dazy" Stuffed cloth arms and legs. Vinyl hands and head. Rooted blonde hair. Dark blue sleep eyes/lashes. Closed mouth with overhanging upper lip. Marks: 1971/Ideal Toy Corp/Ideal LB-12-H-197/Hong Kong, on head. Tag: Lazy Dazy/Ideal, in an oval. Orig clothes. $4.00.

Ideal's Shirley Temple Doll

The Shirley Temple doll was designed by the famous doll designer, Bernard Lipfert. Bernard Lipfert also designed many, many other dolls for almost all toymakers of his time. These included such dolls as Alexander's Dionne Quints, Effanbee's Dy Dee, Patsy, Lovums, and Bubbles. He also designed many "look-a-likes", copies of the originals of a good seller. For example he designed E.I. Horsman's "Baby Dimples", a copy of Effanbee's Bubbles. Hauled into court by Effanbee, Horsman lost their case. Many of the Shirley Temple look-a-likes were designed by him, also.

The first ad to appear on the Shirley Temple doll was in 1934. Altogether there were twelve press ads that showed Shirley and the dolls. Both Shirley and the dolls were dressed alike but not exactly alike. The first was a prototype that had fatter cheeks, a narrower mouth and a much more pointed chin, plus much darker hair, that was not in tight curls. These dolls were made before Mr. Lipfert had completed casting his Shirley head and the early press releases on the prototype dolls had a picture of Shirley's own head superimposed onto that of the doll.

Ideal made the composition Shirley Temple dolls over a period of six years, 1934 through 1940. The favorite size was the 13" introduced in 1935. There are three or four very rare Shirleys: the extremes in size: the 11" and the 27", also the Shirley Babies and toddlers.

There are variations in sizes due to the fact that wood pulp composition was pretty reliable in most ways except for shrinkage and sometimes a 17" mold would produce a 16" or 16½" doll but as a general rule the ten sizes made were, 11", 13", 15", 16", 17", 18", 22", 23", 25", and 27". There were six sizes of the Shirley Baby, at age two, sizes 16" to 25" and all had flirty eyes.

The Shirley Dolls had a variety of markings and the most common is a curled Shirley Temple with Ideal in a diamond on the body. Or a curved Shirley Temple with a mold number beneath that, on the back. Not all the dolls are marked this way but it is the most common.

Sometimes the body or the head was unmarked and as the dolls came down the factory line two of these unmarked sections got together and a genuine "unmarked" Shirley was made.

In 1941 Ideal sold some body molds to Alexander and included were some with the Shirley Temple marked out but the 13 was still visible. But Bernard Lipfert also designed a McGuffey Anna type head for Ideal and some of these are on the Shirley Temple bodies. The doll's name was Nancy and she had human hair braids, an open mouth with four teeth.

A word here: there are cases of someone having an unmarked and a marked Shirley Temple of the same size and they are changing the heads and thereby making two marked Shirleys

Paint finish on Shirleys included a matte to a rosy gloss finish. Some have considerable eyeshadow that is gray to black. Some have a single lash line above and below the eye, along with a few lash strokes. Teeth ran from very well molded ones to just painted with poor outlines. Tongues were of a hard rubber with gloss paint or they are felt. Eyes ran from a pale golded honey to a true brown also a metallic hazel to a true green. Most Shirley Temple eyes tend to cloud over in time as moisture absorbed by the composition tends to change to humidity and enters the eye cases. A few drops of sewing machine or gun oil will help them a lot. The 13" up, came with or without flirty eyes. Wigs were mohair of pale golden yellow, ash blonde and a strawberry blonde.

All the dolls were very well promoted at the time each of Shirley's films were released and there were some extra special issues dolls, in relation to these films or for special events in the life of Shirley, herself. All of Shirley's films are listed:

Little Miss Marker
Blue Bird
Now I'll Tell
Now and Forever
Fort Apache
Honeymoon
Adventures in Baltimore
Story of Sea Biscuit
Kathleen
That Hogan Girl
Kiss And Tell
Young People
Kiss For Corliss
Mr. Belveder Goes To College
Bachelor & The Bobby Soxer
Captain January
Wee Willie Winkle
Heidi
Rebecca of Sunnybrook Farm
Little Colonel
Curly Top
Little Miss Broadway
Baby Take A Bow
Poor Little Rich Girl
Stowaway
Bright Eyes
Littlest Rebel
Just Around The Corner
Stand Up & Cheer
Our Little Girl
Susannah Of The Mounties

Of the special issues, the first was Stand Up and Cheer and is now the famous dancing dress. Next came Shirley's own 6th birthday, in April 1935 and called the Sixth Birthday Doll. There were many contests around the nation before and during the release of this doll.

In April of 1936 came the Shirley Texas Centennial Ranger Doll, or as it is called the Cowgirl doll. 1937 brought out the special "alike" dolls that were awarded to the winners of the national contest conducted to find little girls who most resembled Shirley and her hairdo.

Next came the Wee Willie Winkie doll dressed in Highlander costume, then came Heidi, who was dressed in short and long sleeves, had either cross stitch or rick rack on her costume. After Heidi came the doll with Shirley's own new hair style from the movie Little Miss Broadway, with the curls pulled to the side and tied with a ribbon.

Lucky Penny was next and was for the film called Just Around the Corner, which had formally been named Lucky Penny. The hair style for this doll was two rows of curls in the back instead of the earlier mass of curls from the top of the head.

One special issue was a chocolate brown, painted eyed Shirley called Marama. This doll has black yarn hair, glued on and a picture of one is included in this section. This doll represents the little doll in the movie The Hurricane that the boy Terangi treasured to remind him of his love for the real Marama, which was played by Shirley Temple.

The last movie special issue was the Little Princess Doll for the movie The Little Princess. But there were special releases of the dolls besides promotions in relation for a movie, for example the Storybook series: Snow White, Cinderella and Goldilocks, with a similiar head but it lacks the dimples.

The Shirley Baby came with a cloth body and a composition shoulder plate and head. Some of the arms are all composition and some have cloth upper arms and also some had hard rubber arms and legs. She came with molded, painted yellow hair or had a blonde glued on wig. At first, the wigs had baby thin hair but later they had a mass of curls all over the head. The babies had flirty eyes and more cheek area and a thinner mouth. They all had the typical Shirley dimples.

There is a toddler Shirley Temple and it is rather scarce because not too many of them were made. She has straight legs on a chubby composition body and the dimples are just below the mouth line, on the cheeks. She also had very deeply molded knee dimples. She had a MaMa cryer and is marked with a 73 over the Shirley Temple, on the head and body.

There are foreign Shirleys as the U.S. laws did not cover infringement in other countries. Japan has a composition with molded, tightly curled hair, some were smiling and some had a sober expression but they all had both arms bent. These came in 6" to 10" sizes. Germany had a celluloid Shirley head on a composition body that is marked ST/Germany.

Many, many imitations of the Shirley Temple doll (and some of these were designed by Bernard Lipfert) came onto the market and due to weak U.S. laws of the day and a very competitive market, most of the doll makers got away with it. For example Egee's Miss Charming or Horsman's Shirley (which included a Shirley button and dressed in pantaloons), but the most competitive to Ideal's Shirley Temple was Madame Alexander's The Little Colonel. The Alexander Little Colonel campaign was a tie in with a line of Little Colonel clothes and taken from Anne Fellows Johnston's famous book The Little Colonel but the doll just happened to be released at the same time Shirley Temple's movie the Little Colonel was being promoted. Ideal sued Madame Alexander for infringment but lost the case as Madame Alexander proved she had used the book and had "permission of the heirs of Anne Fellows Johnston".

Another time Madame Alexander appeared to take advantage of the situation was the release of a very lovely Little Princess doll that was 29" tall and put it out at the same time as Shirley Temple's Little Princess movie.

Most of the Shirley Temple look-a-likes had fatter bodies, were of all composition and could have brown, blue or green eyes. Excluding a few major companies, most of these look-a-like dolls were cheaply made.

Shirley Temple and husband John Agar vetoed Ideals plans on releasing a hard plastic Shirley, on the birthdate of their daughter, Linda Susan, in January 1948. But received permission and in the fall of 1957, when the child stars films were being run on TV and with Ideal as one of the sponsors, started promoting the new Shirley Temple doll.

They were of rigid vinyl with rooted saran hair and had pale hazel eyes. The back of the hair was left in a mass of fluff but the front was set in the Shirley type curls. The first was 12", soon followed by a 15", 17", 19" and 36" size. The 36" size did not sell too well so they are pretty scarce. There were people during that time that ordered "replacement" parts from supply houses and strung their own 36" Shirley.

This new Shirley Temple doll ran into 1962 with the 1961 introduction of four specials. The Storybook or Fairyland costumes. Only Aldens featured all four of them. They are Cinderella, Little Red Riding Hood, Alice in Wonderland and Little Bo Peep.

Near the end of 1962 a few dolls were sold in unmarked boxes but all the dolls were marked with an ST followed by the mold size number and then an N. None were marked with the full name of Shirley Temple. A few of the larger sizes had flirty eyes. The dresses came with attached slips and the skirt length was not far above the knees.

1972 brought the re-issue of the vinyl Shirley Temple doll for the 100th Anniversary of the Montgomery Ward Company in the 12" size. Ideal also made a few 17" with an entire new face. This doll is shown at the end of this section. She was sold in a plain white box in 1972 but Ideal plans to issue this doll in 1973 in a very elaborate box, showing Shirley in many poses. The doll will be marked 1972.

Time will tell about the newest Shirleys but collectors will most likely keep the store shelves empty as thought goes back to the most beloved of all child actresses.

Ideal--13" Shirley Temple" All composition with glued on blonde mohair wig. Green sleep eyes/lashes. Black eye shadow. Open mouth with six teeth. Marks: Shirley Temple 13 on back. 1936. $45.00. (Courtesy Allin's Collection)

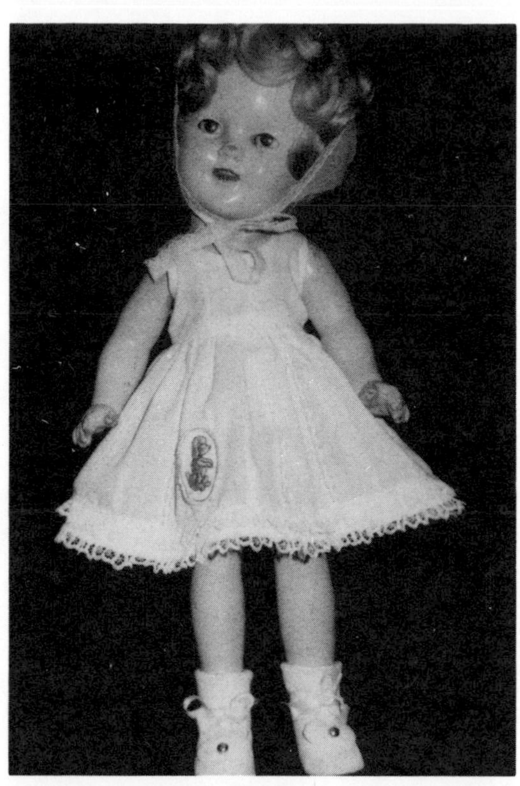

Ideal--13" "Shirley Temple" All composition with glued on blonde mohair wig. Blue sleep eyes/lashes. Open mouth with six teeth and felt tongue. Dimpled cheeks. All fingers molded together and curled. Marks: 13/Shirley Temple, on head. Shirley Temple/13, on body. 1941. $45.00.

Ideal--17" "Shirley Temple" All composition with glued on mohair wig. Green sleep eyes/lashes. Open mouth with six teeth and felt tongue. Dimples. All fingers curled. Marks: Ideal/C OP N & T Co. 1940. $55.00.

Ideal--17" "Shirley Temple" All composition with glued on blonde mohair wig. Green sleep eyes/lashes. Open mouth with six teeth. Marks: Ideal, on head. $55.00. (Courtesy Allin's Collection)

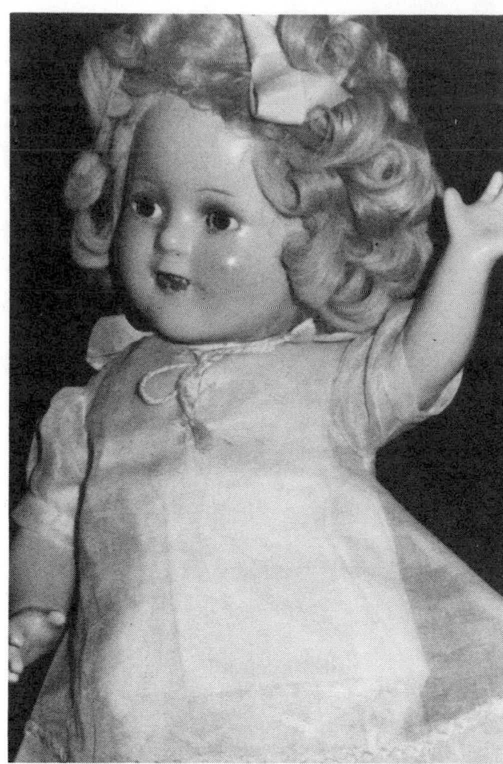

Ideal--17" "Shirley Temple" All composition with glued on blonde mohair wig. Green sleep eyes/lashes. Black eye Shadow. Open mouth with six teeth. Marks: COP. Ideal N & T Co, on head. $55.00. (Courtesy Allin's Collection)

Ideal--16" "Shirley Temple" All composition. Glued on, replaced, blonde wig. Brown eyes/lashes. Open mouth with six teeth. Marks: Shirley Temple, on head. $50.00. (Courtesy Allin's Collection)

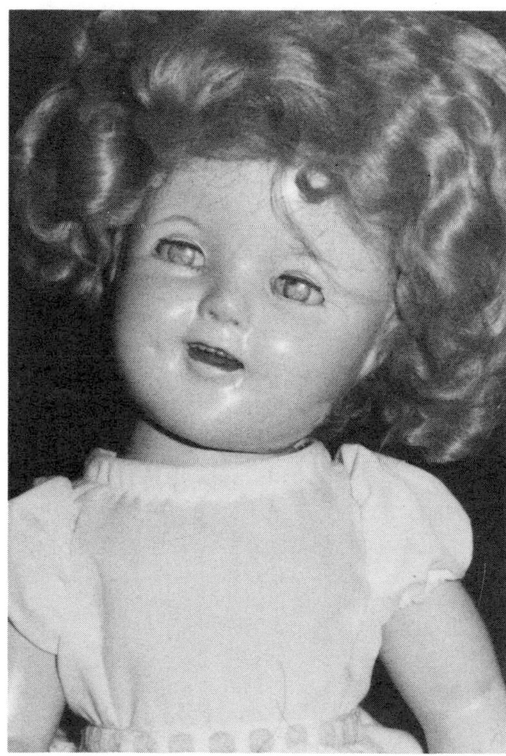

Ideal--22" "Shirley Temple" All composition with glued on blonde mohair wig. Green sleep eyes/lashes. Open mouth with six teeth. Marks: Shirley Temple 22, on back. Shirley Temple Ideal, on head. $65.00. (Courtesy Allin's Collection)

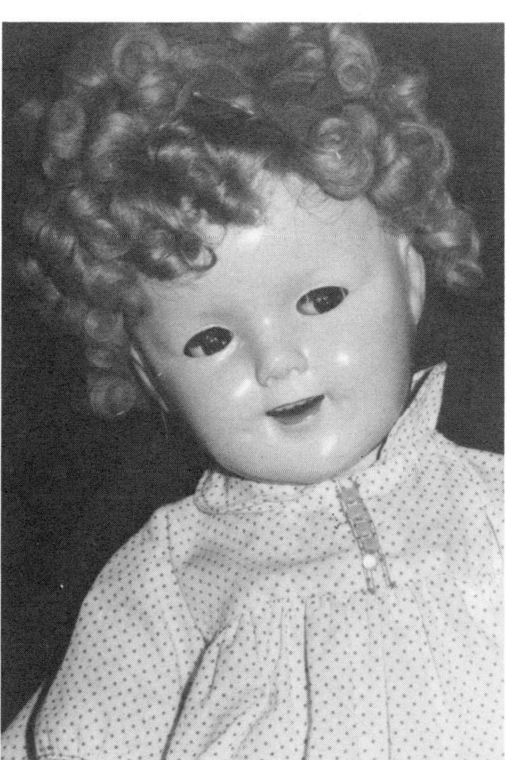

Ideal--27" "Shirley Temple" All composition with glued on blonde mohair wig. Brown flirty eyes/lashes. Open mouth with six teeth. Marks: Shirley Temple, on back. $110.00. (Courtesy Allin's Collection)

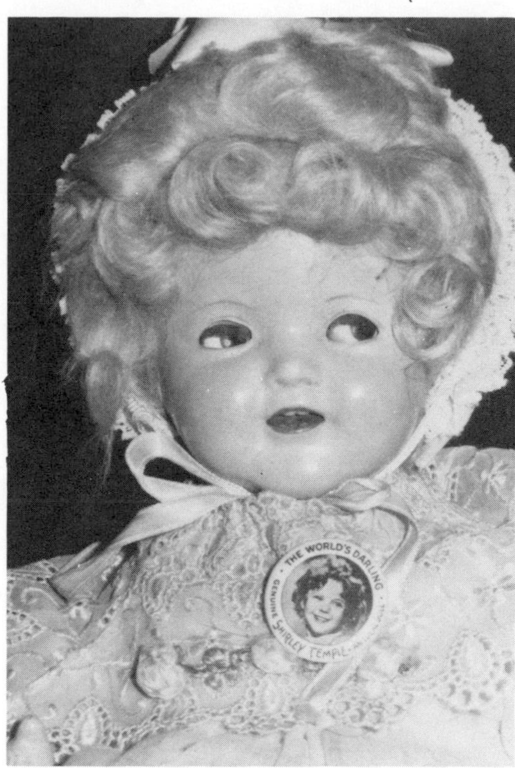

Ideal--17" "Shirley Temple Baby" All composition with glued on blonde mohair wig. Brown flirty eyes, sleep/lashes. Open mouth with two upper and three lower teeth. Marks: Shirley Temple, on head. $120.00. (Courtesy Allin's Collection)

Ideal--18" "Shirley Temple" All composition with glued on yarn hair. Brown complexion. Painted side glancing eyes. Put out as promotion for her movie "The Hurricane" Open/closed mouth with painted upper teeth. Marks: Shirley Temple, on back. $95.00. (Courtesy Earlene Johnston Collection)

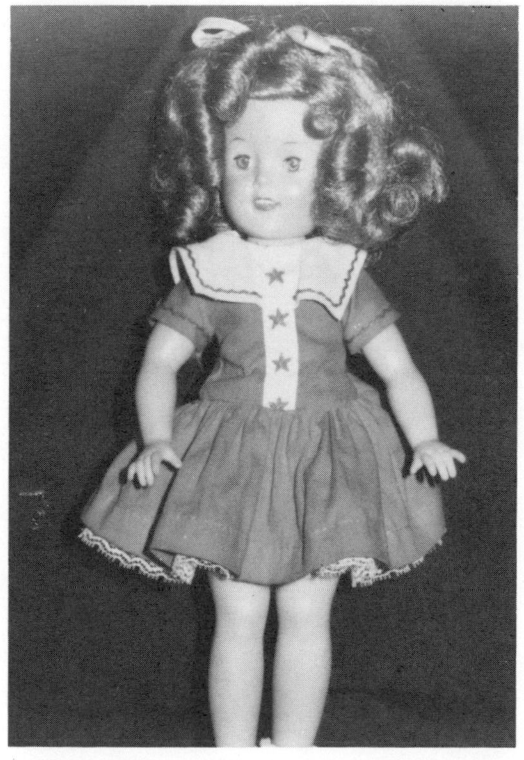

Ideal--12" "Shirley Temple" All vinyl with rooted blonde hair. Brown sleep eyes/molded lashes. Open mouth with four teeth. Marks: ST-12 on head. 1958. $16.00. (Courtesy Allin's Collection)

Ideal--15" "Shirley Temple" All vinyl with rooted blonde hair. Brown sleep eyes/lashes. Open mouth with four teeth. Marks: Ideal Doll ST-15, on back and head. 1958. $18.00. (Courtesy Allin's Collection)

Ideal--17" Shirley Temple All vinyl with rooted blonde hair. Brown sleep eyes/lashes. Open mouth with six teeth. Marks: Ideal Doll ST-17 on head and back. 1958. $20.00. (Courtesy Allin's Collection).

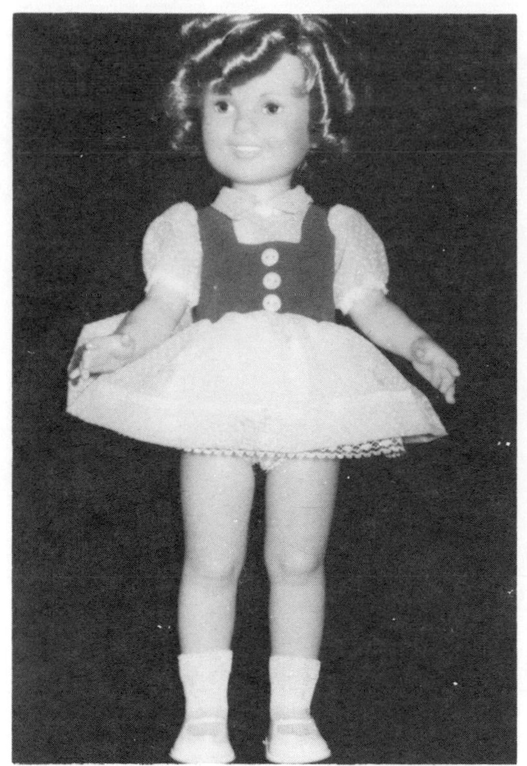

Ideal--17" "Shirley Temple" All vinyl with rooted ash blonde hair. Stationary brown eyes/lashes. Open mouth with painted teeth. Marks: 1972 Ideal Toy Corp/ST-14-H-213 on head. 1971/Ideal Toy Corp/ST-14-b-38 on back. Original clothes. Very short dress. $14.00.

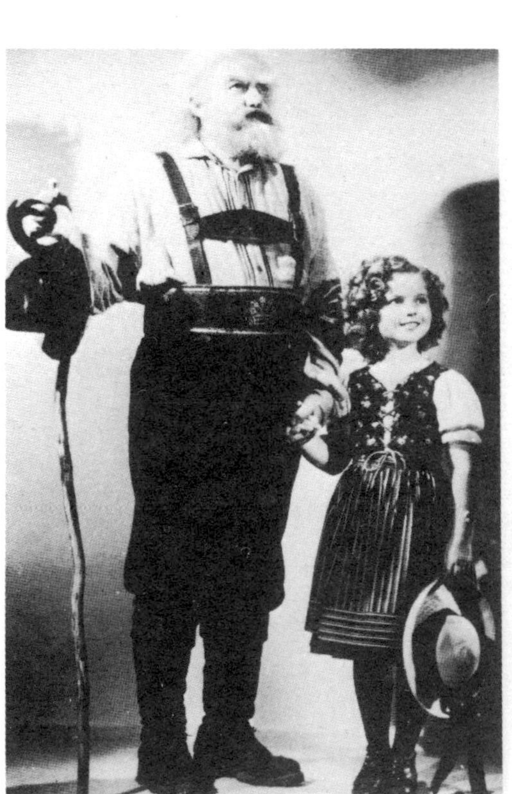

Shirley and Grandfather from the movie "Heidi"

Shirley's Second Best Known Dance Costume.

Shirley Temple dressed as Marie Antoinette

The Hawaiian Shirley, from her movie "The Hurricane" in which she played "Marama".

Shirley Temple and John Boles, one of her favorite "Leading Men"

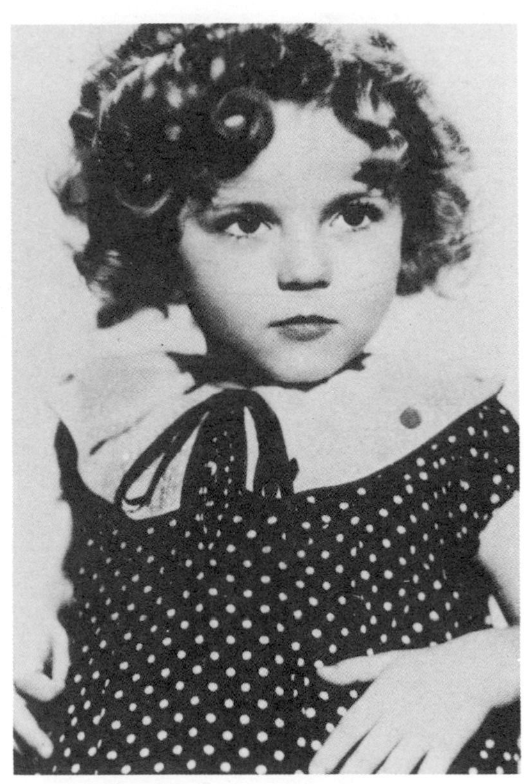

A quiet Shirley in one of her favorite polka dotted dresses.

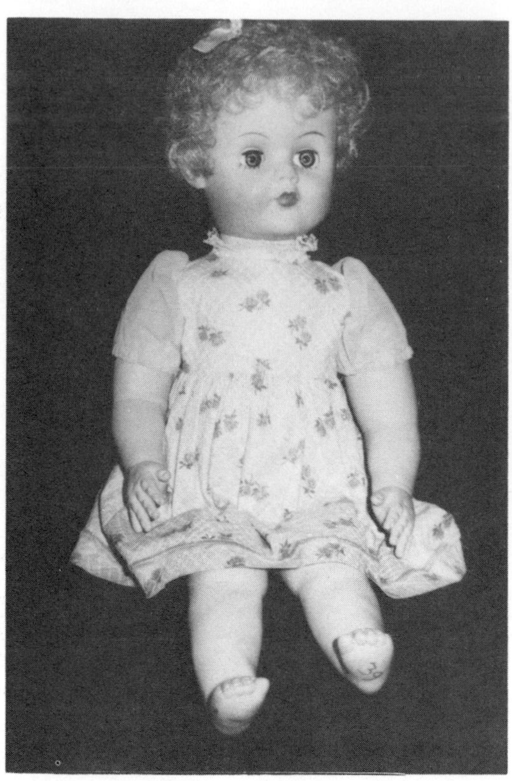

Imco--19" "Love Me" One piece early vinyl body, arms and legs. Vinyl head with rooted blonde hair. Blue sleep eyes/lashes. Closed mouth. Marks: Imco, on head. VS20, on back. 9/V, on lower back. 1953. Original dress. $16.00.

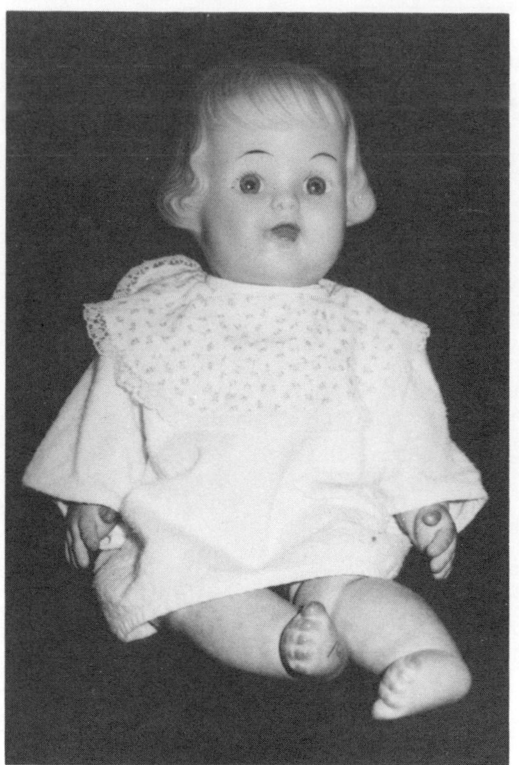

Imperial Crown--15" "Dolly" Latex body, arms and legs. Limbs attached by metal discs. Stuffed vinyl head with molded hair. Stationary blue eyes. Open/closed mouth. Marks: Impco, on head. 1953. Made by the Imperial Crown Toy Co. $4.00.

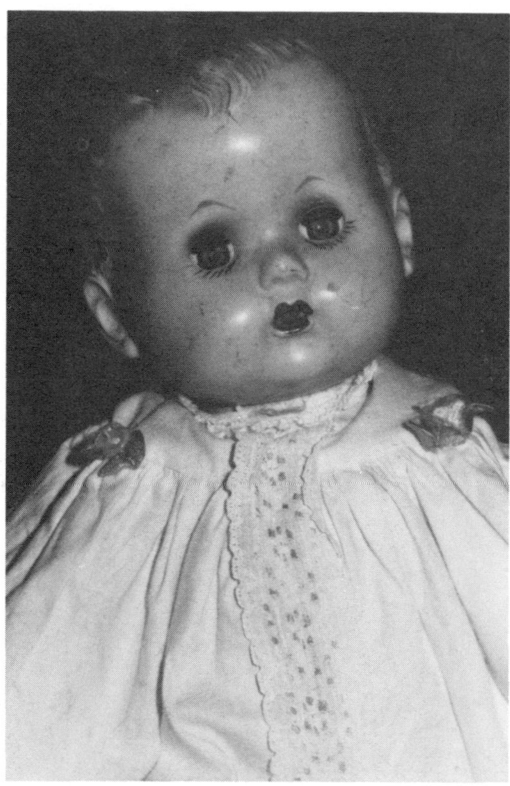

Imperial Crown--14" "Tiny Bubbles" All hard plastic with molded light brown hair. Blue sleep eyes/lashes. Black eyeshadow. Open mouth/dry nurser with small rubber tongue. Baby legs. Marks: Imperial Crown Toy/Made In USA. 1951. $16.00.

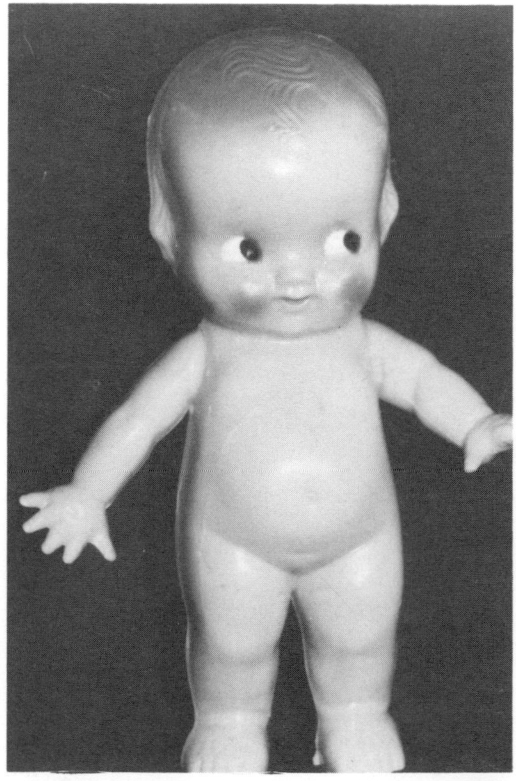

Irwin--6½" "Bashful Boy" All plastic jointed only at shoulders. Painted side glancing black eyes. Closed mouth. Open hands with palms down. Irwin in a flag withing a circle/Made In USA, in a circle. 1950. $3.00.

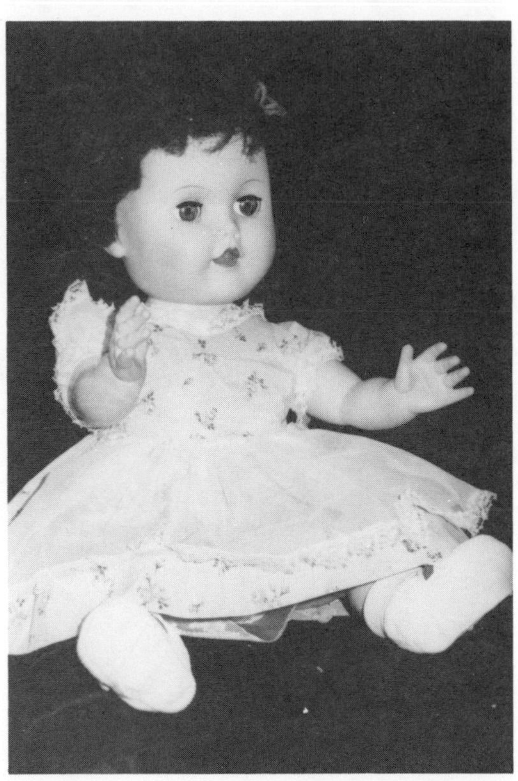

J. Cey--20" "Sherri" All vinyl with rooted black hair. Large blue sleep eyes. Open mouth/nurser. Marks: J. Cey 20, on head. 1961. $8.00.

Jolly Toys--13" "Trudy" Plastic body and legs. Vinyl arms and head. Rooted blonde hair. Sleep blue eyes/lashes. Closed mouth. Marks: Jolly Toy/1962, on head. $8.00.

Jolly Toys--17" 'Pretty Girl" Plastic body and legs. Vinyl arms and head. Rooted blonde hair. Black side glancing sleep eyes/lashes. Closed mouth. Hands open with palms down. 2nd and 3rd fingers molded together. Marks: Jolly Toy Co, on head. 1964. $6.00.

Jolly Toys--16" "Twistee" Molded foam body, arms and legs. Vinyl head with rooted brown hair. Black sleep eyes/lashes. Closed mouth. Marks: Jolly Toy Inc., on head. 1964. $4.00.

Jolly Toys--13" "Nikki" Plastic body, arms and legs. Vinyl head with rooted blonde hair. Blue sleep eyes/lashes. Closed mouth. Marks: Made In Hong Kong/Jolly Toys, on head. Made In Hong Kong, on back. Original dress. 1964. $5.00.

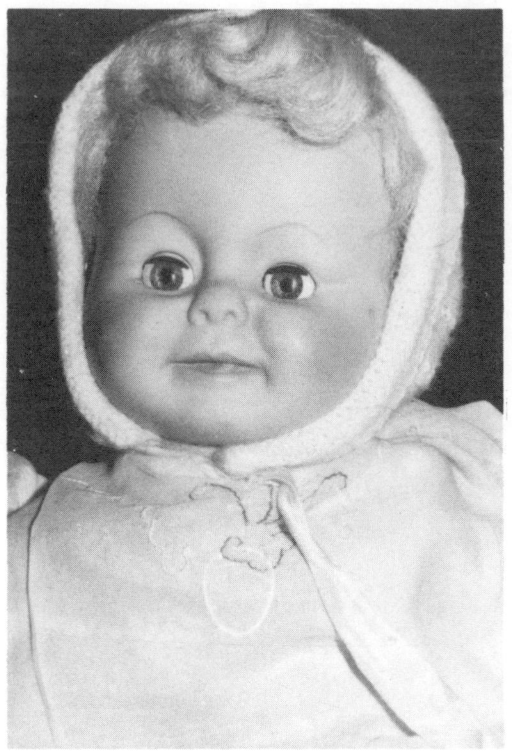

Jolly Toys--17" "Jolly" Cloth body with vinyl arms, legs and head. Rooted blonde hair. Blue sleep eyes/lashes. Open/closed mouth with molded tongue. Right 2nd and 3rd fingers curled. Left thumb, index, 2nd and 3rd fingers curled and molded together. Marks: Jolly Toys, on head. 1965. $8.00.

Jolly Toys--14" "Cutie" All vinyl with rooted hair in twin pony tails. Dark blue sleep eyes/lashes. Large open hands. Stubby legs. Marks: Jolly Toy/1965, on head. Jolly Toy/1966, on body. $8.00.

Jolly Toys--13½" "Judy" Plastic body and legs. Vinyl arms and head. Rooted brown hair. Blue sleep eyes/lashes. Open/closed mouth with two upper painted teeth. Open hands with palms down. Marks: Jolly Toy/1966, on head. $3.00.

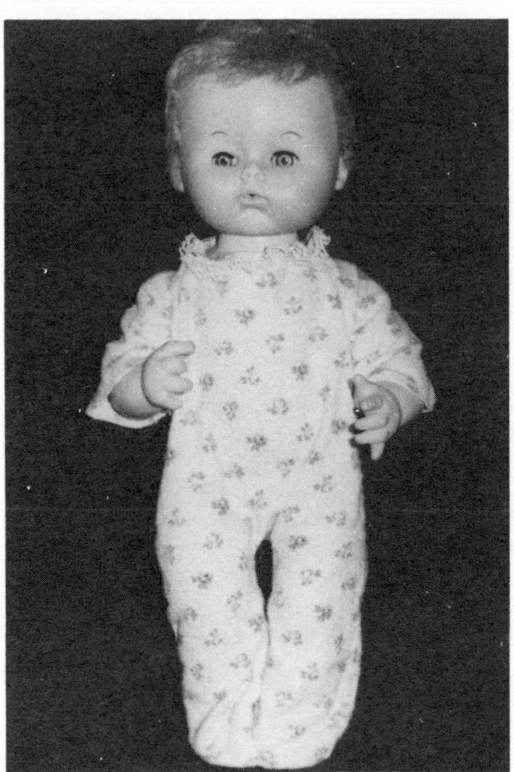

Jolly Toys--14" "Playpen Doll" Plastic and vinyl with rooted dark blonde hair. Blue sleep eyes. Right eye molded smaller than left. Open mouth/nurser. Marks: 26/Jolly Toys Inc/1967. $3.00.

Jolly Toys--11" "Cutie Pie" Plastic body and legs. Vinyl arms and head. Rooted dark blonde hair. Sleep black, side glancing eyes/lashes. Right hand facing body. Left palm down. Short toddler legs. Marks: Jolly Toys, Inc., high on neck. 1967/Jolly Toys Inc, on back. Original clothes. $4.00.

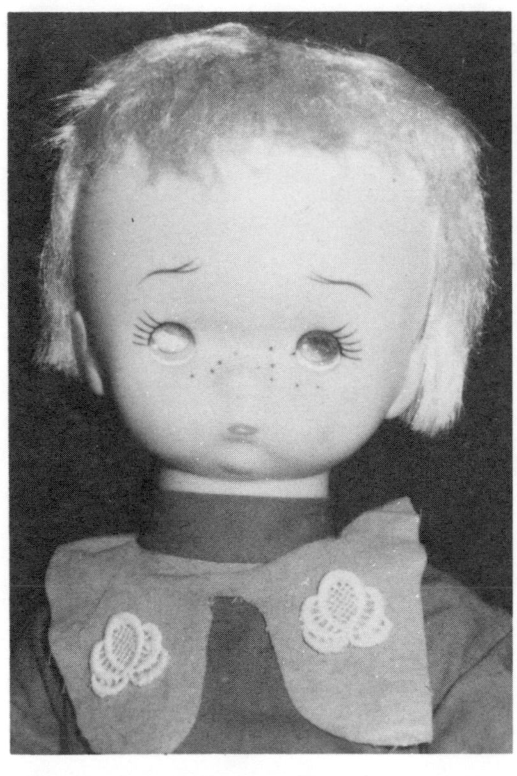

Jolly Toys--14" "Timmy" Foam body, arms and legs. Vinyl head with rooted pink hair. Painted blue eyes. Freckles. Pouty mouth. Vinyl gauntlet hands with left index pointing. Marks: Jolly Toys Inc/1967, on head. $8.00. (Courtesy Allin's Collection).

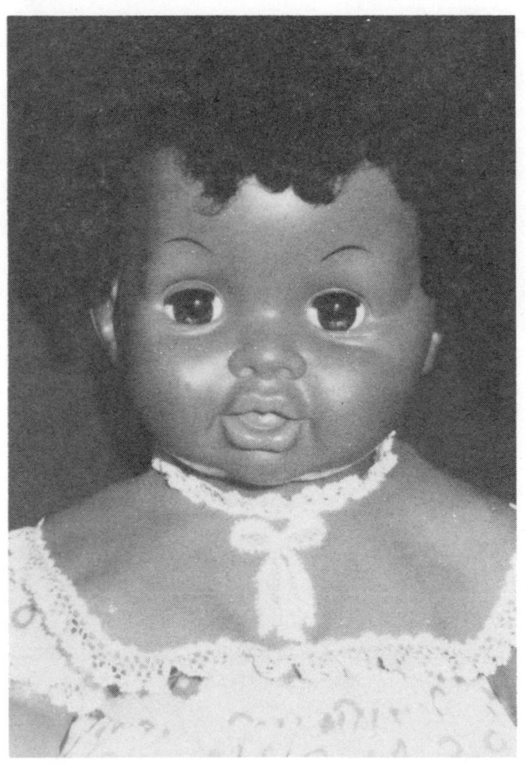

Jolly Toys--20" "Linda" Plastic body, arms and legs. Vinyl head with rooted black hair. Brown sleep eyes/lashes. Open mouth/nurser. Baby legs. Marks: Jolly Toys Inc/1969/16 on head. $9.00.

Jolly Toys--7" "Lil'Lil" Plastic body and legs. Vinyl arms and head. Rooted blonde hair. Painted blue side glancing eyes. Posable head. Original clothes. Set of three girls and one boy. Marks: none. Made In Hong Kong, on clothes tag. Box: Jolly Toys, Inc./1970/Jolly's Lil' Lil. $3.00.

Kay Sam--20" "Catherine" Plastic body and legs. Vinyl arms and head. Rooted light brown hair. Blue sleep eyes/lashes. Blue grey eyeshadow and lash line. Closed mouth. Long thin arms and body. High heel feet. Marks: 4274/K/1961/Kay Sam Corp, on head. 5320/1961/Kay Sam, on body (inside legs). $7.00.

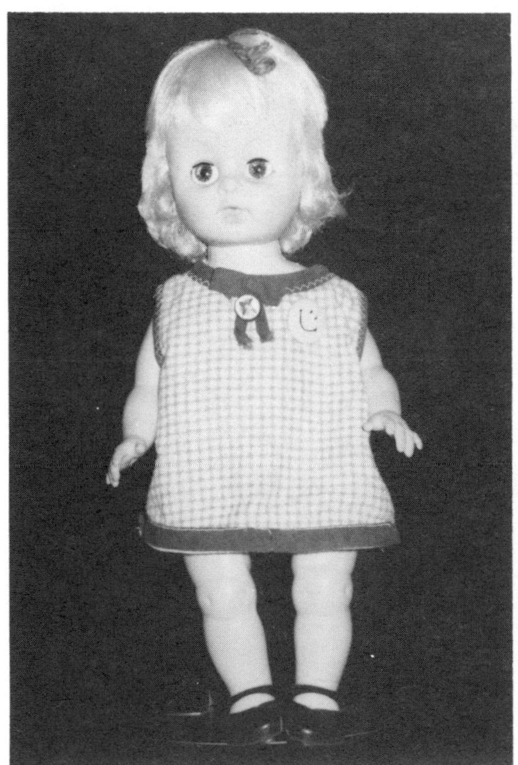

Kay Sam--14" "Miss Sweet" Plastic body and legs. Vinyl arms and head. Rooted white hair. Blue sleep eyes/lashes. Open mouth/nurser. Dimpled knees. Marks: Kll/1963, on head. 6514/Kay Sam, on lower back. $2.00.

Kay Sam--18" "Pumpkin" Plastic body and legs. Vinyl arms and head. Rooted blonde hair. Blue sleep eyes/lashes. Both hands open and extended front and outward. Marks: 4476/Kay Sam 1965/9, on head. $3.00.

Knickerbocher--15" "Snow White" All composition with black glued on wig. Green sleep eyes/lashes. Right arm molded in bent position. Marks: Knickerbocher Toy Co./New York, on back. 1939. $45.00.

Lakeside--5½" Raggedy Andy" 5¾" Raggedy Ann" All vinyl. Bendable all over. Molded and colored on clothes. Painted features. Marks: 1967 The Bobbs Merrill Co, Inc/Mfg By Lakeside Ind. Inc. $4.00. (Courtesy Allin's Collection).

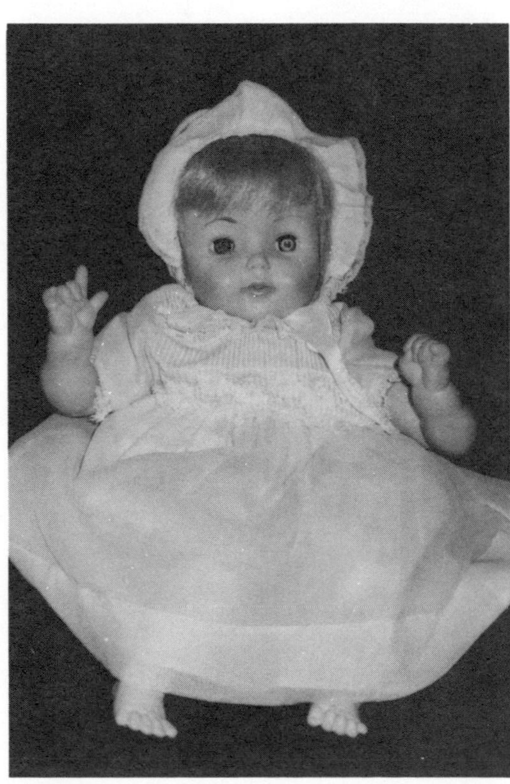

Lorrie--19" "My Baby" Stuffed cloth body. Plastic legs. Vinyl arms and head. Rooted ash blonde hair. Blue sleep eyes/lashes. Closed mouth. Left hand all fingers curled. Right 2nd and 3rd fingers molded into palm. Marks: 1/Lorrie Doll/1960. Made by Eugene Doll & Novelty Co. Inc. $6.00.

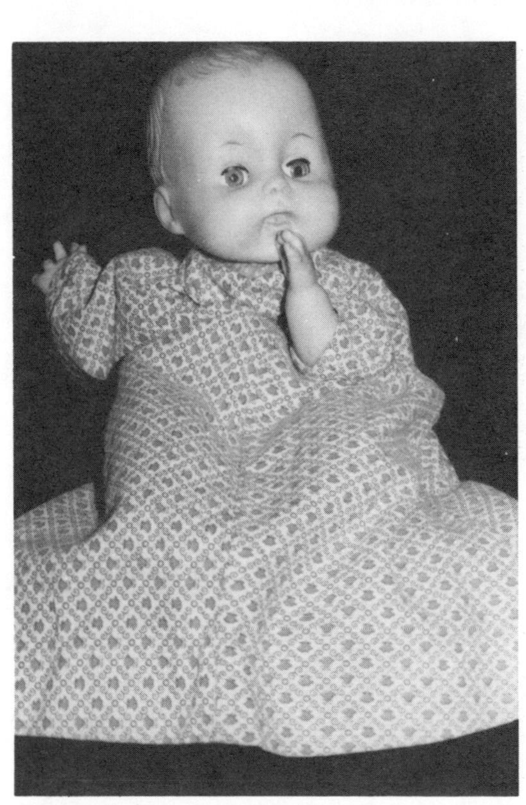

Lorrie--14" "Cuddly Infant" Cloth body of blue/white dot material. Plastic legs. Vinyl arms and head. Molded hair. Blue sleep eyes/lashes. Open mouth. Left thumb, index and 2nd fingers molded together. Right index extended with 3rd finger curled. Marks: 1460T/Lorrie Doll Co/1963 on head. Made by Eugene $3.00.

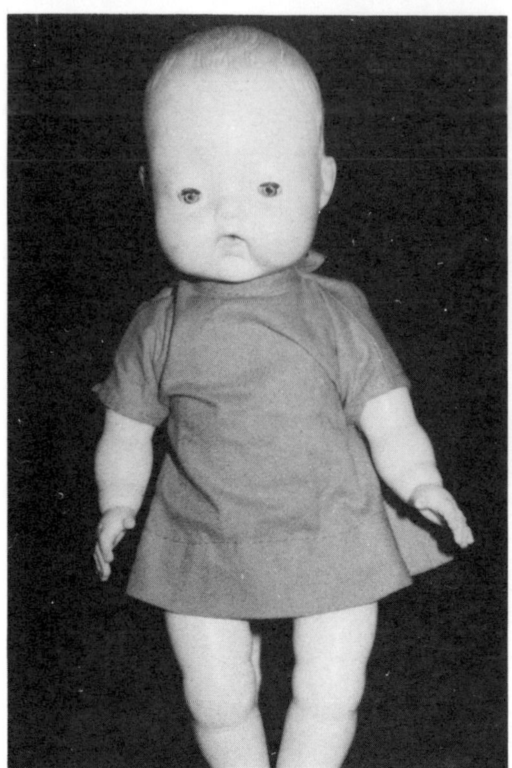

Lorrie--10" "Baby" Plastic with vinyl head. Lightly molded hair. Small blue sleep eyes/molded lashes. Open hands facing body. Baby legs. Open mouth/nurser. Marks: Lorrie Doll Inc/1963, on head. Made by Eugene Doll & Novelty Co. Inc. $4.00. (Courtesy Earlene Johnston Collection).

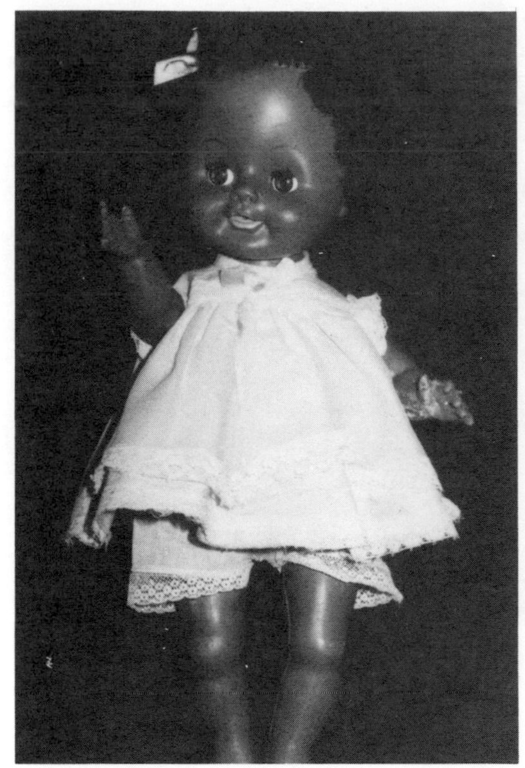

Lorrie--12" "Louise" Plastic body, arms and legs. Vinyl head with rooted black hair. Brown sleep eyes/lashes. Open mouth/nurser. Open hands facing body. Marks: 1250/4/Lorrie, on head. 1964. Made by Eugene Doll & Novelty Co. Inc. $8.00. (Courtesy Allin's Collection).

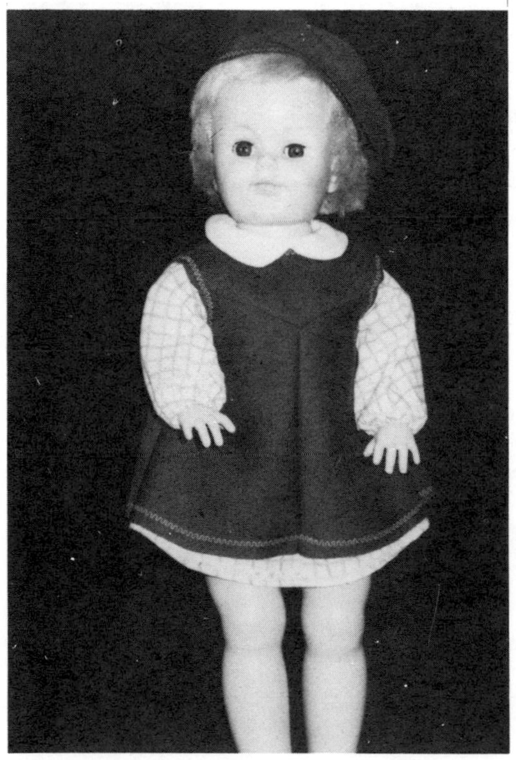

Lorrie--22" "Pastel Miss" Plastic body, legs and arms. Vinyl head with rooted blue pastel hair. Brown sleep eyes/lashes. Dimpled cheeks. Open hands with palms down. Marks: Lorrie Doll/1964. Walker. Made by Eugene Doll & Novelty Co. Inc. $4.00.

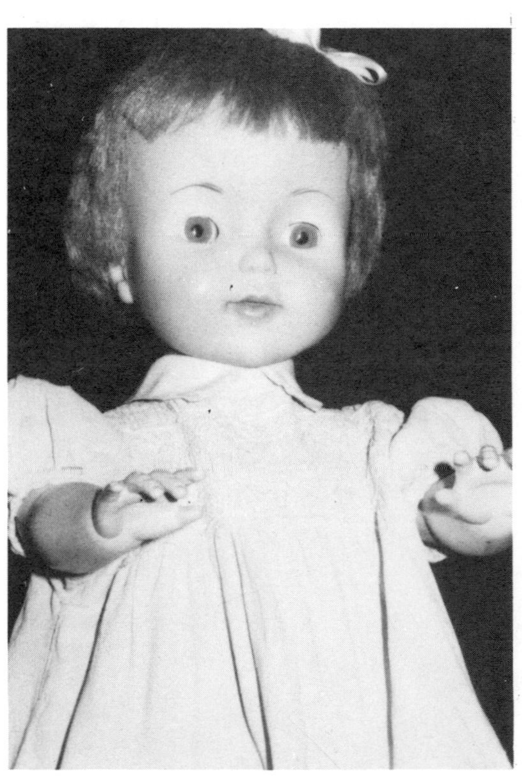

Lorrie--22" "Delightful" Plastic body and legs. Vinyl arms and head. Blue sleep eyes/lashes and light blue eye shadow. Open/closed mouth. Open hands, palms down. Marks: 11/Lorrie Doll/1966, on head. Made by Eugene Doll & Novelty Co. Inc. $7.00.

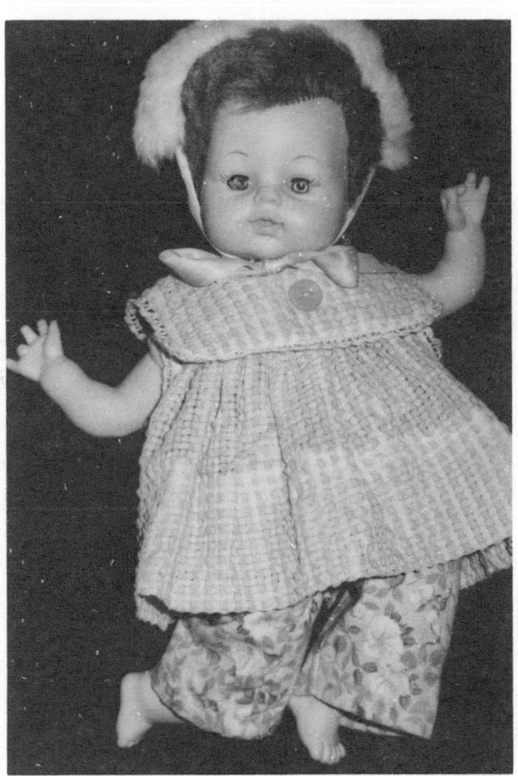

Lorrie--13½" "Lorrie" Cloth body with plastic legs. Vinyl arms and head. Rooted red hair. Blue sleep eyes/lashes. Open/closed mouth. Marks: Lorrie Doll/1968, on head. Tag: Manufactured By Eugene Doll Co/NY NY. $3.00

Lorrie--11" "Marsha" All vinyl with rooted ash blonde hair. Brown sleep eyes/lashes. Open/closed mouth. Marks: Lorrie Doll 1971/Made In Taiwan, on back and head. Made by Eugene Doll & Novelty Co. Inc. $4.00.

Lorrie--9" "Little Linda" All vinyl with rooted yellow blonde hair. Brown sleep eyes/molded lashes. Closed mouth/nurser. Marks: 9/&/11/ Lorrie Doll/1971/Made In Taiwan, on back. 9, on head. Made by Eugene Doll & Novelty Co. Inc. $4.00.

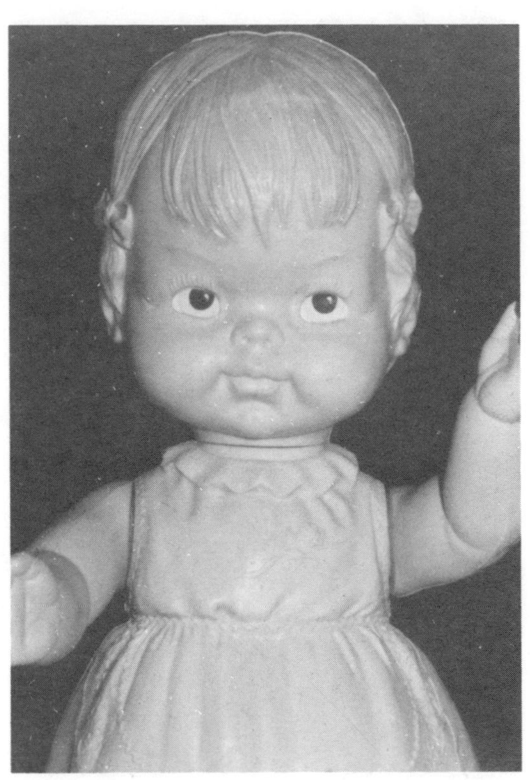

Marx--21" "Miss Toddler" All plastic with molded hair. Paper eyes. Battery operated. Walker. Rollers on bottom of feet. Marks: Louis Marx & Co Inc/MCMLXV/Patent Pending, on back. Louis Marx Co Inc/MCMLXV/Patent Applied For, on bottom. 1965. $20.00. (Courtesy Allin's Collection).

Marx--5" "Twinkie" All vinyl. Painted features, shoes and socks. Soft plastic wardrobe, wigs and acccessories. Marks: Louis Marx & Co Inc/MCMLXV in a circle. $8.00.

Marx--9" "Jamie West on "Thunderbolt" All plastic. Jointed at hips, knees, elbows, neck and wrists. Molded on cowboy suit. Separate neck scarf. Marks: Louis Marx & Co. Inc./ MCMLXVII in circle on back. Horse: same, except MCMLXV on flank. $3.00.

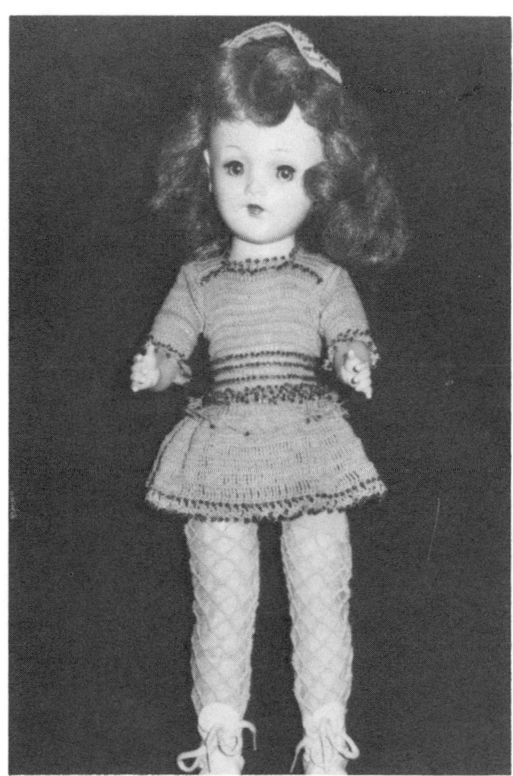

Mary Hoyer Doll Mfg. Co.--14" "Mary Hoyer" All hard plastic with glued on red brown saran wig. Blue sleep eyes/lashes. Closed mouth. 2nd and 3rd fingers slightly curled, molded together. Marks: Original/Mary Hoyer/Doll, in a circle on back. 1949. $30.00.

Mattel Inc.

This company started in 1945 and in 1960 moved their headquarters to Hawthorne, California.

Mattel's research is carried on behind closed doors and has tight security. Research areas are "off limits" and all visitors are screened.This research area is led by a former missile engineer.

One of the founders, Ruth Handler, designed the Barbie doll. Her husband, Elliot Handler, is President of the company.

The Barbie doll was created for Mrs. Handler's daughter, who liked to make clothes for teen-age dolls. Mattel researched the idea and began making Barbies. They were originally and still are produced in Japan.

The sale of apparal and accessories for Barbie dolls, have helped drive the financial boom of this company into the number one toy maker.

In 1960 Mattel introduced a talking doll, Chatty Cathy, which operated without batteries and was another innovation that made this company what it is today.

Mattel is a publicly owned corporation. The corporation has numbered among it's acquistions: Rosebud Dolls, Ltd, England 1967, Standard Plastics Products 1965, Dee & Cee Company of Canada 1962, A doll company in Hong Kong 1966, West Germany 1966, Taiwan 1966, Mexico 1967, Japan (KBK) 1968, Ratti and Mebetoys Italy 1968, and Ebiex Belguim 1968. They also purchased Monogram Models Company in 1968. Mattel is now the largest toy manufacture in the world.

The quality of this company's products is above average but do not expect the mechanisms to work long. Mattel, to date, will not supply replacement voice boxes. You must exchange the entire torso of the doll.

All Mattels are well marked but look on the hips rather than the neck on most of them.

1958: Barbie (5.00)

1960: Chatterbox (Chatty Cathy-9.00)

1961: Babs (10.00), Sister Belle (10.00), Charmin' Chatty (20.00), Mattie (18.00), Ken (4.00), Casper (16.00)

1962: Chatty Baby (8.00), Chatty Cheryl (8.00), Chatty Patter (8.00), Mr. Ed (5.00), Midge (5.00)

1963: Fashion Queen (8.00), Shrinking Violet (45.00), Tiny Brother (8.00), Baby Pat a Burp (4.00), Rickey (4.00), Skooter (4.00), Skipper (4.00)

1964: Baby First Step (8.00), Talking Baby First Step (10.00), Scooba Doo (35.00), Dee Dee (10.00), Tatters (8.00), T-Bone (6.00), Baby Cheryl (16.00), Jet Coder (7.00), Drowsy (15.00), Singin' Chatty (14.00)

1965: Baby Colleen (16.00), Baby Secret (8.00), Patootie (6.00), Tutti (3.00), Todd (3.00), Kiddles (4.00), Little Kiddles (4.00), Baby Biddle (4.00), Fluff (5.00), Puddin' (5.00), Tearful Cheerful (5.00), Milli Middle (4.00), Howard Buff Boodle (4.00), Baby Chatter (16.00), Calamity Jiddle (4.00), Greta Griddle (4.00), Tiddle Diddle (4.00), Lola Liddle (4.00), Florence Niddle (4.00), Dandy (4.00), Bunson Burnie (4.00), Baby Teenie Talk (8.00), Liddle Middle (4.00)

1966: Teachy Keen (8.00), Creeple People (3.00), Buffie (10.00), Christy (3.00), Chris (3.00), Soapy Siddle (7.00), Trikey Triddle (4.00), Sizzly Friddle (4.00), Windy Fliddle (4.00), Baby Step (7.00), Beat A Diddle (4.00), Freezy Sliddle (4.00), Liz Locket (4.00), Lorna Locket (4.00), Lilac Locket (4.00), Lou Locket (4.00), Lola Locket (4.00), Baby Pretty Pout (16.00), Lucky Locket (4.00), Mrs. Beasley (8.00), Kissin Kuzzins (18.00), Major Mason (6.00), Gangy Daglies (6.00), Smiggle Talk (4.00), Storybook Kiddles (4.00), Baby Go Walk (8.00), Babys Hungry (8.00), Baby Say 'n See (8.00), Man From Laser (8.00), Casey (4.00), Francie (4.00), New Barbie (4.00), Julie (7.00), Tiny Tearful Cheerful (6.00), Drowsy (4.00)

1967: Sheila Friddle (4.00), Small Talk (5.00), Sister Small Talk (5.00), Tiff (4.00), Baby Teenie Talk (7.00), Fingles (3.00), Rolly Twiddle (4.00), Baby Teenie Talk (7.00), Fingles (3.00), Rolly Twiddle (4.00), Lenore Locket (4.00), Lambie Pie (8.00), Anabelle (8.00), Jeanette (8.00), Becky (4.00), Randy (4.00), Janet (4.00), Kola Kiddles (5.00), Sherily Kiddle (4.00), Telly Viddle (4.00), Swingy Swiddle (4.00), Cleo (4.00), Carmen (4.00), Laffy (4.00), Olivia (4.00), Petsy Pliddle (4.00), Sweepsy Skiddle (4.00), Slipsy Sliddle (4.00), Lemons Stiddle (4.00), Kampy Kiddle (4.00), Piney Niddle (4.00), Stacy (4.00), Sadie (4.00), Skediddles (3.00), Truly Scrumptous (5.00), Caractacus Potts (6.00), Laverna Locket (4.00), Sylvia Locket (4.00), Sgt. Storm (7.00), Suki Skediddle (5.00), Luana Locket (4.00), Loretta Locket (4.00), Chitty Chitty Bang Bang (6.00), Rosebud (7.00), Bomburst (7.00), Kiddle Kolognes (4.00), Look N' Say (8.00), Doctor Doolittle (8.00 to 25.00), Tippee Toes (6.00), Talking Baby First Step (8.00), Randy Reader (20.00), Sleeping Beauty (4.00)

1968: Capt. Laser (8.00), Harriet (4.00), Holi Diddle (4.00), Anabelle Autodiddle (4.00), Roscoe (6.00), Dick Van Dyke (10.00), Dancerina (8.00), Bouncy Baby (3.00), Sister Small Talk (6.00), Tracy (4.00), Busy Ken (5.00)

1969: Cinderella (8.00), Goldilocks (8.00), Little Bo Peep (8.00), Baby Tenderlove (3.00), Charlie Brown Skediddle (3.00), Beany (20.00), Swingy (6.00), Tiny Swingy (8.00), New Chatty Cathy (6.00), Baby Sing A Song (16.00), Timey Tell (14.00), Chatty Telle (16.00)

1970: Talking Twins (6.00 each), Snow White (8.00), Breezy Bridget (3.00), Talk A Little (5.00)

1971: Dressy (4.00), Big Jack (4.00), Kretor/Zark (8.00), Baby Bye Bye (7.00), Cuddly Beans (3.00), Hi Dottie (7.00), Tearful Tenderlove (4.00), Talking Cynthia (10.00), Baby Tenderlove (3.00), Baby Dancerina (6.00), 11" Valerie (5.00), Baby Walks (7.00), Small Shots Twins (6.00), Baby Love Light (7.00), Pajama Bag Talker (4.00), Shoppin' Sherri (5.00), Talking Twosome (6.00), Pretty Talk Tracy (6.00), Tiny Chatty Baby (5.00), Talking Baby Tenderlove (5.00), Living Baby Tenderlove (3.00)

For Barbie Collectors

1958: Barbie 11½", Blonde and dark hair.
1961: Ken 12½", painted hair.
1963: Midge 11½", Rickey 9¼", Skooter 9¼", Skipper 9¼", long hair.
1964: Allan 12½", red painted hair. Miss Barbie, sleep eyes and bendable knees. Fashion Queen Barbie, with three wigs.
1965: Ken, with bendable knees. Allan, with bendable knees. Skipper, with bendable knees. Midge, with bendable knees. Barbie, with bendable knees.
1966: Francie 11½", bendable knees and rooted eyelashes. Tutti & Todd 6 3/8" and bendable all over. Barbie Color Magic. Barbie Color & Curl. Casey 11", with bendable knees and rooted eyelashes. Julie 11½", with bendable knees and rooted eyelashes.
1967: Barbie Twist & Turn, New standard Barbie, Francie Twist & Turn (also colored Francie), Casey Twist & Turn, Chris 11½", Tutti & Todd, new size of 7 5/8", with rooted hair.
1968: Talking Barbie, Talking Spanish Barbie, Talking Stacy, Busy Ken, Talking Christie (colored), Twist & Turn Stacy, Twist & Turn Skipper, Twiggy London Model.
1969: Twist & Turn Julia Nurse, Talking Julila, Talking PJ, Talking Ken.
1970: Living Barbie, most posable. Living Skipper. Francie, with growing hair. Talking Brad (colored). Twist & Turn PJ. Twist & Turn Christie.
1971: Barbie, with growing hair. Live Action Barbie, on stage. Live Action Ken, on stage. Live Action Francie, on stage. Live Action PJ. Live Action Christie. Malibu Skipper, with tan, bendable legs and Twist & Turn. Malibu Barbie. Malibu Ken. Malibu Francie. Living Fluff. Brad, with bendable legs. Action Big Jack.
1972: Walk Lively Barbie and Friends.

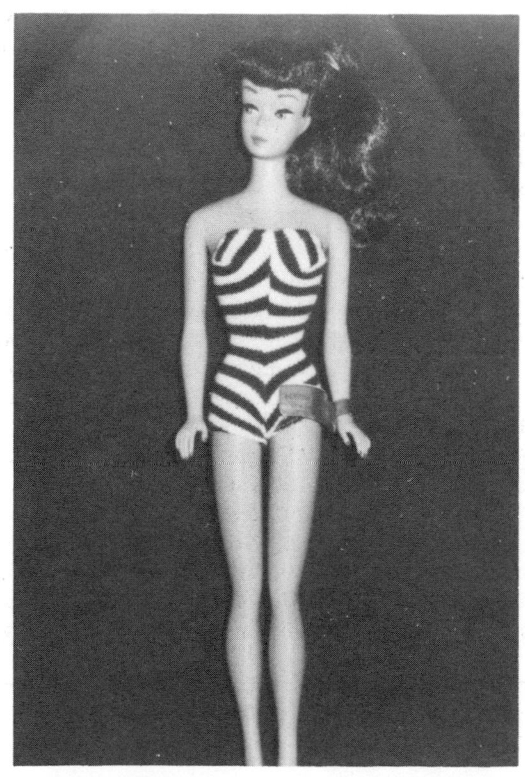

Mattel--11" "Barbie" All vinyl with rooted hair dark brown hair. Painted side glancing eyes. Re-issued for the 100th Anniversary of Montgomery Wards. (Marked "Midge" Original Barbie Doll). Marks: Barbie/1958/By Mattel Inc./Patented. $5.00.

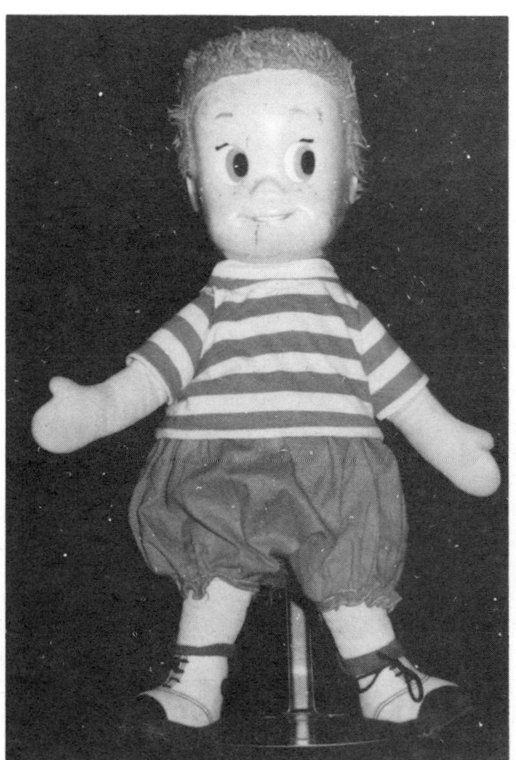

Mattel--17" "Mattie" Stuffed cloth body with mitten hands. Sewn on tennis shoes and socks. Talk pull ring right side of neck. Hard plastic head. Glued on orange yarn hair. Large brown side glancing eyes. Open/closed mouth. Marks: Mattel Inc./Hawthorne, Calif. on head. Small tag on left side says Mattel, Inc. 1961. $18.00

Mattel--17" "Sister Belle" Cloth body arms and legs with sewn on shoes. Hard plastic head with glued on yellow yarn hair. Very large side glancing blue eyes. Closed mouth. Pull ring on right side of neck. Says 11 phrases. Marks: Mattel Inc/Hawthorne Calif. on head. Tag on left hip: Mattel Inc. 1961. $18.00.

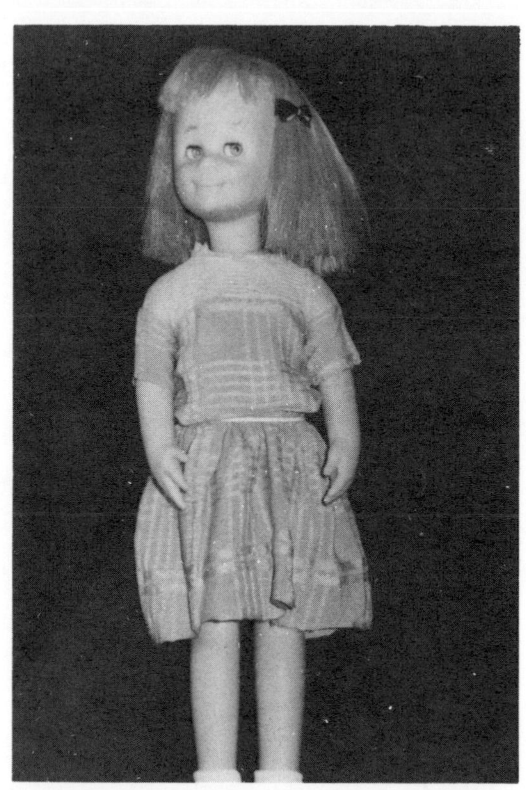

Mattel--25" "Charmin' Chatty" Plastic body and legs. Vinyl arms and head. Rooted blonde hair. Blue side glancing sleep eyes/lashes. Closed mouth. Record fits into slot in side of doll. Pull ring. Marks: Charmin' Chatty 1961 Mattel Inc. $20.00.

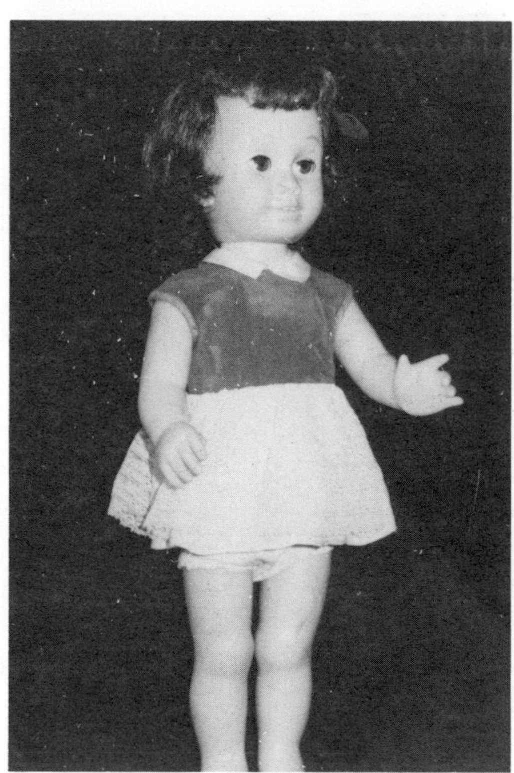

Mattel--20" "Chatty Cathy" Plastic body. Vinyl arms, legs and head. Rooted brown hair. Brown sleep eyes/lashes. Open hands with 2nd and 3rd fingers slightly curled. Marks: Chatty Cathy 1960/Chatty Baby 1961/By Mattel Inc./US Pat. 3,017,187/Other US And Foreign Pats Pend/ Pat'd In Canada 1962. Original clothes. $9.00.

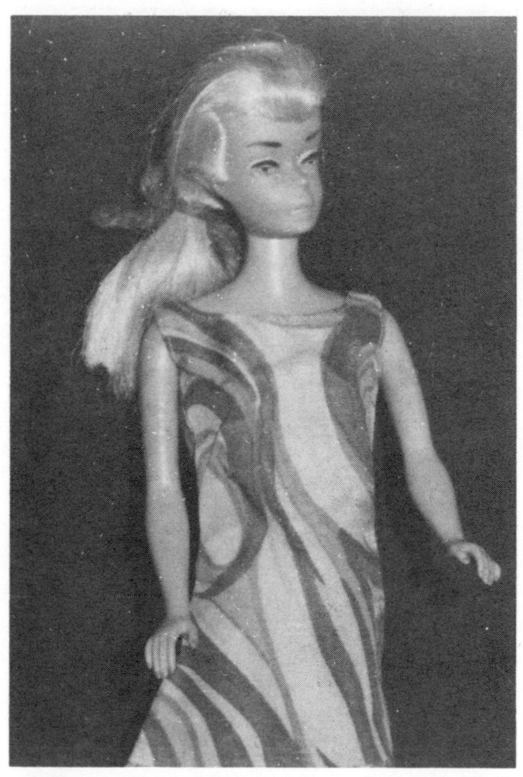

Mattel--11½" "Midge" All vinyl with rooted blonde hair. Painted blue eyes with molded lashes. Marks: Midge/1962/Barbie/1958/By Mattel Inc. $5.00.

Mattel--15" "Shrinking Violet" All stuffed cloth with yellow yarn hair. Felt eyes with movable lids. Movable mouth that is pull string operated. Marks: Mattel Shrinking Violet, other side: 63 The Funny Company/All Rights Reserved Throughout The World With Pat #'s Pat. Canada 1962. $45.00.

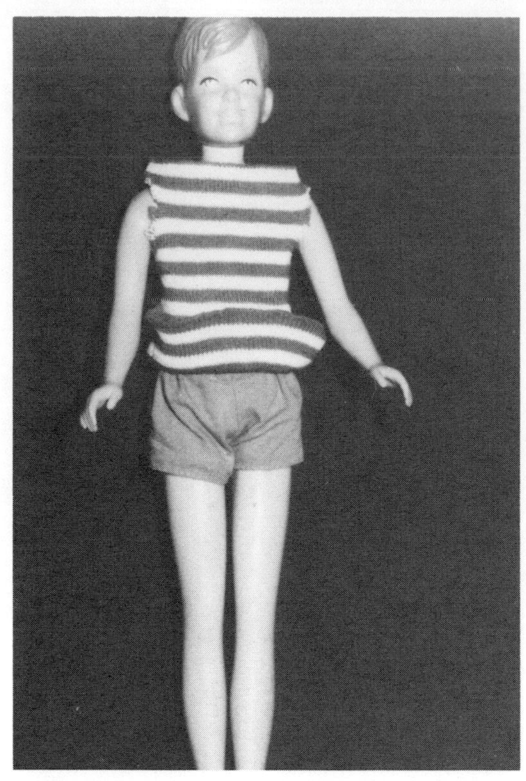

Mattel--9" "Rickey" All vinyl with a suntan. Molded red hair. Painted blue eyes. Marks: 1/1963/Mattel Inc. $4.00.

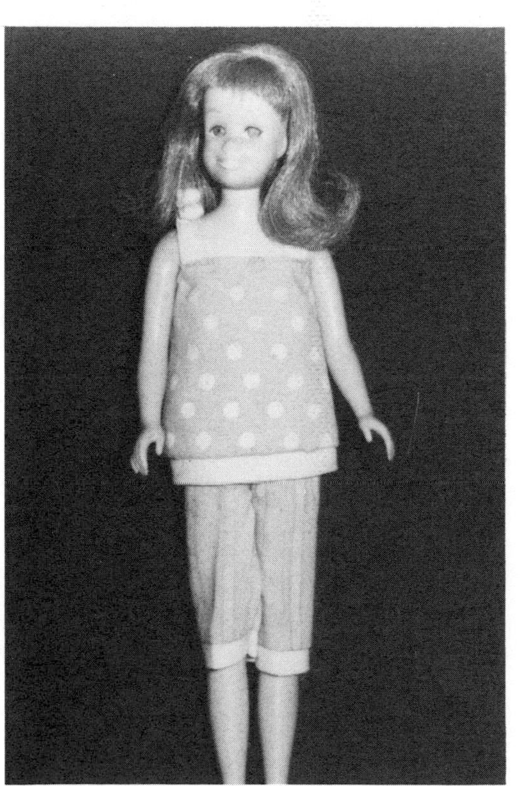

Mattel--9¼" "Skooter" All vinyl with rooted red hair. Painted brown eyes. Freckles. Marks: 1963/Mattel Inc. $4.00.

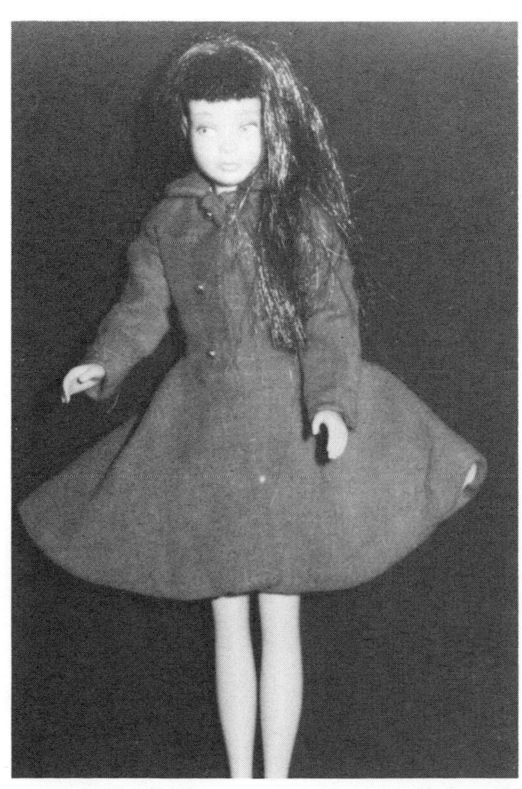

Mattel-9½" "Skipper" All vinyl with suntan. Rooted brown hair. Painted blue side glancing eyes. Marks: Skipper/1963/Mattel Inc. $4.00.

Mattel--13" "Baby Pattaburp" Cloth body. Vinyl arms, legs and head. Rooted red hair. Blue sleep eyes/lashes. Open mouth. Mechanism makes her burp as she is patted on the back. Marks: Tag: Quality Originals By Mattel/Baby Pattaburp/ 1963 Mattel Inc. Original clothes. $4.00.

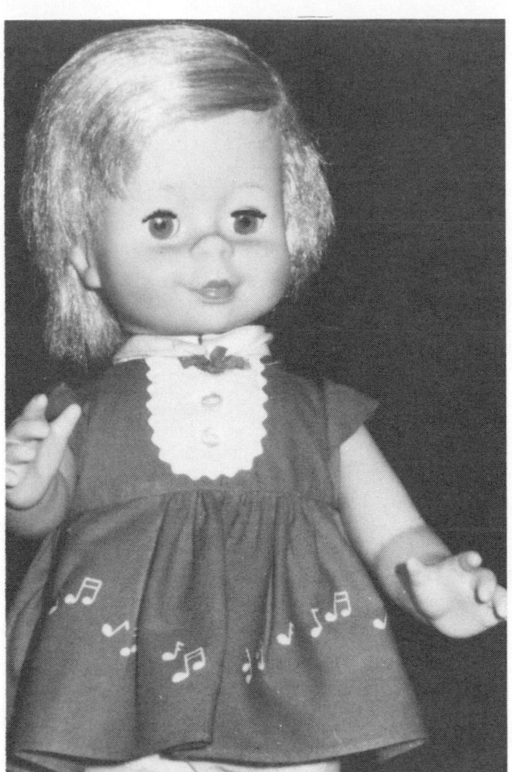

Mattel--17" "Singin' Chatty" Plastic body. Vinyl arms, legs and head. Rooted frosted blonde hair. Blue sleep eyes/lashes. Closed mouth. Freckles across nose. Sings songs by pull string in center of upper back. Marks: Singin' Chatty/1964 Mattel Inc/Hawthorne Calif USA Dress Tag: Singin' Chatty/1964 Mattel Inc. $14.00.

Mattel--18" "Baby First Step" Plastic with vinyl head. Rooted blonde hair. Dark blue sleep eyes/long lashes. Closed mouth. Left hand facing down with all fingers slightly curled. Right hand open and pointing. Walker molded on shoes. Battery operated. Marks: 1964 Mattel Inc/Hawthorne Calif/Made In USA $8.00.

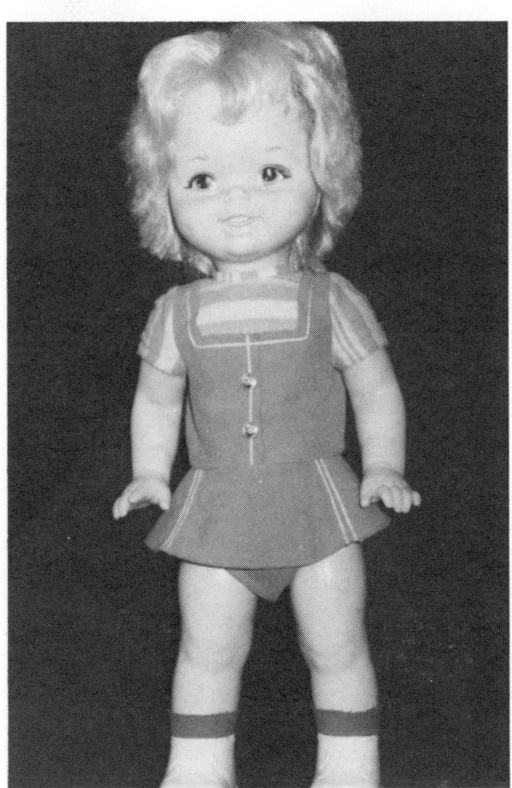

Mattel--18" "Talking Baby First Step" Plastic with vinyl head. Rooted white blonde hair. Blue painted eyes. Open/closed mouth with four teeth. Dimples. Molded on walking shoes/ socks. Marks: 1967 Mattel Inc on head. 1964 Mattel Inc/Hawthorne Calif. on back. Original clothes. $10.00.

Mattel--21" 'Scooba Doo" Cloth body, arms and legs. Vinyl head with rooted blonde hair. Black painted eyelids and eye shadow. Blue sleep eyes/lashes. Closed mouth. Pull string on lower left hip. Marks: Tag: Mattel/Scooba Doo 1964. Original clothes. $25.00.

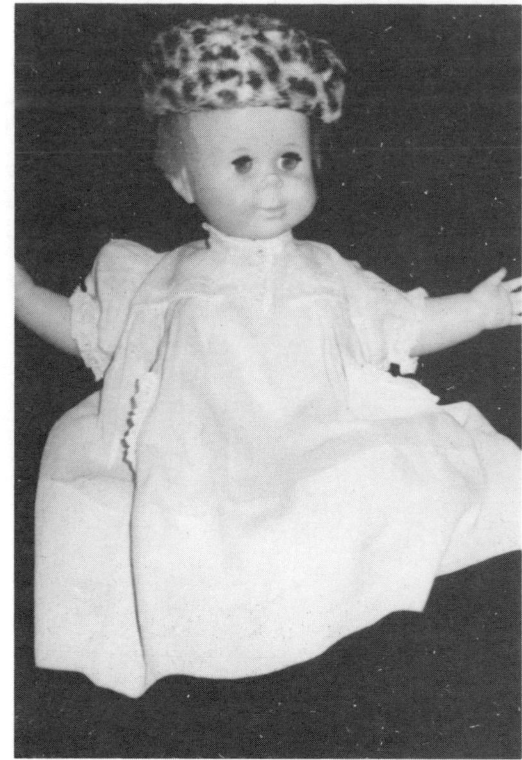

Mattel--16" "Baby Cheryl" Cloth body with vinyl arms, legs and head. Rooted white hair. Dark blue sleep eyes/long lashes. Open hands with 3rd finger on left hand curled. Individual toes. Pull string operated. Marks: Tag: Mattel Inc/Baby Cheryl TM/1964. $16.00.

Mattel--16" "Casper The Ghost" Stuffed body. Hard plastic head with painted features. Pull ring on left side of neck. Says things like "I like you." "Don't be afraid". Marks: Tag gone. 1964. $16.00.

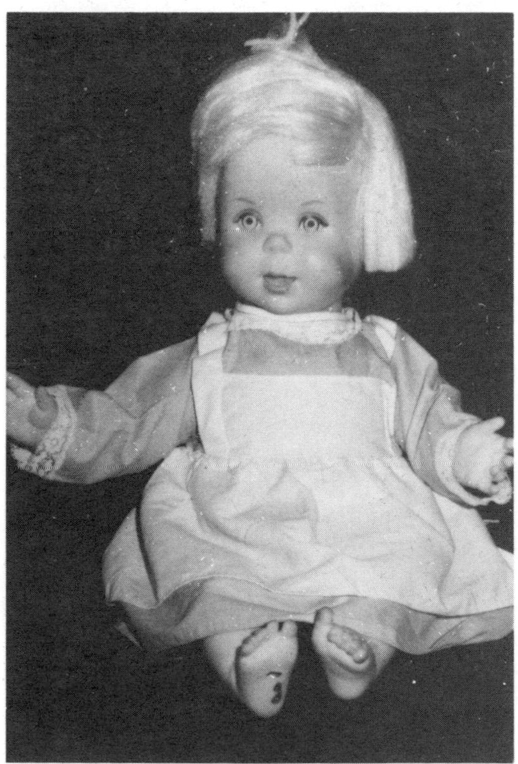

Mattel--17" "Baby Tennie Talk" Cloth body. Vinyl arms, legs and head. Rooted white hair. Painted blue eyes. Open mouth. Pull string on right hand hip. Mouth moves as Baby talks. Marks: Tag: Mattel/Baby Teenie Talk/1965. $8.00.

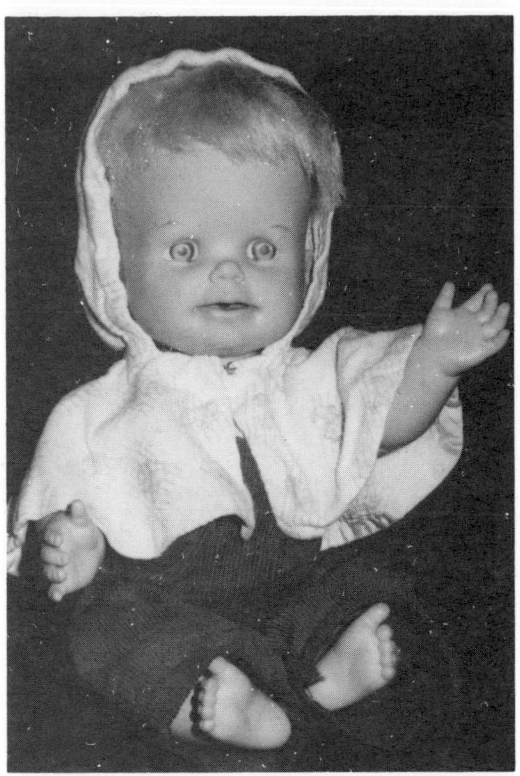

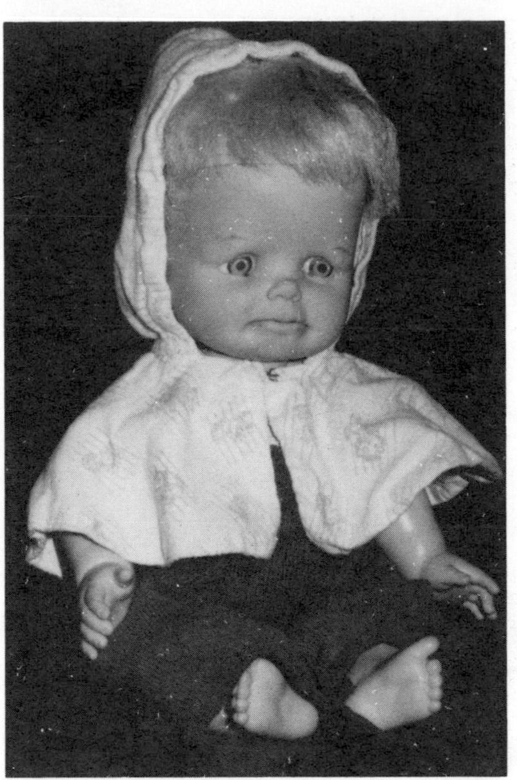

Mattel--13" "Cheerful Tearful" Plastic body. Vinyl arms, legs and head. Light blonde rooted hair. Blue painted eyes. Open mouth. Hands open and facing body. Individual large toes and dimpled knees. Movement of left arm makes face change from sad to glad. Marks: 1965 Mattel Inc./Hawthorne Calif/US Patents Pending/3036-014-1. $5.00.

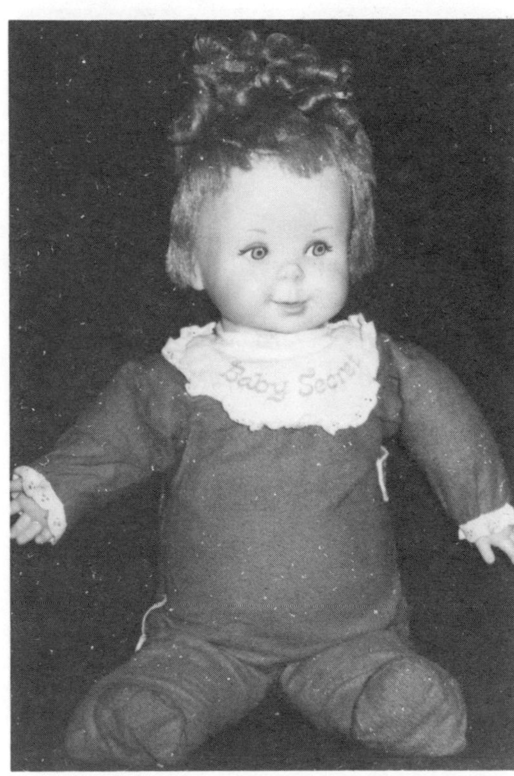

Mattel--18" "Baby Secret" Foam body with vinyl hands and head. Rooted red hair. Painted blue eyes. Open mouth. Chatty ring is located on the right hip. Mouth moves as she says things such as: "Listen, what's that?" and "My name is Baby Secret". Marks: Japan 1965 on head. Tag: Baby Secret/Mattel Inc. Original clothes. $8.00.

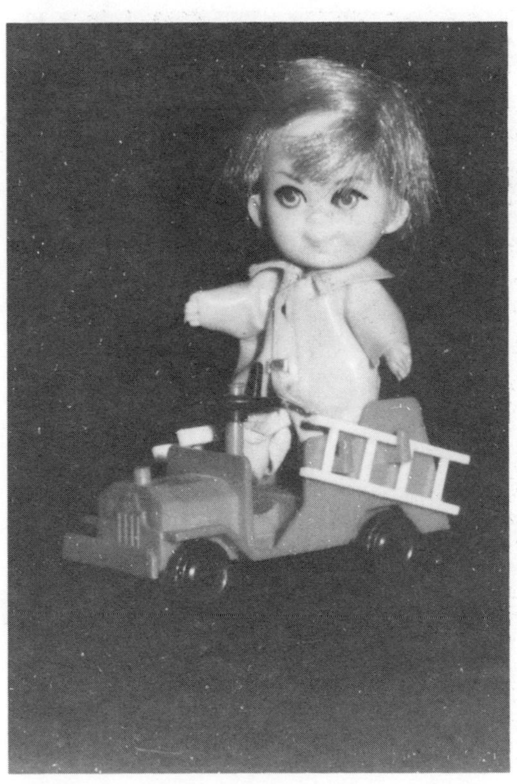

Mattel--3" "Bunson Burnie" All vinyl with rooted blonde hair and painted features. Original. Marks: Mattel. 1965. $4.00. (Courtesy Earlene Johnston Collection).

Mattel--3" "Lola Liddle" All vinyl with rooted blonde hair. Painted features. Original. Marks: Mattel 1965. $4.00. (Courtesy Earlene Johnston Collection).

Mattel--3" "Cinderella" All vinyl with rooted blonde hair. Painted features. Marks: Mattel 1965. $4.00. (Courtesy Earlene Johnston Collection).

Mattel--3" "Liddle Diddle" All vinyl with rooted hair and painted features. One of the "Liddle Kiddle" series. All original. 1965. $4.00. (Courtesy Earlene Johnston Collection).

Mattel-3" "Florence Niddle" All vinyl with rooted hair and painted features. One of the "Liddle Kiddles" series. All original. 1965. $4.00. (Courtesy Earlene Johnston Collection).

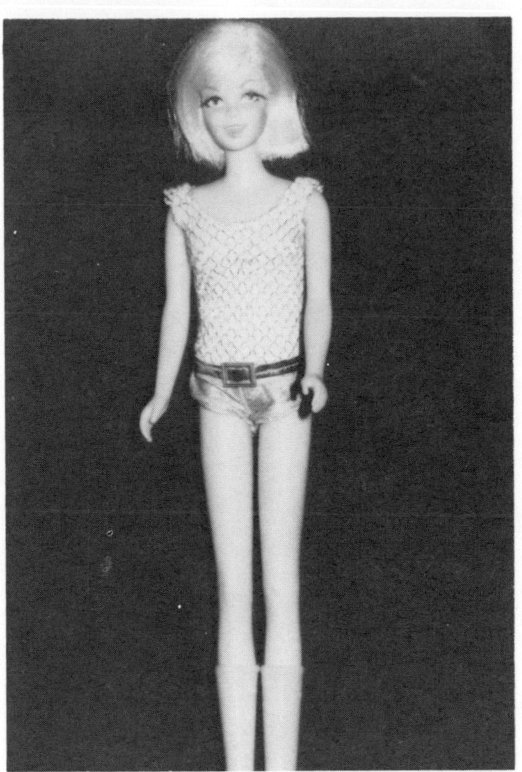

Mattel--11" "Casey" All vinyl with rooted blonde hair. Painted blue eyes. Open/closed mouth with painted teeth. Bendable knees. Marks: 1966/Mattel Inc. $4.00.

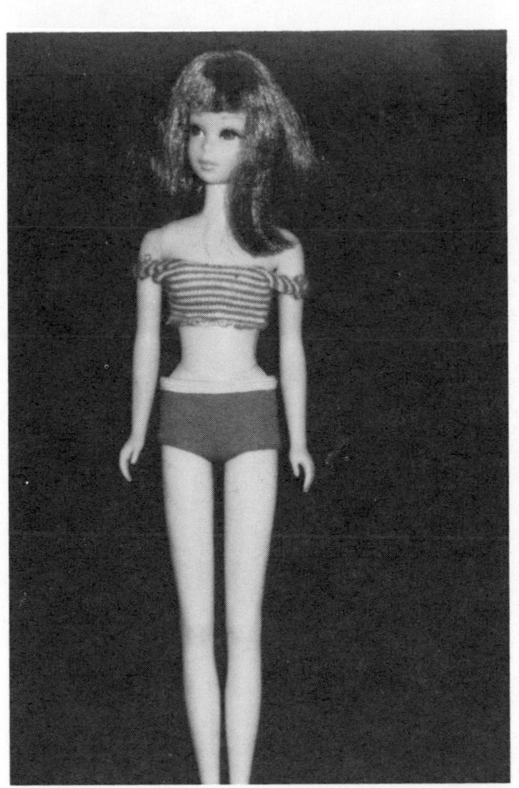

Mattel--11½" "Francie" All vinyl with rooted brown hair. Brown eyes/lashes. Bendable knees. Marks: 1966/Mattel Inc. $4.00.

Mattel--11" "New Barbie" All vinyl with rooted blonde hair. Bendable knees. Marks: 1966/Mattel Inc. $4.00.

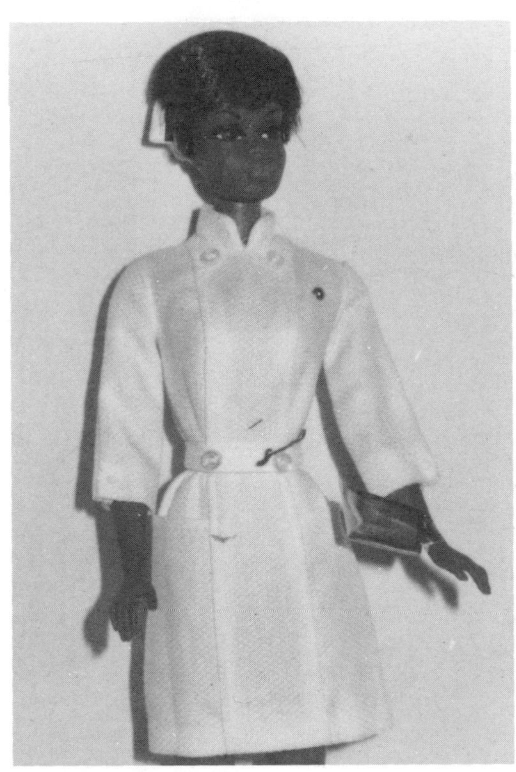

Mattel--11½" "Julia" All vinyl with bendable knees. Rooted black hair. Painted brown eyes. Marks: 1966/Mattel Inc. Original clothes. From TV program "Julia" played by Dianne Carroll. $7.00.

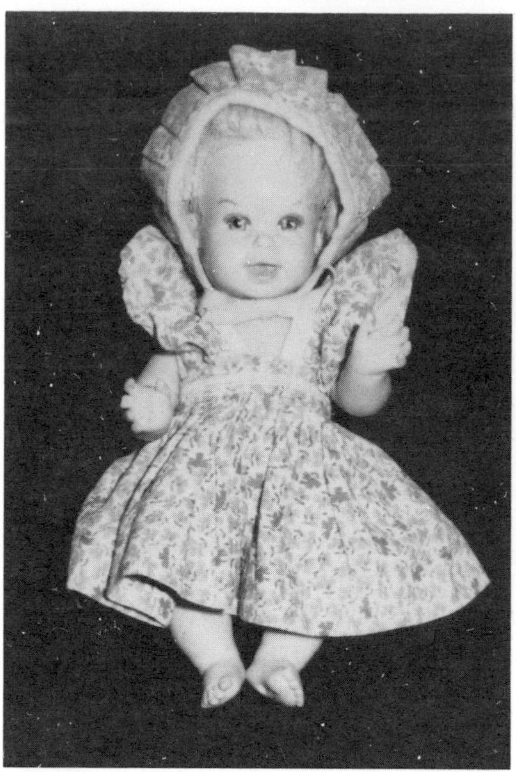

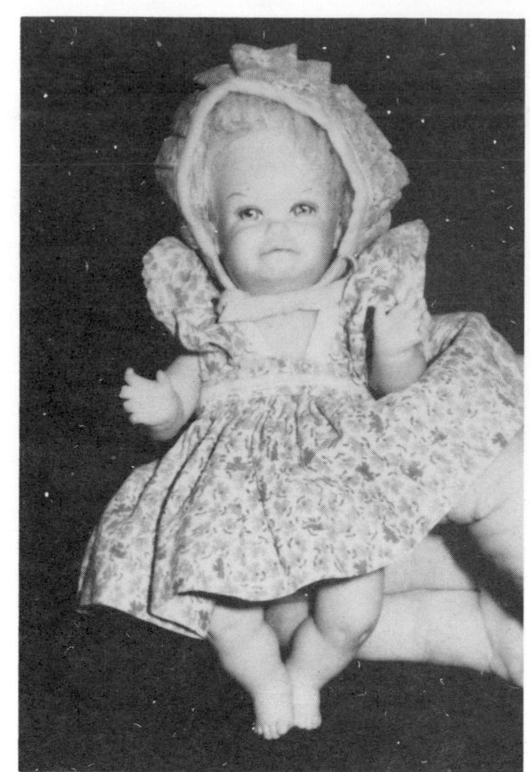

Mattel--6½" "Tiny Cheerful-Tearful" All vinyl with rooted white hair. Painted blue eyes. Open mouth/nurser. Press stomach to make face change. Marks: 1966/Mattel Inc/Hong Kong. $6.00.

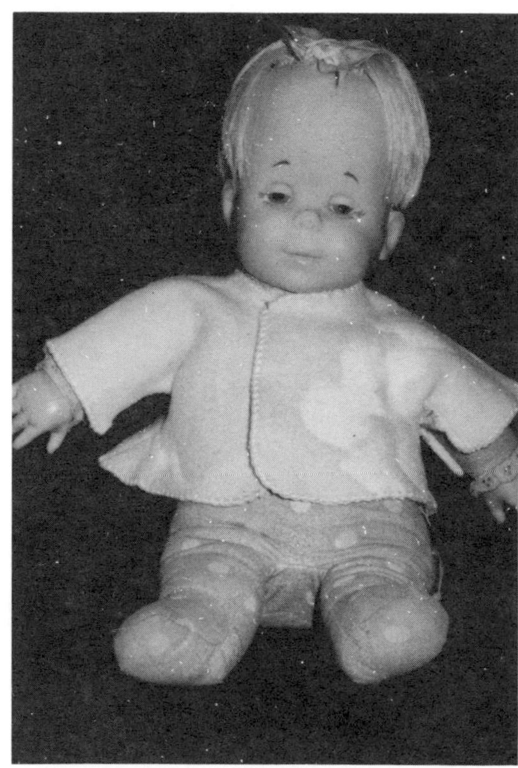

Mattel--15" "Drowsy" Cloth body arms and legs. Vinyl hands and head. Rooted blonde hair. Painted blue sleepy eyes. Closed mouth. Pull ring located on left hip. Says 11 sleeptime things, such as "Mommy, kiss me goodnight" Marks: Tag On Body: "Drowsy By Mattel, Inc. 1966. $3.00.

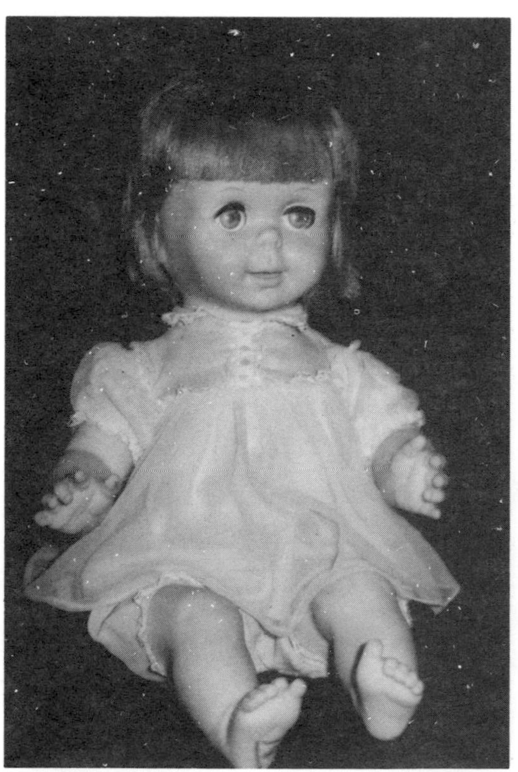

Mattel-17" "Baby Say 'N See" Cloth body. Vinyl arms and legs. Soft, tinted dark pink, vinyl head with rooted dark blonde hair. Blue eyes/molded rubber lashes. Open mouth. Pull ring on left side. Lips move as she talks. Marks: 1966 Mattel Inc USA/US Patents Pending on head. Tag: Baby Say 'N See/1965/Mattel Inc. $8.00.

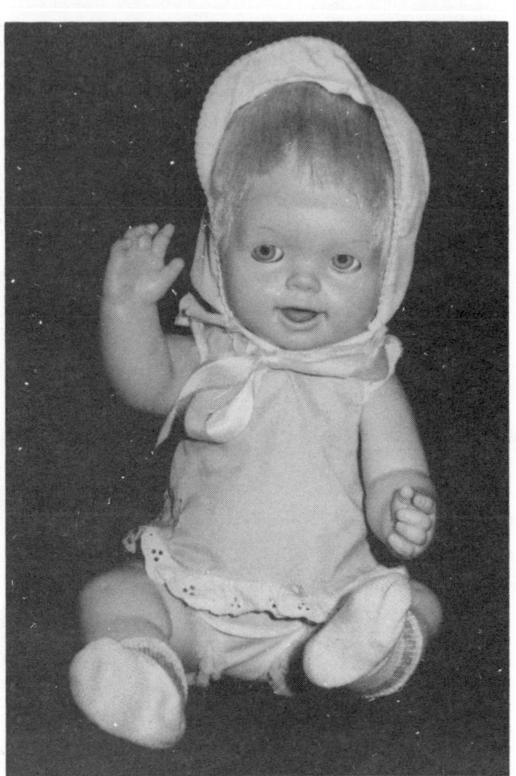

Mattel--17" "Baby's Hungry" Plastic body. Vinyl arms and legs. Soft vinyl head with rooted blonde hair. Blue eyes with molded lashes. Open hands with all fingers curled. Molded toes. Battery operated: eyes roll, sucks on bottle and mouth chews. Marks: 1966 Mattel on head. 1966 Mattel Inc/Hawthorne Calif on body. $8.00.

Mattel-10" "Buffie" Plastic body. Vinyl arms, legs and head. Rooted blonde hair. Painted blue eyes. Open mouth with two painted teeth. Freckles. Open hands with left index extended. Marks: 1967 Mattel Inc/US & For/Pats. Pend/Mexico. 3½" Mrs. Beasley. $10.00 (Courtesy Allin's Collection).

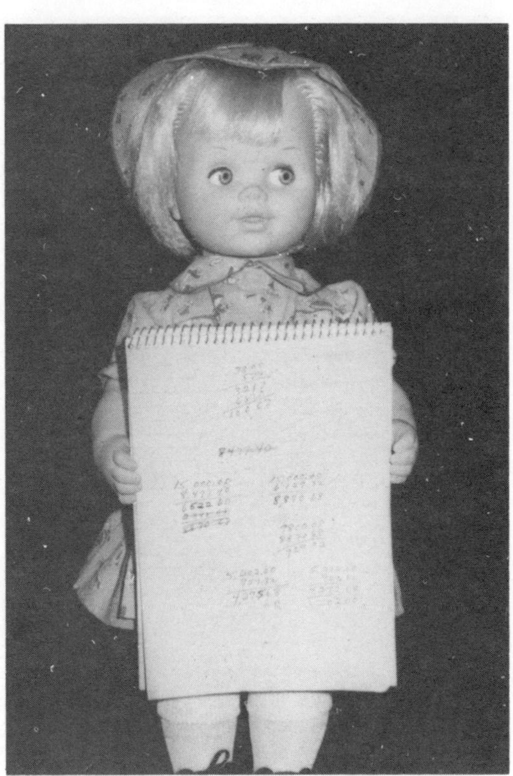

Mattel--19" "Randy Reader" Plastic body and legs. Vinyl arms and head. Rooted white hair. Blue eyes/molded lashes. Hands curled to hold book. Straight chubby legs. Open/closed mouth. Reads nursery rhymes. Battery operated. Eyes move side to side as she reads. Marks: 1967 Mattel Inc/US & For Pats Pend/USA. $20.00.

Mattel--3½" "Sleeping Beauty" All vinyl with rooted white hair. Painted brown eyes. Original clothes. Marks: Mattel, Inc. 1967 Hong Kong, around base of neck. $4.00.

Mattel--10" "Sister Small Talk" Plastic body and legs. Vinyl arms and head. Rooted blonde hair. Painted large blue eyes. Open/closed mouth with painted upper and lower teeth. Left 2nd and 3rd fingers molded together. Marks: 1967 Mattel Inc. Japan, 67/Mattel Inc. US & For Pat Pend. USA on back. Original clothes. $5.00.

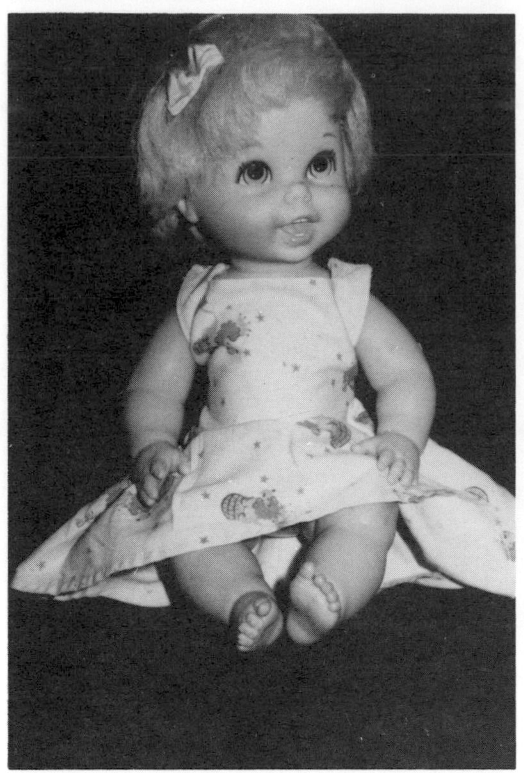

Mattel--11" "Small Talk" Plastic and vinyl with rooted blonde hair. Blue painted glancing upward eyes. Two upper and two lower teeth. Baby crossed legs. Pull ring between shoulders. Marks: 1967-Mattel Inc/Japan, on head. 1967 Mattel Inc/US & For/Pats Pend/USA, on back. $5.00.

Mattel--6" "Doctor Doolittle" All vinyl with molded hair and painted features. Marks: 1967/Mattel Inc./Japan. $10.00. (Courtesy Earlene Johnston Collection).

Mattel--22½" "Doctor Doolittle" Cloth body with sewn on clothes. Vinyl head with molded hair and painted features. Pull string operated. Says things such as "I talk with animals all over the world". Marks: Dr. Doolittle/ MCMLXVII Twentieth Century Fox/Film Corp. Inc. $18.00.

Mattel--4" "Sheila Skediddle" Plastic and vinyl with rooted brown hair. Painted brown eyes. Painted on socks and shoes. Attachment makes doll move. Legs, arms and head move. Marks: Mattel Inc. 1967, on head. Mattel Toymakers, on Skediddle machine. Original clothes. $3.00.

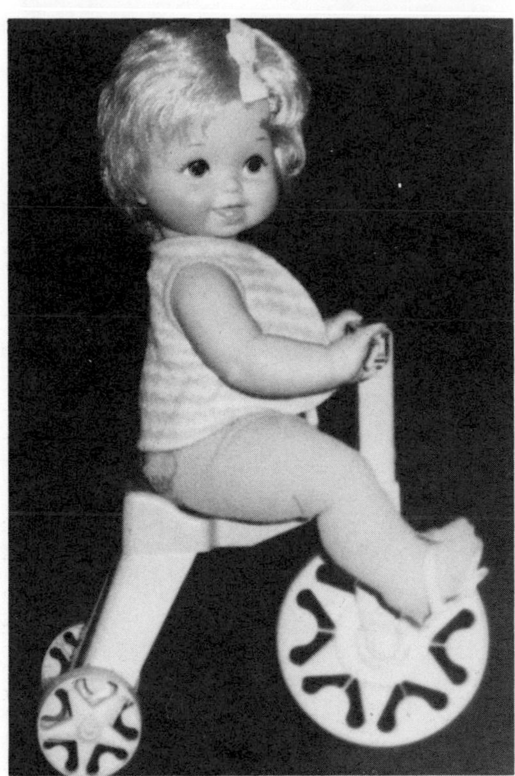

Mattel--16" "Tippy Toes" Plastic body and legs. Vinyl arms and head. Rooted blonde hair. Painted blue eyes. Open mouth with two molded and painted lower teeth. Battery operated. Marks: Mexico, on head. 1967/Mattel Inc/Hawthorne Calif/Made In USA, on body. Original clothes. $6.00.

Mattel--12" "Busy Ken" Plastic and vinyl with molded brown hair. Painted blue eyes. Open/closed mouth with painted teeth. Elbow and knees bend and wrists jointed to rotate. Snap lock thumbs. Marks: 1968 Mattel Inc, on head. Left Hip: 1968/Mattel Inc/USA & For Pats/Pending/Hong Kong. Orig. clothes. $5.00.

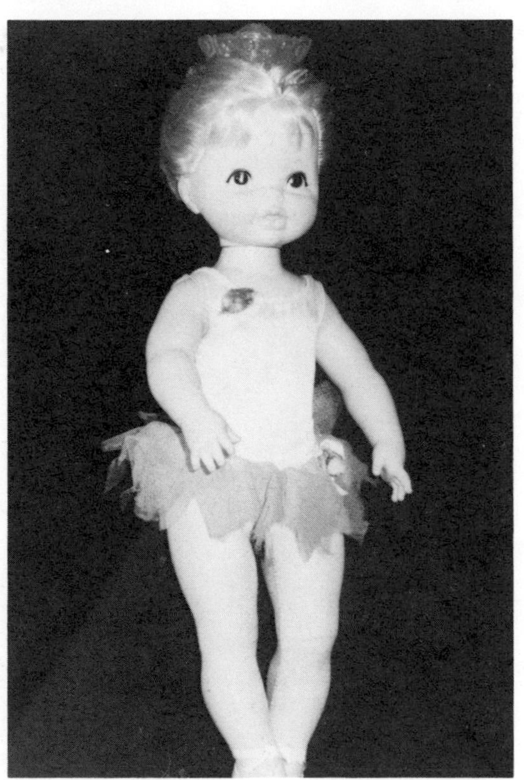

Mattel--24" "Dancerina" Plastic body and legs. Vinyl arms and head. Rooted white hair. Blue painted eyes. Open/closed mouth. Battery operated. Knob on top of head. Marks: 1968/Mattel on head. 1968 Mattel on body. Original clothes. $8.00.

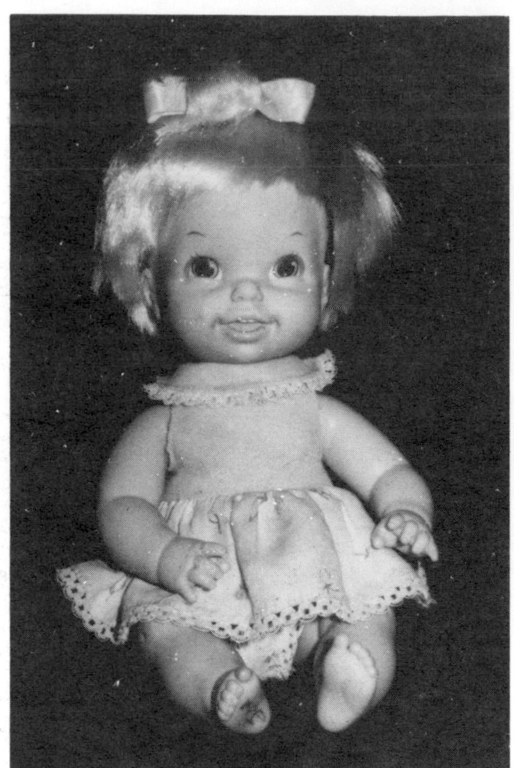

Matel--11" "Bouncy Baby" Plastic body. Vinyl arms, legs and head. Rooted blonde hair. Painted blue eyes. Open/closed mouth. Two painted upper teeth. All fingers curled. Spring action arms, legs and head. Marks: 1968 Mattel Inc/Mexico/US Patent Pending. Dress Tag: Bouncy Baby/1968 Mattel Inc/Hong Kong. $3.00.

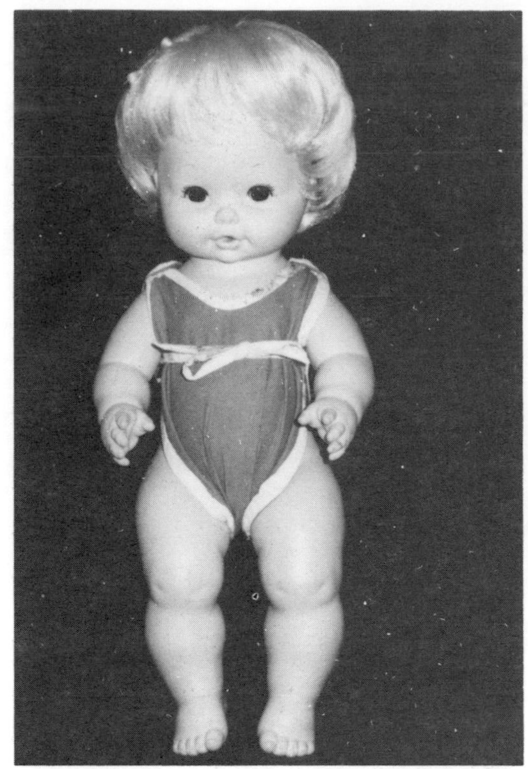

Mattel--15" "Baby Tenderlove" All one piece dublon foam. Rooted white hair. Painted blue eyes. Open mouth/nurser. Marks: 652X/1969 Mattel Inc. Mexico. $3.00.

Mattel--17" "Chatty Tell" Plastic body. Vinyl arms, legs and head. Rooted blonde hair. Painted blue eyes. Closed mouth. Marks: 69 Mat. Inc Mexico on head. 1964 Mattel Inc/Hawthorne Calif/Patented USA Patented In Canada 1962 Other Pat. Pend/Made In Mexico. $16.00.

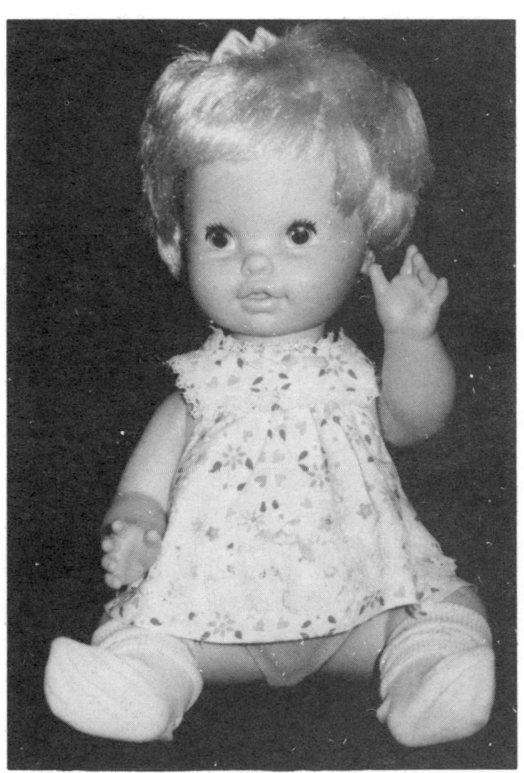

Mattel--16" "Baby Sing-A-Song" Plastic body. Vinyl arms, legs and head. Rooted white hair. Painted blue eyes. Open/closed mouth. Individually molded large toes. Marks: 1969 . Mattel Inc-Mexico, on head. 1964 Mattel Inc, etc., on body. $16.00.

Mattel--18" "Beany" Foam stuffed body with vinyl shoes, hands and head. Three fingers and thumb on both hands. Molded yellow hair. Painted blue, side glancing eyes. Open mouth with molded tongue. Pull string on hip. Marks: Mattel Inc. Toymakers/Bob Clampett-Hong Kong on shoes. Mattel/1969 on tag. $20.00.

Mattel--5" "Charlie Brown Skediddle" Plastic and vinyl with painted features and shoes. Attachment in back makes feet "walk". Marks: 1969 Mattel Inc/Hong Kong/1950 United Features, on head. Mattel Toymakers on Skediddle machine. Original clothes. $3.00.

Mattel--3½" "Breezy Bridgit" All vinyl with molded/painted orange hair. Painted side glancing blue eyes. Freckles. Comes with weighted roller skates and coaster. Marks: 1970/Mattel/Inc., on bottom of left foot. Hong Kong on bottom of right foot. Original clothes. $3.00.

Mattel--4" "Dressy" Vinyl body, arms and legs: one piece and unjointed. Plastic head with glued on paper face. Pull string talker. Pull up head and as it returns to body says, "Here comes my body" and "I've lost my head over you." Marks: 1971 Mattel/Hong Kong, on head and back. Original clothes. $4.00.

Mattel--9½" "Big Jack" Plastic body and legs. Vinyl arms and head. Molded painted hair. Painted brown eyes. Jointed neck, shoulders, wrist, waist, hips, knees, ankles. Marks: 1971 Mattel Inc/US Patent Pending/Hong Kong. Paper Tag: Big Jack. $4.00.

Mattel--7" 'Kretor and 12" Zark" Plastic shark (Zark). Vinyl man (Kretor). Under water, Zark swims and carries Kretor under him. Pull string wind. Marks: Bottom Of Kretor's Left Foot: 6389-0150/2 Right Foot: 1970 Mattel Inc/Hong Kong/US & For/Patented/Patented In Canada 1970. Zark: 1970/Mattel Inc/Hong Kong/US Patent Pending, on the under side of jaw. $8.00.

Mego--11½" "Haddie Mod" Plastic and vinyl with rooted yellow blonde hair. Brown painted eyes. Open/closed mouth with painted teeth. Dimple in right cheek. Jointed shoulders, waist and hip. High heel feet. Marks: Mego MCMLXXI/Hong Kong on back. Dress tag: Mego/Hong Kong. $3.00.

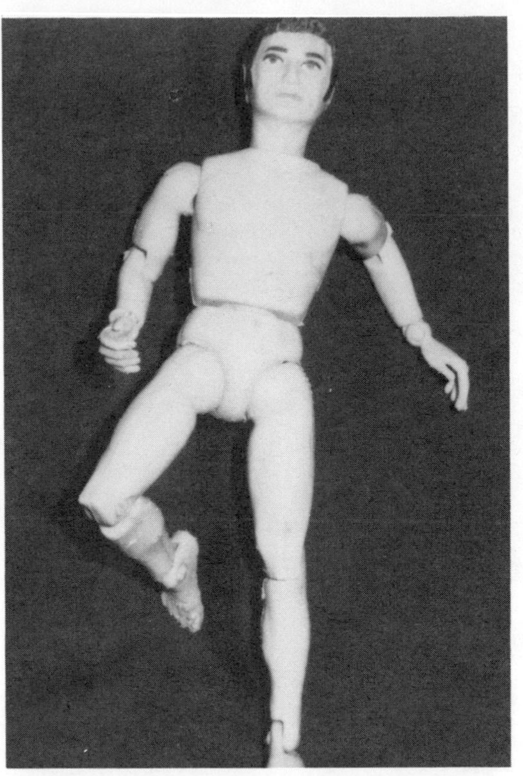

Mego--7½" "Joe Namath" Plastic body, arms and legs. Vinyl hands and head. Molded black hair. Painted features. Jointed neck, shoulders, elbows, wrist, hips, knees and ankles. Marks: Mego Corp/Reg US Pat Off/Pat Pend/Hong Kong/MCMLXXI. (Princess Grace Doll, Inc.). $5.00.

Midwestern Mfg. Co--12" "Nun Nurse" All hard plastic. Blue sleep eyes/molded lashes. Walker, head turns. Marks: On Box: Midwestern Mfg Co/St. Louis 3 Mo. 1958. All original. $5.00.

Molly E Co.--8½" "Molly" Plastic body and legs. Vinyl arms and head. Rooted white hair. Blue sleep eyes/molded lashes. 2nd and 3rd fingers molded together. Marks: Molly E, on head. Part of original clothes. 1957. Made by the Molly E Goldman Company. $4.00.

Monica Studios--16" "Monica" All composition with human hair embedded in scalp. Light blue painted eyes, brown eye shadow. Closed mouth with full lips. Adult hands with painted nails. Jointed, but unmovable head. Marks: none. Original clothes. $45.00.

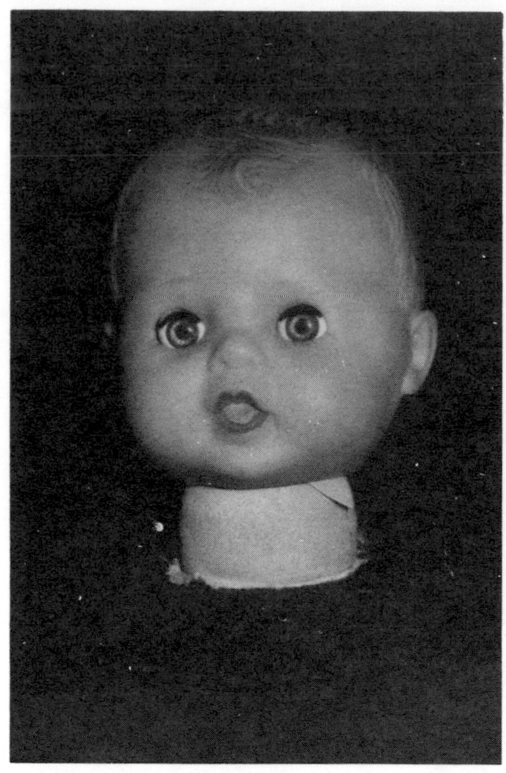

M.R.P.--18" "Christening Baby" One piece latex body, arms and legs. Vinyl head with molded hair. Blue sleep eyes/lashes. Open/closed mouth with molded tongue. Marks: M.R.P., on head. 1952. Made by the Miller Rubber Products Company. This is the company that made the rubber bodies for the Effanbee Dy Dee $15.00.

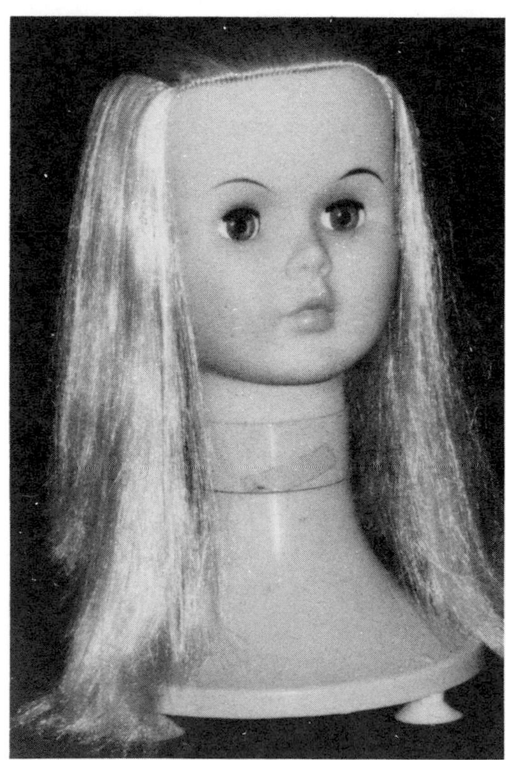

Nabco--13" "Claudette" Plastic base with a vinyl head. Rooted white hair. Blue sleep eyes/lashes. Marks: Nabco Doll, Inc./Pat. Pend, on head. $4.00.

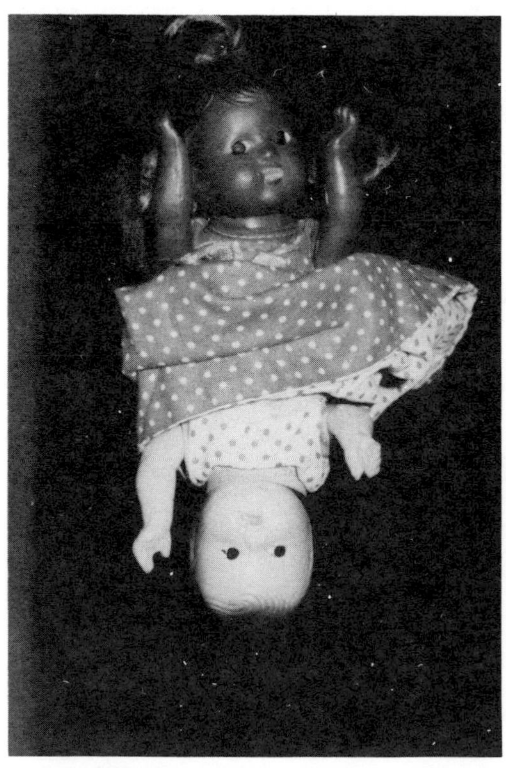

7" "Topsy-Turvy" All composition with molded hair and painted features. Marks: none. 1935. $16.00. (Courtesy Fye Collection).

16" "Happy Toddler" All composition with glued on blonde mohair wig, pulled to sides. Green sleep eyes/lashes. Open mouth with 2 teeth, felt tongue. Wide open hands with right 3rd finger slightly curled. Marks: None. 1936. $16.00.

20" "Walker"--All composition. Glued on blonde mohair wig. Brown tint sleep eyes/lashes. Walker with attached wooden peg upper legs. Head turns as she walks. Open mouth with six teeth. Marks: None. Open crown allows access

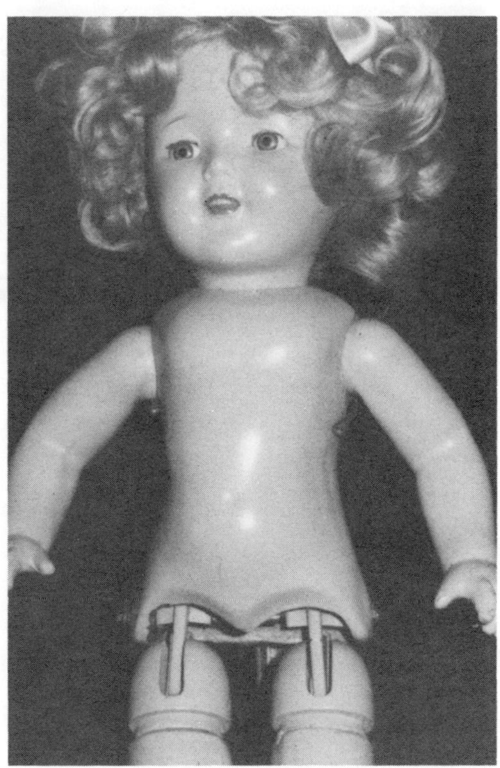

to walking mechanism. Was sold to present owners as Shirley Temple Walker and has also been identified as the Walking Little Colonel by Madame Alexander. 1937. $65.00. (Courtesy Allin's Collection).

22" "Lone Ranger" Cloth body, arms and legs. Gauntlet composition hands and feet. Excellent, high polished composition head with painted features. Marks: None. Original clothes. 1938. $110.00. (Courtesy Fye Collection). Back view on Page 214.

22" "Lone Ranger"

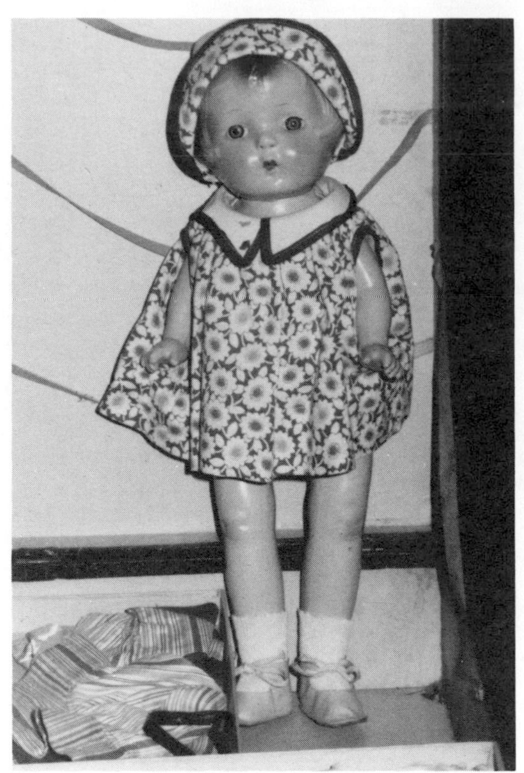

18" "Eva" All composition with molded hair. Blue sleep eyes. Closed mouth. Original clothes and trunk. Marks: None. 1939. $20.00. (Courtesy Fye Collection).

19" "American Child" All composition with glued on human hair wig. Blue decal sleep eyes/lashes. Marks: None. Appears to be a poor copy of DeeWees Cochrans American Children Series made by Effanbee Company. Ca. 1939. $35.00.

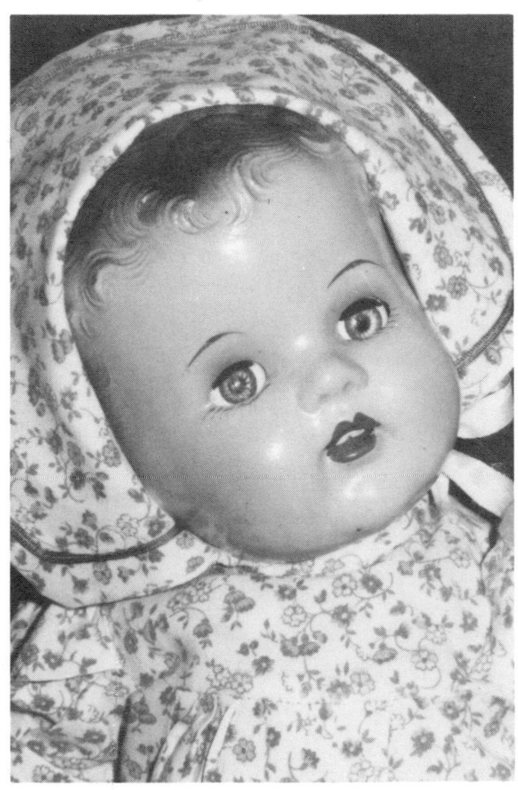

19" "Lois Jane" All composition with molded hair. Blue sleep eyes/lashes. Blue eyeshadow. Open mouth with two teeth. Marks: None. 1940. $42.00. (Courtesy Allin's Collection).

10" and 8" "Dutch Girls" All composition with one piece body and head. Jointed shoulders and hips. Molded hair. Painted features. Marks: None. 1939-1943. $6.00.

21" "Betty Grable" All composition with glued on blonde mohair wig. Blue sleep eyes/lashes. Closed mouth. Posable legs. Marks: 22 over 8 under arms. 22 back of legs. This doll has been

shown at doll conventions as Betty Grable but unless one is found with tag, this is uncertain. Original dress. 1940's. $45.00.

Betty Grable in one of her famous "pin-up" bathing suit poses.

13½" "False Snow White" All composition with painted and molded hair. Molded ribbon. Side glancing painted blue eyes. Closed mouth. Their clothes were stapled on. Marks: None. 1940. $10.00.

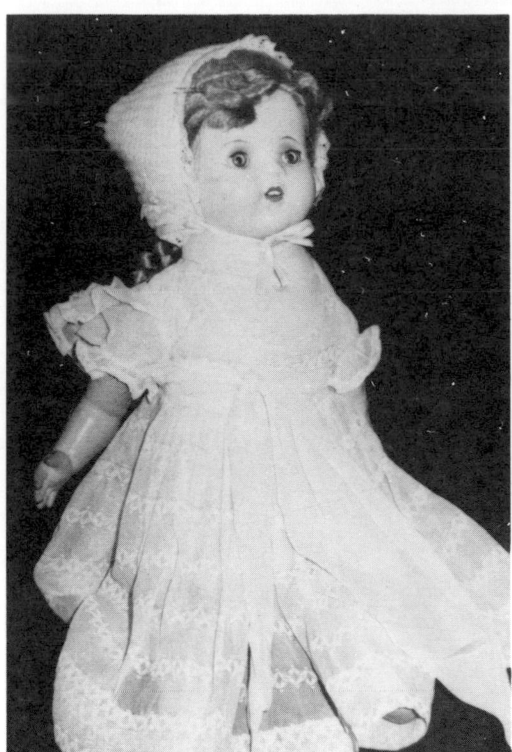

25" "Happy Baby" Cloth body. Latex legs and arms. Composition head with glued on dark blonde wig. Blue sleep eyes/lashes. Open mouth with two teeth. Cryer. Marks: None. 1942. $8.00.

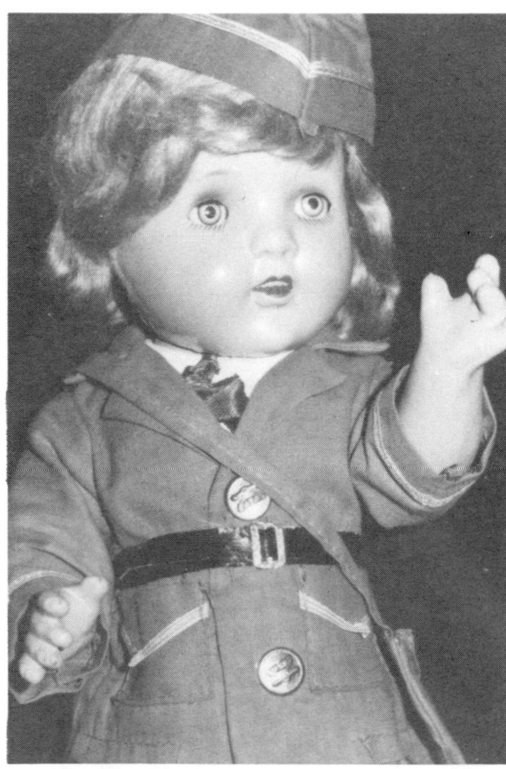

16" "Air Force" All composition with glued on blonde mohair wig. Blue decal eyes/lashes. Open mouth with six teeth. Marks: None. 1942. $35.00. (Courtesy Allin's Collection).

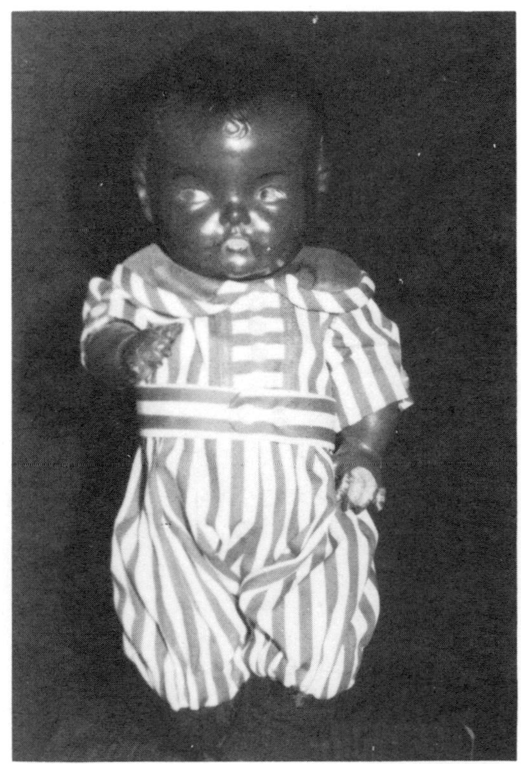

12" "Henry" All composition. Jointed neck, shoulders and hip. Painted side glancing brown eyes. Molded painted black hair. Dimples. American made. 1944. $25.00. (Courtesy Earlene Johnston Collection).

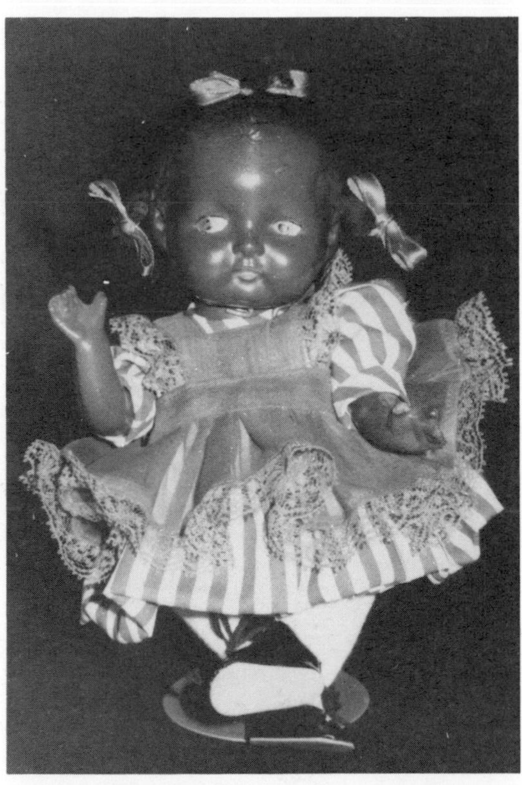

9" "Henrette" All composition with jointed neck, shoulders and hips. Painted brown side glancing eyes. Molded painted black hair with three yarn inset pigtails. American made. 1944. $25.00. (Courtesy Earlene Johnston).

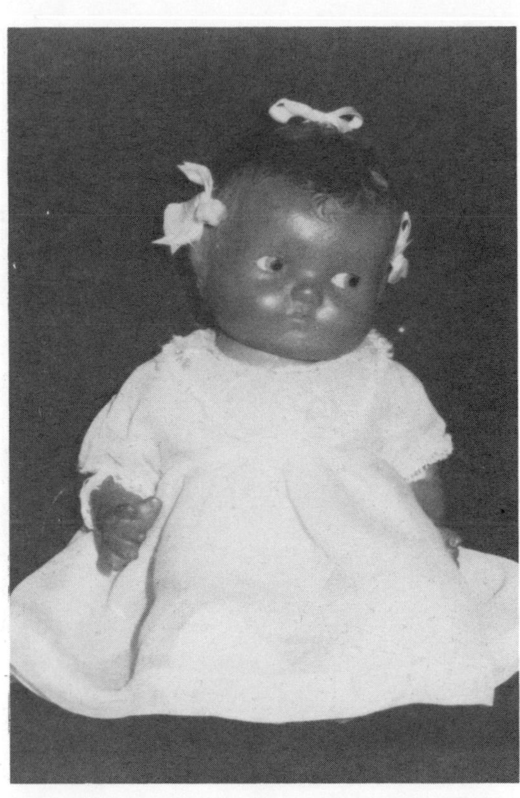

11" "Topsy" All composition with molded and painted black hair. Painted brown side glancing eyes. Closed mouth. Bent and crossed baby legs. 2nd and 3rd fingers curled. Marks: None. 1944. $15.00.

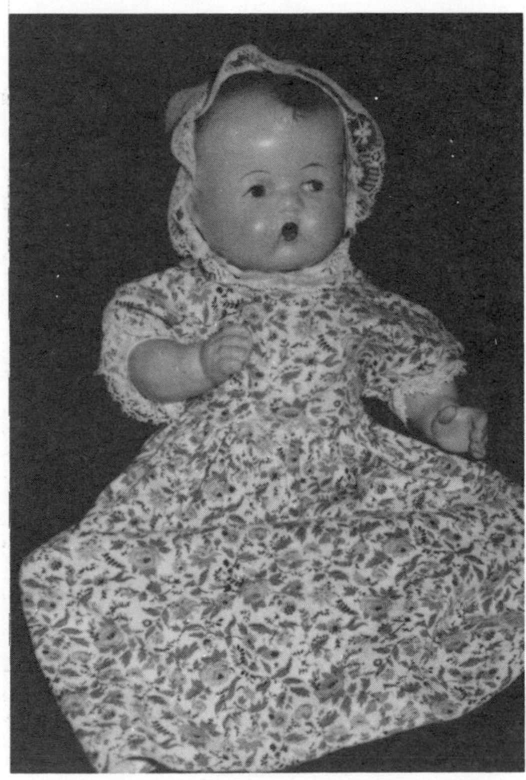

14" "Big Boy" All composition with molded hair and painted features. Molded bent arms. Toddler legs. Marks: None. 1944. Original clothes. $10.00.

17" "Gingham Gal" One piece stuffed body, arms and legs. Composition head with molded hair. Large plexiglass covered eyes. Eyes move within holder. Marks: None. Original. 1945. $25.00.

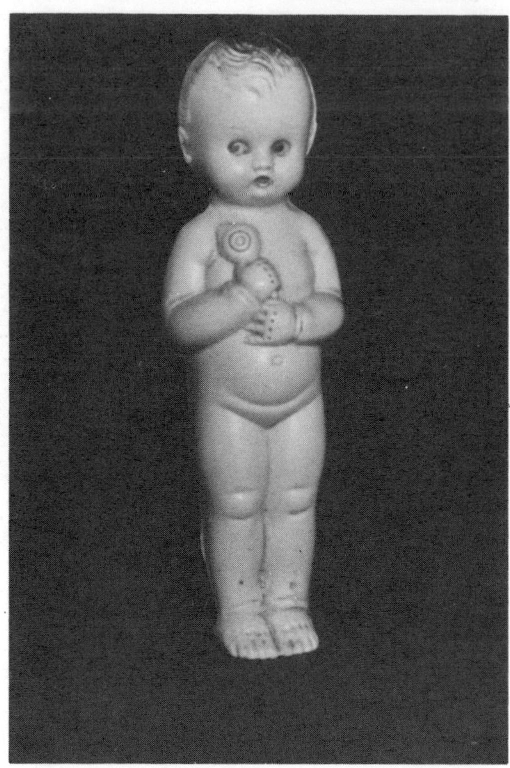

4½" "Lollypop Kid" All hard plastic "Frozen" type. Molded hair and painted features. Marks: None. 1948. $8.00.

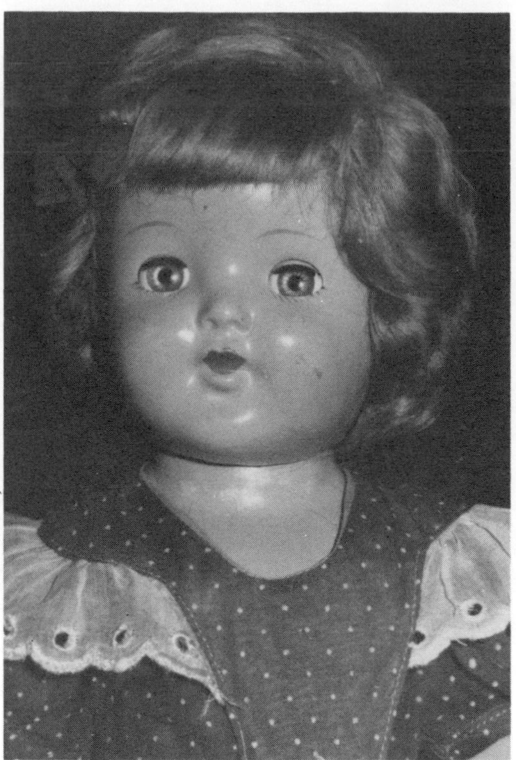

19" "Abbi-Gail" All composition with glued on light brown mohair wig. Blue sleep eyes/lashes. Closed mouth that was later molded open. Open hands, palms down. Right 2nd finger slightly

curled with 3rd finger curled deeper. Left 2nd finger curled and little finger extended. Marks: None. 1948. $40.00.

22" "Dream Doll" Hard plastic head. Glued on yellow mohair wig. Blue intaglio eyes/lashes. Open mouth with two teeth and felt tongue. Lightly dimpled cheeks. Latex body, arms and legs. Marks: 20, on head. 1948. $16.00.

18" "Pauline" Hard plastic head with glued on blonde mohair wig. Blue sleep eyes/lashes. Cloth body with latex arms and legs. Open mouth with two teeth and felt tongue. Marks: None. 1949. $18.00.

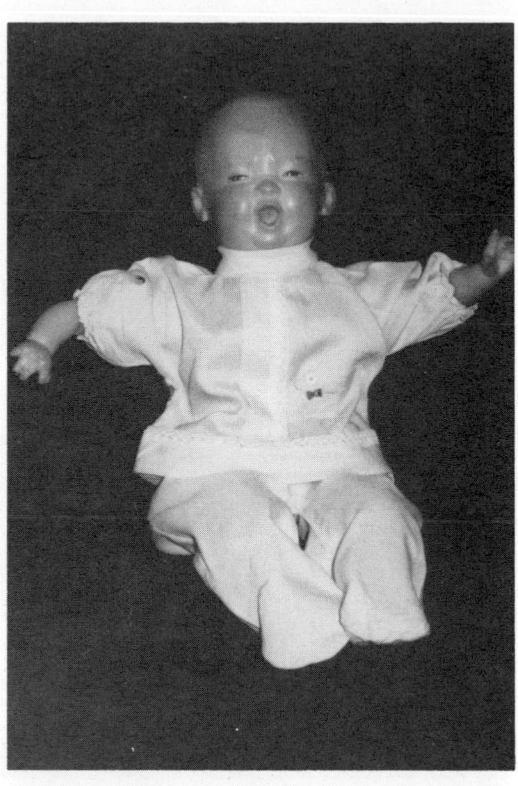

16" "Crying Baby" Cloth body. Early vinyl arms, legs and head. Lightly molded brown hair. Blue painted eyes. Open mouth with molded tongue. 2nd and 3rd fingers molded together. Marks: a V in a diamond. Horsman says this is not their doll. A second exact doll marked: Copr. Lastic-Plastic '49. $10.00.

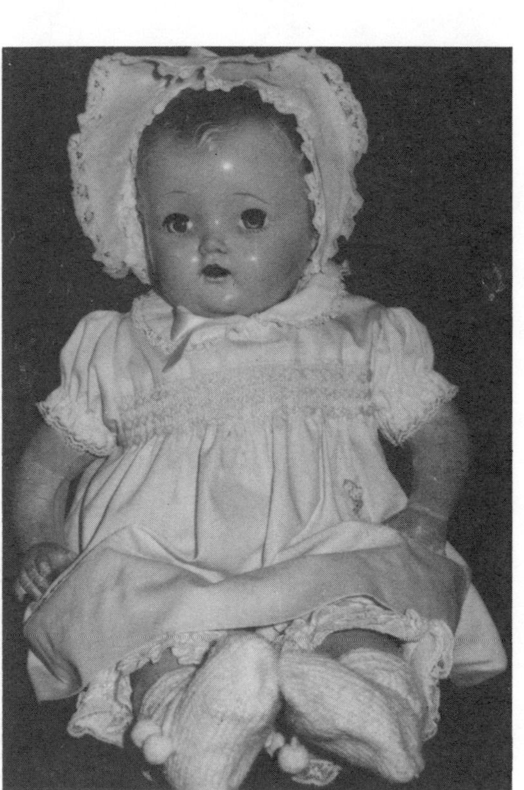

20" "Pretty Baby" Cloth body. Composition arms and legs. Hard plastic head with molded painted brown hair. Blue sleep eyes/lashes. Open mouth with two teeth, felt tongue. Marks: None. 1950. $15.00.

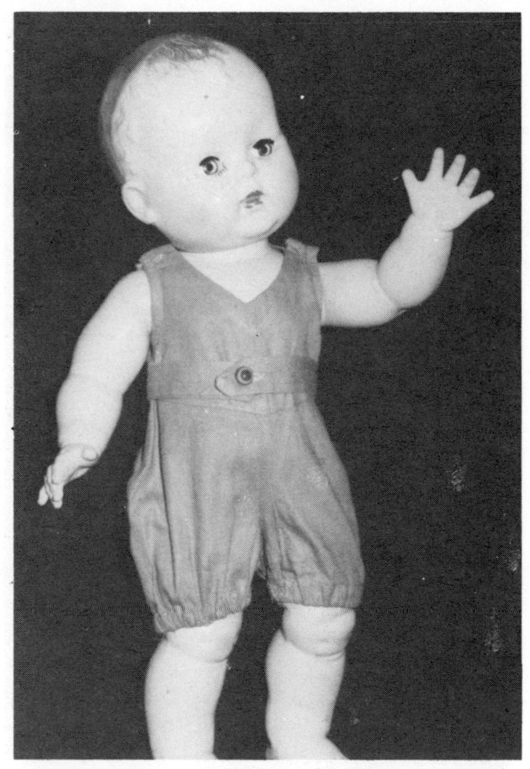

14" "Baby Benny" All hard plastic with molded hair. Blue sleep eyes/lashes. Open closed mouth. Marks: Made In USA, on back. 1950. $20.00.

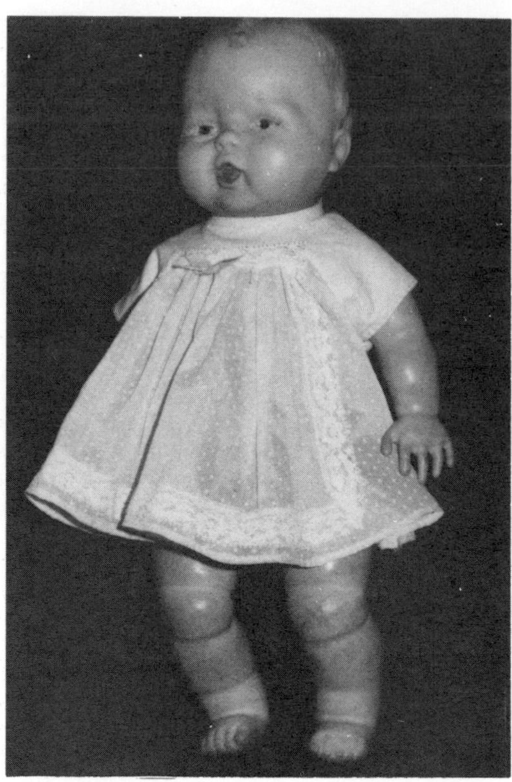

11" "Bendee" Stuffed latex one piece body, arms and legs. Vinyl head with molded and painted hair. Painted side glancing eyes. Open/closed mouth with molded tongue. Puckered expression. Marks: None. 1951. Wire enclosed in legs, body and arms. $14.00.

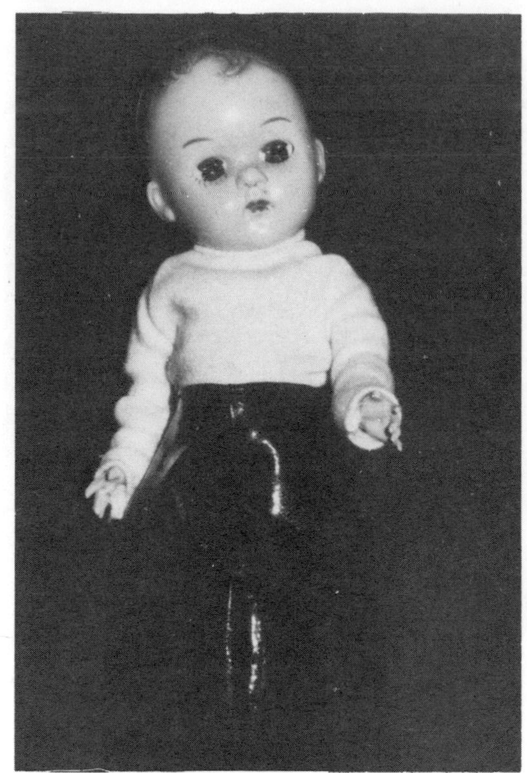

7" "Johnny" All hard plastic with molded and painted hair. Sleep blue eyes/lashes. Molded and painted on shoes. Marks: None. 1951. $5.00.

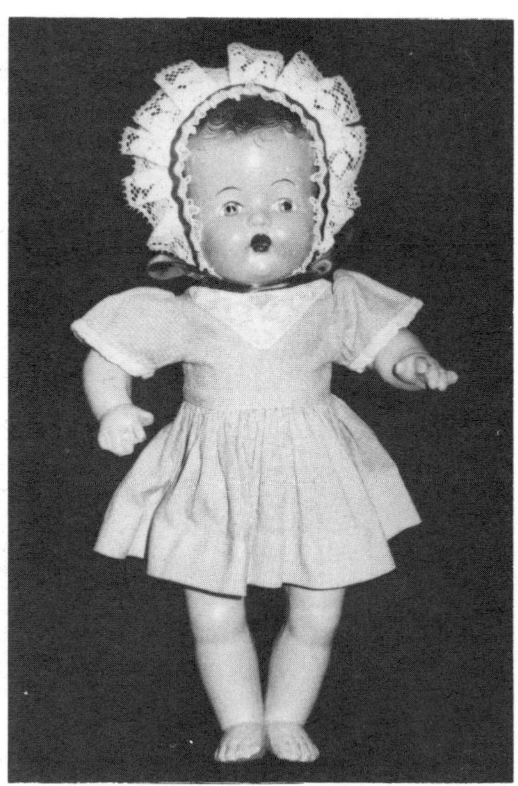

12½" "Dimply Baby" All composition made in one piece head and body. Curly molded hair. Painted features. Crossed baby legs. Marks: None. 1951. $8.00.

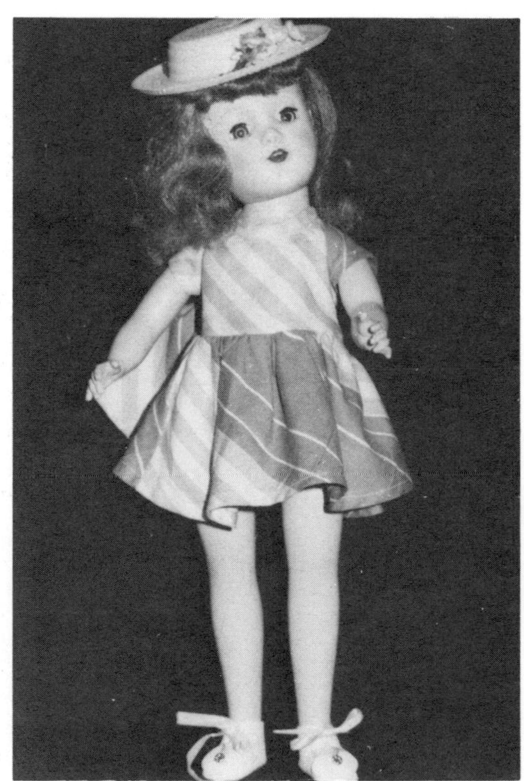

14" "Polly" All hard plastic with glued on light brown hair. Blue sleep eyes/lashes. Open mouth with three teeth and felt tongue. Open hands with left 2nd and 3rd slightly curled. Right 2nd and 3rd fingers molded together and slightly curled. Marks: Made In USA, on body. 1952. $18.00.

10" "Little Traveler" All hard plastic. Glued on dark blonde wig. Blue sleep eyes/molded lashes. Closed mouth. Jointed knees. Marks: None. 1953. $9.00.

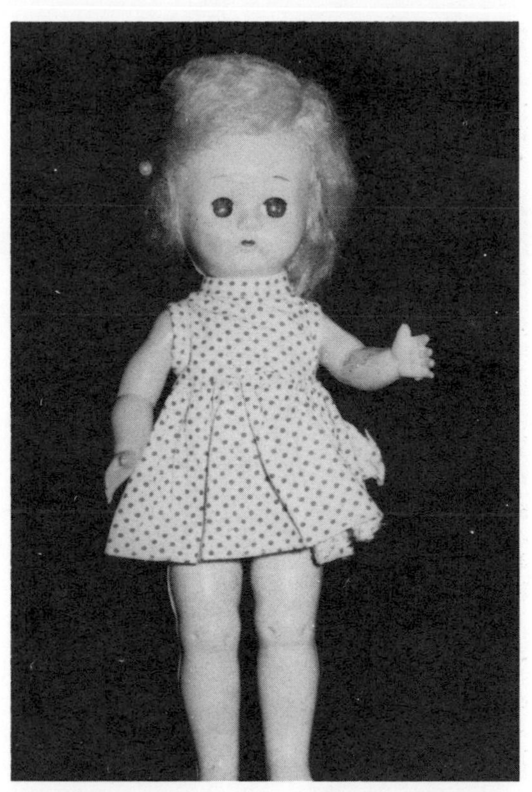

11" "Janie" Hard plastic. Early walker with turning head. Glued on blonde mohair wig. Blue sleep eyes/molded lashes. Closed mouth. Marks: None. 1953. $4.00.

11½" "Teena" All hard plastic with glued on blonde mohair wig. Blue sleep eyes/lashes. Hip socket walker. Jointed knees. High heel feet. Marks: Pat. Pend., on back. 1953. $5.00.

Ideal--7" "Miss Curity" All hard plastic with one piece body and legs. Painted on stockings and shoes. Open hands with 2nd and 3rd fingers curled. Glued on blonde saran hair. Sleep blue eyes/painted lashes. Closed mouth. Uniform and cap made of thin oilcloth. Marks: None. 1953. Trademark Kendall Co. Original clothes. $7.00.

19" "Little Sister" One piece, unjointed, early vinyl body. Vinyl head with rooted ash blonde hair. Blue sleep eyes/lashes. Open/closed smiling mouth. Open hands with palms down. Marks: AE, on head. Came as twins, other with brown hair and brown eyes. 1953. $12.00.

7" "Nun" All hard plastic. Blue sleep eyes. Painted shoes. Marks: None. 1954. $5.00.

15" "World Traveler" All hard plastic. Glued on saran wig. Blue sleep eyes/lashes. Open mouth with four teeth and felt tongue. Marks: Can make out an R, the rest is chipped off. 1954. Sold with trunk and wardrobe. $22.00.

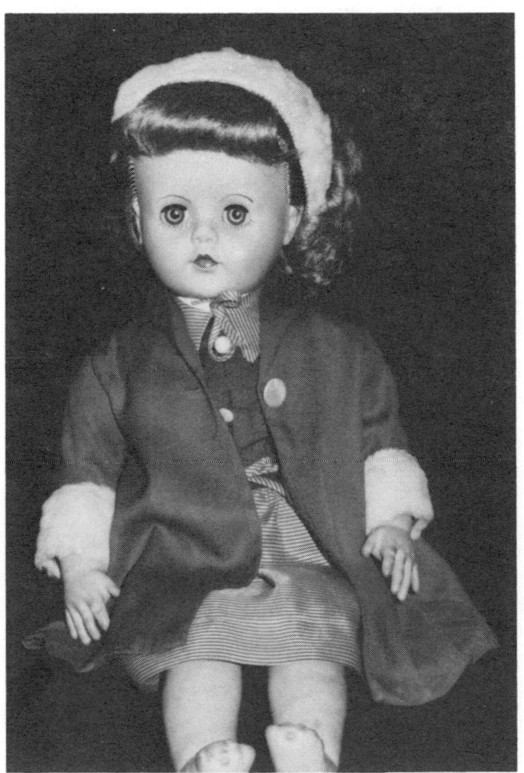

26" "Mary Lou" Soft vinyl head. Big glassene, blue sleep eyes/lashes. Latex body, arms and legs. Rooted dark blonde hair. Marks: X, in a circle, on head and a large A on lower back. Madame Alexander does not claim these X marked dolls. $20.00.

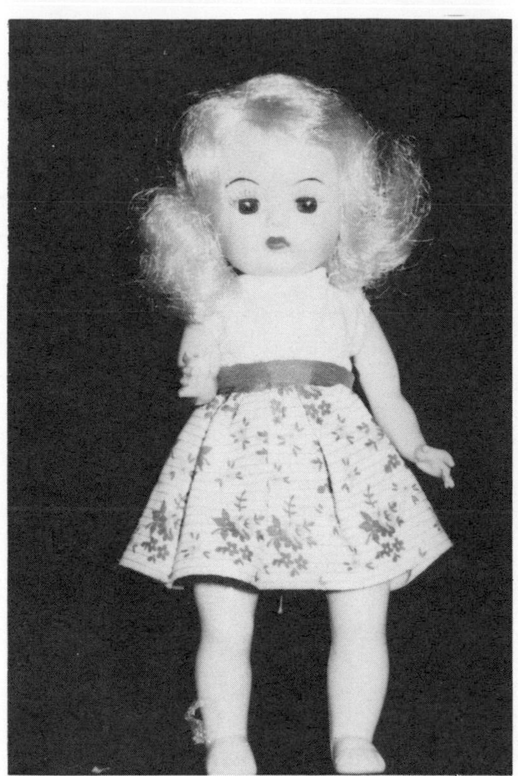

7" "Ninette" All hard plastic with glued on blonde saran wig. Dark blue sleep eyes/molded lashes. Closed mouth. Fat face and legs are far apart. Head turns as she walks. Marks: None. 1955. $5.00.

31" "Rosy Walker" Hard plastic body and legs. Walker with jointed knees. Vinyl arms and head. Rooted dark brown hair. Blue sleep eyes/lashes. Closed mouth. 2nd and 3rd fingers slightly curled. Marks: None. 1956. $30.00.

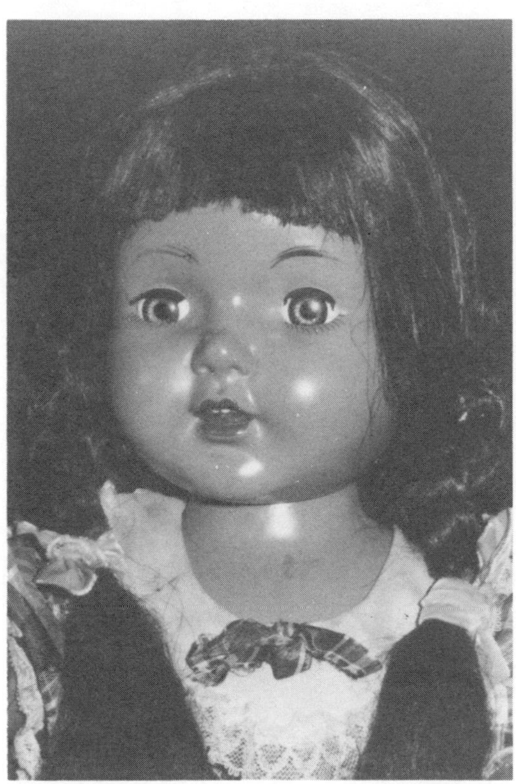

27" "Amy Louise" All hard plastic with glued on black wig. Brown sleep eyes/lashes. Open mouth with four teeth and felt tongue. Walker. Marks: X, in a circle, on head. Original clothes. 1956. $30.00.

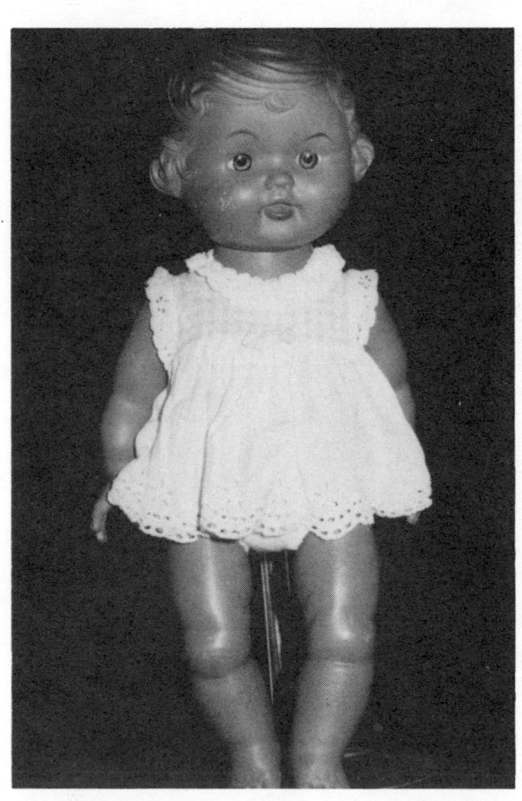

12" "Pansy" Plastic body. Vinyl arms, legs and head. Molded, painted black hair. Brown stationary eyes. Open/closed mouth. Marks: Unable to read mold marks. 1956. $9.00. (Courtesy Earlene Johnston Collection).

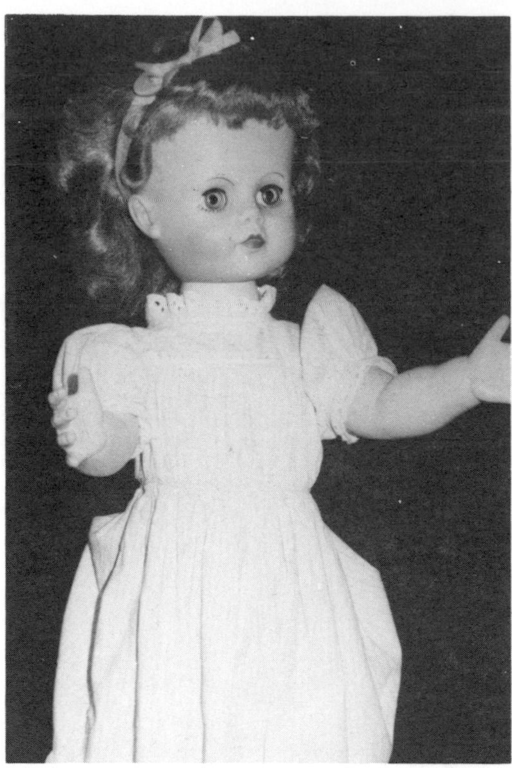

30" "Sweet Lou" Hard plastic body, arms and legs. Stuffed vinyl head with rooted dark blonde hair. Blue/green sleep eyes/lashes. Right arm socketed so it will rotate but left arm will only go straight down to shoulder high. Jointed knees. Marks: X in a circle, on head. 1956. Madame Alexander does not claim these X marked dolls. $22.00.

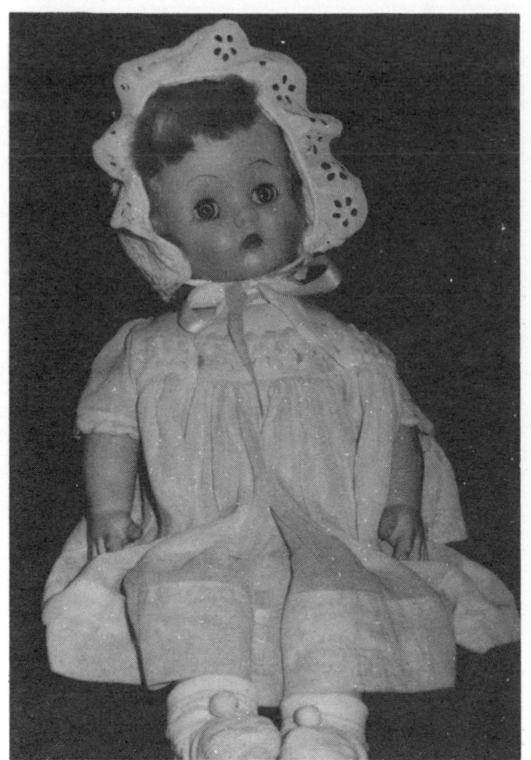

17" "Cuddly Kathy" Latex one piece body, arms and legs. Early vinyl head with rooted yellow blonde hair. Blue sleep eyes/lashes. Closed mouth. Marks: a 3, in a circle on head. 1956. $9.00.

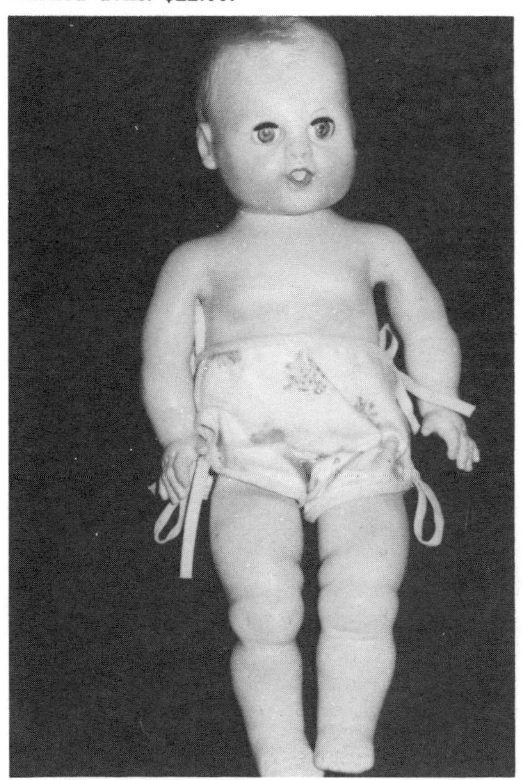

14" "My Baby" Latex, unjointed body, arms and legs. Stuffed latex head with puckered up features. Blue sleep eyes/lashes. Open/closed mouth. Marks: Can not make out except ARR. 1957. $24.00. (Courtesy Earlene Johnston Collection).

15" "Pert & Sassy" All vinyl with rooted brown hair. Pierced ears. Blue sleep eyes/molded lashes. Closed mouth. 2nd and 3rd fingers slightly curled. Medium high heels. Marks: None. 1957. Original dress. $6.00.

19" "Miss Glamour Ann" Hard plastic body, legs, with early walker mechanism. Legs are two positioned and have jointed knees. Vinyl arms and head. Rooted blonde hair. Blue sleep eyes/lashes. 2nd and 3rd finger slightly curled on both hands. High heel feet. Pierced ears. Marks: None. 1957. $8.00.

13½" "Kleenex Baby" Rigid vinyl body, arms and legs. Vinyl head with molded hair. Large blue sleep eyes/lashes. Open mouth/nurser. Open hands, palms facing body. Dimpled knees. Marks: Cannot make it out. 1958. $3.00.

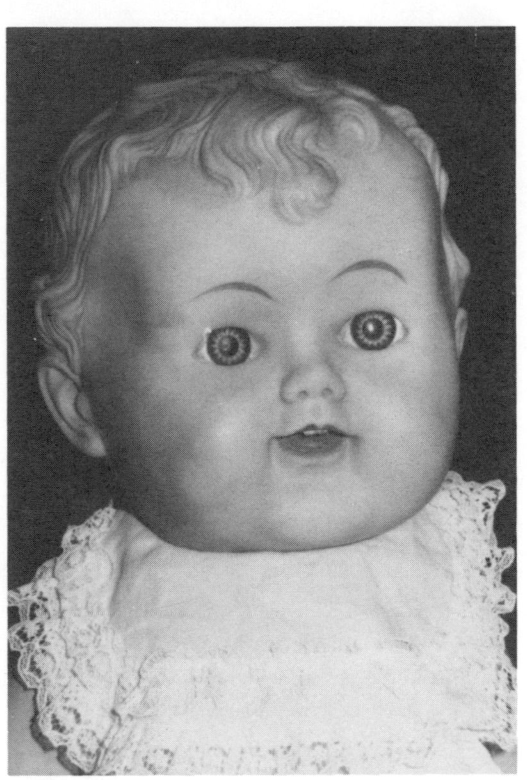

18" "Baby Bunting" Latex, one piece body, arms and legs. Vinyl head with molded hair. Inset stationary blue eyes. Open/closed mouth with two teeth. Marks: None. 1957. $15.00.

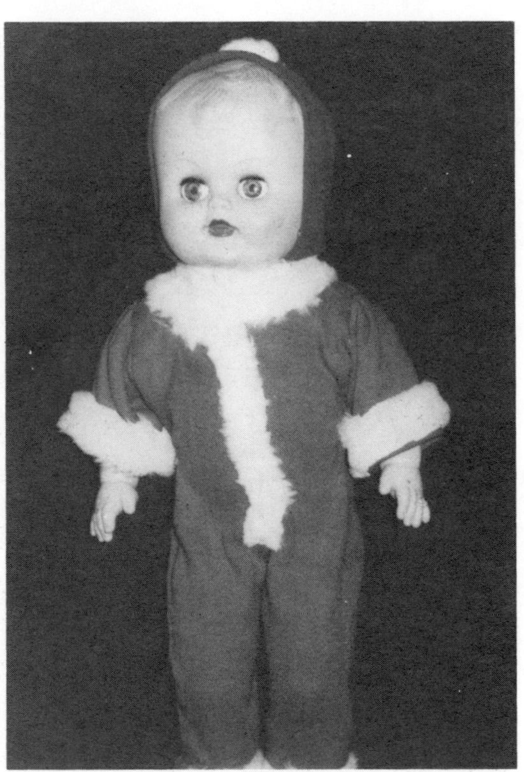

16" "Dream Doll" One piece body, arms and legs. Vinyl head with molded hair. Large blue sleep eyes/lashes. Open/closed mouth. Marks: 15, on head. VS-17/41, on back. 1958. $4.00.

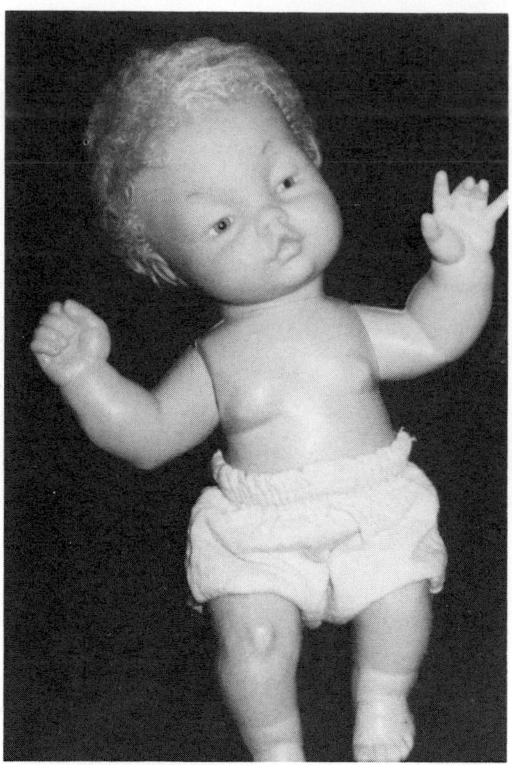

12" "Yuletide" All soft plastic with vinyl head. Rooted white hair. Stationary blue eyes. Pursed mouth that is open/closed. Jointed, rigid arms. Left hand open. Right thumb over curled fingers. Legs rigid with right knee pulled up. 1958. $15.00.

11½" "Angel" All vinyl with molded painted black hair. Inset stationary eyes. Marks: None. 1958. $7.00. (Courtesy Allin's Collection).

19" "Pert Teenager" Solid vinyl body, arms and legs. Vinyl head with rooted dark brown hair. Blue sleep eyes/lashes. Closed mouth. Jointed waist. High heel feet. Painted toe and fingernails. Marks: None. 1958. Original dress. $7.00.

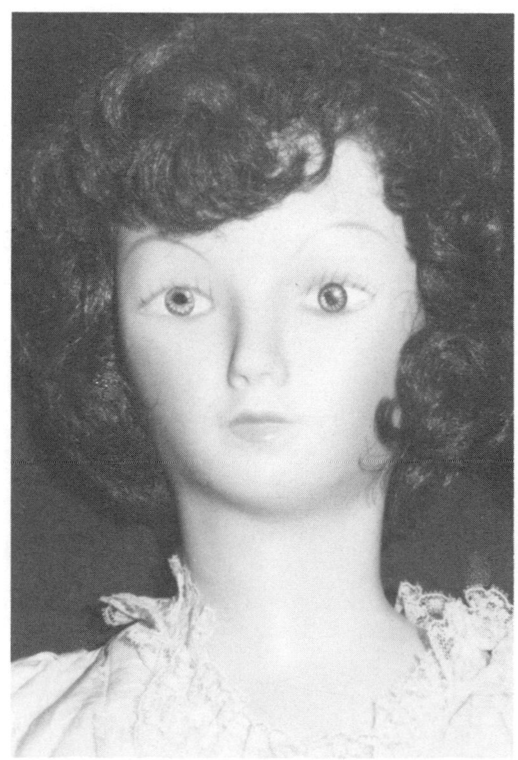

27½" "Bed Doll" Cloth body and legs. Plastic gauntlet feet. Plastic arms and head. Rooted dark brown hair. Inset stationary blue eyes. Marks: None. 1960. $20.00.

25" "Stunning" All vinyl. Rooted ash blonde hair. Blue sleep eyes/lashes. Closed mouth. Jointed waist. High heel feet. Marks: None. Original dress. 1961. $30.00.

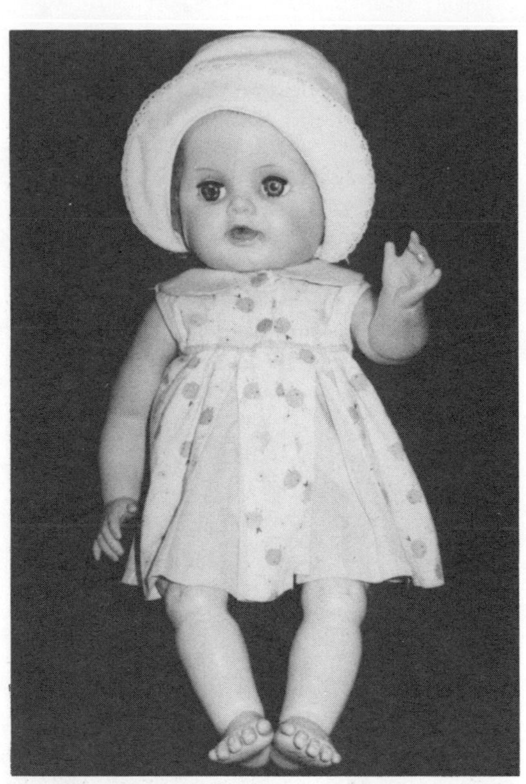

20" "Baby Beth" Plastic body. Vinyl arms, legs and head. Rooted light brown hair. Large blue sleep eyes/lashes. Open mouth/nurser. Open hands with 2nd and 3rd fingers curled. Individually molded toes. Marks: 20-7, on head. 1961. $6.00.

12" "Sugar & Spice" All vinyl with rooted light brown hair. Blue sleep eyes/lashes. Closed mouth. Marks: 4193/K4, on head. 12-3, on lower back. 1961. $3.00.

19" "Trousseau Bride" Hard plastic body, arms and legs. Vinyl head with rooted red hair. Blue sleep eyes/lashes. 2nd and 3rd fingers molded together. Jointed knees and ankles. Marks: AE and something that can't be made out. 1961. $14.00.

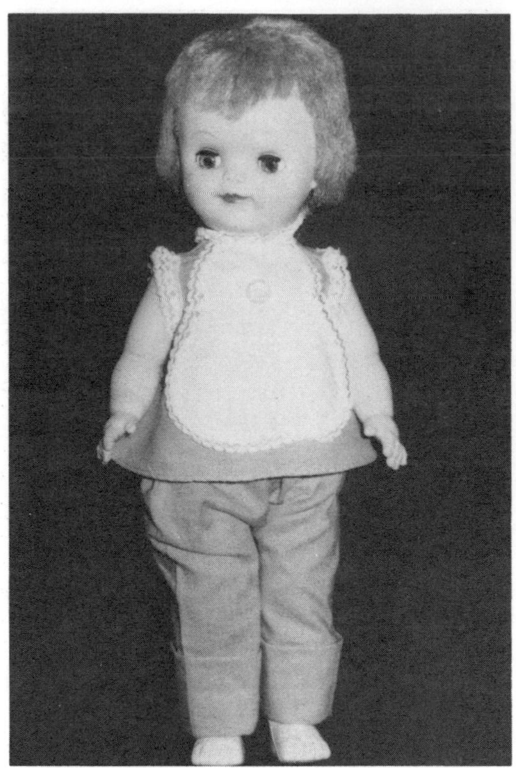

13" "Peggy Ann" Plastic body and legs. Vinyl arms and head. Rooted blonde hair. Blue sleep eyes/lashes. Marks: None. 1962. $3.00.

8" "Bee Bee" All vinyl with rooted dark blonde hair. Painted side glancing blue/black eyes. Closed mouth/nurser. Separate toes. 1963. $2.00.

10" "Campbell Kid" All vinyl with yellow blonde molded hair. Painted features. Jointed at neck, shoulders and hips. 1963. Premium doll from the Campbell Soup Co. $4.00.

11" "Bonny" Plastic body and legs. Vinyl arms and head. Rooted blonde hair. Blue sleep eyes/lashes. Closed mouth. Freckles across nose. Open hands with palms down. Marks: 4092/K53, on head. 1961. $4.00.

8½" "Mattie-Mame" All vinyl with rooted black hair. Painted green/black side glancing eyes. Arms molded in a bent position. Large toes curled up. 1964. $4.00.

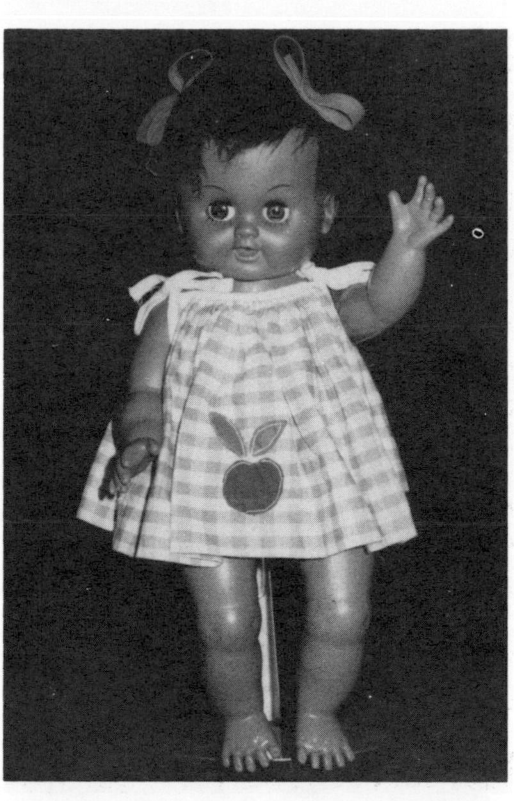

14" "Pretty Girl" All vinyl. Rooted black hair. Brown sleep eyes/lashes. Open mouth/nurser. Open hands with wide spread fingers. Wide spaced toes. Marks: None. 1964. $5.00. (Courtesy Earlene Johnston).

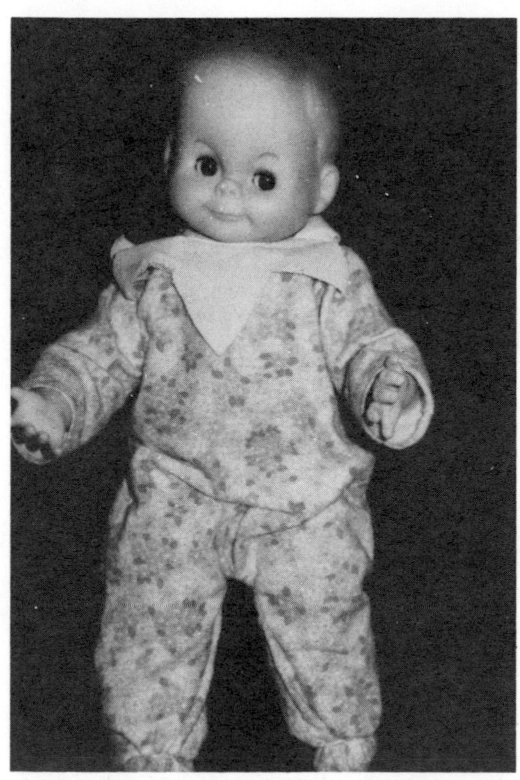

12" "Pixie" Foam body, arms and legs. Gauntlet vinyl hands. Vinyl head with molded blonde hair. Black side glancing eyes/molded lashes. One piece sewn on sleeper. Marks: 2271, on head. 1965. $4.00.

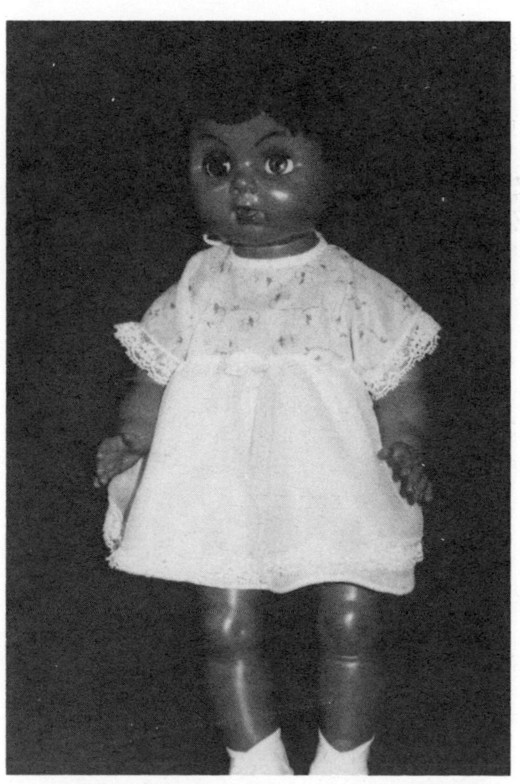

17" "Pixie Haircut Baby" Plastic body and legs. Vinyl arms and head. Rooted black hair. Brown sleep eyes/lashes. Open mouth/nurser. Marks: F-AE378/6. 1965. $6.00.

7" "Imp" Plastic body, arms and legs. Vinyl head with rooted black hair. Painted features. Right hand balled into a fist. Marks: None. 1966. $3.00.

24" "Suzy Smart" Plastic body and legs. Vinyl head and arms. Rooted blonde hair. Blue sleep eyes/lashes. Talk box in center of back. Battery operated. Jointed knees. Marks: D3/450, on head. 1966. $15.00.

22½" "Valerie" Plastic body, arms and legs. Vinyl head with rooted dark brown hair. Large black sleep eyes with black and grey eyeshadow. Closed mouth. Side glancing eyes. Marks: KT, on head. 1967. $8.00.

5" "Amish Boy and Girl" All hard plastic. Glued on dark brown hair. Painted blue, side glancing eyes. Closed mouth. Open hands facing body. Painted on socks and shoes. Marks: None. Original clothes. $16.00. (Courtesy Fye Collection).

8" "Jockey And Fox Hunter" All vinyl with painted features. Jointed neck, shoulders and hips. Marks: Unable to make out mold marks. Original clothes. $10.00.

8" "African Native" Plastic body, arms and legs. Vinyl head with glued on silk thread wig. Painted side glancing eyes. Closed mouth. Right hand curled to hold spear. Left hand palm down. Stubby short, wide spread legs. Marks: None. 1960's. $6.00.

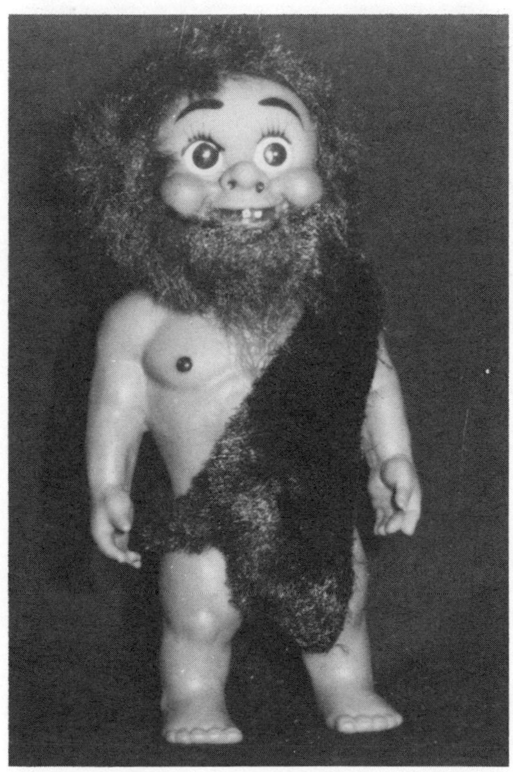

6½" "Sexed Caveman" All vinyl one piece body, arms and legs. Jointed neck. Glued on red hair and beard. Painted brown eyes. Two painted teeth. Marks: None. 1971. $5.00.

Nancy Ann Storybook Dolls

Nancy Ann Abbott started her business in 1941, which grew to a three story factory located in California. At the peak, the factory turned out over eight thousand dolls a day. All the dolls were based on Miss Abbott's own imagination or well known nursery rhymes.

At first Miss Abbott bought doll bodies from Europe and Japan but they had to be repainted in the USA and out of every 100, about 60 had to be discarded as defective. At this point, Miss Abbott and her partner, A.L. Rowland, began to import clays from England and started making their own dolls.

During World War II, when rationing made many materials difficult to get, Nancy Ann Abbott still made dolls by having a strong will power. For example, when she could not get materials for shoes, the toes of the dolls were dipped into black paint.

The Nancy Ann Storybook Doll is being re-introduced, using the original doll complete with movable eyes and a soft china like finish. They are packaged in the traditional polkadot boxes by Nancy Ann Storybook Dolls, Division of Giant Consolidated Industries of Salt Lake City, Utah.

The following are not all the dolls made by this company.

All Bisque Storybooks - 9.00 each

All Hard Plastic Storybooks - 6.00 each - Big Sister/teen size - 9.00

All Vinyl Storybooks - 4.00 each

1941: Gerda & Kay, Sunday's Child, Goldilocks, Polly Put The Kettle On, Little Bo Peep, December's Child, Little Joan

1943: Monday's Child through Saturday's Child, January through November's Girl, Little Miss, Roses Are Red, Over The Hill, School Days, To Market, Loves Me, Merrie Maid, When She Was Good, Sugar & Spice, Ring Around The Rosy, Princess Minon, Minette, Prince Souci, Boy Blue, Mistress Mary, Alice Sweet Alice, Annine At The Garden Gate, Elise Marley, Lucky Locket, Curly Locks, Queen of Hearts, Pretty Maid, Jennie, Princess Rosanie, Little Miss Donnett, Lady In Waiting.

1944: Mary Had A Little Lamb, Little Miss Muffet, Alice Through The Looking Glass, Little Miss Sweet Miss

1946: Birthday Dolls

1947: Fairyland Series, Fairytale Series, Goose Girl, Majorie Daw, Nellie Bird

1952 to 1959: Hard Plastics and Vinyls: Nancy Ann, Little Sister Series, Big Sister Series, Commencement Series, Religious Series, Bride Series, Mother Goose Series, Seasons Series, Fairytale Series, Fairyland Series, Nursery Rhyme Series, Dolls of the Day Series, Dolls of the Month Series, In Powder and Crinoline Series, All Time Hit Parade Series, Nancy Ann (vinyl), Lori Ann (vinyl), Miss Lori Ann (vinyl), Miss Nancy Ann (vinyl)

Nancy Ann--5" "Little Joan" All bisque with glued on blonde wig. Painted features. One piece body, legs and head. Marks: Mold marks so worn, they can't be read. Box: Here Am I, Little Joan. When Nobody's With Me, I'm Alone. 1941. Original clothes. $9.00.

Nancy Ann--6½" "A Flowergirl For May" All bisque with glued on blonde wig. Painted features. One piece body, legs and head. Original clothes. Marks: None. Box: A Flower Girl For May/191. 1943. $9.00.

Nancy Ann--5" "Queen Of Hearts" All bisque with brown glued on wig. Painted features. Original clothes. Marks: Wrist tag: 117/Queen Of Hearts. 1942. $9.00.

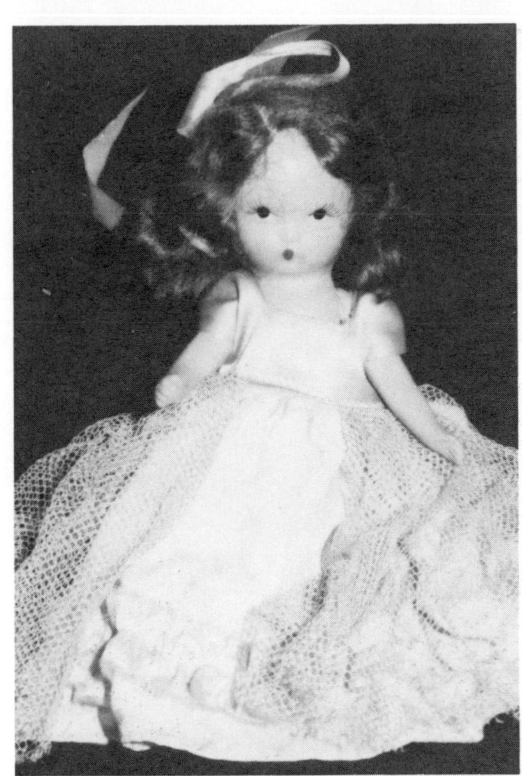

Nancy Ann--5½" "Elsie Marley" All bisque with glued on red wig. Painted features. One piece body, legs and head. Original clothes. Marks: Box: Elsie Marley's Grown So Fine, She Won't Get Up Till Eight Or Nine./31. 1942. $9.00.

Nancy Ann--5½" "Seasons Series-Winter" All hard plastic with glued on brown wig. Painted features. Fully jointed. Original clothes. Marks: Storybook/Dolls/USA/Trademark/Reg. 1952. $6.00.

Nancy Ann--5½" "Daffidown Dilly" All hard plastic with blonde glued on wig. Painted features. Fully jointed. Original clothes. Marks: Box: Daffidown Dilly Has Come To Town, In A Green Petticoat And A Yellow Gown/171. 1952. $6.00.

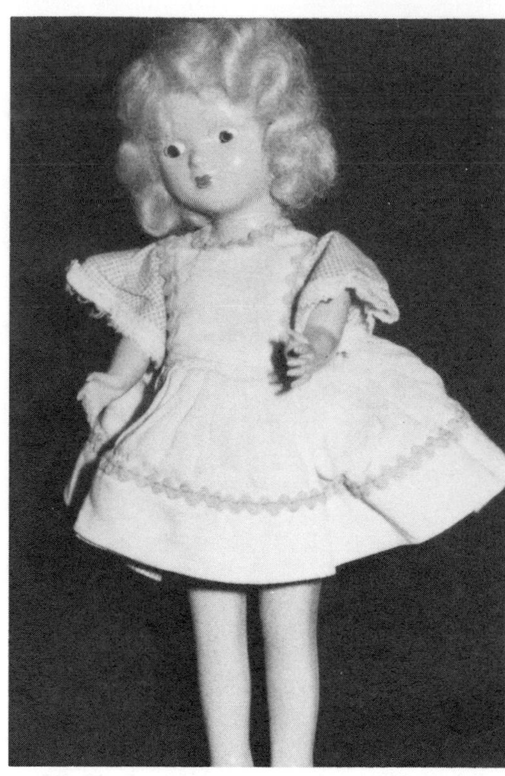

Nancy Ann--7" "Miss Muffet" All hard plastic with glued on blonde mohair wig. Blue sleep eyes/lashes. Jointed at neck and shoulders. Original dress. Marks: Tag: Styled By Nancy Ann/Nancy Ann Storybook Dolls/San Francisco. 1956. $6.00.

Nancy Ann--5½" "Bride Series" All hard plastic with glued on brown mohair wig. Black sleep eyes. Marks: Storybook/Dolls/USA/Trademark Reg. 1952. $6.00.

Nancy Ann--5½" "Doll Of Days Series" All hard plastic with glued on brown mohair wig. Black sleep eyes. Marks: Storybook/Dolls/USA/Trademark/Reg. 1952. $6.00.

Nancy Ann--5½" "Bride" All hard plastic with glued on mohair wig. Black sleep eyes. Closed mouth. Painted on shoes. Marks: Storybook/-Dolls/USA/Trademark/Reg. Original clothes. 1952. $6.00.

Nancy Ann--6" "Commencement Series" All hard plastic with glued on blonde wig. Black sleep eyes. Marks: Storybook Dolls/USA/ Trademark/Reg. Original clothes. 1952. $6.00.

Nancy Ann--5½" "Little Sister" All hard plastic with glued on black mohair wig. Black sleep eyes and painted on shoes. Marks: Storybook Doll/Reg. Trademark. 1952. $9.00.

Nancy Ann--7½" "Diller A Dollar" All hard plastic with glued on blonde mohair wig. Black with blue background sleep eyes. Marks: Storybook/Dolls/USA/Trademark/Reg. 1952. $6.00.

Nancy Ann--7" "Muffie" All hard plastic with glued on brown wig. Blue sleep eyes/lashes. Head turns as she walks. Marks: Storybook Dolls/California/Muffie, on back. Original clothes. 1952. $6.00.

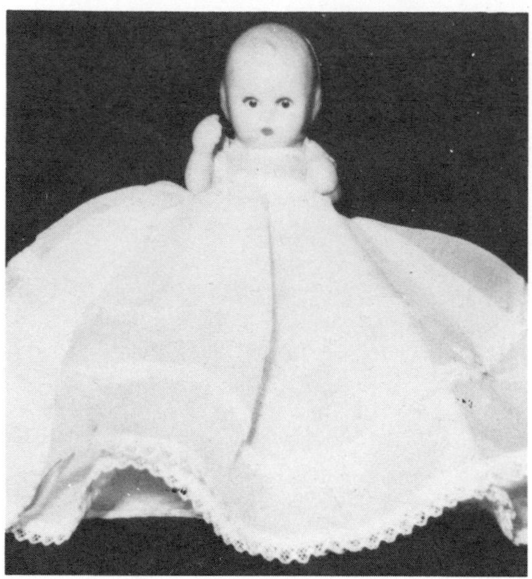

Nancy Ann--3½" "Christening Baby" All hard plastic with molded painted yellow hair. Black sleep eyes. Closed mouth. Right hand fingers curled except index. Left all fingers curled. Both arms molded in a bent position. Straight baby legs. Jointed shoulders and hips. Marks: Storybook Dolls/USA/Trademark/Reg. Original clothes. 1952. $9.00.

Nancy Ann--6" "Valentine" All hard plastic with glued on blonde mohair wig. Black sleep eyes. Marks: Storybook Dolls/USA/Trademark/Reg. Original clothes. 1952. $6.00.

Nancy Ann--10" "Nancy Ann" All vinyl with rooted blonde hair. Blue sleep eyes/lashes. Closed mouth. Pierced ears. Open hands, palms down. Jointed waist. High heel feet. Marks: Nancy Ann, on head. Dress Tag: Nancy Ann Storybook Dolls Inc/San Francisco, Calif. 1959. Original clothes. $4.00.

Natural--14" "Linda Williams" Plastic body and legs. Vinyl arms and head. Rooted dark brown hair. Blue sleep eyes/lashes. Open/closed mouth with six painted teeth. Open hands with extended little fingers. Marks: Linda Williams, on head. 1959. $12.00.

Natural--14½" "Dolly Ann" Plastic body and legs. Vinyl arms and head. Rooted orange hair. Green sleep eyes/lashes. Open/closed mouth with six molded and painted teeth. Freckles. Marks: Linda Williams marked out of mold but still visible. 1963. $10.00.

P & M Sales--19" "Jo Ann" Plastic body and legs. Vinyl arms and head with rooted dark brown hair. Black sleep eyes to side. Black eye shadow. 2nd and 3rd fingers on right hand molded together. Marks: AE-1/P & M Sales Inc./1966, on head. AE, on upper back. A backward AE, on lower back. $6.00.

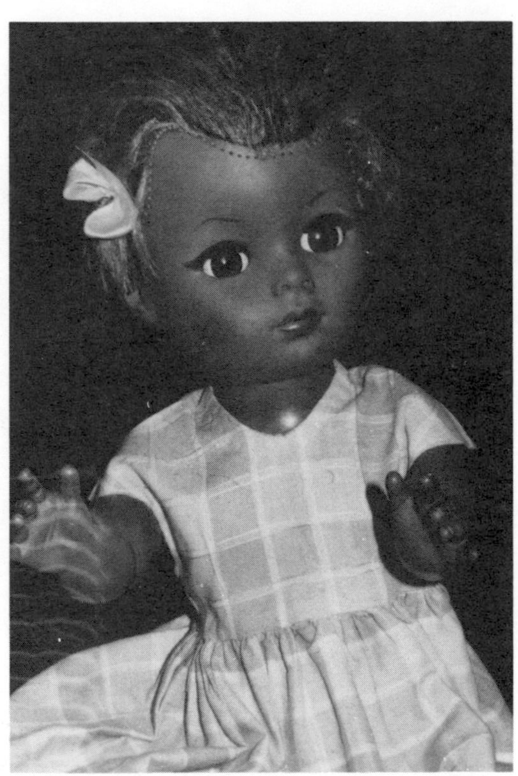

P & M Sales--23" "Belinda" Plastic body, arms and legs. Vinyl head with rooted frosted hair. Brown sleep eyes/lashes. Black eye shadow. 2nd and 3rd fingers molded curled and close together. Marks: P & M Sales Inc/1966/BD/19, on head. $7.00.

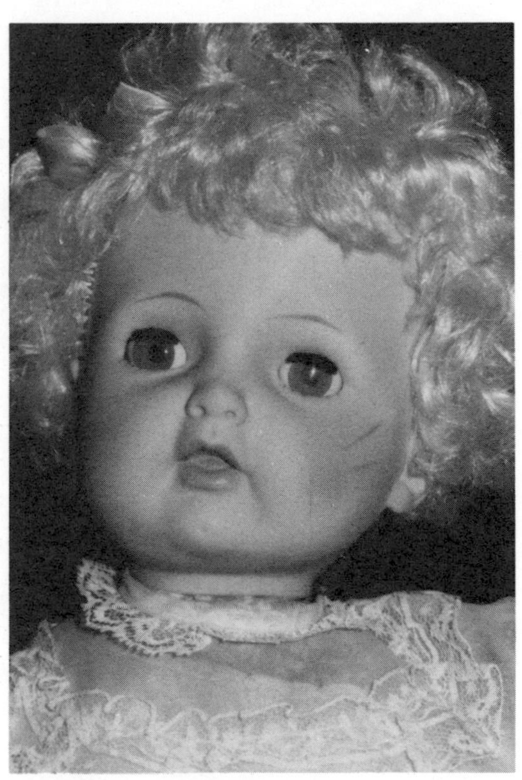

P & M Sales--21" "Baby Princess" Cloth body. Vinyl arms, legs and head. Rooted, tightly curled white hair. Sleep blue eyes/lashes. Open/closed mouth. Dimpled chin. Left thumb, index and 2nd fingers molded together. Right 3rd finger molded into palm. Marks: P & M Doll, on head. 1966. $16.00.

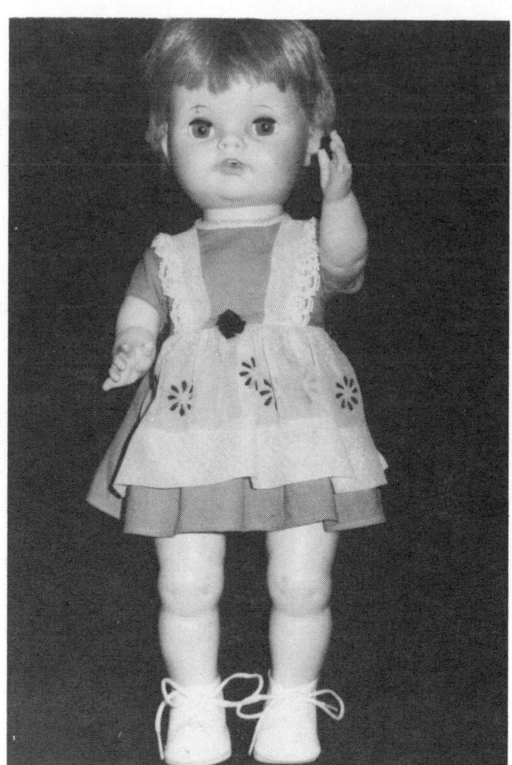

P & M Sales--17" "Royal Princess" Plastic body and legs. Vinyl arms and head. Light brown rooted hair. Dark blue sleep eyes/lashes. Open mouth, two upper molded and painted teeth/nurser. Marks: 17EYE/1967/P&M Doll Co. $5.00.

Pillsbury--7" "Poppin' Fresh" All soft vinyl with painted features. Marks: 1971/The Pillsbury Company/Minneapolis, Minn. $3.00.

Plastic Molded Arts--10½" "Flowergirl 1946" All hard plastic with glued on mohair wig. Blue sleep eyes/lashes molded. Painted on shoes. Marks: Plastic Molded Arts Co/Lic New York, on back. $3.00.

Plastic Molded Arts--11" "Bride" All hard plastic with glued on blonde mohair wig. Blue sleep eyes/molded lashes. Painted on white shoes. Marks: Plastic Molded Arts Co/Lic New York, on back. 1947. Original clothes. $3.00.

Plastic Molded Arts--7½" "Captain Hook" All hard plastic with painted hair. Right arm is a hook. Painted on boots. Marks: None. Original clothes. 1949. $5.00.

Plastic Molded Arts--7½" "Nun" All hard plastic with blue sleep eyes/painted lashes. Painted shoes. Marks: None. 1949. $5.00.

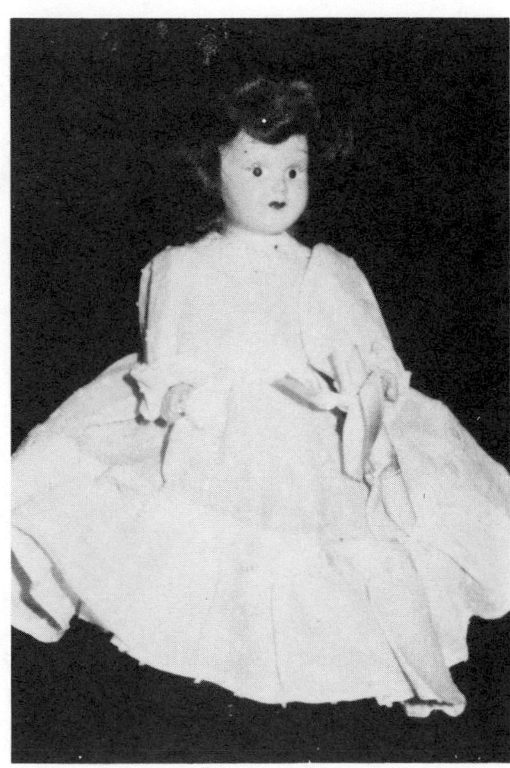

Plastic Molded Arts--7½" "Graduate" All hard plastic with glued on brown mohair wig. Painted side glancing blue eyes. Painted on shoes. Marks: None. 1949. Original clothes. $3.00.

Plastic Molded Arts--7½" "Bride" All hard plastic with glued on blonde mohair wig. Blue sleep eyes/molded lashes. Painted on shoes. Marks: None. 1949. Original clothes. $3.00.

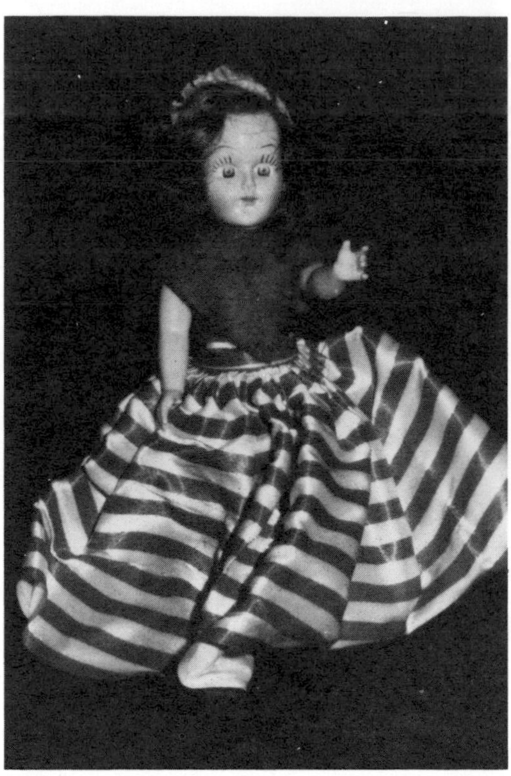

Plastic Molded Arts--6" "Miss America" All hard plastic with glued on brown mohair wig. Blue sleep eyes/painted lashes. Marks: Plastic Molded Arts/Lic New York. 1950. Original clothes. $3.00.

Plastic Molded Arts--7½" "Lady Ravencroft" All hard plastic with glued on black mohair wig. Blue sleep eyes/molded lashes. Painted on shoes. Marks: Plastic Molded Arts/Lic New York. 1950. Original clothes. $3.00.

Plastic Molded Arts--7½" "Miss Valentine" All hard plastic with glued on blonde mohair wig. Blue sleep eyes/molded lashes. Marks: None. 1950. Original clothes. $3.00.

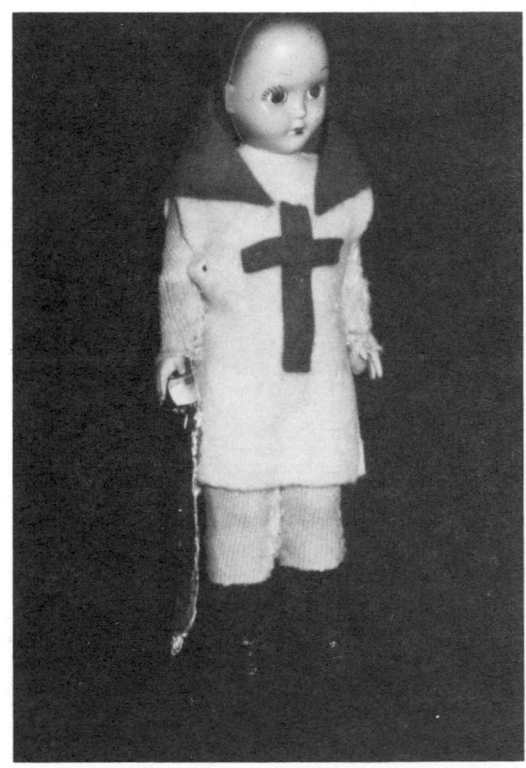

Plastic Molded Arts--7" "Crusader" All hard plastic with painted black hair. Blue sleep eyes. Closed mouth. Marks: Plastic Molded Arts/Lic New York NY. 1950. $3.00.

Plastic Molded Arts--7" "Polish Girl" All hard plastic with glued on blonde mohair wig. Blue sleep eyes/painted lashes. Painted on shoes. Marks: None. 1952. $3.00.

Plastic Molded Arts--7" "Lady Hampshire" All hard plastic with glued on blonde mohair wig. Blue sleep eyes. Painted on shoes. Marks: None. 1951. Original clothes. $3.00.

Plastic Molded Arts--7½" "Miss 1953" All hard plastic with glued on red mohair wig. Blue sleep eyes/molded lashes. Painted on shoes. Marks: None. 1953. Original clothes. $3.00.

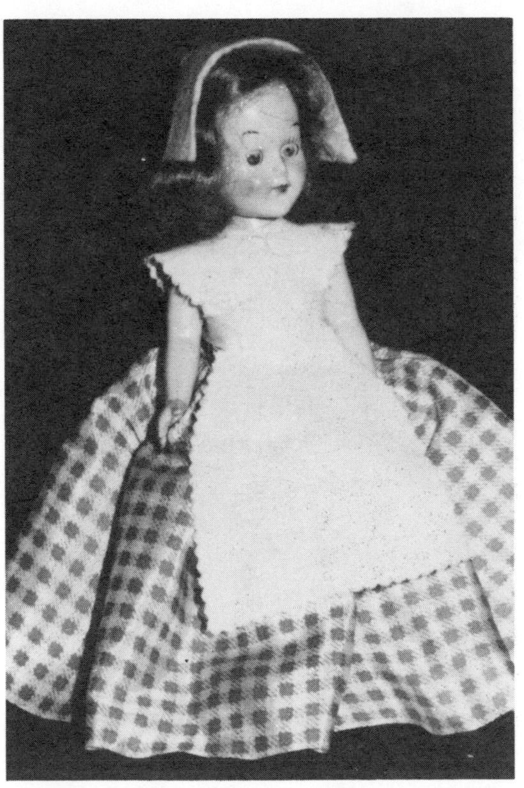

Plastic Molded Arts--6" "Priscilla Alden" All hard plastic with brown glued on mohair wig. Blue sleep eyes. Marks: Plastic Molded Arts/Lic New York, on back. 1951. Original clothes. $3.00.

Plastic Molded Arts--12" "Bride" All hard plastic. Glued on dark red mohair wig. Blue sleep eyes/molded lashes. Closed mouth. Painted on flat shoes. Marks: None. 1951. $3.00.

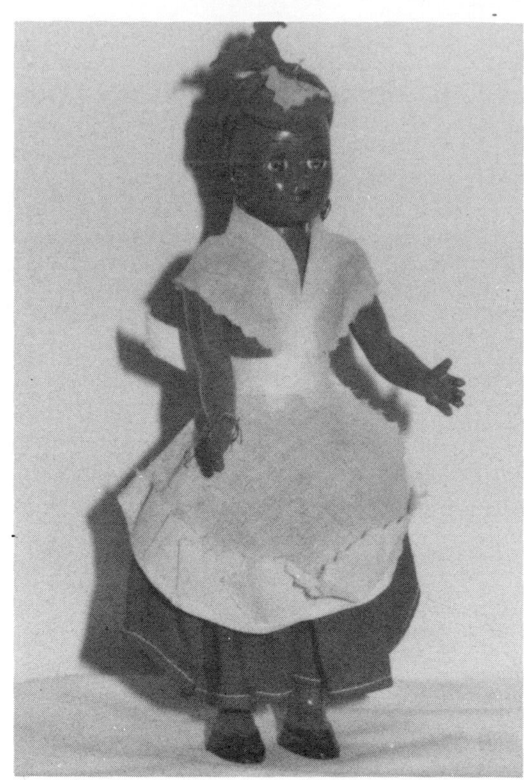

Plastic Molded Arts--7" "Greenbrier Maid" All hard plastic with sleep yellow eyes/molded lashes. Copper bracelet and earrings. Painted shoes. Dress Tag: Greenbrier Maid. 1955. $5.00.

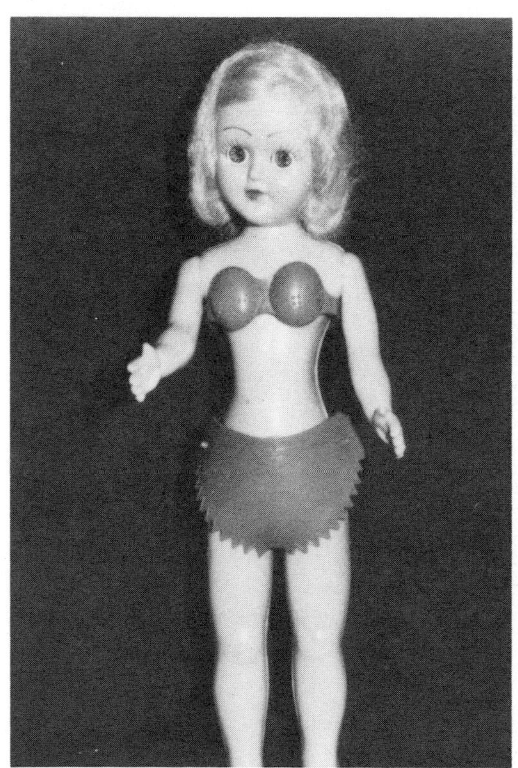

Plastic Molded Arts--7½" "Dress Yourself" All hard plastic with blonde glued on mohair wig. Blue sleep eyes/lashes. Separate plastic pantie and bra. Molded painted shoes. Marks: None. 1955. $3.00.

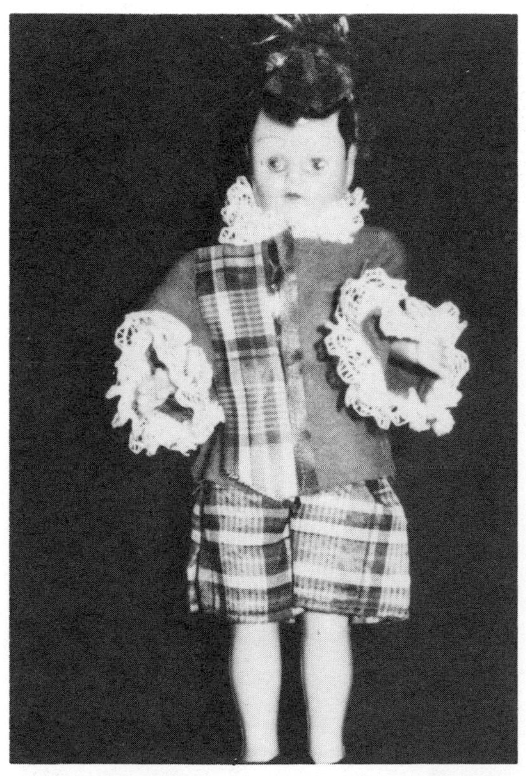

Plastic Molded Arts--7½" "Scotch Groom" All hard plastic with painted black hair. Blue side glancing sleep eyes. Painted shoes. Marks: None. 1955. Original clothes. $3.00.

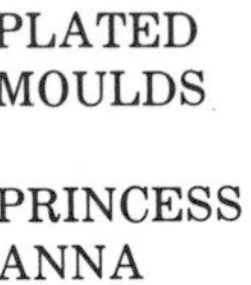

Plated Moulds--15" "Nelly" Cloth body. Plastic legs. Vinyl arms, legs and head. Painted side glancing black eyes. Open/closed mouth with molded tongue. Left thumb, index and 2nd fingers molded together. Right 3rd finger curled into palm. Marks: U/Plated Moulds Inc/1961, on head. $4.00.

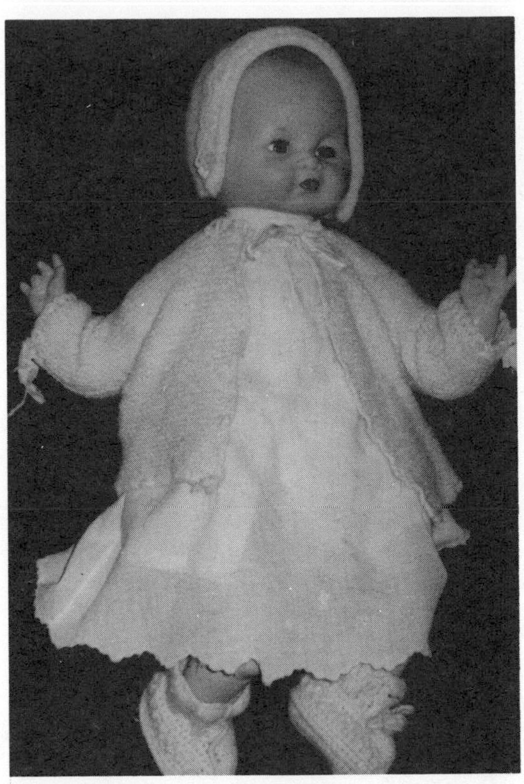

Plated Moulds--20" "New Baby" Head mounted on a wooden block, encased in a red checkered cloth body. Vinyl arms, legs and head. Rooted blonde hair. Very real skin color. High forehead and large shaped head. Blue sleep eyes/lashes. Open mouth/dry nurser. Marks: Plated Moulds Inc/1961 PLS or 5, on head. $6.00.

Princess Anna--6½" "Glorious Gold Princess" All composition with glued on blonde mohair wig. Painted side glancing brown eyes. One piece body, head and legs. Jointed shoulders. Painted on black shoes. Marks:PrincessAnna, on back. Original clothes. 1942. $5.00.

Princess Anna--7½" "Flirtatious Flowergirl" All hard plastic with glued on red mohair wig. Painted features. Molded and painted on shoes. Marks: PA/1947, on back. Original clothes. $3.00.

Princess Anna--7½" "Bride" All hard plastic with glued on brown mohair wig. Side glancing blue eyes. Marks: PA/1947, on back. Original clothes. $3.00.

Princess Anna--7½" "Polish Girl" All hard plastic with glued on blonde mohair wig. Blue painted side glancing eyes. Painted on shoes. Marks: PA/1949, on back. Original clothes. $5.00.

Princess Anna--7½" "Pert Pierrette" All hard plastic with glued on blonde mohair wig. Painted side glancing eyes. Marks: PA/1951, on back. $3.00.

Princess Anna--7½" "Red Riding Hood" All hard plastic with glued on blonde mohair wig. Marks: PA, on back. 1950. Original clothes. $3.00.

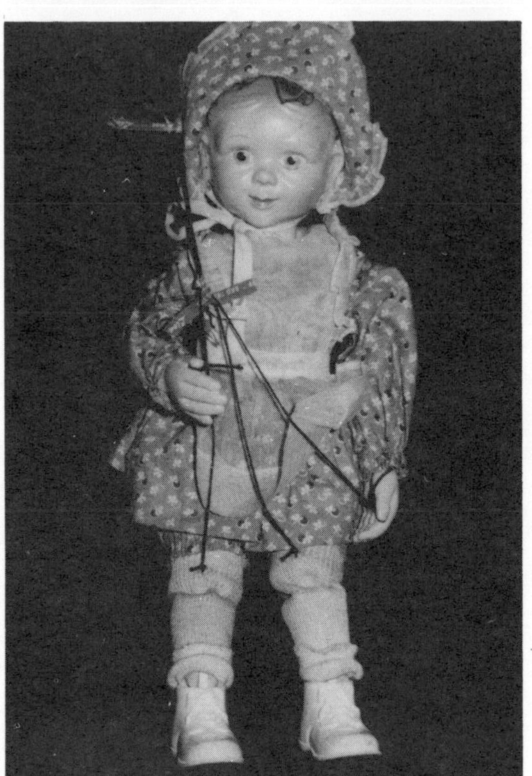

Puppet--13" "Emily Ann" All composition. Molded hair. Painted eyes. Designed and copyrighted by Virginia Austin. One of the Clippo the Clown series marionettes. Marks: Emily Ann/V. Austin/Effanbee. 1938. $40.00 (Courtesy Earlene Johnston Collection).

Puppets--14" "Marie" Wood block bodies. Composition arms, legs and head. Painted features. 1940 Perez, Mexico. $5.00.

Puppets--14" "Tomas" Wood block bodies. Composition arms, legs and head. Painted features. 1940. Perez, Mexico. $5.00.

Ideal Puppet--20" "Howdy Doody" Cloth body with gauntlet hands. Hard plastic head. Blue sleep eyes. Freckles. Open mouth puppet with seven teeth. Marks: Ideal Doll, on head. 1950. $8.00. (Courtesy Allin's Collection).

Puppet--7" "Poodle" Wood with Caracul fur. All puppet strings are color coded to match colors on control board. Marks: None. Imported. By Pelham Co. 1958. $7.00.

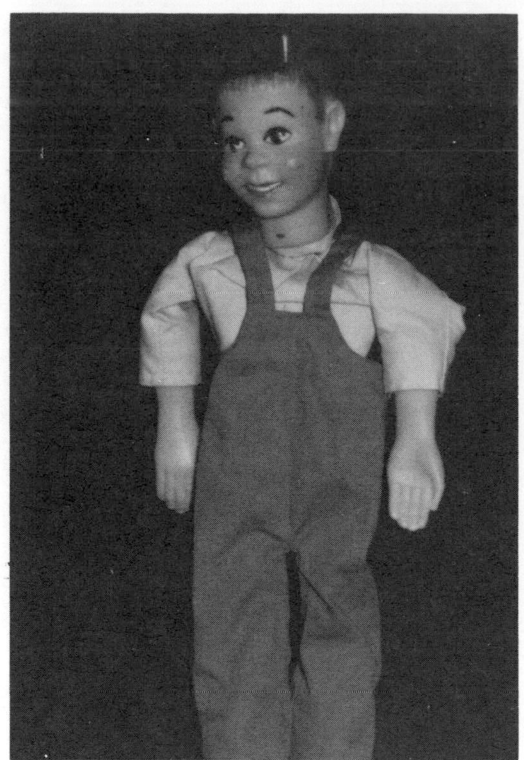

Puppets--12" "Dick & Sally" Vinyl head with molded hair. Vinyl hands and feet. Wood block bodies. Marks: None. 1961. Made by Hazelle. $6.00.

12" "Sally" by Hazelle

Puppet--12" "Woody Woodpecker" Cloth mitt with talk box. Vinyl head with painted features. Pull string operated. Marks: Mattel/Woody Woodpecker/1962. $3.00.

Hazelle Puppet--15" "Teto" Hazelle Clown" "Tenite" head, hands and feet. Two wooden blocks make up body. Wooden pegs for legs and short wooden dowels for arms. 1961. $3.00.

Puppet--21" "Puppetrina" Plastic legs and torso. Foam over springs upper body. Jointed waist. Vinyl arms and head. Rooted blonde hair. Blue sleep eyes/lashes. Open/closed mouth with painted lower teeth. Hand pocket in back, to move arms and head. Marks: 1963/Eegee Co/Pat Pend/17, on head. $35.00.

Puppet--10" "Jiminy Cricket" Cloth mitt with vinyl head. Molded on hat. Painted features. Marks: Tag: Jiminy Cricket/Copyright Walt Disney Prod. Reverse side Gund Mfg Co. 1964. $2.00.

Puppet--11" "Donald Duck" Wooden block upper body. Stuffed lower body. Plastic feet and hands. Vinyl head with painted features. Marks: W.D.P. on head. Tag: Donald Duck/Copyright Walt Disney Prod. Reverse side: Gund Mfg. Co. 1964. $4.00.

Puppet--9" "Yogi Bear" Cloth mitt with vinyl head. Painted features. Molded on hat. Marks: Yogi Bear/Knickerbocker. 1964. $2.00.

Puppet--10" "Pluto" Cloth mitt with vinyl head. Printed body, arms and legs. Painted features. Marks: Tag: Walt Disney/Character/Copyright/Walt Disney Prod. Reverse side of Tag: Gund Manufacturing Co/Made In Hong Kong. 1964. $2.00.

Puppet--10" "Donald Duck" Cloth mitt with printed features. Vinyl head with painted features. Marks: Walt Disney/Character/Copyright/Walt Disney Prod. Reverse Side Of Tag: Gund Manufacturing Co/Made In Hong Kong. 1964. $2.00.

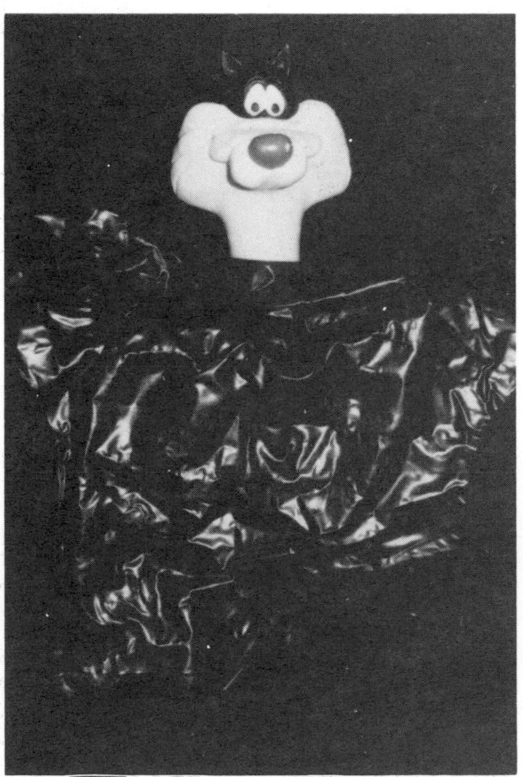

Puppet--9" "Sylvester" Plastic mitt with vinyl head. Painted features. Marks: Sylvester/Warner Bros. Seven Arts Inc. on back of neck. 1964. $2.00.

Puppet--12" "Tom" Cloth mitt with voice box. Vinyl head with painted features. Pull string operated. Marks: Tom & Jerry 1965/Goldwyn Meyer Inc. Mattel, on tag. $3.00.

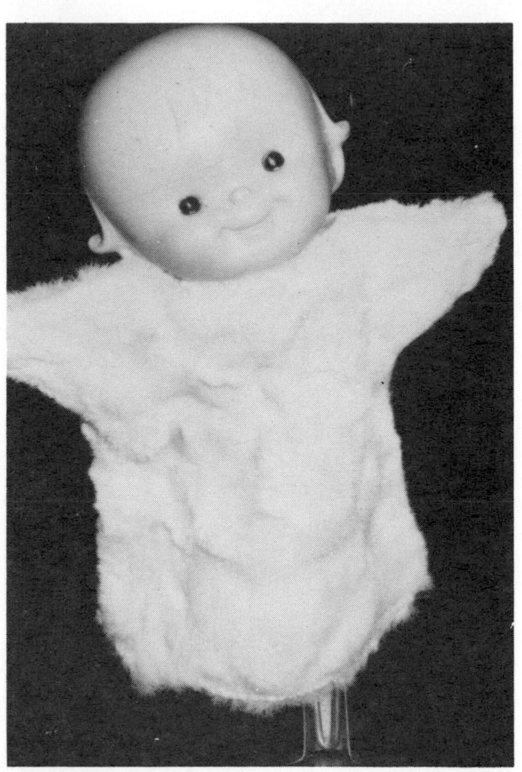

Puppet--9" "Baby" Plush cloth mitt. Vinyl head with painted features. Marks: 1965/Elka Toy. $2.00.

Puppet--30" "Charlie McCarthy" Cloth body, upper arms and feet. Plastic gauntlet hands. Plastic head. Painted features. Marks: Juro Novelty/1965. Original clothes. $50.00. (Courtesy Allin's Collection).

Remco Puppet--5" "Betty Ballerina" Vinyl finger puppet. Yellow rooted hair. Painted black eyes. Fingers placed in dolls legs make her a puppet. Marks: 2504/Remco Ind Inc/01966 on head. Original clothes. $2.00.

Puppet--12" "Popeye" Cloth mitt with voice box. Vinyl head with painted features. Pull string operated. Marks: Tag: King Features/1967. Mattel. $3.00.

Puppet--12" "Dr. Doolittle" Cloth body with printed on features. Vinyl head with molded hair and painted features. Pull ring operated. Says things like: "Did you know animals all speak a language?" Marks: Tag: Doctor Doolittle/Mattel Inc. 1967. $4.00.

Mattel Puppet--7" "Happy Me" Plastic with vinyl head. Molded yellow hair. Large blue painted eyes. Open/closed mouth with painted teeth. Marks: 1968 Mattel Inc/Mexico/US Patent Pending and 1968/Mattel Inc/Taiwan. Original clothes. $3.00.

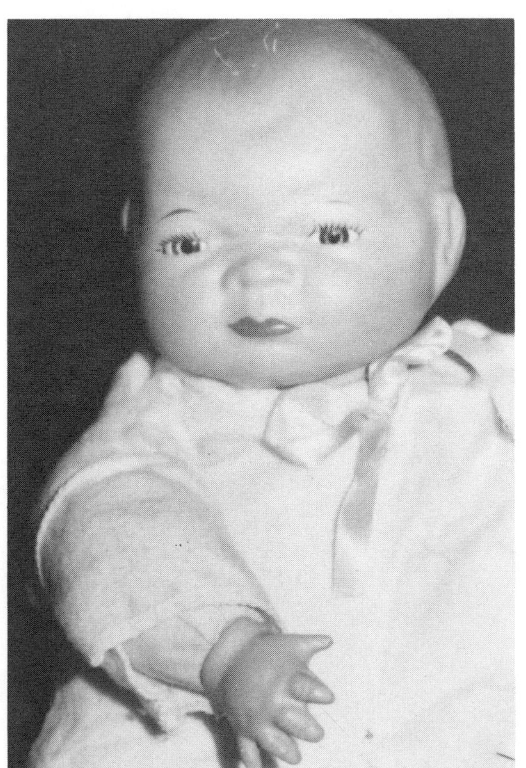

Grace Storey Putnam--12" "Bye Lo" Cloth body, upper arms and legs. Composition gauntlet hands and head. Lightly molded painted hair. Inset blue stationary eyes. Marks: Grace Storey/Putnam, on head. $65.00. (Courtesy Allin's Collection).

Rag--17" "Charlie Chaplin" All cloth with painted face. Wool hair. Floppy feet. Marks: Made By Louis Amberg & Son/Charlie Chaplin, on botton of feet. Original clothes. $75.00. (Courtesy Earlene Johnston Collection).

Rag--11" "Ling Toy" Stuffed cloth body, arms, legs and head. Black yarn hair. Removable clothes. Marks: Made In Hong Kong, bottom of left foot. Sold in Chinatown, San Francisco 1941. $8.00.

Rag--8" "Chi-Lu" Excelsior filled with painted features. Forehead hair painted with small tufts of human side hair. Sewn on clothes. Marks: Paper tag: Japan/10/1940. $8.00.

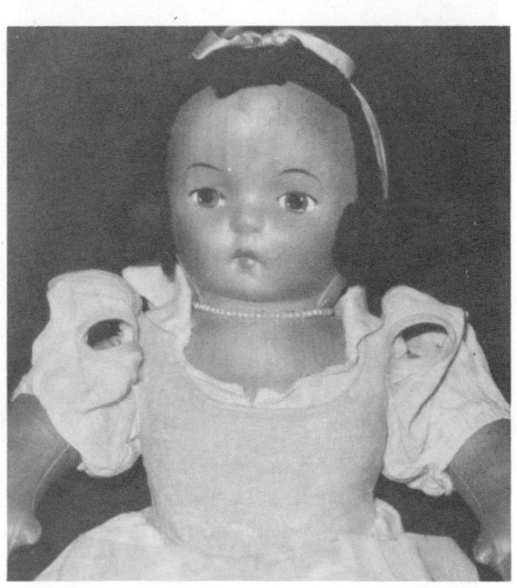

Rag--18" "Snow White" All one piece cloth. Mask face with painted brown eyes. Black yarn hair. Marks: None. 1939. $35.00. (Courtesy Allin's Collection).

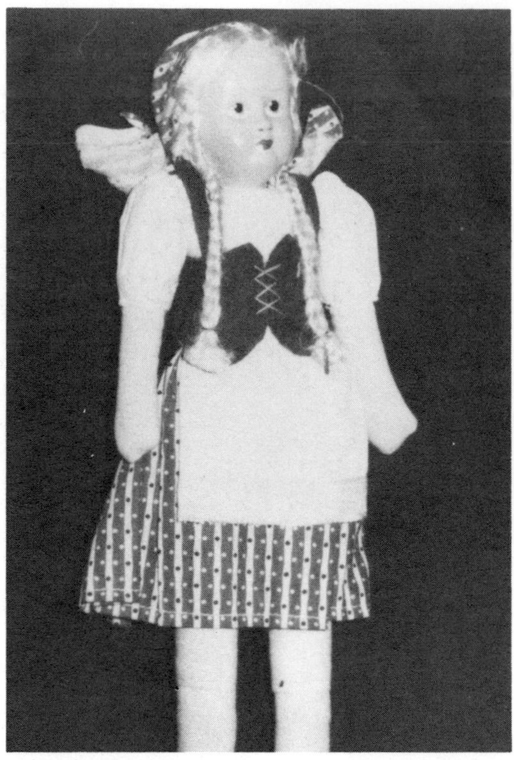

Rag--11½" "Polish Girl" Cloth body, arms and legs. Plastic mask face with painted features. Mohair sewn in wig. Poland, stamped high on right leg. 1940. $6.00.

Rag--12" "Mammy's Baby" Excelsior filled cloth body, arms and legs. Tuft of black mohair sewn on. Pressed, painted mask face. Celluloid earrings. Marks: None. Purchased in 1940. Original clothes. $9.00.

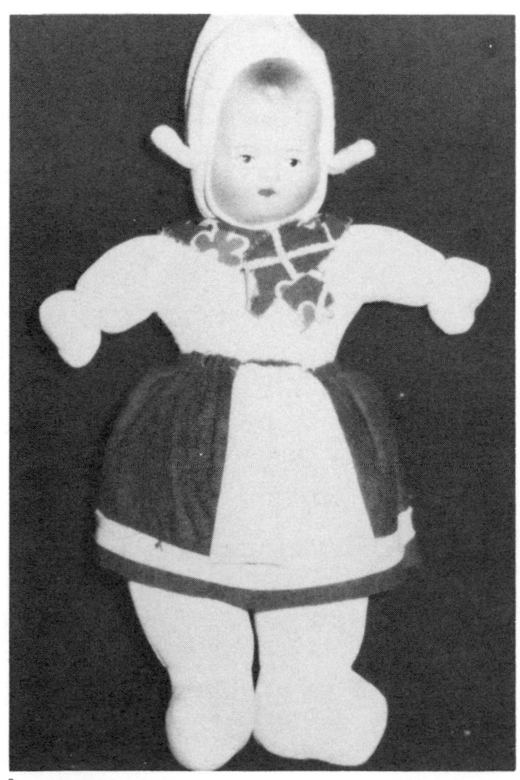

Rag--10½" "Dutch Girl" All one piece sockingette of jersey. Plastic face with painted features. Marks: None. 1949. $7.00.

Rag--9" "Mammy" Cloth, one piece body, arms, legs and head. Sewn on clothes, earrings and head scarf. Made in New Orleans, 1941. Marks: None. $7.00.

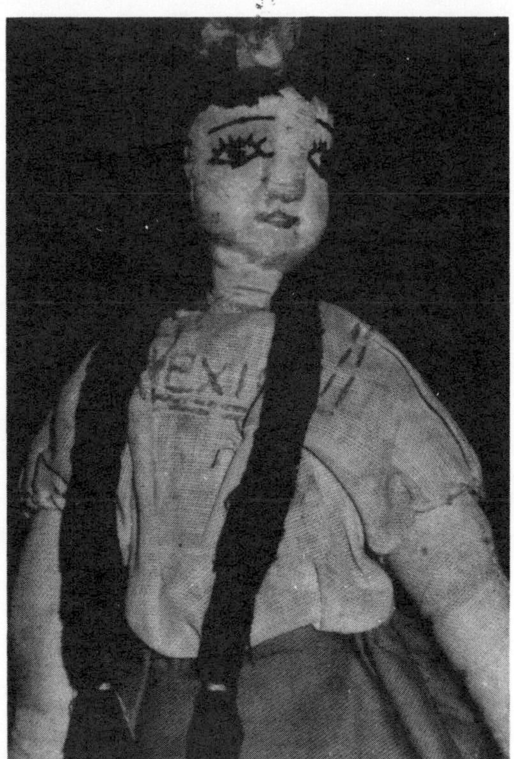

Rag--12" "Marie" All handmade cloth filled. Sewn on features and hair. Brought home from Mexico, in 1939, for a childhood doll of Earlene Johnston, by her father. Marks: Mexico across front of dress. Name given doll by owner. $6.00. (Courtesy Earlene Johnston Collection).

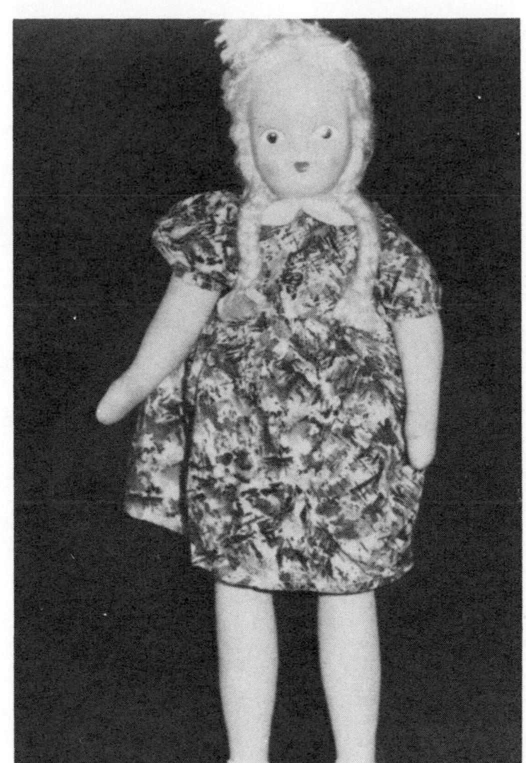

Rag--17" "Abby" Cloth body, arms and legs. Pressed mask face with painted features. Brown eyes. Blonde mohair wig sewn on. Sewn on arms. Legs jointed by pin to lower third of torso. Dimpled cheeks. Marks: None. 1941. Original clothes. $4.00.

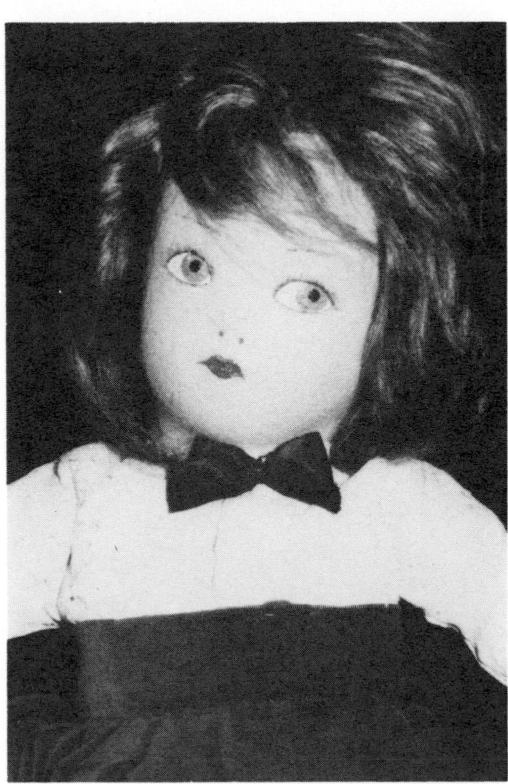

England--15" "Norah Sue" Velvet stuffed body, arms and legs. Felt mask face with painted features. Sewn on human hair wig. Jointed neck. Marks: Tag on right wrist: Made In England/By/Norah Wellings. Original clothes. $32.00. (Courtesy Earlene Johnston Collection).

Rag--8" "Miss Smith" All cloth with sewn on arms and legs. Sewn on mohair wig. Painted side glancing blue eyes. All original. Marks: Tag On Foot: Made In England/By/Norah Wellings. $18.00.

Rag--17" "Tak-Uki" All cloth with rooted skull cap wig. Inset stationary brown eyes. Open mouth/painted teeth. Marks: Tag: Made In England/by/Norah Wellings, on bottom of right foot. $48.00. (Courtesy Allin's Collection).

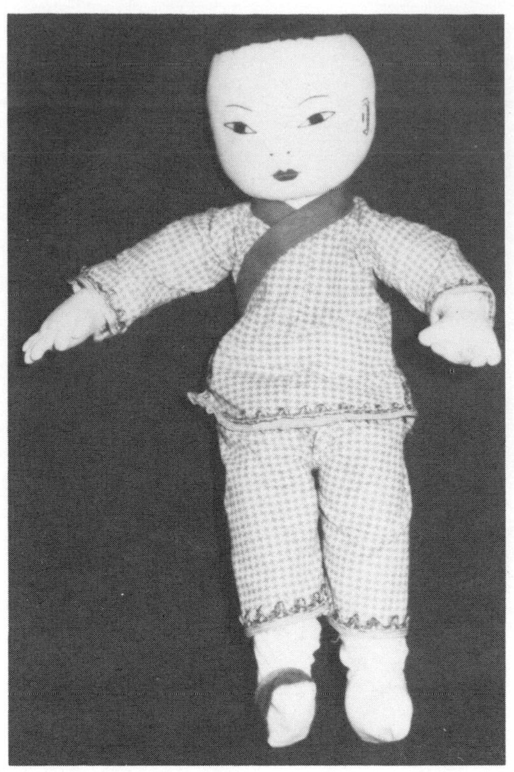

Rag--12" "Soo Ming" Cloth stuffed body, arms and legs. Tightly filled cloth covered head with machined features. Individual fingers. Black yarn hair. Removable clothes. Marks: None. 1950. $5.00.

Rag--8" "Dutch Boy And Girl" Stuffed cloth. Glued on yellow mohair. Plastic, painted faces. Sewn on clothes. Marks: None. 1950's. $4.00.

Rag--10" "Girl And Doll" All sockenette with yellow yarn hair. Felt features and clothes. Marks: None. 1953. $9.00.

Rag--36" "Dancing Partner" One piece cloth body, arms and legs. Plastic face with painted features. Sewn on yellow yarn hair/bonnet. Elastic bands on right hand and both feet. Marks: None. 1954. Original clothes. Made By Etone Company. $16.00.

Rag--15" "Santa Claus" Polyfoam filled body, arms and legs. Gauntlet vinyl hands. Right hand holding bottle of "Coca Cola". Left hand curled, facing body. Vinyl boots. Beautifully molded vinyl face. Painted features. Marks: The Rushon Co, on base of neck. The Rushon Co, on bottom of right foot. 1956. $20.00.

14" "Little Lulu" All cloth with molded and painted features. String hair. 1958 to 1961. Marks: None. The comic strip character by Marjorie Henderson Buell. $35.00.

King--10" "Sweet Pea" Cloth plush body, arms and legs. Vinyl head with molded hat. Painted black eyes. Closed mouth. 1959. Marks: King Features Sy. Inc./Sweet Pea, on head. $9.00.

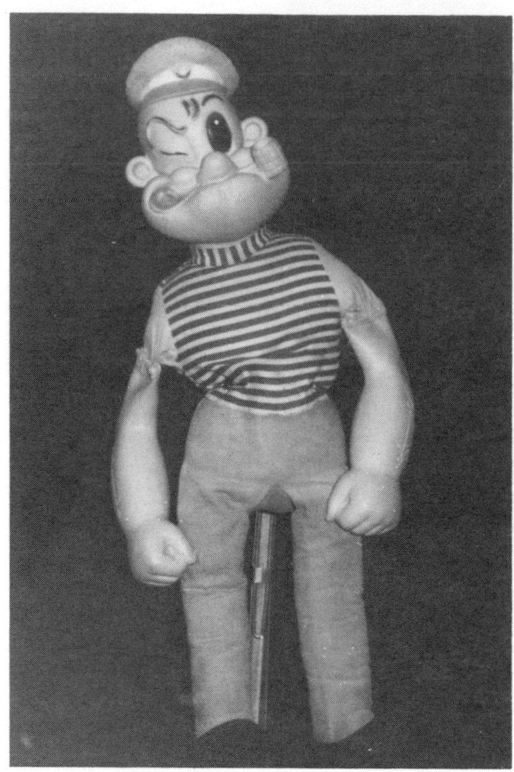

King--21" "Popeye" 1960 cloth filled body and legs. Sewn on vinyl arms. Vinyl head with painted features. Marks: 411/King Features Sy. Inc/Popeye. $16.00.

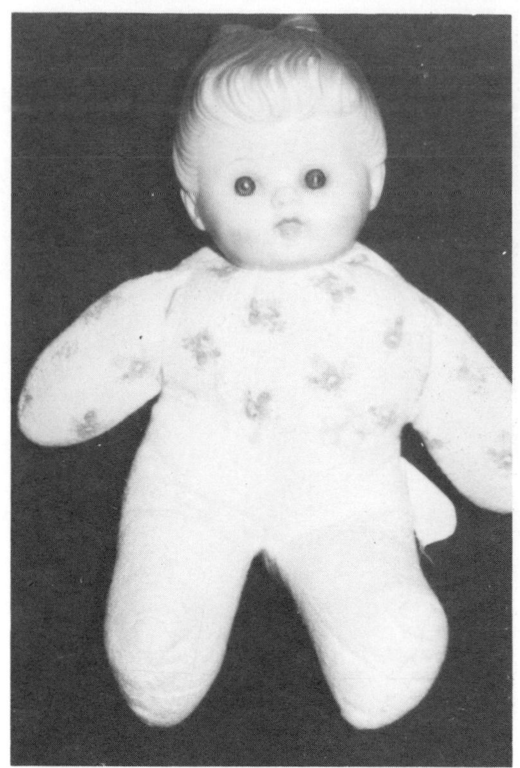

Rag--8½" "Baby's Doll" Cloth body, arms and legs. Vinyl head with molded hair. Blue stationary eyes. Open/closed mouth. Marks: Styled By Stuart/St. Paul Minn., on tag. 1961. $4.00.

Rag--16" "Daisy" Cloth body, arms and legs. Vinyl face mask with painted features. Orange yarn hair. Sewn on shoes. Marks: None. 1961. Original clothes. $7.00.

Rag--15" "Flip The Football Doll" Stuffed body and feet. Vinyl hands and head. Right hand holding vinyl football. Head is stuffed and has molded helmet. Painted features. Sewn on clothes. Marks: 1961/Roko, on head. Mfg'd By Columbia Toy Products Co. $6.00.

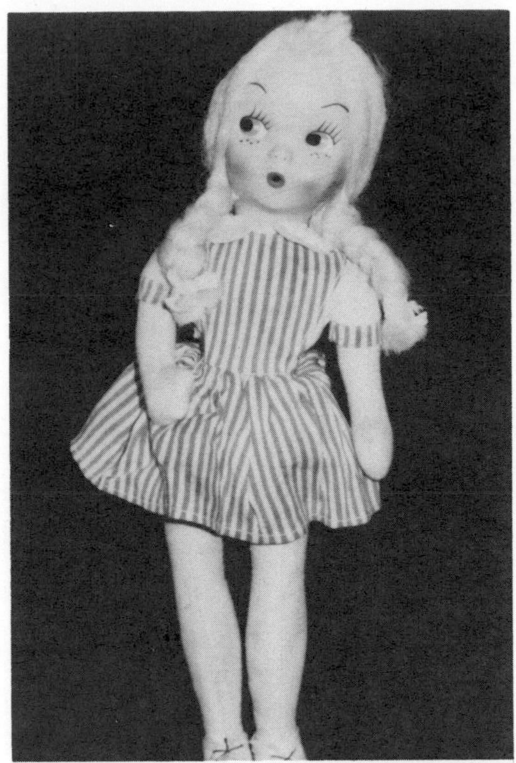

Rag--15" "Candy Striper" Tightly filled cloth covered body, arms legs and head. Plastic face mask. Painted features. Green mohair wig. 1961. $4.00.

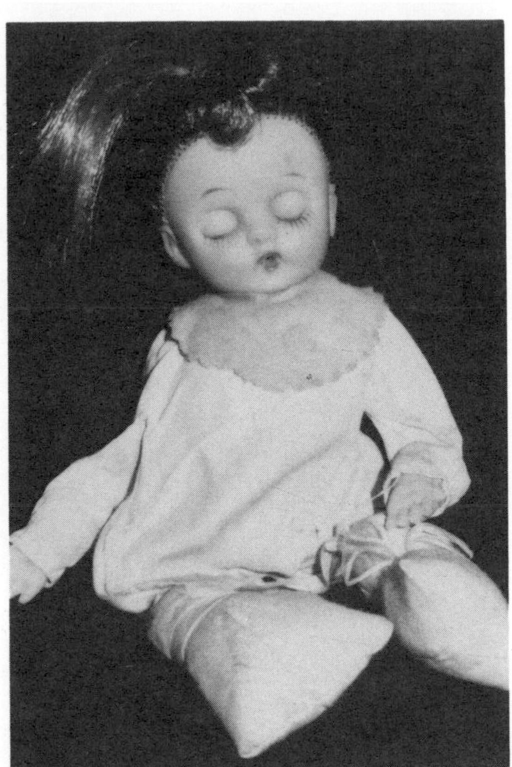

Rag--9" "Cindy" Cloth body, arms and legs. Plastic gauntlet hands. Vinyl head with rooted light brown hair. Painted features. Open mouth/dry nurser. Marks: None. 1961. $2.00.

Rag--17" "Mickey Mouse" Cloth body, arms and legs. Suede mask face with painted features. Marks: None, name tag gone. 1962. $6.00.

Rag--16" "Mr. Magoo" Vinyl head and hat. Open/closed mouth with molded tongue. Foam mixed with cotton stuffing in body, arms and legs. Marks: 1962 UPA Pictures, Inc./All Rights Reserved, on head. $8.00. (Courtesy Allin's Collection).

Rag--15" "Eskimo Pie Boy" Lithographed on cloth and foam filled. Ordered from coupon in box of Eskimo Pie Ice Cream. Trademark of Eskimo Pie Corp. Manufactured by Chase Bag Co. Marks: None. 1962. $3.00. (Courtesy Allin's Collection).

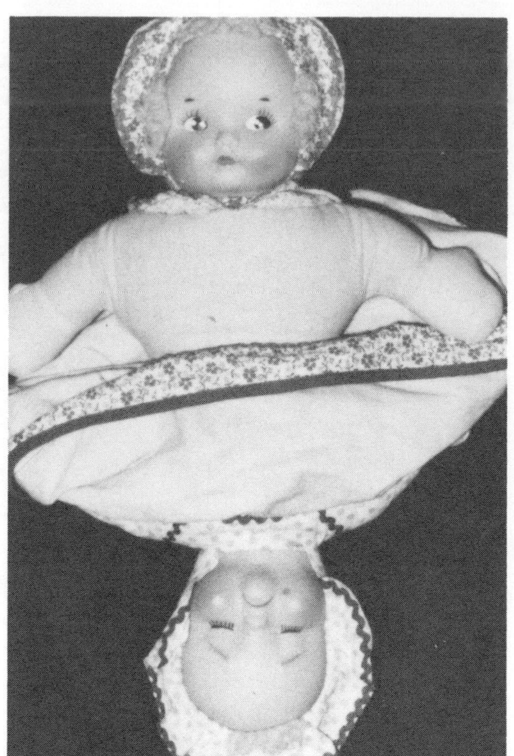

Rag--12" "Multi-Face" Cloth with vinyl heads. Painted features. Tufts of yellow yarn hair. Marks: Knickerbocher Toy Co., on one head. Nick, on other. 1962. $5.00.

Rag--10" "Sleepyhead" Plush body, arms and legs. Vinyl face mask with painted features. Key wind musical. Marks: Tag: Bantam US Toys Inc. 1962. $3.00.

Rag--13" "Pinocchio" Cloth body, arms and legs. Vinyl head. Molded hair and hat. Painted blue eyes and freckles. Marks: Video/Craft Ltd/1962 Japan, on head. Tag: Pinocchio/Vidio Craft Ltd/1962. Reverse side: Knickerbocher/Made In Japan. $5.00.

Rag--15" "Little Bo Peep" Stuffed cloth body, arms and legs. Vinyl hands and head. Painted features. Key wind music box. 1964. Set of five included: Jack, Jill, Little Boy Blue, Mistress Mary. $32.00. (Courtesy Fye Collection).

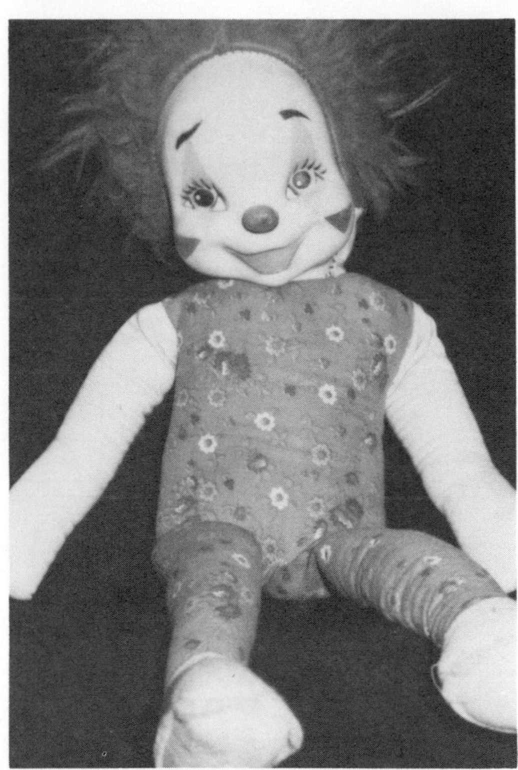

Rag--18" "Clown" Cloth body, arms and legs. Vinyl face mask with sewn on red wig. Sewn on felt feet. Painted features. Marks: Gund, on base of neck. 1964. $6.00.

Rag--12" "Mickey Mouse" Vinyl head with painted features. Plush body, arms and legs. Marks: None. 1964. $7.00.

Rag--23" "Purina Scarecrow" Cloth, lithographed, body, arms and legs. Vinyl head with painted features. Used in Purina's TV commercials. 1965. Marks: R.P. Co., on head. $8.00. (Courtesy Allin's Collection).

Rag--17" "Ronald McDonald" All cloth with printed features. Offered by McDonald Twin Golden Arch Restaurants. 1967. $2.00.

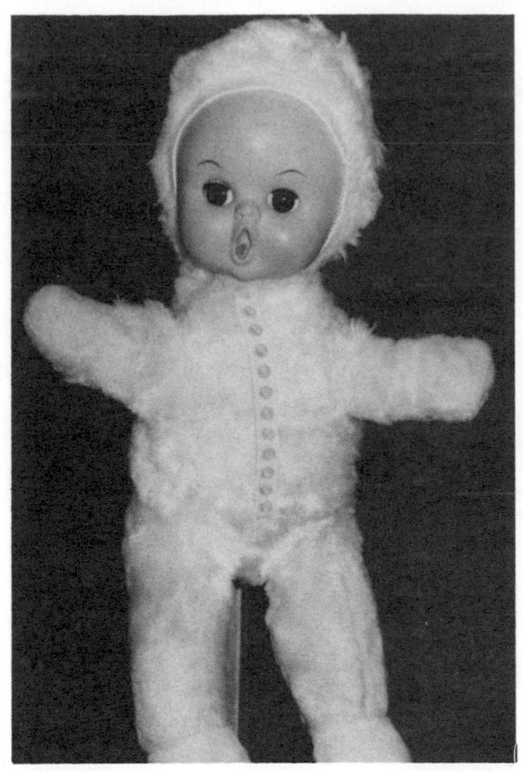

My Toy--16" "Oh My" Stuffed body, arms, legs and head. Vinyl face mask. Large brown sleep eyes/lashes. Open yawning mouth with tongue. Marks: 1967: 1967 My Toy/, on base of neck. $5.00.

Rag--16" "Little Orphan Annie" All cloth with glued on orange yarn hair. Marks: Tag: 1967/Remco In. Inc. Other side: Little Orphan Annie. $15.00.

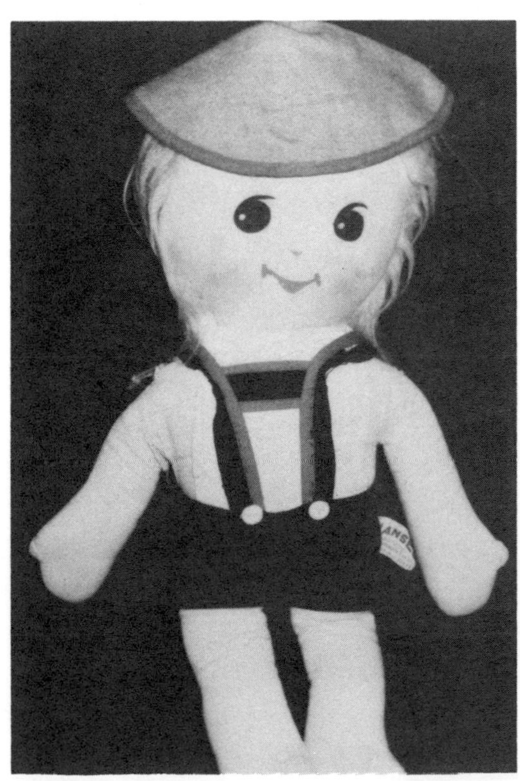

Rag--17" "Hansel" Wool dust filled, cloth covered body. Sewn on clothes. Painted features. Blonde mohair sewn on wig. Tag: Hansel/Rag Doll/Knickerbocher Toy Co. 1969. $4.00.

Rag--9½" "Li'l Soul" Cloth, one piece body, arms, legs and head. Black yarn sewn on hair. Printed features. Removable clothes. Sewn on socks with printed shoes. Marks: 1970/Shindana Toys/Div. Of Operations Bootstrap. $5.00.

Mattel-Rag--8" "Talk-A-Little" Cloth over foam body, arms and legs. Printed features, shoes and socks. Orange yarn hair. Pull string on right side in back of head. Says things like "It's such fun to be cute" "My smile is stuck". Marks: Tag: 1970/Mattel Inc/Hawthorne, Calif/Talk A Little. $4.00.

Rag--19" "Holly" Stuffed body, arms and legs. Styrofoam cloth covered head. Pink yarn hair. Eyes, tear and smile mouth are felt, the rest of features are painted. Marks: Tag: Holiday Fair/Manufactured For Holiday Fair Inc/NYC 1008/1971/Made In Japan. $3.00.

Rag-Amsco--19" "Gramma" Cloth body arms, legs and head. Glued on black/grey/white yarn hair. Painted features. Sewn on black shoes. Marks: Tag: Amsco Toys/Made In Hong Kong. Raggi/Gramma. 1971. $8.00.

Rag--13" "Doughboy" All cloth. Stuffed. Stamped features. Sewn on cap. Marks: Pillsbury, on cap. 1967. $4.00.

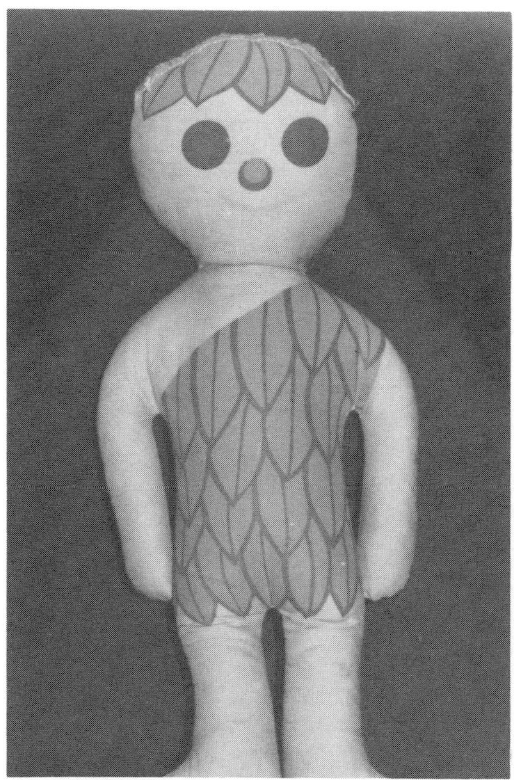

Rag--16" "Jolly Green Giant" Pre-stuffed lithographed rag doll. 1960's $5.00.

Rag--20" "Mr. Peanut" Pre-stuffed, lithographed cloth. Trademark of Planters Peanut Co. 1960's $5.00.

Rag--11" "Eskimo" Plush body, arms, legs and head. Plastic face with painted features. Marks: Tag: Unable To Read. 1960's. $3.00.

Rag--12" "Louise" Nylon covered body over excelsior. Jointed shoulders and hips. Nylon covered arms and legs. Nylon over plastic face mask. Glued on wig. Plastic button eyes. Felt mouth. Glued on shoes. Marks: Dress Tag: Ideal Toy Corp/Hollis 23 NY/Made In Japan. Original dress. 1960's. $5.00.

Remco--5½" "Jan" All vinyl with rooted black hair. Side glancing black eyes, painted. Open/closed mouth with painted teeth. Button in center of stomach makes arm raise. Marks: 2/FJ2-112/Remco Ind Inc/1965, on head. Remco/Industries/Inc., on back. Original clothes. $3.00.

Remco--5½" "Heidi" All vinyl with rooted white blonde hair. Painted side glancing black eyes. Open/closed mouth with painted teeth. Dimpled cheeks. Button in center of stomach makes arm raise. Marks: 1965/Remco Ind Inc, on head. Remco/Industries/Inc, on back. Original clothes. $3.00.

Remco--15" "Baby Stroll-A-Long" Plastic body, and legs. Vinyl arms and head. Rooted white hair. Large blue sleep eyes/heavy lashes. Puckered, closed mouth. Attached molded shoe and socks. Walk mechanism in bottom of shoes. Battery operated. Marks: S2/Remco Ind Inc/E177, on head. 1966. $5.00.

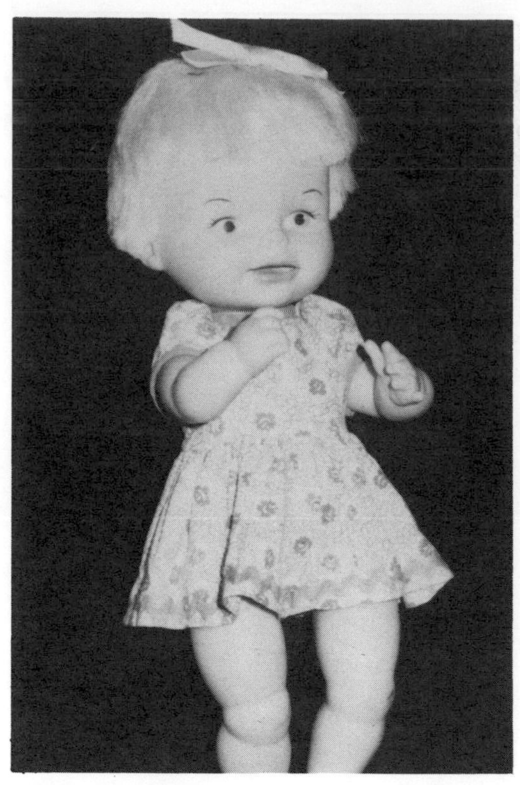

Remco--14" "Baby Sad And Glad" Plastic and vinyl with rooted white hair. Blue painted eyes. Wide open mouth. Deeply molded ears. Left thumb goes into ear and right thumb into

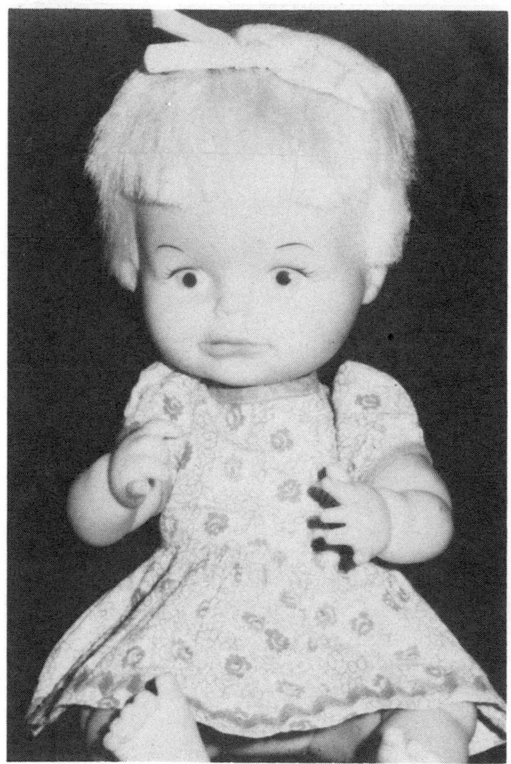

mouth. Left leg opens and closes mouth. Marks: Remco Ind Inc/1966, on head. Remco Ind Inc/1966/1-M, on body. $6.00.

Remco--16" "Snugglebun" Plastic body and legs. Vinyl arms and head. Rooted blonde hair. Dark blue sleep eyes/lashes. Open/closed mouth. Marks: Remco Ind Inc/1965, on head. $8.00.

Remco--16" "Tippy Tumbles" Plastic body and legs. Vinyl arms and head. Rooted red hair. Stationary blue eyes/lashes. Is remote controlled with plug in, in ankle. Battery operated with control box held by operator and attached to doll by cable. Marks: SM/E-32/Remco Ind. Inc./1966. $6.00.

Remco--6" to 7" "Heidi That Grows Up" All vinyl with painted features. Freckles. Hole in head for wigs (two). Waist extends for growing action. Marks: Remco Ind Inc/1966. An original dress. $3.00.

Remco--4" "Bottle Baby" "Cowboy & Grandma" All vinyl with painted features and no hair. Jointed only at neck. Holes in bottom of feet for stand. Marks: Remco Inc/1967, on back. Original clothes. $3.00.

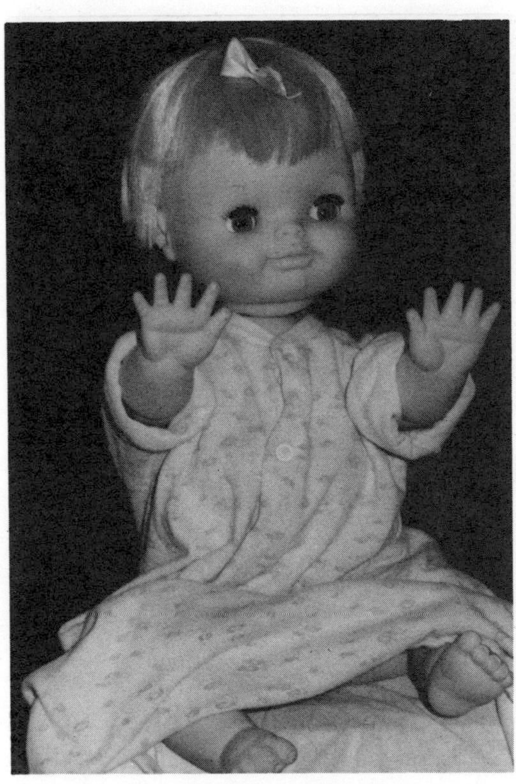

Remco--20" "Baby Crawlalong" Plastic body, arms and legs. Vinyl head with rooted blonde hair. Sleep blue eyes/long lashes. Head mounted on ball socket. Fiber plastic sheath around waist, protects mechanism. Left toes curled. Marks: New/R11/Remco Ind./67,on head. $9.00.

Remco--10" "Linda Lee" Cloth body, arms and legs. Sewn on shoes. Vinyl gauntlet hands. Vinyl head with rooted blonde hair. Blue painted eyes. Open/closed mouth with painted teeth. Dimpled cheeks. Left 2nd and 3rd fingers molded together. Marks: Tag: 1970/Remco Ind . Inc. Harrison NJ. Remco Ind. Inc./1970/66, $6.00.

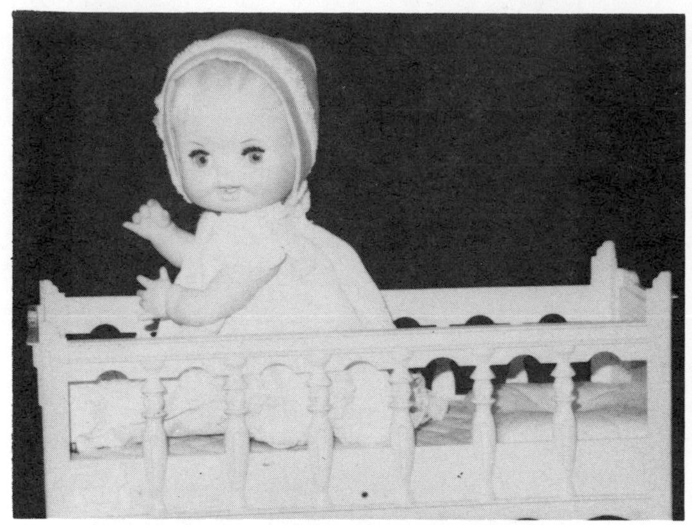

Remco--14" "Baby Grow A Tooth" Plastic body and legs. Vinyl arms and head. Rooted blonde hair. Green sleep eyes/lashes. Open mouth with one tooth. Comes in cradle and is battery operated. Magnets on back of shoes holds her in crib. She sits up, in the crib. Thumb or pacifier makes tooth release when removed from mouth. Marks: Remco Ind Inc/1969 on head. Remco Ind Inc 1966/1-M, on back. $12.00.

Remco--16" "Tumbling Tomboy" Plastic body and legs. Vinyl arms and head. Rooted white hair. Green inset and stationary eyes. Freckles. Dimpled cheeks and chin. Marks: 2000/17EYE/New/E27/Remco Ind. Inc/1969, on head. Original clothes. $6.00.

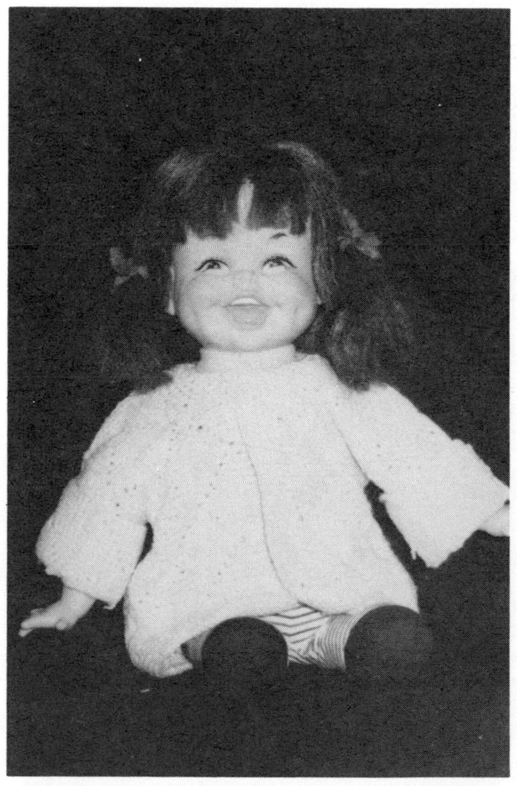

Remco--16" "Baby Laugh A Lot" Cloth body. Vinyl head with rooted dark red hair. Blue painted eyes. Wide open laughing mouth. Six painted teeth and molded tongue. Left 2nd and 3rd fingers molded together. Pull string. She laughs. Marks: 3066/33/Remco Ind Inc/1970, on head. 1970/Remco Ind. Inc/Harrison JN, $8.00.

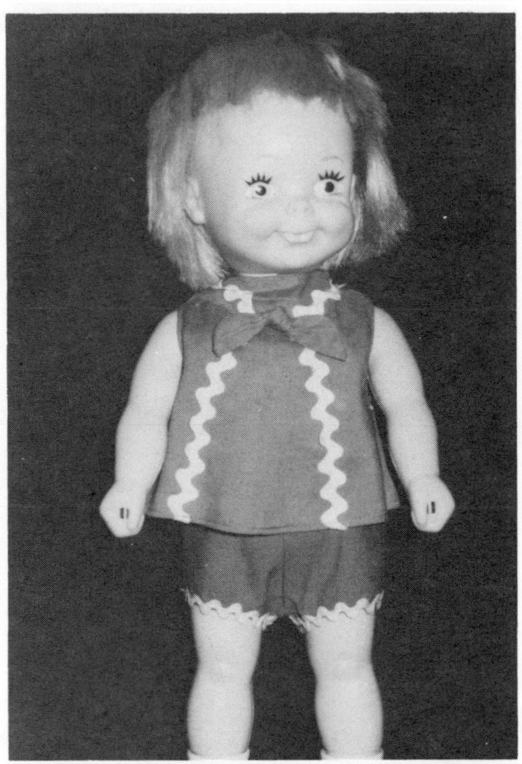

Remco--14" "Jumpsy" Plastic body, arms and legs. Vinyl head with rooted blonde hair. Painted blue eyes. Closed mouth. Battery operated. Holes in hands to hold jumprope. Separate shoes are glued on. Marks: Remco Ind. Inc/1970, on head. $7.00.

Remco--14" "Whistler" Plastic rocker. Foam filled body, arms and legs. Gauntlet vinyl hands. Vinyl head with rooted yellow blonde hair. Blue painted eyes. Puckered mouth. Marks: Remco Ind. Inc./1970, on head. $4.00. (Courtesy Allin's Collection).

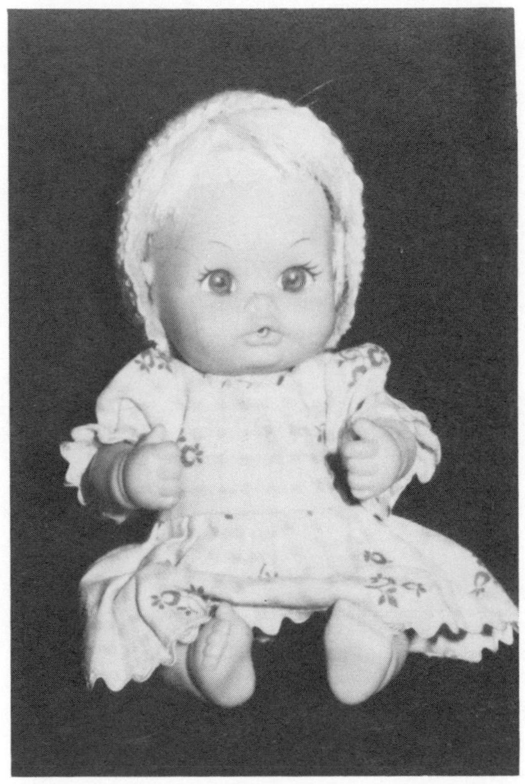

Remco--5½" "Sweet April" All vinyl with rooted blonde hair. Inset stationary blue eyes. Open mouth/nurser. Crossed baby legs. Button in center of back makes arms move up and down. Marks: 3339/Remco Ind Inc/1971, on head. Cries tears. $3.00.

R. Dakin--6" "Funny" Plastic body, arms and legs. Vinyl head with rooted brown hair. Side glancing brown eyes. Closed mouth with one painted tooth. Marks: 1965/R. Dakin & Co/Prod. Of Hong Kong, on head. Tag: Fun Farm/San Francisco/Made In Hong Kong. $3.00.

R. Dakin--7½" "Rosa" All vinyl with painted features. Large side glancing brown eyes. Rooted black hair. Marks: R. Dakin & Co/Copyright 1967/Prod. Of Japan. $4.00.

R. Dakin--7" "Elmer Fudd" All vinyl. No hair. Painted eyes. Jointed shoulders and hips. Marks: Warner Bros. Seven Arts Inc/1968, on head. Warner Bros. Seven Arts Inc/1968/R. Dakin & Co/Product of Hong Kong, on tag and bottom of both shoes. $8.00. (Courtesy Earlene Johnston Collection).

R. Dakin--6½" "First Date" Plastic arms, body and legs. Vinyl head with rooted yellow hair. Painted, closed eyes. Closed mouth. Marks: R. Dakin & Co./Prod. Of Hong Kong. 1970. $4.00.

Royal--20" "Lonely Liza" Cloth over lightly packed, shredded foam body, upper arms and legs. Wire through body so arms and legs are posable. Vinyl lower arms and legs. Vinyl head with rooted blonde hair. Large painted brown eyes. Original clothes. Marks: 1964/Royal Doll. Made In Europe. $25.00.

Royal--11" "Joy" All vinyl with rooted blonde hair. Large painted brown eyes. Closed mouth. Palms down with 2nd and 3rd fingers molded together. Marks: A Royal Doll/'65, on head. 1965/A Royal Doll, on back. $15.00.

S & E--5½" "Valentine Bonnet Toddler" All plastic with blonde glued on wig. Painted side glancing eyes. Jointed at shoulders. Wide open hands with palms down. Marks: S&E, on back. 1952. Original clothes. $8.00.

S & E--5½" "St. Pat's Day Bonnet Toddler" All plastic with glued on wig. Side glancing painted eyes. Hands facing body. Marks: S & E, on back. 1953. Original clothes. $8.00.

S & E--5½" "Easter Bonnet Toddler" All plastic with glued on wig. Painted side glancing eyes. Open hands facing body. Marks: S & E on back. 1953. Original clothes. $8.00.

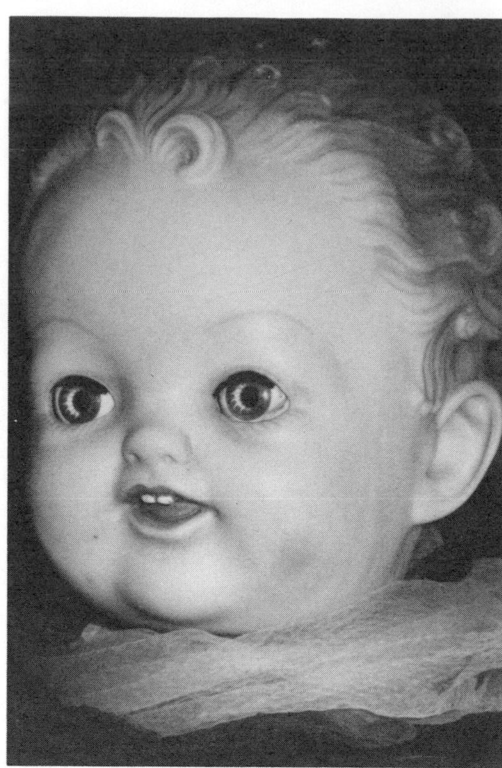

Sayco--25" "Billy Joe" Early vinyl, stuffed head. Latex body. Molded hair. Sleep blue eyes. Open/closed mouth with two molded and painted teeth. Marks: Sayco/25 F. 1950. Sayco is trade name for the Schoen-Yondorf Co. Trade name for this company's latex was Skin-Tex. $25.00.

Sayco--18" "New Happytime Baby" Latex one piece body. Early vinyl head with rooted hair. Blue sleep eyes/molded lashes. Marks: B-17 Sayco. 1956. $7.00. (Courtesy Earlene Johnston).

Sayco--25" "Walking Bride" Hard plastic body, arms and legs. Vinyl head with rooted dark blonde hair. Blue sleep eyes/lashes. Closed mouth. Walker. Cryer. Marks: None. 1956. $9.00.

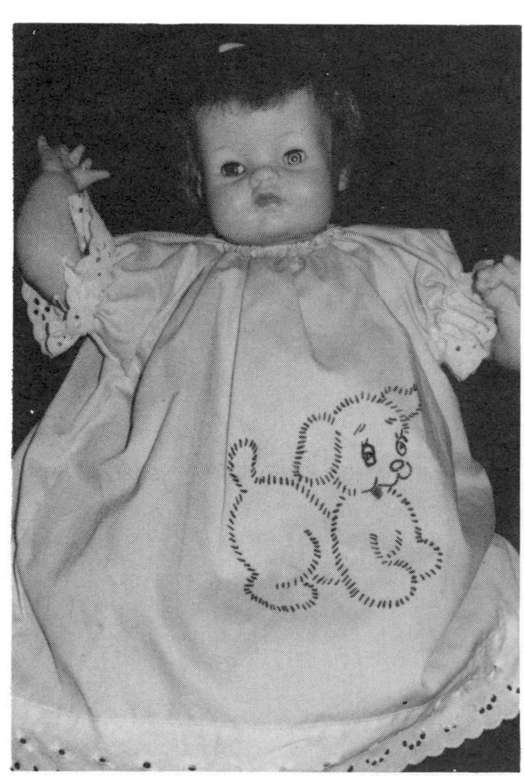

Sayco--18" "Mommy's Baby" Stuffed cloth body. Vinyl arms and legs and head. Rooted blonde hair. Dark blue sleep eyes/lashes. Right hand 3rd finger curled. Left hand thumb and index fingers molded together. Bent baby legs with individual molded toes. Closed mouth. Dimpled. Marks: Sayco Doll Corp/1961, on head. $9.00.

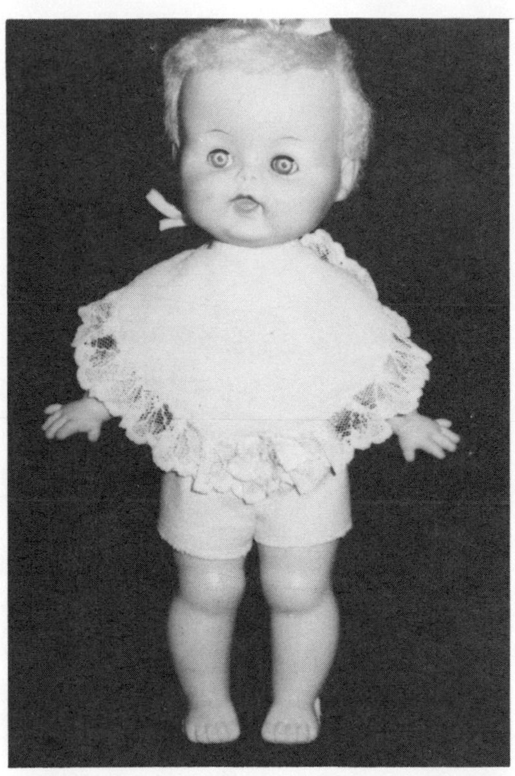

Sayco--11" "Adorable" Plastic and vinyl with rooted blonde hair. Sleep blue eyes/lashes, molded. Open hands with palms down. Marks: K-27/Sayco Doll Corp, on head. $4.00.

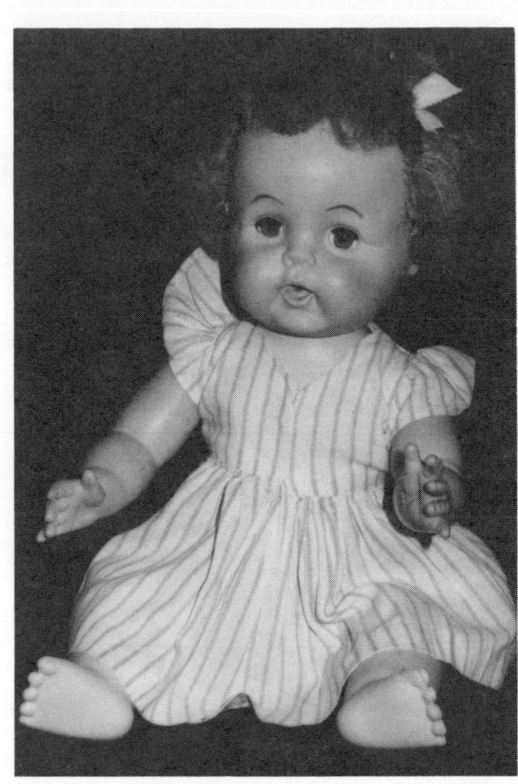

Sayco--15" "Bubble Bath Baby" Plastic body and legs. Vinyl arms and head with rooted dark blonde hair. Dark blue sleep eyes/lashes. Open mouth with molded tongue/nurser. Marks: Sayco Doll Corp, on head. 1964. $5.00.

Scanda House--3" "Indian Troll" All vinyl with rooted orange mohair. Inset, stationary green eyes. Original clothes. Marks: Scanda House/1965/True Troll. $2.00.

Scanda House--3" "Nurse Troll" All vinyl with rooted pink/black mohair. Inset, stationary blue eyes. Marks: Scanda House/1965/True Troll. Original clothes. $2.00.

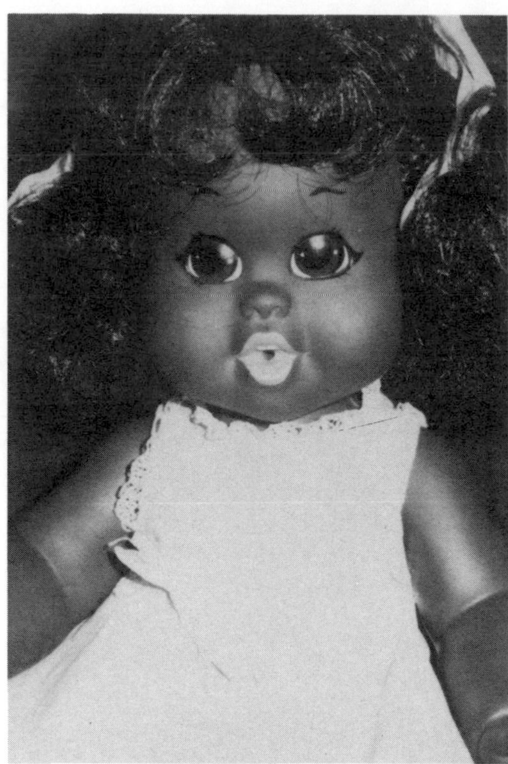

Shindana--13" "Baby Janie" Plastic body and legs. Vinyl arms and head with black rooted hair. Large painted brown eyes. Open mouth/nurser. Painted two upper and one lower teeth. Marks: Div. Of/Operation Bootstrap Inc USA/1968 Shindana. Original. $10.00 (Courtesy Earlene Johnston Collection).

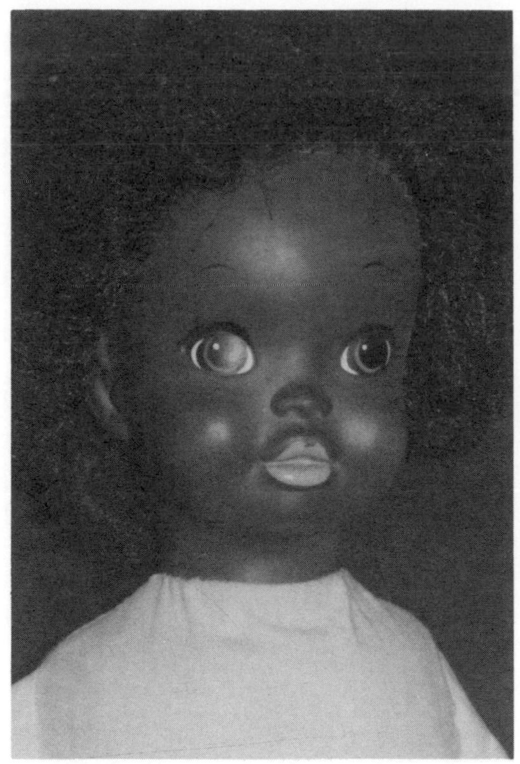

Shindana--15" "Tamu" Cloth body, arms and legs. Gauntlet vinyl hands. Vinyl head with rooted black hair. Painted brown eyes. Talker. Says things like "Let's play house", "My name is Tamu", "Do you like my dress?" Marks: 1969 Shindana/Div. Of Bootstrap Inc. $10.00.

Shindana--16" "Flip Wilson-Geraldine" Foam stuffed cloth covered. Pull string talker. Marks: 1970/Street Corner Productions Inc/Operation Bootstrap Inc/Los Angeles, Calif 90001/Skin Made In Taiwan. 1970. $22.00.

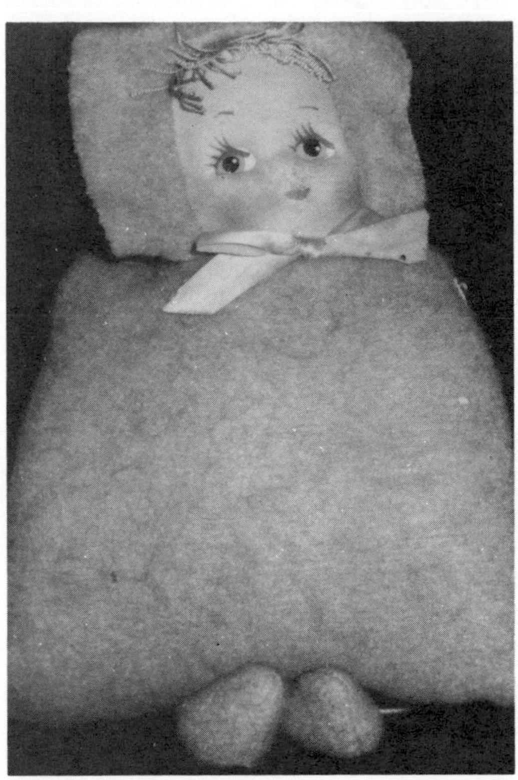

Stuart--10" "Muff Doll" Cloth mask face with painted features. Yellow cord hair. Marks: None. 1939. $10.00.

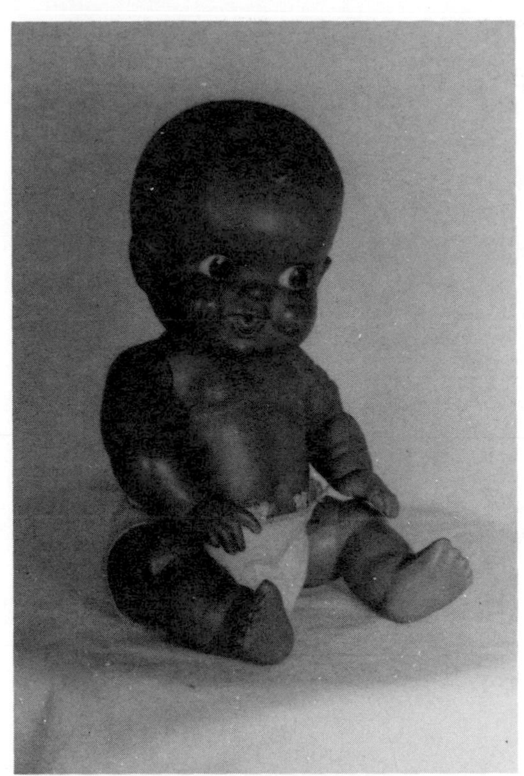

Sun Rubber--10½" "Amosandra" All rubber with painted features. Open mouth/nurser. Baby from radio series. "Amos and Andy" Marks: Amosandra/Columbia Broadcasting/ System Inc/Designed By/Ruth E. Newton/Mfg By The Sun Rubber Co/ Barberton/USA/Pat 2118682/2160739. 1949. $9.00.

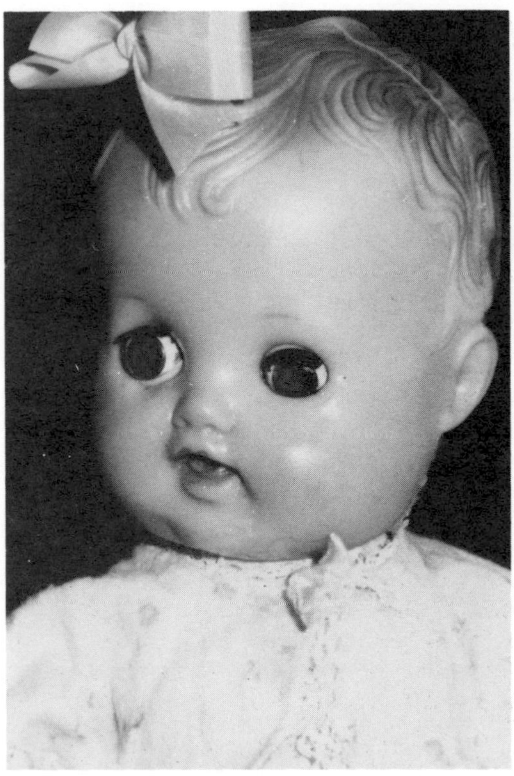

Sun Rubber--12" "Betty Bows" All rubber body, arms and legs. Vinyl head with molded hair and hole for ribbon. Blue sleep eyes/molded lashes. Open mouth/nurser. Crossed baby legs. Marks: Betty Bows/The Sun Rubber Co, on head. Mfg By/The Sun Rubber Co/Barberton USA/Pat 2118682/Pat 2160739. 1953. $6.00.

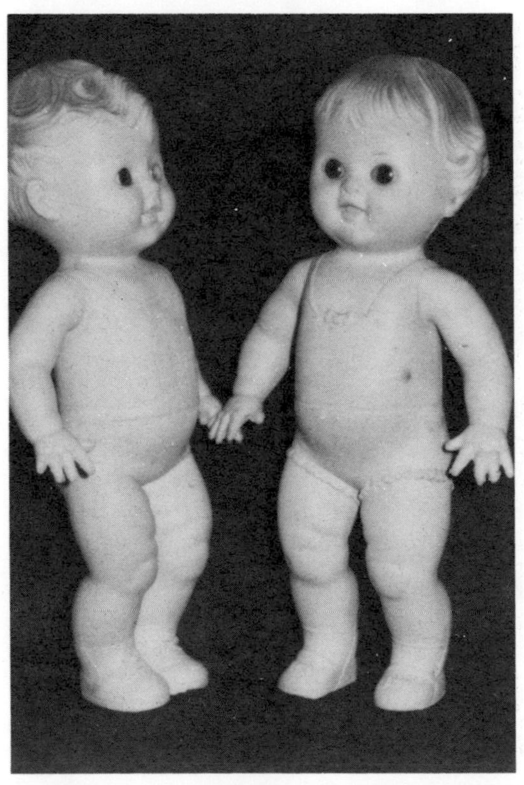

Sun Rubber--10" "Tod-L-Dee & Tod-L-Tim" All one piece latex with inset stationary eyes. Open/closed mouth. Molded on clothes. Marks: Tod-L-Dee/The Sun Rubber Co/50, on bottom of right foot. Tod-L-Tim/The Sun Rubber Co/43, on the bottom of right foot. 1953. $7.00.

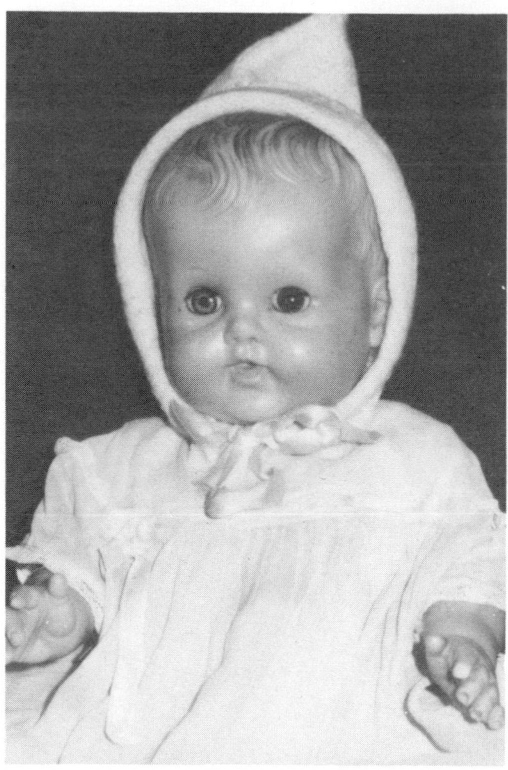

Sun Rubber--17" "Bannister Baby" All "Lastic Plastic" vinyl with molded hair. Blue sleep eyes/lashes. Open mouth/nurser. The doll molded from photo by the famous photographer, Constance Bannister. Marks: Constance Bannister New York, New York, on head. Mfg By Sun Rubber Co/Barberton Ohio $40.00.

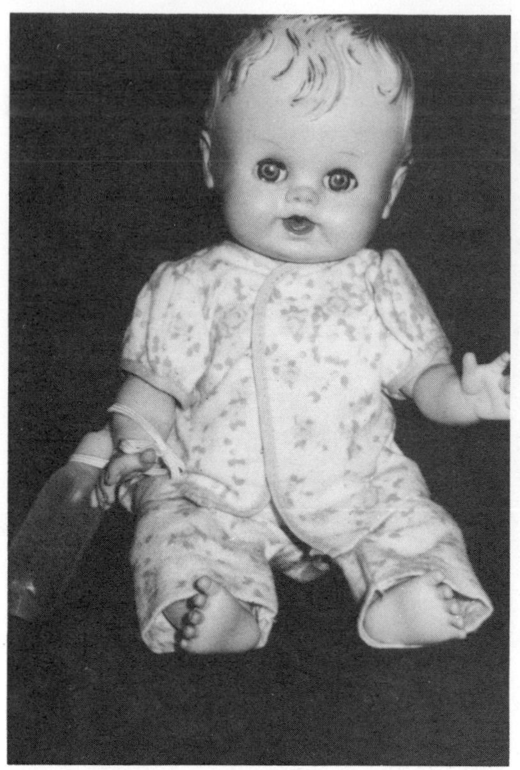

Sun Rubber--12" "Babee Bee" All vinyl with molded hair. Blue sleep eyes/lashes. Open mouth/nurser. Separate toes. Marks: Sunbabe/ Babee Bee/Ruth E Newton/New York NY, on head. 1954. $8.00.

Sun Rubber--8" "Chunky" All vinyl with molded hair. Painted blue side glancing eyes. Open/closed mouth. Molded and painted dress, shoes and socks. Marks: Mfg By/The Sun Rubber Co/Barberton Ohio/Made In The USA/Ruth E Newton/New York Ny/7, all on back of neck. 1954. $3.00.

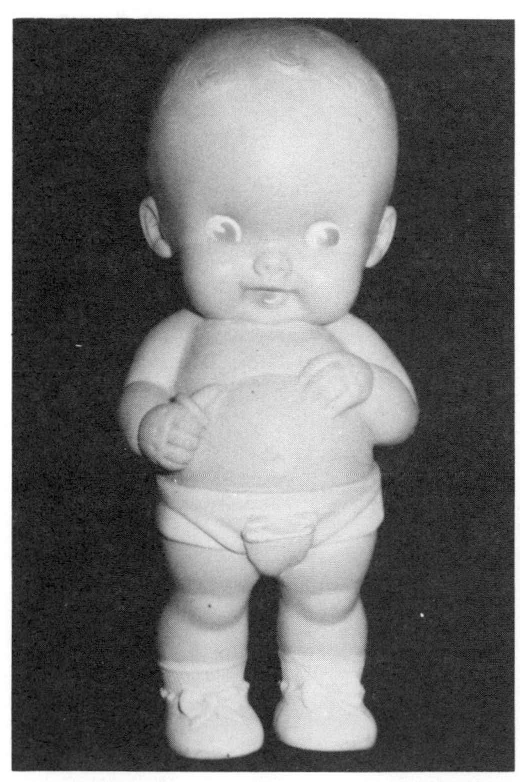

Sun Rubber--8" "Baby" All one piece vinyl. Molded on diaper, socks and shoes. Painted features. Marks: Ruth E Newton/Sun Rubber Co. 1956. $3.00.

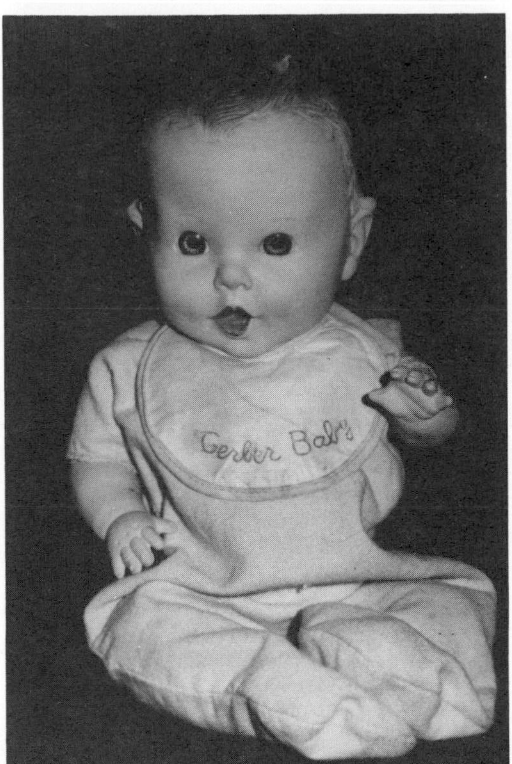

Sun Rubber--11" "Gerber Baby" All rubber with molded hair, painted brown. Inset stationary eyes. Open mouth/nurser. Dimpled cheeks. Crossed baby legs. Marks: Gerber Baby/Gerber Products Co, on head. Mfd By/The Sun Rubber Co/Barberton Ohio USA/Pat #, covered by squeeker, on body. 1956. $9.00.

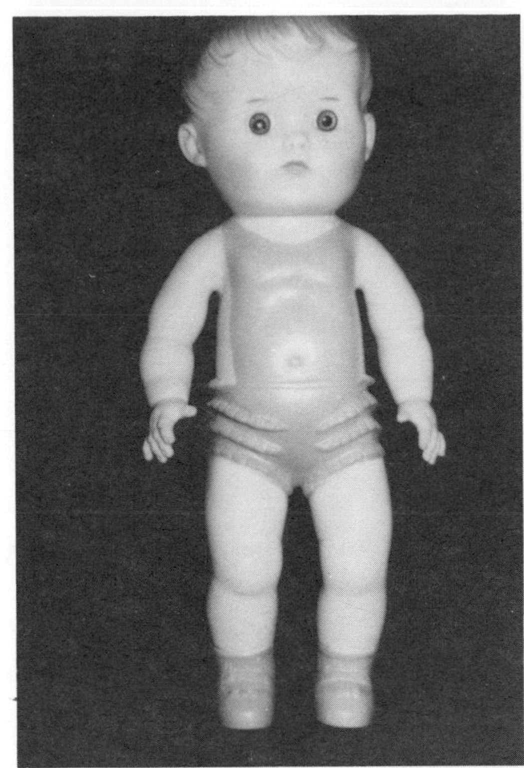

Sun Rubber--10" "Tod-L-Tee" All vinyl with molded hair. Blue stationary eyes. Molded and painted on sunsuit, shoes and socks. Closed mouth. Jointed at neck. Marks: Sun Rubber Co. 1956, on head. $3.00.

Sun Rubber--10" "So Wee" All vinyl with molded hair. Blue stationary eyes. One piece body, arms and legs. Marks: Sunbabe/So Wee/Ruth Newton/New York Ny, on head. The Sun Rubber Co 1957, on back. $5.00.

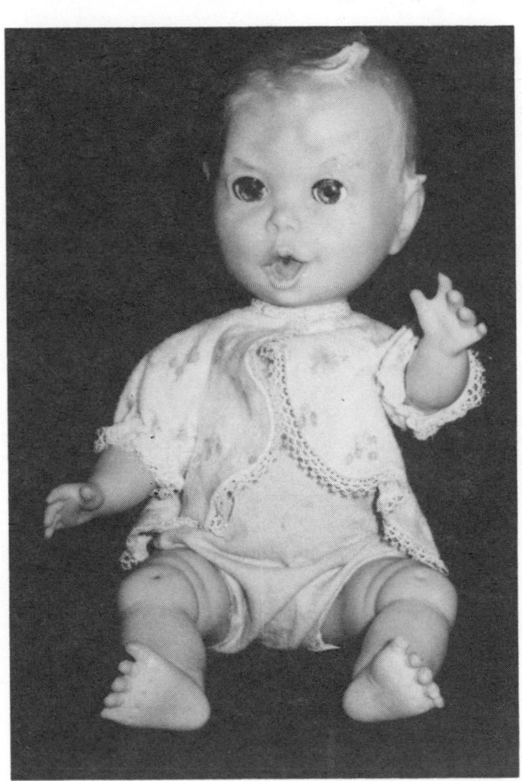

Gerber Products--14" "Gerber Baby" All vinyl with molded light brown hair. Molded eyebrows and eyelids. Blue sleep eyes/lashes. Wide open mouth/nurser. Marks: Gerber Baby/Gerber Products Co 1965, on head. Offered for a very short time as a mail premium from Gerber Baby Foods Co. $10.00.

Super Doll--16" "Little Debbi Eve" Plastic body and legs. Vinyl arms and head. Rooted blonde hair. Blue sleep eyes/lashes. Closed mouth. Marks: Super Doll Inc/1963, on head. $9.00.

Super Doll--17" Melody Baby Debbi" Cloth body with vinyl arms, legs and head. Rooted blonde hair. Blue sleep eyes/lashes. Open/closed mouth. Music box in center of back. Marks: SD, on head. 1965. $8.00.

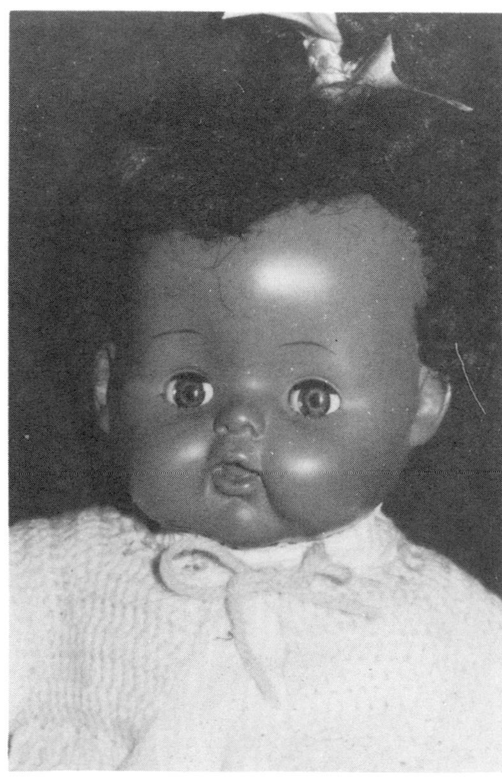

Super Doll--16" "Baby Debbi" Cloth body with vinyl arms, legs and head. Rooted black hair. Sleep brown eyes/lashes. Open/closed mouth with molded tongue. Marks: None. 1965. $10.00 (Courtesy Allin's Collection).

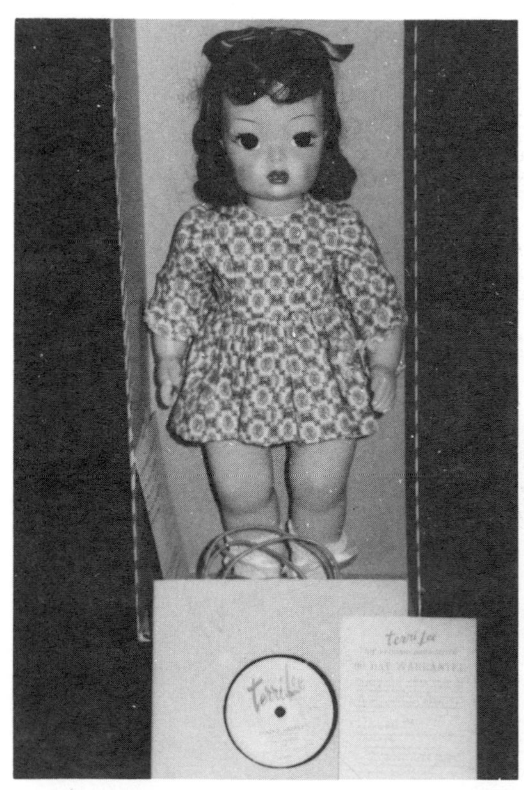

Terri Lee--16" "Talking Terri Lee" All hard plastic. Glued on dark brown wig. Painted features. Attachment at base of neck for "phone jack" to record player. Marks: Terri Lee on back. Mar-Fan Inc. 1708 Standard St. Glendale 1, Calif. on box and record. 1950. Original clothes. $50.00. (Courtesy Fye).

Terri Lee--18" "Terri Lee" All early hard plastic. Glued on white hair. Painted features. Marks: Terri Lee, across back. Original clothes. 1950. $35.00.

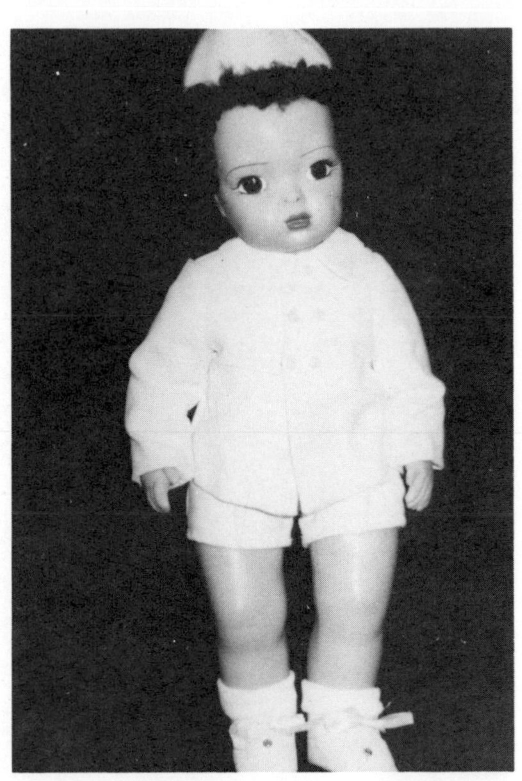

Terri Lee--18" "Jerri Lee" All early hard plastic. Inset scalp with black caracul fur hair. Painted features. Marks: Terri Lee Across Back. Original clothes. $48.00.

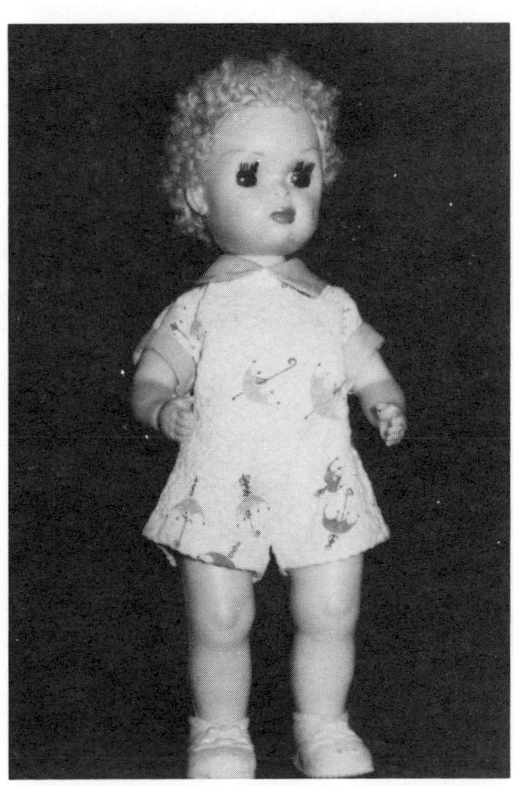

Terri Lee--10" "Walking Tiny Jerry Lee" All early hard plastic with glued on blonde caracul hair. Brown sleep eyes/long lashes. Head turns as he walks. Marks: C, in a circle on back. Original sunsuit. 1950. $25.00.

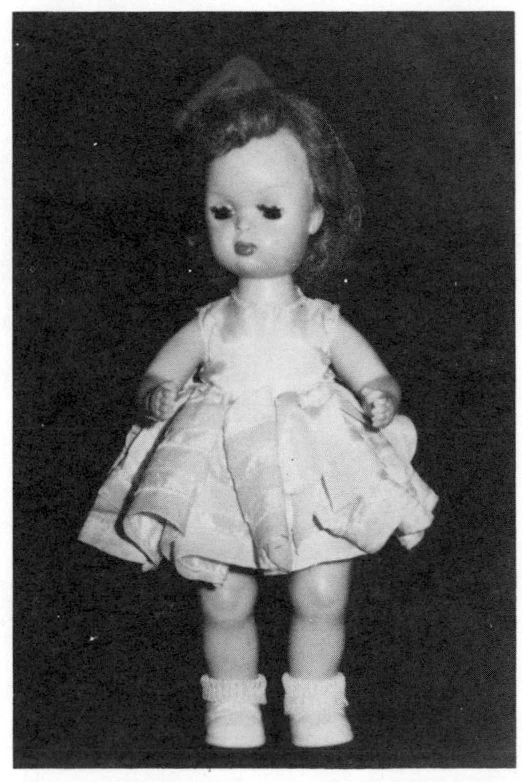

Terri Lee--10" "Walking Terri Lee" All hard plastic with glued on wig. Brown sleep eyes. Marks: C, in a circle on back. Original dress. 1950. $25.00.

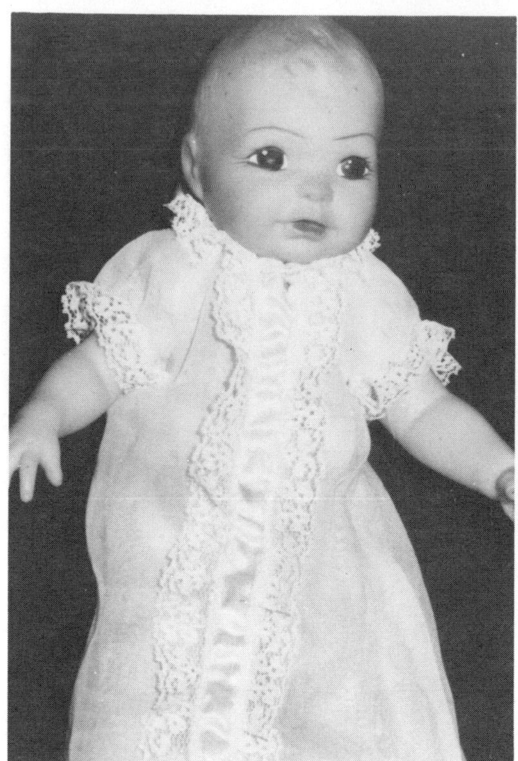

Terri Lee--9" "Baby Linda" All vinyl with molded, painted hair. Painted black eyes. Open/closed mouth. Marks: None. 1951. $36.00. (Courtesy Allin's Collection).

Transogram Co Inc--10" "Mannequin" All composition. Jointed at shoulders only. Molded hair, shoes and socks. Painted eyes. Marks: Transogram Co Inc/New York on back. Box: Designers Wardrobe Trunk Sewing Set. 1947. $18.00. (Courtesy Earlene Johnston)

Transogram Co Inc--9" "Dawk" All plastic with yarn hair. Plastic glasses. Carried different signs such as: Organize Vanilla Ice Cream Haters. Came with 21 changeable signs. Marks: 1965/Transogram/Company/Inc. $6.00.

Uneeda Doll Company

This company began making dolls in 1917. They are also known as the Tony Toy Company, Hong Kong and some of their dolls are marked with a "U", a number, "UD" and "UF".

The following are not all the dolls made by this company.

1942: Miss Ducky Deluxe (20.00)
1948: Carmen (Rita Hayworth 95.00)
1951: Needa Toddles (8.00)
1953: Sweetums (8.00)
1954: Baby Trix (8.00), Surprise Doll (16.00)
1955: Baby Trix (8.00), Dew Drop (8.00), Princess Bride (10.00)
1956: Country Girl (6.00)
1957: Dollikins (10.00), Debteen (8.00)
1958: Pri-thilla (9.00), Baby Dollikins (16.00)
1959: Wiggles (45.00), Betsy McCall (22.00)
1960: Pollyanna (20.00), Freckles (18.00), Bunting Baby (8.00), New Baby Trix (6.00), Blue Fairy (3.00), Tinyteen (5.00)
1961: Baby Talks (20.00), Sunny Face (7.00), Patty Kix (8.00), Dolly Pep (8.00), Purdy (16.00), Yummy (16.00), Princess Doll (8.00), Cuddly Baby (3.00), Babes in Toyland (10.00), Princess (8.,00), Princess Bride (8.00)
1962: Blabby (18.00), Bundle of Love (4.00), Miss Debutante (8.00), Toothums (3.00), Baby Sweetums (5.00), Miss Debteen (8.00), Debteen Toddler (16.00), Magic Bottle Baby (5.00)
1963: Weepsy Wiggles (8.00), Beau (8.00), The Worlds Fairest (6.00), Wishmaker (5.00), Coquette (6.00), Bare Bottom Baby (8.00), Bob (6.00)
1964: Wipsy Walker (7.00), Wish-Nics (3.00), Slugger-Nik (3.00), Piddles (3.00), Pokey (3.00), Elfy (3.00), Posey Elfy (3.00), New Betsy McCall (10.00 to 30.00), Little Coquette (4.00), Debuteen (8.00), Posable Baby Trix (4.00), Needa Toddles (4.00)
1965: Ugh Nik (3.00), Maver-Nik (3.00), She-Nik (3.00), Hula-Nik (3.00), Politik-Nik (3.00), He-Nik (3.00), Wee Nik (3.00), Pretty Portrait (5.00), Bride (6.00), Pixie Haircut Baby (4.00)
1966: Pee Wee (2.00), Impish Elfy (3.00), Years Ago (15.00), Tiny Toddles (3.00), Pretty Portrait (5.00), Moonmaid (8.00)
1967: Miss Modern (4.00), Plum Pees (3.00), Dolly Walker (3.00), Baby Sweetums (4.00), Tiny Trix (3.00), Secret Sue, the girl from U.N.E.E.D.A. (8.00), Baby Bumpkins (5.00), First Born Baby (3.00), Tiny Toddles (3.00), Tiny Teens (4.00), Flower People (5.00 each), Special Limited Edition Golden Anniversary Doll (35.00), Little Sophisticates (3.00)
1968: Miss Modern (4.00), Bundle of Love (4.00)
1969: Balletina (4.00), Bathtub Baby (3.00), Pillow Baby (3.00), Baby Weepsy Wee Walker (4.00), Debteen (5.00), Adorable Cindy (3.00), 11" Dollikins (4.00)
1970: Baby Sleep Amber (8.00), New Born Yummy (2.00), Kim (3.00), Twins (12.00 pair), Dolly Dress Ups (6.00), Lovable Lynn (4.00), Infant Jumper (3.00), Bitsy Bathtub Baby (2.00), Tiny Trix (2.00)
1971: Jennifer Fashion Doll (6.00), New Gerber Baby (5.00), Happy Pee Wee (2.00)

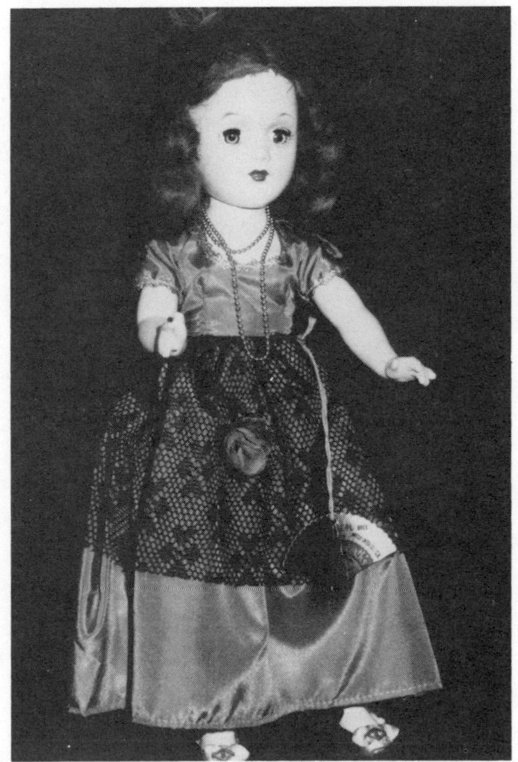

Uneeda--14" "Rita Hayworth As Carmen" All composition with glued on red mohair wig. Adult figure. Stapled on under clothes. Original clothes. Marks: None. Tag & Box: The Carmen Doll/W I Gould & Co, Inc./Inspired By Rita Hayworth's/Portrayal Of Carmen In "The Loves/Of Carmen"/Made In USA. A Columbia Technicolor Picture/A Beckworth Corp. Productions. 1948. Film also starred Glenn Ford. $95.00.

Carmen Box

Rita Hayworth showing off her famous "gams."

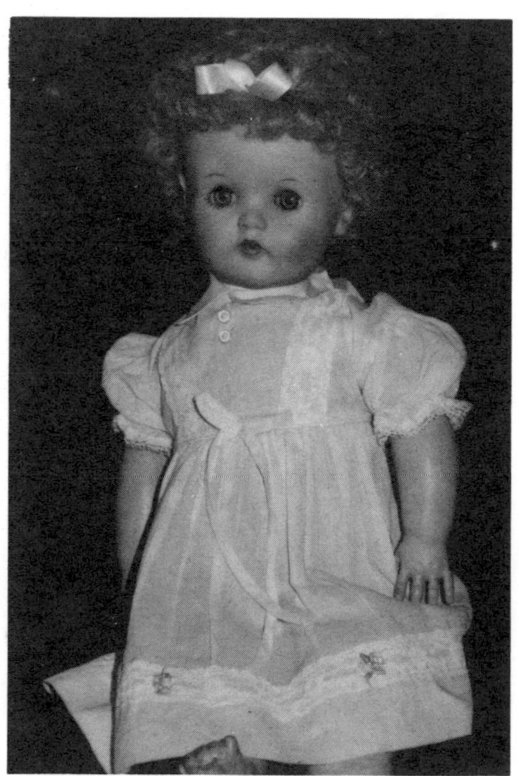

Uneeda--22" "Sweetum" All one piece, unjointed latex body. Vinyl head with rooted blonde hair. Blue sleep eyes/lashes. Open/closed mouth. Marks: Uneeda, on head. 1953. $18.00.

Uneeda--16" "Surprise Doll" All early vinyl with rooted light brown hair. Pin and disc jointed. Open mouth nurser. Blue sleep eyes/lashes. Mechanism in body, makes head nod, feet kick and arms go up, when doll is pressed on stomach. Marks: Uneeda, on head. 1954. Also known as "Baby Trix." $22.00.

Uneeda--20" "Princess Bride" Hard plastic body, arms and legs. Vinyl head with rooted blonde hair. Sleep blue eyes/lashes. Walker, head turns as she walks. 1955. Marks: 3 (in a circle) Uneeda. $10.00.

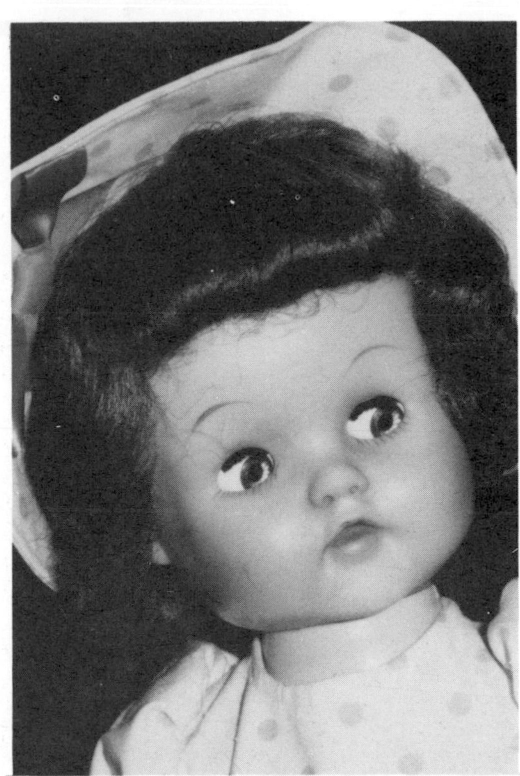

Uneeda--22" "Country Girl" Hard plastic body, arms and legs. Jointed knees walker, head turns. Vinyl head with rooted hair. Flirty blue eyes/lashes. Open/closed mouth. Marks: Uneeda, on head. 1956. $16.00.

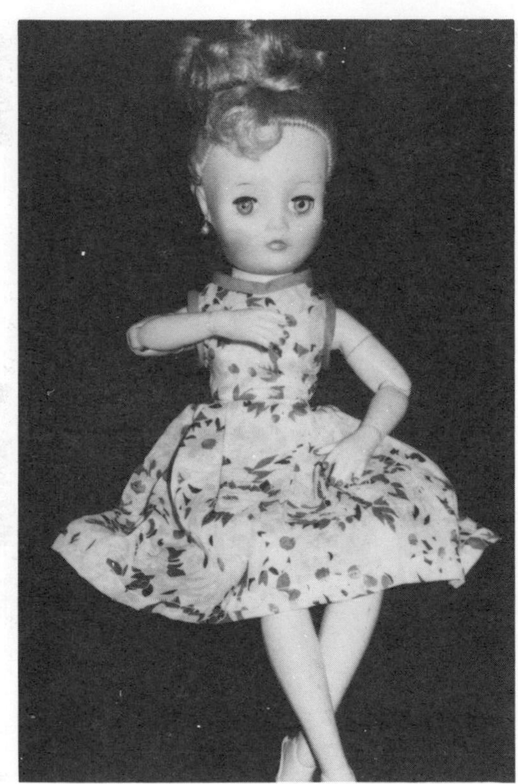

Uneeda--19" "Dollikins" Hard plastic body arms and legs. Jointed at shoulders, upper arms, elbows, wrists, waist, hips, knees and ankles. Vinyl head with rooted ash blonde hair. Blue sleep eyes/lashes. Closed mouth. Pierced ears. Finger and toe-nail polish. Marks: Uneeda/2s, on head. Original dress. 1957. $10.00.

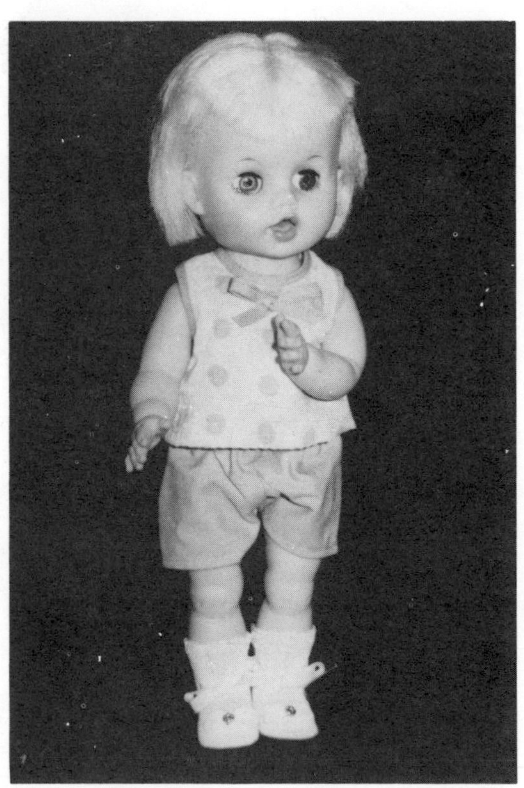

Uneeda--12" "Pri-Thilla" All vinyl with blonde rooted hair. Blue sleep eyes/lashes. Wide open mouth. Left arms molded bent at elbow and curved toward body. Toddler legs with dimpled knees. Sucks thumb. Blew up balloons in 1961. Marks: 4, on head. 1958. $9.00.

Uneeda--20" "Baby Dollikins" Solid vinyl arms, legs and body. Vinyl head with rooted white hair. Blue sleep eyes/lashes. Dimples high on cheeks. Open Mouth/nurser. Jointed at neck, shoulders, elbows, wrists, hips and knees. Marks: Uneeda, on head. Uneeda Doll Co Inc, on back. 1958. $16.00.

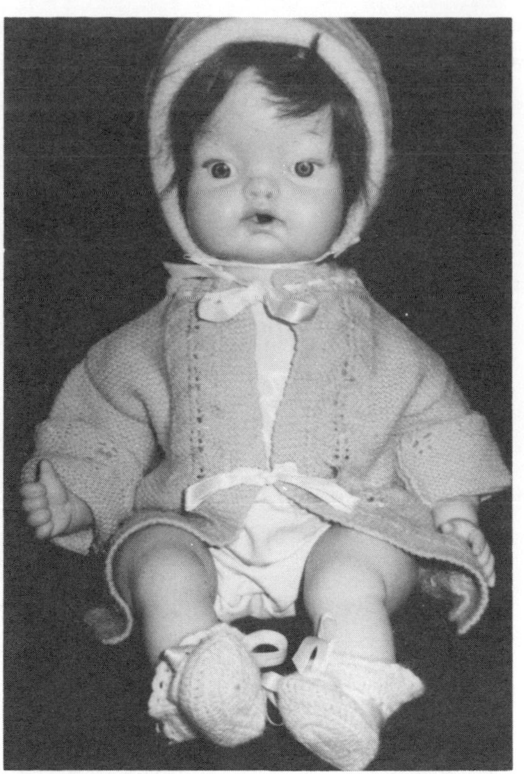

Uneeda--19" "Wiggles" Oil cloth outer body covering with vinyl arms and legs attached. Vinyl body and head. Rooted dark brown hair.

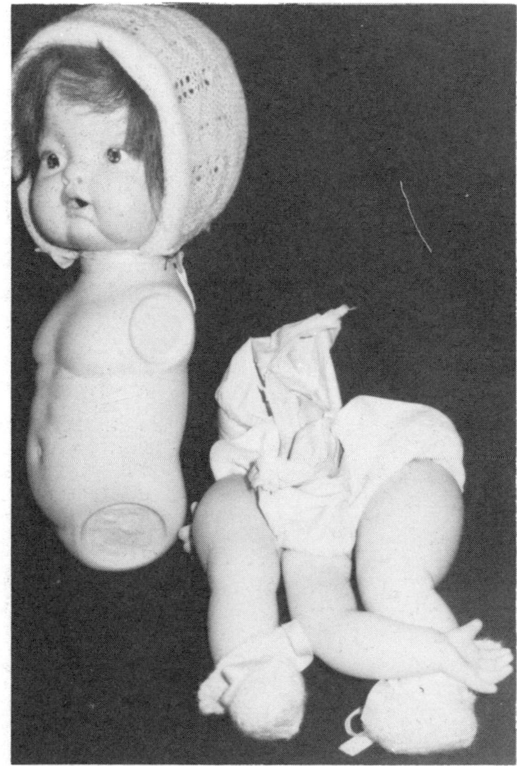

Stationary blue eyes. Open mouth/dry nurser. Mama cry voice. Marks: Uneeda Doll/NF 21, on head. Uneeda Dolls Inc, on back. 1959. $45.00.

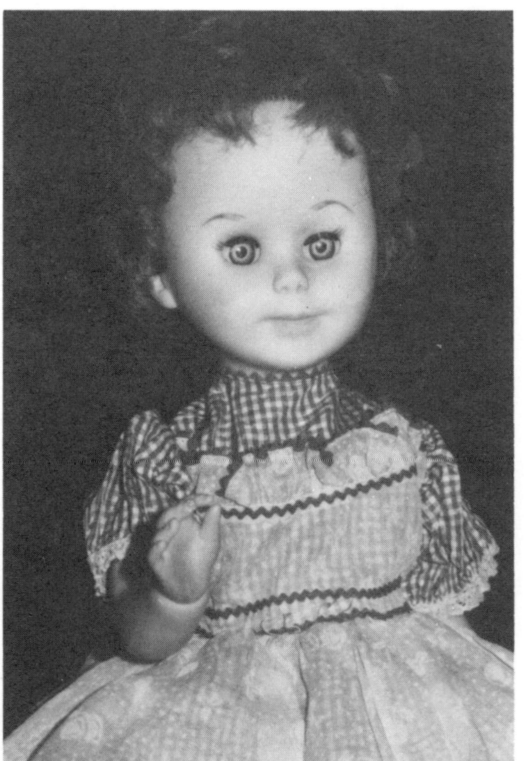

Uneeda--22" "Betsy McCall" Plastic body and legs. Legs jointed high above knee. Vinyl arms with jointed wrists. Vinyl head with rooted ash blonde hair. Blue sleep eyes/lashes. Feathered eyebrows. Jointed waist. Posable head. Marks: None. 1959. $22.00.

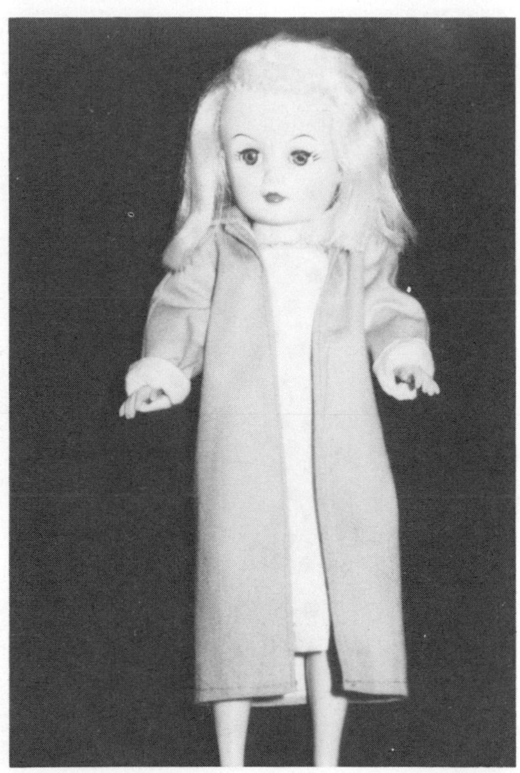

Uneeda--10" "Blue Fairy" Plastic body and legs. Vinyl arms and head. Rooted white hair. Blue sleep eyes/molded lashes. High heel feet. Marks: Uneeda, at base of neck. Originally dressed in blue gown. From Pinocchio. 1960. $3.00.

Uneeda--32" "Freckles" Plastic body and legs. Vinyl arms and head. Rooted red/brown hair. Large blue flirty sleep eyes/lashes. Open/closed mouth with four molded painted teeth. Left 2nd and 3rd fingers curled. Right 3rd finger curled. Marks: 22, on body. Original dress 1960. Freckles across nose and cheeks. $18.00.

Uneeda--31" " Pollyanna" Plastic body and legs. Vinyl arms and head. Rooted white hair. Blue sleep eyes/lashes. Eye liner. Open mouth with painted teeth. Character from Walt Disney movie "Pollyanna" played by Hayley Mills. Marks: Walt Disney Prod./Mfd By Uneeda/NF. 1960. $20.00.

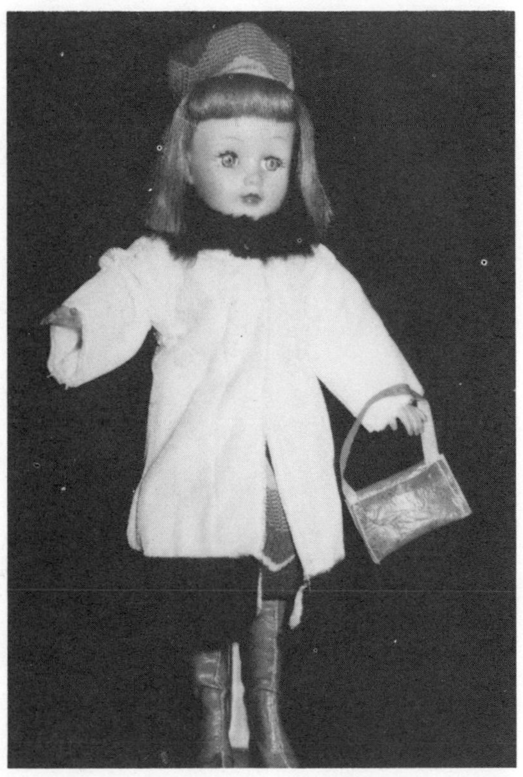

Uneeda--10" "Tinyteen" Plastic body and legs. Vinyl arms and head. Rooted dark blonde hair. Blue sleep eyes/molded lashes. 2nd and 3rd fingers molded together. High heel feet. Jointed waist. Marks: Uneeda, on head. 1960. $5.00.

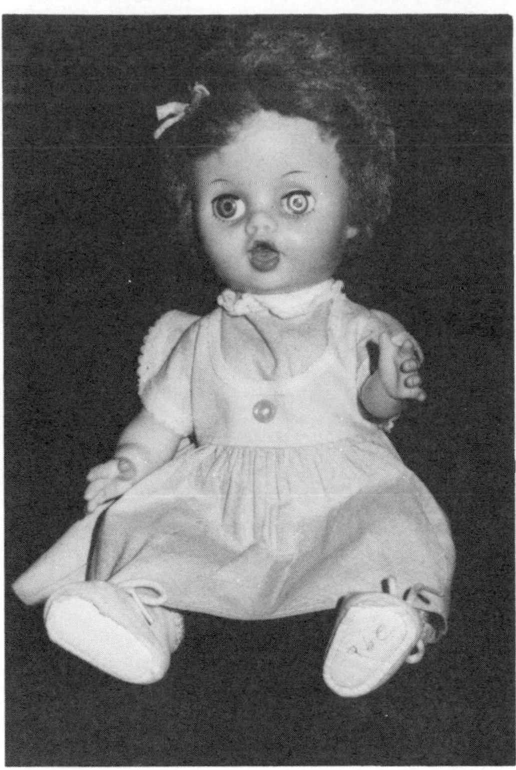

Uneeda--12" "Yummy" All vinyl with rooted light brown hair. Blue sleep eyes/lashes. Wide open mouth. When stomach is pressed, mouth moves with a sucking sound. Marks: None. 1961. Original clothes. $16.00.

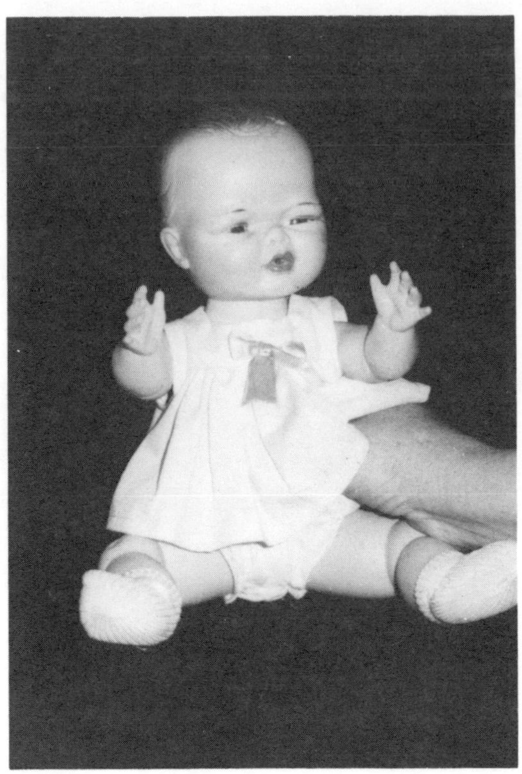

Uneeda--15" "Purty" All vinyl with molded and painted brown hair. Inset blue eyes/painted lashes. Open mouth/nurser. Baby legs. Dimpled knees. Squeeze stomach and eyes squint. Head

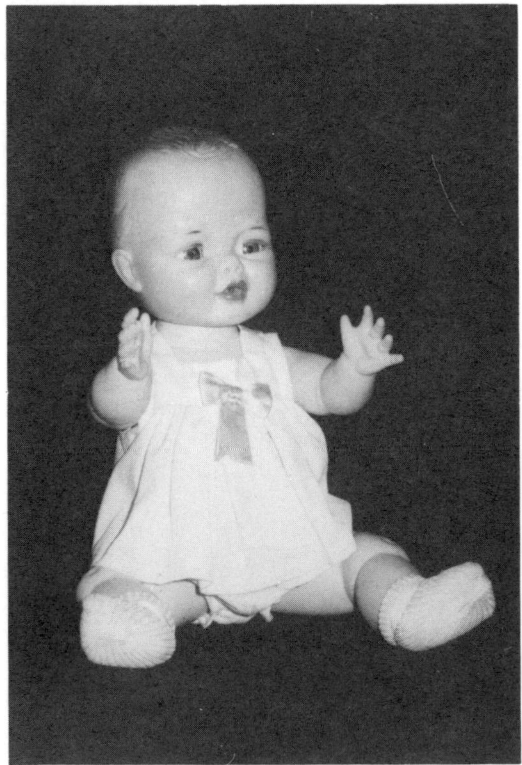

turns and has a "coo" voice as she cries. Marks: Uneeda, on head. 516-42/Uneeda, on back. 1961. $16.00.

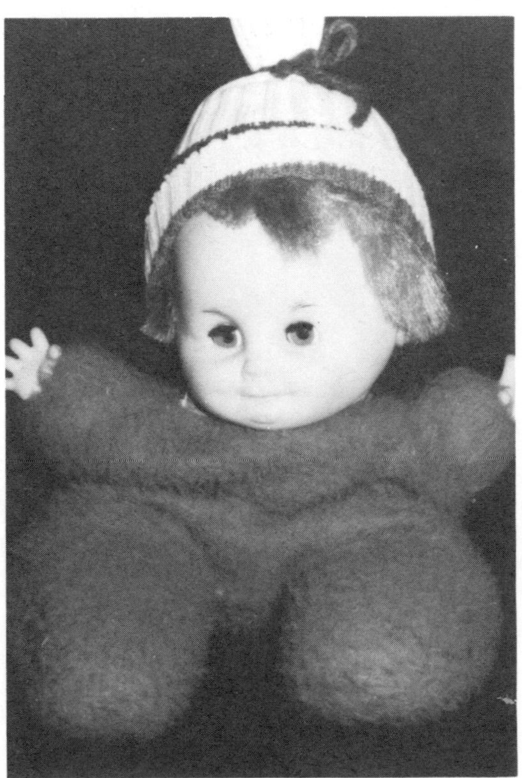

Uneeda--10" "Cuddly Baby" One piece plush filled body, arms and legs, Vinyl hands and head with rooted blonde hair. Blue stationary eyes/lashes. Dimpled cheeks and chin. Marks: 1961/Uneeda Doll, on head. $3.00.

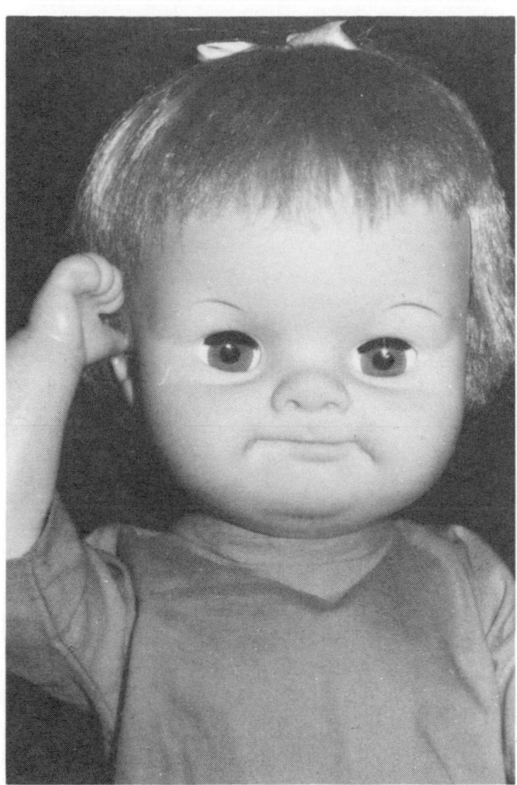

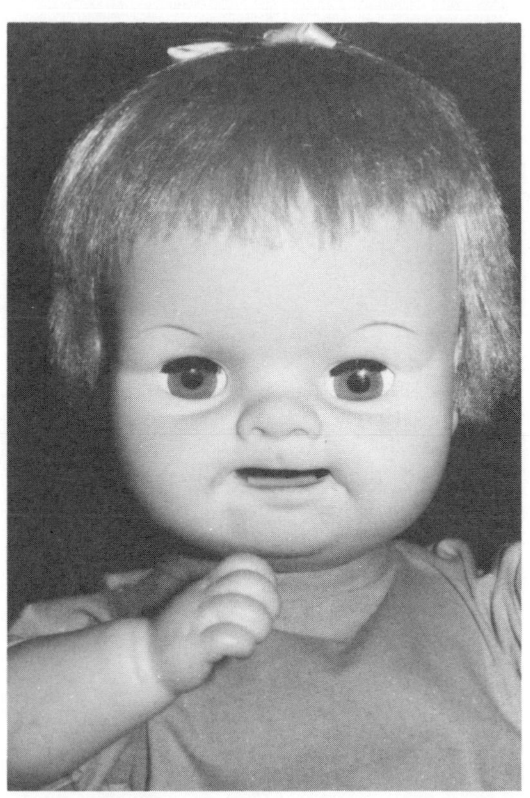

Uneeda--18" "Blabby" All vinyl with rooted dark brown hair. Blue sleep eyes/lashes. Upper lip over lower. Press stomach and mouth moves with cryer voice. All fingers of right hand curled. Sucks right thumb. Marks: Uneeda Doll Co/Inc. in a circle/1962 beneath. Uneeda Doll Co Inc, on back. $18.00 (Courtesy Allin's Collection).

Uneeda--23" "Miss Debteen" Plastic with vinyl head. Rooted blonde hair. Bright blue sleep eyes/lashes. Eyelids are yellow hard plastic. Marks: U, on back of head. 1962. $8.00.

Uneeda--21" "Debteen Toddler" Plastic with vinyl head. Rooted long blonde hair. Blue sleep eyes/lashes. Dimples. 2nd and 3rd fingers slightly curled. Talking mechanism in stomach. Marks: Uneeda Doll Co Inc./1962, in a circle on head. $16.00.

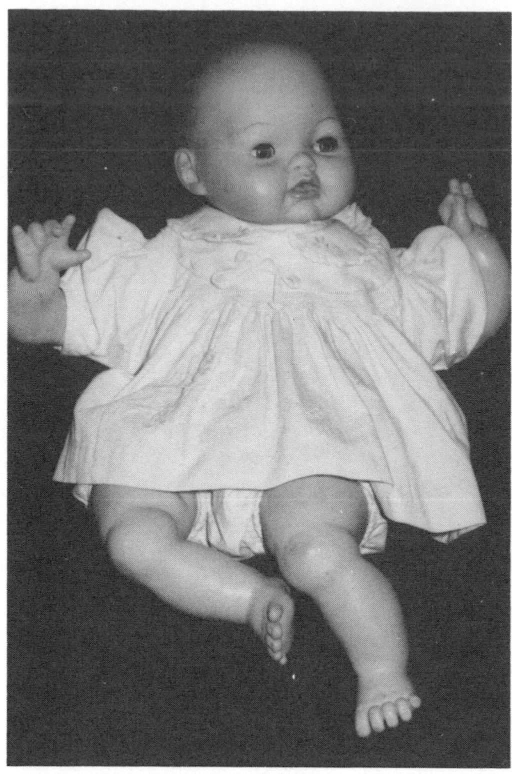

Uneeda--20" "Baby Sweetums" Stuffed cloth body with plastic arms and legs. Vinyl head with molded hair. Blue sleep eyes/lashes. Open mouth/dry nurser. Marks: 1962/Uneeda Doll Co., in a circle on head. $5.00.

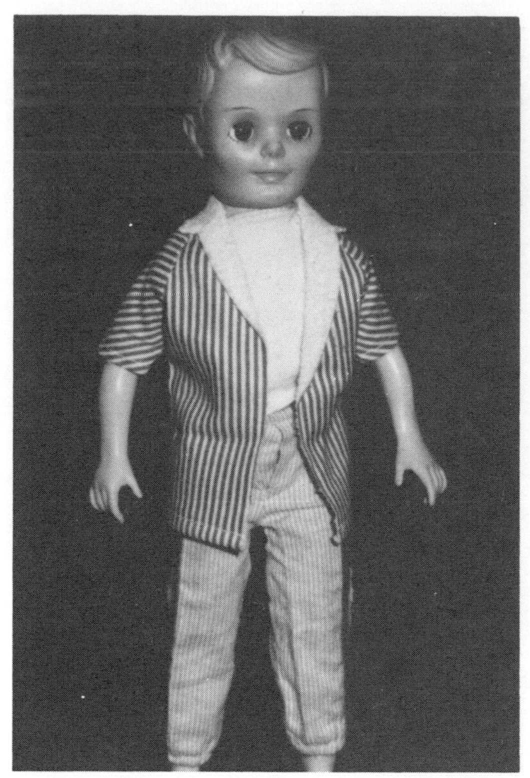

Uneeda--10½" "Bob" All rigid vinyl with more pliable vinyl head. Molded blonde hair. Brown sleep eyes/molded lashes. Marks: Uneeda, on head. Uneeda, on body. 1963. $6.00.

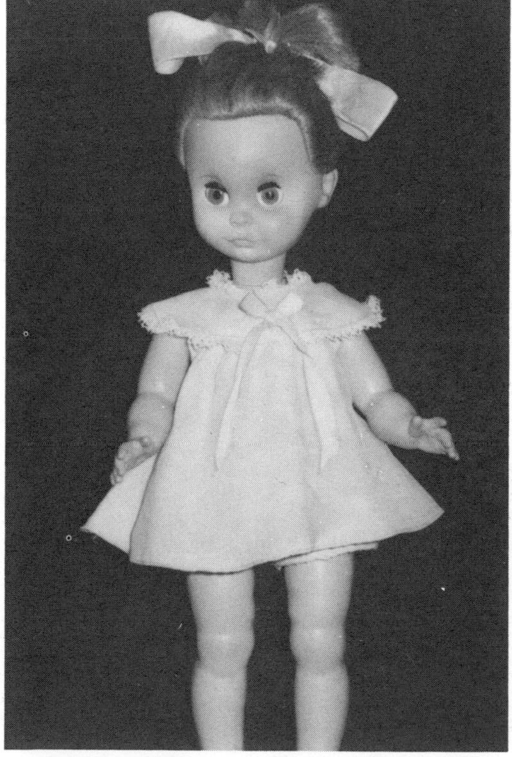

Uneeda--16" "Coquette" Plastic body and legs. Vinyl arms and head. Rooted blonde hair. Blue sleep eyes/long lashes. Dimple in chin. Marks: Uneeda Doll Co. Inc. 1963. $6.00.

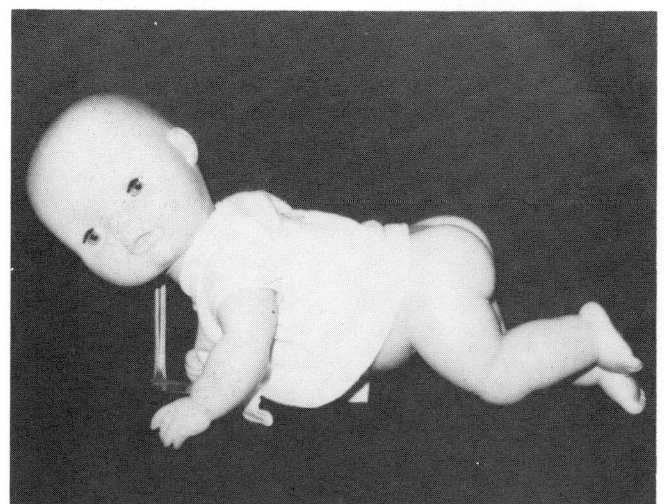

Uneeda--12" "Bare Bottom Baby" All vinyl with molded brown hair. Blue sleep eyes/lashes. Open/closed mouth. Molded bent arms with right fingers curled. Left hand open. Swivel waist with lower body and legs molded in one piece. Neck ball jointed so head will tilt. Marks: Uneeda Doll Co Inc/1963, Orig. clothes. $8.00.

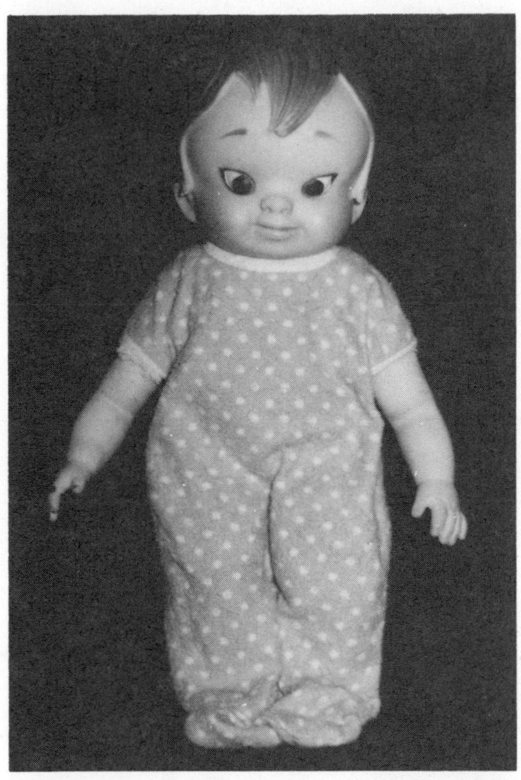

Uneeda--10½" "Posin' Elfy" One piece vinyl body, arms and legs. Crossed and slanted painted eyes. Molded hair. Marks: Uneeda Doll Co Inc, in a circle with a 5 to the right and a 1964 beneath. $3.00.

Uneeda--21" "Debteen" Plastic body, arms and legs. Vinyl head with rooted blonde hair. Blue sleep eyes/lashes. Closed mouth. Marks: Uneeda/1964, on head. $8.00.

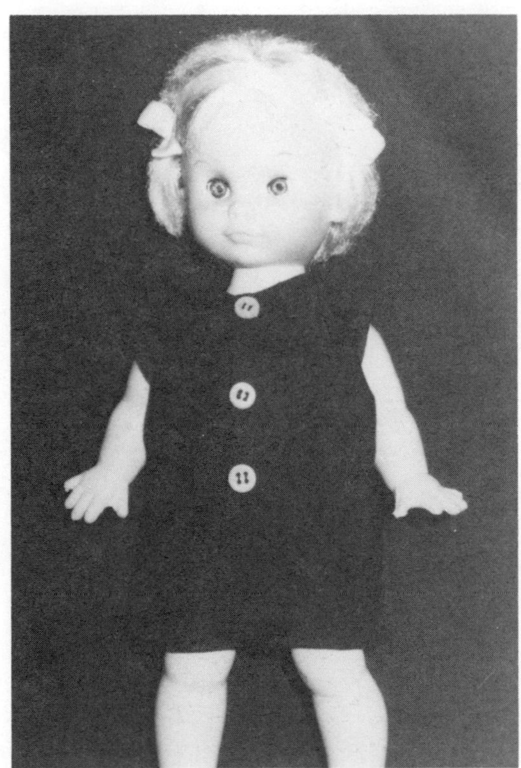

Uneeda--11" "Little Coquette" Plastic body and legs. Vinyl arms and head. Blue, slightly slanted, sleep eyes/lashes molded. Rooted frosted blonde hair. Closed mouth. Dimpled chin. Marks: Uneeda Doll Co 1964, in a circle on head. $4.00.

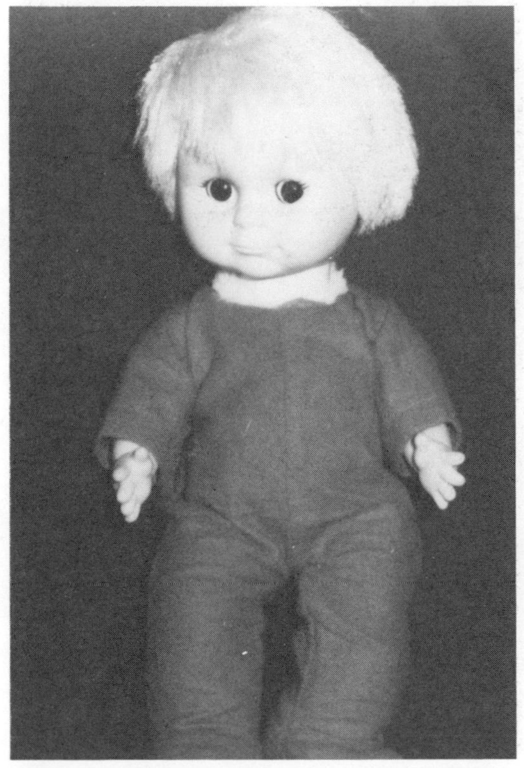

Uneeda--10" "Posable Baby Trix" Foam body with vinyl gauntlet hands. Foam and wire formed feet. Vinyl head with blonde rooted hair. Black sleep eyes, side glancing. Marks: Uneeda Doll Co Inc/3, in a circle, on head. 1964. Original clothes. $4.00.

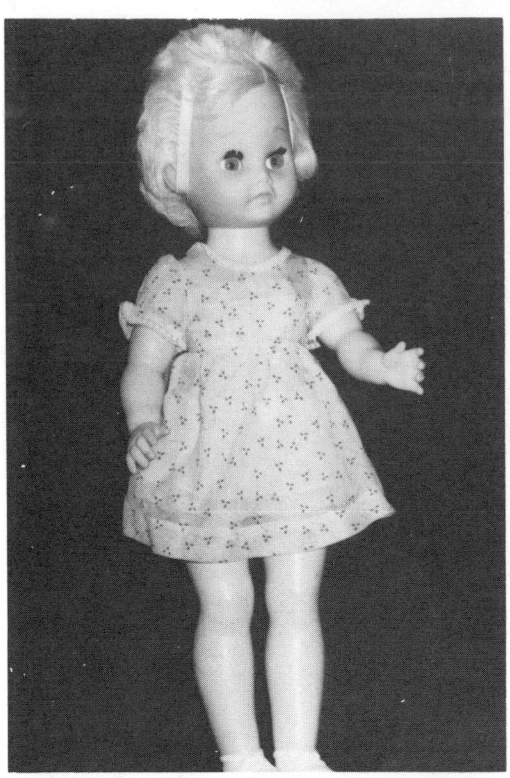

Uneeda--19" "Needa Toddles" Plastic body and legs. Vinyl arms and head. Rooted blonde hair. Blue sleep eyes/long lashes. Marks: Uneeda/ 1964, on head. $4.00.

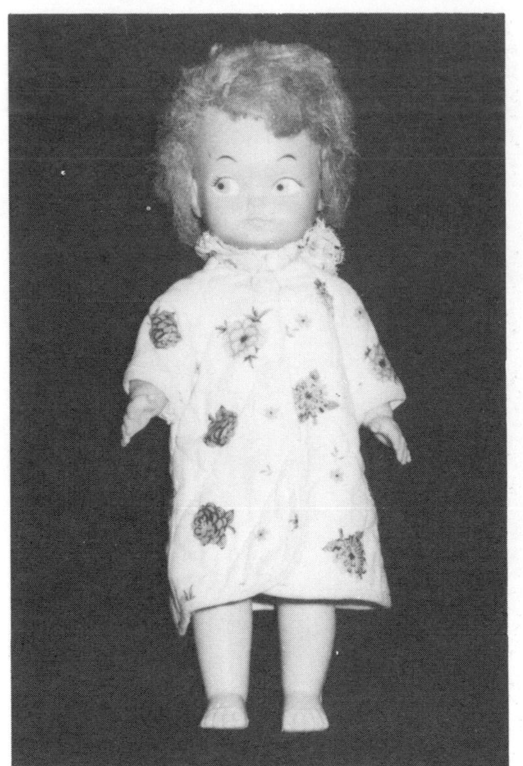

Uneeda--11" "Tiny Toodles" Plastic body and legs. Vinyl arms and head. Rooted ash blonde hair. Painted blue, side glancing eyes. Marks: Uneeda Doll Co, Inc., in a circle with 1966 beneath. $3.00.

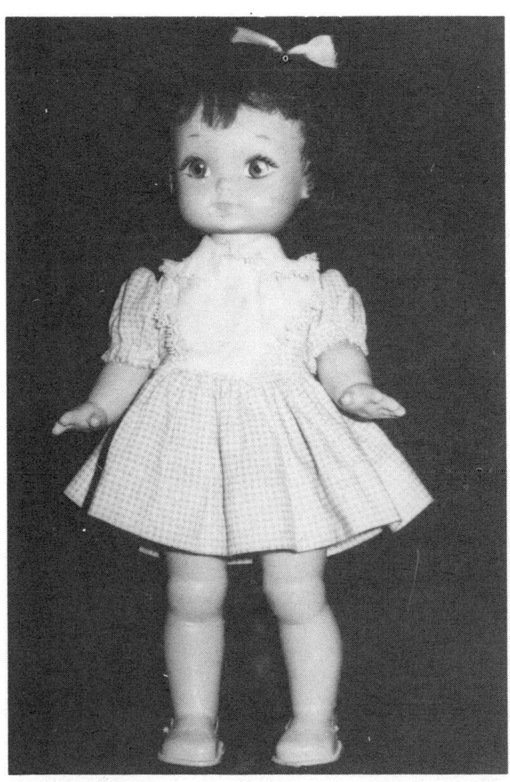

Uneeda--"Pretty Portrait" Plastic body and legs. Vinyl arms and head. Rooted black hair. Painted brown side glancing eyes. Marks: Uneeda Doll Co Inc, in a circle. 11, on the right side and 1966, beneath. Came in own storage frame. $4.00.

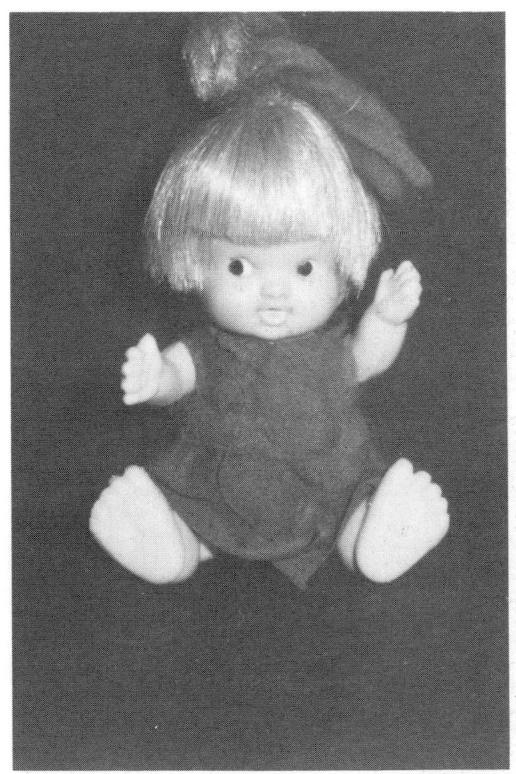

Uneeda--3" "Baby Peewee" Plastic body, arms and legs. Vinyl head with rooted blonde hair. Painted features. Open mouth/nurser. 1966. $2.00. (Courtesy Earlene Johnston Collection).

Uneeda--11½" "Secret Sue" Plastic body and legs. Vinyl arms and head. Rooted orange hair. Painted black side glancing eyes. Advertised as "Girl From U.N.E.E.D.A. Original clothes. Marks: Uneeda Doll Co Inc, in a circle. 1966 underneath. $8.00.

Uneeda--25" "50th Anniversary Antebellum Southern Belle" Plastic body and legs. Vinyl arms and head. Rooted reddish brown hair. Amber brown eyes (sleep)/lashes. Eyeshadow. Limited edition Golden Anniversary Doll. Marks: 8/Uneeda Doll Co/1967. $35.00.

Uneeda--8" "Penelope, Little Sophisticate" Plastic body and legs. Vinyl arms and head. Rooted dark brown hair. Closed eyes with long lashes. Marks: Uneeda Doll Co, In. 1967/Made In Japan. Set of six: Rosanna, Suzanna, Georgina, Marika, Kristina. $3.00.

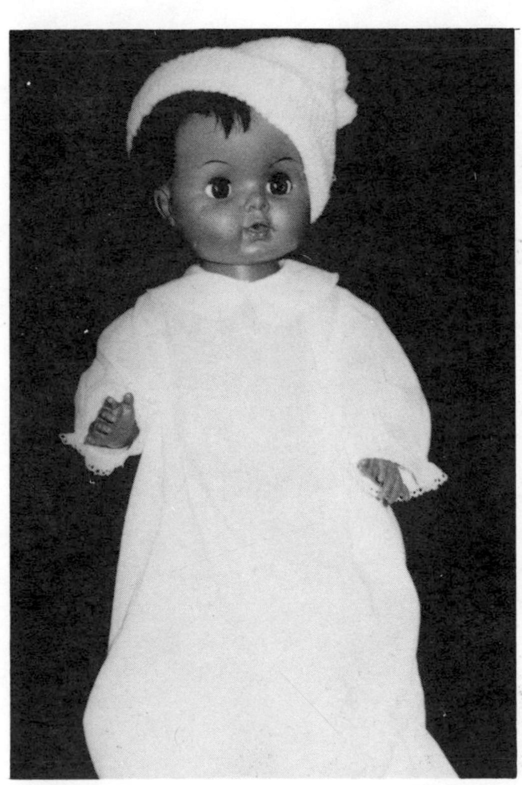

Uneeda--20" "Baby Sweetums" Plastic with vinyl head. Rooted black hair. Brown sleep eyes/lashes. Open hands with 2nd and 3rd fingers curled. Open mouth/nurser. Dimples high on both cheeks. Marks: Uneeda, on head. 1967. $4.00.

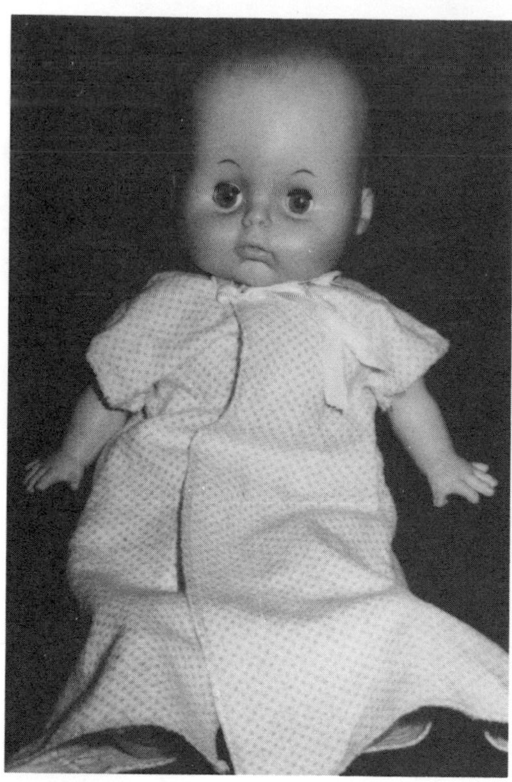

Uneeda--13" "First Born Baby" Cloth body. Plastic arms and legs. Vinyl head with molded hair. Dark blue sleep eyes/lashes. Marks: Uneeda Doll Co Inc/1968/1468, on head. Tag: Made By/Uneeda Doll Co Inc. $3.00.

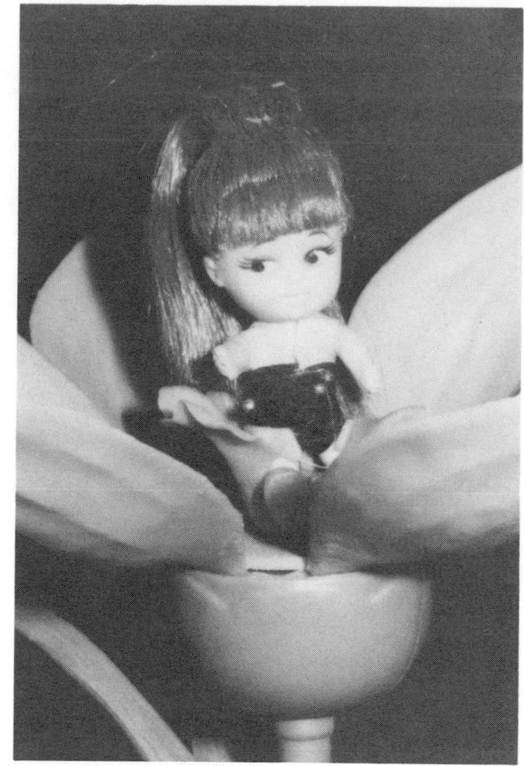

Uneeda--3" "Daffi-Dill" 11" Pot" Pot is of plastic with vinyl leaves that open and close. Doll is all vinyl with rooted light brown hair. Painted side glancing eyes. Set of six: Rosy Rose, Polly Poppy, Dissy Daisy, Sunny Flower, Tiny Tulip. Marks: Hong Kong, on head. 1968. $5.00.

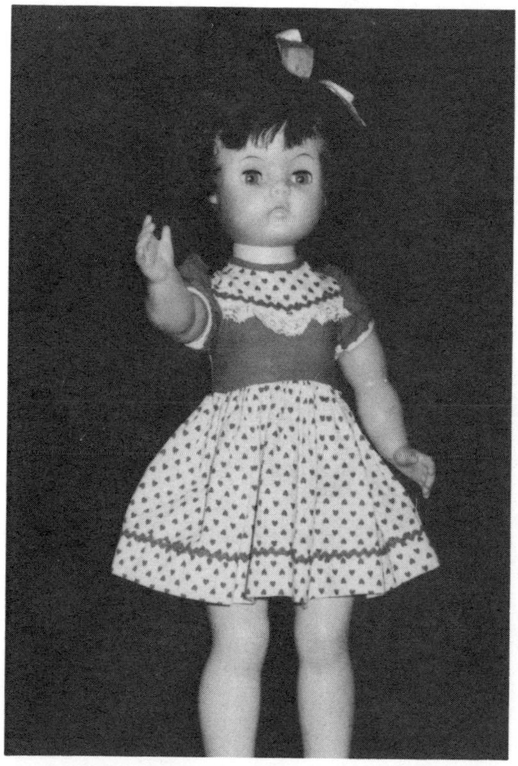

Uneeda--19" "Dolly Walker" Plastic body and legs. Vinyl arms and head. Rooted dark brown hair. Blue sleep eyes/lashes. Marks: U 17/13, on head. 1968. $3.00.

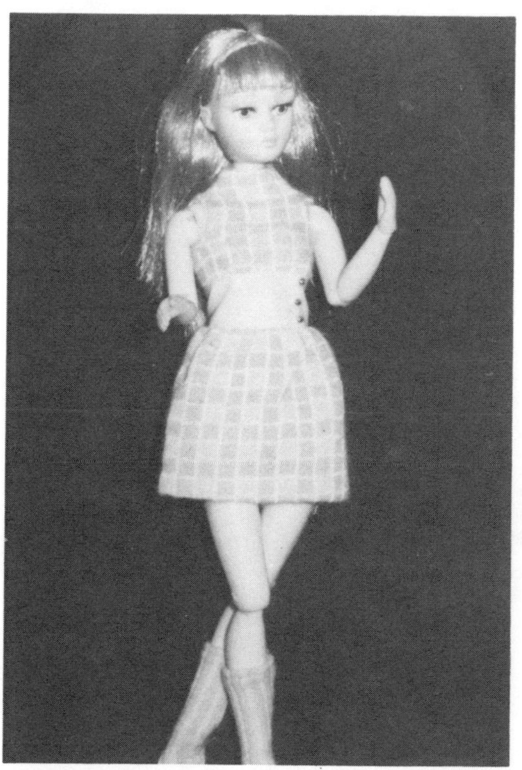

Uneeda--11" "Dollikins" Rigid vinyl arms, legs and body. Vinyl head with rooted blonde hair. Painted eyes. Closed mouth. Jointed neck, shoulder, elbows, wrists, waist, hips, knees, ankles. Marks: Uneeda Doll Co/MCMLXIX/ Made In Hong Kong, on head. Dollikin/US Pat. 3,010253/Other US And For Pat. Pend. $4.00.

Uneeda--16" "Bathtub Baby" Plastic body and legs. Vinyl arms and head. Rooted light brown hair. Blue sleep eyes/lashes. Open mouth/nurser. Marks: 3TD11/Uneeda, on head. 1969. $3.00.

Uneeda--13" "Adorable Cindy" Plastic body, arms and legs. Vinyl head with rooted hair. Sleep blue eyes/lashes. Open mouth/nurser. Right 2nd finger curled deeply into palm. Left thumb, index and little finger extended. Marks: Uneeda Doll Inc/MCMLXIX/Made In Hong Kong, on head. $3.00.

Uneeda--19" "Debteen" All plastic with vinyl head. Rooted red hair. Blue sleep eyes/lashes. Open hands with 2nd and 3rd fingers molded together. Marks: Uneeda Doll Co Inc./1969/ 1970, on head. $5.00.

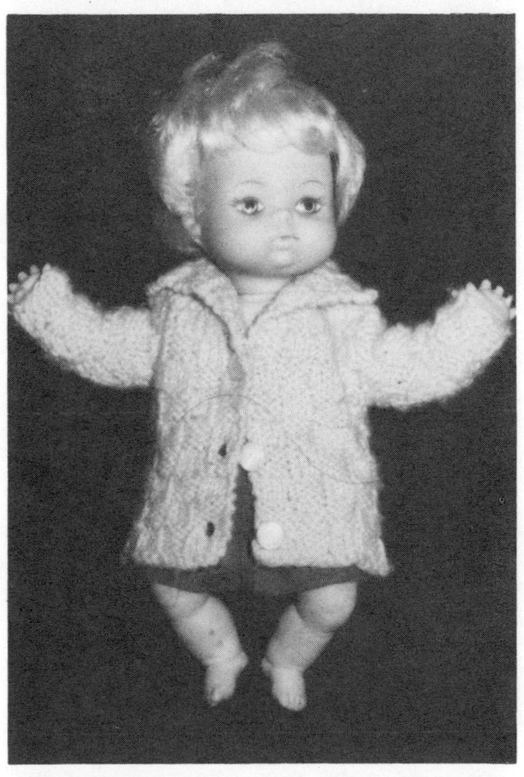

Uneeda--6½" "New Born Yummy" Cloth, foam filled body. Vinyl arms, legs and head. Rooted white hair. Painted blue eyes. Open/closed mouth. Marks: UD Co. Inc./Hong Kong, on head. 1970. $2.00.

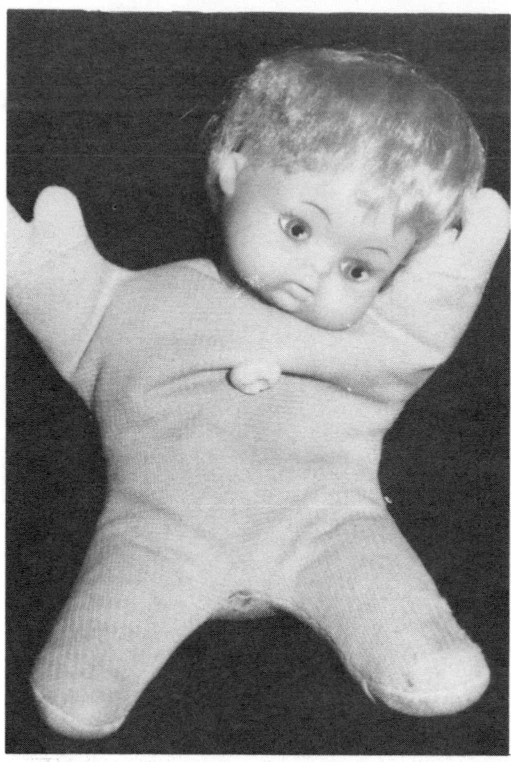

Uneeda--7" "Tiny Trix" Bean bag body, arms and legs. Vinyl head with rooted blonde hair. Painted blue eyes. Open closed mouth. Marks: UD Inc/Hong Kong, on head. Tag: Tiny Trix/UD Co Inc./Made In Japan. 1970. $2.00.

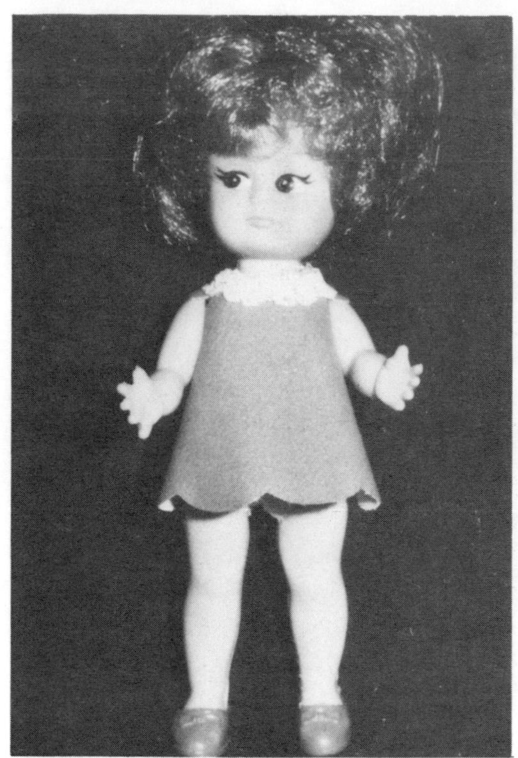

Uneeda--5" "Kim" All vinyl with rooted red hair. Painted side glancing eyes. Closed mouth. Hair grow feature. Marks: UD Co Inc/MCMLXX/ Made In Hong Kong, on head. UD Co Inc/Made In/Hong Kong/Pat. Pend., on back. Original clothes. $2.00.

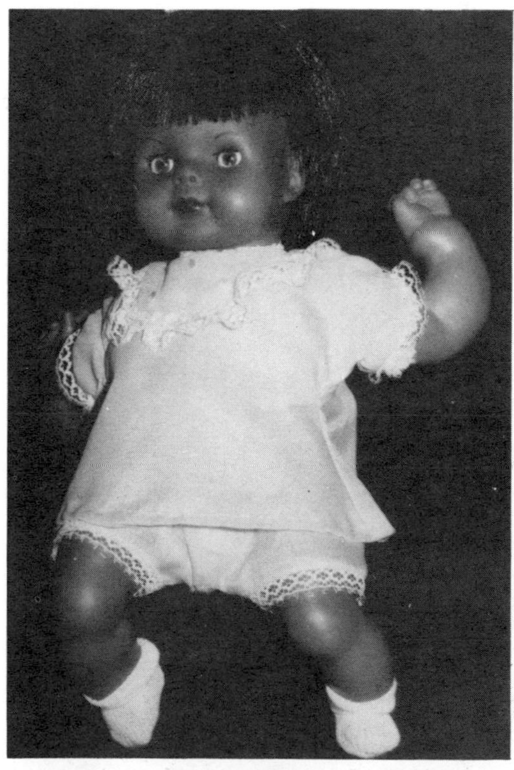

Uneeda--11" "Baby Sleep Amber" Cloth body. Vinyl arms, legs and head. Rooted black hair. Amber sleep eyes. Marks: Tony Toy/1970/Made In Hong Kong. Box: Uneeda Doll Co. Original clothes. $8.00.

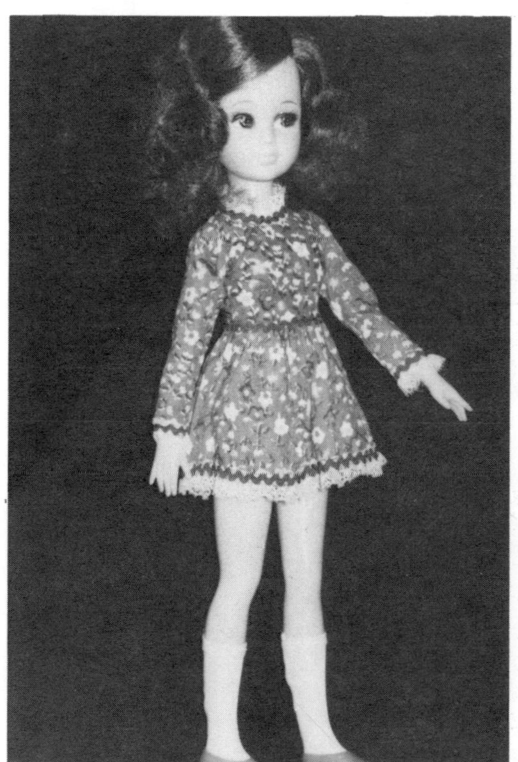

Uneeda--18" "Jennifer" Plastic body and legs. Vinyl arms and head. Rooted brown hair. Painted, side glancing brown eyes. Closed mouth. Open hands with fingers in formal "fashion model" position. Marks: None, on head. Made In Taiwan, on body. 1971. Original clothes. $6.00.

Uneeda--11" "New Gerber Baby" All vinyl with molded blonde hair. Painted blue eyes. Open mouth nurser. Original clothes. Mail order premium. Marks: The Gerber Baby/Gerber Products/1971. Made by Uneeda Doll Company for Gerber Products Company. $5.00.

Uneeda--3½" "Happy Pee Wee" One piece plastic body, arms and legs. Vinyl head. Painted features. No hair. Original clothes. Marks: Uneeda Doll Co Inc/MCMLXXI Hapee Wee, on head. $2.00.

Valentine--19" "Toe Dancing Ballerina" Hard plastic body, arms and legs. Vinyl head with rooted brown hair. Blue sleep eyes/lashes. Closed mouth. Jointed at neck, shoulders, hips, waist, knees and ankles. Wears real Capezio slippers. Marks: None. 1958. Original clothes. $25.00.

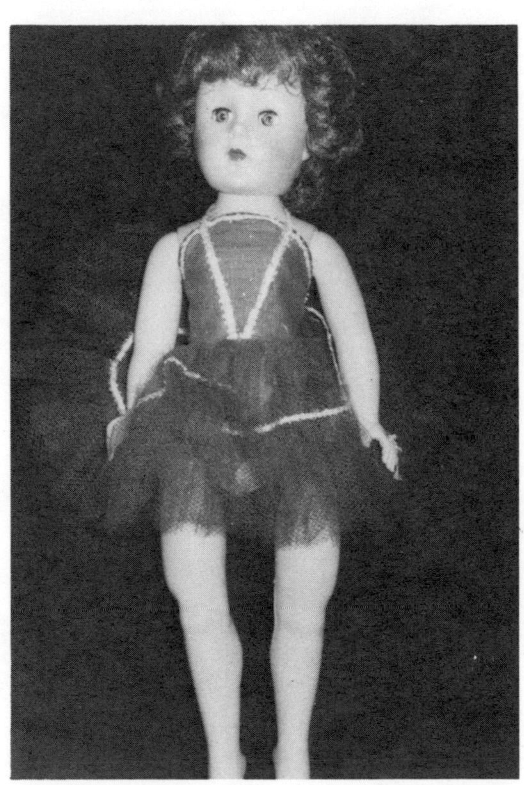

Valentine--18" "Ballerina" Hard plastic body, arms and legs. Vinyl head with rooted light brown hair. Blue sleep eyes/lashes. Feet molded to toe dance position. Marks: None. 1957. Original clothes. $9.00.

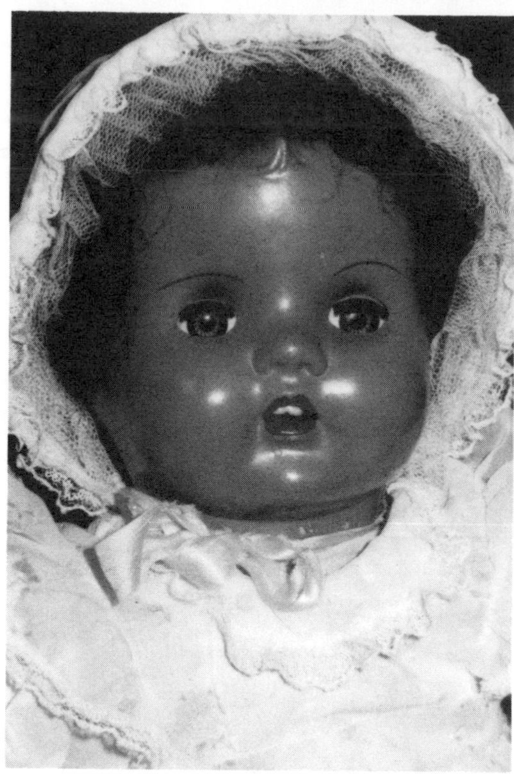

Vanity Doll Co Inc--23" "Big Girl" Hard plastic head on cloth body. Latex arms and legs. Black mohair wig. Brown sleep eyes/lashes. Open mouth with two teeth. Marks: None. 1949. $35.00. (Courtesy Allin's Collection).

Vogue Doll Company

The founder of Vogue was Mrs. Jennie Graves and she began by making doll clothes. Her company struggled and grew into itself through the introduction of the 8" Ginny doll in 1948. The first Ginny was made in composition, then hard plastics and finally in vinyl. In 1951 Ginny had a complete wardrobe, jewelry and furniture. Vogue developed the "Family" idea and introduced 8" Baby Ginnette (Ginny's baby sister), 10½" teenage Jill (Ginny's big sister), 12" Jan (Jill's girl friend) and 11½" Jeff.

In 1960 Mrs. Graves brought out the floppy 18" Baby Dear molded after a real live one month old baby. This doll was designed by Eloise Wilkin. In 1962 a new Baby Dear was introduced and continues to date. Mrs. Graves retired in 1960 and the company has continued under the supervision of members of her family.

Vogue purchased the Arranbee Doll Company (R & B) in 1959 and discontinued the use of that name in 1961. They have continued and very successfully, the Angel baby, Littlest Angel, etc. line.

1973 will end this independent company as Vogue will be purchased by Tonka Corp. Vogue plans to operate the same as in the past.

Dolls designed by Eloise Wilkin for Vogue: Baby Dear marked on leg, 1960/E. Wilkin, Dear One, marked on head, E. Wilkin/Vogue Dolls, Too Dear, marked on head 1963 E. Wilkin/Vogue Dolls.

1948: Ginny (9.00 to 20.00)
1956: Jeanette (8.00), Ginnette (8.00)
1957: Jill (7.00), Jeff (7.00), Jan (5.00)
1960: Baby Dear (18.00), Brickett (25.00), Lil Imp (8.00), Little Baby Dear (6.00)
1961: Littlest Angel (8.00)
1962: Ginny Baby (16.00)
1964: Posie Pixie (10.00), New Baby Dear (8.00), Open Mouth Baby Dear (16.00), Ginnette (8.00), Lil Imp (8.00), Sweetheart Jan (9.00), Miss Ginny (8.00), Too Dear (22.00), Bunny Hug (16.00), Lil Cuddly Dear (8.00), Jama Baby (15.00)
1965: Picture Girl (9.00), Angel Baby (8.00)
1966: Star Brite (25.00)
1967: Little Miss Ginny (6.00), Dearest One (22.00)
1968: Love Me Linda (9.00)
1969: Ginny Baby (8.00)

Vogue--7" "Ginny" All composition with glued on blonde mohair wig. Painted side glancing eyes. Closed mouth. Marks: Vogue, on back. Original clothes. 1948. $20.00.

Vogue--7½" "Ginny" All hard plastic, jointed knee walker. Glued on blonde wig. Green sleep eyes/molded lashes. Freckles. Open hands with 2nd and 3rd fingers molded together. Marks: Ginny/Vogue Doll Inc/Patent No 2987594/Made In USA, on back. Dress Tag: Vogue Dolls Inc. $16.00.

Vogue--7" "Ginny" All hard plastic with glued on lambs wool wig. Blue stationary eyes. Marks: Vogue, on head. Vogue Doll, on back. $16.00. (Courtesy Earlene Johnston Collection).

Vogue--7" "Ginny" All early hard plastic with glued on brown wig. Red/brown sleep eyes. Marks: Vogue Doll, on back. 1953. $18.00. (Courtesy Earlene Johnston Collection).

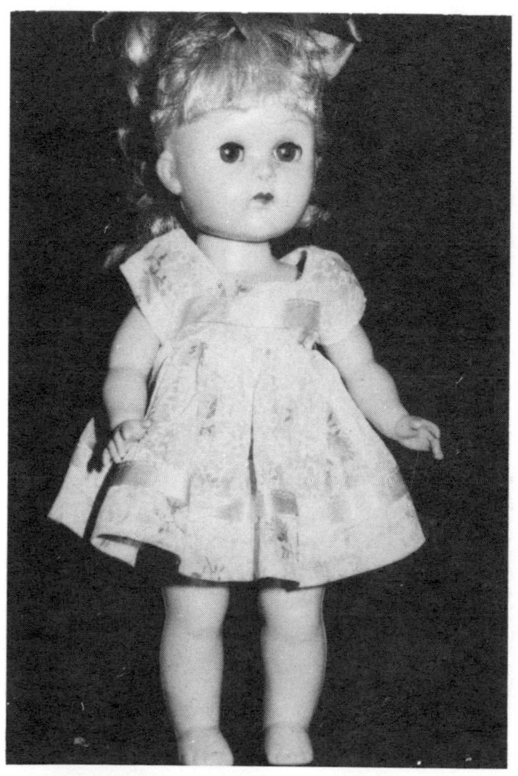

Vogue--7½" "Ginny Walker" All hard plastic with glued on mohair wig. Blue sleep eyes/molded lashes. As she walks, head turns. Marks: Vogue, on head. Ginny/Vogue Dolls Inc./Pat. No. 2587594/Made In USA, on back. 1955. Original clothes. Dress tag: Vogue Dolls Inc./Redford, Mass.USA/Reg. US Pat. Off. $9.00.

Vogue--7" "Ginny Baby" All hard plastic with glued on lambs wool wig. Red/brown sleep eyes/no lashes. Bent baby legs. Original clothes. Marks: Vogue, on head. Vogue Doll, on back. $18.00.

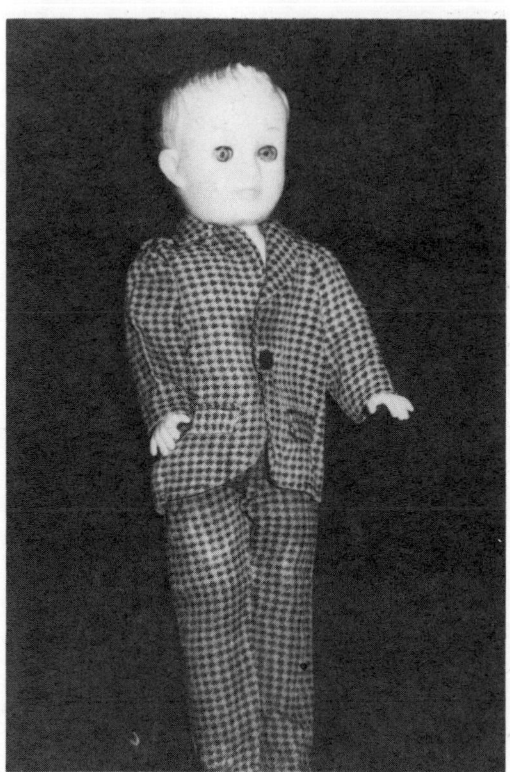

Vogue--10" "Jeff" Plastic body and legs. Vinyl arms and head. Molded and painted brown hair. Blue sleep eyes/molded lashes. Closed mouth. Open hands with palms down. Marks: Vogue, on head. Original clothes. 1957. $7.00.

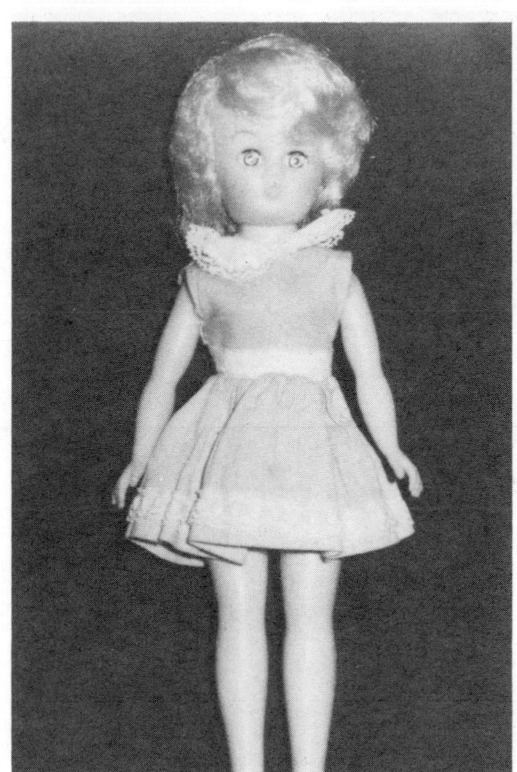

Vogue--10" "Jan" Plastic body and legs. Vinyl arms and head. Rooted blonde hair. Blue sleep eyes/molded lashes. High heel feet. Original clothes. Marks: Vogue, on head. Vogue Doll, on dress tag. 1957. $5.00.

Vogue--10" "Jill" All hard plastic with dark skin tones. Glued on brown wig. Blue sleep eyes/molded lashes. Pierced ears. Jointed knees. High heel feet. Painted fingernails and toenails. Adult figure. Marks: Vogue, on head. Jill/Vogue Doll/Made In USA 1957, on body. Original clothes. $7.00.

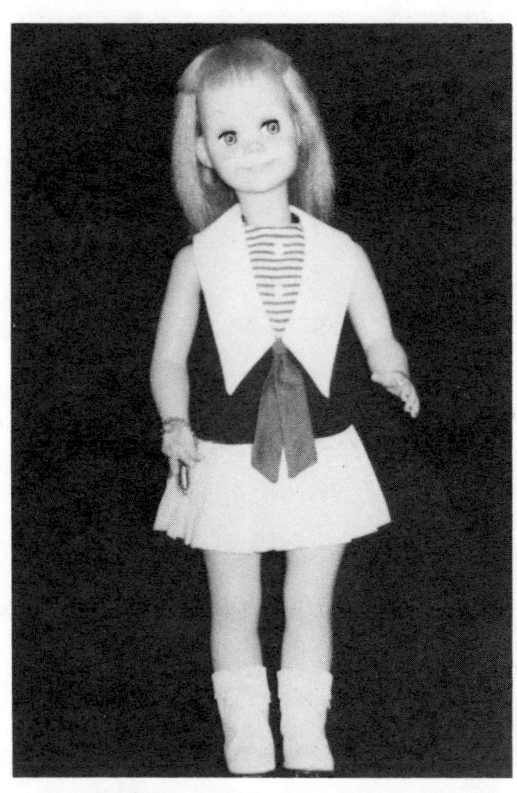

Vogue--22" "Brickette" Plastic two piece body, ball jointed at waist. Plastic legs. Vinyl arms and head. Rooted orange hair. Green sleep, flirty eyes/lashes. Original clothes. Marks: None. 1960. $25.00.

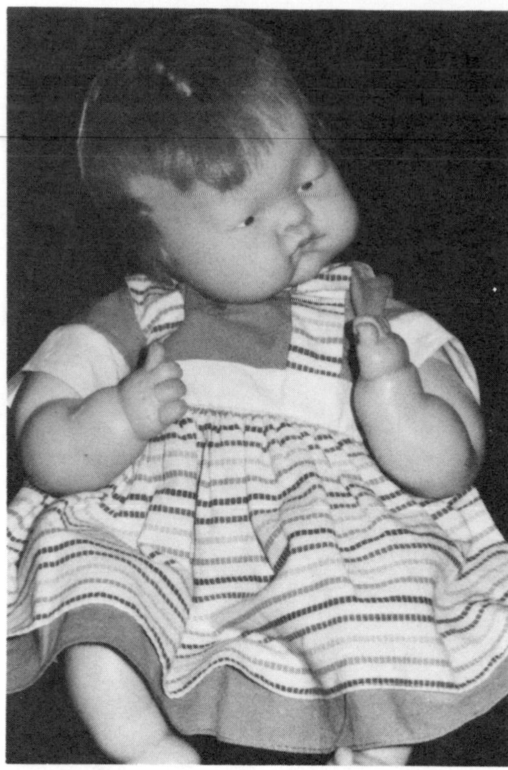

Vogue--17" "Baby Dear" Cloth filled body. Vinyl arms, legs and head. Rooted dark blonde hair. Painted blue eyes. Marks: Tag On Body: Vogue Dolls Inc. Back Of Left Leg: E. Wilkins/1960. $18.00.

Vogue--8" "Little Baby Dear" Cloth body. Vinyl arms, legs and head. Rooted blonde hair. Blue sleep eyes/molded lashes. Open mouth/dry nurser. Marks: #38 on head. Tag: Vogue Dolls Inc. 1960. Original clothes. $6.00. (Courtesy Earlene Johnston Collection).

Vogue--7½" "Ginny" All vinyl with rooted blonde hair. Blue sleep eyes/lashes. Marks: Ginny/Vogue, on back. Vogue, on head. 1960. $8.00.

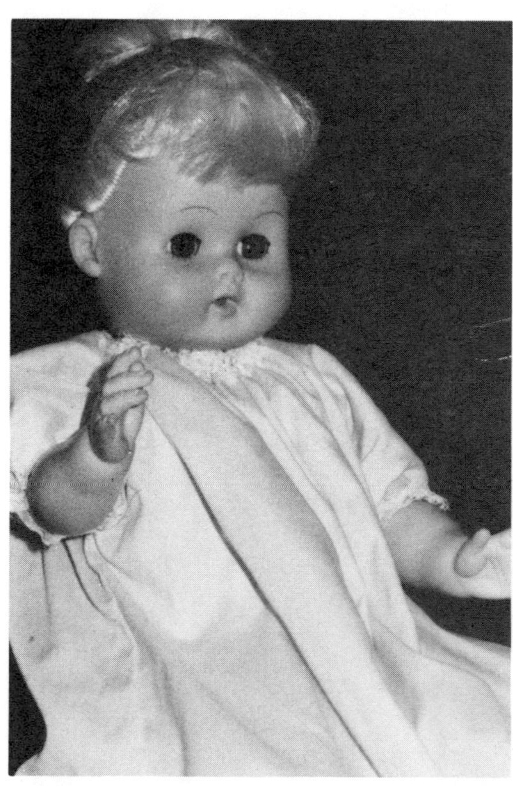

Vogue--20" "Ginny Baby" All vinyl with rooted white hair. Blue sleep eyes/lashes. Open mouth/nurser. 2nd and 3rd fingers curled. Marks: Ginny Baby/10/Vogue Doll Inc, on head. 1962. Rare size. $16.00.

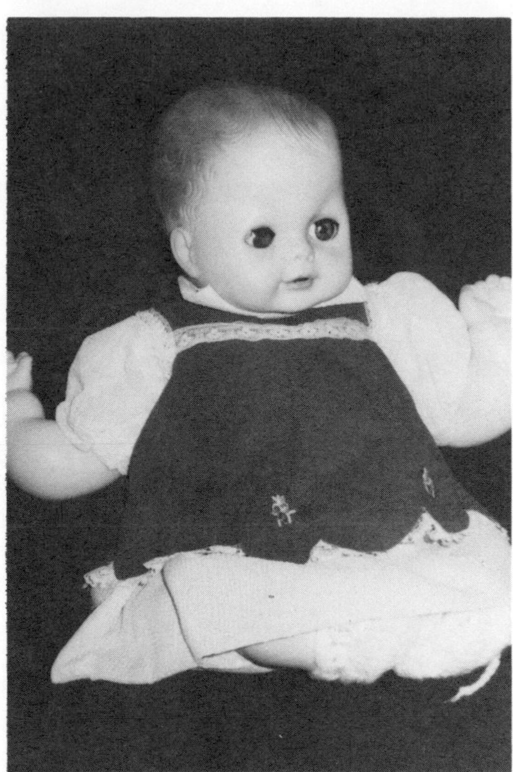

Vogue--18" "Baby Dear" Cloth body. Vinyl arms, legs and head. Molded, painted brown hair. Blue sleep eyes/lashes. Open mouth. Marks: Vogue Doll/1964, on head. Tag: Vogue Doll Inc. Original clothes. Rare open mouth. $16.00.

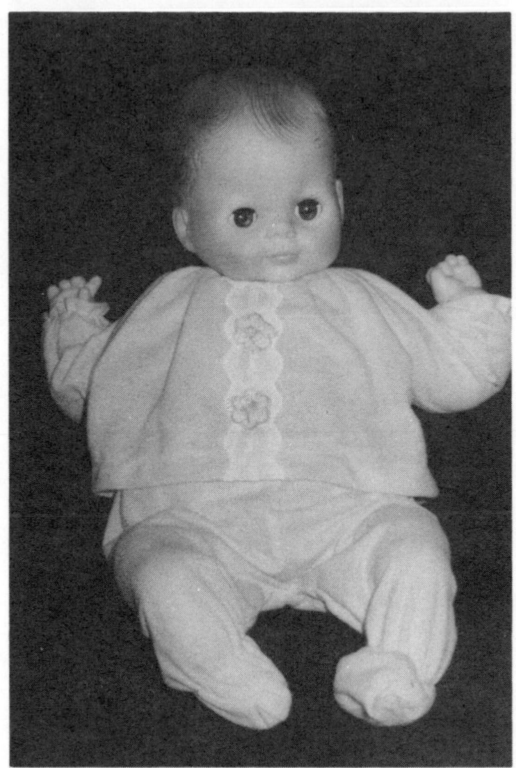

Vogue--18" "Baby Dear" Cloth body. Vinyl arms, legs and head. Molded hair. Blue sleep eyes/lashes. Open mouth/nurser. Right index finger extended. Left hand thumb over index finger. Marks: Vogue Doll/1964/6, on head. $8.00.

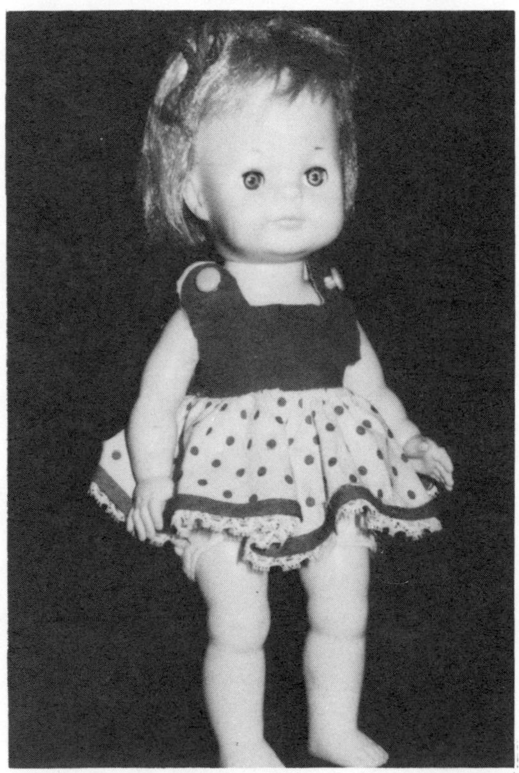

Vogue--11" "Littlest Angel" All vinyl with rooted dark blonde hair. Sleep blue eyes/lashes. Closed mouth. Toddler legs with dimpled knees. Marks: Vogue Doll/1964, on head. $8.00.

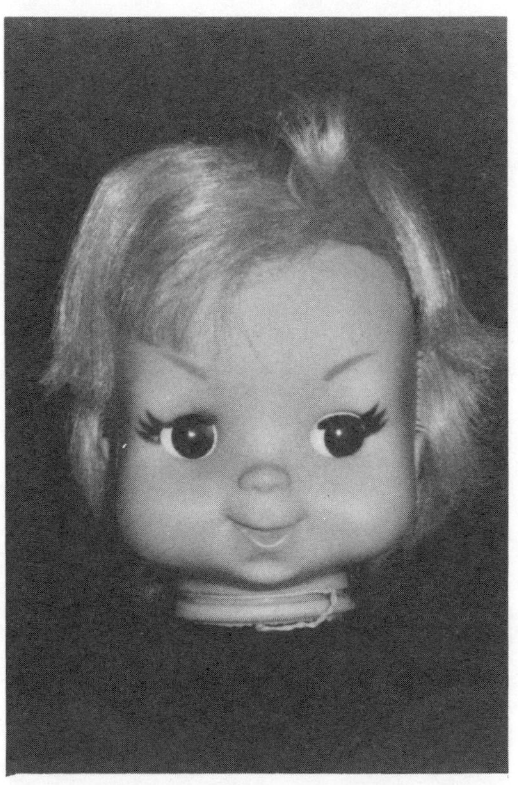

Vogue--17" "Posie Pixie" Foam body, arms and legs. Vinyl head and gauntlet hands. Rooted white hair. Black side glancing eyes/lashes. Open/closed mouth. Marks: 1964/Vogue/71, on head. $10.00.

Vogue--14½" "Littlest Angel" Plastic body and legs. Vinyl arms and head. Rooted dark blonde hair. Blue sleep eyes/lashes. Left hand open, palm down. Right hand open palm down with 2nd and 3rd and little fingers curled. Marks: Vogue Doll/1965, on head. $8.00.

Vogue--13" "Angel Baby" All vinyl with rooted blonde hair. Large blue sleep eyes/long lashes. Closed mouth. Stocky body. Marks: Vogue Doll/1965, on head. $8.00.

Vogue--14½" "Picture Girl" Plastic body and legs. Vinyl arms and head. Rooted ash blonde hair. Painted large black eyes. Open hands with 2nd and 3rd fingers curled. Came with own framed portrait. Marks: Vogue Doll/1965, on head. Original clothes. $9.00.

Vogue--17" "Star Brite" All vinyl with rooted dark brown hair. Big side glancing painted brown eyes with stars. Closed mouth. 2nd and 3rd fingers curled into palms. Marks: Vogue Dolls/1966. This doll was made for only one year. $25.00.

Vogue--11" "Little Miss Ginny" Plastic body and legs. Vinyl arms and head. Rooted dark blonde hair. Blue sleep eyes/molded lashes. Open mouth with two painted upper teeth. Open hands palms down. Flat feet. Marks: 2701/9Eye/Vogue Doll/1967, on head. Vogue Doll, on body. $6.00.

Vogue--17" "Dearest One" All vinyl with rooted dark blonde hair. Black sleep eyes/lashes. Open mouth/nurser. Posable head. Doll is strung. Marks: Vogue Doll, Inc./1967, on head. Vogue Doll, Inc/1967, on body. $22.00.

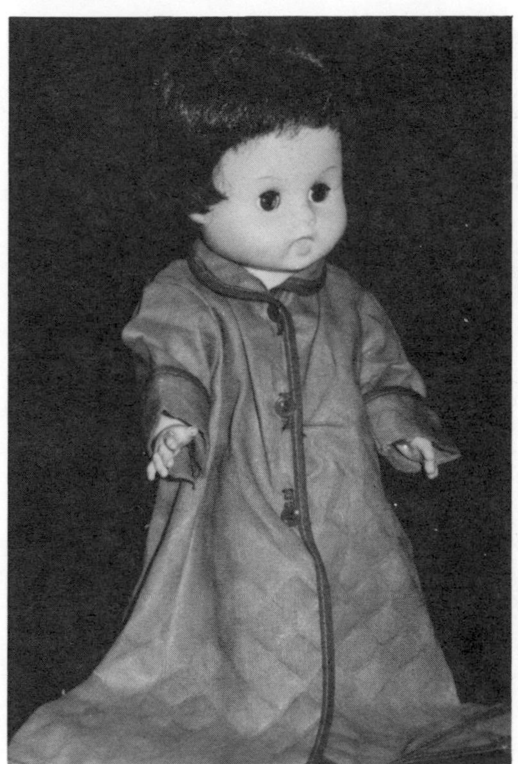

Vogue--11" "Ginny Baby" All vinyl with dark brown rooted hair. Brown sleep eyes/lashes. Open mouth nurser. Marks: Ginny Baby/Vogue Dolls Inc. 1969. $8.00.

Walt Disney 11" "Pinocchio" Composition head, neck and body. Wood arms, legs and feet. Painted hair, features and clothes. Marks: Ideal, on head. Tag: Pinocchio/Des. & Copyright By Walt Disney/Made By Ideal Novelty & Toy Co. 1940. $35.00. (Courtesy Earlene Johnston Collection).

Walt Disney--8½" "Bashful" All composition with glued on beard and painted features. Marks: None. Made By Knickerbacher Toy Company. 1939. $30.00. (Courtesy Fye Collection).

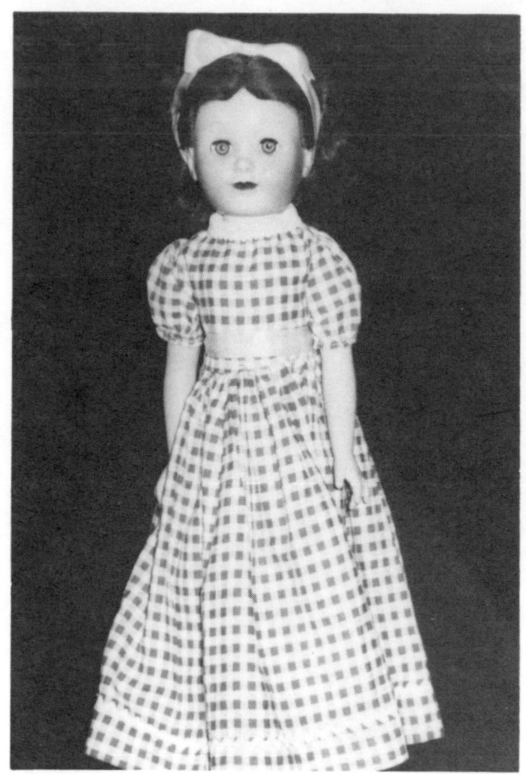

Walt Disney--21" "Snow White" All early vinyl with rooted dark brown hair. Blue sleep eyes/lashes. 2nd and 3rd fingers curled. Turned up "pixie" nose. Unusual hairline. Marks: Walt Disney Prod., on bottom of right foot. Snow White, on head. Made By Sayco. 1950. Sold through grocery markets. $38.00.

Walt Disney--12" "Tinker Bell" All soft vinyl with rooted blonde hair. Stationary blue eyes. Closed mouth. Open hands facing body. Marks: Walt Disney Prod., on bottom of right foot. Molded flange in center of back for string. Replaced Wings. Sayco. 1950. $9.00.

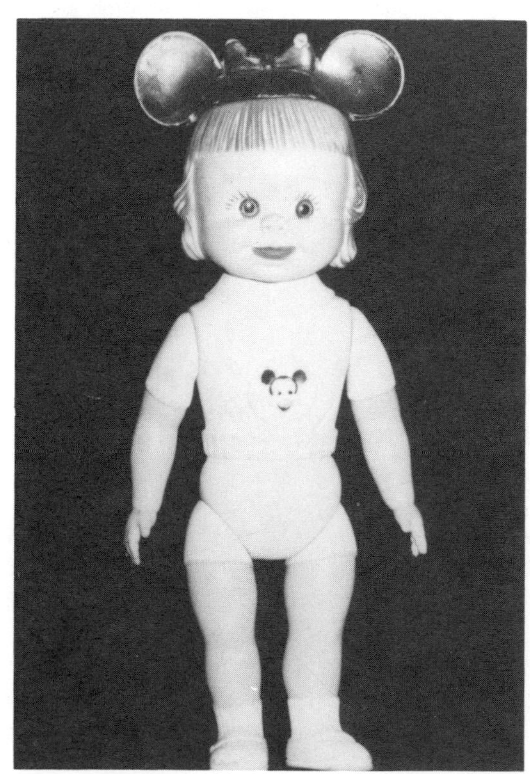

Walt Disney--12" "Mousketeer" All vinyl with molded brown hair. Inset stationary, side glancing eyes. Open mouth with tongue. Molded on hat, socks and shoes. Marks: Walt Disney Prods., on cap. Mickey Mouse Club, around picture of Mickey Mouse on front. 1957. $16.00. (Courtesy Allin's Collection).

Walt Disney--10" "Christopher Robin" All polyfoam and wire. Painted hair, features and clothes. Marks: Bendy/Made In England/Walt Disney/Productions. 1966.

6" "Winnie The Pooh" All vinyl painted yellow. Marks: Walt Disney Productions/1966 Holland Hall Prod. $8.00.

Walt Disney--5½" "Jiminy Cricket" All plastic with painted features and glued on clothes. Marks: Marx Toys/Made In Hong Kong/Walt Disney Productions. 1963. $4.00.

Reference and Bibliography

Schoonmaker, Patricia N. "The Effanbee Patsy Family And Related Delights".
Burdick, Loraine. "A Doll For Christmas". "Child Star Dolls & Toys."
Fawcett, Clara Hallard. Hobbies Magiazine (May, July, September, December 1967.)
Hart, Luella. Spinning Wheel (July/August 1963) "Part IV Directory Of United States Doll Trademarks" (2nd Revised Edition)
Coleman, Dorothy, Elizabeth, Evelyn. "The Collector's Encyclopedia Of Dolls"
Cooper, Marlowe. "Dimples & Sawdust, Volume 2"
Johl, Janet Pagter. "Your Dolls & Mine"
Freeman, Ruth. "Encyclopedia Of American Dolls"
Anderton, Johana Gast. "Twentieth Century Dolls"
Christopher, Catherine. "Doll Making And Collecting"
Doll Collectors Manual by the Doll Collectors Of America, Inc. Several Issues.
Western Auto Supply Catalogs: 1949, 1950, 1951, 1957, 1960, 1961, 1963, 1966.
Macy Catalog: 1960
Holiday Gifts Catalog: 1942
Rohde-Spencer Catalogs: 1935, 1936, 1937, 1938, 1939, 1940
Walt Disney Archives Report For; 1938, 1939, 1940.
Slack Mfg Co Catalog: 1940
Sears & Roebuck Catalogs: 1935 through 1971.
Montgomery Wards Catalogs: 1936 through 1971
Continental Products, Inc Catalog: 1942
John Plain Catalogs: 1942, 1946, 1949.
Hagns Catalogs: 1943, 1946.
Brecks Catalogs: 1950, 1956.
Effanbee Doll Company Catalogs: 1952, 1954, 1958, 1959, 1966, 1968, 1969, 1971
Womens Home Companion Magazine: December 1946, December 1951, December 1953
Celebrity Doll Club Journal: 1st Year, 2nd Year, 3rd Year.
World Wide Doll News: August 1969.
McCall Needlework Magazine: Fall/Winter 1952-53.
Toy Yearbook: 1953, 1954.
Life Magazine: April 1939, October 1953
Alexander Company Catalogs: 1953, 1954, 1956, 1961, 1962
Toy Trader Magazine: May 1955.
John Wanamaker Catalog: 1956.
Woolworths Catalogs: 1956, 1957.
Nirisk Catalog: 1957.
Strawbridge & Clothier Catalog: 1957.
Coast to Coast Store Catalogs: 1957, 1959, 1960.
Toy Fair Catalogs: 1957, 1961
F.A.O. Schwartz Catalogs: 1945, 1949, 1950, 1952, 1956, 1957, 1958, 1969, 1971, 1972.
Franks Children Center Catalog: 1957.
Time And Toys Catalog: 1959.
Toyland Catalog: 1960.
Uncle Harry's Corner Catalog (Billy & Ruth, Inc) 1960
Midwestern Catalog: 1961
Toy Partners, Inc Catalog: 1961
McCalls Magazine: November 1961
Dolls & Toys Catalog: 1962
S & H Stamp Catalog: 1964
National Bellas Hess Catalogs: 1964, 1967.
Topper Toy Company Catalogs: 1964, 1965.
New York Times Newspaper: November 1964, November 1965.
Sunday Bulletin Newspaper: Philadelphia: November 1964.
Top Value Stamps Catalog: 1965.
American Character Article: 1965.
Remco Company Catalog: 1966.
Philadelphia Inquirer Newspaper: December 1967, August, October, November 1969.
Fortune: December 1936, October, December 1940.
Doll Castle News Magazine: July and August 1968.
Uneeda Company Catalogs: 1968, 1969, 1970.
Look Magazine: December 1969.
Bennett Bros. Catalog: 1969.
Altman's Catalog: 1969
Buchsbaum Co. Catalog: 1957.
Goodhouskeeping Magazine: December 1971.
Playthings Magazines: February 1963, March, April, May, August, September 1964,March, August 1965, March, April, June, September, November 1966, January, February, April, September 1967, March, April, June, July, August 1968, March, April, June, August, December 1969, March, July, August, September 1971.
Toy & Novelties Magazines: April, May, July, November, December 1966, February, March, June, July, August, December, 1967, March, April, August 1968, April, May 1969, January, March, May 1970, February 1971.

Price Guide Information

The prices shown are based on the condition of the dolls shown in each book. If a doll is in a more perfect state, has original clothes, does not have a replaced wig or an item missing, then the price will be higher than shown. If the doll is in a lesser condition, the prices will be lower.

The following letters denote a certain condition of dolls shown in this book that are other than mint:

N.O. .... Not Original
F .... Fair Condition
B. .... Bad Condition
R.W. .... Replaced Wig
I.M. .... Item Missing
B.K. .... Bend Knees
S.A. .... Still Available
I.A. .... Item Added (mostly hats or shoes)
N.P.A. .... No Price Available

There are three major eras of modern dolls: composition, hard plastics and vinyl/plastic. The condition of each is important in pricing.

COMPOSITION: Rarely will a composition doll be found in a box, and to be mint on top of that is just as rare, so you will not find a mint in the box doll very often. MINT means that there are no cracks or crazing, the doll is extra clean and unplayed with, plus has all its original clothes and tags. EXCELLENT: there may be very light craze, the clothes may have been washed but otherwise it is as a mint doll. GOOD: means the doll may have a couple of small cracks. light craze, original clothes are dirty, and it can be with or without original tags. FAIR: the doll is not original, the wig may or may not be original, it has very extensive crazing, but only small cracks, and the shoes may be gone. POOR: The doll may be nude, have severe crazing and several deep cracks.

HARD PLASTICS: Once in a while a mint in the box doll will be found. MINT: An unplayed with doll, completely original and with original tags. EXCELLENT: The wig may be slightly messed up, clothes original but washed and doll still has original tags, if any. GOOD: The original clothes may be dirty, wig mussed and undies may be missing. FAIR: The clothes may be dirty, or the doll not original, the wig may be replaced, and the hard plastic shows slight wear at the joints, and may even be slightly soiled. POOR: The doll may be nude, no wig, or a replaced one and doll may be dirty.

VINYL/PLASTICS: Many will be found mint in the box. MINT: Same as being in the box, but the box missing. All original with original tags and unplayed with. EXCELLENT: Hair may be slightly mussed, clothes are original, but may have been washed, but doll has original tags, if any. GOOD: Hair may be mussed, or slightly trimmed, clothes may be dirty, and she has no tags, or perhaps undies and shoes. FAIR: Dressed nicely, but not original, hair needs a lot of work, and the vinyl/plastic may be dirty, but washgable. POOR: The doll may be nude, hair cut, and can have felt tip or lipstick marks on the head or body.

A price guide is just that – a guide and should be used as a guide so the collector will be able to see what area of prices his dolls fall in. A guide is not meant to be "to the penny" in pricing, as prices will constantly change with desire and supply. In some areas of the country, prices are higher on some dolls, and may be lower on others. The collector must use his own judgement on any price guide.

Modern Collector's Dolls I

Page	Description	Price
14	7" Dionne Quints	set 1250.00 up
15	14" Dionne Quints (N.O)	each 425.00
15	McGuffy Ana (N.O.)	400.00
15	Princess Alexandria (B)	185.00
15	Butch (N.O.)	165.00
16	Snow White	400.00
16	13" Snow White (N.O.)	350.00
16	Princess Elizabeth (R.W)	375.00
16	McGuffy Ana (N.O.)	350.00
17	Flora McFlimsey (N.O.)	575.00
17	Kate Greenaway	600.00
17	Sonja Henie	375.00
17	McGuffy Ana (N.O.)	200.00
18	Sonja Henie (N.O.)	375.00
18	WAAC (I.M.)	400.00
19	Scarlett O'Hara	475.00
19	Margaret O'Brien (N.O.) (R.W.)	450.00
19	Baby Genuis (N.O.)	125.00
20	Kathy	400.00
20	Alice	400.00
20	Maggie Mixup	475.00
20	Annabelle	500.00
21	McGuffy Ana (N.O.)	350.00
21	Cissette	225.00
21	Dumplin Baby (N.O.)	165.00
22	Rosebud (N.O.)	100.00
22	Cry Dolly (N.O.)	110.00
22	Bonnie (N.O.)	175.00
22	Cissy	450.00
23	Marme	350.00
23	Kathy Cry Dolly	125.00
23	Princess Ann (I.M.)	1200.00
23	Bonnie Prince Charles (I.M.)	1200.00
24	Elise	325.00
24	Shari Lewis (N.O.)	365.00
24	Kathy	125.00
24	Little Genius (I.M.)	195.00
25	Little Shaver (N.O.)	265.00
25	Marybel	200.00
25	Edith (I.M.)	375.00
25	Kathy Tears (N.O.)	95.00
26	Genius Baby (N.O.)	150.00
26	Little Cherub	125.00
26	Queen	450.00
26	Melanie	525.00
27	Godey	525.00
27	Chatterbox	285.00
27	Melinda	365.00
27	Laurie	75.00
28	Little Huggums (N.O.)	35.00
28	Big Huggums (Happy - 1970)	200.00
28	Sugar Darlin' (N.O.)	125.00
29	Sweet Tears (N.O.)	100.00
29	Bo Peep (B.K.)	125.00
29	Pussy Cat (N.O.)	85.00
29	Sugar Darlin' (N.O.)	125.00
30	Alice In Wonderland (N.O.)	45.00
30	Leslie	365.00
30	Scarlett O'Hara	95.00
30	Storybook Doll	175.00
31	Hansel & Gretel (B.K.)	each125.00
31	Hungarian (B.K.)	125.00
31	India (B.K.)	125.00
31	Spanish Friend (B.K.)	125.00
32	Elise	350.00
32	Rebecca	200.00
32	Betsy Ross (B.K.)	125.00
32	Degas(S.A.)	55.00
33	Happy	300.00 up
33	Grandma Jane	225.00
33	Blue Boy	85.00
33	Red Boy (B.K.)	125.00
33	Cinderella	125.00
35	Dandy	25.00
35	Little Love (N.O.)	65.00
35	Miss Chicadee	50.00
35	Tiny Tears 13"	95.00
36	Baby Lou	15.00
36	Sweet Susanne 17"	200.00
36	Sweet Sue 19"	265.00
36	Tiny Tears 16"	145.00
37	Bride 18"	225.00
37	American Beauty 22"	250.00
37	Sweet Sue 24"	300.00 up
37	Sweet Susanne 17"	200.00
38	Peek A Boo Toodles (N.O.)	145.00
38	Toodles (N.O.)	125.00
38	Sweet Sue (N.O.) 17½"	200.00
38	Betsy McCall	100.00 up
39	New Born Baby	45.00
39	Tiny Tears	100.00
39	Astronaut	110.00 up
39	Graduate	110.00 up
40	Whimmsie (N.O.)	110.00 up
40	Hedda Get Bedda	85.00
41	Betsy McCall	145.00
41	Toodle-Loo (N.O.)	145.00
41	Butterball	165.00
41	Talking Marie	85.00
42	Tressy	35.00
42	New Tiny Tears (N.O.)	50.00
43	Nancy	185.00 up
43	Debu-Teen (N.O.)	165.00 up
44	Little Angel (N.O.)	45.00
44	Sonja Henie	175.00
44	Snuggle Doll	35.00
45	Snuggle Bun	20.00
45	Peachy (N.O.)	20.00
45	Judy	200.00 up
46	Angeline	200.00
46	Nanette	185.00 up
46	Nanette	175.00 up
46	Dream Bride	225.00
47	Taffy (N.O.)	175.00
47	New Happytot (N.O.)	25.00
47	Nanette	200.00 up
48	Francine	200.00
48	Littlest Angel	50.00 up
48	Prom Queen	200.00
48	Littlest Angel	50.00
49	My Angel	65.00
49	Littlest Angel Freckles	65.00
50	21" Skookum	185.00
50	14" Skookum	100.00
50	Playful (N.O.)	12.00
50	Bye-Bye Baby (N.O.)	25.00
51	Baby Doo (N.O.)	25.00
51	Candy	4.00
51	Pretty Lady (N.O.)	45.00
51	Pouty	22.00
52	Cindy	8.00
52	Master	6.00
52	My Friend	4.00
52	Little Miss Gadabout (N.O.)	250.00
53	Raving Beauty (N.O.)	250.00 up
53	Lov You (N.O.)	22.00
53	Miss B (N.O.)	5.00
53	Ballerina Belle	25.00
54	Belle-Lee	5.00
54	Jimmy	9.00
54	Timmy	8.00
54	Babies First Doll	9.00
55	Rock-A-Bye Baby	5.00
55	Perky Bright	12.00
55	Poor Pitiful Pearl (N.O.)	65.00 up
55	Rusty	60.00
56	Liza (I.M.)	9.00
56	Tim	8.00
57	Plum	90.00
57	Miss Peep (N.O.)	45.00
58	New Born Miss Peep (N.O.)	35.00
58	Scootles	175.00
58	Ragsy	60.00
58	Kewpie	12.00
59	Kewpie Gal	65.00
59	Kewpie (Anniversary)	50.00
59	Sad Eyes	10.00
59	Cleaning Day	4.00
60	Bride	12.00
60	Gloria	100.00
60	Emily	75.00
60	Pam (N.O.)	75.00
61	Paula Marie	55.00
61	Baby Bright	20.00
62	Penny Brite (I.M.)	8.00
62	Bonnie Bride	25.00
62	Susie Cute (N.O.)	12.00
62	Baby Boo (N.O.)	30.00
63	Baby Magic (N.O.)	35.00
63	Cool Cat (I.M.)	10.00
63	Baby Tickle Tears (N.O.)	25.00
64	Susie Homemaker	25.00
64	Party Time (N.O.)	25.00
64	Little Miss Fussy	30.00
65	Tickles (N.O.)	25.00
65	Bikey (I.M.)	15.00
65	Baby Catch A Ball (N.O.)	40.00
65	Baby Peek 'N Play	30.00
66	Baby Bunny (N.O.)	25.00
66	Dawn	8.00
66	Smarty Pants	40.00
67	Sunny	225.00
67	Prince Ranier	350.00
67	Liz Taylor	400.00
68	Gypsy Mother & Child	900.00
68	Uncle Sam	135.00
68	Little Women	set 125.00
69	Little Women	set125.00
69	Boy	20.00
70	John Kennedy	35.00
70	Good Luck Troll	12.00
70	May	3.00
70	Cinderella	5.00
71	Scotch Miss	3.00
71	Martha Washington	3.00
71	Scarlett	3.00
71	Carmen	3.00
72	Tinker Bell	9.00
72	Peter Pan	9.00
72	Miss Hollywood	3.00
72	Danny Groom	9.00

Page	Description	Price
73	Miss Tastee Freeze	6.00
73	Miss North America	6.00
74	Miss Charming	250.00 up
74	Gigi Perreaux	200.00 up
75	Bobby	35.00
75	Robert	45.00
75	Lil Susan	25.00
75	Grace	30.00
76	Luvable Susan	25.00
76	Little Debutante	85.00
76	Baby Susan	10.00
76	Tina	25.00
77	Lil Susan (N.O.)	8.00
77	Tandy Talks	65.00
77	Andy	30.00
77	Little Miss (N.O.)	15.00
78	Gemette	22.00
78	Daisy Darlin (N.O.)	25.00
78	Flowerkin (N.O.)	35.00
78	Sandi	18.00
79	Bundle of Joy (N.O.)	8.00
79	Pix-I-Posie (N.O.)	6.00
79	Annette	32.00
79	Musical Baby	18.00
80	Susan	18.00
80	Bundle of Joy (N.O.)	6.00
80	Adorable	6.00
80	Baby Sniffles	4.00
81	Sleepy	15.00
81	Posi-Playmate	16.00
81	Softina	5.00
81	Baby Softina (N.O.)	3.00
82	Cuddlekins	4.00
85	Patricia	250.00
85	Anne of Green Gables (N.O.)	225.00
85	Ann Shirley 20"	300.00
86	Suzanne 14"	225.00
86	Little Lady 18"	250.00
86	Candy Kid	250.00
86	Patsy Joan (N.O.)	300.00
87	Dydee Baby (N.O.)	100.00
87	Lil Darlin' (N.O.)	50.00
87	Honey Girl (N.O.)	165.00
87	Tintair (N.O.)	200.00
88	Mommy's Baby (N.O.)	45.00
88	Baby Cuddle Up	60.00
88	Fluffy (N.O.)	45.00
88	Polka Dottie	185.00
89	Candy Twins	set 65.00
89	Mickey (I.M.)	90.00
89	Fluffy	20.00
89	Katie (N.O.)	25.00
90	My Fair Baby (N.O.)	20.00
90	Twinkie (N.O.)	20.00
90	Patsy Ann (N.O.)	50.00
91	My Precious Baby	20.00
91	Suzie Sunshine (N.O.)	25.00
91	Gumdrop	30.00
91	Precious New Born	30.00
92	Baby Butterball	12.00
92	Baby Sweetie (N.O.)	10.00
92	Babykin	18.00
92	My Fair Baby	10.00
93	Miss Chips	75.00
93	Peaches	45.00
93	Thumpkin' (N.O.)	15.00
93	Chipper	35.00
94	Pum'kin	25.00
94	Half Pint (I.M.)	20.00
94	New Dy Dee Baby	28.00
94	Honey Bun (N.O.)	12.00
95	Lil Sweetie (N.O.)	30.00
95	Tiny Tubber (N.O.)	18.00
95	Baby Face (N.O.)	10.00
95	Button Nose	40.00
96	Butterball	15.00
96	Little Luv	15.00
97	Color Me	6.00
97	Personality Playmate	225.00
97	Sandra	225.00
97	Precious	45.00
98	Curly	8.00
98	Winkin'	4.00
98	Sissy (N.O.)	4.00
99	Fredel	20.00
99	Trudila	20.00
99	Bettina	20.00
99	Jamie	42.00
100	Dee Dee	6.00
100	Nantoc	16.00
100	Eskimo	25.00
100	Col. Saunders	10.00
101	Swimmer	65.00
101	Janie	15.00
101	Rosette	10.00
102	Mariann (I.M.) (N.O.)	10.00
102	Flirty	10.00
102	Cindy	6.00
102	Rose (N.O.)	8.00
103	Beatles	125.00 up
103	Sonja	35.00
104	Andra	15.00
104	Jumeau	650.00
105	Lorraine	80.00
105	Bella Bee	22.00
105	Lynette	13.00
105	Gege (I.M.)	18.00
106	Polly	18.00
106	Soupee	25.00
106	El Soupee (N.O.)	25.00
106	Soupee Bella (N.O.)	25.00
107	Rosemund	22.00
107	Michella	25.00
107	Claudette	30.00
107	Pretty (I.M.)	12.00
108	Pauline	525.00
109	Crawler	15.00
109	Katinka	22.00
109	Peasant Family	set 25.00
109	Gura	30.00
110	Gretchen	22.00
110	Barbel	15.00
110	Pride	225.00
111	Lonee	8.00
111	Freckles	4.00
111	Beebee	4.00
111	Lovely (N.O.)	3.00
112	Eggie (N.O.)	3.00
112	Jane	2.00
112	Lily	2.00
112	Clown	2.00
113	Junie (N.O.)	6.00
113	My Little Girl	2.00
113	Mod	2.00
113	Lil Bit	2.00
114	Little Guy	2.00
114	Baby Jane (N.O.)	2.00
114	Liza	2.00
114	Picture This	3.00
115	Miss India	14.00
115	Red Riding Hood	4.00
115	Carolina	15.00
115	Angelica (I.M.)	12.00
116	Betta	3.00
116	Sweet Adraina	65.00
116	Bride	70.00
116	Valentina	35.00
117	Anita 14"	65.00
117	Guilietta	35.00
117	Alicia 20"	80.00
117	Gabriella 16"	70.00
118	Florenza 14"	65.00
118	Bonomi	18.00
118	Venessa	30.00
119	Nina	15.00
119	Lizza (N.O.)	18.00
119	Mariella	15.00
119	Christina	25.00
120	Dama	25.00
120	Mia	6.00
120	Kitten (N.O.)	15.00
120	Christina	50.00
121	Bed Doll	75.00 up
121	Kewpie	15.00 up
121	Playmate	9.00
121	Sailor	12.00
122	Monkey	15.00
122	Baby	20.00
122	Kewpie Type	6.00
122	Indy (N.O.)	2.00
123	Santa Claus	20.00
123	Eskimo & Party	2.00
123	Kutie (N.O.)	2.00
123	Edy	2.00
124	Swimmer	6.00
124	Doris	8.00
124	Mary Mary (N.O.)	3.00
124	Crawler	15.00
125	Tiny (N.O.)	2.00
125	Brat	4.00
125	Charleen	40.00
125	Wind Song	40.00
126	Cisco Kid	20.00
126	Romona	20.00
126	Americana	15.00
126	Juanita	15.00
127	Pam	22.00
127	Cowgirl Pam	35.00
127	Sleepy Head	3.00
127	Soul Sister	9.00
128	Huggles	2.00
128	Chubby Kid	85.00 up
128	Emerald	30.00
128	Dress Me Doll	3.00
129	Buddy Lee, Hard Plastic	200.00 up
129	Buddy Lee, Composition	275.00 up
130	Doll House Mother	3.00
130	Poodle-Oodle	6.00
130	G.I. Joe	45.00 up
131	Sunday	4.00
131	Little Miss No Name	75.00

Modern Collector's Dolls I

Page	Description	Price
131	Flying Nun	20.00
132	Sleeping Beauty	30.00
132	Rumplestilskin	30.00
132	Goldilocks	30.00
132	Snow White/Dwarfs	40.00
133	Prince Charming	35.00
133	Michelle	30.00
133	World of Love	12.00
133	Baby Ruth	8.00
134	Little Miss Muffet	20.00
135	Masquerade	20.00
135	Bonnie Blue Bell	20.00
135	Red Riding Hood	20.00
135	Sweet Janice	12.00-14.00
137	Jojo	165.00
137	Baby Chubby (N.O.)	30.00
137	Shadow Wave Baby	25.00
137	Cindy Kay	75.00 up
138	Betty Ann	25.00
138	Little Sister	28.00
138	Dolly	75.00 up
138	Gold Medal Doll	165.00 up
139	Pretty Baby (I.M.)	15.00
139	Chubby Baby (N.O.)	10.00
139	Betty (N.O.)	8.00
140	Cindy Kay (N.O.)	45.00
140	Little Miss Betty (N.O.)	8.00
140	Baby Precious (N.O.)	10.00
140	Peggy	85.00
141	Ruthie (N.O.)	12.00
141	Cindy	45.00
141	Fair Skin Doll	25.00
141	Ruth's Sister	75.00
142	Flopsie	15.00
142	Little Happy Fella	20.00
142	Kathy	10.00
142	Betty Jo	35.00
143	Grown Up Miss	15.00
143	Gloria Jean (N.O.)	5.00
143	Princess	30.00
143	Poor Pitiful Pearl (N.O.)	45.00
144	Buttercup	8.00
144	Thirstee Baby	10.00
144	Tynie Toddler (N.O.)	6.00
144	Lullabye Baby	7.00
145	Baby Buttercup	4.00
145	Betty (N.O.)	6.00
145	Mary Poppins	25.00
145	My Ruthie (N.O.)	15.00
146	Softie Baby (N.O.)	4.00
146	Toddler Baby	6.00
146	Sleepy Baby	45.00
146	Answer Doll (I.M.)	15.00
147	Baby Darling (N.O.)	6.00
147	Teensie Baby	4.00
147	Ruthie	15.00
147	Tuffie (N.O.)	55.00
148	Mommy's Darling	25.00
148	Ruthie (N.O.)	10.00
148	Ruthie Baby	14.00
148	Walker Ruth	10.00
149	Baby Tweaks (I.M.)	40.00
149	Lullabye Baby	15.00
149	Songster	15.00
149	Twistie	4.00
150	Athlete	5.00
150	My Baby	4.00
150	Lil Softee (N.O.)	4.00
150	Softee Baby (N.O.)	5.00
151	Love Me Baby (I.A.)	3.00
151	Pooty Tat (N.O.)	4.00
151	Bootsie	8.00
151	Cindy (I.A.)	5.00
152	Buttercup	5.00
152	Bi Lo	30.00
154	Deanna Durbin (N.O.) 17"	350.00
154	Deanna Durbin 21"	500.00
155	Judy Garland Teen Doll 14"	165.00 up
155	Magic Skin Baby (N.O.)	15.00
155	Gorgeous (N.O.)	50.00
156	Magic Skin Doll (N.O.)	22.00
156	Miss Deb	125.00 up
156	Flexy Soldier	165.00 up
156	Sparkle Plenty (N.O.)	45.00
157	Baby Coos	45.00
157	Tickletoes	20.00
157	Tickletoes (R.W.)	20.00
157	Plassie	35.00
158	Magic Skin Baby	12.00
158	Toni 14"	135.00 up
158	Toni 15" (N.O.)	145.00 up
159	Toni Walker 21"	200.00 up
159	Tiny Girl	9.00
159	Pete	5.00
159	Saucy Walker 22"	135.00
160	Kiss Me (N.O.)	60.00
160	Bonnie Braids	45.00
160	Miss Curity (I.M.) 14"	200.00 up
160	Betsy McCall(N.O.)	150.00 up
161	Saucy Walker 22"	135.00
161	Harriet Hubbard Ayers	175.00
161	18" Harriet Hubbard Ayers	200.00 up
161	Baby Big Eyes (I.A.)	55.00
162	Princess Mary	50.00
162	Saucy Walker Vinyl Head	90.00
162	Betsy Wetsy 13" vinyl body	65.00
162	Magic Lips	75.00
163	Miss Revlon	125.00
163	Baby June	50.00
163	Betsy Wetsy	25.00
164	Little Miss Revlon	75.00
164	Miss Revlon (N.O.)	125.00
164	19" Miss Revlon (N.O.)	60.00
164	Mrs. Revlon	70.00
165	Betsy Wetsy	20.00
165	Penny Playpal	150.00
165	Betsy Wetsy (N.O.)	55.00
165	Miss Ideal	150.00
165	Pattie Playpal	150.00
166	Cream Puff	40.00
166	Betsy Wetsy (N.O.)	25.00
166	Dew Drop	25.00
167	Tiny Kissey	55.00
167	Thumbelina	45.00
167	Tammy	35.00
167	Betsy Wetsy	45.00
168	Ted	30.00
168	Pepper	20.00
168	Pebbles	20.00
168	Bam Bam (N.O.)	20.00
169	Pebbles (N.O.)	30.00
169	Cuddly Kissey	60.00
169	Baby Betsy Wetsy	10.00
169	James Bond	50.00
170	Illya Kuryakin	50.00
170	Miss Clairol	45.00
170	Honeymoon (N.O.)	50.00
170	Goody Two Shoes	65.00
171	Betsy Wetsy	45.00
171	Baby Snoozie	20.00
171	Pebbles (N.O.)	12.00
171	Tabatha	45.00
172	Honeyball (N.O.)	6.00
172	Tearful Thumbelina (N.O.)	14.00
172	Baby Giggles	45.00
172	Tiny Baby Kissy (N.O.)	20.00
173	Tubsy	35.00
173	Giggles, White	65.00
173	Giggles, Black	125.00
173	Daisy	15.00
174	Pixie	15.00
174	Newborn Thumbelina (Black)	30.00
174	Newborn Thumbelina (White)	15.00
174	Tearie Betsy (I.A.)	6.00
175	Toddler Thumbelina	25.00
175	April Showers	25.00
175	Little Lost Baby	55.00
176	Crissy, White	50.00
176	Crissy, Black	75.00
176	Velvet	50.00
176	Dale	10.00
177	Kissing Thumbelina	14.00
177	Tiny Thumbelina	14.00
177	In a Minute Thumbelina	14.00
177	Patti Playful	35.00
178	Baby Belly Button (N.O.)	10.00
178	Play N Jane	20.00
178	Dina	75.00
178	Lazy Dazy	12.00
181	13" Shirley Temple	525.00
181	17" Shirley Temple (N.O.)	575.00
182	16" Shirley Temple (R.W.)	525.00
182	22" Shirley Temple (N.O.)	650.00
182	27" Shirley Temple (N.O.) (R.W.)	900.00
183	17" Shirley Temple Baby	900.00
183	Hawaiian Shirley Temple	750.00
183	12" Shirley Temple	150.00
183	15" Shirley Temple	245.00
184	17" Shirley Temple (N.O.)	300.00
184	1972 17" Shirley Temple	175.00
186	Love Me	8.00
186	Dolly (N.O.)	8.00
186	Tiny Bubbles	6.00
186	Bashful Boy	3.00
187	Sherri	10.00
187	Trudy	8.00
187	Pretty Girl	6.00
187	Twistee	10.00
188	Nikki	6.00
188	Jolly	12.00
188	Cuties (N.O.)	12.00
188	Judy (I.A.)	10.00
189	Playpen Doll	5.00
189	Cutie Pie	10.00
189	Timmy	15.00
189	Linda	15.00
190	Lil Lil	3.00
190	Catherine	50.00
190	Miss Sweet	4.00
190	Pumpkin	4.00
191	Snow White	175.00

Page	Description	Price
191	Raggedy Ann & Andy	10.00
191	My Baby	7.00
191	Cuddly Infant (N.O.)	4.00
192	Baby (N.O.)	4.00
192	Louise	7.00
192	Pastel Miss	4.00
192	Delightful	5.00
193	Lorrie (N.O.)	4.00
193	Marsha	2.00
193	Little Linda	2.00
193	Miss Toddler	25.00
194	Twinkie	10.00
194	Jamie West	6.00
194	Mary Hoyer	225.00 up
196	Barbie 1972 (Mint in Box)	300.00
196	Mattie (I.A.)	35.00
197	Sister Belle	35.00
197	Charming Chatty (N.O.)	65.00 up
197	Chatty Cathy	50.00
197	Midge (#12 Barbie)	85.00 up
198	Shrinking Violet	65.00
198	Rickey	75.00
198	Scooter	85.00
198	Skipper	75.00
199	Baby Pattaburp (N.O.)	25.00
199	Singing Chatty	30.00
199	Baby First Step (N.O.)	25.00
199	Talking Baby First Step	35.00
200	Scooba Doo	58.00
200	Baby Cheryl (N.O.)	18.00
200	Casper The Ghost	30.00
200	Baby Teenie Talk (N.O.)	14.00
201	Cheerful-Tearful (I.A.)	20.00
201	Baby Secret	25.00
201	Bunson Bernie	25.00
202	Lola Liddle	25.00
202	Cinderella	45.00
202	Liddle Diddle	45.00
202	Florence Niddle	25.00
202	Casey	65.00
203	Francie	75.00 up
203	New Barbie	35.00
203	Julia	70.00
204	Tiny Cheerful-Tearful (N.O.)	15.00
204	Drowsy (N.O.)	10.00
204	Baby See N Say	20.00
205	Baby's Hungry	25.00
205	Buffie	45.00
205	Randy Reader (N.O.)	30.00
205	Sleeping Beauty	45.00
206	Sister Small Talk	18.00
206	Small Talk (N.O.)	10.00
206	Doctor Doolittle 6"	25.00
206	22½" Dr. Doolittle	65.00
207	Sheila Skediddle	25.00
207	Tippy Toes	25.00
207	Busy Ken	65.00
207	Dancerina	35.00
208	Bouncy Baby	10.00
208	Baby Tenderlove	10.00
208	Chatty Tell	25.00
208	Baby Sing a Song	25.00
209	Beany	25.00
209	Charlie Brown Skediddle	20.00
209	Breezy Bridgit	6.00
209	Dressy	10.00
210	Big Jack	40.00
210	Kretor & Zark	35.00 up
211	Haddie Mod	5.00
211	Joe Namath	30.00
211	Nun Nurse	7.00
211	Molly (I.M.)	15.00
212	Monica	300.00
212	Christening Baby	12.00
212	Claudette	10.00
212	Topsy-Turvy	65.00
213	Happy Toddler	50.00
213	Walker	200.00
213	Lone Ranger	225.00 up
214	Eva	200.00 up
214	American Child	100.00 up
214	Lois Jane	25.00
215	Dutch Girls	6.00
215	Betty Grable	150.00
216	False Snow White (N.O.)	40.00
216	Happy Baby	15.00
216	Air Force	65.00
216	Henry	35.00
217	Henrette	35.00
217	Topsy	20.00
217	Big Boy	7.00
217	Gingham Gal	18.00
218	Lollypop Kid	3.00
218	Abbi-Gail	95.00
218	Dream Doll (N.O.)	15.00
219	Pauline (N.O.)	15.00
219	Crying Baby	45.00
219	Pretty Baby (I.A.)	15.00
219	Baby Benny	25.00
220	Bendee	10.00
220	Johnny	6.00
220	Dimply Baby (I.A.)	8.00
220	Polly (I.A.)	65.00
221	Little Traveler (I.M.)	15.00
221	Janie	4.00
221	Teena	4.00
221	Miss Curity	10.00
222	Little Sister (I.A.)	6.00
222	Nun	5.00
222	World Traveler	65.00
222	Mary Lou	25.00
223	Ninette (I.M.)	25.00
223	Rosy Walker (I.A.)	65.00
223	Amy Louise	95.00
223	Pansy (I.M.)	6.00
224	Sweet Lou	18.00
224	Cuddly Kathy (I.A.)	16.00
224	My Baby (I.M.)	10.00
224	Pert & Sassy	15.00
225	Miss Glamour Ann	20.00
225	Kleenex Baby	4.00
225	Baby Bunting	25.00
225	Dream Doll	6.00
226	Yuletide	25.00
226	Angel	50.00
226	Pert Teenager	25.00
226	Bed Doll	45.00
227	Stunning	60.00
227	Baby Beth (I.A.)	6.00
227	Sugar & Spice (I.A.)	5.00
227	Trousseau Bride (I.A.)	10.00
228	Peggy Ann	4.00
228	Beebee	3.00
228	Campbell Kid (N.O.)	35.00
228	Bonny (N.O.)	4.00
229	Mattie Mame	3.00
229	Pretty Girl	6.00
229	Pixie	6.00
229	Pixie Haircut Baby	8.00
230	Imp	3.00
230	Suzy Smart	8.00
230	Valerie (N.O.)	10.00
230	Amish Boy & Girl	6.00
231	Jockey & Fox Hunter	each 20.00
231	African Native	4.00
231	Sexed Cave Man	20.00
232	Little Joan	45.00
232	Flower Girl	45.00
233	Queen of Hearts	45.00
233	Elsie Marley	45.00
233	Winter	40.00 up
233	Daffidown Dilly	45.00
234	Miss Muffett (N.O.)	25.00
234	Bride	40.00 up
234	Doll of Day	40.00 up
234	Bride	40.00 up
235	Commencement	40.00 up
235	Little Sister	95.00 up
235	Dillar A Dollar	40.00up
235	Muffie	100.00 up
236	Christening Baby	70.00 up
236	Valentine	40.00
236	Nancy Ann	65.00
236	Linda Williams	35.00
237	Dolly Ann	20.00
237	Joann	20.00
237	Belinda (N.O.)	18.00
237	Baby Princess	10.00
238	Royal Princess (I.A.)	5.00
238	Poppin Fresh	3.00
238	Flowergirl	3.00
238	Bride	3.00
239	Captain Hook	6.00
239	Nun	5.00
239	Graduate	3.00
239	Bride	3.00
240	Miss America	3.00
240	Lady Revencroft	3.00
240	Miss Valentine	3.00
240	Crusader	6.00
241	Polish Girl	3.00
241	Lady Hampshire	3.00
241	Miss 1953	3.00
241	Priscilla Alden	3.00
242	Bride	3.00
242	Greenbrier Maid	6.00
242	Dress Me	2.00
242	Scotch Groom	4.00
243	Nelly (N.O.)	3.00
243	New Baby (I.A.)	3.00
243	Glorious Gold Princess	3.00
243	Flowgirl	2.00
244	Bride	3.00
244	Polish Girl	3.00
244	Pert Pierrette	2.00
244	Red Riding Hood	3.00
246	Emily Ann	135.00
246	Marie	6.00
246	Tomas	6.00
246	Howdy Doody	95.00
246	Poodle	20.00

Page	Description	Price
246	Dick & Sally	8.00
246	Woody Woodpecker	4.00
247	Teto	6.00
247	Puppetrina (N.O.)	35.00
247	Jiminy Cricket	4.00
247	Donald Duck	4.00
248	Yogi Bear	3.00
248	Pluto	4.00
248	Donald Duck	4.00
248	Sylvester	3.00
249	Tom	5.00
249	Baby	2.00
249	Charlie McCarthy	75.00
249	Betty Ballerina	3.00
250	Popeye	6.00
250	Dr. Doolittle	22.00
250	Happy Me	3.00
250	Bye Lo	225.00
251	Charlie Chaplin	225.00 up
251	Ling Toy	10.00
251	Chi-Lu	6.00
251	Snow White	125.00
252	Polish Girl	3.00
252	Mammy's Baby	6.00
252	Dutch Girl	3.00
252	Mammy	9.00
253	Marie	6.00
253	Abby	3.00
253	Norah Sue	285.00
253	Miss Smith	65.00
254	Tak-Uki	200.00
254	Soo Ming	10.00
254	Dutch Boy & Girl	each 4.00
254	Girl & Doll	12.00
255	Dancing Partner	18.00
255	Santa Claus	70.00
255	Little Lulu	85.00
255	Sweet Pea	60.00
256	Popeye (I.M.)	40.00
256	Baby's Doll	4.00
256	Daisy	15.00
256	Flip	10.00
257	Candy Striper	4.00
257	Cindy	2.00
257	Mickey Mouse	20.00
257	Mr. Magoo	10.00
258	Eskimo Pie	4.00
258	Multi Face	6.00
258	Sleepy Head	3.00
258	Pinocchio	10.00
259	Little Bo Peep	25.00
259	Clown (I.M.)	6.00
259	Mickey Mouse	45.00
259	Scarecrow	22.00
260	Ronald McDonald	5.00
260	Oh My	3.00
260	Little Orphan Annie (I.M.)	30.00
260	Hansel	3.00
261	Lil Soul	6.00
261	Talk A Little	2.00
261	Holly	3.00
262	Gramma	20.00
262	Doughboy	3.00
262	Jolly Green Giant	6.00
262	Mr. Peanut	5.00
263	Eskimo	7.00
263	Louise	3.00
263	Jan	8.00
263	Heidi	6.00
264	Baby Stroll Along	15.00
264	Baby Sad N Glass (N.O.)	18.00
264	Snugglebun (N.O.)	10.00
265	Tippy Tumbles	12.00
265	Heidi	6.00
265	Bottle Baby	4.00
265	Baby Crawalong (N.O.)	16.00
266	Linda Lee	16.00
266	Baby Grow A Tooth	20.00
266	Tumbling Tomboy	15.00
266	Baby Laugh a Lot	18.00
267	Jumpsy (I.M.)	10.00
267	Whistler	12.00
267	Sweet April	5.00
267	Funny	2.00
268	Rosa	3.00
268	Elmer Fudd	6.00
268	First Date	2.00
268	Lonely Liza	50.00
269	Joy (I.A.)	30.00
269	Valentine Bonnet Toddler	4.00
269	St. Pat's Day Toddler	4.00
269	Easter Bonnet Toddler	4.00
270	Billy Joe	35.00
270	New Happy Time Baby (I.A.)	5.00
270	Walking Bride (N.O.)	6.00
270	Mommy's Baby (N.O.)	4.00
271	Adorable (I.A.)	3.00
271	Bubble Bath Baby (I.M.)	3.00
271	Indian Troll	9.00
271	Nurse Troll (I.M.)	9.00
272	Baby Janie	30.00
272	Tamu	30.00
272	Flip Wilson	20.00
273	Muff Doll	15.00
273	Amosandra	55.00
273	Betty Bows	15.00
273	Tod-L-Dee & Tod-L-Tim	8.00
274	Banister Baby	50.00
274	Babee Bee (N.O.)	20.00
274	Chunky	3.00
274	Baby	3.00
275	Gerber Baby	40.00
275	Tod-L-Tee	8.00
275	So Wee (N.O.)	8.00
275	Gerber Baby (N.O.)	38.00
276	Little Debbie Eve	5.00
276	Melody Baby Debbi (N.O.)	4.00
276	Baby Debbie	6.00
276	Talking Terri Lee	300.00 up
277	Terri Lee	185.00
277	Jerri Lee	200.00 up
277	Tiny Jerri Lee	195.00
277	Tiny Terri Lee	145.00
278	Baby Linda	150.00
278	Mannequin	22.00
278	Dawk	10.00
279	Carmen	225.00
280	Sweetum	6.00
280	Surprise Doll	15.00
281	Princess Bride	15.00
281	Country Girl	18.00
281	Dollikins	25.00
281	Pri-Thilla	18.00
282	Baby Dollikins	40.00
282	Wiggles	40.00
282	Betsy McCall	150.00
283	Blue Fairy	25.00
283	Freckles	65.00
283	Pollyanna	75.00
283	Tinyteen	40.00
284	Yummy	12.00
284	Purty	20.00
284	Cuddly Baby	3.00
285	Blabby	25.00
285	Miss Debteen (N.O.)	8.00
285	Debteen Toddler	20.00
286	Baby Sweetums	6.00
286	Bob	12.00
286	Coquette	10.00
286	Bare Bottom Baby	20.00
287	Posin Elfy	5.00
287	Debteen	8.00
287	Little Coquette	6.00
287	Posable Baby Trix	10.00
288	Needa Toodles	3.00
288	Tiny Toodles (N.O.)	2.00
288	Pretty Portrait (N.O.)	7.00
288	Baby Pee Wee	3.00
289	Secret Sue	20.00
289	50th Anniversary Doll	50.00
289	Penelope	8.00
289	Baby Sweetums (N.O.)	4.00
290	First Born Baby (N.O.)	3.00
290	Daffi Dill	5.00
290	Dolly Walker	5.00
290	Dollikins	20.00
291	Bathtub Baby	4.00
291	Adorable Cindy	3.00
291	Debteen	5.00
291	New Born Yummy	3.00
292	Tiny Trix	2.00
292	Kim	2.00
292	Baby Sleep Amber	6.00
292	Jennifer	18.00
293	New Gerber Baby	36.00
293	Happy Pee Wee	4.00
293	Toe Dancing Ballerina	40.00
293	Ballerina	35.00
294	Big Girl	40.00
295	Ginny Clown (Toddlers)	225.00 up
295	Ginny Imp (I.M.)	125.00 up
296	Ginny	325.00 up
296	Ginny	250.00
296	Ginny	125.00
296	Ginny Baby	550.00 up
297	Jeff	45.00
297	Jan	50.00
297	Jill	50.00
297	Brickette	80.00
298	Baby Dear (N.O.)	80.00
298	Little Baby Dear	10.00
298	Ginny	30.00
298	Ginny Baby (N.O.)	20.00
299	Baby Dear	15.00
299	Baby Dear	15.00
299	Littlest Angel	12.00
299	Posie Pixie (I.M.)	10.00
300	Littlest Angel	10.00
300	Angel Baby	10.00
300	Picture Girl	22.00
300	Star Brite	25.00

Page	Description	Price
301	Little Miss Ginny	20.00
301	Dearest One	25.00
301	Ginny Baby (N.O.)	8.00
301	Pinocchio	200.00 up
302	Bashful	200.00 up
302	Snow White (N.O.)	45.00 up
302	Tinker Bell	20.00 up
302	Mousketeer	22.00
303	Christopher Robin	20.00
303	Winnie the Pooh	15.00
303	Jiminy Cricket	10.00

Numbers, Letters and Symbol Index

Numbers Index

Letter Index

Patent Numbers

Symbols Index

Schroeder's Antiques Price Guide

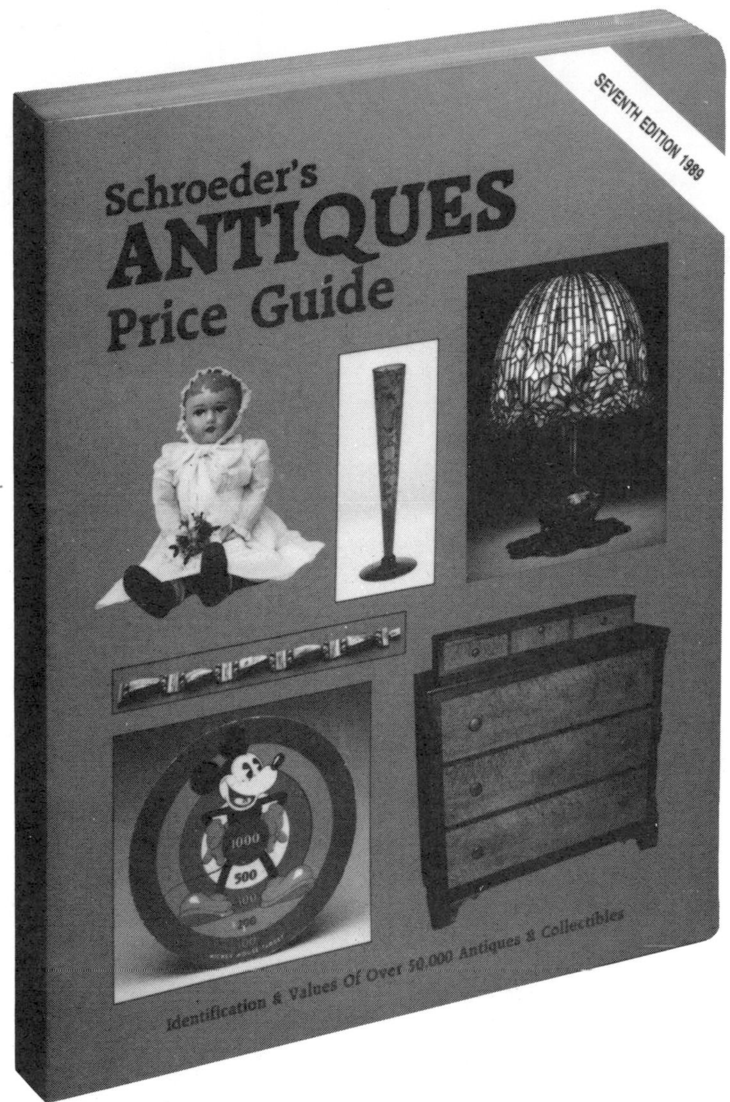

Schroeder's Antiques Price Guide has climbed its way to the top in a field already supplied with several well-established publications! The word is out, *Schroeder's Price Guide* is the best buy at any price. Over 500 categories are covered, with more than 50,000 listings. But it's not volume alone that makes Schroeder's the unique guide it is recognized to be. From ABC Plates to Zsolnay, if it merits the interest of today's collector, you'll find it in Schroeder's. Each subject is represented with histories and background information. In addition, hundreds of sharp original photos are used each year to illustrate not only the rare and the unusual, but the everyday "fun-type" collectibles as well -- not postage stamp pictures, but large close-up shots that show important details clearly.

Each edition is completely re-typeset from all new sources. We have not and will not simply change prices in each new edition. All new copy and all new illustrations make Schroeder's THE price guide on antiques and collectibles.

The writing and researching team behind this giant is proportionately large. It is backed by a staff of more than seventy of Collector Books' finest authors, as well as a board of advisors made up of well-known antique authorities and the country's top dealers, all specialists in their fields. Accuracy is their primary aim. Prices are gathered over the entire year previous to publication, from ads and personal contacts. Then each category is thoroughly checked to spot inconsistencies, listings that may not be entirely reflective of actual market dealings, and lines too vague to be of merit. Only the best of the lot remains for publication. You'll find *Schroeder's Antiques Price Guide* the one to buy for factual information and quality.

No dealer, collector or investor can afford not to own this book. It is available from your favorite bookseller or antiques dealer at the low price of $12.95. If you are unable to find this price guide in your area, it's available from Collector Books, P. O. Box 3009, Paducah, KY 42001 at $12.95 plus $2.00 for postage and handling.

8½ x 11, 608 Pages — $12.95